The Life of St. Mary Magdalen De-Pazzi

Statue of the Saint in St. Mary Magdalen De-Pazzi's (Italian) Church,
Philadelphia.

THE LIFE

OF

St. Mary Magdalen De-Pazzi

FLORENTINE NOBLE

SACRED CARMELITE VIRGIN

Compiled by the REV. PLACIDO FABRINI

❧ ❧ ❧

TO WHICH ARE ADDED HER WORKS, A NARRATION OF THE MIRACLES
WROUGHT THROUGH HER INTERCESSION DOWN TO OUR DAYS
AND PRAYERS FOR THE NOVENA IN HER HONOR

❧ ❧ ❧

Translated from the Florentine Edition of 1852
and Published by the

REV. ANTONIO ISOLERI, Miss. Ap.

Rector of the new St. Mary Magdalen De-Pazzi's Italian Church, Philadelphia, Pa., U.S.A.

❧ ❧ ❧

PART I.

Enriched with New Illustrations together with the Reproduction
of those in the Original Work

❧ ❧ ❧

PHILADELPHIA

1900

Nihil obstat.

J. F. Loughlin, D.D.,

Censor Librorum.

Imprimatur.

+ P. J. Ryan,

Archiepiscopus Philadelphiensis

Philadelphiae, iij Non. Martii, 1900.

207

To the then modest and amiable boy,
the dear Friend of his youth in Savona,
the faithful Disciple of St. Vincent de Paul,
the devoted Son of St. Joseph Calasantius,
the zealous Bishop of Pontremoli,

Monsignor Alfonso Maria Mistrangelo,

now raised to the Archiepiscopal See of St. Antonino
in the noble city of Florence,
where our great and glorious Carmelite Saint
was born, lived, and died,
and where her sacred Remains, still incorrupt,
are venerated,
this Work
is respectfully and affectionately dedicated
by the Translator,

Rev. Antonio Isoleri.

ACCEPTANCE OF THE DEDICATION.

Amico venerato e carissimo

Io sono riconoscente senza fine del pensiero affettuoso di dedicare a me la sua traduzione della Vita di S. Maria Maddalena de' Pazzi. —

Con questo nuovo tratto di benevolenza non solo Ella rinsalda i soavi legami di antica amicizia che ci avvincono, ma mi obbliga inoltre a rivolgere speciali preghiere alla serafica Vergine Fiorentina, affinchè benedica e prosperi le apostoliche fatiche della S.V. in cotesta Chiesa degli Italiani dedicata al suo nome glorioso.

Io le farò con sentimento di gratitudine e, prostrato all'altare ove la Santa, fra i gigli e le rose, sembra ancora riposarsi fra le braccia degli Angeli dopo una delle sue estasi di paradiso, la supplicherò a sorridere dal cielo, a proteggere cotesta popolazione che tanto la venera ed ama e ad imbalsamare, col profumo delle sue virtù, il cuore di tutti; tutti innamoran-

Gù Gesù benedetto

Si uniranno meco nelle preghiere, ne'
voti questa Religione più ferrante e povera, con...
sovente, nelle loro strettezze, soccorse dalla carità generosa di D. Bosco, e gli avrà ottenuto una
dal Signore largissimo guiderdone.

Mentre, cogli auguri d'ogni celeste benedi-
zione, le ripeto le più vive grazie per l'onore
immeritato che da Lei ...... fatto, con
sensi di affetto ed stima mi ripeto

Firenze 1 Marzo 1900

suo devmo
+ Alfonso Maria Mistrangelo
Arcivescovo

TRANSLATION OF LETTER OF MONS. MISTRANGELO, ACCEPTING THE DEDICATION.

Rev. Antonio Isoleri, Ap. Miss ,

Rector of the New St M M De-Pazzi's Italian Church,
710 Montrose (formerly Marriott) Street, Philadelphia, Pa , U S. A

Ven. and Dearest Friend ·

     I return endless thanks to you for your loving thought of dedicating to me your translation of the "Life of St Mary Magdalen De=Pazzi"

 By this new token of good=will not only do you tighten the sweet bonds of the old friendship which bind me to you, but you compel me from henceforth to address special prayers to the Seraphic Florentine Virgin, that she may bless and prosper your apostolic labors in that Italian Church dedicated to her glorious name.

 This I shall do with a sense of gratitude, and, prostrated at the altar where the Saint, among the lilies and the roses, seems still to rest in the arms of the angels after one of her paradisiacal ecstasies, I will beseech her to smile upon you from heaven, to protect those people who venerate and love her so much, and to embalm, with the perfume of her virtues, the hearts of all, enamoring all of Jesus Christ.

 And these very pious but poor Religious, so often relieved in their poverty by the generous charity of Rev A Isoleri, will unite with me in prayers and good wishes and will obtain for you, from the Lord, a very ample reward.

 Whilst wishing you every heavenly blessing, I again tender to you the most lively thanks for the undeserved honor you are doing me, and I again declare myself, with sentiments of loving esteem,

    Your most devoted

     ✤ ALFONSO MARIA MISTRANGELO,

         Archbishop.

Florence, March 1st, 1900.

THE TRANSLATOR TO THE READER.

I undertake the translation of "The Life and Works of St. Mary Magdalen De-Pazzi," by the Rev. Placido Fabrini, for the honor of God and of his servant, St Mary Magdalen De-Pazzi; and, chiefly, to obtain, through her intercession, two graces—one of which is, that I may be able to build a new church under her invocation, to replace the present one, which is old, small, and poorly constructed.[1]

May the necessary light and strength be given to me, so that I shall succeed in accomplishing what I now begin in the name of the Father, and of the Son, and of the Holy Ghost. Amen.

With all but a certainty of not being able to do full justice to the original, and without reflecting on the judgment of translators and publishers, or calling their taste into question, and much less with a view to making comparisons between Saints, but mindful only of A Kempis' advice: "*Noli etiam inquirere nec disputare de meritis Sanctorum, quis alio sit sanctior, aut quis major fuerit in regno cœlorum*" (Lib. iii, cap. lviii, 2)—"Do not inquire nor dispute about the merits of the Saints, which of them is more holy than the other, or which is the greater in the kingdom of heaven;"—I may be allowed to state here that many Lives of Saints have of late been translated from the Italian and other languages into English, and published in this country, which are not half so interesting or edifying as, I confidently hope, this will be found to be, not only by Religious, but by all Christians.

Once for all, I beg an indulgent judgment of this translation and its poor English, in view of the good object and the good will employed to secure it. The original is certainly grand; and, did we but know that another pen was, or soon would be, at work translating it, we would immediately drop our own, thank the Lord, and repent of our presumption.[2]

---

[1] The work of building the new church, a new parochial house, and a school, together with the constantly increasing work imposed by the extraordinary tide of immigration, compelled the interruption of this translation for several years, whilst what was done of it could only be done now and then, at long intervals The church having been completed—one of the graces asked—we have endeavored to complete the work and publish it, in fulfillment of our intention and vow. (1898.)

[2] And, had the magnificent edition of "The Life and Ecstasies of St M. M. De-P" by the Sisters of her Order and Monastery, come out sooner, we would without doubt, have given it the preference. It was issued, Florence, 1893.

7

We earnestly hope that persons living in the world—Protestants as well as Catholics—besides Religious, will read this Life, because we are firmly convinced that it will do all of them some good.   They will find in it much to admire, much to edify them.   There is something for all to imitate.   Through it, our dissenting brethren will know our religion better, and, let us hope, like it more   Who knows, but that such a grand tableau of Catholic sanctity as is presented to them in the Life of St. M. M. De-P., who lived at a time when "the utter degeneracy and corruption" of the Catholic Church was so loudly proclaimed and made a by-word and a pretext for a notable and noble part of Catholic Europe to separate from her bosom, may not only win their admiration, but also draw them into the fold, to become, as their forefathers were, children of that Church which alone is the *Mother of Saints*, which alone can lead them to salvation , so that they, one day, may sing with us : "*Quam dilecta tabernacula tua, Domine virtutum ! concupiscit et deficit anima mea in atria Domini* "—" How lovely are thy tabernacles, O Lord of Hosts ! my soul longeth and fainteth for the courts of the Lord " (Ps. lxxxiii).

ANTONIO ISOLERI, Ap. Miss.,

Rector of St. M M De.P.'s Italian Church.

PHILADELPHIA, July 1st, 1881.

INTRODUCTION.

In consequence of many requests for the "Life of St. Mary Magdalen De-Pazzi," which could not be met on account of the scarcity of copies still extant,[1] the importance of supplying this want was felt by many, and some were about to have another edition issued, when, being spoken to by one of them, I, though the least skilled in the literary art, very gladly undertook with all possible speed to write a work so dear to my heart.

Repeating faithfully all that is believed to have been done by the Saint, gathering all that the writers of her life said that is interesting, and bringing to light unedited documents, with notes for their better understanding, I hope to have satisfied the desire not only of devout persons, but of those who will value this as an historical work

I will say, moreover, that, as all the lives of Saints embrace two parts—the one that we may imitate and the other admire—therefore their publication tends principally to produce these two relative effects, the second of which is a consequence of the first   If we read them without having in us at least a portion of that foundation from which they were reared to the apex of virtue, the *wonderful part* especially will become for us the mysterious volume under seal which human wisdom will try to penetrate in vain   Here is the school of the Gospel, here is the science of God; and, to profit by it, one must approach it with a humble and pure heart.   The proud and worldly man finds in it all impossibility, all darkness, and in his wickedness and ignorance he sometimes goes so far as to deny that God could be so good as to communicate Himself to His creatures in a manner so wonderful.   Let us read with faith and humility the achievements of those who knew how to sanctify their lives; let us walk with them along the path of virtue, and then we will not wonder at the prodigious blessings God granted them.   The Gospel in practice, the gifts of God as a reward ; behold all in the lives of the Saints.

For the first, in all the lives of the Saints we find something to learn, no matter what our social position is.   True virtue is common to

---

[1] In ten years I could not procure a copy of this "Life" in English, except a very small sketch taken from Butler's "Lives of Saints," printed by Henry McGrath, Philadelphia, and the loan of the Life of our Saint by Father Cepari, an English edition out of print.—*Note of the Translator.*

all. From the example of St. Mary Magdalen De-Pazzi, not only persons who, like her, live consecrated to God in the cloister, but all others, can derive benefit. Model of sanctity, she was a teacher of it, and by her example encouraged it in all states of life Separated from the world, buried in her monastery, she teaches that Religion, having apparently in view the happiness of the life to come, promotes at the same time in the best way the happiness of the temporal life As a sufficient proof of the efficacy of her example, it will suffice to point out the peculiar characteristic by which she is distinguished even among the most perfect souls—that of her most ardent desire to suffer, which made her so often repeat, "*Non mori, sed pati*"—"Let me suffer and not die" Our utmost care is to avoid the sufferings of our mortal career, but as they are inevitable, our distress and—in the sight of God—often our faults, too, are doubled by our being at permanent war with ourselves. Man is born to suffer, as birds to fly His life on earth is a contrast, a combat, a struggle. As man gets strong and able to carry his cross, he advances equally in perfection The cross is the seal of virtue Thus, our Saint renounced every delight, not only of earth, but also of heaven. No adversity could trouble her, nay, the more the pain, the greater the joy of her heart, so that, having vanquished the world and conquered the flesh, she did not see nor know aught but her God crucified, for whom she became enraptured with love. Oh ! if but a spark of that divine love which filled her would penetrate our hearts, how much more justly would we value the vanities of the world and the ignominies of the cross ! But our self-love is too strong an obstacle, let us divest ourselves of some of it, at least, to please God ; and He, being so solicitous for our welfare, will not fail to give us a foretaste of the sweetness and amiability of the science of the Saints, by progressing in which our intellect will apprehend those ideas and immutable hopes which acquire no value from human conversations, depend not upon a passing opinion, suit all needs and circumstances, the days of prosperity and those of adversity, and, being at once our encouragement and our guide, they alone form the hero of humanity. Profane histories give us but deeds of ambition, of despotism, based nearly always on the ruin of others ; whilst Religion shows us, in her Saints, the triumph of sacrificing self for the benefit of others. We will see in our Saint, how, having attained to the sublime observance of the first precept, "*Love God above everything*," she knew with equal perfection how to fulfill the second, which is like to it, "*Love thy neighbor as thyself*" Always seeing in her neighbor the image and the child of God, she fulfilled one precept by the practice of the other. There is no better argument than this by which to know the true lovers of God. While this is an indispensable duty for us all, it must at the same time be admitted that the fulfilling of it is oftentimes very hard, and demands of us magnanimous sacrifices. That neighbor whom we must love as ourselves, is not infrequently an indiscreet person, turning upon us the malice of his tongue; an odious rival, raising himself at our expense; a false friend, who betrays our confidence; perhaps our neighbors are impious men, who live by doing harm daily to their fellow-men. And we must love them;—this is the new commandment which Jesus Christ sanctioned by His death on the cross. Our obligation is binding, and the fulfilling of it is all the law. From which it will evidently appear how important is the reading of this history, which offers the most valuable stimulus to practice these virtues, and thus to attain perfect rectitude of spirit.

In the second place, there were very many wonderful traits in St. M. M. De-P. She might be called, with good reason, the *Seraphic*, the *Ecstatic* of the Carmel, as her spirit was almost continually rapt in ecstasy and led to contemplate and enjoy the most sublime perfections of the Godhead Now, Christian admiration for this must proceed from a state of the soul excited by lively faith in the all-powerful goodness of God, who operates in a supernatural manner on the nothingness of the human creature From this will spring a greater fervor to adore, serve, and love so good a God. No one should doubt the truth of the marvelous things contained in this book, as I will relate neither fact nor saying which has not been examined in the processes of her beatification and canonization; and so the conscience of all believers may be at rest The wonderful graces obtained afterwards, and herein narrated, have been examined and approved by learned theologians deputed to investigate by ecclesiastical superiors. This should be sufficient to secure the assent of every prudent man It may be well to add here, that the Saint, being very near death, asserted that "all she had said in ecstasy or privately, or related to the Sisters under obedience, had been the pure action of the Holy Ghost, not interspersed with anything of her own interest." The truth of this assertion appears even on the strength of human reasoning alone In fact, a maiden who knew no more than what was needed by a simple nun, could not have explained the most sublime mysteries of our holy faith with such profound doctrine as she did, unless directed immediately by supernatural light If, in reading, you sometimes find repeated in one part what has already been said in another, it must be observed that, in the Life, all those ecstasies were related which it did not seem proper to separate Some were, in the order of the history, hinted at, which are afterwards related more at length in the Works. As the Saint had different ecstasies on the same subjects, it is probable that she said the same or similar things several times. The ecstasies are faithfully described as spoken or related by the Saint. The periods interposed denote the longer or shorter pauses she made during the spiritual excesses. In this book will also be found some revelations she had, contrary to the opinions of some theologians, which discordance need not surprise, because private revelations have no more weight than a mere opinion. Such is the judgment of the Catholic Church on the revelations of the Saints, so that the Church never intends to raise them, with her approbation, above probability. And I here profess my particular submission to the same Church, fully complying with the Bull of the Sovereign Pontiff Urban VIII in regard to the virtues, miracles, and everything else superhuman of which mention is made in this book. ·

The letters of St M. M. De-P which are appended, are scarce in number, because the Saint was very much opposed to receiving and answering letters. She experienced great aversion to entering into confidential relations, even spiritually, with any person whatsoever; and when she brought herself to write, she was induced thereto by obedience to her superiors. But the few letters we have breathe the fire of divine love into the soul, and are in themselves rich with the best and most efficacious lessons. In the simplicity of their style they secretly bear the mark of the unction of the Holy Ghost, and work miraculous changes in the hearts of their readers. Finally, one can see in them the character of her who composed them, and the fervor of her who wrote them.

The entire book is divided into two volumes: the first contains the Life and Miracles of the Saint; the second, all the Works, that is, those productions of her spirit which we find in existence. Read these pages, faithful Christian, to instruct thyself in piety and to excite thy heart to devotion towards a Saint noble by blood, nobler by virtue, simple by study, but very learned in the school of the spirit; to whom her most adorable Spouse, Jesus Christ, was a teacher. Here, reader, thou wilt find all that is necessary to fulfill those duties which every one owes to God, his neighbor, and himself. Practice with fidelity these useful teachings, and thou wilt become just, humane, charitable, a good citizen, and a fervent Christian. Live up to the exhortations given by St. Mary Magdalen De-Pazzi, and to what she herself practiced, and thou wilt be happy on earth and blessed in heaven.

P. FABRINI.

The Life of St. Mary Magdalen De-Pazzi.

CHAPTER I.

OF THE PARENTS, BIRTH, AND INFANCY OF ST. MARY MAGDALEN.

IN the city of Florence, prolific and happy mother of children praiseworthy for all kinds of virtue, two most noble families, the De-Pazzi and the Buondelmonti, enjoy a most honorable rank for antiquity and nobility of blood, because for many centuries they have counted among their ancestors men remarkable in arms and letters. In the year of our Lord 1559, these two families were united by the marriage of Camillo di Geri De-Pazzi and Maria di Lorenzo Buondelmonti; and as they were of equal nobility of blood, so were they also similar in nobility of mind and love of Christian piety. They lived in the perfect harmony of conjugal affection, without any quarrel on account of domestic differences. They honored one another with reciprocal respect, and foremost in the economy of their family was the piety and the fulfillment of all duties to God which they exacted from their servants, and the benevolence they always exhibited towards each and all of them. On account of their goodness, the nobility of their conduct, and the affability of their conversation, they were not only beloved by their servants, but honored as models by the other families in Florence. In fact, from their house were banished plays and worldly pastimes; frequenting the sacraments on all festivals was commanded; uniting together to hear the word of God and visiting the churches were the usual employments of that devout family. It pleased God that from such pious parents a child should be born who would shed immortal lustre on her parentage; the splendor of whose lofty sanctity increased the glory of the fatherland; and who is now a star of primary magnitude in the illustrious Carmelite Order. Even during pregnancy her mother had reason to foresee what precious fruit she was to give to the world; because she never felt the labors and annoyances usually inseparable from that state. Thus peacefully progressing in it to perfection, on the 2d of April, 1566, she happily gave birth to the

seraphic virgin Mary Magdalen, who, the following day, was born again spiritually unto God by holy baptism in the Oratory of St. John the Baptist in Florence. The sponsors were Pandolfo Strozzi and Fiammetta Minorbetti, both Florentine nobles. The name of Catherine was given to the child, and perhaps not without a divine dispensation, because, in celestial favors and virtuous deeds, she was to be very much like St Catherine of Siena, towards whom she had a particular devotion all her life. Soon after the birth of the child, the mother began to notice the excellent character of Catherine, as during her infancy she caused none of the trouble which nearly all children give to those who nurse them, nay, her mother felt as much delight in doing this as if she were feeding an angel in the flesh. In all this the mother used to take great pleasure, and justly so; she was wont to speak of it to her relations and other persons, who have left formal testimony of it. As the little girl was happily developing, the nature of her character manifested itself in the best and rarest ways. One could easily guess, even at that early age, what she would be when adult. She had a most beautiful mind and a singular brilliancy of talent. This was not joined, though—as often happens—to a certain impulsiveness of nature that finds vent in insolence of manners, affected gestures, and the continuous motion of the body, but was rather coupled with such modesty and meekness as to make her appear serious and majestic, like a lady of advanced age. She was the admiration of all, and the girls of her condition, especially, who sometimes used to be with her, had great respect for her, and proposed her to themselves as an example. Within sight of her, they did not dare to be discomposed nor engage in puerile plays. The charm of her face attracted the love of all those who beheld her, as they could perceive in it the angelic purity of her heart. In conversation she was affable with all, ready to do the will of others whenever it would not be improper for her state. She repaid with fervent thankfulness all favors offered her, and was to all—even the servants—reverent, obedient, and humble. But the most wonderful thing at that early age was the inclination she manifested, almost from her cradle, for spiritual and divine things. Though incapable of understanding them, yet she used very much to enjoy hearing anybody talking about them; and, therefore, when her mother being in company with devout persons used to make spiritual discourses, she would not part from her a moment, as she was thirsty to drink at the fountain of the divine word. As this word fell not in vain into her soul, she began even then to find her delight in retirement and solitude, so that very often she withdrew all alone to some corner as if to meditate on the things of God. She had scarcely learned the rudiments of the Christian doctrine; in fact, she was barely able to read, when she found in an office of the Blessed Virgin, the Symbol of St Athanasius, an abridgment of the sublime mysteries of our faith, and especially of the Most Holy Trinity. Though she did not understand the words, except, as she afterwards said, by a certain spiritual instinct with which her affection was entranced, she read it all with great devotion, and, judging it to be an object of inestimable value, with the greatest joy she brought it to her mother to read. She was struck with admiration, and

Not without Divine dispensation, the name of Catherine was given her at Baptism (page 14).

could see that God even then prepared her tender child for understanding the most sublime mysteries. Not to do anything at random, but with care and reflection, would have been a very rare thing
for a child of her age , and yet this was truly her deportment in all, and
none of those inattentions so frequent to children happened her.
Whatever savored of virtue was in her superior to her age , to religious
and spiritual persons she would present herself with such questions on
the divine attributes that all who heard her were greatly astonished. . On
account of her fervent and assiduous care in learning the mysteries of
the Christian faith, and of her excellent disposition of heart and
intellect, she became so possessed of the knowledge of it that even in
her infancy she could teach others the most difficult doctrines found in
the catechism of our religion. She also manifested at that tender age
the beginning of her holy vocation to the religious state, because she
rejoiced exceedingly, in reciting her prayers, to veil and dress herself as
well as she could in the costume of a nun She was but seven years
old when her mind was opened to the celestial light , in her heart,
before the love of the world appeared for an instant, the love of
God had already kindled in an ineffable manner that immense flame,
which, destroying by degrees the earthly life, was one day to lead her
soul to heaven as a seraph She progressed rapidly in the exercise of
prayer ; she would give herself to it always with new pleasure ; and she
was truly looking for every opportunity quietly to withdraw to the feet
of Jesus. As if she had learned by experience that all worldly conversations were a great impediment to union with God, she would avoid,
as much as possible, talking with anybody on vain subjects Often,
when her people looked for her in the halls and chambers of the palace,
she was found behind some door or bedstead, or in the most remote parts
of the household, with a blissful mien, all rapt in God Moreover, she
knew so well how to guide herself in the practice of prayer that the
most select teacher of the spiritual life would not have known how to
better instruct her. In fact, as could be gathered from her discourses,
it was known afterwards that, in praying during her childhood, she had
practiced the most exact rules which have been suggested by teachers
of the spiritual life. She would remove from around herself whatever
might be the cause of wandering or distraction ; select the most obscure,
retired, and suitable corner of the house, determine the time, and prope
to herself the end of her prayer ; and in it, as she afterwards said, s
purely sought God in order to learn to fulfill His holy will I c
severance was not wanting to her prayer, as nothing contrary or pleasi
could divert her from the daily hours which she had proposed to herse.f
for praying Even in time of aridity of spirit, which is a very strong
temptation and hard to overcome, she was perfectly unalterable till the
completion of her holy purpose Prayer, therefore, had become her
most dear delight and her principal entertainment. Thus is God sometimes wont to plant in some of His chosen souls these precocious flowers,
as a prelude of the fruits of that extraordinary grace which, at the proper
time, He intends to grant them ; so that those who see these flowers
may divine the future, and understand afterwards that from Him alone
so great a virtue has proceeded.

Catherine having persevered in so excellent a disposition till the age of nine years, Father Andrea De-Rossi, a Jesuit, her mother's confessor, thought he would take special charge of her, and first gave her for meditation the Passion of Jesus Christ, appointing for her use the "*Meditations of Father Gasparo Loarte of the Society of Jesus*" In consequence of this direction, she applied herself so constantly to meditation on the passion of Jesus that she would long remain in it motionless,and almost ecstatic ; though sometimes during her prayer she was not able to avoid open and noisy places, she was not dispirited in consequence thereof, but, being all absorbed in God, she seemed to see or hear nothing   In order to remove in advance all causes of distraction, she selected the early morning to pray, so that at this tender age she arose daily from her bed, at a very early hour, and, for fear her mother might forbid her, she earnestly recommended herself to the servant-maids, who were the witnesses of her great diligence, begging them very affectionately not to reveal it to her mother or anybody else She was so constant and well ordered in the prosecution of this holy exercise that she would spend in it one hour every morning, and never omitted it all the time she lived in the world.   When, on account of her infirm health, she had to take iron, and, in consequence of this medicine, some exercise, as soon as she would return to her seclusion she would eagerly give herself to prayer.   In a word, a day did not pass without her employing three or four hours in prayer, and very often she would pass entire nights in meditation and prayer.   If, during them, nature demanded the comfort of sleep, she would take this at very short intervals, and on her knees, with her head leaning on the bed.   Rare example and lesson to those who give up or shorten their prayer for every light cause!

CHAPTER II.

HOW FROM HER INFANCY SHE MANIFESTED HATRED FOR HERSELF AND LOVE FOR HER NEIGHBOR.

HE passion of Jesus Christ kindled in Catherine, though yet of tender age, an ardent wish to suffer for her Saviour. It was a wonder to see so small a creature, delicate and gentle, a strong warrior against her flesh, showing so much resolution to subject it to suffering, which is so inimical and repugnant to nature. She regarded as just the sufferings of the senses; and, as children invent plays and amusements by the instinct of their age, so she would find new ways of afflicting her delicate limbs. Her ardent desire for suffering was not appeased by the discipline—a common instrument of penance—but, in addition, she would make crowns and girdles out of the thorny stems of orange trees, and, imitating the passion of Jesus, she would encircle with them her head and sides. Thus encircled and crowned, she would lie in bed at night, not sleeping, but bitterly suffering. She frowned at homage, and complained greatly of being too much caressed. She would beg the servant-maids, with tender love, not to warm her bed, even in the most rigid winter, from which she would sometimes secretly remove the mattress in order to sleep on the bare straw bed. Her mother noticing this, and, fearing that her daughter's delicate constitution might suffer too much, made her sleep in her own bed, in order to prevent her from practicing such penances. The temperance she practiced in taking nourishment was so exceedingly great, that it might better be called a rigorous and continuous abstinence. She never asked for anything, as children are wont to do, but was satisfied with whatever was given her; and she took so little of it that to her mother, who watched her, it seemed impossible that she could sustain herself. She knew so well how to mortify her appetite for food, which is generally a master over children, that at such a tender age, being invited during the day to take fruits or other things, she would not do it, except when compelled in obedience to her mother. If it had not been for the continual vigilance of others, in order to make her take the ordinary nourishment, she would have utterly extinguished, with her abstinences and fasts, that little vigor of health which nature granted her. When not yet a religious, as we will see, she was placed by her parents in the monastery of St Giovannino in Via S Gallo of Florence, where the Gerosolimitan Sisters are. Here having an opportunity, with holy liberty, to satisfy her love by abstinences, she was reduced to such weakness that she scarcely had sufficient strength to sew. Thus the holy child, with voluntary sufferings, trained herself to combat the devil, hating her own flesh, according to the Gospel teaching. Being asked in her mature age why in her childhood she had treated her body so severely, she answered that she did it in order to render herself better able to pray, as he who hates not himself cannot remain united with God, and cannot be the disciple of Jesus Christ. Thus did she speak, because she was enlightened by celestial light. And that this was the truth, is proved by the charity which she felt very intensely for her neighbor She looked upon the poverty and miseries of others as her own She melted with compassion, and felt moved with sorrow, when she could not assist the poor, whom she regarded as dear to her Jesus, and she looked upon them with as great a love as if they had come out with her from her mother's womb. She reflected, even then, that the charity which is practiced with some sacrifice of necessary things, is dearer to God ; hence the breakfast and the afternoon luncheon which her mother gave her, as a child, she, with great joy, would distribute to the poor, and particularly to the poor prisoners, when, on her way to school, she passed in front of the prisons. Therefore, her parents, seeing how she delighted in works of mercy, when poor people came to the door, gave them the alms through her hands. Her charity did not stop at the visible object of bodily miseries ; but, with greater compassion, penetrating to the spirit, so great was the zeal she felt for the souls of others that she would inconsolably weep for the sins she saw committed, and for those in particular which offended the charity of her neighbor. In fact, having once heard words of grave offense to a neighbor, she passed the whole night without taking rest, buried in grief and tears She wished so ardently to benefit souls, that at such a childish age her greatest delight was to teach children the *Pater Noster*, the *Ave Maria*, and the *Credo*, with the rudiments of our faith. Whilst other children were highly pleased to go from the cities to the villas for sport, she also was delighted, but from a higher motive, that is, because she went there to find scope to satisfy her charity by giving religious instruction to the children of the peasants. This was her entertainment at the villas ; and on feast-days she would gather the little girls of her age, not to play together, but to teach them Christian doctrine. If they were poor, too, she would also practice maternal charity, and assist them, with her mother's permission, in the necessities of life—now with food, now with clothing. She was so much attached to these works of charity, that when she had to return to the city she felt so sorry that she could not be consoled Her parents noticed this, and having compassion for so holy an affliction, and wishing to satisfy such pious sentiments, they brought to Florence a little daughter of one of their farmers, called Giovanna. They raised this child in their own palace in company with Catherine, who continued, to her great delight, to give her instructions in the Christian faith.   As true love is communicative and operative, and such was that of Catherine, not satisfied with instilling in her neighbors that good which perfects the intellect, but desiring also to promote that which perfects the will, she tried to draw not only Giovanna, but also the other servant-maids of the house, to pray with her.   To induce them to do it, she had no regard for her nobility, nor the delicacy of her constitution, nor for her youthful age, nor the weakness of her body ; but, made strong and vigorous by the zeal she felt for the good of souls, she would undertake to do house-work with them, help to sweep the rooms, to make the beds, and provide the needs of the house, so that the sooner they were free from these occupations the sooner they might with her employ the remaining time in prayer.   Thus God united to her charity manifest signs of that great humility which she was to practice.

CHAPTER III.

OF HER DEVOTION TOWARDS THE BLESSED SACRAMENT, AND OF
HER FIRST COMMUNION.

IN the heart of Catherine, inflamed with divine love, God infused so high an esteem of the Sacrament of the Altar, that, before being humanly invited to it, she longed with holy impatience to be admitted to feed upon the Bread of angels. Her age prevented her from receiving in reality her Jesus in the Sacrament; but, with the most intense desire and most ardent love, she rejoiced in the hope of one day obtaining such a grace, and then, as she could do nothing else, she took pleasure in seeing others receive the most sacred Eucharist. She, therefore, almost importuned her mother to take her, not only on festivals of obligation, but also on those days which, without obligation, are solemnized by the piety of the faithful. It is hard to say with how much devotion, on her knees, she would fix her eyes for the whole of the morning on those persons who received Holy Communion; and, almost carried away by holy envy, she would sometimes complain because so great a gift of Heaven was not granted her. On her mother's returning home from Holy Communion, Catherine, as a butterfly in love with the light of the heavenly Spouse, would not separate herself from her, but, scenting with the soul the suavity and spiritual fragrance of Jesus in the Sacrament, who feeds among the lilies (*pascitur inter lilia*), she would draw nearer than usual to her and would not part. When questioned by her mother, she would answer: "Because you smell of Jesus."

To her intense love for this most divine Sacrament was joined a supreme reverence, with which she honored the same with unspeakable humility. One feast-day morning she was late, and, the weather being rainy and the streets muddy, her parents requested her to take breakfast before going to Mass and then to go in a carriage; but when she heard it she burst into bitter weeping, saying it did not behoove her to go to see Jesus in such a manner. In order to quiet her, it was necessary to let her go to the church fasting and on foot. She would beg her spiritual director and her mother with importunity and ardent desire to grant her the consolation of being admitted to the Holy Communion; hence the director, Father Andrea De-Rossi, knowing that her desire emanated from a knowledge and affection superior to her age (ten years), promised to satisfy her on the feast of the Annunciation of the Blessed Virgin. With how much and with what heavenly joy Catherine received this promise, no one whose heart is not as thirsty for Jesus as hers was can imagine.   In all the days which preceded the great solemnity she thought of nothing but the Blessed Sacrament; she never tired speaking of it. She was always in prayer; she was always practicing penance, chastising herself, an innocent virgin, with fasts.   All the years of her life might be called years of innocence, of piety, and a continual preparation for Holy Communion.   Finally, the happy day for Catherine burst forth— the day longed for by her fervent heart, on which, for the first time, at the age of ten years, she received the most holy Sacrament in the Church of St. Giovannino, then belonging to the Fathers of the Society of Jesus.   God not permitting Himself to be surpassed in love by His creature, the greater the wish and devout preparation of this innocent soul, the greater, no doubt, was the consolation with which He filled her soul in Holy Communion, and such was the sweetness she experienced in that sacramental union with God that she used to say she never felt a greater in her lifetime.   Having tasted and felt how sweet and delicious her Lord in this Sacrament was, she became inflamed with a parching thirst often to approach that prodigious fountain of grace, and therefore her spiritual father, seeing in her such great virtue and knowledge superior to her age, properly decided to satisfy her every eight days. God having granted her holy wish, she would await the whole week, with holy sighs and tears of tender love, the happy day for her soul; and every day—nay, every hour—seemed to her a very long time to pass in order to arrive at the moment of her spiritual consolation.   Such was her spiritual delight, her heart being filled by Holy Communion with so many gifts of celestial comfort, she felt as though melting with love, and, this holy fervor showing in her exterior appearance, she became a source of wonder and edification to all those who beheld her so collected and devout.

CHAPTER IV.

SHE MAKES A VOW OF VIRGINITY AND EXPERIENCES AN EXCESS
OF DIVINE LOVE.

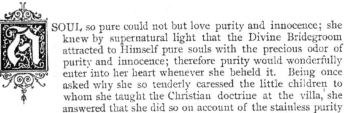 SOUL so pure could not but love purity and innocence; she knew by supernatural light that the Divine Bridegroom attracted to Himself pure souls with the precious odor of purity and innocence; therefore purity would wonderfully enter into her heart whenever she beheld it. Being once asked why she so tenderly caressed the little children to whom she taught the Christian doctrine at the villa, she answered that she did so on account of the stainless purity she perceived in them ; as, not having yet committed sin, they had not stained the white robe of baptismal innocence, and because they represented the Child Jesus of that age. From the same love of purity she ardently desired the monastic state, and even from her childhood she had a resolute and constant will to make it her choice. Enlightened by celestial light and drawn by the high idea she had of holy purity, she thought the offering of perpetual virginity a gift she ought to make to God. On Holy Thursday of the year of our salvation 1576, the tenth of her age (wonderful thing!), meditating on the infinite love with which the Eternal Father loved the world, in giving to it His only-begotten Son, who left Himself, His body and blood, His soul and Divinity, as a food for us miserable mortals, inflamed with the desire of responding with gratitude to so great a love, she thought of making to God the worthiest return possible for her to make. After receiving Holy Communion, the same day, full of divine love, she consecrated her virginity to God by a perpetual vow, and in the same act she plighted her faith and word to her beloved and loving Jesus, that she would have no other spouse but Him. Jesus accepted the offer, and in token of it placed on her finger a most precious ring, which she then neither saw nor felt, but afterwards it was shown her by her Divine Spouse.

If the heart of this tender virgin was ever burning with love for Jesus, in this act she felt such flames of it that, unable to contain them within her breast, she was soon compelled to manifest them exteriorly, and this happened on the feast of St. Andrew the Apostle, whilst she was at the villa with her mother. Her spirit being overcome by an excess of divine love, she felt within such strong ardor and faintness that she

Though only a little girl as yet, she questions her mother and the
Religious concerning the mysteries of our faith (page 15).

was excited almost to frenzy, could find no place to rest, could not speak a word, and seemed almost overwhelmed on all sides. Her mother, believing her to be afflicted with some bodily ailment, did not omit to apply convenient remedies, but human skill was not and could not be of any benefit to her; and well did the sufferer know it; but she said nothing of it to her mother, both through an exercise of humility and for greater correspondence to the love of her Spouse, who was pleased to relieve her on the following day, when her body, yet tender, could not have endured any more. Yet God willed, for a useful manifestation of the truth, that she once would declare the supernatural cause of this. This was done in a case similar to it, which happened her several years later, when she was already clothed in the habit of a Religious, and, being rapt unto ecstasy, she spoke these precious words: "O Love, what Thou makest me feel now is like unto what Thou didst communicate to me on the feast of him who so loved the cross,[1] when I was not yet dedicated to Thee in the sacred Religion,[2] and my mother thought it was bodily sickness." Which being made known to the mother, and she comparing one case with the other, testified to Sister Vangelista del Giocondo and other nuns, that what had happened her daughter at the villa was from a supernatural cause. If she had not declared it before then with such positive certainty, she was none the less convinced of it, since God was not slow in offering to her mind other indications by which to repute her daughter as privileged by Heaven.

---

[1] St. Andrew.

[2] "Religion" here, as in many other places in this book, is used in the sense of "Religious Order."—*Note of the Translator.*

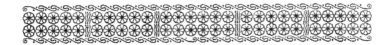

CHAPTER V.

PLACED IN THE MONASTERY OF ST. GIOVANNINO OF THE KNIGHTS
OF MALTA, SHE GIVES EDIFICATION TO ALL THOSE NUNS.

IT was the year 1580, when the most serene Grand Duke of Tuscany, Francis de Medici I, chose as commissary of the city of Cortona, Camillo De-Pazzi, the father of Catherine. It was customary to put in such an office a Florentine noble whose wisdom would equal the splendor of his birth, that he might secure loyal veneration from the people. And the gifts and virtues of Camillo were to amply correspond to the expectation entertained of him. Therefore, having to go there and remain for the course of a year, he resolved to take his family with him, Catherine excepted, whom, not without a heavenly disposition, he entrusted to the care of Sister Selvaggia Morelli, her cousin, a nun held in high esteem in the monastery of St. Giovannino of the Knights of Malta. We will not say how Catherine rejoiced at such a determination on her father's part, whilst, on account of her great care in removing everything that might distract her from her union with God, she certainly saw in it the greatest convenience to attend, while in the monastery, to prayer and other devout exercises. The nuns also rejoiced in their turn, and, on account of the high opinion of the virtue in which they heard she was generally held, they eagerly wished to enjoy the experience of it. Our Catherine then entered the monastery, and her first thought was to obtain permission to freely receive the sacred Bread of angels on all feasts of obligation. This she did while there, with unalterable frequency and always with lively devotion. Two affections were enkindled in her heart by this exercise—one of charity, the other of humility; by charity, she fervently wished that all souls would be partakers of the blessings she found and enjoyed in the sacramental union with God; and by humility, in order not to be singular (as in that monastery such frequenting of the sacraments was unusual), she procured and proceeded with such pious exhortations and examples that some nuns at first, and then all, followed her habit constantly.

The eye of her mother (who, being too jealous of her temporal good, watched her assiduously) not being on her, though in the monastery somebody was always at her side and she also had more opportunity to converse than at the parental house, she cared for nothing but what could promote the perfection of her spirit. Therefore, letting loose the rein of her desire to pray continually, she became so absorbed in this holy exercise that, besides the regular times, during which she often retired to the choir, she would employ three hours regularly every day in it—two in the morning and one in the evening, so that, between these and the *interrupted* times, the nuns saw that most of the day was spent by her in mental prayer. But her fervid spirit did not feel sufficiently satisfied, and therefore even during the night she often left her bed and prostrated herself before God in prayer. On account of her pressing requests to her cousin and teacher, she was often permitted to go at night to the choir for Matins with the other nuns, and when refused she arose at the same hour, and, hidden in her room, she knelt at the foot of the bed and prayed till the morning bell called all to hear the Holy Mass. Her meditations were in a special manner on the current gospels. She took (as those nuns testified), on Saturday evening, the gospel for the following Sunday, and, extracting some points from it, made her meditations on them during the following week. The same nuns also left testimony to the effect that they saw her several times so absorbed in meditation that she seemed to them an angel of paradise. They saw her as if alienated from her senses, her face red as a rose, with her eyes as resplendent as luminous stars; and especially her remaining thus, firm and fixed like a statue for whole hours on her knees, without moving her eyes, caused them great surprise. Whilst they were in the choir reciting the Divine Office, such was her modesty and composure that the nuns, some in wonder, others with delight, and many out of the devotion it would cause them to see her, could not take their eyes away from her.

To make herself even better able to perform this holy exercise of prayer, profiting here also by the great advantage the monastery offered her, as she doubled her prayers, so she also did her penances. Besides taking short rest, on account of the long time employed in meditating, she frequently slept on the bare straw bed, which, though she tried to hide it from her, was often noticed by her guardian. Zealous in her abstinence, Catherine multiplied her fasts and disciplines so that she was reduced to a state of bad health, and yet she was so much opposed to any bodily comfort that she was never sad, except when by the direction of her teacher she was compelled to take something more than the ordinary nourishment.

As in the world she had given edification to many by her virtues, so also in the monastery she was, by the same, a source of great edification to the Religious, who particularly, besides the other things aforesaid, gave testimony of the retirement, modesty, charity, obedience, and humility which they noticed in her. In fact, as they relate, she was never found with the other girls that were kept there or with the younger members of the monastery for recreations and pastimes, but she was only seen with the others in the choir, in places of devotion, or near the sick, and sometimes with some whose conversation seemed to her more spiritual, or with those whom she knew to be better disposed to become more retired and devout. She spoke of spiritual things only, and she studied always to excite the nuns to the religious observance, and all the persons in the monastery to the frequenting of the sacraments. She was never heard to utter a word of vanity, of levity, or idleness, she was never seen excited or restless, but always benign, serious, and meek. Not a hint of murmuring or lamentation came from her lips, and though, on account of her retired and singular mode of living, particularly her frequenting the sacraments, which, at first, was not approved by some, she sometimes encountered opposition, yet she took nothing in evil part, but always covered the faults of others, and with unalterable firmness she advanced in her devout exercises. In visiting the sick of the monastery she would manifest toward them the greatest affection, exhort them with sweet and charitable words, read spiritual books to them, encourage them to patience and other virtues, and administer to them all those charitable offices which were permitted and suitable for her; and thus she occupied her recreation time. Hence, any one looking for Catherine, not finding her in her cell or in the choir, would go straight to the bedside of the sick, sure to find her there   As for the obedience she practiced in this monastery, her teacher asserted, with formal testimony, that Catherine never showed any repugnance to do anything that would be commanded her, but she did everything with promptness and rectitude   Not only to her teacher, but also to all the other nuns, she showed great veneration and sincere obedience   On account of her great love of charity and humility, she desired to be employed in the lowest and most menial occupations of the monastery; hence, she seemed to feel happy when she was permitted to do some servile work. Because of the low esteem in which she held herself, and the respect she had for the religious state, she considered herself unworthy of living with the nuns , and sometimes she excused her keeping at a distance by saying to them   " You are the brides of Jesus, by your religious profession , but I am not, and therefore I am not worthy to stay with you "

The nuns, seeing these rare qualities and singular virtues, conceived the thought that she was not an ordinary creature, but another St. Gertrude or St Catherine of Siena, as they asserted that they had never known a girl endowed with so much goodness ; therefore, such was their respect for her, that some did not dare to converse with her, others never had enough of seeing and talking with her, and all very much desired that she would become a nun in their monastery   This desire was so ardent that, knowing her to be opposed to it, because she was inclined to choose a more severe rule, they declared themselves ready to allow her to lead them to that observance and mode of life which would better please her ; but, humble as she was, she considered herself wholly inadequate for such an undertaking, and, prudently, would not rest assured of the uncertain success of such promises. Therefore, her parents, having returned from Cortona, brought her back again to the ancestral residence, after fifteen months' stay in the above-named monastery. The good nuns were exceedingly disconsolate on account of the departure of a soul so chosen and favored of God, and lamented because Heaven had not permitted them to enjoy her as their sister ; but, at the same time, they remained particularly edified by the example of her piety and holy conversation, and very much pleased at having had among them, during that time, a youthful virgin who, in the first dawn of her life, so to say, gave promise of a noonday of sublime sanctity.

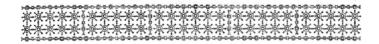

CHAPTER VI.

SHE DESIRES TO RECEIVE THE RELIGIOUS HABIT, AND OVERCOMES
THE DIFFICULTIES WITH WHICH SHE MEETS. SHE CHOOSES THE
MONASTERY, ENTERS IT ON TRIAL, AND, GIVING PROOF OF
HER VIRTUES, IS RECEIVED THEREIN TO BECOME A NUN.

HE holy impatience of this chosen bride of the Lord would not permit her to refrain long from stealing away from the world, to live permanently in the religious cloister, united to her Divine Spouse. Even from her infancy, God had inspired her with the desire to part from the world by becoming a Religious ; though she could not then understand the difference between living in the world and in the monastery. Corresponding faithfully to this inspiration by the very devout life which we have thus far described, she had deserved that God would show her, with a brighter light, the value of religious life, and, with greater impulses to her heart, excite her to make up her mind to embrace it. Hence, in the past she had prudently concealed this desire under a careful silence, as a thing that could not be accomplished at so tender an age, speaking of it only to her spiritual father, to whom she made everything clear. Now, however, she felt ready to execute the Divine will, which corresponded so closely to her own, and she looked for an opportune moment in which to speak of her desire to her parents. Though they could not but have taken notice of such a disposition in their child, yet, she being their only daughter, and being charmed by her character, her features, and her noble manners, they had absolutely made up their minds to have her married. Without anything else, without even asking her once about it, they suggested now one party and now another, as he seemed to suit better the virtues of their daughter and the nobility and wealth of the family. In the meantime, to cure her of the weakness caused by the harshness of her penances and the austerity of her fastings, they conducted her to the villa, where her health was restored by the change of air, restorative medicines, and nutritious food. Her parents, well pleased at it, returned with her to Florence, and renewed their endeavors towards hastening a convenient occasion for the proposed marriage. The mother of the marchioness, dexterously and without showing her the motive, stimulated her, from time to time, to exquisiteness, refinement, and sprightliness, both in her manners and in her dress, only giving as reasons therefor, civility, honor, family, and the like, which, nevertheless, savored of the world. She, though unwillingly, out of respect and obedience to her mother, would, to some extent, concur in these things But God wanted her for a different purpose, and wanted her soon. Hence, Catherine was no longer capable of resisting the fire of Divine love, which consumed her with the desire of becoming a nun. She was now sixteen, and, as she noticed a deep silence on her parents' part, she became prudently suspicious lest they would not allow her to become a nun, as she was passing the age when, according to custom, girls are wont to consecrate themselves to God Therefore she opened her heart to her spiritual director, and felt, in consequence of his approval, more certain of the will of God in this, her insuperable tendency.

Not long afterwards she went to her father and humbly manifested to him her deliberate intention of becoming a nun, and begged him, as well as she could, to be pleased with it—nay, to help her to carry it out. Her father, although a good Christian, yet being great according to the world and penetrated by the maxims of high society, could not sufficiently appreciate those greater joys the soul and heart of his daughter were seeking after He consequently looked no further than to the high standing of his family, and almost got angry at the determination announced to him by Catherine. He told her abruptly that he was far from seconding her, at which she, finding herself in danger either of disobeying her father or becoming unworthy of God, replied with great courage, but not without dutiful respect, that she would rather let her head be cut off than give up her idea of becoming a nun. Her father, seeing such determination, did not dare to repeat his refusal, but sent Catherine to her mother, who, knowing her disposition better and having more intercourse with her, he thought, would perhaps dissuade her, or at least obtain some delay which might serve to do away altogether with her fixed purpose. But everything was useless, as Catherine, being assured of God's will in it, had already put away every human affection and consideration. She rightly perceived that her mother's tenderness would be a greater obstacle to her than her father's opposition, hence she tried with all strength to overcome it, making use of these two means· First, she had recourse to prayer, fervently begging of the Lord to be pleased to take from her mother's heart so much love for her, or diminish it so that it would not be an impediment to the entire fulfillment of the heavenly decrees concerning her, especially in the selecting of her state of life; and, after this, she began to uproot this maternal love, practicing every art, without failing in the honor and respect due her, so that her mother might detach her affection from her. She not only failed to please her in ornamenting and dressing herself as her mother wished, but she avoided also, as much as she could, conversing with her When she was obliged to be in society, she did not deport herself with her previous courtesy and cheerfulness, but with studied rusticity of manner and always appeared afflicted and melancholy. Her mother did not yet understand from whence so great a change proceeded, and therefore did everything to make her affable and pleasant as before. She caressed her with increased tenderness and showed herself affectionate to her, she conversed on spiritual subjects according to her tastes, questioned her about her meditations, and used all possible means to make her again cheerful and content. Catherine resisted with virtuous indifference all these new incitements of the maternal love, which in effect tended to imprison her more safely in the world; for which, as she afterwards confessed to her nuns, she suffered doubly, both because this proceeding was contrary to her inclination and the nature of her heart, and because, loving her mother tenderly, she regretted very much having to grieve her in this manner—hence she lived in a state of permanent combat with herself. She also feared that some other sudden storm might intervene to oppose her firm purpose of consecrating herself to God in the monastery. Her delicate health again succumbed, because of so great and so many distresses. But the painful experiment God wanted His beloved servant to undergo, before introducing her into the garden of consolation, was near its end In fact, her mother, having found out the cause of the unusual behavior of Catherine and her sufferings, conferred about it with the same spiritual father, and received from him the confirmation of the truth She became solicitous of affording her daughter the most valid comfort. She soon called her to herself, and when she modestly approached, ignorant of the cause for which her mother summoned her, she did not dare to raise her eyes from the ground, always fearing more trouble to her greatly afflicted soul The marchioness did not remain sitting as usual; but, as soon as her daughter approached her, she arose to embrace her, and, in a rather subdued tone, assured her that the idea of giving her in marriage was altogether gone from her mind and that of her father. Nay, they were determined fully to second her desire of becoming a nun If she would think about the choice of the monastery, they would please her in everything. She would thus become guarantrix for her husband's will, as, since he had entrusted this affair to her, she felt sure no opposition would come from him. It is not easy to imagine how pleased Catherine was at this news, and how warmly she thanked God in her heart for it. In all her actions she manifested the contentment of her spirit. She uttered a few words of gratitude in answer to her mother, but, being overcome by interior delight, she was unable to express her joy, and, having taken leave, she retired to a dark chamber, where, with sighs and tears of tenderness, she gave way somewhat to the great joy by which she felt herself overwhelmed Then, taking a respite, she showed herself to the family all courteous and pleasant. At the same time, she seriously applied herself to making the choice of the monastery that would be most convenient for her; and as neither by the coaxings of her parents, nor the attachments of the world, nor human regrets, had she been shaken or stopped in her holy resolution, so, in this choice, she would only look to Heaven for light. She had recourse to prayer, the usual manner of the Saints in holding converse with God; she doubled her spiritual exercises, sure means of securing the alliance of Heaven, in order to know the place in which God wanted her heart to serve Him Such being her tendency, and the better to assure herself of the Divine will, she resolved to enter a monastery where community life would be

observed in retirement and complete religious observance. She wished
to be a nun , but of facts and works ; for though yet in the world, she
well understood of how great importance for all in a religious order
these requisites are. Looking at all the monasteries then existing in
Florence, and noting in each the reasons for and against, and very studi-
ously looking for the best, her thoughts rested on three of them.
Speaking of it to her spiritual father, she mentioned them to him with
her reasons. One was the monastery of the Crocetta ; another, of St.
Clara ; and the third, of Santa Maria degli Angeli   In the first, under the
patronage of the glorious St. Dominic, the nuns never see, and are never
seen by, the seculars ; in the second, under the rule of St. Francis, they
were living in the greatest poverty and asperity of penances ; and in
the last one particular attention was paid to interior perfection, and
they received Holy Communion daily—a rare thing in those times.   Her
desires were captivated by every one of these holy places. She also
greatly desired to withdraw bodily from the world as much as possible,
as she was entirely detached therefrom in her soul , and, therefore, she
wished very much never to see, nor to be seen by, the world.   To live
a despised and abject life, and to suf for God's love, was a very strong
craving of her heart, which would have wished to suffer everything
for the sake of her crucified Spouse, Her hunger for the eucharistic
food attracted her with inexpressible force, because by means of it she
could foster, with her Divine Spouse, the purity of the soul, and with
paradisiacal husbandry adorn it with various flowers of religious perfection.   Thus were the affections of Catherine divided, and continuing
to present the reasons for each to her spiritual director, it seemed as if
all the religious requirements she loved and admired in the other two
were united and combined in the monastery of St. Maria degli Angeli;
hence, without any further delay, moved also by a ray of heavenly light,
she resolved to consecrate herself entirely to God in the last named.
The community life which was practiced in very rigorous perfection,
obliging the members to live in true religious poverty and subjection,
the retirement from the gratings and the few visits from seculars ; the
assiduous application of mind to celestial things, a primary characteristic
of the Carmelite Order ; the frequenting of the Most Holy Sacrament,
by which those holy souls became adorned with singular perfections,
rendered the above monastery—degli Angeli—a model for virgins dedicated to the Lord God
    Having told her parents of the choice of the monastery, they
applied themselves to the obtaining of due approbation from the
ordinary, and this obtained, and having prepared everything else for
the purpose, they took her directly to Santa Maria degli Angeli, in
Borgo San Frediano, in order that she might there make her first trial
for the space of ten days, according to the practice and the order of the
superiors   Being introduced there, she was welcomed with great
pleasure by the nuns.   According to their rules, she was given in charge
of those who dealt with the strangers—that is, those whose office it was
to guard and direct the seculars who entered on trial.   They, watching
very closely the qualities, the inclinations, the words, and the deportment of Catherine, soon wondered at the perfections with which she

Being rapt in ecstasy at a very tender age, she is discovered by
her parents (page 15).

was enriched, and esteemed hers to be more than ordinary goodness. From the modesty of her discourse, the gravity of her behavior, the humility and purity of her bearing, the respect and submission she manifested for all, they were able to bear the best testimony to the confessor and the rest of the nuns that she was not only worthy and deserving of their habit, but they should very much wish and yearn for the acquisition of a girl of such noble and distinct prerogatives of blood, education, and most perfect virtues.   They related having observed in her in a very special manner the excessive desire to become a Religious, and her stability and assiduous frequency at prayer.   Some remarked that while praying she would not move in the least, and that from such immobility it was easy to perceive how highly fixed in God her soul was, and how she was already wonderfully habituated to it.   In the monastery, as under the paternal roof, she would arise early in the morning and immediately go to the choir, to remain there for one hour in serious meditation, and throughout the day, whenever possible, she would very gladly return to the same exercise.   From her constancy in prayer, and from the light she manifested about the spiritual life, and from her esteem for the religious exercises, the mother—Sister Vangelista del Giocondo—was induced to make an experiment on the spirit of Catherine, who, although a girl of only sixteen years, an age when nature generally shows more liveliness, yet seemed so advanced in perfection as to be a woman in years.   To ascertain whether this assiduity at prayer proceeded from her own will, or was joined to some human complacency or sensible delight, she told her that if she would receive the habit of a nun she could not recite the prayers she did when secular, and that she would be bound to conform with the others to the practices of the community.   To which she promptly replied " Mother, this does not trouble me in the least, because I know that all things done in obedience to religion are prayers "   The venerable mother had no reply to make, and was sufficiently informed of how enlightened in the ways of God this good child was, and how detached from her own will, and, therefore, most suitable for religion.   Catherine gave also a solemn proof of her mortification, and the mastership she held over her senses and her whole self in this regard.   One day, finding herself with the other nuns in the workhall, some things suddenly fell, making so great a noise that all the nuns were greatly frightened, she alone did not even raise her head or turn her eyes to see what had happened, thus restraining in an exemplary manner the curiosity of apprehension which generally, in such cases, possesses every person, especially if a woman and inexperienced on account of her youthful age.   Therefore, because of all these exterior qualities, which were a sure earnest of her sublime interior perfection, the nuns, by unanimous consent, not only judged her worthy of their order, but eagerly wished for her, and regarded it as a most singular favor of Heaven to have her among them   Therefore, all hailed her with great joy as their sister in Jesus Christ, who would receive the veil in their monastery, at the time they would appoint, with the permission of their superiors

In these few days Catherine observed diligently the orders and the mode of life of the monastery, read the rules and the constitution, and accurately took notice of how they were obeyed. She was so well satisfied and pleased with everything that she could not wish for anything more; and having conceived so high an opinion of the nuns that she reputed herself unworthy to live with them, she said, through her humility, that she would have been pleased to be the lowest menial in the monastery. The nuns therefore longing for her, and she being highly pleased with their goodness and exactitude in obeying the rules, she would have become a nun at once, but by the disposition of her parents and the prudent custom of the monastery she returned for a short time to her father's palace.

CHAPTER VII.

HOW SHE DESPISED BODILY ORNAMENTS AND THE VANITIES
OF THE WORLD.

ATHERINE DE—PAZZI was pointed out by mothers of families as a model to their daughters, when they were carried away and hallucinated by vanity, whilst, through her simple way of dressing, ornaments of a higher value were shining out. Virtue puts on no other dress than that of modesty and simplicity, because it has no need of borrowed lustre. In those who desire to follow Jesus Christ the wish to ornament the person cannot exist. Dress was introduced as a shield from the severity of the seasons and as a help to modesty. To depart from this principle, immovably based on natural rectitude, is to fall into illusion and hypocrisy; and it is for this reason that the grand world of to-day appears to be and is in truth a theatre of falsehoods. Those polishings in the habiliment, especially in the female sex; those insatiable yearnings for the fashions, for the newest and best style; those affected tendernesses and wantonnesses in words and actions, are but the signs of a deceitful and foolish spirit. The audacity with which some cover themselves with a seducing display, even in the church, which is the asylum of innocence and piety, where everything inspires compunction and reminds us of the solemn promises made at our baptism—this is, to say the least, an indication of corruption, unless we call it an indication of a faith nearly extinguished. Hence, before leaving the secular life of Catherine, let noble maids especially consider for a while how she acted in it, and let them not bring forth, as a pretext for not imitating her, new reasons of social convenience; because a Christian's principles admit of no exception of person and submit not to the whimsical changes of the world.

Catherine, then, imbued with the supreme truth, even from her childhood always greatly abhorred everything that savored of worldly ornament—always refused to adorn herself with jewels, rich apparel, embellishment of face, and affected hair-dressing; and in nothing was she so restive in obeying her mother as in fixing her hair and dressing as became her. She loved a modest and simple appearance, would not have silk dresses, nor too showy ones. She put on costumes of inferior quality, without any ornament and always appeared as a poor working girl rather than a rich gentlewoman. Neither did she care to go abroad to festivals, or tournaments, or other shows of the world; nay, she so wearied of them that, although her residence was at the corner called De-Pazzi, where the horse-races were held, and though it was at these times filled with gentlewomen who wished to see them, she knew so well how to mortify herself that during all the time she was a secular she never once looked out of the window on such a noisy occasion—a thing truly worthy of admiration in a girl. The abuse of the world in adorning the new brides of Jesus Christ like earthly brides with excessive artifices, and taking them, as to a scene of pomp, to promenades, vain entertainments, theatres, and other worldly allurements was despised by Catherine, who used to say she could not understand how girls could have a desire to be religious and brides of Jesus, and yet enjoy seeing themselves and being seen vainly ornamented. So, when her mother, soon after taking her from the monastery of St Giovannino de' Cavalieri, made her a white silk dress, even though it was simple in style and without any gold or silver, she had great difficulty in persuading Catherine to put it on. All the day on which, out of obedience to her mother, she wore it, she wept copiously On being asked the reason, she answered. "Because it becomes not a girl who dedicates herself to God, to dress so as to become conspicuous in the eyes of His creatures." And she would add no other ornament to it afterwards. If she condescended to keep that silk dress, it was because of its simplicity of workmanship, and because in its whiteness it offered her the symbol of holy purity. From this fact originated the custom of those girls expecting to receive the habit in her order, who, in the interval when they remain in the world before entering the cloister, absolutely refuse vain ornaments, dressing in a modest manner, and appear, the day they exchange the world's goods for the blessed poverty of Religion, before the priest in a white dress similar to that which was presented to their holy mother when she received the habit of the Carmelite Religious Neither did she distract herself in secular visits nor feed on worldly sceneries before she entered the sacred enclosure, but only visited religious places and devout persons, to whose prayers she earnestly recommended herself And curiosity about the furnishings, or anxiety about those things which of necessity she had to bring along, did not distract her. She left the care of all this to her mother, without even selecting or seeing anything, her thought and her affection being solely occupied in hastening her withdrawal from the world, wholly to unite herself to her Spouse Jesus Let this be an example also to those girls who, in becoming nuns, though they have a real vocation for the life, show themselves anxious to have an abundant and suitable equipment, either for their own pleasure or lest they appear more humble than others in Religion.

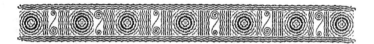

CHAPTER VIII.

HOW SHE ENTERED THE MONASTERY PERMANENTLY, AND WITH
WHAT PREPARATION AND DEVOTION SHE THERE
RECEIVED THE HABIT OF A NUN.

ON the Saturday previous to the First Sunday in Advent, in the year 1582, which was the first day of December, Catherine bade that long-wished-for adieu to the world and entered, rejoicing, the centre of her rest, her paradise on earth—the monastery of St. Maria degli Angeli, of the Sacred Order of the Carmel, in Borgo San Frediano, which was afterwards transferred, as it exists to-day, to the Borgo di Pinti.[1] Before leaving her father's house, she knelt at her parents' feet, asking forgiveness of them for anything displeasing to them she might have done during the whole of her tender life, and earnestly begged that they would impart to her their parental blessing. With tears of true love, she was blessed—not forgiven, though, for she had never been guilty of any fault. She also took leave of her other relations and some persons who, on account of particular friendship, frequently visited the house, and, finally, of all the servants of the house, speaking to everyone words of respect, of humility, of prayer. In this last separation the strength of grace and divine love became more manifest in her. Amidst the tears of her parents and the manifestations of sorrow from her relations and the servants, Catherine bore herself with such fortitude of spirit and firmness of countenance, that she seemed not to feel it. This could not have been the case with that heart so gentle and loving, if the strength of divine charity had not wholly mastered her.

Thus having secured victory over all earthly affections, she was received by the nuns at this second and final entrance with those sentiments with which they were inspired by the general opinion they entertained of her and the trial they had made of her singular virtues during the few days of her first stay with them. For some reason, not unusual in such cases, she did not take the religious habit until the following January. In the meantime, God desired from her another proof of her contempt for the vanities of the world. Whilst she, with all the affection and pleasure of her heart, was preparing to be received into the Order,

---

[1] Public improvements have since made necessary its removal to the Piazza Savonarola, where a new monastery has been built.

she had to endure the temptation of vainglory Her parents, as good
Christians, and in order not to oppose the divine will, so clearly manifested, submitted to the sacrifice, most painful to their hearts, of consecrating their only daughter forever to God.   They had entertained such
delightful hopes of seeing her married into one of the most prominent
families and one day hearing her praised as a model among the mothers
of families and the most noble matrons.   Ordinarily, the perfection of
the secular, especially if persons of wealth, does not go beyond the letter
of the divine precepts.   The spirit which animates the word is not penetrated by them.   The evangelical counsels are a superfluity for them.
Yet, would to God that all would fulfill to the letter what is prescribed
by the divine precepts!
     Catherine's parents still cherished an ardent love for her, hence her
absence caused them great pain; and, in some measure to alleviate their
grief, they resolved to have her portrait at home   The prioress of the
monastery, on being asked, did not oppose a wish so natural to the
hearts of a father and mother, so that, appointing the day, the famous
painter, Santi di Tito, repaired to the monastery in order to paint Catherine's portrait   When she heard this, as she was penetrated deeply by
the spirit of perfection, she cried exceedingly, and would in no way
submit to it.   Being asked the reason for such a firm refusal, she replied
"I came out of the world to return to it no more, and not to be seen in
these dresses again."   It would have been impossible to obtain her consent had not the orders of the superioress and her father confessor
obliged her to give it   Through obedience alone, then, she submitted
to it.   During the time that Santi di Tito, with his colors, was bringing
her back to the midst of the world, she was constantly weeping and
lamenting with these words of humility. "Is it possible that of a creature
so vile as I am, and of a handful of dust, a remembrance will remain in
the world?" This occurrence, however, did not distract her from the
fervent preparation in which she was then occupied for the reception of
the sacred habit.   Her parents obtained in her portrait the only possible
satisfaction which could be granted to them.   They held it very dear,
recommended it to their survivors, and the latter to their successors; so
that it is preserved even to-day, in the same distinguished family, as a
relic of great veneration, of great glory, and of the truest affection   Of
this family I only said a few words in the beginning, to describe the
station and early education of Catherine; I will not fail to return to
it at an opportune point with a more extended notice
     Catherine was more and more animated by contempt of the world
and love of God during the days that followed   Until she received the
religious habit she remained in the department of strangers, renouncing
the customary pastimes and worldly visits which are permitted in the
monasteries to those who are about to receive the habit of nuns.   On
the day before receiving the habit, particularly, she would not go down
to the gratings, and the superioress did not order her to the contrary   She
spent the entire day in fervent prayer, meditating on the great work which,
with sover.... charity by the goodness of God it was granted her to
undertake   To her relations and others who, out of courtesy or because
of great a... desire, came to visit her, she sent a message by the mis-

tress that such a day was not to be spent at the gratings nor in prattling; therefore, they had to depart without seeing her. She would not even look at anything that was sent to her Having spent the night in spiritual contemplation rather than in bodily rest, the following morning, with that fervor and recollection which one can imagine from what we have thus far narrated, she received sacramentally her Divine Spouse Jesus, and, remaining immovable and penetrated by a deep feeling of gratitude till the moment of the sacred ceremony, she experienced in it one of her dearest consolations—nay, the greatest of her whole life After the celebration of Holy Mass by the father confessor of the monastery, Rev Agostino Campi, the ceremony of giving the habit was immediately performed by him, according to the rubrics and the custom of the Order The promptness, the joy, the devotion, the sublime affection that were noticed in Catherine's manner and behavior during this ceremony drew the admiration and the tenderness of those present, even to making them shed tears There was a girl in particular, who, at the sight, wished immediately to give up worldly ornaments, and, following Catherine's example, put on the simple religious garb. That this wish did not proceed from the ordinary volubility of imagination in women, but really from the impulse of divine grace, which offered to that girl the means to obtain her own best interest, was shown by the fact that, shortly afterwards, she became a nun and a companion of Catherine's in the same habit and monastery

Though the ceremony was a long one, the newly-made bride never once turned her eyes to satisfy the natural curiosity of seeing who had come to the church. She remained so imbued with holy thoughts, that even to those who assisted her in taking off the secular dress and putting on the habit given her by the priest, she seemed as if alienated from her senses. Consequently, they felt an embarrassment in touching her, fearing that they would cause her pain by thus distracting her After she had become a nun, she said to some of her devout companions that when the confessor put the crucifix in her hands, the sisters singing "*Mihi absit gloriari nisi in Cruce Domini nostri Jesu Christi*"—"But God forbid that I should glory, save in the Cross of our Lord Jesus Christ" (Galat. vi, 14)—she felt her soul become united to Jesus with such a force of love and sweetness of spirit, that it was a miracle that her body did not succumb from the separation. With a renewal of grateful protestations, of loyal and spiritual offerings, her heart completed this ceremony with God. Now we shall no more see the maid who had to fight at least the fickleness of the world and of nobility; we shall no more see Catherine, but Sister Mary Magdalen, thus newly baptized and dressed in a habit wholly of God

To pursue my object, which is to lead the reader from time to time to make those reflections which may be profitable to both his mind and heart, I would like to show here a little of the importance and value implied in this passing from the world to a religious order It is of no use to describe the value and efficacy of this new baptism to worldly souls, who, if not all, certainly for the most part, regard the religious vocation as a choice of caprice, of egotism, or, at the i. .. of a naturally pious tendency. They do not realize what the effect is to a human soul of feeling its body clad in a habit which, in quality, color, shape, uniformity, in everything, inspires most significant ideas. This total cutting off from the world—nay, this stamping on the world—that is, on all its regards, on all its maxims, its falsehoods, its ribaldries, its abuse of power; this finding of oneself protected by four walls, which form the true home of the Saints, always being a sister or brother to everybody for the love of Jesus Christ, but without any capricious love of the flesh; this victory over the three capital enemies of the soul, which brings back human nature to its true liberty and dignity —all this is not truly understood except by those whom God has admitted into a cloister to enjoy such privileges. I can only repeat to them St. Paul's exhortation—namely, worthily to proceed in their vocation lest they render it useless. The people of the world, in pursuing with hatred those who follow the Gospel, may only do so on account of their own wickedness, according to the solemn sentence of Jesus Christ.

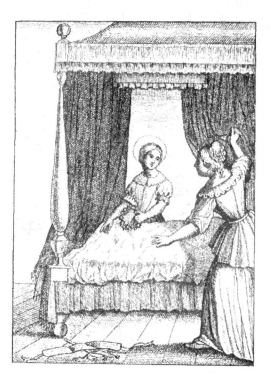

Having made some instruments of penance, she put them on when
going to bed [page 17]

CHAPTER IX.

IN HOW SAINTLY A MANNER SHE SPENT HER NOVITIATE, AND HOW DURING THAT TIME SHE FELT AN EXCESS OF DIVINE LOVE.

IF the joy of Mary Magdalen in receiving the religious habit was great, no less great was the perfection and the sanctity which she manifested during her novitiate, to the amazement of all the nuns and her spiritual father, who acknowledged her as a perfect religious, even from the beginning of her probation. Sister Victoria Contugi, a nun of no ordinary virtue, used to say that Sister Maria Maddalena should have been her mistress rather than her novice, as she noticed in her so great a perfection that most willingly she would have subjected herself to her as a disciple. On the day of her taking the habit, Mary Magdalen fell at the feet of this sister—her mistress—and, in an act of humility and sincere affection, wholly resigned herself to her will. She told her that she gave herself to her as dead, and, therefore, she should do with her what she pleased, because she was most ready to obey her in everything. She begged of her to humiliate and mortify her, without any consideration, whenever God inspired her to do so. She afterwards renewed this act of humble and entire resignation into the hands of Sister Vangelista del Giocondo, who succeeded said Sister Victoria in the office of mistress of novices. Sister Mary Magdalen, even before entering the novitiate or being instructed in it by cloistered persons, well knew, as we have hinted above, that religious perfection does not consist in protracting prayers, multiplying penances and fasts, or distinguishing oneself in works of singular virtues, but rather in the exact observance of the rules, and the faithful execution of everything else prescribed by the voice of the superiors, as the most safe oracle of the divine will. Therefore, not only did she never oppose any orders of her mistresses—not only did she most promptly obey their every wish, but rather most judiciously tried to anticipate their will, so that often she was more prompt in obeying than they in signifying their intention. As to the faultlessness with which she obeyed her mistresses of the novitiate, suffice it to say that, no matter what diligence they employed, they asserted that they could not find out the things which Mary Magdalen liked or those for which she felt repugnance. She was young and of such an ingenuous character as to easily manifest itself, especially when under the assiduous vigilance of persons whose duty it was to watch the simplest word from those novices under their care. During the novitiate, too, the simplest tendencies are remarked; therefore, one can judge whether more can be said of the renouncement and submission of

our Saint's will   And to this submission is chiefly due the observance
of the rules, to which she conformed even to being scrupulous.   There
was not a rule among them, even trifling as it might be, that she did
not appreciate or obey ; and, with equal perfection, she venerated and
observed also those practices of supererogation she found in use in the
community.   Every day she read and studied some point of the rules
and constitution of the monastery, that she might fully and firmly keep
it in her memory.   For greater facility, she would often ask her companions to remind her of the duties and customs of their order, and if
they noticed her failing, to use with her the great charity of warning
and correcting her.   On account of her evident and exceeding fondness
for prayer, her mistress would sometimes give her liberty to retire to
pray at those times when the novices had to be occupied in manual
exercises.   She would not use such permission, protesting that she
would rather be employed in any work determined by obedience than in
the most sublime contemplation of her own choice , because, in fulfilling
the obligation of religion and obedience, she was sure of doing the will
of God ; but not so in the prayers and other exercises, though good and
holy, chosen by her own will.   She said : " If I would pray well at the
times permitted by the religion it would not be little." Lowly and menial
occupations were her delight, and she was the first to submit to the most
laborious ones   The more austere and heavy they were, the lighter and
sweeter they seemed to her.   As a combined exercise of humility and
charity to the lay-novices who were especially entrusted with keeping
the novitiate in order, she used to try and lighten the weight of their
labor.   Sometimes she would secretly take the linens they had to cleanse,
and wash them ; sometimes she would sweep the corridors, the dormitory,
and the other places of the novitiate for them ; sometimes she would
clean the lamps and make the beds ; in a word, she would do everything
she could to help others, considering herself the least of all, greatly rejoicing
to become a servant to the others.   With this same feeling of charity and
humility she preferred to converse with the novices who were most ignorant and least talented, choosing for herself the lowest place among them.
Even here she judged herself the most lowly and least fit for Religion.
She tried to learn something to her benefit from all, and would accept
advice and admonition from everyone, not only with serenity, but with acts
of thanksgiving and gratitude; and to obtain it, she very often prayerfully
urged her mistress and even her companions in the novitiate.   She always
showed herself undisturbed in her peace, and, as she wished all the
others to be so, she became comfort, help, and consolation to them in
their times of sadness   What she observed in others she always interpreted in the best sense ; and, if sometimes anybody's defect would
appear too evident, she rather used the oil of gentleness and prudence
than the vinegar of backbiting   Her conversation was such an
efficacious spiritual lesson to the other novices—her discourses, illustrated by ideas of the eternal life, penetrated the heart so deeply, and her
words were uttered with such fiery zeal, that she inflamed the lily-like
hearts of those virgins with a great love for God, and an ardent desire
to please Him   The novitiate thus became like a paradise of angels on
earth.   This light and these flames of St Mary Magdalen dazzled

almost instantaneously and miraculously the hearts of those girls who used to go and see the monastery with a desire of becoming nuns Without knowing her, they became attached to her, regarding her as an angel in 'the flesh, and wished not to have to part from her any more. The virtues of the other novices emanated in some measure from the perfection of St Mary Magdalen—let us freely call her Saint, as she already truly was, even from that time—hence, she shone above all ; and everybody, with the greatest veneration, stood gazing at her example These efficacious influences, then, had their origin in that familiarity with prayer by which she remained united to God in love, so strongly and constantly, that no occurrence, however strange, could attract her from it for the shortest time. If, awhile ago, we saw her preferring manual work to the retirement of prayer, we must not think that on that account she would be distracted from the holy exercise of interior recollection She well knew how to couple the active with the contemplative life Moreover, she was so industrious in cultivating her spirit that, having completed the manual and the charitable exercises, she would spend in prayer all the remaining time which was freely given to the novices for their recreation. Not satisfied with this, she would steal some hours from her sleep Having no permission from her mistress to arise in the night at unusual hours, she would place herself on her knees on the bed, in which position she was often found, and there, hiding her singular devotion, and rejoicing more in being than only appearing pious and devout, would give vent in some manner to that divine flame which was burning within her breast, and of which, even from this time of her novitiate, God willed that all the nuns should have an undoubted evidence During Advent, one evening, this incident occurred· Our Saint having remained alone in the oratory, after the prayers in company with the novices, she became so red and inflamed in the face that she seemed to be burning with a most scorching fever, and, as if frantic, could find no means to calm herself. She unfastened and violently tore her dress, as if to make an opening for the interior fire to escape, seeming to be consumed and melting away. On the mistress' noticing it, and calling the other nuns, they were all highly surprised at such a novelty. They could not at first imagine the cause of it; but some of them, recalling to mind what the lady marchioness had told them as having happened to her daughter at the villa, and hearing her now pronouncing some divine words, became assured that this was an excess of the love of God Interruptedly and with tears, she exclaimed in these words "O Love, how much offended Thou art ! How much offended Thou art, O Love ! O Love, Thou art not known nor loved !" And in this loving complaint, she moaned with anguish for the offenses committed against God. Forced by obedience to her mistress to enter the bed, having already been led perhaps unconsciously to the dormitory, she said: "Will it be possible that I enter this bed whilst God is so grievously offended? O Love, I will do it through obedience ," and thus she obeyed For about two hours she experienced this excess of love, and then she resumed her natural state The love of God is a fire which burns, but does not consume. unlike our passions, which afford fuel to a fire that will consume out elves and all we possess.

CHAPTER X.

NOTHING was wanting to her heart for a perfect union with God, both on account of her never-stained purity, and of the vow of virginity she made when yet a secular, and also on account of the entire consecration of herself in the act by which, stripping herself of the garb of the world, she put on that of a nun. She sighed, nevertheless, with holy impatience for the time when she would also formally bind herself to God with the loving tie of holy vows in the religious profession. She complained of the length of the time, and measured with loving weariness the passing of the year, because she did not wish to wait till the end of it. It happened that, eight months after her taking the habit, some novices—her companions—were about to make their religious profession, and she asked with great earnestness that she might be admitted with them to witness the solemnity of this act. This being refused her, she grieved much over it, thinking through her humility, or rather the poor opinion she entertained of herself, that the superiors refused her the dispensation because they found her unworthy of this favor. She was so much imbued with this idea that she did not dare to speak or converse with these professed sisters, who remained for some time in the novitiate, as was the custom. So highly did she venerate the religious state, that she excused herself in these short but sincerely humble and affectionate words: "You are the brides of Jesus, and I do not deserve to be one." Her heart had no rest until she was assured that the ordinary superiors had no authority to dispense in such cases. She then patiently awaited the end of her spiritual probation. When this came, she imagined in advance how she, too, would have enjoyed this happy lot; but God wished to try still further this, His beloved bride, and seemed delighted in leading her longer by the road of desire. There being no other novices ready to profess, the superioresses thought they had better join this one to the others; and in this way the profession of Sister Mary Magdalen was deferred. In quietly submitting herself to this postponement she had to perform one of those acts which are by no means

easy for those who are not possessed of the most pure and divine love.
But she, inspired by God Himself, who wanted to try her further, said to
the prioress and to the mistress. "I will not make my profession with
the rest, but you will be obliged to have me make it alone, to your
sorrow" The mothers paid no attention to these words, judging them
to proceed from her great desire, but what followed proved them
to be a most certain prophecy. About the end of March, of the year
1584, nearly two months longer than the year of her probation, on
a Friday morning, the seraphic virgin received a great spiritual consolation, with infinite bodily torment She was attacked by a most
violent fever, with chills, and such a severe cough that her breast
seemed about to burst. The nuns feared lest a vein might break; therefore, they quickly had recourse to human art, under the direction of
Messer Jacopo Tronconi, a most skillful physician, who immediately
opened the vein and then prescribed some medicine. He used all the
other remedies that his knowledge could suggest to him in the case;
but the illness obstinately increased and the seraphic patient was continually agitated by the most cruel and dangerous attacks Eight days
after, being attacked two or three times daily by these pains, the illness
became alarming. The doctor then decided to touch her on the nape
of the neck with a button of fire, which lightened the illness to some
extent, but did not remove it, nor diminish the fever or the cough.
The catarrh increased, and reduced her to such a state that she could not
take any nourishment without great effort, and scarcely had it reached
her stomach before she was taken with a desire to vomit, and being
unable to give way to it by the pressure of the stomach, she was forced
to send forth cries and shrieks which pierced the ears and hearts of
persons afar off. The physician himself, who was often the witness of
this sad spectacle, feared that some breast vein might burst. He saw
her attacked and overcome by the cough three and four times an hour
She became unable to lie on the bed, because as soon as she would lie
down she felt smothered, neither could she stand up, on account of her
weakness Day and night she suffered; dressed and sitting on the same
bed, without rest and without respite.

Forty days had passed since her illness began, and it was still growing worse and more violent. The attending physician agreed with the
nuns to call in for consultation three of the chief doctors of Florence.
These physicians having carefully examined the patient, and prescribed
and applied to her those remedies which, by common consent, they
regarded as the best, seeing their uselessness, became discouraged and
confessed their inability to locate the seat of the disease In the meantime, the patient was gradually getting worse, until the twentieth of the
following May. She became then, by a new and strange change,
unable to take anything, not even fluids If she took but a mouthful
of water, she would faint with pain. Every way, then, being barred
against her support, the physicians themselves despaired of her recovery.
As an extreme experiment, they prescribed for her the water del Tet-
tuccio, which, being taken in a small quantity by the patient for two
mornings, and with the greatest pain, had to be given up. God's
servant was placed in the hands of God, to suffer for three months

the most severe and cruel sickness. The simplicity of the last remedy
used by the physicians must astonish everybody to-day, when medical
science furnishes better remedies than a natural water. In this we have
an evident proof of the progress of this science, for the reason that
greater study and experience give it new and better acquisitions   Let
us reflect, to our profit, that the same thing cannot be said of the
science of the soul's salvation; because this, in its principles, excludes
all doubts, all changes and human experiments. It is all heavenly, all
divine, and consequently altogether invariable; hence, he is not only a
fool and an impious man who attempts to lay hands on it, but he
also is one who pretends to improve it and build it up by substantial
reforms.   That Sister Mary Magdalen should continue to live without
nourishment, and so violently sick, seemed entirely supernatural; but
no less wonderful appeared to be her constancy and firmness, since,
although assailed and oppressed by so many torments, there was never
noticed in her an act or sign of complaint to indicate an impatient
spirit.   She always, even during the inevitable sufferings of nature,
kept her usual calmness and grace; always was most obedient to those
who attended her, and to the physicians, though she did not hope for
health through human skill.   Illness is apt to be the thermometer of
one's virtue and the occasion of reporting victory over one's self, because
when the body is weakened and troubled by sickness, the soul is also
more depressed and enervated by it   If by long-continued and strenuous
acts of virtue in the past it has not contracted strong habits and fixed
the will firmly in the love of virtue, the soul is easily overcome and vanquished, both by the weariness and the pains with which it is troubled
Alas ! most people, far from profiting spiritually by the infirmities of the
body, become worse   This they plainly show afterwards, when they
have recovered, by their sinking deeper into their vices, as if death had
gone far off from them, because they had come out victorious in that combat.   Sister Mary Magdalen in this illness not only gave proof of full
control over her passions, keeping herself constantly tranquil, but with
an over-abundance of divine love she showed that the torments which
assailed her were like so much fuel placed on the fire of her love for
God, or like the blowing of a strong wind, which kindled more and
more the celestial flame in the recesses of her heart   Every natural
hope of recovery having, therefore, disappeared, and everybody thinking
that only a few days of life were left her, the spiritual father and the
mothers of the monastery, not being willing to let her die without the
advantage of the sacred vows, resolved to admit her alone to the profession, as she had previously with a prophetic, but not understood spirit,
foretold.   The seraphic virgin gave thanks to God, who had made use
of such an excruciating sickness to make her enjoy more quickly,
by the tie of the vows, the union with her Divine Spouse   As she was
unable to make her profession in the customary place, and wishing to
do it with all possible reverence and devotion, she implored the nuns
to fix a little bed for her in the choir before the altar of the Blessed
Virgin.   This request was granted her, because of the knowledge she
manifested of the character and importance of this religious undertaking.   She was taken to the choir on the morning of Trinity Sunday,

which in that year, 1584, fell on the twenty-seventh day of May. There, having made her confession to the usual father confessor, Rev. Agostino Campi, and, having received Holy Communion from him, with great animation and fervor she made, at his hands, her regular profession What a deluge of celestial graces, what consolation overflowed the innocent and seraphic soul of Sister Mary Magdalen in that religious and so-much-wished-for act cannot be described, because the happiness of souls that, though traveling on earth, yet are blessed in God's love, cannot be expressed in words. She herself, when brought back to her bed, manifested to some extent what new vigor her spirit had derived from it. She asked as a favor from the nurse that the bed-curtains be lowered and that she be permitted to rest a while Longing more for the rest of the spirit than that of the body, when she found herself alone, she became so fixed in the consideration of the grace received from God, and the union made with Him by means of the holy vows, that she remained motionless, without being troubled by the cough, and in deep rest The nurses, who, of course, had not departed, but had only placed themselves in a position to notice, from time to time, what she would do, perceived that, being rapt in divine thoughts, she was alienated from her senses. Her countenance had assumed an air of paradise; the ashy paleness had given way to a clear, bright color, and her eyes, flashing and most resplendent, were looking fixedly at an image of the Crucifix. Being amazed at such a sight, they called in the rest of the nuns, all of whom greatly marveled, and, becoming at once edified and moved, gave thanks to the Divine Goodness who worked so prodigiously in their dear sister. She remained in that state about two hours, and then, returning to her senses, again resumed the attenuated and pale countenance, and again felt the torments of the fever, the cough, and the pains. This was the first rapture noticed in this ecstatic servant of the Lord, who was so highly favored by God with a most sublime knowledge and wonderful frequency of such graces, the effects of which we shall see at length in the faithful narration of the second volume, viz , in the Works of this Saint.

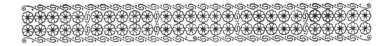

CHAPTER XI.

SHE IS CURED OF HER ILLNESS IN A WONDERFUL MANNER BY THE
INTERCESSION OF THE BLESSED MARIA BAGNESI, WHOM SHE
AFTERWARDS SEES GLORIFIED IN HEAVEN, AND FROM
WHOM SHE RECEIVES SUBLIME KNOWLEDGE;
ON WHICH A REMARK IS ADDED.

HE knowledge of Sister Mary Magdalen's sanctity kept the hearts of the nuns greatly agitated with the ever-increasing fear of losing her. Her illness was, from day to day, growing worse, and the strength of the Saint perceptibly diminished. At the beginning of July the obstinate illness showed not the slightest sign of improvement. It was a miracle how she continued to live, because she would but seldom take any nourishment, and then only in very small quantities and with the greatest difficulty, nay, with a positive effort of nature. The nuns redoubled their prayers, sighs, and tears, and practiced some devotions in common that God might be pleased to give back to them in good health this sister so valuable to them. As the moment appointed by Divine Providence to work new wonders in this, His most beloved servant, was approaching, the souls of the nuns who were to be the witnesses thereof were prepared accordingly. In the year 1577, in Florence, the noble Maria Bartolomea Bagnesi, a sister of the Third Order of St. Dominic and illustrious for her sanctity, departed this life. At the fervent request of the nuns of Santa Maria degli Angeli the body of the sister was given to them, and, therefore, carried with great pomp to their monastery. It was deposited in a sarcophagus and privately kept by them with ever-increasing devotion, until, on account of the many miracles wrought through her intercession, the great and glorious Pontiff Pius VII was pleased to raise her to the honors of the altar, with the title of Blessed. In consequence of this, the sacred sarcophagus was exposed to public veneration. Then a lay-sister, named Sister Maria Dorotea, who knew how our Saint venerated the now Blessed Maria Bagnesi, and how frequently, when in good health, she visited her sepulchre, made a vow one Friday evening that, when able, Sister Mary Magdalen would visit the body of the venerable mother three times reciting each time three *Pater Nosters* and three *Ave Marias*; and that she, Sister Dorotea, would fast for three

She instructs country youths in the rudiments of the faith, and also distributes various alms to them (page 18).

Tuesdays, and on the day of the death of the Blessed Maria Bagnesi, and have three Masses offered in honor of the Most Holy Trinity. She did not make this vow known to anybody Not even the Saint knew it then ; and yet, by disposition of the Divine Goodness, it happened at the same time, that the ordinary confessor, Rev Agostino Campi, entered the monastery to restore the holy patient with the Eucharistic Bread. He told her that he wished her, when able, to go and visit the body of the Venerable Sister Maria Bagnesi, together with Sister Veronica, a novice, and Sister Dorotea, a lay-sister. At these words, as she afterwards related to the nurse, the Saint suddenly felt the catarrh cease, the cough stop together with the shortness of breath, and she found herself free from illness and pain ; so that she promptly, and with a cheerful countenance, answered him "Yes, Father, by the grace of God, I will be able to go" She said nothing then about her feeling healed, perhaps on account of her deeply-rooted humility, or because she was not sufficiently certain of having been favored with such a prodigy. Her confessor having left her, and she knowing positively that she had been restored to health by a supernatural agency, said to the nurse "I want you to know that I am cured, and that I will suffer no more cough or pain, and you will see that taking my dinner will not annoy me." These words, though pronounced with great energy and firmness, amazed the nurse, but did not altogether reassure her The newly-recovered one, who saw that the moment for glorifying God had arrived, and who could see the hesitation of spirit in her assistant, added with an irresistible tone of voice: "Pray, get my dinner ready" It was ready in a moment, and it consisted of light soup and cooked fruit Whilst formerly, on account of her cough and pain, she could ordinarily swallow but a small portion of it, and that with the greatest difficulty, this time—free from pain and without moving herself from side to side—she ate the little she had as if in perfect health, and hungered for more. The nurse raised and lowered her eyes, clasped both hands, and, as if ashamed of herself, dared not move nor speak. In the meantime, the confessor having called Sister Dorotea, ordered her, together with Sister Veronica, to take Sister Mary Magdalen to the sepulchre of Sister Maria Bagnesi Imagine how the lay-sister wondered at the confessor's having the same thought that she had. She acquainted him on the spot with the vow she had made the evening previous and renewed the following morning. Knowing nothing yet of the grace already obtained, she had come with her novice companion in great faith and with a wonderful coincidence of thought to take the Saint to the tomb of Sister Maria Bagnesi. But as they approached the bed of Sister Mary Magdalen, they found they had no longer to deal with a sick person, because she was full of joy and vigor. As if to presage the happy news, she opened her arms to the two sisters, and they embraced one another in the Lord They afterwards made known the cause of their coming, and they saw, to their unspeakable surprise, the Saint arise immediately from her bed and prepare to join and lead them quickly to the sacred sarcophagus of Sister Maria Bagnesi. There, kneeling with her companions, after having prayed together for some time, she begged them to leave her by herself. When she was alone she prayed continuously for three hours, that is, from the eighteenth to the twenty-first hour,[1] with that fervor of devotion which certainly was not wanting in her, and which was called for by such a wonderful occurrence She returned to the infirmary alone, ate some food very naturally, recited some prayers before the Crucifix, and, bidding good night to the nurse, undressed and went to bed, and passed the night in quiet rest   In the morning the nuns, who, even if they had wished to, could not doubt the evidence of the miracle, gathered around her, and turning on her looks which showed all the powers of amazement, all the forces of surprise and tenderness of affection, spoke to her words of the highest veneration and heartfelt satisfaction.   To the joy they felt for their dear sister, who had just passed from a dangerous illness to perfect health, they united the greatest devotion and gratitude towards the Venerable Sister Bagnesi, who had obtained such a providential favor for her who was the ornament and the model of the monastery, on account of her great sanctity.   They all thanked her with feelings of most sincere and deep gratitude   But it behooved Sister Mary Magdalen to do her share towards her own benefactress, and we believe she knew how to acquit herself with exactitude and perfection.   On account of the frequency, the zeal, and the grateful and constant love with which she betook herself to the tomb of her beneficent mother, a few days after she recovered her health, that is, on the eleventh of July, 1584, she enjoyed the following remarkable privilege there.   Whilst with great emotion of heart, at the foot of the sepulchre, she was gratefully meditating upon the favor received, she felt her soul being carried away by superhuman force through the celestial regions.   She was made worthy to behold there the soul of the Venerable Bagnesi surrounded by great glory, and, through the obedience she was under to reveal what she saw in her ecstasies, she related this vision in the following words. " I saw in Paradise a most beautiful throne of incomprehensible light, on which, all resplendent and full of the greatest majesty, the blessed mother, Sister Maria Bagnesi, was sitting, and I understood that this throne was due to her virginity and purity, which were to her very great ornaments.   I also perceived that this throne was adorned with jewels, and these were all those souls she had led to the service of God, and who, encircling her all around like a crown, added to her ornamentation and beauty."   In consequence of the particular devotion she entertained for this servant of God, she was favored, even before her illness, with some sublime visions.   We report them here for the sake of the continuity of the argument.

During the night of the twelfth of February, 1584, being at prayer, and engaged in it with redoubled fervor, her mind was elevated to a very high contemplation.   She seemed to see in heaven the soul of the Blessed Mother Maria Bagnesi, in the bosom of the Word Incarnate, as a precious gem, with which the Divine Word was as well satisfied as a bridegroom with the most valuable jewel with which he may be adorned She understood that the Word kept this beautiful gem on His breast not only to delight in it, but also that it might be seen by all   He desired

---

[1] According to the old Italian way of counting the hours of the day which has lately been revived   *V . at the Translator.*

it to be like a mirror for all who would gaze on it, so that, noticing in it her virtues—charity, purity, humility, patience, modesty, benignity, the sweetness of the love she felt for God and her neighbor during life, and for which she now enjoyed the reward—they would be gently attracted to imitate her, at least in part, thus in some measure satisfying God, as she constantly gave Him delight. Whilst she was contemplating this Blessed soul, God gave St. Mary Magdalen to understand that, on account of the special affection He bore to her monastery, He had predestined two great luminaries for it—as it reads in Genesis, that when He created the world, "*fecit in eo duo luminaria: luminare majus ut praeesset diei, et luminare minus, ut praeesset nocti*"—"God made two great lights: a greater light to rule the day, and a lesser light to rule the night" (Gen 1, 16). The one was the Blessed Virgin, the other the Blessed Maria Bagnesi. The Blessed Virgin is the great luminary, similar to the sun, because she is the special Mother of the monastery, under whose banner they enlist. Therefore, she sheds light like the sun, and on the day of grace, viz, during the present time, she, the Mother of purity, continues to enlighten the souls that are found in her dwelling-place, strengthening them that they may walk in the path of God, making known to them the deceits of the enemy, and all the impediments that those who oppose them may cast in their way She assists them to triumph over such obstacles, and, with maternal affection, she enlivens the sterile ground in the hearts of her beloved daughters with the fire of divine love, so that, through her, they blossom and bring forth flowers of just desire and fruits of good works and holy virtues Again, this holy Mother performs loftier operations in those daughters who have the good disposition and prepare themselves, more and more, by faithful correspondence to grace ; she produces in them those greater spiritual effects which the sun is wont to produce materially in a cultivated garden after a beneficent dew.

The minor luminary, which is the venerable mother, Sister Maria Bagnesi, placed through the love of God over her monastery, is like a moon, which, when the sun withdraws its rays, reflects its light. When, at times, the Mother of God is offended by her daughters because of their negligences and imperfections, and withdraws the rays of her splendor, leaving them in utter darkness, this blessed soul with pious affection enlightens the spirits of those wanderers in the obscurity of the night She offers them efficient help to learn the cause of this darkness, excites them to true repentance, and, with urgent prayers, compels—so to say— the Mother of God to overlook the faults committed by these ungrateful, but repentant, daughters Ah ! if the daughters of Mary could see how much help comes to them from this minor luminary when they find themselves in the obscurity of error, how much more they would profit by it than they now do ! Not only does she protect us in Heaven before God and His Holy Mother, but in the rare example of her virtues she has left us on earth a guide most useful, undoubtedly, for all, but in a special manner for the souls consecrated to God in the cloister, if they would profit by it, following faithfully in her footsteps

Again looking at these two heavenly luminaries, St Mary Magdalen saw that both were continually infusing light into those conse-

crated souls   She saw, moreover, that those who lead an imperfect life
in Religion obscure these luminaries with something like clouds; and
though they cannot take away the splendor from the sun and the moon,
yet they darken them and obscure their rays, preventing them from producing the desired effects in the individual.   Souls who lead an imperfect life in a sacred place not only prevent the operations that these
luminaries would produce, but lessen their influence on all the rest.
With great emphasis, she pronounced these words "Even the faults
committed through weakness become clouds before these luminaries."
But afterwards she was comforted on seeing the Divine Spirit clearing
and casting away all the clouds made by the faults of those souls; so
that the operations of those two divine luminaries were being wonderfully performed and their effects brought to perfection.   She saw some
souls like very thick clouds, which did not disperse, neither at
the light of the second luminary nor at the breath of the Divine
Spirit   They would certainly have prevented the above effects, but the
same Holy Ghost, with an extraordinary wind and great force,
drove them away and confined them to a corner; so that, though they
were present, they did not at all prevent the Mother of God and the
Blessed soul from freely performing their operations upon all the inmates
of the monastery,   The clouds were those souls that refused to remove
the impediments so that God's grace might work in them, and, therefore, they remained with their imperfections   She also understood to
her great joy how the Blessed Virgin adopts, with ineffable love, as
her own daughters, all those who choose to dedicate themselves to God
in this monastery, and spiritually gives birth to them in the sight
of the Word.   When they are born, she presents them to the Blessed
soul of the mother—Sister Maria Bagnesi—who, like a loving nurse,
raises them, and nourishes them spiritually   Because of what she had
learned, having returned to her senses, our Saint was extremely pleased
and thankful to the Divine Providence for so efficaciously watching over
the monastery she had selected

Another time, on the 14th of June, 1584, St. Mary Magdalen, with
two other nuns, visited the body of the Blessed Bagnesi, in order to return
thanks for the health so miraculously recovered through her mediation
While praying, she was led in spirit to the same blessed one in paradise,
standing at the right hand of Jesus, between Jesus and the Blessed
Virgin, clothed in a silver dress with gold and brown embroidery, gold
for her charity, and brown for her great patience.   She had palms in her
hand as do the martyrs, and she was beautifully and grandly adorned
She saw also that Jesus took out of His most sacred hands large and
beautiful jewels, filling the hands of Mother Maria Bagnesi with them,
that she might dispense them   These jewels were of four kinds, viz,
white, red, violet, and brown, white for purity, red for the love of God,
violet for humility, and brown for patience   While the mother dis-
pensed them, she saw her giving many of them, especially the white
and red ones, to the nuns   She herself was given the four kinds, but a
greater number of white and red ones, comes or was given the
four kinds, were of the red and abundance of the brown, because
of the sover and manner of her office required   She

also saw her giving some of them, the most of which were violet and brown, to lay persons Then it was presented to her imagination how the Blessed Bagnesi was gloriously drawn in a chariot of fire, like Elias, the father of the Carmelites, and she understood that chariot to be of fire because of her great charity in spiritual and temporal things The four wheels signified the four cardinal virtues, viz., justice, fortitude, temperance, and prudence, practiced by her during her life. Here ended the second vision St. Mary Magdalen had of Blessed Maria Bagnesi.

We will frequently note similar visions in our Saint, some of which were accompanied by revelations of hidden things or predictions of things to come I have alluded, in the Introduction, to the kind of belief which we should give them At this first, and perhaps not so favorable, impression that may have been made on the mind of the reader, it seems to me opportune to add some remarks which may better satisfy him. Immediate answers have the greatest weight, and more easily recur to memory in similar cases, so that, if one wants to, he may apply them for his own benefit. The Church, unlike secret societies, is wont to work in full light and the evidence of facts She fears not the enmity of man, because she has no need of man The history of virtuous and holy persons should not hide their imperfections, if they exist; nor should it inspire the reader with an uncertain and, perhaps, erroneous piety The exposition of facts is not a panegyric nor a legend Truth is never the loser; and it alone can convince and improve people I am pleased, therefore, in spite of anyone who may be opposed, to quote the words Ludovico Muratori left us in his book on *the strength of human imagination* In it he says: " When some virgins and other souls enamored of God give themselves up to meditate on the life of our Divine Saviour, or other truths of religion, it is proper to suppose that they have already filled their minds with sacred doctrines and devout ideas by the continuous reading of ascetic books, the sermons they have heard, and the instructions given them by learned and pious men. Materials are not wanting to their imagination for the forming of long, ingenious colloquies in their mind, and for the imagining of new ideas by the help of those preceding, deducing one from the other, and representing the actions of God, the angels, and other blessed spirits as their devout affection deems more appropriate and suitable to the subject of their contemplation. All this can take place without any miracle—without particular cooperation of God; I mean to say, naturally. A soul full of sacred affection, with an imagination rich with so many ideas, is sufficient for it. * * * Then the habit of becoming ecstatic is formed, so that at the sight of the divine mysteries, or on returning to their usual meditations, their mind sees itself easily absorbed in these thoughts ; and they seem really, in imagination, to have Christ our Lord present to them, to embrace Him as a child, to accompany Him to the passion, and to do other like things. * * * Ecstasies and visions, therefore, being uniform in their substance, in the absence of an evident intervention of divine action, there must always remain some diffidence lest what appears to be God's work may not be truly so, and a doubt that it may be but a natural phenomenon of persons who are ardently tending to God. Mystics themselves avow that in this matter a soul is subject to many deceptions * * * This is said, nevertheless, not to condemn entirely all apparitions and revelations, because, if to believe too much is an excess, it is no less of an excess to believe nothing."

Behold, then, the plain talk of a writer who, certainly unsuspected of exaggeration in matters of piety, yet knows how to respect what appertains to the all-powerful goodness of God. As for ourselves, let us beware, lest in wanting to be free, we become unjust and unreasonable. Let us freely admit that our Saint was sometimes transported by her imagination to see what did not exist, or to modify the existence of it These fanciful productions, when they are not in opposition to the fundamental maxims of the faith, and, better, if by them a soul profits in piety, may be regarded as a means of Divine Providence more suited to such a person, as Jesus Christ Himself made use of parables and sensible signs to adapt Himself to the common intelligence. We cannot conceive what is above our senses, except by comparison with what is really subject to us The grace of God instructs us according to our capacity, leading us, like children, by external signs, to represent to ourselves the formal existence of the invisible. Our imagination corresponds to it with more or less liveliness, according to our nature, education, and habits, hence, ignorant and simple persons, females particularly, have been and always will be more prolific in forming fanciful ideas; because the stronger they are in imagination, the weaker are their reasoning powers But God, who is so good, sometimes communicates Himself to them in preference to very learned men, for the well-known reason that imagination accompanied by humble devotion is more susceptible to such communication, than an intellect which, though sublime, is puffed up by vain haughtiness. In regard to this science we all have equal strength of mind, and the virtue of our heart alone can make us more apt to attain it, so that the opinion of a poor, ignorant woman may be preferable in this to that of a distinguished theologian Moreover, when the ecstasies, visions, or revelations have the supernatural element required by the above-quoted writer, and certainly by every good Catholic—that is, when we see in them some sure evidence of a prodigy, such as an instantaneous cure, an ecstasy, an elevation of the body from the ground, a revelation of things hidden or far off—we should venerate them as the works of Divine Omnipotence Of such a character are nearly all the marvels of our Seraphim of the Carmel; hence, in venerating these by an indispensable duty of our faith, we should not refuse our assent to others of the same Saint, even if they do not appear so evidently marked Let us, at least, acknowledge them as natural effects either of reason or of fancy, associated with God's ordinary grace The incontestable proof of one fact is a guarantee for a thousand others in the same person, though the cause may not appear of equal credibility every time Every good logician will teach us thus. It is truly a breach of faith when men want to take exception to this unavoidable principle only in matters of religion, as the wicked Jews, who, at the sight of so many and such amazing miracles wrought by Jesus Christ, suppressed what might have convinced them of their own malignity, and would themselves study, and make others also study, the works of Christ from that side only from which they thought they would have a good chance to deny and calumniate. After all, I will grant that some acts in this history, not accompanied or directed by divine grace, might be said to be the consequence of exaltation of mind, or rather a slight excess in piety; but more than this cannot be granted. Even supposing this to be the case, when the Church has not condemned, will we dare condemn it as an excess of virtue, whilst in ourselves we tolerate, and wish others to tolerate, such excesses of vice? I will say, once and for all: Let, at least, the essential virtues of the Christian be possessed by us—let God be within our hearts—and we will know how to judge with equity the actions of the Saints; otherwise our consciences will be tribunals without judges. St. Paul, writing to Titus, has left us this comment: "All things are clean to the clean: but to the defiled, and the unbelievers, nothing is clean; but both their mind and their conscience are defiled" (Tit. i, 15). Let us impress this well on our minds, and apply it efficaciously to our hearts.

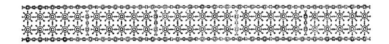

CHAPTER XII.

SHE RETURNS TO THE NOVITIATE, WHERE SHE GIVES NEW PROOFS
OF MORTIFICATION AND SANCTITY, AND IS SEVERAL TIMES RAPT
IN ECSTASY, DURING WHICH SHE LEARNS THAT IT IS GOD'S
WILL THAT SHE SHOULD LIVE ON BREAD AND WATER.

HE superioress, having detained her in the infirmary for a few days longer, thought, as did likewise the spiritual director of the monastery, that she would not send her back to the novitiate, but rather leave her free with the other professed nuns, that at her pleasure and convenience she might better satisfy her spirit of contemplation. She spoke to her about it, but the humble daughter feared that if she satisfied her self-love by allowing this, she might render herself less acceptable to God, so she began to plead with the superioress to place her again in the novitiate, where, on account of the subjection and mortification especially practiced there, she would feel more certain of divine approbation. She was consoled in her pious desires, and so were also the other novices. She, because of her great love of humble suffering, and also to avoid the privilege of associating with the professed mothers before the completion of the usual time spent by all in the novitiate ; they, on account of the companionship of so beautiful a soul, who could instruct them by words and by her exemplary life efficaciously lead them to religious perfection. As if favored of God with a great gift she returned many thanks, and by way of gratitude gave herself up, more than ever, to the observance of the rule and the practices of Religion. She occupied herself in the exterior exercises with such great consolation to her soul and with such an upright intention toward God, that in no case was she ever distracted by them from her interior recollection. When at prayer, which would be as soon as she had finished her manual work, she would immediately be alienated from her senses and wholly rapt in God. It oftentimes happened that in the very act of manual exercise she was overtaken by an ecstasy. It was also an inconceivable wonder to the sisters to see that this holy child, privileged of God with such distinct favors of ecstasies and revelations, not only would derive from them no self-complacency or esteem, but on coming to herself, as if those things had been rather a fault in her, she would humble herself to the least of the novices—even lay-novices. As if

When her mother approached Holy Communion, she drew nearer
to her, as if she " tasted " the fragrance of the
sacramental species (page 26).

mortified, she would return to her other companions to fulfill with additional solicitude the orders and customs of the novitiate, as if to make amends for a time unduly spent. It occasioned them equal wonder to hear her talk to her companions with so much charity and humility, and of herself so basely and contemptuously, whilst a few moments previously she had been heard and seen talking so sublimely on exalted subjects.

Though the pains of her illness, above described, had been so long and excessive, not only did they not extinguish in her the desire she felt of suffering for the love of God, but it seems, having thus tasted suffering, she yearned more and more for it. The kind superioress tried to make sure of the preservation of her health by particular diligence in the use of restoratives and by keeping far from her anything that might cause her pain ; she, on the contrary, tried in every manner and devised every means to suffer much, but without being noticed by anyone There was a lay-novice of great simplicity, and our Saint, ingenious in her holiness, made good use of her in the exercise of her own sufferings The mistress would order this lay-sister to prepare a specially tasty pottage for Sister Mary Magdalen ; but she would persuade the lay-sister to bring her, instead, a small slice of bread in boiled water without salt, telling her that this was better for her. She would also have her bring to the doorkeepers the collation that was sent her, that they might give it to the poor, for the love of God, and she would take for herself a bitter drink made from herbs, saying that this was better for her stomach Perhaps the Saint wished by this suffering to experience in herself the passion of her Divine Spouse, embittered in His last hours by gall, whilst He was dying on the cross for the redemption of souls. It was only after the death of the Saint that the simple lay-sister told of her condescensions Sister Mary Magdalen devised also, about that time, a kind of suffering, by her called *hidden*, which she continued throughout the course of her life It was that, noticing how the superioresses studied to please and satisfy her every wish or desire, not to say need (they so much valued her preservation), she, with virtuous industry, or rather with marked victory over herself, would pretend that what she liked and preferred gave her annoyance and pain ; and, on the contrary, that a thing would please and delight her for which in reality she felt repugnance and antipathy. It happened very often that things were done for her, or ordered, that she very much disliked, and things forbidden her which would have been very much to her taste. Hence, she was living in a continuous act of mortification and abnegation of her own will, and frequently in bodily pain and travail. What crowned this heroic exercise was the virtue of humility, by which this would have remained unknown (as the nuns never noticed it) if she had not indirectly betrayed herself to the other novices by suggesting to them this means of suffering for their greater perfection. They well understood that, before proposing it to others, she had long adopted and practiced it. It is to be remarked that in hiding the truth Sister Mary Magdalen De-Pazzi was very careful not to offend against it in any way, because if we are not always bound to manifest the truth, we are never permitted to advance falsehood ; hence, that language of the world (sometimes adopted, alas ! even by those whose strict duty it is to diffuse the sovereign, unfailing light) which openly says *yes* for *no*, and *vice versa*, is at variance with the Gospel and with God. Consequently, it takes from society the foundation of justice, the only bond that makes compacts inviolable, insures friendship, guarantees peace, safety, and public weal, and everybody, especially if weak and poor, has to-day cause for deeply regretting it.

The light of Sister Mary Magdalen's great sanctity shone in her works, and even from her countenance some ray of God's spirit was apparent. By simply seeing her face, strangers judged her to be a nun of rare perfection. Hence, those girls who entered the monastery on trial, as we have seen happened at the beginning of her novitiate, felt irresistibly drawn towards the Saint by a hidden force of affection and reverence, and if any one of them, as also happened, had entered with a doubt of her vocation for becoming a nun, by dealing with her she would feel her will become prodigiously deliberate and firm to remain there and not to serve God by the religious vows elsewhere. So powerful with the Saints is divine virtue, that it preaches by the actions and the very presence, no less than by words. A wonderful thing happened to a mere country girl who took on the habit of a lay-sister in this monastery. That she might more easily and efficaciously become instructed in the duties of a Religious, the confessor often exhorted her to stay in Sister Mary Magdalen's company; but, on account of her ignorance and simplicity, she could not remember her name, though she greatly wished to. She could not distinguish the Saint from the rest, though, as she afterwards confessed, her face indicated to her a virtue altogether singular. She would ask the sisters to point her out to her, and they, pleased at such marked simplicity, refused to comply; but God, who has a predilection for a simple and ingenuous heart, consoled the lay-sister, and gave a new manifestation of the sanctity of His seraphic bride. One morning, whilst that religious community was hearing the Holy Mass in the choir, the lay-sister had a great desire to know which of the nuns was our Saint. Looking first at one and then at another, she saw a great light suddenly surrounding one of them; and in that light she perceived a most beautiful child, who caressed the nun. From this she became assured that this was the Saint; and, not doubting but that the child was Jesus who so favored His beloved one, she was so overcome by sacred fear that, unable longer to endure such a sight, she was compelled to leave the choir, frightened, not even knowing whither she was going. In the corridor which led from the interior sacristy to the choir, she was met by two nuns. They were surprised at her strange and uncertain movements, and stopped her to ask the cause of her conduct. She openly related to them what she had seen and experienced, and then, having become quieted, she returned with them to the choir, where with great fervor she thanked God, who, by means of divine light, had assured her recognition of the person, and now reminded her of her name, Sister Mary Magdalen, in such a way that she would never forget it again. The simplicity of this lay-sister gained for her at other times similar favors, and especially when the Saint was making bread with the other nuns this lay-sister saw Jesus around her in the same form, who would make light for her when she through her humility would carry the bread to the bakery She also saw an image of the Virgin in relief, in the choir, raising her hand and blessing the Saint. These visions which God made use of to confirm her in her opinion of Sister Mary Magdalen's sanctity, caused her always to venerate the Saint with special respect and distinct and affectionate devotion But the Lord God was not satisfied with decorating His servant with these splendors ; He wanted to form her entirely according to His own heart

On Tuesday, May 21st, 1585, our Saint was busy working in the monastery, when, feeling an extraordinary throbbing of the heart, she resolved to return to the novitiate. She had scarcely arrived when she was thrown to the ground by an unseen force, and remained there a long time as if dead   Then she uttered these words· "Lord, what dost Thou want of me? perhaps the exterior for the interior?" And she understood that God desired that in future she should feed on bread and water only, except on feast-days, when she was to have lenten fare, and this was to atone for offenses which sinners offered to God. God then showed her the reward prepared for those who, for His love, deprive themselves of the pleasures of the world, and, continuing in the ecstasy, she exclaimed with an accent of astonishment: "Oh ! how sweet and charming is the place, and great are the works that must be performed by those who wish to reach there " As the fast prescribed for her seemed to her but a small work compared to the happiness she saw prepared for her soul, she added . " If it were sufficient, O my God, for the salvation of creatures, I would live a thousand years in this world, and I would think myself happy. Thy Word made me ask that I might suffer some pain for Thy creatures , Thou art satisfied with this ; so be it." She continued, then, to speak in this way· " Thou art truly powerful, O my God, as, if Thou hadst not called me thus, and also thrown me to the ground, I would not have answered Thee. May Thy will always be done. I wish rather to die than to offend Thy exalted purity But I wish to rest all in Thee , as, by remaining united to Thee, I know that nothing will trouble me Grant me, then, this favor, O my Jesus, that I may continually rest in Thy divine will." On the following Thursday, as she was reciting the divine office with another sister, she was again thrown to the ground , and being immediately rapt in ecstasy, flushed in the face, and with her eyes fixed on heaven, she said with trebled force: "*Adsum, adsum, adsum*"—"I am present," and, in the person of the Eternal Father, she added : " I call thee that thou mayest follow My vocation and request, as I have already shown thee." And then, in her own person· "Thou art truly great and powerful." After this, she remained over half an hour in silent contemplation, and then came to herself But she remained somewhat perplexed by this vision, as she saw herself in a painful dilemma—not to fulfill, on one side, the Divine will, which she loved greatly ; and not to be able to avoid, on the other side, making herself singular in the community, to both of which her humble spirit was equally repugnant. Reflecting longer on it, she began to fear lest it might not be God who wanted her to lead such a mode of life. She dared not speak of it to her confessor, nor to anyone in the monastery, as she thought they would be opposed to her in this matter. But God, who exacted from her this peculiar mortification, on the following day—that is, on Friday—gave her additional proof of it Whilst she was with the novices, again, and with even greater force, she was thrown to the ground. There she remained speechless for a while ; then, in the person of the Eternal Father, she said . "*Crastina die nihil gustabis, nisi panem et aquam; et si hoc non facies, retraham a te oculos meos*—'To-morrow thou shalt taste but bread and water ; and, if thou failest to do it, I will withdraw My eyes from thee.' But if thou wilt do what I have shown to thee, thus doing My will and that of the Word, who, with so much love gave and gives Himself to thee, I will be pleased in thee, as I have been thus far And if thou wilt that thy work be acceptable to Me, let this exterior action which I demand of thee be wholly voluntary. It will be like a mirror to your mind ; and fear not what thy adversary will do against thee, as I will never let him prevail against thy person. I will give thy mind in charge of angels, that they may guard it. The Mother of My only-begotten Son will be thy guardian, that thou mayst not lose the impress of the passion of the Word, which I have engraved on thy heart ; and be perfectly sure that thy desires will be unknown to the devil, thy enemy, and I will fulfill all thy wishes " Here she became silent; and, for a while, it seemed that her thought was in suspense ; then, sending forth a deep sigh, and crossing her arms, she bowed her head, and said of herself, wholly submissive to the Divine Will: "*Non moriar, sed adimplebo opera tua*"—"I shall not die * * * but will fulfill Thy works" (Ps cxvii, 17). Having uttered these words, she came to herself, and by the command of obedience which compelled her to manifest to some nuns, deputed for that purpose, all she saw or heard during her ecstasy, she at once faithfully related to them what we have said about the above three wonders of the omnipotence and goodness of God Afterwards she spoke of it also to her father confessor, who, in common with the mothers, doubted lest some artifice of the devil might be concealed under such austerity and singularity of fast. Both he and they answered her that they would not permit her to lead such a peculiar life , and that she must submit in obedience, and take the food prepared for the community She promptly submitted to it ; not only with her will, but also with her judgment ; sure that if God wanted it, He would have moved the minds of those who held His place so that they might incline to her favor. In fact, Divine Providence was not slow to manifest in His faithful servant such signs of His supreme will, that no room could be left for anyone to doubt it On the following day, she sat at the table for the common meal, intending, for the sake of obedience, to eat what the rest did When she tried to do so, however, she felt such a revolting feeling at the stomach that she was unable to take even the least amount of soup or a drop of wine. If she would force herself to take even a little, she would be seized with a violent attack of vomiting, with hemorrhages Bread and water only could she take and retain naturally and with ease Because of this, the confessor renewed the experiment, and he and the nuns who had witnessed both the first and second attacks, the latter of which happened on the evening of the same day, thought that to resist this desire of St Mary Magdalen was to resist the pure will of God ; hence they allowed her to follow her will in this new mode of living so divinely outlined And, glad beyond saying, for this concession which freed her from so many anxieties, on the succeeding day, which was the 25th of May, 1585, being nineteen years of age, she immediately began to fulfill the fast imposed upon her, of bread and water on ferial days, and lenten food on feast-days. She persevered in this fast with unalterable fidelity for several years, until the moment when it pleased God to order her to do otherwise.

As far as possible, she took care also to hide the virtue of these acts, saying that God permitted her to do this on account of her sins, because of which she was unworthy to take food like the rest , and, also, that this system was the best for her health—for her humility , in a word, reasons were not wanting for humiliating herself, although it had the opposite effect. The more she humbled herself, the higher grew the good opinion of her in the minds of others, according to the well-known Gospel principle, that he who humbleth himself shall be exalted, and he who exalteth himself shall be humbled. On the 26th, being rapt in ecstasy, the Eternal Father again confirmed the manner of her taking food ; and He told her, moreover, that it was His will that her rest should not exceed five hours, and that the straw mattress alone was to be her ordinary bed. He also wanted her words to be words of meekness, of truth, of justice, her understanding to be as if dead, not only without investigating the things of others, but not even her own , her memory to be forgetful of every other thing except the benefits received from Him , her will desirous of nothing in the world, but only intent on fulfilling what would be pleasing to Him Finally, He wanted her to wholly resign herself to His providence, and place herself in His arms as if dead. And in truth, the life of St Mary Magdalen was so directed by the will of God, and so submitted to the same, that it became a miracle of perfection, and a token of most complete sacrifice to the majesty of the Most High

CHAPTER XIII.

GOD FORETELLS A FIVE-YEARS' TRIAL FOR HER, AND SHE PASSES IT
IN GREAT DESOLATION. VARIOUS TEMPTATIONS, AND THE
REMEDIES EMPLOYED BY HER TO OVERCOME THEM.

O holy souls, not only the consolations but also the aridities of spirit are a heavenly gift, as they firmly believe that both the one and the other proceed from the same Hand that ceases not for a moment to provide for our welfare. Nay, as they draw from the desolations a stronger argument for doing penance, they become united through them with greater sweetness and efficacy to the Divine Goodness. Thus it happened to this great servant of God in the temptations and trials she endured for five whole years, as she therein found the means to conform herself better to the Divine Will, and to obey Him who had so marvelously manifested everything to her. God made known to her that, like Daniel, she would enter the lion's den, viz., that she would be assailed and harassed by most horrible temptations; but in the end, like refined gold, she would come out of the furnace of the tempting devils to become more acceptable to her most pure Spouse, Jesus. On the feast of the Holy Ghost, God revealed to her the great number of temptations she was to endure, and the Saint saw legions of devils under the form of most horrible beasts. She grew pale and trembled with fright at this monstrous spectacle; but strengthened by virtue she offered herself to the Eternal Father, ready to drink the bitter chalice and ascend to Calvary, to consummate there the sacrifice of tribulation. After this offering she recovered from her ecstasy, which had lasted two hours. During this time, though she heard painful news, she was not, on the other hand, left without a sure and sweet token of her Spouse's love. She learned that on the same feast of the Holy Ghost He would infuse Himself into her soul, to render it, with an infusion of sweetness, strong against the pains of her assailed spirit; and that the Eternal Word would be her guardian, together with the great Mother of God, Saint Augustine, Saint Angelo the Carmelite, and Saint Catherine of Siena, her tutelary Saints; and that she would be strengthened with spiritual comforts drawn from the Humanity of the Word, by whose perfection, being made constant, she would gain a splendid victory in all those most bitter combats, and triumph most gloriously and completely

over hell. In the evening of that same day, having reentered the
ecstasy, she again saw appearing before her a group of devils, who, with
tremendous shouts and terrible antics, as though they were wild animals,
threatened to kill and devour her. In the meanwhile, they suggested
to her mind the most impious and wicked temptations, so that she
became extremely sad and afflicted thereby. She uttered touching words,
called upon heaven and earth and the inhabitants thereof to come to her
rescue. Turning to God, she asked. "Where is the sun of Thy justice?
To me it seems obscured. * * * Hast Thou, perchance, withdrawn Thy
goodness from me? I feel abandoned—like a body without limbs, which,
on account of all it suffers, cannot of itself procure any relief" The Lord
gave her to understand that she was to endure these sufferings for the
sake of her neighbors, as she could not, then, be of any advantage to them
otherwise Hence, she replied· "The accursed heretics, for I cannot
call them by any other name, will cause me most cruel pain, because
though they have once received Thy Spirit, O my God, yet they do not
walk in it Many brides also, weary of Thy restraint, will provoke these
most ferocious devils to assail me and increase my torment If, O Word,
these souls should return to Thee, I would be happy; and I would be
satisfied if the devils should come and torment me a thousand times. I
see myself surrounded on every side by horrible monsters, and, hearing their roars, I cannot keep myself from raising my voice also
Should I be forbidden to do it aloud, nobody will be able to prevent me
from crying internally to my God, so that I shall be heard. These
diabolical spirits would like, O my Jesus, to throw faith to the ground, do
away with humility, scorn purity, and place in my heart, instead of
resignation to Thee, a wicked will I do not wonder, that, being unable
to succeed in it, they return to attack me with such fierceness, and try
to make so great a noise that I may not notice the inspiration which proceeds from Thee, O my God. My feelings are like those of one condemned to death, who endures as much pain at the sight of the axe that
is to cut his head off, as at the very moment he receives the fatal stroke
I know very well, O my Lord, that if Thou shouldst lessen the power of
Thy hand, they would take my life. They would truly take out my
very entrails, therefore they rush furiously against me, but my Spouse
has put within me His spirit and heart, and, having thus placed me
in this hard trial, wishes me to suffer for His creatures, that they may
be converted to Him. I recollect, O Word, some few shades Thou
gavest me, under the cover of which I must remain for some time that
I may not hear such dreadful roars and terrible yells, and that I
may not behold the horrible sight of the devils. But, O Eternal Word,
I can find no escape from this lake, no matter whither I fly What
shall I do, then? * * * Better it will be if I arm myself with courage
and glory in suffering *Redime me a calumniantibus me! Gene-
atio mea ablata est et convuluta est a me Oportet contristari in variis
tentationibus Timor et tremor venerunt super me, et contexerunt me
tenebræ Æstimatus sum tanquam mortuus a corde*—'Redeem me
from those who calumniate me (Ps. cxviii, 134) My generation is at
an end and it is rolled away from me (Isai xxxviii, 12) Now you must
be made sorrowful in divers temptations (1 Pet i 6). Fear and

trembling are come upon me, and darkness hath covered me (Ps. liv, 6)
I am deemed as one dead from the heart' (Ps. xxx, 13).   Stretch Thy
right hand over me and give me strength.   I know, O Word, that Thy
goodness is pleased that I should not be deprived of the sense of grace
till the coming of Thy vision (she meant the feast of the Most Holy
Trinity), but that I should rather contemplate Thy greatness and that
of Thy Holy Spirit"   In fact, during the whole octave of Pentecost this sense of grace remained in the ecstatic soul of the Saint;
but on the morning of Trinity Sunday, being still in ecstasy, she
began to exclaim: "O loving Word, the time in which light will fail
is drawing near, and darkness approaches.   The light comes also,
but is dark; the darkness comes, too, but it is clear.   I see the adversaries with their temptations getting together, one by one   Alas! like
bees around the flowers, they seem to surround the soul.   But Thou, O
Word, pressing down Thy hand a little, dost not let them rise, and
Thou sendest those Saints chosen by Thee to introduce the soul under
the most sweet shades already shown to me.   Alas! it is one thing to
hear a thing spoken of and another thing to suffer it   It is meet, O
Word, that Thou, on the day on which we celebrate the feast of the
union—I mean of the Most Holy Trinity—shouldst prepare for thy
bride an unusual and unknown union   *Sufficit mihi gratia tua.*"
During these ecstasies she also understood that she would have to
endure not only the assaults of the devils, but that she should also prepare herself to suffer not a little from her own nuns; as some of them,
seeing her so different from her former condition, would rise against her;
and the others, at least losing the favorable opinion they had of her,
would abandon her, as the apostles abandoned Jesus in His passion
One of the principals of the monastery being present and hearing this,
said with firmness: "If all should abandon thee and turn against
thee, I will never forsake thee."   The Saint answered thus: "Thou
shalt be the first one, and thou shalt not leave this room before thou
shalt already be changed and turned," and it so truly happened.   For some
time she uttered no other word.   Showing great sadness in her countenance, she gradually entered into a mortal lethargy, then, as if with
the effort exerted shortly before final dissolution, with open arms and
with eyes looking as those of one suffering the last agony, she sent forth
a cry of fright at the moment when she had to succumb to the taking
of the sense of grace from her.   Here her ecstasy ended, and our Saint
passed from it to a life of desolation and dryness, in which she remained for five years as though she had never tasted anything of God,
but tasted all the enormity and horribleness of the temptations
which it seems opportune here to describe separately, as follows:

FIRST TEMPTATION.

CONTINUOUS SIGHT OF THE DEVILS AND ARIDITY OF SPIRIT.

The more Sister Mary Magdalen's soul remained void of heavenly
comforts the more her imagination became filled with phantoms and
infernal spectres   Day and night, wherever she found herself, in
whatsoever service, even of piety, her mind was pained by the sight of

At the age of ten, she receives for the first time the Most Holy
Communion (page 21).

he devil, who, appearing to her in the most horrible and diverse forms,
lways persistently tried to frighten her. Hence, the bride of Christ
emained so afflicted, that, as she said, the pain of death would have
)een more bearable to her. She seemed to be in a veritable lion's den,
vhere, being made a target for all the diabolical rage, there was no
nsult that could be contrived in hell which she was not made to suffer. In
act, there is no torment of spirit imaginable that this soul, though most
innocent, did not endure during this hard trial Sometimes she felt so
trongly tempted that, against her will, she would struggle outwardly
lso, and her discourse was not always reasonable What caused her the
greatest pain was the thought that her acts of resistance to the
emptations were not sufficient to save her from sin It seemed to her
is if her will seconded the wicked suggestions, and she were continually
)ffending God (and let anyone who feels any great love for God say
vhat anguish the fear of offending Him causes a soul!). Hence, these
vere her words: " I have become a pit of iniquity, the cause of all the
·vils and offenses which are committed against God; so that I know not
how Jesus and my fellow-creatures tolerate me on earth." Another time,
the said that her mind appeared to her like a great dark and obscure
·hamber, in the midst of which could be seen the light of a very
mall lantern, that is that indefinable trace of good-will which cannot
)e so easily extinguished in one who has been penetrated by the
hivine flames During this privation of intellectual light and devout
·ensibility, all the exercises of the Religion weighed upon her so much
hat she had to act by obedience in order to go to the choir, the
efectory, and all other places, according to the orders of the community,
vhilst before she used to be naturally anxious and happy in obeying
hem She continued the holy habit of private prayers, but she
lerived from them no comfort. Being found at prayer by a nun in a
oom next to the kitchen, and used as one, among pots and pans, with
)pen doors and windows, and being asked by the nun why she had
)laced herself there in prayer rather than in a more convenient place,
vith great submission and bitterness of soul, she answered " It is the
;ame to me whether I pray here or elsewhere ; as, at any rate, I find
nyself much like these earthen pots ; I have no more strength to
aise my mind to God; I have become as a worm " This desolation
)f spirit would not have troubled or robbed her of her peace, only that
the believed it a sign of God's anger As to its being troublesome
ind painful, she was most ready to suffer everything to please God.
Hence, on account of her being in such a condition and her inability to
ree herself from it, with incessant tears and sighs she would accuse
herself of being utterly guilty. The continuous presenting to her
imagination of all the offenses offered to the Divine Majesty—as God had
foretold her during her eight days' ecstasy, when she was about to enter
this lake of anguish—was the cause of the greatest affliction to her.

Now she saw the wicked insults offered to God by heretics,
now those of bad Christians, now the perfidy of the Jews and the infidels ,
but, above all, the monstrous ingratitude of those Religious who observe
not the rules At times, she felt the horror of the blasphemies
uttered against God and the Saints ; at times, the odor of lascivious-

ness and impurity; the black cloud of pride; the execrable stench
of sacrilege, the bitterness of enmity and strife.   She saw these
and other consequences of the passions, leading man to rebel, even
against that God from whose power every impulse to our well-being
essentially comes.   All these things deeply wounded to the quick the
heart of this innocent victim.   Thus God wished to try the fortitude conferred on her by the almost continuous heavenly vision which she enjoyed
in the foregoing contemplations, so that no grace granted to her would
remain without its exercise and test of virtue.

SECOND TEMPTATION.

SHE IS TEMPTED AGAINST FAITH—ARTIFICE OF THE DEVIL TO HINDER HER FREQUENTING THE MOST HOLY EUCHARIST

The devil assailed the unconquerable faith of this great Soul with a
snare which was as impudent as it was foolish   He wanted no less than
to convince her that there was no God, nor after-life besides the earthly
one, transitory and frail, and that, therefore, it was vain and superfluous
to suffer for the love of One who does not exist, and useless to labor for
an eternal life which was purely imaginary, as everything ends with
man's death.   She felt this erroneous idea becoming so deeply impressed in her mind that she became so confused as to be incapable of
recalling any of the many powerful reasons to dissipate it   Though her
will was ever ready to give up life in any painful way for the confessor
of the faith, yet, not feeling the former ardor and light she wished to
still have, it seemed to her as if she seconded the temptation, which
pained her heart exceedingly   Moreover, the enemy's cunning was re
markable in the peculiar choice of the object of these assaults, which
was the august Sacrament of the Altar.   He is not ignorant of our
having in the Eucharist every weapon to win any combat—every good to
enrich our souls.   The frequency and the devotion with which St Mary
Magdalen made use of it displeased Satan very much; hence he gathered
about him all his diabolical forces to distract the mind and the heart of
our Saint therefrom   He wished to destroy in her altogether the
faith in this most august Sacrament, suggesting to her that it was
idolatry and foolishness to adore what was introduced by the fanaticism
or the interest of men, and that, as a wise woman, she should rather
despise than use a superstitious food.   He then filled her with such
repugnance against approaching Holy Communion, that, while formerly
she found in it all her comfort and delight, now she felt the pain of
death.   The temptations against faith molested her more and more in
the act of receiving the Blessed Sacrament; and the devil, unable to
subdue her to this unbelief, as the father of lies and contradiction,
afflicted her on the other hand by inspiring her with the fear of receiving
Holy Communion without being in a state of grace   It was easier to
persuade her of this on account of her great humility—her desolation
and sadness of spirit—of which she was not relieved, even when receiving
Holy Communion.   Her soul, therefore, was sorely afflicted; because,
in the very source of her delight she found so many reasons for grief.

But the enemy of souls failed to make her diminish the usual frequency, nay, to render herself stronger in such a war, she then made use of a remedy which had been suggested to her by the Queen of Heaven. It was to have it imposed on her by obedience never so much as to think of omitting Holy Communion. Having obtained this from the superioress, she answered her with promptness and joy. "I will try, with the help of Jesus, to do what has been imposed on me." From this act, she derived so much strength against the temptation that she felt some respite from it. But the devil seeing that this means robbed him of the hope of victory, made use of external means to frighten the humble maid As she approached the small window to receive Holy Communion, a horrid monster appeared to her imagination, which—full of wrath and fury, its eyes flashing fire, its mouth vomiting flames, a naked sword in its hand—threatened her with death if she dared to approach. At this sight, she became so dismayed that she had not strength to move a step farther; and it became necessary that the spiritual director should encourage and exhort her to approach without fear As he saw the temptation did not cease, he prudently thought of giving her Holy Communion by herself until he knew her to be free from this trouble. Though the Communions of St. Mary Magdalen were deprived of spiritual light, yet they were not without profit, as she would draw from them great courage and an invincible constancy to fight against such fierce adversaries. Though so long assailed, she never gave up the field to the enemy, nor did she doubt the Divine help. This, at times, made itself powerfully felt, and occasionally, in the course of those five years, even ineffably sweet , so that, as a restorative of the spirit, it reinvigorated and stimulated her, even causing her to wish for new difficulties and new pains for the love of God.

THIRD TEMPTATION.

SHE IS TEMPTED TO BLASPHEMY AND CONTEMPT FOR SACRED IMAGES.

The above temptation against faith was accompanied by the most horrible one of blasphemy; for in the very act when the devil tried to make her disbelieve in God, he impiously excited her to blaspheme Him. This was not a mere suggestion, but was so live and fierce that she seemed to hear, as if they were present, the voices of the most wicked and impudent blasphemers who crowd together in a tavern and appear to vie with each other to see which of them can best turn himself into a Satan. This happened to her more particularly when reciting the divine office Though she tried with all possible care to apply her mind and heart to sing the divine praises, the envious enemy, to prevent her doing this good, filled her ears with such execrable blasphemy that she was not only compelled to distract her attention, which was intent on doing contrary things, but, even in pronouncing the sacred words, it seemed to her that she pronounced, instead, those very blasphemies, so sharply was she tempted. All sorrowful and with a most touching expression she used to say to her companions : "Ah! sisters, pray to

Jesus for me, lest, instead of praising God, I blaspheme Him!" It is useless to attempt to prove what painful torture this temptation was to her heart; she who was so inflamed with the love of God and full of zeal for His glory that she would have submitted to the most severe labors, to the most cruel torments, even to be thrown alive into the fire, that God might be loved, blessed, and glorified Let anyone think how deep a wound is naturally inflicted on one's heart by the hearing of calumnies and maledictions uttered against the visible object he loves and worships, and, worse, to find himself provoked to become an accomplice in them. Then comparing this earthly object, this worm crawling along in the mud, filthy in the extreme, with the God of majesty, of love, of glory, in whom all the beauties, and riches, and perfections of creation are united, let him judge, as far as possible, of the intensity of the sorrow that the above temptation caused to a soul like that of Saint Mary Magdalen De-Pazzi. Hence, she continually practiced acts in opposition to that inward temptation, and outwardly recited, as well as she could use her voice, praises and benedictions to the Lord

Following the temptation of blasphemy, another, one of contempt for sacred images, came to assail her, the devil presenting to her all that seems most silly and ridiculous in them, so that she had to make a great effort to look at them with patient eyes. The enemy was vanquished by her constancy. Whilst she not only venerated them more fervently and contemplated them with presence of mind, praying before them,—God, to the greater triumph of His invincible heroine, wrought several miracles, through her intercession, on her behalf, or for others, as we shall see in the course of this history, making use of the sacred images, that is, of those very means of which the malignant enemy made use to assail and fight her.

FOURTH TEMPTATION.

OF DESPAIR AND OF ABANDONING THE RELIGIOUS STATE.

The sagacious enemy of souls did not fail to take advantage of the desolation and aridity of St. Mary Magdalen to assail her with a masterstroke on that side where she least suspected an attack. On account of her excessive humility, as we have already seen, she readily believed herself unworthy of the Divine favor, and rather deserving of any punishment. Many of the beautiful communications, and many marked privileges by which God had favored her in the preceding years, had become like so many sharp thorns to her heart. She feared all might have been illusion with her, and that now she was justly punished for them by the Divine Justice. Hence the devil redoubled his malign forces, supposing it to be very easy to lead her, as if by the hand, and by the road she herself had opened, though innocently and virtuously, to the depths of the abyss of despair. He suggested to her the most gloomy images of deceit, of terror, of vengeance. All was lost to her, he told her, and any effort to raise herself to God was useless, since He had irrevocably rejected her; useless all prayers to appease Him, since the sentence of reprobation had already been pronounced against her, and it was impossible to have it revoked, useless all sacrifice, as God does not accept the offerings of reprobate souls. Satan told her that Jesus, whom she called her Bridegroom, and in whom she delighted so much, was but her enemy; the most shameful and terrible consequences of His wrath she would soon feel, in the everlasting punishment of her hypocrisy, her false devotion, and her continuous sinning. Distressed and torn with anguish by such painful thoughts, especially by that of being, through her own fault, separated from her good God, and, seeing that her protestations of confidence and resignation were not responded to as she wished, on account of the barrenness of her spirit, she fell into such an excess of bitterness and discouragement that she positively regarded death to be a lesser evil than the continuance of such a bad life. "How," she would say, "can I live, being an enemy of God, and a scandal to the monastery and the whole world?"

Thus she gradually came to wish for her death. Hotly pursued more and more by her enemy and her own imagination, which at this time was fully a prey to the phantom of terror, the thought made its way into her mind that the best thing for her would be to put an end to a life which had become to her wholly unbearable. It was the night preceding the feast of St Andrew, Apostle. Sister Mary Magdalen was in the choir with the other sisters, reciting matin, when, carried away by the vehemence of the temptation, she suddenly came out of the choir, and, quickly crossing part of the corridor and some cells, reached the door of the refectory towards which she was going. The pale light of a community lamp, placed at the end of the corridor, shone into it through two windows. The door of this room was not closed tightly, and allowed a glimmer of light to reach the wash-room, which adjoined She entered this room, led more by her knowledge than by the feeble light. Stopping at the first table she grabbed a knife, and, with it in hand, she ran back to the choir so as not to give in to the infernal suggestion, but rather to obtain a more complete victory over the enemy, for which end God permitted this aberration in her. In fact, she did not perceive that she was noticed by all the nuns, and did not pay any attention to them. They, naturally amazed at such a strange occurrence, anxiously asked her the reason for it, but without answering she swiftly ascended the Blessed Virgin's altar. There, placing the knife in Mary's hands, she knelt and prayed before her for some time with the most touching expressions, asking her the grace to triumph over such a temptation. Then descending to the ground and having placed that same knife under her feet, she trampled upon it several times with the greatest contempt, subduing by this act of strong determination the enemy and his arms. When she came to herself she continued with the nuns the recital of the divine praises. Another time, in order that the like temptation would not go so far, she asked to be imprisoned in the cell of the mother prioress, where God, to reward her humility, granted her something of the old consolation, and strengthened her with new vigor to resist victoriously in this spiritual combat. She well needed it, as Satan was to attack her again, though less audacious in appearance, yet more dangerous in his true nature. Without openly offending her faith the enemy infested her mind, about the religious vocation, with such thoughts as these "Thou art damned by thine own will only; thou didst mistake thy vocation, and, therefore, thou walkest over a road which for thee is all ruin   God wanted thee in the world, where thou mightest have done much good for thyself and thy fellow-creatures. Being a good mother of a family, thou wouldst have been the comfort of thy partner, the salvation of thy children, the edification of all.   See, O wretched one, how much thou hast forever left behind thee! Buried in this monastery, thou losest thyself, and savest nobody.   Repair, therefore, whilst thou art able, at the present time, an evil which is about to become irreparable   Divest thyself of this habit; leave this monastery, go back to worldly society, enter at once that road which Providence has traced for thee "   So sagaciously importunate was this infernal enemy becoming in order to seduce the Virgin of Christ; but he found her to be so strong a bulwark that the arrows sent against it returned with double fury to the point of starting.   One day, in order to overcome the attack, which was unusually overpowering, with a rope around her neck and her hands tied behind her, like one condemned to death, she went to the mother prioress, and in the presence of some sisters, asked, for the love of God, the religious habit.   At another time, on a similar occasion, and perhaps a graver one, as she was particularly tempted to go to the main door to leave the cloister while the doorkeeper was absent, she ran to take the keys of the monastery, and, to confound the devil more, went to lay them at the foot of the Crucifix   Thus she baffled the artifices of hell   She wept inconsolably over the sins she feared she was committing, judging herself to be the greatest sinner in the world, and, therefore, unworthy of living in the sacred cloister. She used to wonder why the earth did not open under her feet, especially when she was approaching Holy Communion   For all this God rewarded her, and gloriously placed her above all snares, no matter how malignant and formidable.

FIFTH TEMPTATION.

OF PRIDE AND DISOBEDIENCE.

The arm of terror having proved of no avail to overthrow this valiant servant of Jesus, Lucifer turned his efforts to inspire her with his dearest sentiment, by which he sits over all, as prince in the kingdom of darkness, crowned with a crown of ignomy, of opprobium, and of torment.   Always a liar, and inconsistent, as are also all his followers in this world, he pretended to make her grow proud by the very means he had used to draw her to despair   He would place under her eyes the many gifts with which God had endowed her, both in nature and in virtue, the many celestial and extraordinary favors which proved her sanctity beyond a doubt, the many communications of special love given her by her Divine Spouse; everything, in a word, that could stimulate her self-love to delight and glory, and believe herself superior in merit to the others.   He suddenly filled her with a repugnance to submit to the will of another, as if she were one who, being guided by supernatural light, needed no human counsel, nor to strictly follow the orders of the Religion, which savors too much of materiality, and, therefore, suits but souls and imperfect souls   it   oh! how

Lucifer deceived himself when he hoped to shake and vanquish St. Mary Magdalen, in humility and obedience, virtues that were so deeply and firmly rooted in her that she seemed confirmed in them by the divine grace, as the Apostles were confirmed in all of them after the descent of the Holy Ghost. In fact, though strongly molested, it was not difficult for her to oppose contrary acts, as her habits naturally and easily led her to them. There was no case in which she was led to transgress the least rule or order of the superioress; nay, by the very reason of being tempted, she became more solicitous and exact, both in humbling herself and in obeying. Sometimes she would renew in the presence of the other nuns the vow of obedience to the superioress; often she would have her command her, in virtue of this obedience, to do all that was prescribed for her, and especially that towards which she had felt a repugnance She submitted herself to all, and begged of all to humble and mortify her, in order, she said, that her pride might not be lifted up In a particular manner, in order to derive from it the most legitimate and prompt effect, she requested it of the superioress, who, to please her in so holy a desire, and that her soul might be enriched more and more with celestial riches, now ordered her to ask pardon of the nuns, sometimes separately, sometimes all together in the refectory, now she ordered her to discipline herself or be disciplined by others; now, with a rope around her neck and her hands tied behind, she directed her to kiss the nuns' feet under the tables of the refectory. At times, she would make her get up from her seat and go around begging a little bread from the others for the love of God, and, having got it, eat it in the middle of the refectory. Knowing that from being thus mortified she truly derived great spiritual benefit, the superioress would address her with words of reproach and contempt; she also charged other sisters to do the' same When they did this, out of obedience, the Saint stopped and listened to them with great modesty. Kneeling at their feet, and calling herself a sinner, she asked their pardon, ending with this motto, as humble in her sentiment as she was sincere: "May God count it as merit for you." Though the superioress knew that some apparent faults during the time of such a terrible combat were, in our Saint, rather the consequence of the fierce temptations assailing her, yet, for such faults, though they were most trifling, she bitterly reproached her before all She imposed public penances on her, as, for instance, making her stretch herself on the floor before the doors through which all the nuns had to pass, they carefully trampling upon her, tying her, with her hands behind, in some part of the monastery, where, all meeting, every one of the sisters said something to mortify her. Moreover, keeping her continually occupied in the low duties of the kitchen, carrying hot coals or wood, drawing water, making fire, fixing and sweeping, or doing any other humiliating thing in the monastery, such as is imposed on the least of the servants. In a word, either by the direct will of God, or by His permission, this rather trying proceeding of the sisters, and the still more trying one of the superioress, were for her efficacious fires in the crucible of spiritual perfection on which she rested for these five years She, who really felt in her soul the benefit of it, so cheerfully accepted all such things, that she seemed to have no other comfort in all trials than to be humiliated and despised ; and she so truly delighted in them, that, being without them, she would seek after them, and sometimes take them of her own choice.   On the eve of All Saints, in the year 1588, feeling herself greatly tempted to be disobedient, she blindfolded herself, and got a lay-sister, who supposed she had the permission of the superioress to do it, to tie her hands behind her with a rope, and then fasten her to some posts in the neighborhood of the choir.   Being seen in such a condition by the mother prioress, and asked the reason why, she replied that she had done it because she had felt some difficulty in obeying; and, as her will was against binding herself to the sweet bond of obedience, therefore it was proper that her body should be bound by these ropes.   With great fervor, she then begged that she would charge all the nuns, on entering the choir, to say these words to her, for her greater confusion: " Sister Mary Magdalen, learn to do as thou pleasest " The prioress did this, and all the nuns obeyed, though much confused and touched by the heroic virtue their dear sister practiced in that act, at the end of which she thanked them all and asked their forgiveness Thus do the Saints act   God would not leave without some immediate reward a work of such marked perfection in His most faithful champion. No sooner was the bandage removed, and the rope loosened, than— turning her eyes for a moment to that part of the choir which was visible, seeing a Crucifix, and thinking of how much He suffered for our salvation—she was rapt in an ecstasy, during which she was wonderfully consoled, instructed, and strengthened by the divine love. Another time, in the same manner, and for the same end—self-abase- ment—she got some one to fasten her to the grates of the choir, and obtained permission from the superioress that all the sisters should say to her · " Sister Mary Magdalen, this has befallen thee on account of thy faults, and because thou wantest to act too much according to thy will." Again, on another day, while she was contemplating—ecstatically—the ex- cessive pains of the Divine Saviour, and becoming inflamed with the desire of imitating Him, she had an inspiration that it would be pleasing to Him if she were voluntarily to lie stretched across the door of the choir by which the nuns, who were inside, would necessarily have to come out.   She did this with all solicitude and fidelity; and the nuns, in customary obedience imposed by the superioress, became to her a repeated instrument of mortification   Thus, then, would she be humbled and despised, who, among them all, was a mirror of obedience, and thus the temptations, far from being to her a cause of loss, increased her merit and strengthened her in virtue.

SIXTH TEMPTATION.

OF GLUTTONY AND .OF IMPURITY—TO CONQUER THIS LATTER SHE THROWS HERSELF AMONG THORNS.

That instinct of nature which leads us to wish for what we have not yet tasted, now troubled our Saint in a persistent manner . and he who tempted Christ in the desert presented to her imagination whatever was most pleasing to the palate to induce her to wish for new and delicate

In the same year in which she makes her vow of virginity, she
receives a precious ring from her Divine Spouse (page 22).

viands, but, much more, to make her break the rule received from God, of living only on bread and water So rigid and constant a fast displeased the enemy too much. If the body be well fed, he well knows how to use it to the detriment of the soul He occupied himself, therefore, with great skill in entering this door, which, being the least suspected of possible danger, made the access easier Very often during the day, when Sister Mary Magdalen, on account of her excessive abstinence, though approved of by God, felt a natural need of better nourishment, the enemy would inflame her with so violent a desire for some food, that sometimes she would show all those restless motions of the tongue and mouth that are wont to seize an extremely hungry and impatient person Sumptuous tables and exquisite viands would then present themselves to her imagination, and particularly in passing the cupboards in which the supplies for the community were kept under key, she was so vividly affected that to her it seemed as though everything were exposed, and she even felt some sensations gratifying to her taste. With such sights and imaginary tastings she continued to be molested, even in the act of prayer, and sometimes in the very act of receiving Holy Communion ; so that it was most painful for her, in so far as it was not only contrary to the virtue of abstinence, so much practiced by her, but also to her natural inclination, by which, to say the least, she always abhorred gluttony She said once to a sister, that God would not let her be troubled by the devil in anything that would molest her so much as this ; because gluttony seemed to her so unbecoming and ugly a vice, that she felt that no other temptation would humble and degrade her so much as this one But the enemy, with all his violence, could not succeed in making her appetite for eating and drinking prevail and overcome our abstinent and mortified Magdalen Even in regard to natural needs, she knew so exactly how to keep herself within the rule God had given her, that the devil came out of the combat confused and ashamed, and she with a new source of merit. The malign suggestion thus progressing by the way of the senses, he, who was not allowed to tempt Christ, because He was God, against so delicate and noble a virtue, did not let this sacred virgin go without making her pay the tribute almost common to human flesh. Though God had privileged her with so many favors, He would not have her altogether exempt from the struggle in which the children of men have to engage, for this angelic virtue of chastity This is the most familiar, powerful, and efficacious arm the enemy finds in us against ourselves. This is the bait, by the seducing force of which, unfortunately, many persons illustrious for talent, learning, courage, and also for virtue, have succumbed. This is the passion which, exciting the lower part of our nature so unbecomingly, causes such a disorder and darkening of the powers, such enervation of the natural virtue, that it almost leads man to the brute state ; and, therefore, this is the road by which the greatest number of souls are irreparably lost. The impure enter not the Kingdom of Heaven, and to the nuptial chamber of the Lamb of God only the virgins have access, and they accompany Him whithersoever He goeth, singing with Him that celestial *epithalamium* which they alone have learned These virgins are particularly the chosen ones, the flower of the Church of Jesus Christ, by whom He g'ives Himself, and

who will ever be found in this, His earthly paradise, and will afterwards
adorn the heavenly one.

Sister Mary Magdalen was certainly a precious plant of this paradise,
and the Divine Bridegroom gave evident signs of the delight He took in
her virginity. Now, in order that her victories might be complete, and the
triumph over this strong antagonist would be another gem in her crown,
God permitted that for two years, that is, from 1585 to 1587, she would
suffer in her body spurs of impure sensuality, and in her mind, impure
fancies. But being generally accustomed to opposing and denying in
herself even every desire and the least satisfaction of the sense, bound by
a particular vow to this celestial virtue, even from the age of ten years,
having guarded this virtue both in her mind and in her body with a
perfection more angelic than human, she knew so well how to shield
herself from the spurs, though most vehement, of concupiscence, that
not only her pure soul was not stained by it in the least, but she
did not even apprehend what the devil wanted with such temptations.
In the midst of them and during all her lifetime she always maintained
herself in such simplicity and innocence, that when advanced in years,
nay, being near to death, she said, as a solemn proof of the all-powerful
virtue of the grace of Jesus Christ, which alone supports and strengthens
corruptible human nature, that she ignored everything that sullied
chastity. This was said in answering a novice who spoke to her in confidence, fearing that she had contracted some stain From this we infer
as certain, either that God by a singular favor would not permit that
so pure a soul, accustomed to raise itself and dwell among elevated
and divine things, should be oppressed by such vile objects, or that she,
by the divine grace, was so careful and prompt in rejecting the imaginations, and did so much violence to her mind in quenching the impure
flames of sensuality, as not to permit herself to make the shortest reflection on them, or give them the simplest thought. Though she apprehended them as an evil thing, yet she never came to understand their
object, or their intrinsic malice—a rare privilege that God grants only to
those souls that are destined to enjoy the rest of contemplation on the
very breast of the Divine Love, as was the case of John alone among
the Apostles. But this bride of Christ, extremely jealous of the integrity
of her purity, was not satisfied with the opposition she offered to these
temptations by her intellect and will, and, feeling that a vice of sense
and flesh proceeded from them, she began to chastise her own flesh with
renewed zeal and excessive rigor. Besides taking but sparingly of bread
and water, besides sleeping on the bare straw-bed, and this only for a
short time, besides doing the daily work of the servants of the monastery, in which she engaged day and night, very often she would scourge
herself piteously with iron instruments, gird herself with a very sharp
cilicium, and treat her body in the worst and most excruciating manner
She even made herself a girdle of nails set in canvas, the points of which,
projecting, horribly pierced her bare body, on which she wore that
instrument of penance invented by her taste for suffering All this was
a great, but not altogether unusual, torment for her body. A wonderfully extraordinary one was that which she devised and executed on the
eighth day of September, 1587 Feeling tempted in the flesh by a strong

fire of impure sensuality, and as it seemed to her that she did not wholly quench it with all her inward efforts, she entered the room where the wood was kept, picked out the thorns and sticks she found there, and making a bundle of them, carried it to a more remote room. Shutting the door, she undressed, and like the glorious St. Benedict, placing it on the floor, she laid on it, and with great courage rolled her body over it, so that she was all scratched and wounded to such an extent that not only the thorns but also the floor was red with her blood, as the nuns witnessed, who found her there dressing herself. Thus those thorns, blossoming through her pure blood, became a crown to her virginity and infrangible arrows that subdued the enemy of purity and made him blush for shame on account of the intrepidity and heroism with which he was vanquished When I think of the example she has left us, I cannot understand why we feel such little shame as we look at our mode of life, so much opposed to this virtue Most Christians, not to speak of unbelievers and bantering philosophers, who yet wish to be saved, pretend to use such different means in defense of this virtue—so delicate as to be likened unto a looking-glass, which is tarnished by the lightest breath I do not know how they regard this virtue, who, professing to follow it to the most severe perfection, yet live among the comforts of gluttony, of sleep, and of soft feathers, and place themselves among so many attractions, of movements, of forms, of graces, of words which are most powerful incentives to lust. Quite opposite was the view that the Saints took of it ; and of truth, we must all be out of the right path, if we pretend to say that they deluded themselves in their excessive zeal, or that God, contradicting Himself, wishes to save anyone who throws himself among the impure flames of sin and lives in the midst of them. Different by far, from the life led to-day by their respective followers, were the lives of the Apostles, their disciples, the primitive Christians, the inhabitants of the desert, the founders of the Religious Orders, and their first followers ; of so many martyrs, confessors, and sacred virgins of centuries gone by

SEVENTH TEMPTATION.

SHE IS VISIBLY ASSAILED AND TORMENTED BY THE DEVIL, AND COMES OUT VICTORIOUS.

Before proceeding to describe the personal and visible assaults St Mary Magdalen had to endure from the devil, it behooves me to declare what the profession of faith of every Christian must be in regard to such things Let not the pious reader regret this deviation from our history, little opportune though it may be for him, as it is very important that we blunt the cynical sneer by which most people in our days answer the narration of diabolical influences, when they do not go so far as to openly deny them It will be better for this book to be at times not altogether meant for the man more learned than devout, rather than to come to be considered as nothing more than a work worthy only of going through the hands of nuns and devotees, and no farther. Now Moses, the oldest of history.   .. .   '   ' . ... .he wisest of legislators, in presenting to us the grand spectacle in which God by His word created heaven and earth, and made man to His own image (and in man all mankind is included), paints for us the original state of innocence and happiness, and then the malice of the spirit tempter, and his appearance under the form of a serpent, and the fall of Adam and Eve, most fatal to their posterity   From Adam to Moses it was believed, at least by Abraham's descendants, that God having from the beginning—viz., before He made man—created His angels pure spirits, and free from all matter, and having placed them in a condition in which they were free to secure their eternal happiness by voluntarily submitting to their Creator, some of them permitted themselves to be seduced by their self-love, so that from luminous spirits they were changed into spirits of darkness   Such belief was more clearly expounded from the epoch of Moses to that of Jesus Christ   In the Paralipomenons, in the Psalms, in Isaias, in Zacharias, and more distinctly in Job, we read of the apparitions and the power of Satan, prince of demons, to harm us mortals   Thus in the same book, and again in Daniel and in the book of Wisdom, open and clear mention is made of a place of eternal torment destined for rebellious angels and wicked men.   Though at times idolatry deluged the earth, and ignorance and blindness enveloped men in numberless errors, still the idea that between God and man there were intermediate spirits, good and evil, was not obliterated by the Pagans, as we are assured by the authority of Plato, of Xenophon, of Apuleius, of Ptolemy, and other Pagan writers   The existence of a future life was also universally felt, though man was forgetting himself in a thousand vagaries by imagining it to be such as to suit his senses   The dreams of the metempsychosists, the court of justice of Minosses and Radamantes, the occupation of Charon, the Elysium and the Tartarus of mythology, are so many evident witnesses of the belief of all nations in the existence of beings superior to us by nature, and of a justice without appeal awaiting us at the end of this life.   But whatever preceded the coming of Jesus Christ was but the effort of that insuperable tendency impressed by the Creator on the human soul, which could not and should not have its completion until the appearance of the splendor of divine revelation   No sooner did Jesus Christ appear on earth in His mortal flesh than those sparks of eternal truth, which had predisposed the human soul to it, became shining torches, at the light of which the entire world bowed its head   The doctrine of Jesus Christ, announced by example before it was by word, and afterwards confirmed by miracles, was destined to convert the universe.   The Apostles preached it everywhere, and sealed it with their blood.   During the persecutions by the emperors, whose pride was wounded to the quick by the principles of Christian equality, the followers of Christ died for the faith, and, by their example, hundreds and thousands of idolaters were awakened to profess the doctrines received from the Apostles.   The more tyrants invented tortures, the more was the courage of the martyrs increased against the fury of their persecutors

The Church, already formed with St Peter as the legitimate successor of the Divine Master, passed triumphantly through the space of centuries   For eighteen centuries, from age to age, from people to people, she brought everywhere the name and the glory of her Founder. And we have her to-day as Jesus Christ established her. The sacred deposit of the Gospel, during the succession of two hundred and fifty-nine Pontiffs, through the most extraordinary vicissitudes, was not altered one syllable. Anyone can convince himself of it by a comparison with the oldest code. The Gospel, then, so much extolled to-day even by laymen and politicians, assuring us of the existence, sometimes even visible, of the good angels, clearly describes in the Apocalypse the fight which took place between the Archangel Michael and Lucifer, and the victory of the one over the other. It also describes hell, the place of all torments, into which the angels who rebelled have been thrown, and to which all who die in mortal sin shall be condemned. Giving to Lucifer the name Dragon, it will lead us to understand that his celestial knowledge and that of his followers was changed into ambitious cunning; that a malign envy took in them the place of charity, and their natural greatness was turned into pride. Their happiness then became the sad satisfaction of securing companions for the abyss of miseries to which they had been sentenced, and then occupation the vile employment of seducing the universe. St. Peter represents the devil to us as a roaring lion going around to devour souls. St Paul exhorts us with the most ardent zeal to stand prepared against the snares of Satan, the prince of this world—that is, of all the wicked. All the four Evangelists unanimously relate many facts in which the devils visibly used their malice to the damage of humanity. Besides the audacity of Satan in presenting himself to Christ in the desert, and taking Him by the hand to tempt Him repeatedly, they relate how the same Divine Redeemer, in the presence of the multitude, delivered, not by any chemical or magical preparation, but by a simple word, by His command, various persons possessed and ill-treated by the devil. In some persons, He added to this the miracle of an instantaneous cure from an antecedent illness or defect of nature, as in the lunatic, in the deaf and dumb, and in the blind and dumb. Whilst these miracles could not be wrought to confirm an illusion, they stand as a most evident proof of the existence and the power of the devils. Besides, these miracles were of such a Divine character, that out of so many eyes riveted upon Christ, and so many ears attentive to His words, and so many enemies striving to charge Him with being an impostor, there was not one who succeeded in raising a doubt as to their reality. The Gospel goes on to relate how the Apostles and the disciples, in the name and by the virtue of their Divine Master, delivered many others possessed of the devil, sometimes accompanying this with miracles, for another end. In the annals of the Church we find no person of any virtue who had not to endure terrible combats with the devil; and we read of many instances in which the devil, assuming a visible form, attacked and tormented persons of a holy life, but who, triumphing through the Divine assistance, exercised also on behalf of others the power of delivering those who are possessed, which power Christ left to His bride, the Church. From the beginning of the Christian era down to the last century, many have been the heretics, who, with their false doctrines tried to destroy Christianity; many have been the dogmatical errors against Christian faith. But among so many enemies and so many heresies, the existence and the nature of pure spirits, the distinguishing of them into good and wicked, the condemnation of these latter ones to eternal torment, their sway over us,—all these ideas which we derive from tradition, inspiration, revelation, and experience have been almost universally respected. This deceitful triumph was reserved to the blind and proud delirium of the revolutionists of the last decade of the past century, who, combining in themselves all errors, tried to uproot and annihilate all truths, establishing the worship of the goddess Reason. What neither Celsus, nor Porphyrius, nor Julian the Apostate dared to impugn, they all denied What always existed, and, consequently, what alone had the character of truth, they pretended utterly to destroy. Everything was to give way to Reason. And this worship, having degenerated into the most monstrous tyranny, left such horrible traces of itself that everybody abhorred following it. Terrorism having been assuaged, and more moderate, though not less pernicious, maxims adopted, Rationalism, that, is, the system of believing only what one understands, sprang up What a discordance of opinions this has necessarily caused, is evident and palpable from the enormous gradation of human intelligence. We may compare the light by which Catholicism triumphantly shines to the mid-day sun Some persons pretend to look at it as they would at a lantern, through the corporal eye. Consequently, their sight is dazzled, and error takes possession of them It is a sad misfortune that on this the indifference and unbelief of to-day are based Everybody wants to see, everybody wants to reason, and with no other guide than that of caprice, interest, or ambition The sun of the Church of Christ, that measures its existence from the birth of the world, is considered to-day as being unable to guide the steps of man And with a calm mind, even by persons of otherwise moderate opinions, the existence of spirits, the power of the devils, hell itself, and, consequently, the justice of God, and whatever belongs to this most essential attribute, are denied The excess of ignorance and contradiction lies in the audacity of those who boast of being followers of the Gospel, whilst they believe of it only what they suppose will favor their mode of thinking and living. To see Jesus Christ communing with the plebeians, exhorting the masses, sitting at the table with the publicans, picking out, as His first disciples, some fishermen—that is, free men in the midst of the ocean, where no other law is known but that of heaven, to see, in a word, Jesus Christ always pleasant, always meek with the poor and afflicted, and, on the contrary, always severe with the rich, the ambitious, the hypocrite,—all this pleases the world of to-day, that would propose the Divine Redeemer as a model of democracy This I hold to be the only reason why such people believe in the sacred Gospel Hence, they reject severity of morals and purity of heart, because these cost something to the appetites of carnal men. They reject what the Divine Wisdom placed beyond the limits of human comprehension, because earthly pride is unwilling to give way to mystery. They reject the diabolical assaults and possessions, and the miracles, because to-day *they* do not see the former, and the latter are not wrought as those same unbelievers would like to see them. They are similar in this to the Pharisees of old who asked Christ to confirm His works by showing them some celestial prodigy. Finally, they reject the authority of the Church, because her ministers, they say, are men of vices and crimes Which, alas! being sometimes true, instead of hurting, offers one of the most convincing proofs of the infallible and perpetual government of God over the Catholic Church A moment's reflection will show how repugnant to good sense is this injustice of refusing to admit alike all the facts which proceed from the same principle of authority. As the faith of Christ tolerates no compromise, and as there is no article in the Gospel which claims our submission less than another, it follows that, if we refuse belief in the existence, the power, and even the visible work of the infernal spirits against man, in so far as God permits, we will be heretics and infidels, like those who deny all. If our belief in what remains proceeds not from God, it must simply be an illusion that will inevitably make us the victims of eternal misfortune In so far as our dignity inspires us with hopes above those of the brutes, let us, at least, keep our faith intact, not going forward into it with that fatal *why* which caused the apostasy and condemnation of so many illustrious men. Let us also appreciate what is suggested to us by the divine poet.—

> " Mortals, remain contented at the *Quia*,
> For, if he had been able to see all,
> No need there were for Mary to give birth "
> —DANTE, *Purg*., C. III.

From the fierce persecutions with which hell assaulted St. Mary Magdalen De-Pazzi let us learn how precious virtue is, and how important the salvation of a soul washed in the blood of Jesus Christ.

To our Saint it was also reserved to suffer torments in her body at the hands of the devil, in order that, like wheat chosen for paradise, she should pass through the hardships of all kinds of suffering, and, like gold well refined in the crucible of torments, she should become more purified for the glory of heaven, there to shine with most brilliant splendor God gave liberty to the devils to torment her in all her senses, and they did so with so much vehemence and fury, that particularly through the eyesight, the hearing, and the sense of feeling, they persecuted her greatly above the ordinary strength of human nature They appeared to her in horrible forms—now of lions or rabid dogs, now of serpents or savage animals, and always in the act of assailing and devouring her. These assaults would leave her livid and chilled as if in agony "O Sister," she said once to a confidant of hers, "just imagine how much this horrible sight of the devils must grieve my soul!" Another time, while she perspired excessively on account of the agitation caused her by the devil appearing to her in a monstrous shape, she called to her help St. Michael the Archangel, and then, turning to a Crucifix, she exclaimed. "O Word, O Word! *In te, Domine, speravi, non confundar in æternum!*"— "In Thee, O Lord, I trusted, I shall not be confounded forever" (Ps lxx, 1). Then turning to the enemy: "What dost thou want of me, horrible beast? *O bone Jesu!* by the sight of the offenses offered to Thy Divine Majesty, and by this of my adversaries, I seem to taste hell. But if you devils swallow me, you will be compelled to throw me up" Again, finding herself alone in a room she was heard to combat with the devil saying when Dare from rage, what dost thou want of me?" And, as if he attempted to insult her, she would again repeat: "Depart and do not approach me; I tell thee to take thyself away in the name of Jesus, and if I can order thee to do it, I order it." And then she prayed to God to lend her assistance She was over two hours in this contest. Being asked by the superioress about what had happened, she told how the devil, in the form of a frightful beast, threatened to devour her. She was a martyr because of the torment with which her hearing was afflicted, as we have already said in the Third Temptation, for howls, roars, and blasphemies continually resounded in her ears, with such force and persistence that often it was found necessary to shake her bodily, that she might hear the human voice. The psalmody of the choir was heard by her only as a confused murmur.

But the sense of feeling was the one which was to bring her the first palm of martyrdom. The devils threw to the ground that noble and tender body, weakened by her penances, in such a violent manner, that, to anyone who saw her, it was a wonder that she remained alive The nuns who witnessed her actions were amazed at seeing her thrown to the ground, her body prone, making gesticulations and motions—now with the head, now with the arms, now with the feet—as if she were being struck, and then—all sadness—become pale and trembling. After having continued for three, four, or even five hours in this agony, she would appear with wounds and bruises, or, at least, extraordinarily weak in body. She herself would then relate, in obedience to the interrogation of the superioress, how the devils, having thrown her to the ground, struck and scourged her with hard sticks, or, turning themselves into vipers and serpents, entwined themselves around her, and bit her, so that she could not keep from writhing, as she felt such pain as though they were tearing her limbs to pieces. Neither time nor place gave truce to so painful a struggle. Sometimes in the choir she was thrown to the ground and struck during the recital of the divine office and in assisting at Holy Mass One day in particular, she was struck so heavily in the face that it swelled, and it became necessary to doctor it for some time. Several times she was thrown down the stairs, and especially whilst she was going to Holy Communion, or to do some charitable deed In this, though, the wonderful and miraculous assistance of God was made manifest Being precipitated with great violence down a flight of twenty-six stone steps, it repeatedly happened that the nuns who had run at the noise, instead of finding her mangled would see her, to their ineffable wonder, safe and sound, arising in all tranquillity and continuing her occupation. It also happened that the devils dragged her through the choir, the corridors, and the cells of the monastery; but to the sisters who witnessed such struggles, it was not given to see the hand that produced them, nor to afford opportune help to the sufferer. One evening, the Saint was in the room of the prioress when she was suddenly thrown to the ground Her throat and face began to swell, and being forced to cough, as if she were being choked, profusely perspiring, she was heard to say "I die! I die! I am choked!" This stra⋯ ⋯ ⋯ ⋯ ⋯ ⋯ work of diabolical artifices on this meek ⋯ ⋯ three hours After that time she was free from pain ⋯ ⋯ ⋯ ⋯ ⋯ ⋯ der the eyes of the nuns All she outwardly suffered from terrors, torments, and contests, she made sufficiently clear when she said that, between the interior temptations and the external combats, she was so much occupied that time was not left her to offer herself to God Most wonderful mystery of the Divine Will in so innocent a creature!

As this noble virgin entered with invincible spirit this den of infernal lions, boldly answering to the first assault—"*Sufficit mihi gratia tua*"—so she persevered in it for five years, never yielding to fear or diffidence. She unflinchingly resisted, with vigor and valor, all the conspiracies of hell against her The serenity of her countenance did not grow cloudy in the midst of so many sorrows and shades of evil suggestion, her heart did not grow despondent when seized by so much aridity of spirit and in the absence of spiritual consolation, she did not complain of the bitterness of the pains she felt in her body, made a target for Lucifer's hatred Always meek and peaceful amidst all manner of snares, always full of hope in God, and always firm and constant, even in the greatest and most dangerous struggles—a lament never escaped that angelic mouth, a motion was never noticed which might impair the equanimity of that spirit, always immovable in its resolution to please God whether in consolation or in affliction Though from the physical torments she would grow pale and tremble in the heat of the fight, yet, with a more heavenly than earthly countenance, she would utter these words "My Jesus, where art Thou?" The nuns sometimes insisted on affording relief to her in the excess of her suffering, but she would peacefully answer them "Do you not remember that these things must be, and that it is the Divine Will I should pass through these temptations? Let the devils do what they will, I know the Lord will not permit them to do more than my spirit can bear." Sometimes smiling at the very torments, she would say to the devil "And after thou shalt have tormented me as thou wishest, what shalt thou have obtained? At any rate, *Benedicam Dominum in omni tempore, semper laus ejus in ore meo* "—"I will bless the Lord at all times; His praise shall be always in my mouth" (Ps xxxiii, 1) One day, to reproach them for their impotence, after she had been thrown twice to the ground, she said to the devils "You can only do to me what my Spouse permits you to do." And she said particularly to one devil· "I do not deny thy being strong, horrible beast, and my being, of myself, weak, but the Lord is near me, who is infinitely more powerful than thou " And, addressing them all, she said "Do you not perceive, foolish and ignorant, that I am with my Jesus, and you can do me no harm? Do you not perceive, also, that with all your attacks you will make me a more glorious victor?" Encouraged by celestial protection, she showed herself to them in the act of triumphing When she saw them in the choir trying to suggest vain thoughts to the minds of the nuns, to distract them from the divine praises; when in the Communion chapel, to prevent their being recollected in God for that great act, and, in hearing God's Word, to distract them with untimely ideas; when in the refectory, to stimulate their sense of gluttony to cause illness, and to withdraw their attention from the ſ⸺ ⸺ ⸺ ⸺ ⸺ ⸺ ⸺ or in other places of or⸺ ⸺ ⸺ ⸺ ⸺ ⸺ ⸺ ⸺gel t. she, intrepid, the cross in one hand and the discipline in the other, was chasing them all around, saying to the nuns "Don't you see that all the monastery is infested by devils, who stay around us to tempt us?" Being asked why she made no effort in the direction of the chapter, to shake the devils from it, she replied that they did not enter that place because of the acts of humility and mortification that were performed in it.

We being docile, therefore, to the suggestions and teachings of the Catholic doctrine about the existence, nature, and condition of the infernal spirits, the facts of St. Mary Magdalen De-Pazzi's life thus far narrated are for us an ulterior confirmation of these things, as may be seen by the most obvious reasoning. In a soul naturally so good, so well cultivated by education and virtue, so favored by divine grace, such a contradiction of sentiments could not, of itself, appear so suddenly. Neither could that principle of sin, which unhappily is rooted in our hearts, pass to the act of molesting us, except by the force of exterior seducing circumstances, or by one's own wicked will. This is afterwards followed by fanaticism, as a consequence of it, and, at the same time, a cause of irregular and perverse imaginations. Outside of these causes, every movement arising in us which is opposed to the eternal law can be caused but by the external suggestions with which the devils go about seeking our ruin. Hence, this creature, ever innocent, protected by the sacred cloister and the devout practices, in common and in private, which she performed in it, with the most firm and constant disposition to throw herself into the fire rather than to commit sin, had an imagination which, if capable of excess, must be of virtue, and not of vice. These wicked tendencies, especially to blasphemy, cannot be attributed to anything but to the art of the devil. Nor can the sad phenomena of her body be explained by any other cause. Her physical condition, according to the testimony of the first doctors then in Florence, was not subject to any organic affection; and the faculties of her soul, whose witnesses were her spiritual directors, who carefully studied everything extraordinary that happened in her, were never diverted from their freedom of action, though their activity sometimes would not correspond to her desire. Finally, in addition, the fact that she specifically foretold this infernal combat, determining even the time, which, having been literally verified, seals the truth of the things above related with a most marked divine character. It remains now for our instruction, that in the incontestable evidence of this personal struggle, excited by hell more as a revenge than a simple temptation, and perceiving the rare sanctity of our Magdalen, we learn what power the devil has over us, and what and how great is the assistance of God in our behalf, whenever we do not render ourselves unworthy of it. And if such excessive and extraordinary aggressions are not heard of in our days, and we have no reason to fear that we may suffer them ourselves, we should fear none the less the ordinary temptations tending more adroitly, though less openly, to lead us to perdition. Especially should we fear the living persons of whom the devil commonly makes use to interfere with our welfare, to divert us from the right path, and to ruin us utterly.

EIGHTH TEMPTATION.

SHE IS MOLESTED AND CONTRADICTED BY HER NUNS.

Unhappy is the man who fastens all his happiness to the opinion or the plaudits of the world. He lies down in the evening with but one thought, awakes in the morning with but one hope, and passes the day in seeing the dreams of the night vanish one by one And if sometimes worldly laurels carry one triumphantly to the summit of the Capitol, ordinarily this serves but to hasten the ignominy of the Tarpejan rock Well does the Holy Ghost warn us that cursed is the man who puts his trust and his happiness in another man. When we base our judgment on the estimation of others, in most cases our logic gives way to incoherence and folly. Our soul, created to the image of God, cannot be judged but by principles proceeding from God Himself; otherwise, we will estimate one another with the most monstrous injustice and unreasonableness. Experience teaches us this every day To-day we raise to the sky what we shall to-morrow cast into the abyss, to-day we erect the gibbet for him whom but yesterday we placed on the throne. The thousand motives which now incline us in favor of a person, are shortly afterwards turned into so many motives to condemn him, without the least remembrance of his worth. What more powerful and efficacious example of this can be found, than that which Jesus Christ Himself wished to leave us in His own person? He, acclaimed by the people as the new King of Israel, made His triumphant entry into the earthly Jerusalem, where everybody vied in addressing Him with words of joy and acclamation His most innocent life, His most wonderful doctrine, His modesty, benignity, meekness,—all His virtues and His many miracles had finally brought the people to acknowledge His mission But as those men still looked at Jesus Christ with a carnal eye, therefore, by the volubility and inconstancy of earthly vision, a few days afterwards the most horrible, the most execrable, and the most monstrous of crimes was committed by those very men against the sacred person of the Divine Redeemer. They had forgotten everything that a few moments before had moved them in His favor Even the Apostles, already well purified in the spiritual sight, forgot somewhat the virtue of their Divine Master, although they had been for a long time the eye-witnesses thereof The prophecies were thus fulfilled, and the way of light and truth was thrown wide open to us. Walking in it, let us not look for any reward from the world other than that of ingratitude and calumny. "Every man," even Seneca says, " who walks in the right path must never get discouraged, nor stop at the shocks of falsehood that will assail him without fail " Our Saint, being so zealous an imitator of the sufferings of our Divine Saviour, was to partake also in some manner of the mortification of the unjust judgment of the world Domestic demons— demons clothed in human flesh—were to make her feel their wickedness She had, inspired by her Spouse Jesus, foretold to the sisters, as Christ did to His Apostles, that in the time of her tribulation they would turn against her, as we have already seen in the beginning of this chapter, and to the nun who, like Peter, declared herself the most firm and faithful, she answered that before the rest did so, she would have given up her favorable opinion of her. The sisters saw that what she had foretold about this tribulation had come to pass; they were cognizant of the exquisite virtues which adorned her soul, they knew that the spirit of God guided her constantly, even in the midst of the fiercest enemies They could not, in the least, doubt that she would valiantly resist all the infernal assaults, or that her pristine purity would suffer the least taint. Notwithstanding this, they all waged such war against her, that no matter how much we wish to ascribe this to Divine permission, it was nothing, in fact, but the immediate effect of human ignorance and perversity. She was no more, for them, the former Magdalen; the austerity of her past savored of ostentatious piety, and some even doubted that it might be but apparent, as the under-cook one day, being in the adjacent room for the purpose of preparing fruits for dinner, saw a sister who perfectly resembled Sister Mary Magdalen enter the kitchen, and, approaching the pot, take therefrom a piece of meat, with the appearance of a desire to eat it. She was so scandalized at it, that, having spoken of it with very little discretion, she raised in a short time a great prattle at the expense of our Saint, and, out of about eighty female and claustral tongues composing that religious family, every one had to utter her word of criticism about this occurrence   Likewise, another time, at night, a sister of the appearance of Sister Mary Magdalen was seen to steal into a room and take something to eat. But in the first and in the second case the nuns were quieted down, though not all of them were convinced until an eye-witness asserted having seen Sister Mary Magdalen elsewhere at the time of the above-related occurrences, viz   at the time of the first one, in the chapter; and at the time of the second one, in the oratory of the novitiate   So that all those who had no difficulty in lending belief to such an assertion, and, on the other hand, would not countenance a mere calumny, had to infer that the devil, in both cases, had assumed the form of our Saint, and thus shown himself in those actions to discredit her   The fact is, that out of so many nuns, only two remained constant, that is, receded less than the others from the favorable opinion they had of this holy and noble virgin. The ecstasies and the extraordinary favors which had appeared so evident in her that there was not the least reason for doubting them, were now reputed to be mere frauds and diabolical illusions   Her many sufferings during this time of desolation and trial were now believed to be consequences of ill-will, or caprice, or, at least, negligence, because of which such strange things justly happened to her. The very miracles, as we will see, wrought through her at that time did not suffice to make the sisters hold the requisite good opinion of her. Hence, those among the sisters who were inclined to judge her with more benignity, and not to treat her as a hypocrite or a dreamer, considered her guilty of sloth   We may infer from this how many afflictions and what ill-treatment Magdalen had to endure for so long a time, and in so numerous a gathering of religious persons When it is a question of hunting up the peculiarity of anyone living with them, who may be a standing reproach to their tepidity, they are worse than any class of lay-persons   Just as the Pharisees cried out "Blasphemy!" when Christ forgave sins, pronounced it abasement, when

He consoled sinners, declared it revolting and notorious impiety, when He healed the sick on the Sabbath-day,—they are capable, being animated by the same Pharisaical spirit, of clothing with malice the most holy actions of their neighbors. It is not improbable that among so many sisters in the monastery there should be some of this description

But this sacred virgin, having triumphed over all the infernal fury above described, triumphed no less over all that these, her domestic devils in the flesh, could invent to her dishonor and torment. She, like the woman eulogized by the Holy Ghost, opposed silence, meekness, and benignity to the persecutions. Constant in her devout proceedings, she loved and venerated all, prayed for all, did good to all, but neither wished nor hoped for anything from any living person. She served God, like St. Paul, in good and bad renown alike, and, leaving us the example of how a good name is to be preserved, she secured a true victory by faith, which places the whole world under our feet, as St John teaches us: "*Hæc est victoria quæ vincit mundum, fides nostra*"—"And this is the victory which overcometh the world, our faith" (1 John v, 4) There is no kind of temptation over which faith cannot triumph. Not by a cynical sentiment, which faces public opinion with contempt and derision, but, convinced that the scourge comes to us from the loving hand of God, who strikes us, as His children, for our best welfare, and makes us happy by placing us under an unjust persecution, we triumphantly ride over all our enemies. Justly is the Christian's victory attributed to faith, because this shows us the joys we must hope for, excites us to the acquisition of them, and teaches us whence we must expect the help necessary to win and what motives we have for trusting in such help, because manifestly loyal is He who fights for us and with us. To faith, as to a root, hope and charity must be united, which three virtues assure us, according to St. Paul, that neither life nor death, neither men nor angels will separate us from the charity of Christ. By the Cross, invoked by us with a lively faith, all the infernal spirits are dispersed or rendered impotent to hurt our soul. By practicing the principle which faith proposes to us, that "he who is smitten on one cheek should turn the other to the smiter," we radically remove from our heart everything that may be opposed to our own good and that of society, and thus implant in the soul of the offender the most noble thoughts, unlike that inhuman principle of the world, that "he who receives a blow on the face, unless he takes revenge for it, is dishonored." By this principle the greatest infamy and degradation is wrought on the Christian and the man, as on their skill, or rather the hazard of the point of a sword, they place the honor, the blood, and the life of man. If then, as believers in God, we wish not to be indifferent to our eternal destiny, let us reflect well on the fact that nobody shall be crowned unless he shall have legitimately fought in the necessary fight of this life, that is, with the arms of faith, left us by Jesus Christ, and employed by all the Saints

St Paul, chosen by God as the first proclaimer of this truth, had experienced in himself more than others the dangers which, at every step, threaten us with ruin —the most powerful enemies who incessantly work our perdition, and he ever moved to the sure guide in the path of our welfare, tells us distinctly: "*Non coronabitur, nisi qui legitime certaverit*"—"For he also that striveth for the mastery, is not crowned except he strive lawfully (2 Tim. ii, 5). If we also have the ambition to leave behind us an honorable name, let the truth be impressed on our mind that by no other path will we come to it but by that of virtue, though the world may follow the opposite. To immortalize the memory of anyone, we speak but of his moral and Christian virtues. To exalt a genius in art or science, if not possessing virtuous qualities, historians assiduously study to present him with some invented ones. To praise a sovereign, they begin with his beneficence; a magistrate, with his rectitude; a rich man, with his liberality; a poor man, with his patient submission. So that at the very moment when the world with its maxims is persecuting virtue, it finds it necessary to acknowledge it in the initiative of any glorious undertaking. Therefore, by an irresistible logic, it venerates the Saints above all; and justly venerates Mary Magdalen De-Pazzi with a eulogy superior to that which will ever be given to those personages who become celebrated by despotism, by power, by war, by riches, by science—proving every day that, as Fenelon says, "Man is always small when he is not great except by vanity."

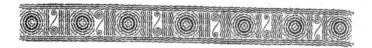

CHAPTER XIV.

OF SOME SPIRITUAL COMFORTS GRANTED BY THE DIVINE GOODNESS TO ST. MARY MAGDALEN DURING THE ABOVE-DESCRIBED FIVE YEARS OF PROBATION.

HE SEES JESUS AS WHEN PILATE PRESENTED HIM TO THE PEOPLE.—He who carries his cross for the love of God never succumbs to its weight. Deified, so to say, by the merits of Christ, it contains in itself so much sweetness and relief that it often infuses into the soul of the patient sufferer the most lively consolation. This faithful Bride of Christ for whom tribulations were like fuel that kindled in her more and more the fire of Divine love, during those five years, was comforted and consoled in various ways. Now by means of the Most Holy Sacrament; now by being raised into ecstasy, and thus partaking of the celestial secrets; and now by joyous and wonderful apparitions, either of her Divine Spouse, or of the Blessed Virgin, the angels, or her patron Saints; but especially by the following occurrence: On February 5th, 1585, which, in that year, was Shrove-Thursday—that is, the last Thursday of carnival—the nuns were making, as was customary, a devout exercise, to atone for so many offenses which in those bacchanal days were wont to be offered to the Divine Majesty, when she, considering such offenses in the bitterness of her heart, was rapt in ecstasy, and the suffering Jesus appeared to her in the act and under the form in which the impious Pilate showed Him to the Hebrew people, saying: "*Ecce Homo.*" At such a sight, inflamed with the most fervent desire to suffer, she exclaimed: "My Jesus, why cannot I be the one who suffers as many pains, derisions, and abuses as those traitors make Thee suffer when Pilate shows Thee to the people? Why cannot I remove from Thy head that piercing crown that pains Thee so much, and put it on my own, as it is for me Thou wearest it, and for me Thou sufferest these pains and torments?" Then she understood that Jesus, to comply with her virtuous wish, would give her a precious gift, full at once of sadness and sweetness—that is, the little packet of myrrh of His passion, such as St. Bernard had been favored with. Hence she, gladly and with sentiments of affection, begged of this Saint to prepare her to receive it, sanctifying her in the blood of Jesus. After this, naming separately the instruments of the passion of her Divine Spouse, whilst seeming to be in His embrace, she extended her hands as if in the act of receiving that great gift, and then, as though she had received it, pressed her hands closely to her breast and said : "*Fasciculus myrrhæ dilectus meus mihi, inter ubera mea commorabitur*"—"A bundle of myrrh is my beloved to me: he shall abide between my breasts" (Cant. 1, 12). Saying this, she fell to the ground, trembling, with manifest signs of great suffering ; and, in fact, as she afterwards related by obedience, at that moment, not only in her mind, but also in her body, she felt the most excruciating torments. Having come to herself shortly after, filled with fervor and stronger and more courageous than ever, she continued her combat against the devils.

2. SHE ENJOYS THE SIGHT OF THE INFANT JESUS.—A few days after it pleased the Divine Goodness to favor this Virgin Saint in a manner not less precious and effectual She had anxiously wished for a long time to see the Infant Jesus as He looked when He came from the immaculate womb of the most holy Mary. This wish was fully gratified when, being rapt in ecstasy, the Blessed Virgin appeared to her with the Divine Child as she wished to see Him, and placed Him in Mary Magdalen's arms. The Saint was overcome with delight and joy, and seemed to melt with love. Words could not express the emotion and sentiments of tenderness to which she gave vent in this contemplation of the Infant Jesus.

3 SHE IS COMFORTED BY THE GLORIOUS APPARITION OF ST. THOMAS AQUINAS —On the 7th of March of the same year, 1585, the feast of St. Thomas Aquinas, as she was contemplating the glory of her patron Saint, she was rapt in an ecstasy, during which she saw him surrounded by a glorious light, and, being by him encouraged to persist dauntless in the combat, she was informed that her aridity of spirit was still to increase Hence, recommending herself with great energy to the intercession of the Saint, she seemed to see and feel as though, before leaving her, he had anointed her heart and all her senses with an odorous and precious liquid, which left her spirit very cheerful and reinvigorated.

4. SHE DRAWS CONSOLATION AND PROFIT FROM MEDITATING ON THE MYSTERY OF THE WORD INCARNATE.—Moreover, on the feast of the Annunciation of the Blessed Virgin, in the same year, meditating on the most profound mystery of the Incarnation, she remained ecstatic for six whole hours, deriving therefrom very great spiritual comfort, as by means of celestial revelations she felt her understanding enlightened and her will strengthened, both of which in the darkness of the temptations she seemed to have lost.

5. HER PAINS FOR SOME TIME GIVE WAY TO CONSOLATIONS, AS IT HAD BEEN FORETOLD TO HER.—On the twentieth day of July of the following year, 1586, being the feast of St Margaret, Virgin and Martyr, whilst she was in the choir reciting the divine office, her spirit was carried out of her senses, and she understood how God would be pleased to slightly mitigate that spiritual conflict until the following month of October It so happened, for. during that time, she was left unmolested by the diabolical vexations, enjoyed more tranquillity and consolation of spirit, and had more frequent and remarkable ecstasies.

She receives the holy habit of the Carmelite Order (page 37)

6. SHE IS ASSURED OF NOT BEING DELUDED IN REGARD TO THE SUPERNATURAL GIFTS.—But the following month of August was chosen by Divine Providence to calm and strengthen, in the most marked and efficacious manner, the troubled spirit of Mary Magdalen. On the eleventh day of the month she entered into a wonderful ecstasy, in which state she remained until the fifteenth, returning to her senses for but two hours each day, to say the divine office and take a little nourishment of bread and water. Little did she talk during these four days, and very much did she enjoy the highest communication between God and herself. As the sentiment of despair was the most apt to depress her spirit, for, on account of her humility, she continually feared to be deluded in her ecstasies and revelations, the benign Lord, who does not allow the humble of heart to be dejected, but rather wishes for their exaltation, came to her rescue and reassured His beloved in her great affliction in a wonderful way. During the same month she had two ecstasies, one on the sixteenth and the other on the twenty-fifth, during which she was distinctly assured that the revelations and supernatural occurrences she enjoyed were not delusions of the devil, but pure consequences of God's love for her In the meantime, God let her know that He wanted her, for fifteen days, to take nourishment but three times, namely, on the two Thursdays and the Sunday intervening, taking on each Thursday, in the evening only, a little bread and wine, and Lenten diet on Sunday This confirmed her more and more in regard to what was now made manifest to her She made this injunction known to her spiritual father and the mother prioress, and, as they also wished to have some guarantee of the truth of these visions, they gladly granted her permission to follow it. In order to faithfully comply with the Divine will, manifested to her on a Sunday, and having at the same time obtained permission, on the following Monday she undertook this fast, so that she was without any nourishment at all until the evening of Thursday, when she took a small quantity of bread and wine; and from then until the evening of the following Sunday, and so also during the second week she did not even take a drop of water, except what God had ordered her to take The most holy Eucharistic Bread, which she received every morning, was the true and only restorative that helped her to pass through the fifteen days, even more active than usual at all the exercises of Religion To the great astonishment of the nuns, they never saw her tired or pale, nor showing a sign of weakness, much less of succumbing or giving way, on account of her excessive abstinence, as some of the nuns supposed would happen The Lord, to reward such loyal and complete correspondence, confirmed her in the assurance of not being deceived, so that the enemy lost all hope of seducing her in this manner, and likewise her confessor and the nuns, not being able to doubt such a sign's being from God, subdued to a great extent the fear they had begun to entertain about the truth of her actions and visions

7. JESUS APPEARS TO HER IN HIS GLORY, AND SHE SEES ALSO ST. JOHN THE EVANGELIST AND ST. CATHERINE OF SIENA —While she was in a most humble posture with a rope around her neck, as was said above, she kissed the feet of all the sisters Afterward, full of

spiritual joy, she withdrew to the choir, and there, being rapt in ecstasy, Jesus, glorious and resplendent, appeared to her, and, to reward this humiliation, lovingly received her into His arms, and with a kiss of divine love inebriated her with such sweetness that she gave evidence thereof in her countenance and her whole person. In the same ecstasy she saw St John the Evangelist and St. Catherine of Siena, who, by means of strong chains, bound the devils she had vanquished and overcome

8. SHE SEES JESUS SCOURGED, AND SHE HEARS HOW HER HUMILIATION IS PLEASING TO GOD.—Having procured somebody to tie her behind the book-stand of the choir, to her humiliation, in such a position she was rapt in ecstasy, and then she saw Jesus tied to the pillar and scourged. She was wonderfully consoled by this vision and encouraged to suffer every pain for the love of the suffering Jesus. Another time, after the act of humiliation in which she caused herself to be bound blindfolded to the grates of the choir, she, when loosened and unveiled, prostrated herself before the altar of the Blessed Virgin. Here she immovably fixed her eyes on the image and was raised into an ecstasy, during which the Lord told her that this action had pleased Him very much, as He regards closely and with love all acts of humility, and distantly and with contempt all acts of pride. She also understood how the devils were confused at it; and she seemed to hear their roars, as if they could not endure her humiliations

9 SHE SEES THE GLORY OF ST AUGUSTINE.—On the eve of St Augustine's day, 1587, as she was reciting some psalms in honor of this Saint, she felt a great desire to see his glory. God complied with her desire. On the evening of the same day, as she was in the choir for the recitation of compline, she was rapt in ecstasy, and the vision of St. Augustine, in his most refulgent glory, was presented to her imagination; by which, as if that glory in some way redounded unto her, her eyes became brilliant with celestial joy, and in her countenance shone a certain divine beauty. She then addressed to the Saint most affectionate words. The following night, being also in the choir for matin, she saw, ecstatically, St. Augustine as glorious as the preceding night; and, remaining for a while in this contemplation, she finished the office by herself, in such a way that reciting one verse she would pass over the other in silence lasting as long as would be required by its recital. It was concluded from this that the Saint himself was her partner in the psalmody. She also gave evidence of hearing at the same time the angelic melodies, as, listening very attentively, she burst into these words "These songs are far different from those we engage in on earth!" Having ended thus the recital of matin, she remained in ecstatic contemplation until the time for Holy Communion, when, having received with ineffable sweetness and fervor the Eucharistic Bread, she came to herself from the ecstasy. In customary obedience, she related how God in this instance increased the strength of her spirit to overcome her enemies and advance in spiritual perfection

10 THE BLESSED VIRGIN PUTS ON HER A WHITE VEIL.—The ecstasy she had on the 17th of September of the same year, 1587, was very wonderful and effective. Being fiercely attacked in the virtue of chastity, as was related, and forbidden by her confessor and her mother

superioress from again throwing herself among thorns, or doing any other injury to her body, she, by way of compensation, gave herself up to prayer with redoubled fervor, imploring above all the assistance of the Queen of virgins. On the same day, it happened that, having withdrawn to a remote chamber, by prayers of a most suppliant devotion, and by most touching tears, she turned to the most pure Mother of God, that she might obtain for her such a victory over the impure temptations, that her virginity would not be stained in the least thereby. Having just made the request, the Blessed Virgin appeared to her in the form of a noble and tender mother, and, consoling her, told her to be calm, as in all such temptations she had never offended God, nay, by her courageous fight with the impure spirit, she had come out completely victorious, and, as a reward therefor, the Blessed Virgin put on her a pure white veil, and told her, moreover, that in future she would not again have to suffer the temptations or suggestions of impurity. At this moment, Mary Magdalen interiorly felt as if all appetite of carnal concupiscence was being reduced, and that all the disordered fire of sensuality had been extinguished in an ineffable manner. In fact, during all her life, this angelic soul was not again molested by a desire of the flesh, nor even by any imagination or the least thought contrary to holy purity.

11. JESUS CLOTHES HER WITH AN INVISIBLE RELIGIOUS HABIT, AND FROM HIM SHE RECEIVES SACRAMENTAL COMMUNION —During the temptation of forsaking the Religious habit, on the 5th of August, 1588, after having resisted it with great strength, in order the better to remove it, she began to read attentively the life of St Diego, her particular protector. While reading, she was alienated from her senses, and saw, in spirit, this Saint showing her a pure white habit which came out of the side of the Divine Redeemer. Magdalen being charmed with it, felt an ardent wish to be clothed with it, and, with great warmth, supplicated her Celestial Spouse to give it to her, and through the merits of St. Albert, Carmelite—whose feast was being celebrated on that day—to condescend to clothe her interiorly with it, that she might more efficaciously imitate the Saint whose life she was reading Panting for it with all her heart, and keeping her eyes fixed on a Crucifix that stood before her, she saw, coming out of His side, a tunic even more beautiful and precious than the habit mentioned above; He had in his right hand a scapular, in His left, a cincture, on His head, crowned with thorns, a white veil, and, coming out of the wound in the neck, caused by carrying the cross, a shining mantle. This sight having filled her with the liveliest enthusiasm, she suddenly leaped upon the altar where this Crucifix was, and there, performing all the acts which are wont to be made at the first reception of the Religious habit, and pronouncing the appropriate words, manifestly demonstrated that she received from the hands of Jesus that habit of religious form and divine origin And, as if already dressed, she proceeded through the ceremony, giving evidence that the Queen of Heaven placed the garland on her head, and the light and the Crucifix in her hands, as is usually done with the new Rel ... The ... well attended to the singing of the customary vers ... the dressing, nor

was sacramental Communion wanting in this ecstatic ceremony, as, at that point, she said the *Confiteor* and *Domine, non sum digna*, &c., and, in the attitude of receiving the Bread of Angels, she showed that Jesus Himself gave her Holy Communion. Being thereby overcome with joy, she addressed these affectionate words to the Divine Spouse whom she had received: "*Dilectus meus candidus et rubicundus*"—"My beloved is white and ruddy (Cant. v, 10) . . . "*Speciosus forma præ filiis hominum*"—"Beautiful above the sons of men" (Ps. xliv, 3) . . . "*Electus ex millibus*"—"Chosen out of thousands" (Cant. v, 10). "*Diffusa est gratia in labiis tuis. Collocavit se in anima mea.*" Then, being excited by the greatest desire to lead everyone to this divine Sacrament, she subjoined: "*Dilata, Domine Jesu, cor meum, ut inducam omnem creaturam ad communionem corporis et sanguinis tui.*" And, giving vent to the sentiments she felt in her heart towards the Divine Goodness, she exclaimed: "*Quam bonus Israel Deus!*" Then, taking the Crucifix out of which she had seen the habit come, and having thanked the Lord for all the graces with which He had favored her, and recommended to Him the salvation of all souls, she gave it to all the nuns present, that they might kiss it. Finally, coming to herself from the rapture, she placed before the superioress the plain manifestation of the above-mentioned favors which she had enjoyed ecstatically for the space of three hours.

CHAPTER XV.

SHE SEES THE SOUL OF ONE OF HER BROTHERS IN PURGATORY, AND UNDERSTANDS THE EXCESSIVENESS OF THE PAINS BY WHICH SOME VICES ARE PUNISHED THEREIN.

N June of 1587, a brother of the Saint died. Whilst she was praying to God for his soul, she was transported in imagination into purgatory, where she saw that soul suffering unutterable torments. At such a sight she prayed with redoubled fervor to the Divine Goodness for its deliverance; and having remained in devout prayer for over half an hour, she came to herself, much terrified. Then, with her eyes filled with tears of sadness, she went to the superioress, and, falling on her knees at her feet, said in a tone of amazement and sorrow: "O Mother! great, indeed, are the pains which the souls suffer in purgatory! I would never have thought them to be so intense, had God not given me some light in regard to them." Also, on the day following, meditating on those pains, she fell into a painful alienation from the senses, during which, turning to heaven, she exclaimed: "O my God, my heart cannot bear to live on earth and converse with creatures after such a sight." But on the evening of the day following, whilst she was in the garden with the other nuns, her spirit wandered at greater length, and more distinctly among the various conditions of the suffering souls. With a sad and pale countenance, her eyes showing the sorrowful object which absorbed her, with a grave bearing, she started and at a slow pace went around the garden, and, stopping now here and now there, gave evidence of seeing most excessive and diverse pains. From the words she uttered, it seemed as if in one place she saw the pains of the Religious; in another, those of the hypocrites; then those of the ignorant; then those of the disobedient; here, those of the impatient; there, those of the liars; besides those of the ambitious, the proud, the avaricious, and, lastly, those of the ungrateful. Such was the terror that seized her on beholding this sight, and such the compassion she felt for the sufferings of others, that, because of the intensity and variety of feeling, now she would stoop down to the ground, now sadly shake her head, now clasp her hands, now, raising her eyes to heaven, with deep sighs, address to God the most fervent prayers for the suffering souls, and now invite heaven and earth to share in her distress. She would also turn herself to the poor souls, now addressing words of compassion to them; now reproaching them for the sins for which they were tortured, and now comforting them by the hope of the joy they expected. So lively

were the acts she performed, so fervent and resolute the words she uttered in this ecstasy, that she actually appeared to see those torments with her corporal eyes, and she so touched the nuns present as even to make them shed tears, and enkindle in all in the monastery a permanent fervor of praying to God for the souls in purgatory. Among the remarkable things she said about these pains, was that "all torments endured by the martyrs are like being in a delicious garden, compared to what the souls in purgatory suffer," and then, when out of the rapture, she added that "those pains were so terrible that if in seeing them she had not had the assistance of her guardian angel and St Augustine, who continually accompanied her in that place, she could not have endured such a sight" From this vision she learned how to understand and better venerate the perfection of the purity of God, who does not permit to enter into His kingdom any but souls purified and cleansed of even the least stain of guilt; and she resolved to hate sin more, resist the temptations with greater strength, and with frequent prayers and expiatory deeds relieve the suffering souls. Among these, cutting off by the arm of faith all the doubts that audacious and foolish unbelief present to us, we should reflect that there are now, also, our relatives and friends, who anxiously await our mercy. Oh, if it would only be given us to hear their plaintive appeals! Like St. Mary Magdalen, let us also revive our faith and fervor on behalf of those blessed souls! None of us are free from at least some obligation towards the dead The strictest duties of acknowledgment, of gratitude, of justice call upon us to help them. Nor can we flatter ourselves that we have nobody there belonging to us by some title; as it is very seldom that one may leave this mortal life having no need of purification. "No man is without sin," teaches the Apostle "No creature can justify herself before God," says Job The mercy of God, it is true, forgives all, but His justice retains some part of the debt, which we must pay in the next life before our souls can sit at the banquet of the Lamb, like immaculate daughters of Zion. Hence, it is also to our own interest to relieve the suffering souls, as it being almost inevitable that we will pass through or rather remain for some time in that place of sighs and desires, by shortening for them the road to heaven, we make it easier for ourselves; and by obtaining for them the possession of the sovereign good, we render ourselves less unworthy of possessing it, and consequently we diminish the amount of our debts and shorten the time of our deliverance. "Do good unto the just soul," says the wise man, "and thou shalt be rewarded for it." It is not faith alone, nor the Church only, that reminds us of the needs of the dead; but a universal custom, as old as the world, plainly proves that God Himself has implanted in man such pious and noble sentiments for the memory of the departed, as if to admonish us of the future survival, to which we are immortally privileged. The Church proposes several means of fulfilling so solemn and sacred a duty, as suffrages of piety; but our heart has full liberty of choice among all virtuous works. Even the merest thought directed to good, God accepts in expiation of the faults of others Let us, then, remember to place, with Tobias our bread and our wine on the sepulchre of the just, that is, to offer daily for them some sacrifice to the Lord.

CHAPTER XVI.

BY THE WILL OF GOD SHE TAKES OFF HER SHOES AND STOCKINGS AND PUTS ON THE POOREST TUNIC.

POPE ST. GREGORY, commenting on these words of the Divine Master—"*Qui non renuntiat omnibus quæ possidet, non potest meus esse discipulus*"—said that he who undertakes to fight the devil must put off the vestments of earthly things: "*Qui contra diabolum ad certamen properat, vestimenta abiiciat, ne succumbat.*" Thus God, who wished the greatest perfection for this fighting soul, having placed it in this fight as if in an encounter with the devil, notwithstanding her being divested of every earthly thing—that is, of all attachments to this world, which are just the vestments meant by the above text—yet He also imposed on her the literal observance of such a precept, so that the lightness of the body might correspond to the prompt attitude of the spirit in victoriously fighting all her enemies. It was the 5th of July, 1587, when God, having taken this faithful servant into ecstasy, gave her to understand it to be His will that she should go barefooted, choose the meanest among the habits of the Religious, and take for herself the poorest cell and the most wretched bed. She, without interposing a single thought of delay, being still in ecstasy, took off her shoes and stockings, and, going to her cell, removed therefrom every object, even the least one, with the exception of a Crucifix on the little altar; she also stripped the bed, leaving only a straw mattress and a board. Then, going to the room where the nuns' habits were kept and repaired, she opened the closets to see what tunics they contained. Selecting the most worn and patched one, she withdrew to another room, where, taking off the one she had on, she put on the other. The contentment and joy of her heart at seeing herself so meanly clad for the love of God was so great, that, fixing her eyes on heaven, she thanked Divine Providence for it as for a special benefit, and, with unutterable emotion of affection, recited the *Te Deum*. After this, making a bundle of her former habit, she brought it to the room of the mother superioress, and, taking an inkstand, with pen and paper, immediately went to the choir, and then ascending the altar of the Blessed Virgin, and kneeling down, placed the paper in the bosom of the sacred image, with her profession renewed in writing upon it, in these words:

"I, Sister Mary Magdalen, make profession of and promise to God—to His most pure Mother, the Virgin Mary, to St. Catherine of Siena, and to Francis the Seraphic, and to all the celestial court—obedience, chastity, and poverty in the manner in which God at this moment makes me understand and know, with a firm purpose of never leaving it unless I should have a true light, making me know that it is pleasing to Him, as I now understand that it is truly Himself who wants me to observe this poverty; hence, confiding in His help and mercy, I make this profession—*in manu puritatis Mariæ* "—" in the hands of Mary's purity."

Whilst she wrote this spontaneous formula, she kept her left hand continually on the hands of the image. Then laying down the pen, with her right hand on the inkstand, and gravely stretching out her left hand on the paper, and, finally joining both of them with energy, she said with a firm voice "If anybody shall tell me that I invent a new rule, I will answer that it is no novelty, but simply perfecting my rule, as all should do." She then spoke of holy poverty in such a manner as to excite in all the sisters who heard her a great desire to observe it minutely. Finally, turning again to the Blessed Virgin, with affectionate and pressing words, she begged that she would take her under her constant and particular protection, and help her to do all that God had manifested to her that she should do. Then, coming to herself from her rapture, she went to the mother prioress, and falling on her knees, with her hands joined, entreated her in the name of God not to prevent her following that mode of life which Heaven so evidently dictated for her. The prioress answered at the moment, with all prudence, that it was necessary to inform the spiritual father, and then all should submit to his advice. Her desire having been made known to the confessor, before he granted the permission he wished to assure himself, by a new trial, of the obedience of Sister Mary Magdalen, thinking also that he thereby would ascertain whether there was any diabolical deception in it. Hence he positively commanded her to put on her shoes and stockings, and clothe herself with her usual vestments. The Saint felt an extreme disappointment in finding her spiritual director differ from the revelation just narrated, and the doubt arose in her mind that perhaps she had been deceived, as she could not believe a decided opposition in her spiritual father possible, if what she intended doing were from God. This grave doubt caused her to burst into tears; still, wholly resigned, she obeyed. But the Lord did not cease to inspire her with her former sentiment, as He wished it carried into effect absolutely. He repeated it to her several times; and on the 2d of the following month, August, raising her into ecstasy again, He made her feel an irresistible tendency to repeat the above-described action. Actually unable to overcome the divine impulse, she took off, as before, her shoes and stockings, looked for the poorest tunic, which, for the sake of obedience she had left off, and, in taking it up again, said with a tremulous voice · "My God, when I shall be with Thee, I will obey Thee; when I shall be with them, I will obey them. Give us light here below." The mother prioress saw and heard her and, showing herself to her with an imposing appearance, thus spoke to her · "Sister Mary Magdalen, for obedience' sake, give me those vestments, and do not

Whilst reciting the Divine Office in the choir, she receives the blessing of the Blessed Virgin (page 57).

clothe yourself with them; put on your stockings and shoes again."
At this voice of obedience, the Saint came again to herself from her
rapture, and promptly gave up to the superioress the tunic asked for,
and put on the stockings and the shoes; but something wonderful followed. Her feet began to swell, and they pained her so that she could
not stand on them. She could not walk except on her hands and
knees; consequently, she was compelled to move in this way on the
ground, and when she was to receive Holy Communion she had to be
carried on the arms of the other sisters. Having continued several days
in this distress, the spiritual father thought it a sufficient indication that
it was the will of God that she should follow such a mode of poverty.
He, therefore, gave his affirmative notification to the mother prioress,
and she said to St. Mary Magdalen: "If you believe this to be God's
will, the spiritual father gives you permission to go barefooted, according
to His command." Immediately Magdalen took off her shoes and
stockings, and at the same time—no less wonderful than in the preceding occurrence—all pain in her feet ceased, and the sisters noticed
the swelling effectively decreasing. She was now ready to move and
walk without pain; and, in fact, she went quietly and without delay to
the choir, where, before the usual altar of the Blessed Virgin, she gave
to God the most fervent thanks for having thus made His Divine Will
manifest to her superiors. After this, she began to obey this command
of God in a most severe manner, dressing herself in the patched and
wornout tunic, and going barefooted continually for three years, suffering
such cruel pains in winter that, sometimes, when walking on the
ice in the garden, blood would flow from her feet, because of the
delicacy of her skin. But she never spoke a word of complaint, nor did
she ever adopt or accept any relief. At the end of the five years of probation, having, as we shall see, an inspiration from God, she again put
on her shoes and slippers, but not her stockings, except during her last
illness. She practiced the same poverty with regard to her cell and
habit until her death, in reward for which she was introduced into
heaven to enjoy unfading delights.

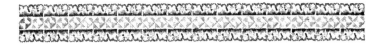

CHAPTER XVII.

BY SOME MIRACLES WROUGHT DURING THIS TIME, GOD CON-
FIRMS THAT SUCH A PROBATION CAME FROM HIM.

HE better to convince those spirits who doubted the sanctity of Mary Magdalen, of their injustice, God determined by the following miracles to manifest to the eyes of the world, even in the very midst of her trials, how much her spirit was adorned with it.

1. SHE RESTORES TO HEALTH A LAY-SISTER WHO WAS ALMOST DYING.—In 1587, Sister Fede de Domenica da Legnaja, a lay-sister in the monastery of St. Maria degli Angeli, was suffering from the contraction of her limbs, and was swollen from head to foot, her left side having become a span shorter than the other. In consequence of this contraction she could neither move her hands nor her head, and suffered most cruel pains throughout her body, which gave her not a moment's rest. Troubled for several months by this ever-increasing malady, she had such little hope of life that the physicians, considering any further visit useless, abandoned her altogether to Divine Providence. The sufferer, in the absence of all comfort from human science, felt a great confidence in the virtues of her fellow-sister, Mary Magdalen, arise with unusual strength in her soul. It was the month of July of the above year. Our Saint, counseled by the spirit of God, instead of immediately granting the request, as according to her natural piety she would have done, said: "Tell Sister Fede that to-day is not the time; let her have patience and prepare for to-morrow at Vespers' time, when I will visit her." The next day, at the time appointed, the Saint, being in the oratory of the novices in ecstasy, kneeling before an image of the Virgin, suddenly arose to her feet, and taking the image in her hands, she went with it to the bed of the sick sister, placed the image on her, and kneeling, with suppliant hands, addressed to Heaven in the meanwhile the most fervent prayers for the health of her sick fellow-sister. But a few minutes elapsed before the sick sister moved her arms, which before she could not do at all, took the image between her hands and kept it there firmly; and then our healer arose, pronouncing with great feeling these words: "O Lord, Thy will be done;" and made the sign of the cross on the patient with the image. Suddenly all the nerves of the contracted limbs extended, the swelling disappeared, the pains ceased, and she was wholly cured, so that she would have left the bed at once, had not the sisters prevented

hér doing so then. On the following morning, meeting with no opposition, she arose fully cured, and a few days afterwards (it was not permitted her before by obedience) this Sister Fede who had been almost dying, returned to her usual exercises, which were the most laborious in the monastery.

2. SHE FREES A GIRL WHO WAS POSSESSED BY THE DEVIL — Catherine, daughter of Carlo Spini, a noble Florentine maiden, being possessed by a wicked spirit, went with her mother, one day in 1588, to visit Sister Mary Magdalen De-Pazzi, her relative   As the three were conversing at the grates of the parlor, the Saint was raised into ecstasy; at the sight of which the devil began greatly to torment the girl, throwing her to the floor, making her throat swell, and causing her to roar and bellow, with frightful contortions   This sight moved Magdalen to the tenderest compassion towards this unhappy creature.   She sent for the father confessor, who was then in church, and as soon as he came to the parlor, begged of him that he would command that spirit to depart immediately from the girl's body.   But the confessor, who trusted more in the sanctity of St. Mary Magdalen than in himself, answered her. "I order thee, by holy obedience, that thou thyself command him to do this." Then the Saint, with majestic demeanor, full of confidence in God, said to the spirit. "I command thee, on the part of God, that thou depart from this body," and made the sign of the cross on the girl possessed, who was immediately left free and at rest from all trouble, as if she had never suffered it, and never more in her life was she molested by that spirit

3. BY THE SIGN OF THE CROSS SHE CHANGES SOME SPOILED WINE IN A KEG INTO GOOD WINE, DRINKING OF WHICH A SICK NUN REGAINS HER HEALTH —In August of 1588, the wine in a keg in the monastery having become sour, and the mother prioress having no means to provide good wine, she ordered Sister Mary Magdalen to pray to Jesus that He might be pleased to turn the spoiled wine again into good wine   Then our Saint, strengthened by obedience, took a little framed picture which represented St. Diego, and going with it to the wine-cellar, after a short prayer, made the sign of the cross over the keg   After this, the sister-butler came to draw wine, and found it, in fact, restored to its former good taste   The nuns gave thanks to God, who had so miraculously provided for their needs   A fellow-sister, Mary Angiola Santucci, was then confined to her bed by a serious illness, and, on hearing of this miracle, asked for a drink of the wine   No sooner had she tasted it than she felt a notable relief from her illness, and, feeling her hope of ultimate recovery increase, she wanted to taste more of it on the following day   After this, she felt better, and on the third day, taking the same small quantity, she recovered her health entirely, to the inexpressible wonder of the sisters, who could not help being cognizant of the double prodigy worked through the virtue of our humble and holy virgin.

4. SHE LICKS WITH HER TONGUE THE CONTAGIOUS SORE ON A NUN AND HEALS HER —For many years. Sister Barbara Bassi, a nun in said monastery had been suffered for a time terrible disease that, according to the doctors verdict the most of the body having become

infected, the acid humor gradually gnawed her flesh, and consequently diminished from day to day the efficacy of any medicine. In 1589, she had come to distrust her health so much that, seeing herself covered with sores and scabs, with a perceptible wasting of her body, she had given up the use of all remedies, and was not even taking care to guard herself in her room, but wandered through the monastery a prey to thoughts of sadness and despair   Sister Mary Magdalen, returning one morning after Holy Communion to her cell, met this poor sick sister in a very retired place.   On account of the great charity with which her heart was burning for her neighbor, and the compassion she actually felt, she began to lick with her tongue the hands, the arms, and the limbs infected with the disease, saying to the sufferer that, if she should have faith and trust in God and the Blessed Virgin, she would recover   In fact, two or three days afterwards, she unexpectedly found herself wholly healed, her flesh being as pure and clean as if she had never suffered any illness, and she was never again attacked with such an infection

5. SHE REANIMATES THE PARALYZED LIMBS OF A LAY-SISTER BY MAKING THE SIGN OF THE CROSS.—In the same year, 1589, Sister Pace Colombini, a lay-sister of the same monastery, being struck with apoplexy and having lost the feeling in her left side to such an extent that she did not feel the least pain from a long pin's being thrust in by the physicians   Mary Magdalen finding herself one day in the room of this sick sister, the mother prioress asked her to pray for her and bless her. Our Saint, on account of her humility, refused to do this for a while; but, conquered by obedience and charity, she made the sign of the cross over the sick nun, who immediately felt that some life was returning to the dead side   Being animated to hope well from her great benefactress, she begged her, with the greatest fervor, that she would continue to pray for her and visit her.   On the following day, Magdalen was anxious to comply with the patient's wish, and visited her, and again made the sign of the cross over her   The paralytic felt likewise a new vigor in her limbs, so that she began to move them a little   On the third day, repeating the visit and the blessing, our Saint accomplished the prodigy of a perfect cure, so that Sister Pace Colombini said with a firm voice : "I am healed"   Shortly after, she got out of her bed to the great amazement of all the nuns, and much more of the doctor, who, having been unable to see, according to his science, any hope of recovery from such an illness, could not assign a human reason for seeing her well and occupied, like any other lay-sister, in the housework of the monastery. This lay-sister was never more overtaken by this illness as they generally are who have once had a stroke.

Thus did God at once humble and exalt this, His handmaid, who, by her sanctity, confounded the rebellious and proud Lucifer; condemned the world in its false glories, its ridiculous pomps, and its vices, condemned also her fellow-sisters of the monastery in their unjust doubts; and glorified more and more the holy Name of God, furnishing in herself a new proof of the truth of that evangelical principle. that "triumph belongs to him who is the most sincere," in opposition to the political sophism that "the right belongs to him who is the shrewdest."

CHAPTER XVIII.

BEFORE THE END OF THE FIVE YEARS' PROBATION, SHE PERFORMS
A MOST SEVERE PENANCE OF FIFTY DAYS, AFTER WHICH
GOD REWARDS HER WITH SEVERAL FAVORS.

HE end of the five years ordained by God for the probation of the Saint was drawing near, when, on Easter Sunday, the 22d of April, 1590, being raised out of her senses, she understood it to be the will of God that she should undertake a new Lent of rigid penance, to last until the next Pentecost, when the combat would cease. This penance she was to perform in atonement for all the faults she had committed during those five years, assigning ten days for each year. Hence, most faithful to the divine inspirations, with His permission, she fasted all the fifty days on bread and water, slept on the bare floor, except Sundays, when she would rest a little while on the ordinary straw-bed. Besides many mortifications, spiritual exercises, and other penances which she ordinarily practiced, not a day of these fifty passed without her cruelly scourging her flesh with an iron discipline, keeping before her a human skull, a cross, and a clepsydra indicating the half-hour, which she would very often overstep, and sometimes even double in scourging herself.

Having reached through such austerity the 9th of June, the eve of Pentecost, and feeling in the morning unusually afflicted from an unknown cause, she withdrew to a place apart and used the discipline on herself for the space of almost an hour; then she went to the oratory of the novices, where, praying before the image of our Lady, she had an ecstasy of nearly two hours. The superioress, in order to get a new proof of her obedience, called her during that time, ordering her to present herself to her. At the voice of the mother, quickly returning to her senses, with deep humility she knelt at her feet, and, in obedience, related all she had understood during this ecstasy. It was that the Lord was pleased that in future she should go barefooted no more, as she had been doing for three years, but should put on her sandals, though not her stockings; that on the following three feast-days of the Holy Ghost she should conform herself to the life of the community, eating meat and whatever else the mon s cry all aved; and t'is, every year on this solemnity, as a joyous remembrance that on this reast her painful probation

had ended by God's taking her victorious out of the den of infernal lions
As the Jews yearly celebrated the remembrance of their having been
freed from Pharaoh's slavery, so she was to do likewise at Pentecost,
giving also to the body, as a companion in these sufferings, some lawful
comfort.   From that hour forward, she was also permitted to drink some
wine every Thursday evening in memory of the most sacred Eucharist.
Likewise, having desired and often asked our Lord not to grant her
so manifest and frequent supernatural favors, that she might not appear to be an object of admiration and singularity, she understood in
this ecstasy, that in future she would be less favored exteriorly with
them than she had been before her probation.   At the same time, her
soul would be even more strongly united to God, in such a manner
though, as not to prevent her from working and conversing, except
on the three days of Pentecost, when God wanted her all to Himself.   On
the first day, that she might rejoice and feast in God alone for the
victories obtained over the devils during the five years past ; on the other
two days, that she might hear what the Divine Will demanded of her
for the future   Here her interview with the mother prioress ended.

When the evening came, she quickly hid herself in her little room,
where, instead of taking rest, she passed the night in prayer till the sign
of matin, at which, going to the choir, she recited there the divine office
with the other sisters, till the *Te Deum*.   This being commenced, she
was rapt in ecstasy, and the Lord, by means of St Angelo the Carmelite,
revealed to her that He would keep her in the state of grace and
strengthen the powers of her soul and the senses of her body, so that she
might use them only in honor of God and in the service of her neighbor.
She then saw in her imagination, and even somewhat sensibly, that
the above Saint first anointed her eyes, and then her ears, mouth, hands,
and feet, and afterwards purified and strengthened her soul with the blood
of Jesus, for which she said · "*Lavit animam meam in sanguine Sponsi
mei*"   From this vision she drew great strength and much knowledge
God granted her particularly this most remarkable grace—for which she
so ardently wished—that in future she would consider every person as
just and holy, and never would she judge them otherwise, no matter
what fault she might perceive in them.   If the sin were so manifest as
to admit of no doubt, she would have the grace of excusing the intention,
and if the very intention appeared evidently bad, she would blame the
violence of the malign tempter for it, whose snares no mortal can wholly
escape   "If anyone," she said during the same rapture, "shall come to
tell me of any fault of my neighbor, I, my Lord, will not listen, but will
tell her decidedly that she should pray for her neighbor and myself, that I
may correct myself first; and of the faulty deeds witnessed by me, rather
than speak to others, I will advise the delinquent herself, as, otherwise,
instead of remedying the faults, many more are committed, and sometimes greater ones than those of which we speak "   Her spirit of charity
made her earnestly express the desire for the salvation of all souls, including those of heretics and infidels, and that all creatures would love one
another.   Having thus entered the ecstasy at the hour when she was
wont yearly to receive the Holy Ghost, she began with loving and
entreating expressions to invoke the same Divine Spirit; and then,

remaining for a while in silence, her face became at once wonderfully beautiful, her eyes shone with the most fervid joy, and, with a voice of contentment, she repeatedly exclaimed "Behold, He comes down!" Showing that the Divine Spirit, in then visiting her soul, delivered her from the stormy lake of infernal peril, and gave her back the feeling of grace, communicating to her, as an ample reward, His celestial ardor. In the excess of her joy, she uttered some passages of Holy Writ, as "*Eripuit me de manibus inimicorum meorum, et ipsi confusi sunt*"— "He delivered me from the hand of my enemies (Ps. xvii, 18) . . and "they have been confounded" (Ps. lii, 6). "*Transivi per ignem et aquam, et eduxisti me in refrigerium*"—"I have passed through fire and water, and Thou hast brought me out into a refreshment" (Ps. lxv, 12). She then saw the devils holding records of the faults into which she had fallen during these five years, and she said: "These most ferocious beasts hold in their hands old papers, thinking to return with them to their chief devil to tell him of some great gain, but my patron Saints take and tear them, as everything is purified by the blood of my Jesus. They are more grievously tormented by what they had thought would be a conquest, but they return without any victory. Who will understand, O my Lord, that what I thought to be an offense is not an offense, but a joy and glory to my soul? Only he who experiences it. But now an idle word will be for me a more serious thing than what before seemed to me a grievous offense against God, because I enjoy more liberty and can say: '*Servite Domino in timore, et exultate ei cum tremore*'—'Serve ye the Lord with fear. and rejoice unto Him with trembling'" (Ps. ii, 11). Here, turning to the mother prioress and to her mistress, and joining and pressing with her own the hands of both, she told them, with a feeling of real gladness "It came and has passed away (that is, the time of probation). help me, therefore, to thank and magnify my God." After this she recovered from her rapture, and, having partaken of the Eucharistic Bread and heard the Holy Mass, went through some community acts with the sisters, and then took her repast When just out of the refectory, she was again alienated from her senses, and saw in spirit a great light, in the midst of which were her fourteen patron Saints, who, being divided into seven pairs, were in a wonderful manner making a glorious procession. She named them in the following order: St Thomas Aquinas and St. Agnes; St. John the Evangelist and St Mary Magdalen the Penitent, St John the Baptist and St Catherine, Virgin and Martyr; St. Stephen and St Catherine of Siena, St Francis and St. Clara, St. Augustine and St. Angelo the Carmelite, St Michael the Archangel and her own Guardian Angel, who were all going to the Eternal Father, and were drawing precious gifts from His bosom, and coming back with them, in behalf of Jesus, to adorn her and reward her for the pains she had endured during the five years of her probation But as she always, and especially during that time, had lived in great fear of having in many things offended God, moved at once by surprise and joy, she said. "O my God! it looks as if Thou wouldst reward me in some way for the offense I have offered Thee. as it seems to me that I have done nothing else but offend Thee; but as Thou knowest everything." In the meantime, as she related, those Saints, approaching, adorned her with those rich gifts drawn from the bosom of the Eternal Father. St. Thomas Aquinas and St. Agnes placed on her head a beautiful crown, on which was written: *Tu videbis* ("Thou shalt see"), on the right, and *Jugum meum super te est* ("My yoke is upon thee"), on the left, which *yoke* meant the satisfaction of the Word in all His brides. In receiving this crown, she made an outward motion, as if she had fixed a garland on her head, and pronounced these words: "The crown you now give me will not prevent me from wearing that of thorns (given to her by the Lord five years previously), nay, I hope, it will be a greater ornament to the same." Then St. John the Evangelist and St. Mary Magdalen the Penitent gave her a necklace, on which was written *Tu videbis*, on the right; *Verità, Mansuetudine* ("Truth and meekness"), on the left. St. John the Baptist and St Catherine, Virgin and Martyr, clothed her with a pure white habit, which on the breast bore the face of Jesus wonderfully painted, on the right a pomegranate, on the left a lily with three little bells. St. Stephen and St Catherine of Siena adorned her with bracelets on which three eyes were engraved, which signified the Providence, the Mercy, and the Love of God St Francis and St. Clara put on the little finger of her left hand a ring formed of a four-faced diamond, on one face was written· *La salute* ("The salvation"); on the second *Annichilazione* ("Annihilation"), on the third *Individua ed intrinseca carità* ("Individual and intrinsic charity"); on the fourth *Povertà* ("Poverty"). St Augustine and St Angelo surrounded her with a fulgid whiteness, which, covering all, occupied no space, and the top of it represented the Crucifix   Finally, the Archangel St Michael and her Guardian Angel gave her a sword   Whilst she was contemplating with indescribable admiration the superhuman beauty of these, her patron Saints, and delighting in seeing herself so favored by them, transported by an excess of joy, she began to dance with the greatest agility coupled with equal modesty, and it seemed to her that the Saints at the same time were celebrating with celestial melody, in union with her, the victories that the Lord had granted her. Having somewhat subdued this great exultation, standing still, and with a firm voice, she said· "I wish to go to all those places where my adversary tried to harm me, in order to confound him and all his duplicities." In fact, being still ecstatic, she went through all those parts of the monastery where she had been attacked by the devil, and stopping particularly at one place where the fight had been more obstinate, dancing and singing, she began to mock the enemy, saying these words : "In spite of thee, I will keep the feast on the day of my Lord; I will laugh at thee before Him, and will throw myself at His feet" Having knelt there for a moment, she rose to her feet, continuing in a tone of sweet song   "In all that happened to me, O devils, before my God, to your torment, I will glory, and I will make of it a crown to put on my head, and before Him I will humble myself." Again throwing herself on her knees, in an act of adoration, soon afterward she arose, and continued· "O horrible, infernal beasts! Brawl and roar as much as you like; my soul will think no more of you than of a butterfly, but will thank my God for this great gift." In another place, which was also remarkable for the vexations

She receives the Holy Infant into her arms from the hands of the Blessed Virgin (page 86).

which Satan made her endure, she sang the words of St. Paul   "*Quis nos separabit a charitate Christi ? tribulatio, au angustia, au fames ?*"—"Who shall separate us from the love of Christ? Shall tribulation? or distress? or famine?" (Rom. viii, 35). "*Nemo poterit me separare a charitate Christi*"—"No creature shall be able to separate *me* from the charity of Christ" (*Ibid.*, 39). *Omnia arbitratus sum ut stercora, ut Christum lucrifaciam*"—"I have counted all things but as dung, that I may gain Christ" (Philip. iii, 8)   Then strengthening her confidence, she said with the holy prophet: "*Dominus illuminatio mea et salus mea, quem timebo ?*"—"The Lord is my light and my salvation, whom shall I fear?"   Finally, going to the choir, before the altar of the Blessed Virgin, she offered herself to her, with these expressions : "O most pure Mary, I offer and give myself to thee, not only with the purity and innocence I received when I consecrated myself to thee, but with that innocence more adorned and purified. Receive me, then, O Mary, and keep me in thy care." After this offering she came to herself from her ecstasy, which was so extraordinary and delightful, and had been witnessed by nearly all the nuns, who ran to share in the joy of their wonderful sister, then so triumphantly freed from diabolical vexations which had been so lasting and frightful   They could not, from the feeling of affection, of complaisance, and, I will add, from their own mortification, restrain their tears at the sight of this angelic soul, sending forth from her countenance, and especially her eyes, the most ardent sparks of paradise.   Having then returned to herself, she and the nuns reciprocally proffered acts of benevolence, forgiveness, and esteem, and all most gladly returned to God sincere praises and thanksgiving

On the following morning, the second feast of the Holy Ghost, after Holy Communion, the Mass being nearly over, God *sensibly* called Mary Magdalen, who, answered thrice—"*Ecce adsum*"—and was again absorbed in ecstasy, in which she understood how, in future, as a reward for enduring the horrible sight of the devils for the five years past, she would have always before the eyes of her mind the presence of His Divine Majesty. Jesus appearing to her, she was immediately filled with unutterable joy; and, looking steadily at Him, began to say : O my Spouse (as I must so call Thee), the sight of the devil is very horrible but Thine is incomparably more delightful, for Thou art, as the prophet said : "*Speciosus forma præ filiis hominum*" And as in the past there was no time or place in which I had not to suffer the frightful sight of those malign spirits, so now, walking, standing, working, and talking, I shall always see Thee, O my Beloved As they besides showed themselves to my mental view, and sometimes also appeared under various forms to my corporal eyes, so Thou also wilt be present not only to my mind, but also to the eyes of my body, to make me rejoice and exult the more" And Jesus asking her, then, in what form she preferred to see Him, she added : "As Thou art one God in three Persons, therefore I will be well pleased to see Thee in three forms, viz., as Thou wast when Thou didst dwell in Egypt, that is, in Thy Infancy, then as Thou wast when Thy Mother lost Thee in the temple ; finally, as in the days of Thy Passion " No sooner had she said these words than her wish was gratified. The Divine Redeemer showed

Himself to her, first, as He was in His Infancy; and she, all joyous, thus expressed to Him the loving sentiments of her heart "Oh! behold my little Infant just at the age of three or four years, oh! how beautiful Thou art! Thy beautiful eyes, so cheerful and smiling, and at the same time so thoughtful and grave: Thy head encircled by a garland of flowers, the fragrance of which draws one to embrace Thee; Thy tender hands adorned with three most beautiful rings. Oh! what a wonderful thing! Thou art little, and yet art God, but thy littleness makes me know Thy greatness. O greatness and littleness of my God! I could never satiate myself looking at Thee   O little and great God, so beautiful and attractive! I fear that Thy beautiful aspect may make me rejoice so that I may show it exteriorly also" Shortly after, seeing Jesus as in His youth, she continued thus "Oh! behold my Spouse, who shows Himself to me just at the age of twelve, when He was confounding the doctors in the temple. What an admirable countenance! how a meek gravity shines in it! His eyes are not turned to the earth, nor to heaven, but He is all recollected within Himself, to teach His bride that she must not look to the earth, as she must have already overcome all the things therein to be found, and that she must not look to heaven neither, in order not to forget her co-operation on behalf of creatures, but, looking at herself, she must acknowledge the vileness of the body and despise it; the greatness and dignity of souls, and procure, with all her might, their salvation and perfection   This gentle Youth has, in His right hand, a book, not suitable for a tyro, but for the learned and wise, in which He wants me to study in recompense for the time of my affliction and darkness   In His left hand He has a harp, with which to accompany the hymns of love. Oh! what a sweet melody! Oh! how good the Lord is to the souls who seek Him alone!" Having become silent for a while, she then went to kneel before the altar of the Blessed Virgin, and, it being already the hour when she usually received the Holy Ghost, she begged of the Divine Spirit to communicate Himself to her as well as to all the Religious of her monastery   She did not have to pray long, for a short while after she saw how the Spirit was received by the many under the form of a common ray, and by herself under that of a loving dart, which made her feel a new ardor of heavenly flame. In the meantime she came to herself from her rapture, and, having restored her body with some food, was again alienated from her senses and then she saw Jesus in the third manner in which she wished to see Him. Looking at Him in that immovable attitude which is characteristic of one who is struck with the highest amazement, she said to Him. "O my Jesus, in Thy full manhood shall I see Thee, when I am working, when praising Thee, and when toiling in all places but in those in which I have to regard Thee as an infant and as a youth   I will see Thee in that beautiful and graceful age, in which Thou didst leave Thyself as food and suffered the most cruel passion. I will delight very much in regarding Thee as Thou didst show Thyself to me now, sitting at the fountain (the Well of Samaria), asking questions and enlightening the people. Yes, O my God, at the fountain, because I must give glory to Thee alone, the unfailing Fountain of all good   '*Non nobis, Domine, non nobis*'—'Not to us, O Lord, not to us' (Ps. cxiii)   I might go through many places mentally, as Thou didst do so much during that time; but I prefer to stop with Thee at the fountain, and sometimes I will also anoint Thee as Magdalen did. Charity to my neighbor shall be the ointment. The tears with which I shall wash Thy holy feet will be that charity described by St. Paul, which consists in weeping with those who weep, and rejoicing with those who rejoice. The hair, which is regarded as an almost superfluous thing, will be represented by the condescension that a soul, thinking highly of Thee, must use in adapting herself to the frailty and littleness of her neighbors. And still, looking on Thee at the fountain, I see Thou hast a cross at Thy right to show that though the intense suffering of my soul, known to Thee, is ended, nevertheless another cross will be left to me, which consists in seeing that Thou art neither loved nor understood, and that Thy will is not executed. Thou hast written in Thy hands all the words (she meant the works), and how can this be that Thou takest words for works? Ah! yes, I understand; because Thou rewardest more a fervent desire of doing a work when one cannot do it, than the work itself when done without the desire, and if Thy work is not accomplished, it is not because there will not be Thy will, but because there is no disposition in creatures, and there are no generous hearts to make such beginning as would be necessary" After a brief silence, returning to the understanding of what the Lord required of her, according to the order of the life of the Incarnate Word, and having begun at the morning of His infancy and gone through all His life, it was noticed that she entered the passion, Jesus showing to her, under various forms, what He wanted her to accomplish in herself, hence she spoke thus: "When I shall be tired of my labors, I will have medicine and food with which to nourish myself; and it will be a chalice of blood, which is the passion of my Word If Thou wert only a martyr, O my God, I would deem suitable to Thee what I now see on Thy breast; but Thou art even the head of the martyrs, and Thou dost this for my instruction My Spouse has a palm on His breast—of which the leaves and centre are somewhat black, but the extremity is green—to teach me that the beginning and root of all my works must be to do them according to God's will, and they must be done also with some fear, which is signified by the black around the leaves; but it must be a filial fear. The black in the centre indicates that, according to my ability, I must see not only that my works are according to God's will, but conformable to the just who live on earth, as the will of all just travelers can only be but one with God's. The extremity is all green, because these works must be performed with confidence. I see my God with His head not covered with blood, but rather, as the prophet said, '*Sicut unguentum in capite, quod descendit in barbam, barbam Aaron*'—'Like the precious ointment on the head, that ran down upon the beard, the beard of Aaron.' (Ps cxxxii, 2) Every hair has its drop, which does not wait for the other, and as soon as the first one drops, it provokes the second, and this the third, and the third the next: so great is the abundance of dew on His head. The drops are nothing but the knowledge and intelligence which God imparts to the soul, and out of which one draws the other as by accepting one and making it bring forth fruit, God is induced to give more, and continu-

ing in the faithful correspondence, one obtains the whole perfection.
The head of my God is also like a small cloud, which draws to itself
the water already fallen, to again moisten the earth with it, He
gathers the fruit and the work which the soul has done with the intelligence communicated to her, to re-infuse into the same new gifts and
new graces. I do not know, my Lord, whether to-day Thou wilt show
me all the things Thou hast created. He has two tongues on His
sacred shoulders ; one of which is the praise of God, the other one is
charity; and both speak out at one time   Here I must pay attention
and see which one speaks louder, and listen to that, but so as not
to prevent my hearing the other.   If I occupy myself in some practice
of charity, or of Religion, I must be, in desire, praising Thee, and never
leave Thy praise to attend to myself, but if I am praising Thee, I must
not be, except by loving affection, helping my neighbor.   I must foresee well whether I can practice charity before or after praising Thee
But if I see that by delaying some practice of charity, or of Religion,
I may cause scandal and trouble to my neighbor, I must rather delay
the praise of God than become a stumbling-block to the salvation of
the souls of others   Thus shall I hear both voices without preventing
the hearing of the one through hearing the other   Thy Word holds in
His left hand a little bell, by which He wants me to understand that I
must invite His brides to the perfection to which they are called · He
wants this little bell to give a penetrating sound, but without noise,
because I must admonish and speak with sweetness and meekness, and
never with severity of expression or manner, as a sweet and meek
speech does better than a harsh and severe one   He holds this little
bell in the left hand, as that is the side where the heart is, to show me
that the words I speak must proceed from the heart, that is, from a
heartfelt love of God and my neighbor, and that I must say nothing
except what I myself have first practiced.   In His right hand my Spouse
holds a dial ; and yet Thou art God ! but for me Thou holdest this timekeeper with two faces, on one side is the sun, on the other the moon   The
timekeeper denotes to me that I must measure time so that reward and
salvation may not have to be measured to me , for to him who measures
not the time, the reward is measured, that is, he will not be given much
of it · a small thing is easily measured   The moon engraved on one
side shows me the changeableness of earthly and transitory things,
which we should esteem as such   The sun engraved on the other side
represents to me the constant and entire perfection of celestial things,
and of God, for whom and in whom I must give every thought, desire,
and affection   In the same hand He holds a scale, to teach me that
I must do everything thoughtfully, or with prudence , and He also holds
with both hands a very rich sceptre, entirely of gold and adorned with
most precious stones.   What else is this sceptre, O soul, but the honor
and glory due to God in all things?   The stones set in it signify
taking delight in all that God delights in.   He delights in the creature,
in His power, goodness, mercy, and all His other divine perfections;
and the soul must do likewise   He holds this sceptre with both hands,
as the glory to be given Him must proceed from the love of God and our
neighbor.   This God of mine has under His feet a crown that looks

golden, but is not; under the crown are some lilies, under these the devils. The crown is nothing but the glory and the honors of the world; the lilies are the sensual pleasures, which, together with the devil and the wicked flesh, must be kept under foot and trampled on. My Jesus, I understand not why Thou appearest to shut Thy eyes, unless Thou enlighten me in regard to it. By that He wants to teach the Bride-soul that she must shut her eyes and almost fall asleep, in order not to feel the temptations of her passions, which are within, and which are like little children who, when they want anything, make so much ado, with tears, or sweet smiles, or otherwise, until they get it. Our passions often overcome us, either by fear, or by love, or by other innumerable emotions, but the soul must be asleep to them and shut every opening of sensibility against them, raising herself above them and approaching God. And, after having done these things and many more, she must call and intimately believe herself an unworthy servant, and unable to do any good action. Finally, my God gives me three most worthy queens, with their suites, for if they were unaccompanied their dignity and greatness would not be known. He wants me always to follow in their footsteps, that I may not lose the road which leads me to Him, my Beloved. These are three most worthy virtues, in which I must always exercise myself, that is, charity, mercy and purity, or truth and righteousness, as I may call it, together with the suite of holy humility, as the virtues which are not accompanied by humility cannot be truly called virtues, and are of no value before God or for the soul."

Here she became silent for a good length of time; and then, recommending all creatures to God, came to herself from her ecstasy, in which she had been about twenty-one hours. With such bountiful reward of celestial graces and superhuman knowledge did God immediately reward the sufferings of five years, endured with such an heroic constancy and generosity by the noble and holy Mary Magdalen De-Pazzi.

Let us here remark, once for all. She spoke Latin, quoted and applied the texts of the Holy Scriptures with as much skill as if she were a profound theologian. We have had, so far, some proofs of it, and shall have more in abundance as we proceed to relate her achievements. Behold, therefore, a new argument to prove that her spirit was of God, for, uninstructed by human means in this language, and much less instructed in the knowledge of biblical texts, she could not use the former and quote the latter so easily and adroitly, unless by the help of Him who, animating the clay by His simple breath, and forming of it as great a number of vessels as there are individuals in all human-kind, sometimes infuses His wisdom into the weakest of them, that the strong, not to himself, but to the Divine Source alone, may return the honor and the glory of every good thing.

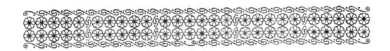

CHAPTER XIX.

GOD REVEALS TO HER THE STATE OF VARIOUS SOULS DEPARTED
FOR THE OTHER LIFE.

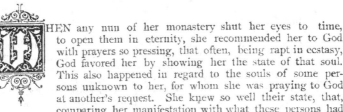

HEN any nun of her monastery shut her eyes to time, to open them in eternity, she recommended her to God with prayers so pressing, that often, being rapt in ecstasy, God favored her by showing her the state of that soul. This also happened in regard to the souls of some persons unknown to her, for whom she was praying to God at another's request. She knew so well their state, that, comparing her manifestation with what these persons had done during life, there was no doubt left of her being inspired of God.

1. SHE FORESEES THE DELIVERANCE OF HER BROTHER'S SOUL FROM PURGATORY.—The first soul known by her while in this life, to be in purgatory, was her brother's, as we related in Chapter XV. Through her most fervent prayers, her brother soon obtained deliverance from that painful prison, and she learned the knowledge of their efficacy, so that, turning her mind to him, she then pronounced these words: "Happy thou, O beloved brother, as thou wilt soon be called to eternal bliss, and, though great and unutterable are the pains, still they are not equal to the future inexpressible and incomprehensible glory prepared for thee in heaven."

2. SHE SEES THE SOUL OF A NUN OF HER MONASTERY, WHO, AFTER SIXTEEN DAYS IN PURGATORY, ASCENDS GLORIOUSLY TO HEAVEN.—On the 3d of February, 1588, whilst alienated from her senses, it was given her to see the soul of a sister of her monastery, who, sixteen days after she had passed out of this life, was going gloriously into heaven; and she understood that for three particular reasons she had been detained during that time in the pains of purgatory: First, because on festival-days (as she was very skillful in handiwork) she had done something not altogether necessary; secondly, because, as a senior mother of that religious family, she failed once, through human respect, to notify the superiors of something which she felt she ought to make known for the welfare of the monastery; thirdly, because she was too much attached to her relatives. Those who preside over a family, either religious or lay, private or public, should not fail to apply to themselves the second case, whence it appears that they must receive with affability, gratitude, and efficacious determination any judicious

person who may reach their hearts by the voice of truth ; but they are often unable to hear this voice, because their sensual appetites are too well fed, they are too puffed up by vainglorious complacency and too much deceived by false adulation   It is the will of God that the great man should sometimes be advised and guided by the inferior, so that, through the elevation of one and the lowering of the other, the human parity established by the eternal law may remain unalterable.   Immediately were revealed to our Saint the three virtues of the same soul, by which she understood that the sufferings of purgatory were shortened for her   The first was the solicitous care with which she always had endeavored to preserve the purity and simplicity of her Religion , the second, the great charity which she practiced for all the sisters during life; the third, having always taken in good part all she saw or heard.   Therefore our Saint saw, afterwards, 'that this happy soul, purified from all stains, and rich in merits, was going to enjoy the Sovereign Good, accompanied by her Guardian Angel and St. Miniato, Martyr, who, according to the custom of the monastery, had been appointed her protector for that year   At such a sight Magdalen was filled with joy, and felt an ardent desire to follow that soul, in order to hasten to the full enjoyment of her beloved Spouse, Jesus.

3. SHE SEES THE SOUL OF ANOTHER NUN OF HER MONASTERY, WHO HAD BEEN BUT FIFTEEN HOURS IN PURGATORY, GOING TO HEAVEN — On the 5th of June of the year 1589, a nun died, in whose behalf St Mary Magdalen had performed very many charitable acts during her last illness.   As they were about to bury the body, Magdalen was looking at it from a church blind, and while doing so she was rapt in ecstasy, and saw the soul of her fellow-sister ascending to heaven , hence she said " Farewell, sister , adieu, blessed soul , thou goest to paradise, like a pure dove, leaving us all here below.   Oh ! how glorious and beautiful thou art ! And who could recount thy beauty ? How short a time thou hast remained in the flames ! Thy body is not yet buried, and thy soul flies to the glory of the blessed   Now thou dost fully understand what I was telling thee while yet on earth, viz., that it will seem to thee as if thou hadst not suffered anything, when thy sufferings are compared to the glory that Jesus hath prepared for thee in paradise " She also understood then that that sister had remained but fifteen hours in purgatory, because she had borne with great patience all the troubles she encountered during life, and especially the very great pains of her last illness   As soon as the body disappeared from the view of those present, Magdalen returned to her senses, saying " At the same time that they give burial to the body, the soul is placed forever in heaven "

4 SHE SEES THE SOUL OF A NUN OF HER MONASTERY SURROUNDED BY FLAMES, ADORING THE BLESSED SACRAMENT, AND SHE UNDERSTANDS THE REASON FOR IT —Another day of the same year, 1589, whilst she was in the choir praying, the soul of a deceased nun of her monastery appeared to her, covered with flames, as if with a mantle, under which a white habit was apparent , and in that condition that soul adored the Eucharistic Sacrament in deep reverence. Magdalen, asking of God the meaning of this understood how the white habit had been given that sister for having preserved her virginity

inviolate until death; the mantle of fire which covered her had been given to her in punishment for some faults, and she was ordered to stay before the Blessed Sacrament covered with that mantle, in punishment for having several times during life omitted Holy Communion, and that, just for this neglect, she had to stay every day for one hour in such adoration till she had wholly atoned for the fault, after which she would fly up to heaven. Accordingly this soul was seen by our Saint, not long after, going to the bliss of eternal rest.

5. SHE SEES IN PURGATORY THE SOUL OF HER MOTHER LOOK-ING VERY CHEERFUL, AS SHE WAS SOON TO GO AND ENJOY THE ETER-NAL GLORY, AND IN THIS VISION MANY THINGS ARE MADE KNOWN TO HER.—In Advent of the year 1590, Maria Buondelmonti De-Pazzi, the happy mother of Magdalen, paying to the Author of nature the common tribute, ended her life of edification, of love, of zeal, and of sorrows When the sad news reached Magdalen, she said she knew it already, as, when her mother breathed her last, she felt an unusual pain in her heart and a strong inclination to kneel and say a *Requiem æternam* for her mother's soul. This she did not do, however, as she was in the presence of many nuns. With all the love with which the filial sentiment inspired her, she quickly withdrew to give vent to her wishes and sup-plications for the salvation of this soul, rather than to lamentations and tears for the loss of the body. In the meantime, reciting the *Miserere*, she was rapt in ecstasy, and then saw in purgatory the soul of her mother, very cheerful and contented, as though little children were removing the flames from around her, and the tears of the poor who were weeping over her death gave her great relief in those pains. The little children, she understood, were those whom, during life, she had taught and led in the way of the Lord, as she had so wisely done by word and example, the tears were those of indigent persons to whom she was wont to distribute help in the true spirit of charity Here, her mother disappearing, her Guardian Angel presented himself to her mind, and from him she understood many things concerning the indescribable glory of paradise prepared for the merits of this soul, particularly because of her works of charity, not so much exterior as interior, on behalf of her neighbors; and that she would shortly pass to enjoy that glory. Mag-dalen said to the angel that she wished to possess three things with which her mother was endowed: her great righteousness, her prudence, and her tolerance and resignation, by which she preserved her equanimity, both in prosperous and in adverse circumstances. After these petitions, she came to herself from her rapture, and then continued to pray daily for the hasty deliverance of her dearly beloved mother. On the eve of the Nativity of the Blessed Virgin, it being just fifteen days since her mother had departed this life, she understood, in a new ecstasy, how her soul on the morning of that same day, at the hour corresponding to that in which it had left her body, had flown up to heaven; and she saw it, all joyful, glancing at the side of the Word, and there it stopped, as at the time of death it possessed God in the act of charity She had already seen how her patron Saints had ⸺ ⸺ her soul into heaven ⸺ ⸺ ⸺ ⸺ ⸺ ⸺ ⸺ ⸺ with a habit of blood, St. Agnes with various flowers and S John the Baptist

The Blessed Virgin puts a spotless white veil on her (page 89).

placed on her head a crown, at which she, greatly wondering, being still in her rapture, uttered these words. "How and why is the halo placed on thy head since thou hast not been a virgin, nor hast thou been numbered among those who had the desire of virginity, as thou hast been satisfied with the state and vocation in which God placed thee?" . . She then understood that her mother had merited that crown for her great suffering, especially interior, on account of some sad causes, which so often exist in the case of those who are obliged to live in contact with society. She also saw how the Blessed Virgin embellished that soul in different ways, because, while in this world, she held her name in great reverence and devotion, to her own great advantage and profit. Having then remained for a while to look at the position of her mother, she received from her the three following counsels First, that she should seek the highest possible degree of humility, secondly, that she should practice obedience with exactitude, thirdly, that in all things she should use prudence. Thus ended the ecstatic vision regarding the soul of her mother Some days after, in another ecstasy, God showed her in heaven, rich in glory, the soul of a priest she had known, and who, during his lifetime, had done much for his own perfection and for the eternal salvation of others

6 SHE SEES THE SOULS OF TWO PERSONS KNOWN TO HER CONDEMNED TO ETERNAL TORMENTS.—In the year 1594, on the 22d of December, her spirit being raised above her senses, she saw the soul of an unhappy man at the moment that he passed from his deathbed to the eternal torments. God revealed to her that the chief cause of his damnation was his having held in contempt the treasures of Holy Church, laughing at the indulgences and all the other graces the Church benignly imparts to her faithful children, which contempt indicates the depth of iniquity into which a wretched man may fall. Again, after a few days, having reentered an ecstasy, she saw the soul of another man surrounded by infernal flames, to which Divine Justice had condemned him At such a sight Magdalen grew pale and became so frightened that she nearly fainted, and, in a piteous voice, she began to say to him: "Unhappy man! Thou hast become a firebrand of hell; soon thy pastimes were changed into horrible and everlasting pains". And, gazing up to heaven, she continued: "O Eternal God! the people of the world do not meditate well on these things." By which words, and the manner of her uttering them, she inspired those present with great fear, and she was left so depressed by the awfulness of the vision, that for several days she was unable to find a thought that would restore her to tranquillity She made known afterwards, by customary obedience, that God had granted her these two visions that she and her companions, the nuns of her monastery, might be more inflamed with zeal for the salvation of souls, and try to appease Divine Justice by their prayers and penances.

7. SHE SEES THE SOULS OF MANY RELIGIOUS DAMNED FOR NOT OBSERVING THE VOW OF POVERTY, AND FOR OTHER SINS —One Sunday, while they were singing vespers in the choir, she was rapt in ecstasy, and the Lord showed her a great number of souls falling down, like

lightning, into hell; and having asked of God who they might be, she was told that they were the souls of Religious who, having lived in monasteries of lax observance, by transgressing their vows, and particularly that of poverty, had been sentenced to eternal torments   This had been done also because they had used the sacred habit to feed their vanity and fickleness, with offense to modesty and religious decorum   Hence, weeping, she said   "O unhappy souls, how much better would it have been for you, if you had remained in the world, than to have bound yourselves by solemn promises in the cloister, without observing them !   Now your torments increase in proportion to your unfulfilled obligations . .   O religious poverty, how little thou art known and practiced !   If thou wert justly appreciated by those who profess to follow thee, the cells would not be seen full of ornaments, the keeping of money to be spent according to one's will would be abhorred like poison, and so many other vain pomps, unbecoming the true Religious, would be banished from the sacred cloisters   Oh ! how the beauty of religious poverty, O my Jesus, has become deformed by the possession of accursed property !   Oh ! how many souls of Religious are burning in hell for not having held in esteem and observed holy poverty !"   Without fathoming the hidden thoughts of an individual, still the world itself has the right to ask of those who profess religious perfection ·   Why so much affectation in a habit which in its form indicates penance, and which even in its color signifies innocence ?   Why that luxury in dwellings, which rivals that of the world?   The pretext for this luxury, that men of great dignity are received therein, is a vain one; as the religious houses should represent the stable of Bethlehem, where the kings and the shepherds alike were received   It is impossible not to be convinced, upon the first accusation, of levity of spirit ; hence, those who are guilty of it, being unfaithful to their assumed obligation, or, at least, incapable of doing all the good which is expected of them, are justly destined to that place where sighs, and cries, and loud lamentations resound through the air, and of whom it was well said .—

> Forthwith
> I understood, for certain, this the tribe
> Of those ill spirits both to God displeasing
> And to his foes —*Dante's* (Carey Trans) *Hell*, III.

But, thanks to Divine Providence, even to-day, in the midst of that class of persons, there are not wanting those who by their example, wisdom, and doctrine, which secure their perfection, lead others also into the path of salvation; and this is particularly the case among the children of St Francis, who follow more strictly the spirit of Jesus Christ, by poverty alone, which their holy founder called *his lady*, and on which he willed that the Order he was erecting should chiefly rest.

> Then, the season come that he,
> Who to such good had destined him, was pleas'd
> To advance him to the meed, which he had earn'd
> By self-humbling , to his brotherhood,
> As their just heritage, he gave in charge
> This vicar t lady, and enjoin their love,
> And faith t er   *Parad.* C · Iro   *ad.* XI.

Another time, likewise in ecstasy, Magdalen saw a great multitude of souls of cloistered persons who were burning in the everlasting flames, because, to the great offense of God, they had abused the time which by the rules is generally granted for the recreation of the body, that afterwards they might, with greater zest, attend to devotions. Here she also wept bitterly, and with a voice of sorrow pronounced these words· "O wretched Religious souls! O great misery, that what is granted to Religious for their recreation should become the cause of their eternal ruin!" And she offered to God the most fervent prayers, that He might condescend to enlighten those souls, bound by solemn vows, and having still time for penance left to them.

8. SHE SEES THE SOUL OF A NUN OF HER MONASTERY WHO, AFTER BEING DEPRIVED OF THE BEATIFIC VISION FOR FIVE HOURS, GOES TO POSSESS THE ETERNAL JOYS.—In 1598, about the end of October, in said monastery, Sister Maria Benedetta Vittori died, young in age, but old in virtue and perfection. Our Magdalen, who never failed to assist in cases of extreme importance, being present at her death, saw a great multitude of angels surrounding her and waiting for her to draw her last breath. The following morning, whilst the body of the deceased was in the church, and Mass was being sung for her soul, she was rapt in ecstasy, and saw the soul of the sister in paradise, adorned with a glory superior to that of any other nun in the monastery who had previously died. Describing the ornaments and delights of that soul, she told how, in reward for her ardent charity, she was dressed with a gilt mantle, and, for having always dealt with her neighbor in loyalty and meekness, a most sweet liquid came out of the mouth of Jesus into her own, and made her taste a great sweetness, and she freely fixed her eyes on the humanity and divinity of the Word. Magdalen, moved by the sight of so delightful an object, exclaimed in a voice of joy and complacency: "O my dove, how beautiful art thou! how resplendent with celestial light! I know that now thou dost not go with thy head bowed down, as thou wast wont to do when amongst us." In the meantime she understood that this soul had been detained in purgatory five hours before ascending to heaven, but had not suffered there any pain of the senses, only the privation of the sight of God, and this for a very slight fault of self-love, which was that on seeing anyone displeased on her account she grieved so much that she was thereby distracted from her recollection in God After this, recommending to that blessed soul herself and her monastery, the sweet vision ceased, and she returned to her senses She had also seen in purgatory the soul of a Florentine gentlewoman, who suffered heavily for having prevented her daughter from becoming a nun

9 BY FORCE OF ENTREATY SHE OBTAINS THE SALVATION OF THE SOULS OF TWO MEN SENTENCED TO DEATH —As human justice was leading two wretches to the last punishment, near the monastery of St. Maria degli Angeli, where they had treacherously perpetrated a murder, our Saint being informed of it, brought into action all the zeal of her most loving heart for the salvation of their souls, and doubled the efforts of her tender and winning mediation with the

Divine Mercy. At the moment in which the life of these two creatures of God was being cut off by the hand of man, Magdalen, rapt out of her senses, understood how the souls of both had passed to a place of salvation : one ascending immediately to heaven, on account of a perfect resignation to die ; the other, after a short stay in purgatory, because less resigned. Which, in fact, corresponded to the disposition of each of them in the different manner of submitting to their sad doom. The Christian death of both was chiefly attributed to the prayers of Mother Mary Magdalen, the assiduity, energy, and efficacy of which, in the eternal behalf of these two unhappy men, were known to all.

CHAPTER XX.

SHE SEES IN HEAVEN THE GLORIOUS ST. LOUIS GONZAGA OF THE SOCIETY OF JESUS.

HE language of the passions and that of ignorance easily lead us to generalize an opinion either in favor of certain classes of society or against them. In the strangest and most illogical manner a uniform character is attributed to all the members constituting a class of persons; and, generally, this is in a bad sense, on account of the evil tendency of man to speak ill of his neighbor and calumniate him rather than to speak well of him and justify him. From the faults of some members the whole body is judged; hence, the most monstrous injustice to the innocent ones. The ecclesiastical congregations, and particularly the regular ones, are subject, more than others, to such wholesale condemnation; and among these none has been or is still so maligned as the Society of Jesus. Men conspicuous for doctrine, power, and wealth joined the rabble; nay, they themselves urged the attack on the Jesuits. Their rich possessions and their supposed meddling in family and political affairs are causes for displeasure, as thereby their spirit seems very unevangelical, viz., little loyal, but rather exceptionally egotistical in regard to other religious corporations. These faults may be the effect of the abuse of individual men, whose passions are never extinguished while on earth; but they can never supply an honest pretext for inflicting a condemnation on the whole moral body. (Some other pernicious things of which the world sometimes complains, blaming the Jesuits for them, are rather to be blamed on those who, not being Jesuits in garb, affect to belong to them by affiliation, taking from them all their faults and none of their virtues; hence, their spirit is moved by false zeal, which gnaws at charity and begets dissension, so that, more than others, these restless proselytizers disfigure and injure both the Company of St. Ignatius and the holy religion of Christ.) On the other hand, the perfection in science and virtue of so many members of this Company, who have spent their lives for the good of society in general, gives it the most legal and sacred right to public esteem and gratitude. To-day they militate under laws wholly identical with those that gave us such advantages; so that there is no reason why the latter should not be reproduced. Therefore, not with contempt, which is ill adapted to persuade anybody, but with words of conviction and the evidence of facts, we must enter into their spirit, that they may lend us their hand to help us to walk steadfastly according to the needs of the day. It is a common saying that ignominious and coercive forms do not suit the present times, nor the ideas thereof. Let us, then, practice with everyone this most sound principle, and let us be convinced that modern society cannot reach its normal state until we uniformly come to an understanding in order to establish the universal brotherhood of man, to which object the wishes of all wise persons tend Intellects have already been shaken, young people, above all, pant after the knowledge of truth. Who gives them the glass in which to see themselves, and learn good morals, philanthropy, uprightness, and all that constitutes a young man such as the country may rest her hopes on? Who but the Jesuit in the person of St. Aloysius Gonzaga, reared and raised till the age of seventeen in a princely family, a model of purity and humility, and who lived in the Company of Jesus till the age of twenty-three? In that year of his age, which was the year 1591, a fierce pestilence broke out in Rome and cruelly scourged all Italy. During this plague, he gave proof of possessing the charity for his brethren of which Christ said there is none greater, viz., that charity which makes one give up his life for others; and thus rendered himself such a model of spiritual perfection that there is no college or society of young people among Catholics, which has not chosen him as a protector and a guide. It is certainly a difficult thing for the Company to give us a second St Aloysius, but it cannot be denied that many of its members have several times since made great efforts to approach, as near as possible, his sanctity. We had an evident proof of this in our own days, when the pestilential scourge in 1837 again struck the lofty countenance of the Eternal City. It was then that the children of St. Ignatius distinguished themselves in a marvelous and singular manner in assisting corporally and spiritually the unhappy ones affected with cholera morbus, when some of the ecclesiastics, even the regular ones, had retired to avoid the contagion. The world, then, may yet look for some good from the Jesuits; and as their social position, in preference to other Religious, enables them to do much good if they are filled with the pure spirit of their founder, just as they might do great harm if this spirit degenerates into a spirit of turbulence, intrigue, stubbornness, hypocrisy, therefore we must exhaust with them all the means of conciliation. And if this should prove to be useless, let us weep over the loss of those who wish to be lost, but let us respect the dignity, the right, the justice of the innocent, whom we will always find amidst all classes of persons.[1]

To our St. Mary Magdalen, who was well disposed towards the Company of Jesus, God wanted to give a fresh proof of the very high perfection of St. Aloysius Gonzaga On the 4th of April of the year 1600, whilst she was praying with a very high degree of fervor, her mind was raised to the celestial beatitude, where she saw this angel of purity, radiant with sovereign splendor, enjoying with a most joyous

---

[1] The reader should bear in mind the prevailing spirit of the times in which the original was written. *Note of the Translator*

and glorious countenance the unutterable reward of his virtues. Dazzled by the sight of this heavenly object, with pauses and interruptions, she uttered these words: "Oh! how much glory Louis, the son of Ignatius, possesses! I would never have believed it, unless Thou, O my Jesus, had shown him to me. . . . It seems to me in a certain manner that there could scarcely be so much glory in heaven as that which Louis enjoys. . . . I say that Louis is a great Saint. . . . We have saints in church (she meant Saints whose sacred relics they had in the church of the monastery) who, I believe, have not so much glory. . . . I would like to be able to go through the whole world, and say that Louis, son of Ignatius, is a great Saint ; and I would like to be able to show his glory to everyone, that God might be glorified. . . . He possesses so much glory because of his interior work. . . . Who could ever relate the value and the merit of interior works? There is no comparison between the interior and the exterior. . . . Louis, whilst on earth, kept his mouth open to the Word " (she meant to say that this Saint loved the interior inspirations of the Word and tried to fulfill them) . . . "Louis was a hidden martyr ; because he who loves Thee, my God, knows that Thou art so great and infinitely amiable, that it is a great martyrdom to him to see that he does not love Thee as much as he wishes to love Thee; and that Thou art not loved, but rather offended by creatures. . . . He made himself a martyr also. . . . Oh! how much he loved Thee on earth! hence he now rejoices in heaven in great fullness of love. . . . While on earth, the heart of the Word pierced him with darts; now that he is in heaven, those darts rest in his heart ; as he now understands and enjoys those communications that he merited by the acts of love and union which he performed, and which were like darts." In seeing that this Saint prayed warmly for those who, during life, gave him spiritual help, she added: "I, too, will try to help souls, that, if any of them go to heaven, they may pray for me, as St. Louis does for those who, while on earth, assisted him." Here the Saint ceasing to speak, the vision and the rapture ended ; but she continued to venerate the Jesuit Luigi Gonzaga with great reverence and with the most tender and constant devotion all her lifetime.

CHAPTER XXI.

SHE SEES AND FEELS FAR-OFF THINGS AS IF THEY
WERE PRESENT.

MONG the supernatural gifts with which God vouchsafed to deck this bride of His, was this one, viz., her seeing and feeling things far from her as if they were present to her. She was several times favored with this gift, and especially in the following cases:—

1. SHE SEES IN SPIRIT AN ANSWER WHICH THE MOTHER, SISTER CATHERINE DE-RICCI, IN ST. VINCENT DI PRATO, WAS GIVING TO ONE OF HER LETTERS.—In 1586, whilst Magdalen was one day in ecstasy in the novitiate hall, she dictated a letter addressed to Sister Catherine De-Ricci, a nun at that time living in the monastery of St. Vincent in Prato, and now enjoying the glory of heaven, and on earth the honors of the altar. The letter being sealed, it was sent to its destination by the steward of the monastery. A few hours having elapsed, and Magdalen still continuing in the same ecstasy, from the words uttered she gave the nuns to understand that she saw the steward handing the letter to Sister Catherine; and shortly after, from the movement of her eyes, she appeared to read what that sister was writing in answer. As this answer did not fully meet her desire, she became somewhat troubled in her appearance; and she also seemed to see the answer handed to somebody. About four hours afterward the steward returned with it, and was questioned by the sisters as to the time and other circumstances attending the execution of the commission. The letter was read by the superioress, who, having received from the Saint, after her rapture, a complete explanation of it, found everything to coincide with what had been ecstatically revealed to her.

2. WHILE IN THE REFECTORY, SHE SAW THAT A NUN OF HER MONASTERY WAS DYING SUDDENLY IN A REMOTE CELL.—In 1591, on a Friday evening, being in the refectory for the purpose of taking some little food with the other sisters, Mary Magdalen suddenly arose from the table, and, swiftly going to the superioress, told her with vehemence: "Mother, that soul passes away!" Without saying anything further, she ran to the room where Sister Mattea Focardi, a lay-sister, was confined, because of a sore on her right leg, which was far from threatening death. By day, although confined to her room

Being rapt in ecstasy, she receives Holy Communion from
Jesus Christ Himself (page 90).

but not to bed, she would work with promptness of spirit and agility of body. When Magdalen arrived, followed by other nuns, by the order of the mother prioress, Sister Mattea was found to be in her last agony; and, the Saint recommending her soul, in a few minutes the dying one expired.

3. FROM AFAR SHE HEARS TWO NOVICES, WHO WERE IN A REMOTE PLACE, MURMURING ABOUT THEIR NEIGHBORS —During the time when our Saint attended the novices in the company of the mistress, Sister Vangelista del Giocondo, she was speaking with her one day on an unimportant subject. She suddenly said, as if she had heard something extraneous to it. "Mother, those two creatures speak not well, I will go and correct them." Guided by the Spirit of God, who, on account of her desire for the perfection of souls, manifested to her hidden things, she went directly to where these novices were, and found her vision to be true, as they themselves avowed both to her and to Sister Vangelista.

4. FROM THE MONASTERY SHE SEES AND HEARS THE FATHER RECTOR OF THE JESUITS IN THE COLLEGE OF FLORENCE CONFERRING WITH HIS ASSOCIATES.—In the year 1600, one Saturday evening about dark, she called to her the novice De-Berti, who in the world had been a penitent of the Rector of the Jesuits, and thus questioned her. "What dost thou think father rector is doing at this hour?" The novice answered: "I think he must be praying" "He is not praying," the Saint replied, "but talking with some of the fathers about such things (she named them); and the Holy Ghost is forming all the words which he utters." On the following day, the above-named father having come, as the extraordinary confessor, to hear the sisters' confessions, she told him what she had seen and heard of him the evening previous, and he declared that her vision corresponded in every respect to the facts.

5. SHE ANNOUNCES WITH CERTAINTY THE DEATH OF A NOBLEMAN OF FLORENCE BEFORE THE NOTICE OF IT REACHES THE MONASTERY.— Pier-Francesco Santucci, of a distinguished Florentine family, was lying grievously ill, though not extremely so He had a daughter, a nun and a companion of Magdalen in religion and in the monastery. The Saint, being alienated from her senses, seeing in spirit his passing, went to his daughter, and, taking her by the hand, said to her: "Sister, weep not; thy father, by the merits of Christ and the intercession of St Francis, for whom he entertained so much devotion, has passed at this moment to a place of salvation." The steward of the monastery was immediately dispatched to the Santucci palace, and in a very short time he returned with confirmation of the above news, and the daughter attested that her father entertained great devotion to St Francis, paying to him daily homage by several exercises of affectionate piety.

6. SEVERAL TIMES SHE SEES IN SPIRIT THE ACTIONS OF HER FATHER CONFESSOR.—The father confessor being in the church, and she in a remote cell, knowing nothing of him, it so happened that she saw him spiritually several times, and she manifested the vision as follows. "I see the blood of Christ dropping from heaven upon souls: the father is in church hearing confessions; I, too, will go and receive this blood." And she went, and found him, in fact, engaged in that

work. It also happened that when he was leaving the house or some other place, or was in the street, coming to the monastery, Magdalen by divine inspiration would speak of it to the nuns, and shortly after they would see him arrive. One day more distinctly feeling a strong desire to speak to her confessor, and being at that time in the refectory for the midday meal, whilst in the act of putting the food into her mouth, she was rapt in ecstasy; and then, seeing in spirit that the father had reached the church, she dropped on the table what she held in her hand, and without delay ran to him. He had, in fact, arrived, and she conferred with him on some of the favors with which God had privileged her.

CHAPTER XXII.

SHE FORETELLS THINGS TO COME AND SEES HIDDEN ONES.

ESIDES the aforesaid gift of knowing things from far off as if they were happening under her own eye, Magdalen had also the other one of foreseeing and foretelling them long before they happened. Whilst praying to God for the happy issue of some future thing, she was nearly always not only heard but granted a prevision of it. The nuns soon became aware with certainty of this most distinct privilege; and, afterwards, even secular persons; so that both the former and the latter, moved by inborn curiosity to know the future, used to go to her, for this purpose, often and with persistence, and would then notice her words and sayings with the greatest accuracy. But she, knowing what they wished, was very cautious in guarding such a precious gift with the virtue of humility, not manifesting her power except to her spiritual director, the superioress, or some sister who enjoyed her confidence. To others, and especially persons in the world, she would give general answers, even when she had a certain and special prevision. This she did on account of her humility, which, by unalterable Divine disposition, was followed by greater exaltation. She was so penetrated by the spirit of prophecy, that often, without wishing it, she manifested to any one future things, especially during her ecstasies, when being filled with a supernatural force, she could not resist, as God then was speaking by her voice. During them, she was often heard to say: "Keep it to Thyself, O Lord, keep it to Thyself:" meaning, by this, to annihilate any possible sentiment of curiosity or of her own worthiness. She considered herself wholly unworthy of such communications; and that they might at least remain unknown to others, she would offer pressing prayers to God. Consequently, as a reward, she had more of them than could be counted, through God's wisdom and liberality. The following are the most remarkable ones:—

1. SHE PREDICTS THAT CARDINAL DE-MEDICI, ARCHBISHOP OF FLORENCE, WOULD BECOME POPE, BUT THAT HE WOULD ONLY LIVE A SHORT TIME IN SUCH DIGNITY.—In September of the year 1586, when the nomination of the new prioress of the monastery of St. Maria degli Angeli was about to take place, His Eminence Alessandro De-Medici,

Cardinal Archbishop of Florence, was coming to preside over the election.
Magdalen was divinely inspired to speak to him on this occasion, about
various things concerning the government of the Florentine Church, and
particularly about that of her monastery. Some persons had so maliciously
spoken to His Eminence about the Father Confessor, that he was almost
resolved to remove him. The Saint, knowing this tendency, and judging
it contrary to the will of God and the welfare of the monastery, felt
determined to speak frankly about it to the Cardinal. But she wished
first to submit her determination to the mother prioress and the confessor himself for advice. Both of them opposed her so much in this
that they were actually thinking of obliging her to hide in her cell during the hours in which His Eminence would hear the opinion of the
nuns. Prudential reasons moved them to this. But man's counsel is
powerless against God's will. On the 29th of September, the day
appointed for the election, Magdalen, having received Holy Communion
early in the morning, became immediately alienated from her senses,
and, while thus ecstatic, stopped at the grate of the chapter, which
looks towards the church, where the superior was to receive the *voice*
(vote) of the nuns, and the virtue of the Spirit of God kept her immovable many hours, that is, until the arrival of His Eminence, so that
not even by force could she be removed or even shaken. At the sight
of the Cardinal this immovability turned into a great animation of spirit,
which made her suddenly utter these words in an ecstatic and majestic
manner: "Alexander, Alexander, *noli tangere christos meos, et in
ancillis meis noli malignari*"—"Touch thou not my anointed : and do
no evil to my *handmaids*" (Ps. civ, 15)—adding afterwards that which
God inspired her to manifest in behalf of the monastery and the confessor. Then she came out of her ecstasy, and left the place. His Eminence, greatly amazed at what he had heard, could not at the moment
answer anything, but that this daughter had spoken well in the person
of the Holy Ghost. He was so touched by it, that, after the ceremony,
he had the Saint called to him and discoursed with her for a while,
drawing therefrom evident proofs of her sanctity, and ineffable consolation for his heart. Before leaving the monastery, he greatly commended the virtue of Magdalen to Sister Vangelista del Giocondo, the
new prioress, telling her that during the private colloquy Magdalen
had foretold him that he was to be Pope. Magdalen corroborated
this fact to the superioress when she asked her about it. When, after
the lapse of some years, the same Cardinal was called to Rome to be
sent to France as a Legate *a latere* of His Holiness Clement VIII, while
going thither, and as he was in the street opposite the monastery of
Santa Maria degli Angeli, Magdalen, who then was contemplating
ecstatically the divine attributes, pronounced these words. "This
Christ (such was the name she gave to the prelates) has received
to-day a great honor, and will reach the supreme one; but it will
not last long, when he will want to embrace his glory, it will disappear." The same prediction she made several times when not in
ecstasy; it was verified in 1605, when said Car... was elected
Sovereign Pontiff, assuming the name of Leo XI and the completion
of this prophecy took place twenty-seven days afterwards, when, leaving

the pomp that the world was prodigally giving him, he returned the dust of his body to the earth, and his soul appeared before that terrible Judgment-Seat, before which no human power can take exception.

2 SHE FORESEES THAT SOME GIRLS WILL BECOME NUNS IN HER MONASTERY.—On account of the love this Saint bore her Religion, she did her best in order that the rules would be invariably observed. thus she constantly prayed to God that he might, for this monastery, select souls endowed with the true spirit, which being granted her by Divine Goodness, several times some girls were made known to her in spirit whom God proposed would become nuns therein, and especially in the following instance: One day in 1590, being in ecstasy, she said that she saw the Blessed Virgin leading a girl from the Indies, to become a nun among them. The sisters present, hearing this news, were troubled, as it would be very much against their wishes to accept foreigners The cause of their trouble becoming known to the Saint, she assured them, that, being led by the Blessed Virgin, that girl would certainly be endowed with all the virtues suitable to this vocation; and said, in particular, that she would be a lover of poverty, of self-abasement, and much enlightened as to the religious life. This prophecy was fulfilled five years afterwards, when, in 1595, Catherine, daughter of Roderigo Ximenez, a Portuguese, having been brought to Florence by her parents to marry into a noble family of that city, refused all earthly espousals, and chose the religious state in said monastery, all of which happened a month after her arrival in Florence She was called Sister Catherine Angelica. On the day of her receiving the habit, Magdalen foretold many things which were to happen to her during her life; and she herself testified in time that these came to pass just as the Saint had foretold.

In 1598, a Florentine girl of the noble family De-Berti, to please an aunt, entered the monastery of Santa Maria degli Angeli for ten days For several reasons she had positively decided to become a nun among the Dominicans of St. Catherine of Florence. But witnessing, during one of these days, a rapture of our Saint, she felt constrained to question her thus: "Dost thou believe, mother, that I am to be a nun in this monastery?" And Magdalen immediately answered: "I not only believe it, but know with certainty that thou shalt be here with us " This seeming impossible to the girl, and whilst she was thinking of some difficulties she foresaw, Magdalen, as if seeing her thoughts, subjoined "Jesus will send down some of His dew on these hearts and will mollify them, and every difficulty will vanish " The same thing she repeated to her another time at the gates of the monastery, when this girl had come out ; and she showed herself so sure of it that, if an angel had told her the contrary, she would have taken him for a demon The prophecy of the Saint was fulfilled, as the De-Berti became a nun in this monastery, and, out of veneration and gratitude, she wished and obtained to be called Sister Mary Magdalen.

At that time there was being educated, in the above-mentioned monastery of St. Catherine, Francesca de Sommai, a noble Florentine girl, who, because of her singular goodness and innocence, being like an angel in the flesh, was greatly loved by the said De-Berti, who had been her companion for some years in the same monastery. Hence, De-Berti, being now a nun in the monastery of Santa Maria degli Angeli, wished very much to have with her so dear a companion in the most intimate and lasting manner, that is, she wished God would lead her to become a nun in the same monastery For this she was always praying to God, and she also often importuned our Saint that she might for this purpose interpose the power of her mediation with God One day, our Saint being in ecstasy, she asked her this question "Mother, dost thou think that Francesca de Sommai is to be a nun with us?" To which Magdalen frankly replied. "Jesus showed her to me with our habit on." Another time she answered a like interrogation as follows: "I doubt not but that Francesca de Sommai will be a nun in this monastery: I know it with certainty." Nothing was yet known about the girl's intention. At the end of two years Francesca came out of the monastery of St. Catherine, and, moved by devout curiosity, for some days entered into that of Santa Maria degli Angeli. All her affection, though, was for the former, where she had dwelt from the age of three years. Nevertheless, inspired in an altogether singular manner, she selected the latter in which to become a nun, and carried out her determination with great solicitude.

3. To a Mother who obstinately refused her Daughter Permission to become a Nun, she foretells Death, in Punishment of this Refusal.—In 1594 a noble Florentine girl anxiously wished to become a nun in the monastery of Santa Maria degli Angeli ; but her mother was inflexibly opposed to it To overcome this opposition, the afflicted girl was having recourse to the prayers of our Saint, who, knowing the obstinacy of the lady, said one day to her daughter that her mother would shortly die and she herself would become a nun in this monastery. Both of which things came to pass that same year.

4. Through her Intercession a Gentlewoman conceives a Daughter, and our Saint foretells that in case the Girl be not consecrated to God in Religion, both Mother and Daughter will have to endure great Trials in the World, and it so happened.—About that time a lady of Florence, much noted for her title and state, was grieving because God had granted her no children. In order to be consoled, she had recourse with confidence to the prayers of our Magdalen; and she was not disappointed. Not many days elapsed before she felt that her ardent wish was about to be gratified. The knowledge of this fact having been imparted to Magdalen, she said: "Tell the lady that she will give birth to a girl , but to remember that she will be a child of prayer and therefore must be dedicated to God in the sacred Religion ; or else great will be the sorrows of both mother and daughter." The birth took place according to the prediction, and the sorrows came also afterwards The mother, forgetful of the warning of the Saint, or too mindful of worldly honor, when her daughter reached a suitable age, married her to a rich marquis, who, having shortly afterward been found guilty of rebellion against his prince, lost his head by the executioner's axe His property was confiscated, leaving his widow in sad desolation and with the indelible mark of infamy on herself and relatives.

5. SHE FORETELLS OTHER CHASTISEMENTS TO A GIRL IN CASE SHE DID NOT FOLLOW HER RELIGIOUS VOCATION, AND TO HER MOTHER IN CASE SHE WOULD OPPOSE HER , AND THE PREDICTION CAME TRUE.— Another girl, a noble Florentine, felt called by God to the religious state; and in fact, in order to try it for a while, she entered, for some days, the monastery of St Maria degli Angeli , but, allured by human interests and considerations, could not bring herself to a final decision, because her mother was unwilling to give her consent to it. The Saint failed not to do her best, in order that the girl would correspond with fidelity to the divine call, but, seeing her still irresolute, she told her frankly that God had chosen her to be a nun in that monastery, and that if she refused to become one she would have to suffer many adversities in the world, and if her mother would dissuade her from becoming a nun she, too, would be severely punished. But neither one nor the other paid any attention to Magdalen's words, which, having been inspired by God, were not uttered in vain, as great family woes befell the daughter after she was married, and the mother was visited by a cancer of such intensity and malignity that in a short time it carried her to the grave amidst the most excruciating pains.

. 6 SHE FORETELLS THE RECOVERY OF A NUN WHO WAS SERIOUSLY ILL, AND OTHER PARTICULAR EVENTS.—Sister Maria Vincenza Dati, a noble Florentine girl, who had been six years a nun in the monastery of St. Maria degli Angeli, and had always been in ill health, in 1592 was attacked by such a violent fever that the physicians thought a pulmonary ailment would soon ensue. She suffered this fever for eighteen months, and her health was wholly despaired of. This nun, knowing her dangerous condition, placed her confidence, which is never totally extinguished in the heart of the living, in the efficacy of prayer, recommending herself particularly to the great charity of our St Mary Magdalen The Saint felt compassion for her, and said to her one morning after Holy Communion· "Sister, have faith, as Jesus wishes to restore thee to thy health." She then prayed before a Crucifix, made the sign of the cross on the sick sister, and added : "Thou shalt recover little by little, so that it will seem as if thou didst recover naturally, as for this purpose I prayed to Jesus. Moreover, I tell thee that thou shalt live many years in Religion in good health, and wilt be able to obey all orders and labor in all offices like the others." This prediction was verified completely, as in the course of three months the patient had entirely recovered her health in a very natural way, and lived a long time afterwards, working with invaluable activity at all things which the rule and obedience imposed on her.

. 7 WHAT SHE ASSERTS TO MARIA DE-MEDICI, QUEEN OF FRANCE, COMES TO PASS. SOME REFLECTIONS ARE PREMISED IN REGARD TO THIS.—After the example given by Christ to His disciples in washing their feet, and the exhortations made to them to imitate Him—the disciples, thinking of the sorrow they should feel for His ignominious and painful death, which was approaching and had been by Him openly announced to them, and detesting the treason which they knew one of them was to commit, and on account of which all were dismayed and full of grief, in fine, after having listened for three

years to His exalted teachings,—forgetful in a moment of all and
little understanding them, they began to contend among themselves
regarding the pre-eminence and the honors of the kingdom promised by the Divine Saviour.   They were so ambitious that each of them
not only burned with the desire to occupy an honorable place in that
kingdom, but wished to be exalted above his brethren, and thus they
were battling among themselves with regard to their greatness or
preference.   So strong is the pride which the first father transmitted
to his children that it could not be kept quiet, even in the hearts of men
on whom the most efficacious graces of divine perfection had been immediately bestowed.   This most hateful sentiment has caused, in every age
and country, the devastation of the most sacred rights of humanity.
Well did Italy experience this, and more particularly Florence, whose
very buildings, according to Sismondi, give a special idea of the individual strength and cupidity of citizens who wish to be great, and of the
haughtiness of the great ones who will not associate with them.   The
fifteenth century witnessed the ill-omened conspiracy of the Pazzi against
the house of Medici, which furnished the most evident proof of the
difficulty of establishing an Italian government, one and national
Everywhere in Italy the factions of those times were rotating like a wind-
mill—now for one, and now for another rival, according to the expression
of the famous emir and marabout, Abd-el-Kader,—but were always
crushing down new victims.   Thus it happened that, the sovereign
power being seized by extraordinary and preponderant forces, every one
had to keep pent up within his breast the noble thought of fatherland—
reputed by those in power to be criminal—and the unhappy Peninsula
was seen—

> . . . . girded, but not with her sword,
> Fighting, but with the arm of foreign people ,
> Ever doomed to servitude, whether victorious or vanquished —FILICAJA

Thus works human ambition, the archenemy of brotherly love.
But, as the Divine Master permitted that His disciples would profit so
little in virtue, that afterwards, being ashamed of their nothingness, they
would become rooted in humility and thereby worthy of the Divine
assistance, with which they were finally so copiously favored, so He
wanted to teach all that ambition, thirst for power, and rivalries originate
purely from man's wickedness, from which nothing better can be
expected, and, *vice versa,* that the forgiveness of injuries, individual
charity for our neighbor, and veneration of innocence are the outcome
of virtue, which, in order to be ingenuous and pure, can have no other
beginning than God   That such was the virtue of St. Mary Magdalen
De-Pazzi, it is superfluous to repeat   I will rather say that we may
believe the virtue of Princess Maria, daughter of Francis, Grand Duke
of Tuscany, to have been true also, as it seems that, the aristocratic
aversions being still alive, she laid down at the foot of the cross every
low rancor, every perturbing recollection, and rendered what was due
respectively to the individual, to crime, and to innocence   She several
times manifested her affection and regard for the D Pazzi family,
and in a special manner for St Mary Magdalen towards whom she
conducted herself in an extremely d cont and affectionate manner.

At different times she went in person to visit her at her monastery The most remarkable thing happened in 1600, when, having been solemnly married to Henry IV, king of France, before leaving Italy she wished to have a confidential and private conference with our Saint. The queen recommended to the prayers of St. Mary Magdalen principally three things: the first, a most important one and worthy of the nobility and piety of her spirit, was, that the temporal kingdom would not be to her the cause of losing the eternal, adding that if she had any doubt of it she would rather have chosen to live poor, and to beg from door to door, than to accept the position of queen. She asked St. Mary Magdalen to pray to God that the high dignity to which Providence had raised her would not make her forget her nothingness—to the detriment of her soul, and the offense of Divine Goodness. Oh! if the princes and the powerful ones of the world would think thus, the submission of others would be more spontaneous and loyal, and they would not for the slightest cause feel the necessity of using brutally coercive force! The second recommendation was, that her husband might love her; the third, that she might have male issue The holy mother promised her to pray to God for these just petitions, and asked her, in return, these three graces. That she herself would interpose with the king in order that he would reëstablish the Jesuits in his kingdom, telling her that it would redound to the very great advantage of France and the great glory of God; the second, that she should try to extirpate heresies, and bring the kingdom to the condition in which it was in St. Louis' time; the third one, that she would be a lover of the poor And the Saint told her that, if she did these three things, God would surely satisfy her wishes, particularly the one in regard to male issue. She also told the nuns several times during this first year of the marriage of Maria De-Medici, that this queen would give birth to several male children, as she was praying to God for this with the greatest fervor, in order that the kingdom would not fall into the hands of heretics. It happened afterwards that the queen had several sons, the first of whom was Louis XIII, for whom she was regent for several years, when he succeeded in 1611 his unhappy father—whose precious days were cut off by the wicked Francis Ravillac, which event filled entire France with inconsolable sorrow—he having been regarded as a good husband, a good father, and a good ruler Even from the year 1604 the Jesuits had been recalled to France, and this by a declaration of parliament, on condition that one of them would remain at court to give an account of the doings of the Society This condition, almost an ignominious one, became for them a marked honor, as they succeeded in being appointed the king's confessors. The queen-mother, after the celebrated Cardinal Richelieu through her mediation was promoted to be the Prime Minister of State, and after having done her best for the welfare of the kingdom, being somewhat displeased about some political affairs, retired to Brussels, and ended her days at Cologne in 1642, leaving behind good reason to hope that she had passed to the permanent enjoyment of that peace which is the fruit of virtue alone, and which is expected in vain from human greatness and glory. Her wise son and good king Louis XIII did not long survive her; and was succeeded in the

kingdom by his son Louis XIV, who, at his birth, was regarded by the
French as a gift Heaven had granted in response to their desires, hence,
they named him *Adeodato* (God-given)   The glory of his government
and his immortal deeds secured for him afterwards the surname of *Great*.

8. A Prevision, manifested to several Persons, in regard to the Time of their Death.—In 1590 there was living
in the monastery of Santa Maria degli Angeli, in perfect health, Sister
Maria Grazia Gondi, as teacher of novices.   One day, our Saint seeing
in spirit that this nun in a short time was to fall sick and die, approaching the mistress of novices, told her: "Mother Mistress, your teacher
will die in a few days."   The mistress was both shocked and grieved at
this news, and, awaiting the confirmation of it, saw the prediction
verified in less than fifteen days, by a terrible and sudden sickness, which
rapidly carried away Sister Maria Grazia.

At the death of a fellow-sister of this monastery in 1594, the Saint,
whilst offering prayers for the repose of her soul, was rapt in ecstasy,
and saw her in the glory of heaven   Remaining for some time in contemplation, she finally uttered, as if in amazement, these words · "Oh !
the pillars of the monastery shake !"   And turning to the mother,
Sister Evangelista, who was present, added : "Thy column shall
remain."   Coming out of the ecstasy, and being asked the meaning of
these expressions, she answered that the Lord had shown her that in
a short time four mothers of the council of that monastery were to die .
who having all been prioresses, had supported, like pillars, the good
government of the community with their wisdom and experience ; and
that she, Sister Evangelista, who had also been prioress, would survive
them many years.   In the course of a few months death truly overtook
the former ones, and the latter survived them for the long space of nearly
thirty years

A young lady of the notable Florentine house of the Gianfigliazzi,
having become a nun in the monastery, · under the name of Sister
Maria Caterina, when the time for her profession arrived, although in
very good health, she was told by the Saint that she would not live long
after her profession , and this was verified at the end of six months
Three days after the death of Sister Maria Caterina, whilst our Saint
was praying for her soul, she saw her in ecstasy coming out of purgatory and going joyously into heaven   She understood during the same
ecstasy that Sister Maria Innocenzia Dati, who also was a young novice,
of florid and robust appearance, would very soon die   Three months
afterwards this novice was no longer among the living   Another young
sister of the same monastery, Sister Maria Benedetta Vettori, being
sick, but not seriously so, our Saint foresaw that she would die of that
illness, and made it known to a sister of hers, a nun also in the same
monastery, in these words . "What wouldst thou say if thy sister
would die ?   This thought cannot but sadden thee , but it is necessary
to conform to God's will "   Within the month Sister Maria Benedetta's
days were ended.   Mary Magdalen foretold, to another nun of her monastery, that she would die without the sacraments.   This sister was
seized with great fear and sadness as she knew how valid these were Sister
Mary Magdalen's predictions, and she went immediately to the superioress

She frees a woman from the devil (page 97).

with the sad news, but the latter told her to keep herself prepared and well disposed. It so happened that, before a long time had elapsed, one of the veins in her breast broke, and she was so quickly suffocated by the rush of blood that it was impossible to administer the sacraments to her

When the Saint was in her last illness, Sister Maria Maddalena Berti, already mentioned, begged her that, if the Lord would call her to Himself, she would come three days afterwards to take her also out of this world, as she did not think it possible to survive her longer, on account of the great affection she bore her. Sister Alessandra del Beccuto, the infirmary nun—young, healthy, and strong—hearing these words, and almost making fun of them, said to the Saint: "Mother, please gratify her; take her along with thee into paradise" At these words, the Saint, smiling, turned to Sister Berti, and told her: "I shall not come for thee; but I shall certainly come for Sister Alessandra." About a year after this prophecy the holy mother died, and two months and a half after her death Sister Alessandra also died

During the last days of the life of St Mary Magdalen, a nun of her monastery, Sister Maria Vittoria Ridolfi, a promising young sister, was sick. Being warmly recommended by the superioress to the prayers of the Saint, that she might regain her health, the Saint replied with this strong assertion. "It is the will of God that she should die, and this will happen a few days after my death" The death of the Saint followed shortly, and that of Sister Maria Vittoria six days afterwards. At that same time, two sick men being recommended to the prayers of the Saint (one of them was Signor Filippo del Caccia) she said. "The Signor Filippo will die, but the other will get well" And it so happened

9 PARTICULAR MANIFESTATION AS TO WHICH OF THE NOVICES WOULD BE PRESENT AT HER DEATH, AND PREDICTIONS ABOUT THE TIME OF THE SAME.—Magdalen being the mistress of novices for the first time, that is seven years before her death, spoke to them one day in such a manner that she named those among them who would be present at her death Those who did not hear their names conjectured that they were to die before she did; hence Sister Elizabeth Rabatti, one whose name had been passed over in silence, to remove all doubts, said to her "Mother mistress, assist me at my death" To which she replied: "I shall be living at the time of thy death, but unable to assist thee" It so happened that all the novices whose names had not been pronounced died before Mary Magdalen did; and Sister Elizabeth died precisely at the time when our Saint was so overcome by her own sickness that she could not render her any assistance. When the physicians, after having given up all hope of recovery, judged that but a few days of life were left to St Mary Magdalen, they requested the prioress to have Extreme Unction administered to her, she, hearing this news and the opinion of the doctors, said: "Be assured, mother prioress, that I shall not die so soon, as my time has not yet come" She survived a year longer than had been thought possible by the erroneous judgment of man's science On the 25th of April, 1607, Sister Orsola died in the same monastery, and as soon as she breathed her last, some nuns went to tell it to the Saint, who was sick in bed, and to them she said: "To-day

a month I will die too." One of them remarking that the Ascension would fall that year on the 24th of May, and thinking that the Saint was to die on that day, added . "I would not like that thou shouldst die on the feast of the Ascension " To which our seer replied in a tone of certainty . "The day of the Ascension I will be here." And her happy death, in fact, took place on the 25th of the following May, one day after said solemnity.

10. KNOWLEDGE OF FUTURE THINGS CONCERNING THE MONAS-TERY.—On the 23d of March, 1584, whilst this chosen soul was alien-ated from her senses after sacramental Communion, there appeared before her mind a beautiful garden with many trees, some larger and some smaller. A skillful and diligent gardener tilled it with the greatest profit, when, behold ! on the third day she saw a squalid and gloomy person, scythe in hand, coming from afar, and striking this good guardian on the legs in such a way that he fell to the ground, seemingly unable to rise. During the period of uncertainty as to whether the gardener would recover or not from his fall, another gardener was pro-posed, who, on account of his apparent good qualities and the protec-tions with which he seemed to be covered, was commonly regarded as very suitable, but some of them having penetrated his spirit and seen and made known something unfavorable, so much opposition was raised to him, especially by twelve of the larger trees, that he was not accepted, nor could he enter the garden. Then another one was pro-posed, who, though good in himself, yet was not suitable for the cultiva-tion of such a garden , hence this one was also rejected. In order to get rid of these two, especially the first one, much energy had to be used. The wise gardener having now recovered from his fall, returned to his former occupation, to the ever-increasing advantage of the garden. The person with the scythe repeated at other times the attacks on him, and finally succeeded in striking him so severely that he did not again recover. Then the greater part of the trees fell, and all of them were shaken, with the exception of the twelve above alluded to, which were so well rooted and fixed that not only did they not shake in the least, but through their influence became of such assistance to the others that in a short time all of them arose who had fallen to the ground. The meaning of the vision was this : The garden represented the monastery; the twelve trees meant twelve Religious who were the most perfect ; the gardener was the father confessor, Rev. Agostino Campi, and the three days signified that he was yet to live three years, at the end of which time he would be struck by so serious an illness as to make one doubt of his recovery ; but that, through the mercy of God, recovering, he would yet live some time to the spiritual advantage of the monastery, though from time to time his life might be in danger. It so happened that, in the midst of frequent dangers, he lived four years longer, that is, until the 5th of June, 1591. During his last illness the Saint, with the warmest fervor, begged the Divine Clemency that he might be spared to her till the feast of the Assumption of the Blessed Virgin After many prayers, she heard interiorly from the Lord, that though he would not be alive on the day of said solemnity, yet he would live as long as would be necessary for the peace and good direction of the monastery

So it happened , as, having received Extreme Unction on the second day of Pentecost, and whilst his loss was commonly regarded as imminent and irreparable, there was danger that he would be replaced by one of those above mentioned, with serious harm to the monastery on account of their relative incapacity. But God, who does not speak in vain to the hearts of his beloved ones, made Campi recover from his illness, and improve so far as to be able to hear the confessions of the nuns on the feast of Corpus Christi, and also give them Holy Communion In the meantime, the monastery was altogether freed from the above-mentioned danger, thus verifying all the Lord had foretold this blessed mother. The vision continued in the following manner: There were rooted in the garden three hearts; but there was only one into which God infused and distilled an agreeable and sweet dew, which thoroughly fertilized it These three hearts, she understood, belonged to three priests, two of whom loved the monastery spiritually, and had much confidence in Campi; and the third one had been the extraordinary confessor of it, by order of the Most Eminent Archbishop. The dew which she saw being infused into this heart was the grace of God, with which he was to nourish and well direct the souls entrusted to him , because of which the holy mother was well pleased, rejoicing in the Divine Providence that with so much art and love had predisposed the spirit of this priest for the benefit of the nuns. During this vision she saw also the soul of Rev. Agostino Campi being raised up to celestial glory, and bearing as a special ornament a red stole, the reward due to a martyr. She understood that such a distinctive mark had been given him for three reasons. first, for the infirmities he had virtuously borne , secondly, for the persecution which he encountered, and which he endured with much constancy and patience, thirdly, for the burning desire which he felt, during life, to submit in reality to the pains of martyrdom. That soul afterwards appeared to her as if addressing to his successor, Rev. Francesco Benvenuti, these words "I labored much to cultivate that vineyard and garden; now it is thy turn." And, turning to the Most Holy Trinity, he paid homage and begged that an abundance of grace would be given to Benvenuti, in order that he also might continue in that spiritual cultivation Here it seemed as if Campi had eviscerated himself in behalf of his successor, and poured into him all the virtues which he had practiced during life in order to bring to perfection all the souls entrusted to him The facts well prove that Benvenuti was moved by an instantaneous and irresistible impulse to conform himself, as far as possible, to the sentiments and practices of his predecessor, especially in regard to the frequenting of the sacraments, although many other interests often called him elsewhere. At another time the Saint saw our Lord, who, from among many priests, was selecting two for the monastery, one of whom He was taking out of the wilderness, and the other from among the people, and both of whom He was holding by the hair The second was given to the monastery before the first one , and this was verified in the person of Benvenuti, who was chosen confessor and director, although he was very much bound to society by many occupations She saw the other one resting in a place where he was doing much good , but he was kept there until the time when he would be given to the monastery This happened in the person of Rev Vincenzo Puccini, a man who was leading an hermitical life, and who succeeded Benvenuti after the latter's death She also understood how these two fathers were to feed the souls of the nuns, and govern the monastery according to the spirit of the Society of Jesus, and so both of them did

She saw, moreover, a most beautiful garden, in the midst of which was planted a noble and resplendent tree laden with divers fruits, some small, some large ; some sour, some neither sour nor altogether ripe, some very beautiful and well seasoned, distilling their sweetness into others, but this was hindered by some cobwebs which enveloped the tree. By the garden-gate someone was coming in with a mattock and a cross on his shoulder, and a game-pouch with many little pockets full of various seeds, which he would sow in the garden with great care and love She understood the garden to be her monastery The tree planted in the midst of it, bearing a variety of fruits, signified the different profits of every nun ; for some, like little fruits, were wanting in those virtues which are required by religious perfection ; others, like sour fruits, would not let the regular discipline make them perfect ; and finally, others, by the continuous exercise of the real and true virtues, and the union with God, were like very beautiful fruits, seasoned and savory, distilling the sweetness of their words and actions into their companions, though some imperfections then existing in the community prevented this distillation from reaching its proper end She understood that he who was entering with mattock and cross on his shoulder was Benvenuti, who again, with the weight of the government of the monastery and the souls in it, was going to cultivate this garden, sowing therein his doctrine, his counsel and advice, both for the general good of the community and the individual need of every one She also understood how those cobwebs,—that is, those imperfections— caused great displeasure to this gardener ; and that, unless they were brushed away, as the Saint afterwards declared to the mother prioress, she feared they might prevent the realization of the ardent and anxious desire of perfection which this father entertained, and that his diligent concern might remain fruitless through the fault of others

The said garden presented two circuits of buildings one very spacious, but not high , the other narrow, but very high The first was the one spiritually built by Father Campi—large and spacious, he having been many years in the government of the monastery ; but not high, as he had to do much in laying the foundations, that is, introducing many things of essential religious obligation ; so that he was prevented from attending as fully as he would have wished to the sublimity of the interior perfection, especially among the generality of the nuns The other circuit was that which Rev. Francesco Benvenuti was to build—not large, for he was not, as the Saint foresaw, to live many years in the spiritual direction of the monastery ; but of a height far superior to that of the first one, as he would lead the souls, already well prepared, to a much more elevated perfection ; and in the meantime, gathering to himself all that the other had formerly built, he would introduce the souls into a general storehouse, and inebriate them with the wine of cheerfulness, which is the divine love; and then he would lead each one into a particular storehouse. He would lead them into the first by the perfect observance of the three vows, through the influence of his zeal; and into the second, by means of the great assistance he would lend to each one that she might correspond with fidelity to her own vocation. Here appeared to the Saint a mountain so high that its summit could not be discerned by the human eye; this was the mountain of perfection, towards which the same father was directing them; and, as they walked towards it, she noticed some moving with great swiftness and without any impediment, others more slowly and interruptedly, others were made to fall by the wind of their passions, and others were drawn back by the weight of their garments, viz., their vicious habits; and those who fell were taken by the same father into his arms, and, with great love, replaced and led up in the direction of the mountain by means of his spiritual help. The Lord gave her to understand how our adversaries, the demons, could not harm said Benvenuti, as he was always accompanied by St. Francis the Seraphic and St. Catherine of Siena, who, on account of the special devotion he had towards them, defended him in a manner wholly insuperable, one with the cross, and the other with the precious blood of Jesus and the crown of thorns.

In the same year, 1591, as Easter was approaching, she saw at another time, in spirit, the garden of her Religion, which, through the care of the gardener, was very prosperous, its trees and fruits being beautiful and exquisite; but one had to take care not to lower the branches to the ground lest they should be gnawed by the grubs, though even for that the gardener had a remedy, as by the burning fire of charity and zeal for the salvation of souls, he killed and exterminated those larvæ. "If I," said she in an ecstasy, "had to paint the gardener of this place, I would not represent him in the habit he wears, but in the garb of the prophets; he who saw them knows how it is; and, as his wishes rest in a firm place, I would give him Nazaritic locks, and put in his right hand a globe, and, instead of those two little points, I would fix there the knowledge of himself and of God, and, instead of the little shovel, which is in the middle, I would put a Crucifix, and instead of the signs which indicate all the movements of the sun around the globe, I would place all the potential virtues, viz., charity, obedience, humility, patience, knowledge of God and one's self, as this is what I am philosophizing about. In his left hand I would put a book full of the various flowers and sweet fruits of the texts and authorities of the Sacred Scriptures, together with the Epistles of St. Paul, in which so many times is mentioned the mellifluous name of Jesus, which he wishes to have impressed in his heart and in the heart of all creatures. I am not afraid of being deceived in judging the inmost desire of this gardener's heart, as I am sure he has no other end in view but the salvation of souls"

Some days afterwards, being rapt in spirit, she saw the demons who had plotted together to attack and destroy this garden; and, as the loving God had increased His gifts therein, and the spiritual means of loving and serving Him, so they redoubled the hatred and the temptations upon the Religious, to prevent, above all, the profit which Benvenuti would have brought to them. Hence, she saw more distinctly than at any other time, as we have said, the monastery filled with devils in every place except the chapter, which they could not enter on account of the acts of humiliation practiced there. They employed all their malignity to harm the sisters. In the room set apart to receive Holy Communion and hear the word of God they interposed many obstructions, that is, they tried to cloud their intellects and to fill their hearts with vain thoughts, so that they might not know the great union which is made with God in that act, and, instead of appreciating the immense grace and the ineffable efficacy of His word, they would go there thoughtlessly and as if from habit. The devils also tempted them, by means of various artifices, to abstain from the Eucharistic Food , and, when any of the sisters would succumb, the demons would make a great feast and swear at them. In the work-hall, besides insinuating negligence and torpor to the detriment of religious poverty, they would incite them to useless discourses, and sometimes even to such discourses as were injurious to the charity of their neighbors. While in the refectory, she saw a demon at the door, who, as the sisters came in, gave them some vials to smell, and many demons incited them to a dislike for mortification, tempting them not to pay any attention to the reading, or else to murmur inwardly about the quality of the food and to desire more delicacies But the strongest and most pressing temptation in all places and at all hours tended to distraction, and consequently to the abuse of speech, resulting in a breach of the most sacred duty binding a person living in a religious community. The victorious demons then seemed to play ball with the vanquished heart

On another day, she saw that, as Benvenuti was nearing the entrance of the monastery to hear confessions or to preach, a demon gave to many of his companions the sign to enter also The office of some of them was to represent his words and the perfection he was teaching as something nearly impossible to practice; others would see that his words were heard as if by chance, without considering them or applying them to one's self, others would see that all the confessor said should be received with contempt But, at the end, she saw that, if many and many more were the demons in every place tempting and trying to distract the nuns from the road to perfection, greater by far was the number of the angels whom the most compassionate God was sending to their help, so that, fighting with undaunted constancy, they might triumph. This victory generally was achieved to the great benefit of those souls, both through the example and the prayers of our Saint, and through the zeal and solicitude of the virtuous Benvenuti

Together with the favor of seeing the state of souls in the future life and things absent and to be, God granted her the gift of clearly penetrating hidden thoughts and secrets of the heart, which gift, on account of the many instances that happened, especially to the novices and the young ladies entrusted to her care in the monastery, was so well known and certain that these and even the professed nuns would examine their consciences before going into her presence ; and whilst before her, they would take the greatest care not to admit a thought for which they might have to blush. They could not, without trouble of mind endure her presence when their conscience reproached them for even the most hidden fault.

Many and wonderful were the instances proving the existence of such a privilege during the time she filled the various offices in Religion, as we shall see in the progress of this Life, limiting ourselves here to relate the following:—

1. To a Gentlewoman, before giving her a Hearing, she manifests in Divers Cases what was secretly felt by her.— Elizabeth Migliorini, a Modenese gentlewoman of exemplary life, and who greatly loved, esteemed, and cherished the sanctity of our Magdalen, at the examination of witnesses for her beatification deposed as follows. A duel had taken place in Florence between persons who enjoyed the confidence of this gentlewoman and were dear to her. One of these persons was fatally wounded, and before he expired Elizabeth anxiously went to the Saint that she might obtain for the unhappy wretch time for repentance, and that, if it pleased God, the deed might remain unknown to the justice of this world. The Saint was called, and as soon as she appeared at the parlor grates was rapt in an ecstasy, during which, seeing in spirit what had occurred and the gentlewoman's object in coming to her, without hearing a word, suddenly spoke as follows: "Elizabeth, fear not, as the Blessed Virgin has covered this sin with her mantle, and the blood of Jesus Christ has washed and forgiven it. Tell them (those between whom the quarrel had occurred) to remain in faith, charity, and humility, as everything is settled." Elizabeth was pleased at hearing this and had the satisfaction of seeing it in fact, as far as could morally be wished for. The wounded man, touched by real repentance, gave the kiss of peace to his adversary; and, having received the sacraments and other consolations of the Church, died in perfect tranquillity. The duel remained so secret that no legal knowledge of it reached the magistrate, and the parties became reconciled and voluntarily extinguished every spark of discord.

At another time a very ugly thing, which used to happen at a devout gathering of pious persons, was related in confidence to this same gentlewoman for her advice. The perpetrators were unknown. Elizabeth was not slow in going to the Saint, who, being called to the parlor and there becoming alienated from her senses, before she heard anything, began to exclaim, with a sad countenance and in a troubled voice, that she was seeing enormous filths and horrid things, smelling the intolerable stench of sin, that God would reveal all, and that she also (Elizabeth) would see the delinquent, and afterwards all would be remedied. The noble Elizabeth, being greatly amazed, gave thanks to God, who so profitably communicated her secrets to St. Mary Magdalen, and became more and more confirmed in her opinion of the sanctity of this venerable mother. Shortly after, the guilty party became known, and a complete cure of the disorder was easily effected

The Pope, not as Vicar of Christ, but as a man armed with a sword,[1] was debating some issues with the Duke of Ferrara. Elizabeth wished to see the end of the disputes, which were inevitably scandalous and harmful to society, and for this object she vowed to visit the miraculous Madonna di Reggio, in Lombardy. Taking counsel from

---

[1] Temporal ruler. —*The Translator*.

the Saint at the parlor grates about the fulfillment of this vow, she saw
her in ecstasy, and heard her saying to herself "On thy return take
care, as the devil wishes to harm thee ;" and she added, that she should
bring back the image of Saint Hyacinthe, to whom she was devoted, and
also some relics. Elizabeth followed the holy counsel, and, having visited
this Madonna, on recrossing the Alps of Bologna experienced the work
of the devil. The horse she was riding, having broken the bridle
through some unknown cause, began to run so wildly that every means
to check him became of no avail, and the unhappy rider was thrown from
the saddle and fell backward, but in such a manner as to remain with a
foot entangled in the stirrup. Thus she was dragged by the horse for
many yards over the uneven and stony ground, so that those who
accompanied her expected to find her, if not dead, certainly badly
bruised   But she did not feel hurt in the least , for which, giving
profuse thanks to God, she acknowledged that the means of her protection were the sanctity and counsel of Sister Mary Magdalen

This lady having resolved, for economic reasons, to settle permanently in Modena, before quitting Florence went to the Saint to bid her
good-bye. Having acquainted her with her intention of leaving
Florence, Magdalen gave her this answer, as short as it was determined :
"Thou shalt go and return." Elizabeth bowed her head like one
resigned to a possibility, but without seeing any reason for its realization   She left for Modena, but, after a year's absence, was recalled
to Florence, by order of the most serene Grand Duchess of Tuscany, to
wait on Lady Irenæa Pica Salviati, sister of the Duke of Mirandola, who
was troubled with sore eyes. Elizabeth therefore having returned,
found that the afflicted Lady Irenæa had lost one eye entirely and the
other was so blackened and bruised that she could see nothing, and
there was no hope of improvement   In the midst of so great an
affliction, having consulted together, both the patient and her assistant
remembered the efficacy of our Saint's prayers   Elizabeth went to her,
and, filled with sentiments of wonder and veneration because of what she
had foretold her a year before, related to the Saint what was then passing,
and very warmly recommended to her the sad case. Magdalen answered
thus : "Tell Lady Irenæa to recommend herself to St. Francis and to
visit the image of the most holy Annunziata. Both of you dress in
gray for a year, out of devotion to St Francis, and the Lord will give
her back the sight of both eyes as formerly " On the morrow both
of them began to follow the advice of the Saint with respectful
confidence ; and on the same day Lady Irenæa began to improve. The
improvement continuing day after day, in a short time her eyesight was
restored and she enjoyed her former good health, protesting herself
eternally obliged to the mother, Sister Mary Magdalen

2. SHE SEES AND MAKES KNOWN THE THOUGHTS THAT A GIRL
WAS HIDING WITH REGARD TO HER VOCATION.—A very marvelous
thing of this kind was that which happened to a daughter of Dr Carlini, of Florence—Leonora, by name. In November of 1501 this young
lady entered the monastery of St. Maria degli Ang... with apparent
curiosity, intending to remain there for a certain ti... ...ed with it
It is true, she wished to become a nun, and that was the real motive for

her entering; but she neither said it then nor had she ever yet manifested to anyone this tendency.   In the meantime, it happened that, on the very first evening after entering, whilst in the company of Sister Mary Magdalen and several other nuns, the Saint was rapt in ecstasy, and in that state began to speak, saying that she had seen the guardian angel of Leonora, holding in his hands a ladder, the top of which reached heaven, but he kept it in suspense, as if not knowing where to rest it, and, as she was thus looking at this angel, she saw at his side St Francis, St. Dominic, and St Angelo the Carmelite, conferring and almost disputing among themselves as to the spot whereon the angel was to lean the ladder, each one of them wishing him to lean it upon his own Religious Order.   The Saint, admiring so amiable and pleasant a dispute, and feeling inclined to see the victory on the side of St Angelo, as the patron of her own Order, heard that the Lord Jesus Christ commanded the guardian angel of Leonora to rest the ladder on the monastery of St. Maria degli Angeli in Florence, therefore, turning to the maid, she frankly spoke to her: "Thy guardian angel has rested the ladder on this monastery, it is the will of God that thou become a nun here, and thou wilt overcome all the difficulties thou wilt encounter." Leonora, confronted with so precise a declaration of God's will, and finding her thoughts so marvelously unraveled, fixed on this monastery and nowhere else the vague idea of becoming a nun.   After a ten-days' retreat in the same, she returned to the paternal residence, where for the first time she ingenuously made known her new resolution   This was so much opposed by her father and brothers that, on an evening of the following January, she thought of relenting and going without delay to her father to attest her submission to him and to place herself entirely in his hands.   But at the moment of passing out of her room with such a thought, she felt herself pushed back by an invisible force   This happened again the second and third time that she made the attempt, so that, acknowledging this as a supernatural opposition, she was more and more confirmed in her intention of becoming a nun, despite all human hindrances   On this same evening, and at the same hour, which was one hour after dark, the mother, Sister Mary Magdalen, alienated from her senses, pronounced these words· "That dove wants to fly; keep her, O Lord;" and three times she repeated "Keep her, O Lord." Having returned to her senses, and being questioned by the usual superioresses, she related that she had seen this young lady, under the form of a dove, about to leave her vocation, but that God had so assisted her that this would not happen. On the following day the nuns sent for the girl, in order to find out what had happened to her the evening previous   When she reached the parlor, she told what has been related above, and the nuns in turn informed her of the contemporaneous vision of Sister Mary Magdalen.   Leonora was most grateful to God for this coincidence and the mediation of the Saint, and she corresponded so faithfully to the divine call, that by means of virtuous acts she succeeded in obtaining the permission of her father and brothers, and in a short time she became a Carmelite nun in the monastery of St Maria degli Angeli

3 SHE ENJOYS A DISTINCT VISION AT THE TIME THAT A GIRL RECEIVES THE RELIGIOUS HABIT – Whilst Mass was being sung for the

taking of the religious habit by a girl, the venerable Magdalen, being rapt in ecstasy, saw the Lord granting this girl many gifts and graces. At every *Kyrie eleison* a choir of angels descended. At the epistle God confirmed all the graces to the Religious which had been communicated to them in the beginning, and even increased them. At the gospel the Lord gave many rich ornaments to her who was about to receive the sacred habit; afterwards she saw a cherub with a book in his hands, who, whilst the novice was singing "*I am the handmaid of the Lord,*" wrote in it these same words and those which she uttered at the end of the ceremony. This, she understood, was done by the angels with all the Religious, in order to show to them, on the day of judgment, to their greater joy or confusion, all that was implied in an act so solemn and important. No sooner had this girl taken the habit, than another angel of the choir of the seraphim appeared, holding in his hands the Life Record of the Religious. This angel reading, related to the Saint all the good this girl had done till that hour, her wish to enter in Religion and become the bride of Jesus, and all her good thoughts, wishes, and affections; then he wrote down the good works and the profit she was to make in the religious life. Finally, in capital letters, he marked the book with the name taken by the novice in this new baptism. Magdalen, having been for a while silent, with a full understanding of the interior dispositions of the soul of this young lady, recommended to God all the Religious, and sinners, and then came out of the ecstasy.

CHAPTER XXIII.

OF THE GREAT PURITY OF HEART AND DELICACY OF CONSCIENCE OF ST. MARY MAGDALEN.

FTER relating the wonderful favors which God granted this holy soul, it is befitting to show with what candor and purity her heart was enriched. It is only reasonable to believe that God does not so intimately communicate Himself except to lilies of immaculate purity and real sanctity. During her whole life Magdalen gave evident proofs of the candor and innocence of her habits and affections. One day she was speaking to a sister of the pleasure and delight with which she used to embrace and hold to her bosom the little children of her tenantry, whom she had instructed in the Christian doctrine, when, while yet a girl, she had visited the villa. The sister, as if jesting, or out of curiosity to hear what answer the Saint would give her, said to her: "Mother, it may have been a fault to have taken so much delight in so doing." At which the good mother, overcome by a holy fear of having offended God therein, asked the sister to tell her frankly of what fault she deemed her guilty. The sister replied: "It depends on the intention thou hadst in it." And then Magdalen, with as much humility as frankness, answered: "For no other reason did I delight in those little children than because they represented to me Jesus at that age, and also because of the purity and innocence which is found in them."

So great was the simplicity, the candor, the humility, the meekness, the sincerity, and the frankness of her words and of her works, and especially the humble and pure faith Magdalen always had, that of a truth a child could not have had more. These dispositions, instead of diminishing, rather increased and became perfect in her as she advanced in years; so that, in her old age and in the maturity of her excellent virtues, her life was an exemplification of the blessed childhood promised of old to the Church of Christ by Isaias the prophet, and commended by our Divine Saviour even to the oldest of His followers; and without which, He asserts, no one can have a place in His heavenly kingdom. Magdalen never had a strong earthly affection, nor hatred, nor rancor, nor love of worldly goods. She always believed everyone, as a child does, even without understanding, and she never contradicted anybody. Her conversation, moved by simplicity coupled with prudence, could not but render her more amiable and estimable every day   Her actions were never over-shadowed by a secondary or worldly end. Sometimes she was heard to say: "If I thought that I might become a shining seraph by speaking a single word with any other purpose than the love of God, even though He would not be offended by it, I would not utter it."   What a sublime sentiment of purity ! And if it occasionally happened that in some of her actions she doubted the purity of the end, she interrupted the work, leav-ing it unfinished until she became certain of having directed it also to the glory of God, as she intended and wished to do absolutely   She was so well used to this rectitude of intention that she could not understand how any gesture, motion, or even raising of the eyes of those souls who con-secrate themselves to God, was not exclusively directed towards exalted and divine purity   She loved no creature except in its relation to God. Those who knew her and conversed with her gave solemn testimony of it ; and she herself, in her last years, whilst familiarly conversing with the sis-ters, said that, though she had borne much affection to creatures, yet she had loved them only because of the precept of charity given by Jesus Christ, and in order to imitate His example of unbounded charity; but that, with the exception of this love, she never had the least attachment to any creature.   During her last illness she also said, with a great sense of gratitude to God, that she did not recollect that her heart ever had taken any pleasure or delight, even for the shortest space of time, except in God , and she added, when near the end of her life, that she found nothing in herself that gave her more peace and comfort than this.   From which we may not only conjecture, but argue with certainty, that this holy soul preserved till death the white robe of baptismal innocence; nay, to give her words their just meaning, it seems that it could also be said that her purity was more angelic than human—as to the angels alone is given by nature what to her was granted by grace, viz , never to take any delight but in God   This, in a human creature endowed with senses, is so wonderful that to our understanding, with some reason, it appears incredible, but it was not so to those who lived with her and saw in fact the continuous absorption of her mind in God.   It was in consequence of such great purity of heart that she perceived the least stain and spot of imperfection in her soul, and kept the strictest account of it; hence, she humbled and accused herself of things in which the other sisters could see no shadow of imperfection; and they remained struck with amazement and confusion at seeing that, amidst the sublime acts of perfection which she constantly practiced, she would find things of which to accuse herself, and to punish herself for.   She sometimes even judged her virtuous actions to be faults—not through that sentiment of scrupulosity which proceeds from pride, as is wont to be found in those persons who follow piety more from ostentation and self-love than to please God—but in consequence of her great purity and humility combined, because of which her heart, placed like a highly polished mirror before the rays of the Divine Sun, regarded itself as dimmed by even the least earthly breath

On the evening of the 6th of April of the year 1 , having placed herself on her knees in the most humble attitude, in order to examine her conscience about the actions of that day, she was rapt in an

By licking the arm of a nun, she heals her of a contagious sore
(page 98).

ecstasy, in which, having first recited the psalms, "*Domine, quid multiplicati sunt*"—"Why, O Lord, are they multiplied," etc. (Ps. iii), and "*Qui habitat,*" etc —"He that dwelleth" (Ps. xc), she thus spoke to her Jesus "O my Jesus, what was the first thought I had on this day? I grieve because it was not of Thee, as I was afraid lest it would be late to call Thy brides to praise Thee, nor did I think of offering myself to Thee or honoring Thee. Then, O my Jesus, I went to the choir to offer myself to Thee, but I did not wholly and in everything resign myself to Thy will   O most benign God, what mercy can I expect from Thee, as I did not place myself entirely in Thy hands?   Have mercy on me, O Lord, though I do not deserve it; as I rather deserve a thousand hells.   When I went to recite Thy praises, I took more pains about those sisters I saw wanting in something while performing this duty and making the necessary inclinations than I did to honor Thee and offer to Thee my praises in union with those of the blessed spirits   Well may I ask for Thy mercy, O great God, as in what belongs to Thee, which is Thy praise, I was guilty of so many imperfections   When I came to receive Thy Body and Blood, which I should have done with all possible affection, I grieve that I had no intention of doing it in memory of Thy passion, as Thou commandedst; and I did not think of uniting my soul with Thee, either; but I thought of how I could give rest to my heart It is true that I first heard the Divine Word, but I thought more of whether we acted as Thou madest Thy *Christ* tell us, than about the love Thou borest to me   Hence, O my Lord, I can ask nothing but mercy of Thee.   When I went to receive Thy blood in the sacrament of penance, I thought more of what I had to say to Thy *Christ* in order to quiet my heart, than of the benefit Thou wert conferring on me by washing my soul in Thy blood, and I did not trust in Thy love to give me grace that would put my heart to rest   O my Lord, what were the words I uttered?   They were of censure (she says this, because being a mistress of novices, she had accused herself of having reprehended a novice), "and my way of speaking, which was not very meek and gentle, caused ·her who heard me to be disturbed; and, what is worse, I failed in charity, for when I saw that her heart was disturbed, I did not try to quiet it, so that, but for this it would unite with Thee.   Behold, O my Lord, what I derive from so great a union and so much light which Thou givest me, if Thou wouldst give some of it to another creature, she would be much more grateful to Thee, whilst I, miserable and un-happy one, do not derive any fruit therefrom, as I fail in charity towards Thy brides.   Forgive me because of Thy passion.   And then, when I went to speak to that creature" (she meant an aunt of hers, to meet whom she went to the parlor grates, and there was rapt in ecstasy), "I regret that I committed an act of great hypocrisy, by causing myself to appear what I am not; and though I beckoned to Thy creatures, I did not merit to be understood by them" (she alluded to the instruction she had given to the sisters, viz., that when they would notice that she was about to remain ecstatic at the grates, they should remove her, lest she might be seen by outside persons —and for this purpose she had given a sign), "as I appeared to keep my soul united with Thee; and yet Thou knowest how many times my mind wandered away from Thee; I appeared to be a true Religious, and yet Thou knowest what I am. I ask mercy of Thee, O my God, for this great hypocrisy, and I offer to Thee Thy blood which Thou hast shed for me with so much love. If Thou, O my Lord, sendest my soul to hell, as I deserve, Thou wilt justly place me below Judas, because I have so much offended Thee. I then went to give the necessary food to my body; but what intention had I of honoring Thee? as I did not remember to offer up to Thee many and many poor people, who, perhaps, had long been knocking at doors to find a morsel of bread, which, perhaps, had not been given them; whilst the monastery, without any work on my part, and, what is worse, without any merit, furnishes me, wretched and miserable, with what I need to sustain my body. Not only did I offer this offense to Thee, but also the other one when I made Thy bride say so many words, and yet I knew it was not lawful to speak in that place. Behold, O my Lord, that in all my doings I find I have offended Thee How then shall I be able to appear before Thee to ask of Thee gifts and graces, and recommend Thy creatures to Thee, since I have so greatly offended Thee that I do not deserve that Thou shouldst show mercy to me? But may the love which moved Thee to come down to the earth and shed Thy blood, move Thee also to show mercy to my soul. Afterwards, when I did not go to praise Thee, together with the rest of Thy brides, it was my fault alone, for, when that soul asked me not to go, I consented immediately not to go O my Jesus, had she requested me to stay for some charitable act, I would not so soon have answered Yes O my Lord, how can I hope to get to that place where I shall have to praise Thee with the blessed spirits, having failed to praise Thee in the company of Thy brides? I offer to Thee Thy blood, that through it Thou mayest be merciful to me Also in that action which I performed, what intention had I of honoring Thee, O my Lord, since I regretted more the time taken away from me in giving than having failed to offer my soul to Thee?" (she meant the time during which the Lord kept her alienated from her senses) "It is true I made a sign to Thy little virgins to keep silence, but I did not consider how much more obliged was I to keep my soul united to Thee. And when I was about to invoke the Holy Ghost, my mind was so far from Thee that I did not remember the manner in which I was to do it, so that those who had been less time in Religion had more prudence than myself See, O my Jesus, how in all my actions I have failed; how then can I appear before Thy Goodness, having so often offended Thee? Again I offer to Thee Thy blood, as through it only do I hope for pardon. Greatly did I fail, O God, when I had to perform the other action, in not enduring a little fatigue by moving faster. I failed, I say, in what I was obliged to do, asking others to do me the charity, in the meantime I failed to do it to my soul. I took more care not to fatigue myself a little than I did that Thou shouldst not withdraw from me. In all my actions I find faults, O my God. But Thou, overlooking so many offenses, by Thy Goodness alone again didst draw me to Thyself and gavest me therein so much light that, if Thou hadst given it to another soul, she certainly would have drawn therefrom more fruit than my self, poor vile creature that I am Again did I give comfort to my body by means of some food, and likewise I did not recollect so many of the poor who have nothing wherewith to feed themselves, whilst for me, O my Lord, Thou hast so amply provided. I offer to Thee, again, Thy blood for so many offenses which I have offered to Thee. Alas! my Lord, we are in darkness, and I have not performed a single work without offending Thee What then shall I do? O my God, I have offended Thee so much on this day, I will not offer to Thee the final offense, which would be not to trust in Thee and in Thy mercy. Well do I know, O Lord, that I do not deserve forgiveness; but the blood Thou hast shed for me will make me so hope in Thee that Thou wilt have to forgive me " At this point of her self-examination, being still in ecstasy, she withdrew to a remote cell, where with merciless *disciplining* she tore her innocent flesh, in punishment of these light and almost unavoidable faults. Such examination, besides furnishing an eminent proof of the more than human purity of her heart, should cause confusion not only to those souls that swim in iniquity as in water and sleep tranquilly in the filth of every intemperance, but also to those who, whilst professing a devout and religious life, regard venial sins as nothing, and but hastily examine their conscience. Moreover, we have in her life another proof of how she regarded even the slightest fault. This was, that, living continually in fear of offending God, and fearful, therefore, in all works of offending Him, as she was one day absorbed in this thought, she was overtaken by such an excessive and devout affection that she fell to the ground before an image of the Virgin, and there remained in ecstasy for the space of two hours, during which time our Lord permitted her to see all the sins and faults she had committed during her lifetime At such a sight, though all were of trifling account, she burst into a copious shower of tears, and with a tremulous voice uttered these words "Willingly would I go to hell, could I but be sure that I never had offended Thee, O my God." Having such a pure soul, the least stain appeared horrible to her, and, on account of the love she bore to God, she considered as deserving of hell the least offense offered to Him.

A strong proof of this great purity of heart was also the love she always manifested for it, both in words and actions The nuns remarked that when Sister Mary Magdalen had occasion to go down to the parlor grates, if little children were there, she rested her eyes on them, and never was satiated with looking at them, and she spoke to them evidently with great pleasure, calling them blessed, because they had never offended God, and wishing them to maintain themselves always pure and innocent. On arriving among the sisters, if it should so happen that they would be speaking of purity of soul, she would gladly say "In this place I shall be pleased to remain, because here they speak of purity." And she would then begin to speak of it with so much fervor that she greatly inflamed the hearts of the sisters with the desire to acquire and practice this virtue. In an ecstasy she had in relation to the mystery of the Incarnation, she thus expressed herself "Purity is so great and incomparable a thing that a creature is not capable of it, nor can she understand it " And, exclaiming, she added: "O unutterable purity, how clean and pure one must be to receive Thee! O Word, how dost Thou regard our affections and purposes before they unite with that spirit of purity! And those worldly and sensual people, after all, with their filthy sensuality and malice, think of reaching this divine and most pure spirit. They are in greater error than the devil was when he wanted to make himself equal to God." At other times she would say: "O purity, how many wonders thou dost reveal to us in the other life, which are utterly hidden to creatures—not to those, though, who seek for thee! For in that life those persons who had seemingly been very exemplary in this world, shall be seen to be inferior to many whom to simply name would make the others smile, but because they were rich in this most precious treasure, and the others most wanting in it, the Lord will magnify the former, and lower the latter" She also frequently said: "At purity-weight, O my sisters, God wants to reward us in the next life." On reflecting in how little esteem this virtue is held by the world, she was wont to say, with deep sorrow. "O purity, O purity, little known and little desired! O my Spouse, O my Spouse! now that Thou art in heaven in Thy humanity, sitting at the right hand of the Eternal Father, '*cor mundum crea in me, Deus*'— 'Create a clean heart in me, O Lord'" (Ps. l, 12) Sometimes whilst with the sisters, she would say, sighing. "We fail to work with purity" Being asked by a nun how one could acquire this virtue, she answered: "If in everything thou wilt seek not to follow thy own will, choosing rather to suffer than to enjoy thyself, thou wilt at the end find that thou didst work with purity, because in truth our own interests have nothing to do with it; hence the road of suffering is safe and very dear to His Divine Majesty" Finally she was so much in love with and thirsty for this virtue, that she asserted that, as far as she was concerned, she would be satisfied if she would remain in the lowest degree as to all other virtues, but as to purity of mind and body she aspired to the highest, and to as much as a human creature may acquire. Hence she felt a corresponding hatred and abhorrence for sin, so that at the mere name of mortal sin she shivered from head to foot, and, transported by the most ardent zeal, at times she would loudly utter against it words expressing abomination, sorrow, and horrible amazement She apprehended its gravity and enormity to such an extent that she could not conceive it possible that a Christian could be found so wicked as to offend God with deliberate intention Fifteen days before her death she thus manifested her ideas on this point: "I leave this world with this one inability —viz., to understand how a human creature can consent and determine to commit mortal sin against her Creator." Hence, seeing the uselessness of her wish, viz., to be able to blot out every sin from the world, she grieved exceedingly, and incessantly shed tears of the greatest bitterness, both for the offenses which were offered to the Divine Goodness and for the unhappy fate of those who committed them and never thought of weeping for them.

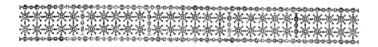

CHAPTER XXIV.

OF HER SINGULAR GIFT OF PRAYER AND HER INTIMATE UNION WITH GOD.

IT would be useless to remark the assiduity of Magdalen in the exercise of prayer; as, besides the hours allotted to it by the rule, which she scrupulously kept, she was nearly always, by an uninterrupted act, so united with God that her life might be styled a continuous prayer, so strongly and with so much delight did God occupy her heart and fill her with the desire for Himself! The actual delight of her mind could be noticed by her abstraction from the senses and the abandonment of the inferior parts by the spirit. In all her actions, either of labor or recreation, she was with God; and not only was she rapt in most happy ecstasies whilst in prayer, penetrating then deeply into the contemplation of the divine attributes, but also in every act and thought of hers, and even in every action she saw others performing; as the attraction of the *known* beauty and goodness of God cannot be intercepted or distracted from a soul that is taken up with it. There was no place in the monastery in which she did not enjoy such a divine favor; in the choir, in her cell, in the refectory, in the hall, in the vege-table-garden, and at all times, the Spirit of God attracted her to Himself in sweet union—sometimes even in the act of her giving to her body the necessary nourishment. We have already seen how several times she was rapt in ecstasy at times and in places when her will would have preferred to have been otherwise; hence, on account of the frequency of such ecstasies, in which she spent the greatest part of her life in Religion, and on account of their evident superiority over her senses, it can be asserted with strict regard for truth that not only had she her mind fixed on God during the time of the ecstasy, but also outside of it, and in a very intimate manner; for, it being an inflexible rule of human logic that it is impossible to reach from one to another extremity without passing through the intermediate space, likewise one cannot from the distraction and vanity of certain thoughts suddenly reach an ecstatic contemplation. It is necessary first to remove the distraction, and turn the mind to the good thought, reflect on the same, and, by means of intellectual reasoning, move the affection so that this may by degrees come nearer to God, until such a depth of penetration be reached that all the powers of the soul are carried along.

Now if St. Mary Magdalen was so easily rapt in God in every place, at all times, and on every occasion she had of seeing, hearing, or speaking, not only can no one deny that her mind was free from all vain and earthly thoughts, but it must be asserted that she was so united with God as to be in a continuous and proximate disposition of ecstasy; as, in fact, every slight increase of spiritual affection used to carry her out of her senses. Moreover, she herself related that the Lord several times assured her that she would enjoy the same spiritual union with Him in her normal state as when in ecstasy, with the single exception that in the former there would be no visible effect. To this fact all her companions in the monastery bore testimony, for, remarking in amazement her extraordinary mode of action, they used to notice her at her exterior occupations with such an abstraction of spirit that she appeared to act mechanically and as if her mind and heart never descended to perceptible things; though, as we have repeatedly said, she was always ready and accurate with her will to accomplish everything in the line of her duties. Noticing that the nuns thought more of the sentiments she expressed during the state of ecstasy than of those uttered while out of it, she said to them : " Hold in the like esteem what I tell you out of the ecstasies, for God gives me the same light and union " Thus she expressed herself, not out of vainglory, but because she was inspired by the light of truth for the advantage of souls In various ways did the nuns notice the absorption of her mind in God Being suddenly asked by the mother prioress, and while she was a young novice by the teachers, about her thoughts and interior operations, she, always most prompt and instantaneous in her answer, manifested with sincerity and ingenuousness her interior movements. They always found her occupied about God; sometimes offering to Him her actions for His glory, uniting them to those which the Word Incarnate had performed on earth ; sometimes thinking of the love God had shown to man ; sometimes enjoying herself in the meditation of the divine perfections or the communication which God makes of Himself and His attributes to creatures ; now she offered up the blood of Jesus for the salvation of mankind, now she busied herself with the desire to labor for souls or to suffer for the glory of God, and then, again, she would dwell on some mystery of Christ's passion, or she would have other similar thoughts, but all would be virtuous and supernatural.

That no exterior occupation was an obstacle to such heavenly communication, she confidentially made known one day to one of her novices " It is the same to me if I am told to go and pray in the choir or to do any manual work, it makes no difference to me in the least ; nay, if I told thee that sometimes I find God more in the latter than in the former, I would think I told thee the truth "

In the refectory, at the community meals, she used to act as follows It was the custom of the monastery to interpose three short stops during the reading at table. During these Magdalen performed some acts which manifested her mind's devotion. At the first stop she kept her hands joined ; at the second, she separated them and rested them on the table, at the third, she crossed them. The nuns being anxious to receive an explanation of these movements, she, in virtue of obedience, declared that at the first she adored Jesus to reverence the honor which His most holy humanity paid to His Divinity before commencing to take the food of His labors, viz , to work for the salvation of souls ; and to reverence that adoration which the Virgin Mary offered when she saw Him born in the stable and placed in the manger ; hence she joined her hands in an act of adoration. At the second stop she thought how pleased Jesus was, when preaching, in giving to His own soul as food the redemption of our souls, as this was His food ; hence she rested her hands on the table. At the third stop she reflected how Jesus on the wood of the cross, having accomplished the work of human salvation, was like one who, being satiated, wishes for no other food ; He was satisfied with the food of our souls and our salvation, and even if He had created new worlds and made an infinite number of other wonderful works, in none would He have been so pleased and delighted as in the human redemption accomplished by Him; hence at this stop she kept her hands crossed One would never be done if he attempted to describe all the mystic thoughts that were gathered from the works and words of Sister Mary Magdalen, and which gave undoubted testimony of her constant union of mind with God. Suffice it to say here, as a seal, that even while asleep she was often heard to utter words of eternal life ; so much was she habituated to think of heavenly things.

Though nothing needs be added now to judge with how much perfection she fulfilled the precept of St Paul " *Sine intermissione orate*"— " Pray without ceasing" (1 Thess. v, 17) Yet some very excellent particulars of this exercise are worthy of being mentioned ; among which are the great esteem in which prayer was held by her, and her invariable perseverance in it Having adopted some devotions, she would continue in them, though her exterior and vocal prayers were very few, as she was chiefly occupied in interior and mental prayer ; and, unless prevented by obedience or some necessary occupation of charity, she never let the time appointed by her for such exercise pass by without it She was wont to spend many hours of the day and night on her knees ; which practice she always faithfully kept. Neither tediousness, nor aridity, nor temptation could ever keep her from her usual prayers Her soul, unless prevented by the needs of this life and the obligations of the community, would gladly have made but one prayer of the entire course of her mortal pilgrimage, joining nights to days, and these again to nights, as she not seldom did, especially during the years of her novitiate These prayers she engaged in with so much affection and reverence towards God that, though not in ecstasy, she always appeared immovable and deprived of bodily sensibility Very short was the rest she took; ordinarily it was not over five hours a night, spending the remainder in prayer ; but often she did not even take these hours, as she either spent them all in praying or only obtained some sleep on a chair or when kneeling with her head resting against it If in the night, by an occupation of obedience or charity, some hours were taken from her, rather than rest, she devoted the remaining hours to prayer , as she preferred that the body should suffer for want of necessaries rather than that her soul should be deprived of its spiritual nourishment. Oh ' how many times her mistresses during the time of her novi-

tiate, and her novices and young girls when she was their mistress, thinking she was taking her rest, heard her, sitting up and sometimes in
the chapel, weeping, sighing, and praying. If the conversion of sinners was recommended to her, if important business concerning the
honor of God and the salvation of souls or the welfare of the Religious was at stake, if any novice was to profess or receive the habit in
the monastery, or if any other circumstance required for herself or her
neighbor more than the ordinary Divine help, she deprived herself of all
rest, and spent the whole night in offering up prayers to God and
afflicting her soul in order to obtain opportune assistance from the
Divine Mercy. Many a time in her life Magdalen made the spiritual
exercises according to the golden rule left in writing by St Ignatius
Loyola. With the permission of the superioress and her confessor, she
would during those days withdraw from all human intercourse, and
pass them entirely in profound contemplation. But what she always
held in greater esteem than every other devotion was the recital of the
divine office, and especially in the choir. She thought, and rightly too,
that no other exercise brought us nearer to the angels than this. Hence,
no sooner did she hear the sign for it, than she would rejoice and, leaving
unfinished whatever work at which she might be occupied, she ran to
the recitation of it with happy solicitude. Even while sick, she used to
make every effort to go to the choir; and, as long as it was physically
possible for her, she never failed to attend the diurnal hours, and even
matin at night When she actually felt herself nailed to her bed, she
there recited the office in company with some sister, making up for
not being in the choir with so much gravity and devotion that she
seemed to be an angel burning with divine fire. If sometimes, on
account of the various offices she filled in Religion, at the time of some
canonical hour she was necessarily detained out of the choir, there also
she wanted a companion to recite that part of the office omitted, giving
her reason therefor in these humble words. "I have little spirit, and in
saying the office with a companion I become a partaker in her fervor
and devotion." Those divine sentiments contained particularly in the
psalms, being by her understood and relished in the highest degree, often
transported her into ecstasy both at the common and at private recitation; and always, of course, she was ablaze interiorly, showing it in the
vivid reddening of her face, and very often her heart was throbbing so
hard that it seemed as if she could not keep it within her breast But
at the moment of the *Gloria Patri* even stranger effects would appear in
her person; bowing the head, she would turn pale, tremble, and was
barely able to utter the words. One morning, the companion who was
reading matins privately with her noticed in her such an extraordinary
change at the above action, that seeing her heaving and unusually short
breathing, she could not but immediately stop and ask her the reason
for this manifest suffering, upon which the Saint made a motion signifying to be patient, and, the matins being ended, made this declaration She said it was her devout custom, on pronouncing the *Gloria
Patri*, to make an offering of herself to martyrdom for the glory of
God; and, being then more than usually recollected in it, it seemed to
her as if she were in effect offering her head to the executioner; hence

nature, frightened by the dread of such apprehension, had caused her suffering. Therefore, in order to satisfy the obligation, she was compelled to moderate and slacken the intensity of her interior acts, that they might not sink too deeply in the knowledge of things divine, causing her to be alienated from her senses and thus preventing her fulfilling her daily duty. O singular gift! acquired, though, and possessed through the habit formed from her very childhood of keeping her mind fixed on God by means of assiduous and fervent prayer.

One year, on the feast of the Ascension of our Lord, Magdalen, being seated at the common table of the refectory, and fixing her thoughts on how she should prepare for the solemnity of the Holy Ghost, which she always longed for and celebrated with particular devotion, was drawn in spirit out of her senses, and in that state manifested her affections and deliberations as follows: "O holy Apostles, when the Lord ascended into heaven, He taught you what you were to do in order to receive the Holy Spirit. Do you now teach me O pure John, O loving Philip, do not refuse me your assistance. Tell me what must be my Cenacle, what my interior and exterior operations, and what the elevations of mind during these few days. It will be well to construct the Cenacle on high, that is, in the side of the Word, to dwell therein in a union of love Tell me what my food and spiritual beverage must be I wish it extremely pleasant and wholesome. The consideration of the great and of the most humble operations performed by the Incarnate Word while on earth will be my food, and the beverage will be the blood which comes out of those four sacred fountains of His adorable hands and feet; and sometimes I may go to that fountain which has so many rivulets— that of His venerable head. O loving Word! thirty-three years Thou didst remain with us, and I must perform thirty-three acts of annihilation between the day and the night, and this will be one of the interior operations. Eight days Thou didst wait to give us Thy blood after Thy birth; and I must examine my conscience eight times between the day and the night, as, unless the soul be well searched into and purified of her faults, she is not apt to give her blood for Thee, viz., to offer herself to Thee in the act of martyrdom; and whenever I go through my examination of conscience, I will add thereto the renewal of the religious vows. Forty days Thou didst remain on earth after arising from the dead; and I must, between the day and the night raise my mind to Thee forty times. Seven years Thou didst remain in Egypt; and I must, between the day and the night, recommend to Thee seven times those who lie in the darkness of sin Forty days Thou didst wait after Thy birth before being offered in the temple; and I must, between day and night, offer myself to Thee forty times in readiness to Thy holy will. The spiritual nourishment will be the daily meditation on Thy most holy passion, accompanying it with the meditation on that ardent love with which Thou becamest incarnate; on that humility with which Thou didst converse; on that meekness with which Thou didst preach; on that cheerfulness with which Thou didst grant the prayer of the woman of Canaan and the Samaritan, the latter did not ask Thee, but Thou didst invite her to ask I will also meditate on these words: ' *Hic est Filius meus dilectus, in quo mihi bene complacui*'--' This is my beloved Son, in whom I am well pleased' (Matt. iii, 17). . . . '*Cibus meus est ut faciam voluntatem Patris mei*'—'My meat is to do the will of Him that sent Me (my Father's)' (John iv, 34). . . . '*Discite a me quia mitis sum et humilis corde*"—"Learn of Me, because I am meek and humble of heart" (Matt. xi, 29). Twelve years Thou didst live on earth before giving any sign of Thy wisdom, twelve interior acts of love for my neighbor must I perform, and ten of humility, likewise interior. Oh! how many opportunities for these interior acts offer themselves to us, how many inducements for the intellect and the will! Seven times must I adore the Most Blessed Sacrament for those who fail to adore Him, seven times must I adore my Christ, who carries the cross with His head bent for all the elect   Three times must I give particular praise to the Blessed Virgin, as Mother and Protectress of all religious souls, that she may cooperate particularly with her assistance in the keeping of the three vows of Religion.   As often as I shall be able, I must perform acts of charity for my neighbor, with all possible love and cheerfulness of soul.   I will always remain in the act of guarding my senses; and in order not to be regarded as singular, I must do this at hours, at times, and in proper ways; for, if I should never take notice, some nun might think that I am angry with her; and if I should not answer questions, I would give occasion for suspicion.   Thrice a day I will remind the sisters with whom I am conversing, of the dignity of the vocation to which we are called, saying something in praise of it; and of this vocation I will remind myself continually.   Whenever the opportunity offers itself, I will console the afflicted, both interiorly and exteriorly; and, in conclusion, I must remain in a continuous act of charity, and guard my heart "   With these ideas and desires of interior and exterior operations she came out of her ecstasy, and endeavored to do all very punctually in order to prepare herself to receive the Holy Ghost   From which we infer that the interior, positive acts of devotion and virtue she performed during these ten days were one hundred and seventy-eight each day, not counting other devout considerations of the love, humility, and meekness of Jesus, the spiritual and corporal works of mercy, and the unceasing watchfulness over her heart which she had previously imposed on herself   Let the reader here reflect and consider what soul clothed in mortal flesh could in a single day perform such and so many interior acts of virtue, except one that had been raised to so divine a union as would befit more an angelic than a human creature   The soul of Magdalen communed with God so closely that nothing but God could she see in every object, in every place, and at all times, and she was simply led by God Himself.

We have already seen in Chapter XII the mode of life which had been celestially prescribed for her   Now it is opportune to relate the twenty Rules of life she received from the Lord after that time, and afterwards, on account of her faithful correspondence, the spiritual exercises, the offerings and protestations of every day; which again very strongly prove how intimately her soul was united to God.   One morning as she was absorbed in the love and gratitude of her Jesus in the Sacrament just received, she heard Him call her thrice times, as foll   "Come, O my spouse, as I am He who extracted thee from My mind and placed thee in the maternal womb, wherein I have been pleased in thee." At such a sensible and distinct invitation, she immediately stood up, and, with a countenance very much inflamed, she moved around to seek Jesus through the monastery. Having gone a short distance towards the lower corridor, she heard for the second time: "Come, as I am He who extracted thee from the maternal womb, and united Myself to thee, being pleased in thee!" And, on her redoubling her zeal, she grew impatient to find the wished-for Bridegroom. She ran through several rooms in a manner both uncertain and rapid; and, when about entering the chapter, she heard for the third time. "Come, my chosen one, I wish to give thee a Rule and put an end to thy passions for all thy lifetime, until I lead thee to see and enjoy Me in the land of the living." Here Magdalen remained motionless, and, receiving the Rules, she thus expressed them, speaking in the person of the Word: "I, Spouse of thy soul and Word of my Eternal Father, give thee a rule in the same act of love in which I made thee partaker of my purity Beloved of thy Beloved, note My and thy rule; Mine, because I give it to thee; thine, because thou must keep it.

"1. First, I require of thee that in all thy interior and exterior actions thou look always to that purity which I made thee understand; and imagine that all thy works and words are to be the last

"2 Try, according to thy ability and the grace which I will give thee, to have as many eyes as I will grant thee souls

"3. Thou shalt never give counsel, nor order, though it be in your power, except after having submitted it to Me, hanging on the cross.

"4 Thou shalt never note any fault of mortal creature, nor reprimand it, except after having first acknowledged that thou art inferior to that creature.

"5. Let thy words be sincere, truthful, grave, and far from any adulation, and thou wilt always point to Me as the model of the works that creatures must perform

"6. With thy equal let not thy amiability surpass thy gravity, nor thy gravity exceed thy meekness and humility

"7. Let all thy actions be performed with so much meekness, and in so humble a manner, that they may appear like a magnet to draw creatures to Me; and with so much prudence, that they may be a rule to my members, that is, to the Religious souls, and to thy neighbors.

"8. Be thou day and night thirsty (as the deer is after water) to practice always charity with My members, holding the weakness and weariness of thy body in as much consideration as the dust which is trodden upon.

"9 Thou shalt exert thyself, in proportion to the ability I will give thee, to be food to the hungry, drink to the thirsty, clothing to the naked, a haven to the imprisoned, and relief to the afflicted.

"10. With those whom I leave in the ocean of this world, thou shalt be as prudent as the serpent, and with my chosen ones, as simple as a dove; fearing the former as the face of a dragon, and loving the latter as the temple of the Holy Ghost.

"11. Hold sway over thy passions, asking the grace therefor of Me, who am the Ruler of all creatures.

" 12 Be condescending with My creatures, as I, while on earth, used with them sovereign charity, always mindful of these words of My Apostle: '*Quis infirmatur, et ego non infirmor?*'—'Who is weak, and I am not weak?' (2 Cor. xi, 29).

" 13 Thou shalt not deprive anybody of anything that thou mayest be permitted to give away, on being asked for it; and thou shalt not deprive any creature of anything that may be granted to her, unless thou hast first borne in mind that I am the scrutinizer of thy heart, and that I will have to judge thee in power and majesty.

" 14. Thou shalt esteem thy Rule and the constitutions of the same, together with thy vows, as much as I want thee to esteem Myself, trying also to imprint on the heart of every one of thy sisters the zeal of the vocation to which I called them and of thy Religion.

" 15. Thou shalt have a great desire to be subject to all, and a horror of being preferred to anyone, even the least one

" 16. Thou shalt not consider thy relief, rest, and delight to consist in anything but in contempt and humility

" 17 On this day thou shalt cease letting creatures know thy desires and My commands, except those I have entrusted thee to and My *christ*.[1]

" 18. Thou shalt be a permanent oblation of all thy desires and operations, together with My elect, in Me

" 19. From the hour when I departed from My holy Mother, viz., from the twenty-second hour[2] until the time thou art to receive Me, thou shalt make a continuous offering of My passion, of thyself, and of My creatures to My Eternal Father; and this will be thy preparation to receive Me sacramentally, and between the day and the night thou shalt visit My Body and Blood thirty-three times.

" 20. The last thing will be, that in all the operations which I will permit thee, both interior and exterior ones, thou wilt be transformed in Me."

After this she remained for a while in silence, then, still ecstatic, she continued in the person of the Word —

" This is the Rule which the Beloved of thy soul in an act of love has given thee. Therefore, thou shalt take it, and thou shalt keep in thy heart the things contained therein, and shalt put them all in practice, except when charity and obedience may deprive thee of visiting My Body and Blood "

Having said this, she came to herself from her ecstasy. How faithful she was in keeping these rules, the course of her life bears infallible testimony. Her zeal to comply with the greatest exactness with the instructions of her Divine Master, suggested this practice to her. She devoted one entire day of every month to the most searching examination of her conscience to see how she had kept these rules, and, for the least fault of which she might deem herself guilty (which never failed to be the case, on account of her most profound humility), with an iron discipline she would unmercifully scourge herself for a whole hour   Besides the exercises corresponding to this divine direction, not a few were the

---

[1] The confessor. *Note of the Translator.*

[2] Old Italian method of computation, again lately revived   *Note of the Translator.*

The time of her probation being over, she is decked with a crown,
a necklace, etc. (page 102).

acts, the offerings, and the protests of piety which she practiced daily of her own spontaneous and particular inclination. Remarkable above all was her exercise every morning, which, the better to execute, she wrote with her own hand as follows :—

"First, thou shalt say three times · '*Benedicta sit Sancta Trinitas,*' etc.—'Blessed be the Holy Trinity,' then thou shalt examine thy conscience, offering the Blood of the Word. After this thou shalt adore the Most Holy Trinity, first adoring the Eternal Father, acknowledging Him as God, offering thyself to Him in this acknowledgment as being ready to give thy life and thy blood. Likewise, then adoring the Eternal Word and the Divine Spirit, thou shalt do the same; praying each of the three Divine Persons that They may be pleased to accomplish in thee Their divine will. Afterwards, thou shalt adore the Beloved Word, confessing Him true God and true man, offering to give thy life and blood for this confession and truth. Thou shalt also adore the unity of the Most Holy Trinity with an act of reverence, making the same offering of thyself. Then thou shalt renew thy profession with the greatest possible purity and simplicity of affection, promising to observe perfectly the rule and constitution. This done, thou shalt consecrate thyself to the Most Holy Trinity, making a perfect oblation and holocaust of thyself, committing all thy intentions, thoughts, words, and works, interior and exterior, to the purity of God, praying to Him that He may fulfill in thee that divine and loving will of His for which He created thee and called thee to the perfect state of Religion.

"Afterwards thou shalt reflect within thyself, knowing that thou art nothing, and then, elevating all thy mind to God, thou shalt rejoice in His infinite perfections and in the thought that He alone is inscrutable and cannot be understood or comprehended by any creature, taking delight in this—that all creatures in heaven and on earth, and all that exist, give Him glory, praise, and magnify Him; thou shalt rejoice at His infinity, which is such that all creatures, though doing what they can, yet do nothing in comparison to His greatness, thou shalt rejoice as much as possible that He is God, as He is, and, knowing Him to be the Sovereign Good, infinitely lovable for His own sake, thou shalt wish to love Him with the perfection wherewith the blessed love Him, and all creatures and the blessed together have loved Him, do love, and shall love Him for eternity; and with all the divine perfection with which He loves Himself, has loved, and will love Himself forever. Thou shalt thank His Divine Majesty, that, loving Himself, God pays the debt we owe to Him.

"Again, humbly adoring the Most Holy Trinity, thou shalt offer to Him, first, all His divine perfections; then the perfection, fullness of grace, and merits of the Incarnate Word, that of the Virgin Mary and of all the blessed, and also of all the elect, wishing thou wert able to suffer and do all that has been suffered and done, and for eternity will be suffered and done, by all creatures for her honor and glory. Thou shalt also wish all thy lifetime, particularly on this day, to be able to exalt, praise, magnify, and honor her as the blessed and all creatures exalt, praise, magnify, and honor her, and as much as God Himself does, in an act of love.

" Again making thy adoration to the Most Holy Trinity with the intensest possible love, thou shalt thank His Divine Majesty for the good that God possesses, rejoicing and delighting in it, and thus thou shalt thank Him for the glory conferred on the humanity of the Word, on the person of Mary, and for that which the blessed have received and all the elect shall receive. Thou shalt also thank Him for the benefits, graces, and communications which He has granted thee and will grant thee throughout eternity. Then thou shalt thank Him for having created thee to His image and likeness, redeemed with the blood of His Only-begotten, espoused and consecrated thee to Himself, and for giving Himself to thee every day; and for all the graces and communications He has granted thee, always crediting them to Him, rejoicing not at seeing thyself enriched with such graces and gifts, but because by means of these benefits thou shalt have greater strength to serve and honor Him, offering the Incarnate Word and His blood in thanksgiving to the Eternal Father for so many mercies

" Here thou shalt enkindle in thyself the fervor of spirit and conceive the desire to unite thyself with thy most loving God, whom thou hast known and knowest to be so great and immense; and knowing and believing by living faith that He through His infinite power and liberality can and wants to unite Himself with the creature, thou shalt be humble within thyself, knowing thy vileness; then thou wilt turn to the Eternal Father, and pray to Him that He may give thee His Divine Word; and when He shall have given Him to thee, thou wilt shut thyself in His heart, and there thou shalt relax thyself in Him, in union with that relaxation which the Word made of His soul on the cross, viz, when He expired. Being united with the Word, thou shalt resign thy will into the hands of the Eternal Father, saying : ' *Fiat voluntas tua*'—' Thy will be done ;' in union with the resignation of the Word in the garden. After this thou shalt pray to Him to grant thee and fix in thee His eternal will, offering thyself to Him as a daughter. Then thou shalt ask the Word to grant thee love, offering thyself to Him for a bride; and thou shalt ask humility of the Divine Spirit, offering thyself to Him as a disciple

" This done, thou shalt offer to the Eternal Father the Word, with all His divine perfections, soul and body, thoughts, words, and works, together with the little bundle of myrrh of His passion and His precious blood, and thyself with Him. This thou must do as if thou wert making said offering in the Divine temple of the Heart of said Word, in union with the offerings He made whilst staying with us on earth. Thou shalt make that offering for all the Church triumphant, militant, and suffering, wishing to do so with the greatest feeling of love with which it may ever have been or may ever be offered by all creatures. As the Eternal Father takes great delight in this offering, thou shalt rest in this delight, and therein thou shalt take the cross together with the Word, with the determination of following Him until death Then thou shalt make to thy God, Spouse, and Teacher the following promises

" 1. I promise to choose the deepest humility L

" 2 To adore and confess the unity of the Most Holy Trinity for those who refuse to do so.

"3. To exalt poverty always and in all things.

"4. To be the favorite of the afflicted and troubled. ⌐

"5. To build all interior and exterior actions in the wounds of Jesus.

"6 To be the atonement for the imperfections which are committed in the dwelling of Mary (viz , in her monastery)

"7. To keep far from the things of the world and from thyself, as the heavens are far from the earth.

"8. To enjoy contempt and humiliation, as God rejoices in Himself

"9. To rejoice in being of God, and in poverty of spirit, and to suffer anything rather than prevent thy neighbor from enjoying God

"10 To condole with God for the offenses offered to His Divine Majesty.

"Having terminated this exercise with thy God, thou shalt go to the Blessed Virgin, to venerate her, in the manner which is due to her Then thou shalt pray to her, that she may obtain for thee that thou may be, with her, Mother, Daughter, and Spouse of the great God; mother, by means of the conformity and uniformity of thy will with that of God ; daughter, by pure and right love ; spouse, by fidelity and the keeping of the promises made to Him. After this, thou shalt offer to her all her dwelling, praying to her to keep it and guard it with that love with which she guarded the Incarnate Word and her own purity and virginity. And, finally, thou shalt make her this protestation, saying I protest to thee, O most pure Mother, and my most amiable Mother, rather to be in hell than not always to have zeal for the observance, and the perfection of myself and all thy dwelling—that is all thy daughters who are now in it and will be in future. And thou shalt say three times the 'Angelical Salutation' in the place in which it shall please thee. Then thou shalt offer thyself to thy guardian angel, praying to him to keep thee always, and thou shalt promise to him to correspond to the interior inspirations and divine illuminations. To all thy patron Saints, and to all the celestial Jerusalem, thou shalt promise that thou wilt honor and revere their feasts and relics, and, above all, thou wilt imitate them in their true and holy virtues "

Analyzing this exercise, we find contained therein seven adorations, ten offerings, eleven petitions, six acts of love of God, five acts of spiritual desire, the same number of acts of thanksgiving, thirteen promises , and the acts of humiliation, promises, renewal of profession, and resignation in God are five in all · which, added to the first, make altogether seventy-two interior acts towards God which our Saint practiced every morning, with singular attention of spirit, before the sign of rising was given to the community.

CHAPTER XXV.

GREAT EFFICACY OF HER PRAYERS, AND SOME WONDERFUL THINGS
WROUGHT THROUGH THEM.   RESIGNATION OF HER
WILL TO GOD'S WILL.

 S we may infer from the foregoing with how much reason Magdalen De-Pazzi might have said, with the Apostle: "*I live, yet not I; but Christ lives in me;*" so also appears of what great value her voice might be before her Divine Spouse. The prayers of this soul were so efficacious and acceptable in the sight of God, that it is not exaggeration to say that no grace she asked was ever refused; which assertion, besides numberless other facts, is also founded on this one, that, in an ecstasy of many hours' duration, she said, in the person of the Eternal Father: "*Sponsa unigeniti Verbi mei, quidquid vis a me pete*"— "Spouse of my only-begotten Word, ask of me what thou wilt." We have already seen that, at the very time of her desolation, God, through her intercession wrought various prodigies. Here it would be proper to relate all the others that were wrought through her agency during her lifetime; but as miracles are the offspring of prayer and of sanctity, we will now relate some of those which belong to the first class, keeping the second for a more advanced stage of the Life, and then leaving it chiefly to the attention of the reader to remark the lesser graces which are spoken of in passing, and leaving also to his conjecture the numerous other graces not reported, as they are well-nigh innumerable. For, though she did her best to hide from the world and live entirely unknown and forgotten by creatures, yet persons afflicted and troubled always had recourse to her, some by word of mouth, some by writing, some by means of a third party—for instance, the nuns—and all recommended to her both their spiritual and temporal needs. Many afterwards returned to present to her their most lively and heartfelt thanks, declaring that through the prayers of our Saint they had been consoled in their afflictions.

1. FOR A NUN OF HER MONASTERY SHE OBTAINS THE MIRACULOUS CURE OF ONE OF HER EYES.—In the year 1592, Sister Cherubina Rabatti was suffering most acute pains from a tumor in one eye, called lachrymose; and as, in spite of all the remedies used, there was no sign of healing, the doctors resolved to burn it. The patient being most afflicted, was recommending herself to the prayers of Sister Mary Magdalen, who, feeling the tenderest compassion for the suffering of her sister, began with all fervor to ask Divine assistance in her behalf. Especially on the evening preceding the day appointed by the physicians

for the operation, between the fifth and the sixth hours of the night, she prayed in a more direct and animated manner for the health of the sick sister. In the meantime, Sister Cherubina, overcome by a greater intensity of pain, was supplicating the Blessed Virgin to grant her patience; when, lo! be it a vision or in sleep, she saw before her the mother, Sister Mary Magdalen, who with a countenance extremely majestic and beautiful, and her eyes raised to heaven, was offering to God fervent prayers. While gazing upon this consoling object, she felt her face pressed suddenly and the eye which was sore opened by force, it having been entirely shut for many days. At this action she felt such pain that she fainted; and on recovering, a quarter of an hour afterwards, she found her eye wonderfully cured and free from pain. Early on the morrow, Magdalen went to pay her a visit, and on finding her cured and cheerful, she congratulated her, but without showing any surprise. The first thing Sister Cherubina asked her was, whether she had been to see her during the night previous, and on the Saint's answering No, but that she had prayed for her at a certain hour, the cured sister revealed what had appeared to her in a vision, and, thankful to her mediatrix, returned also due thanks to God for the recovery He had granted her, the effect of which was so complete and lasting that never more in her life had she to suffer from sore eyes.

2 SHE OBTAINS FROM JESUS FOR THE SAME NUN TO RECEIVE COMMUNION MIRACULOUSLY DURING A SICKNESS.—On another occasion, the same Sister Cherubina, being sick, was complaining to Sister Mary Magdalen that, having to keep her bed, she was prevented from approaching Holy Communion with the rest, as she very ardently desired to do. The Saint, being always efficaciously compassionate for the just wishes of her neighbors, withdrew to pray to Jesus that He might be pleased to console the sorrowing sister; returning to her, as if certain of the prodigy which was to take place, she told her to be on the alert for the next day at the hour when the nuns were wont to go to Communion, and not to doubt but that Jesus would console her. The devout sister had faith in the words of the Saint, so that she prepared her soul as if to receive the Eucharistic Bread at that hour. Now it happened that whilst the priest was giving Communion to the nuns in order of religious seniority, when it would have been Sister Cherubina's turn, the Host disappeared from his hand, and, fearing it might have fallen, he looked and made others look diligently for it, but in vain. Sister Vangelista del Giocondo went shortly after to visit Sister Cherubina, and related to her this inexplicable occurrence, when she heard from her that Jesus had sent her that Host through the prayers of Sister Mary Magdalen, to whom she had recommended herself, and how in that Communion she had felt a joy and a comfort the like of which she had never felt in her life. Hence both of them, with tears of tenderness, gave thanks to God, who in His omnipotence thus manifested the preference of His love for a human creature. Anyone who wishes to doubt the possibility of this fact might as well try to put a limit to the creative power; which would be impossible to do, except by giving up good sense. It remains, therefore, that nothing can contradict the existence of the same, as it was testified to in the process by several persons.

3 SHE DELIVERS ANOTHER NUN OF HER MONASTERY FROM CALCULUS.—Sister Catherine Ginori, after suffering for three years from calculus, was reduced to such a state that the physicians wholly despaired of her life, and the nuns by turn were watching at her bedside every night. Sister Mary Magdalen was there one night, and the patient was more than usually troubled by her pains, so she recommended herself to our Saint that she might obtain for her from God some relief or greater patience. Sister Mary Magdalen began to pray for the afflicted sister, who suddenly went to sleep, and, on waking up shortly afterwards, found herself without the least pain, and so free from the disease that she survived many years in perfect health, keeping all the rules and orders of Religion.

4. THROUGH HER PRAYERS, THE COMMUNITY BEING IN WANT, IS PROVIDED WITH DINNER.—The monastery was so poor that but for the assistance of some benefactors it could not have been kept up. One morning in Lent there was nothing in the house for the sisters but a few herrings—insufficient for their actual needs. Sister Mary Magdalen being in the kitchen, called the lay-sister under-cook to herself and thus said to her· "Let us pray to the guardian angel of Lapo del Tovaglia (a noble Florentine and a benefactor of the monastery) that he may inspire him to send us as many herrings as may suffice for the whole community." A prayer being offered up by both together, behold! an hour later, in spite of a very heavy rain, a messenger of the said Signor Lapo appeared at the monastery gates with a basket of herrings sufficient for the dinner of that day; and all the nuns returned their heartfelt thanks to God for such a providence

5 SHE OBTAINS FROM GOD, THROUGH HER PRAYER, THAT THE WINE OF ONE BARREL, WHICH HAD SPOILED IN THE CELLAR OF THE MONASTERY, BECOMES GOOD AGAIN —In 1602, the wine contained in a large barrel for the use of the monastery was spoiled; and, on account of poverty, could not be replaced The mother prioress, Sister Vangelista del Giocondo, recollecting how in 1588 the prayers of Sister Mary Magdalen remedied a similar defect, now commanded her again to pray to God that this wine might become good once more. The humble maid did not wish to pray alone, but begged the prioress herself to join in this action; hence both, going down to the cellar, prayed for a while together, after which the prioress ordered Magdalen to make the sign of the cross on the keg. This the Saint having done by obedience, and a little wine having then been drawn out, it was found to have regained its former good taste.

But the principal practice of the union with God which gave such efficacy to the prayers of Mary Magdalen was her conformity to the divine will. She never asked nor wished for anything except the will of God. She was wont to say that she would have considered it a notable fault in herself, to ask the Lord, for herself or others, for any grace with greater solicitation than simple prayers, and she protested with these expressions. "I rejoice and glory in my doing the will of God, not in His doing mine ; hence I am under greater obligations to God when He does not hear me, than when He grants me what I ask of Him " Even the sanctity and perfection of her soul she did not want to have according to her desire, but wholly in conformity with the divine will; hence, among several acts of God's love which she had imposed on herself for a daily exercise, this particular one was found written. "To offer herself to God and to wish for all that perfection which He is pleased we should have, and as He wants us to have it" How perfectly this submission was practiced by her became evident on the second of the eight days of that great ecstasy of hers, in which, speaking of the coming of the Holy Ghost and the wish she felt to receive Him, she declared herself one with the divine will in these words, suggested more by the logic of the heart than of the intellect: "I with a desire wish Him and do not wish Him; and well do I know that I must and must not wish Him, and with this desire I wish Him for myself and for all How is this? These are contrary things, to wish and not to wish I say that I do not want to wish by myself, as if by myself, because I do not want to have any desire of my own And I dare say—nay, I will say—that if He were granted to me, that in this my will might be done, and not His as His, and not as mine, though in this there would be His will, but not primarily, I will say finally that in no way would I be satisfied, so much am I determined not to retake possession of and make mine that which I have already given Him and which I want to be wholly His, that I may say with all truth: '*Fiat voluntas tua.*' I speak of my will and of my desire, for the good which comes to me by this channel seems not good to me, and I would rather choose not to possess any other gifts except (and this is also His) to give up all my will and all my desire in them, than to have any other gift according to my desire and my will '*In me sint Deus vota tua, et non vota mea*'—'Let every wish of Thine, O God, be fulfilled by me, and none of mine'" Thus did this holy soul loftily raise her will to conform to God's will. But we should not wonder at it, since the first lesson given her by the Holy Ghost in early life, perhaps in her infancy, and the first grace which she, divinely inspired, asked of the Lord, was to fulfill in everything until death His divine will. Therefore, looking up to heaven, she frequently said. "O Lord, Thou knowest that even from my childhood I desired to please Thee!" Which desire in her finally reached such a degree that many a time with great feeling she protested thus: "If I should here see hell opened, O my Lord, and know it to be Thy will that I should suffer eternally in those flames, I myself would plunge into them, to fulfill Thy holy will." She also protested that if in anything a doubt should have arisen before her, whether that thing was conformable to God's will, though she might have had undertaken it in good faith, yet she would not have continued it, even though it cost her life; and on the contrary, for the same reason, she would not have omitted anything, even the least thing, which she thought to be according to God's will. This disposition she had, not only in consequence of an act which had become generic and habitual, but because in the smallest action she constantly renewed it; so that she was many times heard to say, in speaking of going from one room to another, or the like: "If I did not think that it was the will of God, I would not go from here to there"

What is generally found to be so hard even by spiritual persons— that is, to actually direct every action to God—was to Mary Magdalen so easy and familiar as to make it seem impossible to her that reasonable beings could act inconsiderately; and she wanted by all means that the first consideration should always be for the will of God. She would thus speak to the sisters· "If you wish to reach great perfection in a short time, you must try to perform all your actions in order to fulfill the will of God, as this holy intention is capable of sanctifying the work." On noticing that they did this only indirectly, she used to feel unutterable pain and give vent to these and the like words of complaint· "O Sisters, how much we lose, because we do not understand this traffic!" She was so enamored of doing the will of God, that, at simply hearing it spoken of, she used to sparkle with joy, and her rejoicing soul was some time rapt in ecstasy This took place particularly one evening, when nearly all the nuns having retired to their cells to rest, and Magdalen having remained for a little while in the corridor, she heard some one say that a certain sister felt a great desire to do the will of God, at which, greatly rejoicing, she said. "She has good reason to feel so, as doing the will of God is the most amiable action" She became so glowing with heavenly enthusiasm that she remained alienated from her senses, and, unable to keep within herself the excessive sweetness which the object of her ecstasy caused her to feel, thus ecstatic she ran through the dormitory, exclaiming that the will of God was lovable; and she called the sisters to come together with her to confess that the will of God was amiable. At this cry of God's Spirit in her the sisters felt their hearts touched, and, they also partaking of Magdalen's zeal, came out of their cells and with her went to a small oratory in the interior of the monastery, where, not without tears of devotion, in a loud and unanimous voice they confessed the will of God to be amiable, a great desire remaining in them all to fulfill it.

At other times also she used to say to the sisters: "Do you not feel what suavity this simple expression contains· Will of God?" And it was, in fact, this sentiment which sweetened the numerous afflictions of her life, they being considered as proceeding from God's will, and the adversities and trials of those five years of probation, at the horrible sight of which, foreshown her by God, she said nothing but: "*Sufficit mihi gratia tua*"— "Thy grace is sufficient to me" In this correspondence to the divine will she lived as if dead to herself, and exactly tallying with her was the likeness of a soul which God showed her on the sixth of the eight days of the great ecstasy, and by her described in the following words· "She is walking along behind her Spouse, without seeing, without hearing, without understanding, without knowing, without speaking, without tasting, and, I was going to say, without acting, and altogether as if dead; only intent on following that interior attraction of the Word, in order not to offend Him" Thus exactly did she live, always and altogether surrendered to the wishes of the Most High, and looking upon her own will as her greatest enemy, so that, conversing one day with a sister, she told her that she wished for nothing from the Lord except that He would take her own will away from her, for she knew that even by earnest trying she did not progress as much as she wished in those virtues which make a soul pleasing to God These words she uttered with such a feeling of humility that she had scarcely finished them when she was raised into ecstasy, Jesus showing to her the great harm done to souls by their being led on by their own will. This is the case particularly with Religious, on account of the vow of obedience, by which their own will is already consecrated to God. Having at the same time understood that Jesus did not want her to permit herself to be led in anything by her own will, being still ecstatic, she took the superioress, who was present with the sisters, by the hand and conducted her to the oratory, where she offered most fervent prayers to the Blessed Virgin, ardently supplicating her to be pleased to give her light and help to know and fulfill the divine will. She also prayed with great fervor and with tears for the said superioress, in order that she also would try for the love of Jesus to divest her of her own will, and, as an act of resignation, she prostrated herself three times to the ground, as if to ask forgiveness, and then came out of her ecstasy, leaving to the sisters many lessons of holy life.

On the day following, being occupied with holy exercises of the community, suddenly and with violence she was thrown to the ground, and simultaneously rapt in ecstasy, when Jesus appeared to her with a troubled countenance. At such a sight she became pale and trembled; and, looking for the cause of the anger of the Divine Spouse, she understood that it was this, viz., that having been at other times made to understand how He wanted to raise her to a higher degree of religious perfection, and that her actions were also to be a little singular, she, moved by a desire to avoid such peculiarity, had offered some resistance to this, His divine will, and had given way to the thought of suffering anything rather than pass for a person of singular life before her companions. For this, then, she saw Jesus with a troubled countenance, who imposed on her that both exteriorly and interiorly she should have been grateful to Him, without opposing to Him the least resistance Not many days after, being in the choir, she was again rapt in ecstasy, and saw Jesus still with an angry look, for which she fell, dismayed, to the ground with her arms crossed; and, fearing lest this anger might have been caused by some act of her own will not conformable to God's will, she said with St Paul: "O Lord, what dost Thou will of me? Give me what Thou art pleased in, and I will do everything, provided Thy resplendent eyes may look down on me and Thy face may not appear angry with me "—and she added other words of humility. Having remained thus a little while, she arose from the ground with a cheerful and serene countenance, and, turning to an image of the Blessed Virgin, she said· "O Mary! I see after all the most pure and resplendent eyes of my Spouse, looking down upon me with a countenance no longer troubled but benign —But, pray! tell me, O my Jesus, what did I do in so short a space of time for which I may have deserved so sweet and smiling a look?" And she was answered. "Conformity of will " This, then, is what renders Jesus benign and propitious to us Let us reflect in regard to the above-described facts in the life of our Saint, that no matter how much one may believe himself resigned to the divine will, he will never be truly so until he has succeeded in divesting himself entirely of his own.

CHAPTER XXVI.

SHE MANIFESTS IN DIVERS WAYS HOW HER HEART POSSESSED EMINENTLY THE LOVE OF GOD.

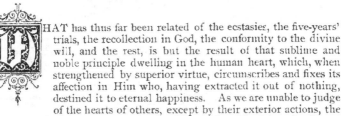

HAT has thus far been related of the ecstasies, the five-years' trials, the recollection in God, the conformity to the divine will, and the rest, is but the result of that sublime and noble principle dwelling in the human heart, which, when strengthened by superior virtue, circumscribes and fixes its affection in Him who, having extracted it out of nothing, destined it to eternal happiness. As we are unable to judge of the hearts of others, except by their exterior actions, the many wonderful occurrences in the life of Mary Magdalen furnish us with ample proof of how justly she is called the *Serafina del Carmelo.* If what is written in the divine book of the Canticle is an excess of the love of the soul towards the Sovereign Good, I am at a loss to know in what Mary Magdalen's love differed from that of such a Bride. Certainly there has never been a person so much in love with another who did or felt in the least what our Saint did and felt for God's love. It has already been said how her mind was continually fixed in God, both praying and meditating, teaching and busying herself about domestic occupations; and how she was so passionately rapt in the contemplation and enjoyment of God, that at the least thing she was taken out of herself and her senses. Moreover, she had during her lifetime such moments of holy inebriety, that her heart was unable to contain the ardor and intensity thereof, and compelled her to act almost as a mad person would, bursting out into words and acts of holy madness. She who was by nature and the austerity of life of a delicate, slim, and attenuated appearance, when overtaken by such excesses of divine love, used to become strong, and her countenance appeared full and brilliant, her eyes reflected celestial splendors, and from every movement of her person appeared singular energy, strength, and vivacity. Hence, to give vent to the exuberant vigor by which she then felt herself permeated, she was compelled to move and stir in an unusual and wonderful manner. She used to run swiftly from one place to another, tear anything that came to her hands, and, as if she were about to burst, unbuckle and wrest off her clothing and run through the monastery, exclaiming with a loud voice: "Love! love! love!" Turning to her God, she used to say with the most lively and heartfelt emotion: "O my Lord! no more love! no more love! the love Thou bearest Thy creature, O my Jesus, 's too much   it is not too much for Thy greatness, but it is too much for Thy creatures, so low and despicable !"   And she acknowledged herself unworthy of this love, saying .   "Why dost Thou give me so much love, who am so unworthy and vile?"   At other times she used to say · "O God of love ! O God of love ! O God, who lovest Thy creatures with a pure love !" and the like burning words.   Sometimes in the midst of these excesses of love she used to take the Crucifix in her hand, and thus go shouting through the monastery : "O Love ! O Love !" And at times she would stop, gazing with ecstatic sweetness at the loving countenance of her beloved Spouse ; or press the Crucifix tenderly to her bosom and kiss it, saying "O Love ! O Love ! I will never cease, O my God, to call Thee Love and joy of my heart, hope and comfort of my soul !"   The sisters derived much pleasure from seeing her in these excesses of love, so that they gladly followed her, also feel-ing a spark of that divine flame.   Magdalen noticing them, used to say to them   "Do you not know, my dear sisters, that my Jesus is nothing but love? nay, He is crazy with love.   Crazy with love, I call Thee, O my Jesus, and will always call Thee so.   Thou art all amiable and jocund, recreating and comforting, nutritive and unifying ; Thou art pain and relief, labor and rest, death and life at the same time.   Finally, what is it that is not found in Thee?   Thou art wise and joyful, sub-lime and immense ; wonderful and ineffable "

At other times during the same ecstasy of love, on account of her ardent wish that God would be known and admired by all men, turning her eyes to heaven, she pronounced these words · "O Love ! O Love ! give me so strong a voice, O my Lord, that in calling Thee Love, I may be heard from the east even unto the west, and in all parts of the world, even in hell, that Thou mayest be known and revered as true love.   O Love, Thou penetratest and passest through, breakest and bindest, rulest and governest all things   Thou art heaven and earth, fire and air, blood and water ; Thou art God and man   And who could ever think of and explain Thy greatness, Thou being infinite and eternal ? " Thus, exceedingly enthusiastic with divine love, she passed whole days, appearing to be an angel on earth feeding on the delights of heaven.

On the 8th of January, 1584, the soul of this, His beloved servant, being rapt in God, after Communion, she felt that her Spouse was greatly complaining to her, because prayers were not offered to Him for the innumerable and grievous offenses that were continually being com-mitted against Him all over the world by sinners, in order that He would not have to give vent to His resentment and anger against them and all other creatures on their account ; and she was given to understand that in God this desire of being forced, as it were, by His elect not to chastise sinners is so great, that to make her the better comprehend it, He Himself condescended to inform her of it by uttering the words of the forty-first Psalm   "*Quemadmodum desiderat cervus ad fontes aquarum, ita desiderat anima mea ad te, Deus*"—"As the hart panteth after the fountains of water; so my soul panteth after Thee, O God "   Not under-standing how there could be any desire in God, she was saying   "Oh ! how can God wish?   No desire can be found in Him.   And how can He say also '*of t*, *Deu* ' being God Himself?"   While perplexed with this thought, her mind was enlightened by her beloved Spouse, and she understood that it was the soul of the Incarnate Word that was speaking to the Eternal Father in such a manner, praying to Him for the conversion of sinners; hence the words *ad te, Deus*, that is: "Eternal Father, I wish for Thy honor and greater glory that all creatures may be converted to Thee, praise and glorify Thee, and enjoy complete happiness, and, as Thou, O Father, hast glorified Me, thus do I glorify Thee on earth, wishing and praying that all creatures may be saved, and may come to Thee, living fountain."

Having remained in silence for a while, she then added: "Yes, O Word, Thou hast already said it: '*Pater, clarifica Filium tuum, ut Filius tuus clarificet te*'—'Father, glorify Thy Son, that Thy Son may glorify Thee' (John xvii, 1); and also: '*Ego clarificavi te super terram*'—'I have glorified Thee on the earth'" (*Ibid.* 4). And her Spouse, enlightening her still more for the full understanding of His above-mentioned desire, told her by a similitude that He was like a father who, having a son guilty of bad conduct, is bound to correct and chastise him; but also, like a father who loves his child and rejoices when a friend interposes between him and his child, and begs him to forgive the delinquent as a favor to him, because in this way mercy replaces justice; likewise to God, Father of mercies, she might be sure, it was infinitely pleasing to be able to grant forgiveness to sinners, when His dear ones ask Him for it with all the affection of their hearts.

During this same ecstasy she was also given to understand how all the sins committed by creatures in the world have their origin in self-love, which multiplies in the soul as weeds do in the ground when not rooted out by the husbandman. Hence she used to see the world as an immense field covered and full of this self-love—the beginning and foundation, she used to say, of every sin; and which, unless it be uprooted, ruins the soul, introducing itself into every action and work So deeply in reality is the secret love of self rooted in man, and so tenaciously is it striking root in most hidden recesses of his heart, that with difficulty it permits itself to be known by man—not to speak of uprooting it all and destroying it so that not even the least root remains. A single root alone would suffice to diminish the price and value of and even corrupt the noblest actions of the greatest Saint Mary Magdalen then continued; "O how much this self-love has been abhorred by my Word, especially at His Nativity, taking the form of a tender child, and resting on hay between two animals in a stable ! In all His other works also He wanted to manifest His opposition to it, loving humility and hating pride and sensuality ; always suffering inconveniences and privations, and finally dying on the hard wood of the cross, between two thieves, without the comfort of a created thing; and He taught his creatures how to come to God, far from this pestiferous love of self." She also understood that two classes of persons possessed by self-love are found in this world. The first are those who are so full of it, that, blinded by it, they see nothing , hence they walk in the most dense darkness, so that at the least obstacle they stumble with serious danger; and moreover, they, like those who are born blind, do not see the misery wherein they find themselves · and, if this is manifested to them, they

She sees many claustrals and ecclesiastics in hell (page 111).

do not believe it ; so that their loss is inevitable and irreparable. The second ones are those who walk as if through a mist, so that, though they may be prevented from seeing many things, yet they see the greatest dangers ; and being therefore easily able to avoid them, they are in a better condition than the first ones. The less self-love a soul has, the more clearly she sees, and the more easily can she reach the port of heaven Having expressed these revelations, she came to herself from her rapture, strongly and efficaciously wishing to uproot from her own heart every feeling of self-love, so as to render herself more and more conformable to the sublime and pure affections of heavenly things

As the love of God is so operative a fire, it not only with hidden flames melts in sweet ardor the hearts of the Saints, but also causes them sometimes to believe that when unable to resist the divine flames they can get relief from such great ardor through natural remedies. It often happened to our Saint, that, having burned for many hours in so great a fire, with a mad restlessness she went to the well, and, though in the heart of winter, drawing out some water, she used to plunge her bare arms in it, drink of it in great quantity, and pour some of it in her bosom, saying that she felt herself burning and consuming. Turning up to heaven with a loving and radiant look, she used often to repeat: "I can no longer endure so great a flame !" On account of the same divine fire it often happened that even in winter she could not wear flannels, nor could she gird her habit as usual, feeling as if she were bursting. Among such excesses of love the nuns remarked the very wonderful one which happened to her on the feast of the Finding of the Holy Cross in 1592 Having received Communion, and being rapt in an ecstasy, whilst remaining in an immovable position, she spoke first with great fervor on the excellence and value of the cross of Jesus ; then, contemplating the Incarnate Word who was nailed to it, she began to exclaim · "O Love, O Love ! how little Thou art considered and loved ! If Thou dost not find where to rest Thyself, come, O Love, all in me, and I will receive Thee well." And complaining of those souls that do not love God, she added "O souls created by Love, why do you not love the Love? What is love but God? 'Deus charitas est.' O Love, Thou makest me melt and waste away : Thou makest me die, and yet I live ; I feel pain when Thou dost make known to me how little Thou art loved and known " Here, on account of the pain she felt, she made very piteous and significant gestures and motions. Now she would raise her hands to heaven, now she would open her arms, now she would clasp the hands in so touching a manner as to excite devotion even to tears in those who saw her, and she never stopped saying · "Come, souls, to love my Love ; come to love your God." And, being unable longer to keep still on account of this desire, she began to run very swiftly through the monastery, it seeming to her as if she were making a tour of the entire world, to seek and unite souls to love God, calling them with the usual phrase: "Come, souls, come to love your God." On meeting some nun she would suddenly seize her by the hand, and, strongly pressing her to herself, she would say to her: "O soul, dost thou love the Love?" And thinking that every nun felt like herself the divine flames, she would reply . "How canst thou live?

Dost thou not feel thyself consumed and dying of love? " Finally, after having long run through the monastery in this state of loving frenzy, and seeing no other way of inviting the souls of the people outside to love her God, once she got hold of the rope of the big bell, and, ringing it energetically, she repeated at the top of her voice "Come, souls, to Love; come to love the Love by whom you have been so much loved!" During this same excess she went to the well to cool the ardor that consumed her, and, plunging her arms into the cold water, she also poured some of it in her bosom.   After which, with wonderful celerity (which the sisters considered supernatural),without ladder, without any support, as if flying, she ascended to the entablature of the choir facing the church, many feet above the floor, to a spot not wider than the third of an arm's length, unprotected on every side, and, as if she were upon a wide and safe pavement, she ran to embrace a Crucifix in relief, which was fastened in the centre of the entablature.   Having removed it from its place, and, carrying it in her arms, she descended with the same agility, and, then going apart in the chapter, there, on her knees, she spent the whole of that day, and some hours of the evening, ecstatically contemplating in that image the love of her beloved Bridegroom, and giving vent to the ardent affection of her heart towards Him   In the meantime, she was also seen by the sisters to press her lips several times to the side of the same Crucifix, like one sucking and absorbing with great relish some sweet liquor, by which, as she said after the ecstasy, she really felt herself very much nourished and strengthened.

No less wonderful did Magdalen appear on another day, when overcome by a similar excess of love   Having ascended again and with the same agility to the aforementioned entablature, and having again taken from it that same Crucifix and made to Him many protestations of the tenderest love, she went to the choir, took Him down from the cross, and invited the many nuns present to kiss Him.   They, being influenced by the example of the ecstatic sister, one after the other approached the devout image, rendering to it this act of Christian piety   When this was done, Magdalen placed the holy image on her lap, and contemplating in it her Jesus dead and taken down from the cross, and looking fixedly at His sacred wounds, it seemed to her as if she saw Him covered with sweat and blood.   Touched at such a sight, she thought of wiping His face and limbs, and, having no linen in her hands, she took the veils from her head, and with loving reverence she touched and wiped the wounds and the limbs of Jesus in the image with them.   Nor was this pious action of hers left without a divine recompense, for, at the end, the superioress taking those veils, she found them really damp, as though some perspiring person had been wiped with them   Which being by the nuns regarded as miraculous, they gave Magdalen other veils, keeping these as precious relics, which was not by any means a vain thought, for, having sent them after the death of the Saint to several sick persons, wonderful effects were wrought and seen

Another time, having entered an excess of the same love, she went in the choir to the chapel of the Blessed Virgin of the Manger, and having opened the railings of the altar (which was not used for the divine celebration) she ascended to it with the same agility, and, having knelt on it, she addressed loving prayers to the Mother of God, that she might give her the image of her Son Jesus, who was there represented with her in relief. Then making a sign of having obtained this favor she took in her arms that holy image, and, stripping it of all its ornaments, she said: "I want Thee stripped, O my Jesus, as I could not bear Thee with all Thy infinite virtues and perfections. I want Thy humanity entirely bare." She then went with the same image to different places in the monastery; in each of them, imitating the priest when he offers the Host, she raised the sacred image, offering it to the Eternal Father, and saying in one place "*Offero tibi, sancte Pater, Filium tuum, quem ab æterno genuisti, et mihi in terram misisti*"— "I offer to Thee, O Holy Father, Thy Son, Whom from all eternity Thou hast begotten and sent to me on earth." In another place she added. "*Vivo ego, jam non ego, vivit vero in me Christus*"—"And I live, now not I; but Christ liveth in me" (Galat. ii, 20). "*Dilectus meus candidus et rubicundus*"—"My beloved is white and ruddy" (Cant. 10); and there she repeated the act of offering, with the following words: "*Offero tibi, æterne Pater, Filium tuum, quem ab æterno in sinu tenuisti, et in sapientia tua genuisti, et propter miseriam meam et misericordiam tuam in terram misisti*"—"I offer to Thee, O Eternal Father, Thy Son, whom from eternity Thou hadst in Thy bosom and didst beget in Thy wisdom, and for my misery, in Thy mercy, Thou hast sent upon the earth" In a third place, using the same ceremonies, she thus expressed herself: "*Offero tibi Filium, æterne Pater, quem post resurrectionem ejus ad te attraxisti et ad dexteram tuam collocasti.*"—"I offer up to Thee, O Eternal Father, Thy Son, whom, after His resurrection, Thou hast raised to Thee and made to sit at Thy right hand." These offerings over, she returned to the choir, and, having reverently ascended said altar, she gave the sacred image to all the sisters to kiss, as they all had gathered to see the wonderful sight; and she offered to some the head, to others the breast, to one the hands, and to another the feet of the Crucifix, as the Spirit of God directed her to do.

The sentiments which Magdalen expressed, whether in ecstasy or not, were always of the highest and most affectionate esteem towards her God. She used to call Him· "God of love, of sovereign goodness, of unutterable power, of ineffable wisdom, the keeper of our hearts, the substance of my being" Turning to the Word, now she would call Him: "Eternal Word, Infinite Wisdom, Sovereign Goodness, Love incarnate, Word become man, Eternal Wisdom, Word, Spouse, O my Spouse." Now she would invoke Him· "O only-begotten Word, O great God, O pure God!" Speaking of His humanity, she added: "O slain Lamb! O profound and admirable Humanity of my Word!" If she looked at His sacred limbs, she called them "loving;" if at His Sacred Heart, she exclaimed· "O most sweet, most merciful, and most loving Heart of the Word made man," if at His Divine Person· "O my Spouse, my beautiful Spouse, O Love, O Sweetness, O Comfort of my soul, O good Jesus, O my Jesus, O my God." If she named the Holy Spirit, she gave Him the epithet of "sweet, "loving," and the like. Besides those above quoted, she was also wont to use the following expressions towards God: "I will never be done calling Him 'Love,' Thee alone I want to love and no other love ; the more I find Thee, O my Jesus, so much the more I thirst to seek Thee," and the like.   But the most powerful testimony of how the divine love was burning in the heart of Magdalen is afforded us in those interior acts, the exercise of which in great part she happily left written.   Among the many remarkable ones during the course of her life are the following, written by her own hands, of which it is opportune to speak here.—

1. She loved to enjoy and take delight in the divine attributes, viz , in the omnipotence, wisdom, goodness, and infinite love with which God loves Himself and all His creatures

2. She wished to God all the good, glory, and honor that He had, and would have throughout eternity

3. She rejoiced at the mutual communications which take place among the three Divine Persons.

4 She rejoiced at the thought that God is so great and infinite that He cannot be understood by creatures

5. She rejoiced at the infinite love with which God loves Himself, has loved and will love Himself for eternity , and she delighted in this, that all creatures and all the blessed spirits are not capable of loving Him as He deserves ; and she thanked His Divine Majesty because God loves Himself infinitely.

6. She rejoiced for all the treasures and infinite graces that the Eternal Father granted and communicated to the humanity of the Word, as for the grace He had of performing miracles and of drawing the hearts of creatures to Himself.

7 She rejoiced that the Eternal Father gave us creatures as an inheritance to the Incarnate Word , and she rejoiced at the delight He takes in such inheritance, and at His complacency in the souls of the just

8. She rejoiced at the love the Incarnate Word bore to virginity.

9. She offered God to God Himself in thanksgiving for all the glory, honor, and happiness He possessed, and in thanksgiving for all the gifts and graces He communicated to all creatures.

10. She used to say to the Lord "If at this moment I could give Thee all the glory, honor, and praise that are given thee at present by all the blessed spirits, and all the just of the earth, I would willingly do it ; but, as I cannot, accept of my good will towards Thy divine Majesty "

11. She offered herself to God, and wished for all the perfection He was pleased she should have, and in the manner He wished her to have it.

12. She inclined her will to love creatures only because God loves them, and to rejoice at the love He bears them and the perfection He communicates to them ; and even granted (which is impossible) that God wanted to permit a creature to offend or displease us, yet she wished this creature to have all the perfection and the glory of the seraphim, even if it was to be employed in offending us, thus uniting with God in not wanting anything but what He wills.

Such was the sweet disposition by which this soul enamored of God was favored, and such were the acts of most intense love which she practiced.

CHAPTER XXVII.

HER GREAT DEVOTION TOWARDS THE MOST HOLY SACRAMENT OF THE
ALTAR; AND HOW SHE RECEIVED COMMUNION SUPERNATURALLY
SEVERAL TIMES DURING HER ECSTASIES. SHE SEES JESUS IN
THE HEARTS OF THE SISTERS WHO RECEIVE HOLY COM-
MUNION, AND EXHORTS THEM TO FREQUENT IT MORE.

LOVE is that sweet movement of the heart which disposes and bends to unite with the loved object; and as it is not the body but the soul that loves, it follows that the soul of the true lover tends to unite himself with the soul of the beloved, and therefore regards the body as an impediment and an obstacle to this union. Because of this impediment lovers get angry, and try their best and would give half their lives to remove it, in order to secure, as from spirit to spirit, an immediate and free union. "Behold," says Cesari, "the ardent love of a mother for her child. In the impetuosity of her tenderness she presses him very closely to her bosom, as if she wanted him to enter her womb again. She stamps burning kisses on his brow, and appears as if she wanted to eat him up. What is this? The soul of the mother, that tries to unite with the soul of the son, finds the body standing between; and she, with such loving frenzy, sucking this body, appears as if she wanted to destroy it, or take it within herself, and almost to absorb it, and thus become one with him, soul and body; or rather, she seems from the mouth of the infant to draw within herself through her mouth the soul of her beloved, that it may become one with her own. See how the nature of love manifests itself! But you can also see how, just on account of the body, this perfect union is not possible among men. Christ alone could accomplish it: He hid in the body His Divinity, personally united to His soul. And moreover, hiding Himself more completely and making Himself smaller under the appearance of bread, He found the way thus to enter—God, soul and body—into our heart, and as true food to penetrate our interior. There He goes to find the beloved soul, and face to face, spirit to spirit, the Divine Word and our soul (which is but a breeze and a breath of the divine substance) drawn by mutual affinity, kiss one another, become as one and the same thing, embodying one another; nay, as the power of the Divinity infinitely surpasses that of the human spirit, the latter is so much more efficaciously absorbed by the former and in a manner which God alone knows and can make known, that loving transformation follows whereby man, coming out of his natural mode of living, acquires a life, a way of working, and a will wholly divine. Hence all the Saints always had for this Heavenly Banquet the most longing desire, both because of the union with the beloved Jesus and the recollection of that night set apart by the same Divine Redeemer in order that He might oppose the most tender demonstration of His love to human perfidy and ingratitude, excessive beyond conception. This testament of living and perpetual love forms the primary object of every soul who, turning her face to her Divine Maker, opposes no obstacle to His divine charms."

What was to become, therefore, of our Magdalen so enamored of her God? By what ardent wishes must she have felt her heart borne away towards the Eucharistic Food? We have already seen how from her tender years she was equally reverent towards It and hungry for It; and that, just on account of the daily reception of the Most Holy Communion therein, she chose the monastery of Santa Maria degli Angeli As the divine love grew in her with age, so, in equal measure, this celestial hunger grew ; so that she came to think it was impossible for her to live, unless she could feed daily on this Angelic Bread , in fact, she never voluntarily omitted to receive it , and, even during her infirmities, she tried, as far as lay in her power, not to be left without it One day during the time of her novitiate, it happened that the father confessor delayed the hour of Communion unusually, so that the mistress of novices, thinking he was no longer coming, obliged Magdalen to breakfast. No sooner did she, against her will and by mere obedience, swallow a mouthful than the father arrived and had the bell rung for Communion The holy novice felt such regret and grief at this, and broke into such bitter weeping, as to make the mistress, who had been the cause of her disciple's being deprived of so much good that morning, weep also. The Saint was so transported by the wish of uniting herself with Jesus by means of this Divine Sacrament, that even the interval between one day and the other was very painful to her; and at the time of Communion it often happened that, being impatiently waiting for her turn in the order of seniority, without thinking, she would go ahead of others, sometimes even the very superioress. The fervor and reverence with which she approached the Sacred Banquet a man could scarcely imagine It can well be said, that strengthened and kindled in the love of God by thus nourishing herself with the body of Christ, and becoming every day more inflamed with it, she was continually in her thoughts, discourses, and most ardent desires sitting at the Celestial Banquet, so that, as a rule, before or after Communion, she was alienated from her senses. Reflecting either on the love shown us by Jesus in the Eucharist, or on His Passion, in memory of which this was instituted, she would first become inflamed with the most loving gratitude, and then, beginning to consider her nothingness in comparison to the infinite divine greatness, she would approach to receive this Sacrament with so profound a reverence and fear that she used to say she was expecting, some time, on account of her unworthiness, that the earth would open under her feet, in the performance of this action. She was so immersed in the consideration of receiving her Jesus in the Sacrament, that every exercise, though laborious and distracting, far from making her mind wander, would rather become for her a proximate preparation for Holy Communion   It happened sometimes that during these very exercises she was rapt in ecstasy, and thus ecstatic went to Communion.   Wonderful in a special manner it was the morning the bell for Communion rang while she was making bread, when, carried out of her senses by an excess of joy, she went to Holy Communion forgetting her arms were bare and that there was flour on both her hands.   Though in far-away cells, wherein it was naturally impossible to hear such a sound, yet there was no instance in which it did not penetrate to her ears ; and it was enough for her to speak of it, in order that the sisters would consent to follow her with firm faith, though they themselves might not have heard the common call.   It also happened that, Magdalen being in ecstasy at the moment the bell invited the sisters to the Eucharistic Banquet, she, as if at the voice of obedience, returned to herself and proceeded with the rest to the Divine Repast.   On account of her thinking so little of herself, she was sometimes seized by so profound a respect that she felt a reluctance to approach Holy Communion, saying emphatically : "Oh! how great a thing it is to receive a God!"

Before the Blessed Sacrament she seemed an angel assisting before the Majesty of the Most High ; and when the confessor exposed It for adoration, her eyes sparkled with joy, and in her voice and the movements of her body she manifested the excess of her contentment   Whenever she knew this before the other sisters, she would run to them, and break the happy news, saying : "Don't you know?   The father wants to expose the Most Holy Sacrament for us."   Thus when the confessor entered the monastery to give Communion to the sick, she, as if attracted by a strong magnet, could not help drawing as near as possible to him, to adore, close by, her Jesus in the Sacrament.   Her devotion to Him was so great that every day (between day and night) she would ordinarily visit Him thirty times, according to the order she had received from Jesus Himself in the twenty rules above mentioned   She used to call Thursday " the day of love," on account of the institution of the Eucharist, which took place on that day , and she felt a special desire that the sisters would receive Communion on that day

During her ecstasies she had most sublime revelations concerning this great gift of God , and especially in one of them the Eternal Father taught her the manner of preparing for Holy Communion She expressed other devout thoughts in another ecstasy, in which she spoke wonderfully of how the Incarnate Word rests Himself in the soul and in the Church   In another ecstasy she spoke with celestial knowledge of the complaisance of God in being united to the just soul, by the likeness the soul has to God, and of the delight the soul feels in remaining united with God.   On account of the ardent wish she felt in her soul, she often manifested in her ecstasies that Jesus, in order to satisfy her, gave her Holy Communion with His own hands   This happened especially during the two ecstasies above referred to, during which she had a taste of the Passion of Jesus ; and contemplating the institution of this great Sacrament, and representing vividly the Divine Saviour in that action, she acted as though she actually received Communion from Jesus, in company with the Apostles. So it appeared to the eyes of the sisters present, and was so understood from the words she uttered in her ecstasy, among which were the following · "*Dilectus meus candidus et rubicundus collocavit se in anima mea*"—"My Beloved, white and ruddy, placed Himself in my soul." Another time—it was the feast of St. Albert the Carmelite,—when she was clothed with the habit that came out of the wounds of Jesus, as has been related in Chapter XIV, in which ecstasy she said the *Confiteor* and "*Domine, non sum digna*," three times, she opened her mouth as if she were receiving Holy Communion, and she continued recollected, as usual, for the thanksgiving. By the like supernatural power, one morning (the confessor having been prevented from coming to give Communion to the nuns, and these being gathered according to the custom in such case in the Communion-room, to supply the deficiency with their desire), Magdalen, rapt in ecstasy, repeated the acts and the words above said, and then, returning to herself, related that she saw St. Albert the Carmelite carrying the Most Holy Sacrament and giving Communion not only to herself, but also to all the nuns who had come there, in token of the delight God took in the practice of spiritual communion   God also granted her to see Jesus in the heart of the sisters after they had received Holy Communion ; and sometimes she manifested in what form she saw Him in each of them— He showing Himself to her in some as a child, in others at the age of twelve, and in others still at the age of thirty-three years, in others as suffering and crucified, and in others as risen and glorious, and this diversity occurred according to the various meditations the sisters were engaged in, or according to the capacity and the merits of each of them.

One morning, it being Easter Sunday, whilst she was mistress of novices, and sitting at the table with unwonted joy and gladness, a novice waitress could not keep herself from asking her the cause of so great a joy. To whom Magdalen made answer: "Because I see Jesus resting in the breast of all the sisters, glorious and risen, as Holy Church to-day represents Him to us ; and His presence is the cause of my being so joyful." Having uttered these words, she remained alienated from her senses, and began a tender colloquy with her Divine Spouse. Thus the company of the sisters promoted in her the presence of God and the love of her neighbors ; and one day, she being in the midst of her sisters, looking at all of them, and particularly resting her eye on one, she thus spoke to her: "Oh! what love do I feel for all these sisters, seeing them all like so many tabernacles and ciboriums of the Most Holy Sacrament they so often receive !"

And the more good she understood to be contained in this celestial gift, the more did she wish the sisters to partake of it, so that, in order that they would approach it often, she was wont to speak of it to them with so much love and esteem that sometimes on such occasions she was by her enthusiasm carried out of her senses   This happened to her one day in a special manner, when discoursing on the "*Consummatum est*"—"It is consummated" (John xix, 30), uttered by Jesus on the cross, applying which to the soul who has fed on the Angelic Bread, she said : "As soon as the soul has received the Bread of Life in the Most Holy Sacrament of the altar, by the close union contracted with God, she can say also: '*Consummatum est*' In that celestial food all good is found, all wishes are fulfilled in God; and what else can the soul want, when possessing Him Who contains everything? If the soul wishes for charity, possessing Him Who is perfect charity, she has also the perfection of charity; the same is to be said of the true faith, of hope, purity, wisdom, humility, and meekness; as Christ in the soul, by means of this food, begets all the virtues. What can the soul want or wish, if all the virtues, gifts, and, graces she might wish are gathered in that wonderful God, who is truly under those sacramental species, as in truth He is sitting at the right hand of His Father in heaven? Ah! Oh! how well then the soul, having and professing this God, can say with truth : '*Consummatum est!*' She wants nothing, she wishes for nothing, she longs for nothing else but Him who then has given Himself wholly to her, communicating to her, together with Himself, all his goods."

At another time, as she was giving the spiritual exercises (availing herself of those of St. Ignatius) to one of her novices, the latter relating to the saintly mother how in her meditation on the Divine Eucharist she had centred her thoughts so much on the love with which Jesus had instituted it, that she could not pass to any other idea, Magdalen, feeling her heart touched by such expressions, replied several times: "When one stops to think on love, she cannot proceed further, but must stop at love ;" and here she went into ecstasy. At another time, being still mistress of novices, she knelt in their midst, and, crossing her arms on her breast, said these words: "O sisters, were we to penetrate deeply into the fact that whilst the sacred species last within us, the Divine Word performs in us those operations which He performs in the bosom of His Eternal Father, and the Word being in the bosom of the Father, and the Father in the Word, and the Holy Ghost in both inseparably, we, in receiving the Word, receive all the Most Holy Trinity: Oh! if we would penetrate it! Oh! if we would know it! we would not approach Holy Communion so much at random, nor would we for such trifling causes neglect to receive it, but we would think well on it before omitting it." Such words, uttered with the greatest fervor, caused in the soul of the novices great desire to frequent the Eucharistic table. Knowing that any one had omitted by her own will Holy Communion, she felt such grief in consequence of it, that it made her weep; and she used to address such a one in words like these: "Thou dost not know, O sister, of how much good thou hast deprived thyself, ah! how much good thou hast lost this morning !" And she added the most pressing exhortations to persuade the frequenting of the Eucharistic Sacrament, demonstrating the advantages it brings to the soul, and the offense offered to the love of Jesus by omitting Holy Communion when one can receive it

One morning, two nuns having been casually left without Holy Communion, and Magdalen being in ecstasy, as soon as she heard some one speaking of that, she came to herself, and, all inflamed with charity, went to call back the confessor, who was about leaving the church, and begged of him that for the love of God he would give Communion to those two sisters; which being done by him, her spirit abandoned itself again to the ecstatic contemplation. She would pray the Divine Goodness, fervently and incessantly, to be pleased to preserve in her monastery, till the end of the world, the practice of frequenting the Most Holy Sacrament; and therefore to grant them spiritual fathers who would feel this desire also, and who would have such light as to worthily admit the sisters to this Banquet. On noticing in any one little fervor and diligence, she was also wont to say: "I am pretty sure that a single Communion made with true spirit and sentiment, is apt to raise the soul to a great perfection of life." Sometimes she called to herself some sister, and with many sighs and tears, told her: "Let us pray to the Lord, sister, that He may grant us light that we may not grow so cold and frozen in His service, and particularly in frequenting this Food of Life."

Among the fruits she attributed to the frequent receiving of Jesus in the Sacrament for the benefit of her monastery, was the detachment and seclusion from the society of seculars, which she remarked in all the sisters, and in which she felt immense consolation. Encouraging those who, through pusillanimity and excessive fear abstained sometimes from receiving their Spouse Jesus in the Host, she used to say to them: "Offer to God in reparation all the actions you perform, and perform them with the intention of pleasing His Divine Majesty, then go to Communion with purity of heart and with humility, in memory of His Passion, as He has ordained." Again. "As a preparation, think attentively and try to penetrate the fact that what you receive is God, Who gave Himself to us, through love; and therefore He wants to be received with feelings of great love and gratitude." Sometimes she suggested that, the better to prepare one's self, a Communion would be offered on behalf of another, as to a frequent communicant one is a preparation for the other; and she taught that from Communion to Vesper time, one should be exclusively engaged in thanking Jesus, Whom one has received, and from Vesper time till the morning following, in preparing, by thinking of Him Who is to be received again in the next Communion. Among other reflections she suggested for this purpose, were the following ones. "Think you have to perform the greatest action that can be performed in this world, that is, to receive within you the great God. Think that whilst you deserve to be hurled into hell, Jesus, through His goodness, shows you so much mercy, that He gives Himself to you in the Most Holy Sacrament: what purity should your heart possess, having to receive the Fount of purity!" Moreover, she regarded it of the highest importance to approach Holy Communion free not only from anger, but even from the slightest bitterness towards our neighbor, as a Sacrament of love should not be received if fraternal charity does not exist. "If you have anything," she used to say, "against any sister, try, before you go to Communion, to feel within yourselves interior sweetness towards all; and when you do not feel it, ask it of Jesus, until He gives it to you. And if you experience a prompt determination to lay down your life and blood for that sister, in case the will of God required it, go then readily to Holy Communion." For the same exercise of Charity, she recommended that, in preparation, one should have a desire to benefit the whole world, and ask God to grant a hunger for this Sacred Food to all faithful souls.

She did not like to see the sisters going to work through the monastery so soon after Communion, but wished them to remain for a while to enjoy the presence of their Divine Guest, making them reflect that this was the most precious time we have in this life, and the most appropriate to treat with God and give Him the opportunity to purify, enlighten, and sanctify our souls. Hence she taught them to employ that time in loving aspirations, praise, thanksgiving, and offering of themselves to God, and that there was no means more efficacious to perfect a soul than the spending of the time after Holy Communion in such pious exercises, as the person who learns from Jesus needs no other books or teachers. What a shower of heavenly sweetness would fall on herself, and what flames of divine love she would send forth to heaven after feeding her soul with the Bread of Angels, he may imagine who reads the history of her life and the sublime knowledge with which she was privileged.

On the 12th of February, 1584, as the nuns could not receive Communion sacramentally, they had come together, according to the above-mentioned custom, for their spiritual communion Magdalen, being very anxious to feed on the Bread of Life, began to pray with the others, and, being soon rapt in ecstasy, was consoled by a joyful vision, in which, with the eyes of her angelic mind, she again saw St. Albert the Carmelite, who held in his hand the pyx of the Most Holy Sacrament, took out the Host and gave Communion to all those *who greatly wished for it*, passing by the others; and, having thus completed the act in that place, he went through the monastery to give Communion to some others desirous of it, but who through obedience were engaged in some community work, giving to them words of consolation, whilst to her he said: "Know that though these brides of God neither feel nor see that I, blessed soul, give them Communion, they are, nevertheless, enriched and favored, through me, with all the gifts and graces they would have received if they had, in fact, received Holy Communion; and though I may not be by them loved as a father and held in that veneration they owe me, as one who has battled under the same banner of the Virgin Mary under which they battle, I would not, nevertheless, keep myself from proving to them a loving father by ministering to them the Food of Life"

On Good Friday of the same year, she understood the new exercises she was to perform when she could not receive Holy Communion; and it seeming to her that her soul was dipped thrice in His sacred side, after a short silence, being rapt in ecstasy, she spoke as follows: "I will not ask Thee, O my God, that Thou come to me sacramentally, as Thy Church ordains otherwise; but rather do I ask of Thee the knowledge of Thee and of myself, for, if I get that, I know I will love Thee, and if I have Thy love, how canst Thou not come to me, that love being the cause of making the soul come to Thee? Should I receive Thee sacramentally without this love, Thou wouldst pass by and wouldst not dwell in my soul What shall I do, O Word, in that day when I cannot sacramentally receive Thee? First, redouble the above knowledge, secondly, multiply prayer, thirdly, examine my conscience more fervently and carefully, and have contrition for my sins and imperfections , fourthly, more often raise my mind to Thee, fifthly, be more sober in speaking; sixthly, more circumspect in temptation ; seventhly, more God-fearing in all my actions and operations; eighthly, more affable in conversation, with a resolution to bear patiently everything contrary, ninthly, in fine, and in conclusion and fulfillment of all other things, be more prompt to obey my superiors, equals, and inferiors.   If Thou dost the will of those who obey, as Thou sayest that Thou dost ; then if I shall be obedient and pray to Thee to unite Thyself to me, Thou shalt do my will   I go to receive Thee, to honor Thee, to unite with Thee, for the repose of the souls in purgatory, and to make a commemoration of Thy Passion in that most Holy Sacrament. If I shall not be able during these days to make this commemoration, I will pass to that which, shortly after, Thou didst make in the garden . "*Non mea voluntas, sed tua*"—"Not my will, but Thine be done" (Luke xxii, 42)   I can also afford relief to the souls in purgatory by performing acts of charity, reciting psalms, and making an offering to Thee of Thy blood."   Here she made in silence a longer pause, after which she ended with these words : "Two more, and then it is done "   She meant to say that Jesus had to dip her twice more in His side, and then the *seven* dips were completed which the Divine Spouse had promised to give to this beloved soul, in order to purify her with His Blood and bring her to the highest perfection that can be attained during this earthly life.

As a reverent desire to frequent the Eucharistic Banquet is a token of conscientious purity, so the nausea and indifference which most people feel for It indicate an impure and guilty heart   He who approaches it simply because he is forced by the precept of the Church, gives evidence of knowing very little of the excellence of this gift; and he who even refuses to comply with this duty, shows a reprobate soul, that to the excess of love opposes the excess of ingratitude   This perfidy was to the Heart of Christ a sword which pierced it and caused it the most acute pain ; of it He always complained . "*Filios nutrivi et exaltavi · ipsi autem spreverunt me*"—"I have brought up children and exalted them ; but they have despised me" (Isai 1, 2).   He wished with the most ardent desire to institute this Fountain of our salvation, in which He gives us to drink His Blood, the Well-spring of all our good   He hunts up men; to them He is longing to give Himself, to them He says from the sacred ciboriums "Come to Me, O all ye who are oppressed by the labors of humanity, and I will give you comfort and strength."   The Eternal Father from above those tabernacles cries out, too   "*Hic est Filius meus delectus. . . . Ipsum audite*"—"This is My beloved Son, hear Him " (Luke ix, 35)   He offers to us His beloved Son, from whom we may learn wisdom, fortitude, and all the virtues we need   In a word, the Communion of the Body and Blood of Christ with His Divinity is the greatest effusion He can make of His goodness, because it is Himself, than Whom no greater good exists.   And thus, on our part, we manifest the most monstrous ingratitude towards this Divine Benefactor, and cause to ourselves the greatest misfortune.   Not a few even go so

She sees the glory that the Jesuit, St. Aloysius Gonzaga, enjoys
in heaven (page 116).

far as to criticise the Church, because she compels her children to receive Holy Communion annually. Besides the total want of correspondence of love towards God, these also manifest that their spirit makes a bad use of the faculty which distinguishes man from other animals. The Church as a society is within her strict right in regard to the test by which she wants to recognize her members; and the act of humility which she orders to precede it is but the foundation of the spirit of the true believer. If she adds the command to a law of love, this results but in the condemnation of the faithful who are reluctant to submit to the sweet yoke of Christ; hence it well accords with reason that for this refusal they are adjudged as members cut off from the Holy Catholic communion.

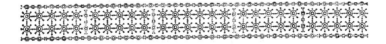

CHAPTER XXVIII.

HER ZEAL FOR THE GLORY OF GOD AND THE SALVATION OF SOULS, AND
HOW FOR EACH OBJECT SHE WISHED TO GIVE HER LIFE.

S is the natural prerogative of perfect love towards God,
Magdalen found her delight not only in contemplating Him
glorified in heaven and praised by creatures, but ardently
wished to diffuse among her neighbors the divine flame
which was burning in her own heart. Every action, affection, and thought of hers had no other object than God's
glory; her fervent sighs flew like darts to this aim. With
a cheerful spirit she undertook every labor for the glory of
God; and for this she asserted that, if it had been possible, she would have
given her life a thousand times a day. Oh! how many times was she
heard to exclaim, during her ecstasies, with glowing fervor: "Blessed
and happy would I be were I to be found worthy of giving my life and
blood for Thy glory, O my God!" At the ringing of the bell calling
the nuns to the choir for the divine praises, she sometimes said to those
who happened to be with her: "Lo! the voice of God calls us; let us
not be deaf to it; let us not fail to do what it demands of us; let us go
and praise God."

The great fervor with which she recited the ecclesiastical prayers,
she wished to see also in all creatures, and above all in her companions of the monastery; to whom, if an opportunity presented itself,
she addressed words of complacency, of encouragement, or reproach,
according to the needs of each one of them, to the end that all would
be as zealous as possible for the honor and glory of God. Though her
voice was weak, yet she made every effort to keep up in the choir the
canonical recitation, when there was need of it; and when unable to do
it, being overcome by the hurry of those who had stronger voices,
she grieved so much thereat that she was compelled sometimes to ask
leave to come out of the choir. At one time, having left her place, she
went before the superioress during the recitation of the office, and, with
humility equal to her zeal, said to her: "Mother, the psalmody is carried
on so hurriedly that one would think that there is something else to be
done which is of greater importance than this." Another day, seeing
that a chorister hurried the office too much, she spoke to her as follows:
"Sister, if thou hast anything to do which is more important than this,
come out of the choir, and go and do it." She gave similar advice to

many, and she used to often say: "I dare not dispatch the divine praises like the other business of the monastery" Thus with her zeal she brought the nuns to recite the divine office very devoutly, and she noticed both in herself and the others even the smallest fault, not only in the recitation but also in the least important ceremonies Consequently, she once accused herself of having paid more attention to seeing that these things were done right, than of having kept her mind fixed in God. This fervent solicitude was born in her because of the high estimation in which she held the Divine Office, the exercise of which she considered the principal one in Religion, after the reception of the sacraments, and, therefore, she was wont to call it "the exercise of the angels" Hence, she used to say that one should assist in it with angelic modesty and reverence; and this she tried to impress chiefly on her novices. As they were going to the choir, she sometimes told them · "Consider that you go to praise God with the angels; that you are in the presence of the Most Holy Trinity, and that you are not worthy of being there; and that at every word you ought, through reverence, to stoop to the ground."

There are other instructions she used to give them with regard to this exercise of the choir, which we will relate when speaking about the zeal for the souls entrusted to her care. She was unable to conceive how the desire and zeal for God's glory should not have been such in all creatures as she felt it in herself; she really could not see otherwise. Hence, she was sometimes heard to say · "It seems strange to me, and I avow it is a thing I cannot understand, why there is such a scarcity of souls that hold the honor of God in high esteem" And she added: "Ah! pray, sisters, let us compel Jesus, with our prayers, always to grant a pastor to this place, who may be zealous of God's honor."

Having in view also the divine glory, this holy soul had the most burning desire for the conversion of heathens and the extirpation of heresies; so that she cherished a special affection for those Regular Orders that tend directly to the greater glory of God and the increase of His kingdom by means of the propagation of faith and the conversion of souls. The same affection she entertained towards those religious persons who labor towards that end Whenever she would hear something read in the refectory in which the gain of some souls to the Christian faith was related, she manifested even exteriorly the joy and happiness of her spirit, and (as she was wont to say) she felt herself burning with a feeling of peculiar benevolence and esteem towards the happy workers of such conversions, and was longing to do the like, herself, for the glory of God The life of St. Francis Xavier, the letters of missionaries from Japan relating the conversion of the people of that kingdom, seemed to melt her with a desire to be there, too, to cooperate in the salvation of those souls and to suffer martyrdom for them She envied, in a certain way, the birds which have a free and easy access to all the regions of the world She wished for wings in order to fly all over the earth to convert souls for the greater glory of God She used to exclaim with an ardent sentiment: "Oh! that it were given me to go among the heathens and even to the Indies, and instruct those little lad an infants in our faith, so that Jesus might have

those souls, and they might have Jesus!" Another day, being in
ecstasy, and speaking in general about the heathens, she thus expressed
herself: "If I could, I would take them all and bring them into the
bosom of Holy Church, there to be by her breath purified of all their
infidelity and regenerated,—as a mother regenerates her little ones,—and
then placed at her sweet breast to feed them with the milk of the most
holy sacraments. And oh! how well would she feed and nurse them at
her breast! Oh! how gladly would I do it if I could!" Thus penetrated by this thought, when asleep she used to dream and speak of the
conversion of the heathens. Being so fixed in this thought, she imagined sometimes that she was in those places laying down her life for
Christ's faith. One day, whilst having her hair cut off according to the
custom of the nuns, she was overtaken by such apprehension that,
thinking she had her head actually under the axe of the executioner,
ready to suffer martyrdom, being alienated from her senses, she began
to say: "Does he not come? Why does he delay so long? . . .
Behold, my head is perfectly ready." And in this wise she was nourishing in the meantime her pious imagination and affection.

In order to realize to some extent her most intense desire for the
conversion of the heathens, very often she would offer to God for them
the blood of Jesus, and apply towards their conversion the works of
Religion, the Communions, and many of the penances which she practiced. She also tried effectually to inspire the same sentiments she felt
in all those who conversed with her, especially those of the monastery
who were committed to her direction. Hence calling the novices often
together to work or various exercises of the community, being intent in
a particular manner upon the conversion of the Indians, she used to say to
them · "Let us offer to God for the heathens whatever we shall do
to-day;" or "Let us ask of God as many of those souls as we shall take
steps through the monastery;" or "Let us ask for as many of them as
we shall say words in the Divine Office " When they were sewing, she
was wont to say. "Let us ask for as many as we will make stitches
with a needle." When washing the linen, she exhorted them to ask for
as many of them as the number of times they dipped their hands into
the water; in a word, she used to take advantage of every exercise to
make such petitions to God

She also grieved greatly because the spirit of innovation was creep-
ing so much among Christians as to plunge many of them into heretical
errors. She was wont to weep because even men of high learning,
beguiled and seduced by strange passions, renounced the purity of the
faith of their fathers, sometimes for the simple reason that the ministers
of the sanctuary were not worthy of their vocation So insane a pretext,
so often thrust forth, is a very evident proof of the association of vicious
morals with willful ignorance in matters of religion. Impiety marks
the soul of him who, being raised in the way of the Lord, as shown us
by revelation—the deposit of which is only in the Church instituted by
Christ—turns elsewhere, either to listen to the foolish derisions of an
apostate or to those of his own intellect corrupted by the passions
Magdalen considering the perverse heresies of such people, and the
havoc they make of souls, used to call them cursed, according to the

language of the prophet—incarnate devils, poisoned tongues, trying, as far as they could by their words and deeds, to rend and tear the garment of Christ, which is the Holy Church. "Our souls ought to be," she used to say, " like so many turtledoves, always grieving and weeping over their great blindness "

No less pain did she feel in seeing Catholics so ill corresponding to the principles of faith which they boast of professing. Very often, and with very great fervor, she used to pray to God that she might revive the faith in the followers of Catholicity, and, with faith, all the virtues it begets In an ecstasy, with feelings of the most bitter anguish, she thus expressed herself: "And of what avail is faith to one who profits not by it? Sow it, sow it, O Word, living and ardent in the heart of Thy faithful ones, after warming and kindling it in the furnace of Thy Heart and Thy infinite charity, so that the faith of Thy faithful ones may correspond to their works, and their works may correspond to their faith Alas! unhappy me! how many shipwrecks in the faith! But why? Because charity was already extinguished. Thy faith makes the journey of the sun; here it was born, there it sets. And what is the sign given of this setting of the sun? The darkness of the sins which are seen committed everywhere." Being stimulated more and more by these sentiments, she used to add: "Oh! that some one would take my life and make me shed all my blood, so that this faith, lit up in Thy Blood and revived in Thy charity, would be propagated *among all those who profess Thy faith!*"

With similar love and zeal, she daily recommended to God the Holy Church and the Sovereign Pontiff, and saw to it that her disciples did likewise. On asking one of the sisters one evening, whether during the day she had prayed for the Church and for the Pope, and the sister answering No, Magdalen, greatly struck with such lack of zeal, told her: " What sort of a bride art thou who dost not recommend the Church to God every day?" Showing by these words that it was a special obligation of nuns to recommend daily the Church to God in their prayers, so that His representative may obtain from her children love, confidence, and union. The desire for the glory of God became, therefore, in the heart of Magdalen one with that for the salvation of souls, in which God seemed to have wholly immersed her; hence, while ecstatic, she spoke one day as follows : "*Collocavit me Verbum in desiderio quod Ipse habuit in humanitate sua*"—"The Word placed in me the wish He had in His humanity." And she felt within herself such a zeal that nothing was wanting, in the limited capacity of a creature, to imitate that which our Divine Redeemer had for the salvation of men.

This zeal was to the heart of Magdalen both a delight and a martyrdom at the same time , delight, because in her trials, temptations, and aridities she found consolation in her being able to offer to God some tribute of expiation and intercession for the salvation of souls. One day especially, being oppressed by the weightiest anguish, it seeming to her as if she were almost forsaken by her Spouse Jesus, at first she thus addressed Him. "O Word, my Spouse, yet Thou art in me and I in Thee! *O bone Jesu*, why dost Thou not help me?" Repeating many times "*O bone Jesu*," but without any relief to her painful situation, she had recourse afterwards to this desire for the salvation of souls, saying: "*Sursum corda: habemus ad desiderium salutis animarum omnium credentium*"—"Lift up your hearts: let us burn with the desire for the salvation of the souls of all believers." And every temptation vanished immediately, her spirit being immersed in light, peace, and joy. On the other hand, this zeal was a martyrdom to her, because, as it never left her heart, it consumed her day and night. In an ecstasy, speaking with God of this desire, she used the expressions of the prophet David alluding to the Divine Redeemer: "*Desiderium animarum tuarum comedit me*"— "Lord, the desire of the salvation of Thy souls has consumed me." And shortly afterward she added · "*Conserva me, Domine, quoniam in desiderio animarum consumpta est anima mea*"—"Keep me, O Lord; as my soul is consumed by the desire for souls." The sisters who conversed more intimately with her testified that *this desire* was so intense and continuous in her, that scarcely an hour passed without her manifesting it by some word or action. Far from its leaving her memory by any exercise whatsoever, it rather happened (and this not seldom) that, whilst in company with the other sisters, she would leave suddenly and betake herself to the choir or elsewhere, to prostrate herself before God and implore the conversion of sinners

As to the offenses offered to God by so many ungrateful Christians, they were the principal cause of her martyrdom   To make reparation for them in some measure, very often she would rise about midnight, and going before the Blessed Sacrament, there prostrated, she was wont to bewail, with the bitterest tears, the offenses offered by sinners to the Divine Goodness, and to humbly plead for their salvation   At the times when God is more offended by men, as in the carnival season, we have already mentioned how she redoubled her prayers and penances for the sinners, and exhorted her companions of the monastery to do the same.   One night preceding Shrove-Thursday, calling, as usual, all the nuns to matin, she asked some to join her, and she and they went through the dormitory scourging themselves, and inviting the others to praise God and to expiate with penances the faults of men. During Lent she also prayed to God with increased fervor, that He would grant light and strength to sinning souls, so that they might profit by so propitious a time.

Notwithstanding so great a zeal, Magdalen grieved very much at being unable to contribute to the conversion and salvation of others, according to her wish.   The great work she was already doing towards that end seemed nothing to her; hence, in an ecstasy, she complained that she could not find anyone to fill the desire of her soul by giving her some opportunity of coöperating with such in the good of souls, and these were her words: "*Considerabam ad dexteram et videbam, et non erat qui impleret desiderium animæ meæ*"—"I looked on my right hand, and beheld (Ps. cxli, 5), and there was not one that would fill the wish of my soul." One day, being found weeping excessively in a remote place, and being asked the reason of her tears, she answered. "I weep, because it seems to me that I am idle and do nothing in the service of God and for the salvation of souls " On being visited by a good servant of God, who labored greatly in Florence for the conversion of sinners, and on his telling her of his many troubles in bringing souls to God, she on the one hand rejoiced very much at this, but on the other hand broke into bitter weeping, considering it to be a great shame for her that a lay-person could be so zealous, whilst she, according to her way of judging herself, did not do anything in this matter. Often would she say to the sisters. "Let us not permit lay-people to excel us," and she would subjoin with great feeling. "We must give an account to God, not only of the evil deeds which we shall have committed, but also of the good we might have performed and which we omitted. God did not separate us from the world that we might be good only for ourselves, but that we might help our neighbors with our prayers and penances, and appease His wrath against sinners, this is our mission." In order the more to enkindle in herself and others the fervor of this desire, she used to often repeat· "Who knows but many souls, perhaps, have failed to be converted because we have not been fervent in praying to God for them?" At other times she used to say, according to the language of St. Catherine of Siena, that God complained at not having in this world anyone who opposed His wrath and appeased Him, and she added: "We, sisters, must render to God an account for many souls that are to-day burning in hell; for, if you and I had been fervent in prayer, and in offering the Blood of Jesus for them, and in warmly recommending them to God, He, perhaps, would have been appeased, and they would not be in the midst of those torments. Let us offer then, daily, to God the Blood of His Divine Son for sinners, and let us undergo any suffering to obtain their conversion." As the delight she felt in asking of God the salvation of souls comforted her in every tribulation of spirit, so it also helped to encourage and comfort her tepid and melancholy disciples; hence, on seeing one of them afflicted, she was wont to speak to her thus: "Thou hast not the love of God, why dost thou remain so? Thou wouldst do better to think about the salvation of some soul, and go and snatch it from the claws of the devil and gain it over to God." And she suggested to her some prayer to be recited for this object, assuring her that she would obtain everything from God, whenever she would supplicate Him with lively faith. "O novices!" she also used to say, "could you see the beauty of a soul in the grace of God, you would become so enamored of it that you could do nothing else but ask souls of God; and, on the contrary, were a soul in the state of sin to be shown you, you would hate sin more than the devil himself, and pray always for the conversion of sinners"

As an infallible proof of the great zeal of Mary Magdalen for the conversion and salvation of sinners, it must be added that she actually martyred her body, and asked God always for infirmities and trials, to expiate the sins and procure the salvation of sinners. Whatever punishment they deserved, even if it had been the pains of purgatory, she wished it to fall on herself. And going farther, she came even to offering herself spontaneously to God to stay in hell to suffer for the salvation of others, provided she would not there curse and blaspheme His Divine Majesty. Hence she once said in an ecstasy, that if a person were to be sent to hell (without offending God), for the sincere conversion of a soul, he should glory in it, as this all tends to the pure honor of God; so great was the esteem in which she held the salvation of souls. For this work she postponed not only all her temporal, but also her spiritual interests; hence when opportunity was offered her to help some soul in jeopardy, she did not hesitate to give up not only every comfort, and frequently the very necessaries of life, but also her prayers and other devout exercises; and for this end also she often protested to God that she would very willingly submit to being deprived of every spiritual sentiment and taste and left only with her will, by which she might love and serve God alone.

Besides the above-described five years of probation, which show how far God answered this desire of His faithful servant, we will see later how her desire was complied with—now by means of serious and long illness, now by means of trials and desolations of spirit. Nevertheless this thirst of hers was never quenched; nay, the more pains she endured for this end, the more she wished to endure, and, as one enamored of suffering, she was wont to say it was her sovereign consolation to suffer, and called this her *glorious pain*. In an ecstasy she also declared that, on the contrary, not to suffer was to her a great torment, meaning that it was a greater torment for her soul to be deprived of suffering for the conversion of sinners, than the enduring of any suffering, no matter how severe; as in this she felt so much delight, that it overcame any pain. At another time, being also alienated from her senses, on fervently recommending to God the salvation of souls, she was heard to say "For whom at all hours and at all moments I would willingly suffer martyrdom, and, if it were possible, even a thousand deaths . . . Oh! how happy and fortunate would I not be, were I granted this grace I so much wish for!" Another day, feeling the same desire of being martyred for the salvation of souls, she said "Martyrdom would not be martyrdom to me, but a paradise." On various occasions she also said that she wished she could die a thousand times, in order to be able (rising each time) to give life to a thousand souls One morning in particular, being inflamed with this holy fervor, she took the Crucifix in her hands, and with the greatest ardor of charity, thus said to Him: "Thou, O Lord, hast wanted to die on the cross and give all Thy blood for sinners, I, too, O my God, would like to give my blood and be deprived of life, that they might be converted." Once, in prayer, God showing Himself to her as angry with sinners, she, wishing to assuage His anger, addressed to the Divine Word these forcible words: "O Word, why dost Thou not make me taste hell and lose my life, so that, at least partially, the wrath of Thy Father may be appeased?" In a word, she never was without these ardent desires; so that like St Paul, in the excess of charity for the salvation of other souls, she postponed her own, and the glory of her soul to theirs; hence in a rapture, asking of God the conversion of some persons, she emphatically said. "Lord, unless Thou grantest me the grace of giving me these souls which I ask of Thee, I will say that I do not want to come and enjoy the glory Thou hast prepared for me." In another ecstasy she protested that if our Lord had asked her, as He did St. Thomas Aquinas, what reward she wished for her labors, nothing else would she have asked Him but the salvation of souls.

Though this zeal was a spontaneous and natural consequence of that divine flame which was burning in her heart, yet she omitted not to apply herself to those peculiar reflections which were most apt to promote it in her and make it of the greatest efficacy in others First, she considered the love God bore and bears to souls, how much the Divine Son suffered for them on earth, and that they are the inheritance given by the Eternal Father to Jesus Christ. Afterwards, she thought how beautiful a thing is a soul in the state of grace, how God likes it, and how great a good it is for the soul itself On the other hand, she would reflect how ugly and horrible is a soul in mortal sin, and what a bad state it is to be in. She plunged herself so deeply in these and the like thoughts, that she often merited in her ecstasies to see souls in one or the other of these states—the beauty of those in the state of grace, and the horrible appearance of those in the state of sin.

To proceed on this subject, putting it all in one chapter, it is necessary to show here at greater length by what anguish her soul was oppressed at the sight of the grave and multiplied offenses which men offer to God, without her having any hope of stopping them, as she wished with an immense desire. In an ecstasy in which God showed to her the hearts of sinners, she broke out in these words: "Who will be able to take away so much malice from the hearts of creatures? It is certain that nothing less than Thy charity and goodness, O my God, is required. . . . Ah! if I were made worthy of giving my life for the salvation of Thy creatures, and in order to remove so much malice, what a comfort it would be to me! A great thing it is to live and yet to die continually. Oh! what a great torment it is to see that I might be of some benefit to Thy creatures, by laying down my life, and yet I cannot do it!" And feeling herself consumed by this zeal, she used to say: "O charity, thou art a file, which, little by little, consumest the soul and the body, and constantly feedest the soul and the body."

She detested the malice of men with the following expressions. "Alas! these men, so full of malice, seem to me not men but demons. And what do the demons practice but malice? Their exercise is nothing but malice in order to deceive truth." Unable to bear the sight of so much iniquity in creatures, she used to say. "Whither shall I go? Whither shall I turn, O my God, so that I shall not see Thee offended? Everywhere, everywhere I see malice abounding." And, praying for the conversion of sinners, she used to repeat: "O Father, O Word, O Spirit, O Triune and One God, grant light to every man, so that by it everyone may know, and partially, at least, comprehend his malice." Feeling the ardent desire to cooperate with this conversion also, she continued · "Grant me the grace that I may satisfy for them by laying down my life for them, if necessary." As the zeal by which she was replenished proceeded from that pure principle which cannot league itself with the sinful desires of selfish man, and knows no other end but justice and truth, she did not like to be alone in this holy work, but wished all the servants of God to unite with her, hence she fervently prayed to the Lord that He might grant to them also the desire she felt for the salvation of souls, and, not finding it in others according to her zeal, with feelings of great affliction, she thus expressed herself: "Oh! why cannot I communicate it to them, so that all, and I with them, might give satisfaction to Thee, O my God, for all the offenses which are offered to Thee? Though Thy goodness alone can satisfy Thyself, yet it would be of some alleviation to me." Knowing the cause of so little zeal to be generally ignorance concerning the offense towards God, she was wont to exclaim. "O malice of creatures, how little and by how few art thou comprehended! Good God! it is not understood! Many say that Thou art offended, but they know not and do not comprehend what *offense* is" Well did she understand the gravity of offending God, and so much so, that in seeing the sins of the world, as they were often shown her by His Divine Majesty, she suffered excessive and extreme pains. Thus during that rapture in which Jesus espoused her, being terribly assailed by great tortures, she repeated from time to time: "*Circumdederunt me dolores mortis; dolores inferni circumdederunt me. Comedit me dolor inferni, præ multitudinem iniquitatum nostrarum*"—"The sorrows of death surrounded me" (Ps xvii, 5). "The sorrows of hell encompassed me" (*Ibid* 6). "The sorrow of hell has eaten me up, on account of the multitude of our iniquities." And on account of the oppression she felt, she breathed heavily, and, with sighs mingled with sad tears, threw herself on the floor, shuddering, whilst a convulsive tremor shook her limbs and the paleness of death appeared on her countenance "O Lord, I can stand it no longer," she said with a faint voice, "and if sinners do not want to remove from themselves so many sins, remove from me, I beg Thee, the sight of such iniquities, as I can bear it no longer." And she remained one hour and a half in this most intense affliction, uttering many other words in detestation of the monstrous ingratitude of man. In another ecstasy, she went so far as to say: "Oh! if there once would be an end, O my God, to the offenses which are offered to Thee! Oh! if for once, the cursed demons had no occasion to trouble me with the sight of the sins of men? But what? It would be too much I would have a foretaste of paradise. Thou wilt always, O my God, that the gall of temptation may be ever mixed with the sweet honey of Thy grace."

It must also be noted that this great and excessive affliction at the sight of the sins committed, which she deemed the greatest of all the many sorrows she endured during her life, she had also to bear very often, since, during those five years of her probation, the devils used it as their chief instrument with which to torture her soul, and after that period of time, God permitted her often to see such sights, so that by the anguish they caused her she might, to some extent, satisfy for the sins of others, and be more and more inflamed and induced to pray for divine mercy, and to do special penance for sinners themselves. Moreover, to grieve for the offenses offered to His Divine Majesty was her daily exercise, as she protested every morning that she wanted to do it with the greatest interest In consequence of this zeal she regretted also seeing so little of it in her neighbors, and especially the superiors, of whom she was wont to say that they ought to be thirsty and anxious for the love of God and the salvation of souls, even as the deer pants after water: and not permit them to perish, through their lack of interest, and r," into the infernal pit, by not wishing, through human respect, to displease them by zealous correction. "Oh! how hateful before God," she ecstaticly exclaimed, "such dissimulation is! though He wishes that in our hearts we feel compassion for the faults of others, nevertheless He likes and wishes also that those who are bound by their office be zealous and severe in chastising the faults, that the hearts may be purified from the cockle and remain pure wheat, worthy of being stored in the barn of God in life everlasting" And she added "If severe justice were thus practiced with sinners, oh! how much greater assistance would be rendered to the Church of God than is now done!"

Another time also, in a rapture, God having manifested to her the coolness of many superiors in correcting and punishing delinquents, she exclaimed · "Ah! how many do I see, who under the cloak of mercy let many of their own faults go unpunished, together with those of their subjects and inferiors! and for this they expose themselves to the great danger of going to hell." Turning to God, she thus continued: "What greater cruelty can there be than to have mercy for offenses which are offered to Thee, without resorting to means which would show the grievousness of these very offenses, and obtain repentance and amendment in the sinners?"

In another ecstasy, speaking in the person of the Eternal Father, she strongly complained of the human respect some priests have in reprehending and correcting, and being desirous of showing that this was the principal cause of so much malice being found in men, she made use of the following expressions: "Even my *christs* do not attend to their work, and do not open their eyes to see what is their duty to correct and amend, permitting poor souls to fall into faults, sins, and blindness, so that they sink into the abyss of all miseries and unhappiness." In order to inflame herself and move others to this zeal for fraternal correction, she used to reason as follows "If I love a sister, I am bound, though I might be engaged in the praises of God, to leave them and go to render assistance to her in her needs; and if bound to do this in exterior things, much more am I bound to enlighten her and warn her about her fault, which is an interior need of the soul, more important by far than the exterior one And if in order to help the body I would stay up one night, or two, or as many as required, much more, if I felt love for my neighbor, I should not regard it as a labor to pass one or two nights in weeping for a fault, though a very small one, of my sister," (which in fact she did).

God, who in His immense goodness, delighted in seeing in the heart of this holy maid the zeal infused by Him so well cultivated, condescended many a time to make known to her by supernatural means how pleasing it was to Him to be appeased towards sinners by the offering on their behalf of the Precious Blood of His Divine Son; and how, on the contrary, it was displeasing to Him that so few engaged in such an office. We shall see in its proper place, viz, in the Works, the description and the effect of this In the meantime let these two most important truths, from which originate so many misfortunes fatal to human society, be a lesson to us. One is the pertinacity and arrogance of him who maliciously sins, and, being plunged into his wicked habits, places these above all things sacred, convenient, civil. The second is the negligence, the indolence, and the weakness of him whom God or men has placed over others, and who thinks but of feeding caprice and ambition in himself. The condition and. the consequences of both were justly bewailed by our Saint. The wicked, who, having freely given themselves away to all the passions, plunge with insolent audacity into a criminal career, harm themselves more than others; for, being condemned by public opinion, their triumph over the just man cannot be but the consequence of brutal force, or of an effervescent seduction, which, if able to contaminate the heart, cannot cloud the intellect. But those especially, who, being seated upon a prominent seat and having the scales of equity entrusted to them, neglect the exercise of the administration committed to them, by not giving to every one justly what belongs to him,—encourage the wicked to usurp and cheat, urge the sinner to plunge himself more into sin, paralyze the just and the innocent man into a painful inaction. In the silence and ill-support of the truth on the part of those who have the official trust of it, others see, at least, a connivance with the darkness, the error, the crime , from this follow the total ruin of social order and the irreparable loss of so many souls, caused by him who did not know how or would not guide others on the road of justice and truth, though he was bound to do it. Jesus Christ, the true and only ruler and guide of the human family, furnished us with the description of such people in the person of the mercenary shepherd. "He," says Christ, "who cares but for his interest and profit, and lives in the fold but to butcher the sheep and feast on their flesh-meat, when he sees the wolf coming towards the flock saves himself, abandons the sheep, and runs away; then the wolf, being left free, snatches or scatters the flock."

The law sanctioned by nature and revelation is above all men. He who administers it is subject to it, the same as he who is but its servant. The force of duty is equal in both ; or, rather, the former is under greater obligation, as being bound to account for himself and for others. Hence he who administers will only be a good shepherd when, having entered into the fold, according to the evangelical phrase, by the door—that is, legitimately—will keep his sheep, viz., the people, subject to him, so as to correct and punish with the most efficacious energy those who transgress, and protect and reward those who are deserving of it, and, as the last proof, will lay down his life for his sheep when the enemy thrusts himself into the flock to scatter it Justice free from the least exceptions is the only foundation of good social order Let superiors be animated and inflamed with the zeal of this virtue; let them practice it without regard to all persons and firmly, both in rewarding and punishing their subjects, and no reasonable man will regret it. Let them give it all their thought and study, even their life, if needs be. By so doing their supreme mission will be fulfilled, and there will be no cause to lament with Mary Magdalen De-Pazzi so many human miseries But, unfortunately, if

> A sovereign hence behooved, whose piercing view
> Might mark at least the fortress [1]

---

[1] The best commentators of Dante by ???? understand ????, as the virtue which is most needed in a prince for the public wea. Justice regts and establishes peace

She foretells the elevation of Cardinal Alessandro de' Medici to
the Sovereign Pontificate (page 121).

188

yet it is very difficult to find a faithful performer of his duty. If determined to find out some trace of constant equity, we will find it only in those States (though somewhat languishing) and in those religious Congregations in which justice is impartially administered by the superiors, who provide in every case, as faithful guardians and unchangeable representatives of the laws. But, taking mankind as a whole, we are forced to exclaim also with the divine poet :

> . . . Laws indeed there are :
> But who is he who observes them? None ; not he,
> Who goes before, the shepherd of the flock,
> Who chews the cud but doth not cleave the hoof.
> Therefore the multitude, who see their guide
> Strike at the very good they covet most,
> Feed there and look no further. Thus the cause
> Is not corrupted nature in yourselves,
> But ill-conducting, that hath turned the world
> To evil.—*Dante's* (Carey Trans.) *Purgat.*, XVI.

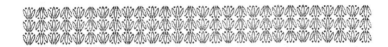

CHAPTER XXIX.

HER SEVERE PENANCES AND THE EFFICACIOUS PRACTICE OF HER
ZEAL IN BEHALF OF SOULS, ESPECIALLY OF THOSE COM-
MITTED TO HER CARE IN HER MONASTERY.

Y reason of the sublime variety preordained by the Divine
Wisdom in the heavenly Jerusalem, not all the Saints have
received the palm of martyrdom; but they all ardently
wished for it and tried to obtain it *in themselves* by the
means which they had at hand. Martyrdom is, truly, that
act of religious heroism which shows the greatest perfection
of a man in his religious faith. But this is none the less
proved by continuous and loyal acts tending to this same
end. Thus in the Christian Religion the constant and unchangeable life
of mortification and penance which holy and devout souls are wont to
lead, is equivalent to a true martyrdom and eminently evinces the perfection of the follower of Christ.

Of the torments with which Magdalen treated her body, thus subduing its senses, we have already said not a little; so that it remains
only just to touch here upon it, making but a short addition to the facts
above related. We repeat then, first, that her throwing herself naked
among thorns was a kind of martyrdom, together with the other severe
penances which she practiced in order to conquer the impure temptations
by which she was molested. Though from the twenty-first year of her
life, by a singular privilege of our Blessed Lady, she was never subject to
feelings or imaginations of impurity; and though the pure candor of her
innocence was never sullied by a voluntary sin, yet, as long as she lived,
she continued with a constant, nay, a progressive austerity in the ingenious manner of chastising her body. All this may also be said to have
been directed to expiate the sins of others, as she herself was not guilty
of anything which might deserve such severe treatment. Which is
also well confirmed by her very ardent zeal for the salvation of souls.

Recalling then to memory her penances of the year 1587, during
which she was covered by the Blessed Virgin with the white veil which
delivered her from the impure stimulus of the flesh, she having, from
the year 1585, subsisted simply on bread and water, except on Sundays,
when she used Lenten food:—she continued the same method till the
year 1590. This year, her probation being over, by divine will she
mitigated such austerity of fasting, taking the community meals on

Sundays, and drinking a little wine on Thursdays, but on the remaining days of the week she made use of but bread and water Thus continuing until 1592, her superiors noticed that her health had deteriorated very much; hence, for fear of losing her, they suggested to her that she should pray to God to permit her to partake of all the community meals Which being done by her, the Divine Goodness condescended to satisfy the wishes of those who had the health of our Saint so much at heart, and Mary Magdalen, submitting to the divine inspiration, adapted herself completely to the food of the monastery; so that, having been remarkable till then for the peculiarity of her life, she became exemplary in conforming herself to the common meals with the rest.   Always very sparing and modest in taking what was offered to her, she was wont to refuse the most delicate viands, taking instead the most coarse and gross ones, making believe, with ingenious virtue, that she relished more the latter than the former.   This she practiced till death.

From the same year, 1587, till 1590 she went barefooted. On account of the delicacy of her flesh and of her working in the kitchen (in doing this work in winter time she exposed herself in the orchard to snow and ice) she suffered so intensely that her feet were wounded and sore and bled copiously.   Her flesh became livid, and at times she trembled so that she was unable to articulate a word; but, never satiated with suffering, one day she remained thus barefooted for many hours on the snow praying.   From the year 1590 till her last illness, by obedience she put on her shoes and slippers, but never the stockings; and for three years previous to 1590 and afterwards until said sickness, she never wore more than one tunic and it became worn out and thin; so that every winter she caught very severe colds.

From the year 1581 till her last sickness she slept in her habit upon a straw-bed, and very often on the bare floor.   Her rest was very short ; and when she protracted it to five hours, she deemed it excessive.   Not seldom she passed the night without taking any rest at all, but spent it in prayers or exercises of pious charity towards her sisters and for the benefit of the monastery.   And if during these exercises she felt herself sometimes constrained to take some rest, she would rest for not more than half an hour, leaning her head against something.

Besides the woolen tunic which, according to the rule of the monastery, she wore during all her lifetime, she sometimes also wore on her bare skin an iron belt, sometimes the hair-cloth, and sometimes the belt of nails she herself had made.   She would very often discipline herself with various instruments, but mostly with an iron chain weighing about three pounds ; and she would do that for whole hours; so that being often heard by some sister, who feared lest she should shatter herself by this hard and prolonged rigor, she would call in the superioress or the mistress of novices, that they might come and stop her. Of this the mother Sister Evangelista del Giocondo left a special testimony, declaring that she found her many a time in the act of most cruelly scourging herself, her flesh livid and bleeding, and even the floor and the walls of the room besmeared with blood.   To these cruel torments she added others which her indefatigable and insatiable zeal suggested and prompted her to invent. It was principally remarked that on lighting a candle, she used to let some of the melted wax drop on her hands and feet, which would be skinned thereby, and she would sometimes be made lame for some days. She would also press her flesh with iron pincers until the blood would flow. In the fervor of prayer, like another St. Jerome, she was wont to strike her breast with a stone. She would gather up a quantity of nettle in the orchard, and, bringing it into her cell, she would rub it over her body. During the time that she went around with shoes or slippers, that the feet might not be without their martyrdom, she used to break some dry cypress berries, and, placing them in her shoes, she would walk about as usual, with great pain. In a word, she regarded her body as a vile beast of burden, as the ground which we tramp upon. She loaded it with all sorts of toils, and reduced it almost to the exhaustion of its last degree of strength.

Now, if so delicate and young a maid, and so innocent withal, was wont to treat herself so cruelly, it must be repeated that she did it not only to preserve, increase, and purify her love for her God, but also to be of benefit to her neighbors, by trying to soothe the wrath of God, satisfy His Divine Justice, obtain the conversion of sinners, the deliverance of the souls in purgatory, and the like graces. The love of God was certainly the greatest mover and the primary object of all her actions, but as it is impossible to love God without loving our neighbor also, because God's love and our neighbor's naturally join and become one, therefore this beautiful soul, as she had the love of God in a supreme degree, so she had also and practiced that of her neighbor. Being prevented from going around the world to convert souls to God, and unable to satisfy in any other way the ardent desire she felt of doing so, except by means of private penances; besides the severe exercise of these, as we have related so far, she would try to put in practice all her zeal for the salvation and perfection of all her companions in the monastery. To all, as needs be, she tried to become useful,—now with prayer, now with counsel, now with advice and lessons, now with reproaches, but always and especially with her example. She used to notice the spiritual needs of each sister so accurately that the most zealous and learned spiritual director could not have known more in that matter; and so efficaciously did she try to provide for the needs she had noticed, that there was not an ignorant sister, who, desiring to receive her help, would not be enlightened; none afflicted, who would not be consoled, none discouraged, who by her help would not be strengthened; none imperfect, that she would not correct and oblige to amend; and none desirous of doing good, that she would not encourage   So that of all those with whom she lived in religion, there was not one who did not receive from her some particular assistance, besides the general help she gave to the monastery and the community She spared no labor or inconvenience, and she even forgot her food, her rest and all other bodily necessities, to assist in some way the spiritual needs of some of her companions   To be of some benefit to souls, she thought it proper to omit even her prayers and forego every spiritual delight; and she held such charitable work in greater esteem than all the ecstasy of spirit which she might have had. She gave this reason for it: "In the ecstasy God helps me, but in helping my neighbor I help God." To have a better chance to instruct and enlighten, she pre-ferred to converse with simple persons, as the minor novices and the lay-sisters. And whenever her parents would send either male or female servants, or peasant maids to visit her, or when for any other business of the monastery she was offered an opportunity to speak to this class of persons, or to children, she would always give them some salutary souvenir and lesson

The mothers of the monastery, having from the beginning discov-ered the useful and extraordinary disposition with which the spirit of Magdalen De-Pazzi was endowed, resolved to give her the opportunity of employing it, and the community the advantage which undoubtedly would be derived therefrom Hence, no sooner was the time ended, during which, after the novitiate, one must remain under another mis-tress, in the juniorate, she was made pedagogue, that is, companion of the mistress of novices, at the youthful age of twenty-three years. Prompt to obey, she accepted this office, but in her humility she feared much, deeming herself unable to keep watch over the new little plants of the Religion, especially because she could not devote to it all the diligence she wished, in consequence of her still suffering the five-years' trial, during which she was so distracted and troubled Notwithstanding this she completely fulfilled the task entrusted to her, and with great profit to the novices ; so that on account of her success during the three years she exercised this office, when she reached the age of thirty-three she was elected mistress of those who come out of the novitiate, and overseer of those who entered the monastery intending to become nuns.

Having passed, with great satisfaction to all, three years in these two offices, she was immediately chosen mistress of novices, which office requires the greatest delicacy of conscience and the most exact perspi-cuity of spirit, and imposes the gravest and most momentous responsi-bility before God and the Religion. The love and interest that Magda-len cherished for these souls committed to her, the zeal for their salvation and perfection, the wonderful ways by which she instructed and exercised them in the way of God, are not easy to tell, as it is very difficult to make those understand them who have not been eye-witnesses. To the very nuns who, having lived with her, gave testimony of what they saw, after relating many things it seemed as if they had said nothing, in com-parison to what they had seen. They strongly asserted that the love which Magdalen showed, and in fact felt, for the persons entrusted to her care, surpassed that of any mother. For, it being free from those vicious excesses to which nature is wont to carry mothers in moments of carnal or maternal fervor, the charitable love of Magdalen was always even and smooth in its intensity, always pure and upright in its aim She herself would protest to the young ladies in her keeping, that she loved them with more than maternal tenderness. Hence, she used to watch over each of them with most efficient solicitude ; and not only had she at heart their spiritual needs, but their corporal ones as well, as if she were the most tender of mothers On discovering some of their needs, either she immediately provided for them herself, or saw that the superioress did so If anyone was too timid to ask anything, or to manifest her troubles or needs, the Saint gave her courage and attended to her with a more watchful eye, and made her companions watch her also, that nothing would be wanting for her comfort She mended and cleaned their habit⸱ ⸱⸱⸱. was always ready to lend any other charitable service needed at th   e. She lightened their labors, and saw particularly to it that they   e equally glad and cheerful both in prosperous and in contrary things. If one of them fell sick, it is hard to tell with how much charity and kindness she stood around her to wait on her, to nurse her, and render her all possible assistance She saw no affliction of spirit or body in those daughters that she did not feel in herself as her own, and she wished to free them altogether from it, in order to take on herself all the pains of others "Ah! if I could but free thee from these pains," said she, with an accent of extreme desire, "how willingly would I do it!" If sometimes, even in the middle of the night, whilst resting on her straw-bed, weakened by her labors, she heard any of them moaning or complaining, she arose at once and ran to the side of the patient, in order to afford her opportune assistance; and both to her and to all she was wont to say, in a beseeching way, that they should not at all spare her, and in whatever need it might be, they should call her freely, waking her up even at midnight. She would have very promptly gone to all; as she always did with a truly jovial disposition, free, at the same time, from all partiality. If, finding herself waiting in the night on some sick nun, she was asked by her to go and take rest, she would reply· "Sister, if thou needest me, I will stand here on my feet till to-morrow morning, and, I trust in God, it will not hurt me in the least."

Once, as a reason for the tenderest love she bore to the sisters and particularly her disciples (whom she loved more than their natural mothers), she alluded to the words uttered by St. Paul in one of his Epistles "Your mothers bring you forth into this world but once, but I bring you forth to God thousands upon thousands of times with pain, as I feel like yourselves whatever sorrows and afflictions I know you to feel" At other times she declared that she felt such a particular love because these souls were by Religion entrusted to her care, and she knew that in working for them she was sure to do the will of God Moreover, it seemed right to her that they should be treated with this, and, if it were possible, with a greater love, for the good of their own souls and of the Religion, in order that they might become attached to the Order ; hence, she was wont to say to the sisters: "These daughters come from the world, leaving father and mother and all the advantages of the world ; hence, it is necessary that they should find in the Religion someone who may induce them to willingly embrace the labors of the same" And to the novices. "Daughters, you have left one mother and have found many; you have left a few sisters and have found here a great number of them, who will love you better than your parents, as they will love you in charity and in God, which surpasses, by far, natural and carnal love." Thus she endeavored with all possible care to divest their spirit of earthly affections, raising it to the celestial ones which are professed and followed in the Religion by those who, being called in by God, lead a life faithful to the supreme light

With a view at the same time to the advantage of the monastery, and thinking, therefore, of the good or evil consequences which may result to the same from the good or evil qualities of the young, whenever a girl entered therein, the Saint minutely observed her steps, her movements, and all her external deportment, in order to find out whether her tendencies and interior qualifications fitted her for the Religion; and, to this end, she particularly studied the docility of her intellect and the flexibility of her will; and, in these, she shrewdly exercised the young postulant on every occasion. Neither did she, for desire of increasing their number, hide from them the rigors of the Rules; but there was no regulation of the monastery, nor rough and laborious work of the community, even of but probable occurrence, that she did not show to them with an unexceptionable sincerity, which leads us to the following remarks. Some think it to be the custom of the Religious, that rather than to manifest the hardships of their state,—in order to raise a desire for it in those who ask to be received, they entice them with the captivating ease of a life not only free from human troubles, but also firm in its tranquil existence, besides possessing the most valid and rich hopes for the life to come. The young person thus may give herself merrily up to a bond now considered of extreme lightness, and which, known afterwards and felt to be of enormous binding force and weight, will make the young person succumb as a victim of despair in the religious house, or return to the world a useless, restless, and sad being. If of this last alternative society has plenty of cause to complain, finding itself troubled by elements so heterogeneous, Religious must not be blamed for it as much as if they had failed to make known to their postulants the state which they were about to embrace. All of them hold it as a constant and essential custom to give to those who wish to receive their habit, the rules and constitutions of the Order, that they may read and know them all, and to explain the spirit and the aim of it, the customs, and everything else that may have been afterwards introduced into them. Ill corresponding to the vocation is the ordinary origin of the sad results in those who vowed themselves to God by a solemn promise. Hence, whilst we recommend to the rulers of religious communities the most severe circumspection in order to satisfy themselves of such vocations, we tell them to employ all their zeal in preventing anyone from falling away from the heavenly call. A longer trial and a wiser age is, of course, the wish of most people to test the religious vocation. This is practiced in some States of secular dominion, and in a manner yet more praiseworthy and useful in the Venerable Society of Jesus, which, being able to glory as one of the foremost Orders because of the number of its members, has also the satisfaction, on the other hand, of having to deplore far less than any other the falling away of those who have solemnly joined it. The sagacity with which the Jesuits study and test at length their alumni before they admit them to the vows, and their promptness in getting rid of them if a doubt supervenes about their vocation, is the reason why one of them very seldom lays down the habit after having made solemn vows.

Magdalen, who in all that was possible to her, modeled herself on the spirit and practices of St. Ignatius and his sons, during the time fixed by her Order for the probation of the young postulants, exhausted all industries, so that if not in the duration, at least in the chief maxim, she might do as is done by the Jesuits. Not only did she open her eyes well on the novices, but wished them also to open their own and wholly on the new state they were to embrace ; and on their giving sign of the least dissatisfaction, she was wont to say frankly to them · " If you do not like this mode of life, you may choose another place, as here we wish to go on in the manner which you see " On a doubt arising about someone's vocation, she was rather inclined to send her back to the world, than to make her embrace a state in the choice of which (these were her words) the highest degree of liberty and free will is required With greater reason, if she judged anyone positively unfit for the monastery, without regard for human respect she would acquaint the superiors so that there might be no occasion of scandal to the rest. On account of the zeal always alive and burning in her heart, whenever a well-disposed girl was to receive the habit of the Religion, or a novice to make her solemn profession, for many days previous she used to offer for this purpose many prayers, penances, and Communions, and she asked the rest to do the same The night preceding the sacred ceremony she took no rest, but passed it all in prayer that the new Bride of Jesus might obtain her light from the Divine Spirit to know the dignity of the state for which she had been chosen and for grace to effectually correspond to such a vocation. With all diligence she endeavored to make those who had received the habit or made their profession attached to the Religion and the customs of the monastery, studying to impress in their souls the benefit received from God, and exhorting them to be thankful therefor not only to His Divine Majesty, but to the nuns also. " Daughters," she was wont to say to the former, " be thankful principally to God, and then to all these mothers and sisters who have received you , as, through them, you have received the most precious gift that, after baptism, God can bestow on His chosen ones in this life The entering of the Religion means that you are bound by gratitude to love and serve all, deeming yourselves unworthy of their company ;" and thus she accustomed them to be also respectful and submissive to the mothers, which is so necessary in the monasteries

God, therefore, who had chosen Magdalen De-Pazzi not only to be holy in the fulfillment of her duties, but also to make others holy, endowed her with so rare a prudence in bringing souls to perfection, that it was a truly wonderful thing to behold Her fine discernment made her adapt herself so well to what was required by the temper of the characters and inclinations of the minds under her, that she did not seem to be a mistress of all the novices, but she appeared to assume many forms of mistress, in proportion to the number of subjects entrusted to her care She used to make, so to say, a minute anatomy of the mind, the passions, and the heart of every one, so that she attained such a perfect knowledge of their interior dispositions as each of them might know of her own Hence she adopted the most opportune and convenient manner of dealing with them—serious or affable, rigid or soft, reserved or open —as the occasion might require · always preserving, though, equal charity for all and keeping her own soul in the fullest calm of affections Of the very many things which could be repeated about this prerogative, we will relate here but a few, from which, though, it will be easy to infer of what ability our Saint was possessed to govern souls. One of the twenty rules God gave her was that she should have as many eyes as she had souls to govern, which she effected so that the more adult and perfect nuns, besides the novices, greatly wondered at it. By a supernatural light she was wont to see the souls of all, so that she could make no mistake in the conduct she observed towards each of them Hence she imposed more on those who were better able, and compassionated more those who comprehended less , she would show more rigor to those who had greater desire and anxiety to learn, and, on the contrary, she encouraged those who were remiss of spirit and timid to walk in the way of the Lord, showing them esteem and affection. Thus she would severely reprehend and punish one for a light fault, and another, for the same or a graver one, she corrected mildly and was patient with her; with some she dissimulated, as though she took no notice of anything ; with others she conferred charitably; and with others still, she avoided even talking, showing herself far different from what she was in reality. But such dissimilar dealings were directed by so great a divine light that none ever suspected her of partiality or entertained a jealous fear lest others were better loved. All declared that she used the mode of direction which was most profitable with each; at the same time that they saw her severe and grave with one, benign and piteous with another, looking at one with a rigid eye, and thus bringing a burning shame to her face and making her lower her head, and turning to another a favorable countenance, thus reassuring her and banishing all sadness from her heart. She restrained the excessive joy of some, so that it would not turn into dissipation , and she alleviated the sadness of others, so that it would not fall into barren desolation. She moderated the too fervent ones, and encouraged the tepid ones Thus she was to all a wise and prudent directress, and always in the act either of helping the spirit or doing acts of charity towards the body, now for one, now for another, now for all together. From everything she took occasion to promote sanctity—reprehending, humiliating kindly, mortifying, teaching. The penances, as a rule, she imposed moderately on those tender plants of the great Householder; and if any, stimulated by more fervent piety, spontaneously asked for extraordinary ones, she did not always grant the permission, thinking that discretion was greatly required in the exterior penances, especially for the beginners in the way of the Lord She did not reprehend anybody if her soul was not altogether in peace , and if anyone in resentment answered her with little respect, she limited herself to gazing at her with a look of compassionating interest, and afterwards, at the moment she considered the most opportune, she proceeded to administer the correction—so highly did she value rectitude in the direction of souls, though the tumultuous motions of irascibility never troubled her mind or her heart. She also awaited till the subjects were also tranquil before correcting them. She tolerated for several months one who, moved by the enemy of all good, was burning with passion against her, and, when she saw her better disposed, she made her profitably conscious of her error. She used to give them frequent advice as to how to dispose themselves to receive mortification with a quiet and submissive disposition, as she knew this to be of the greatest importance for their spiritual advancement. She inculcated in them very frequently that the fruit of prayer was to be in a special manner the acquiring of the virtue to suffer all that displeases self-love "When you," said she to them, "stop praying, you must be ready to receive any reprehension and mortification, let it be just or not; and you must be so firm and fixed in God that nothing can disturb the quiet of your soul" Hence she was wont to impose the penances and other humiliations as soon as prayer or other practices of piety were ended, both because at that time the soul being recollected in God is better disposed to virtue, and because, if any one was deemed to have prayed well, she should humble herself in sight of her faults, and uproot from her heart self-complaisance, which is poisonous to the soul when without the thorns of self-abasement Moreover, on account of the charity with which Magdalen adorned the rigors of the penances or reprehensions inflicted on her subjects, they were not saddened, but were rather drawn to love and revere her the more, and they used to say: "She is truly a mother to us." Such great light and flames did they get from her teachings, that some of them, as they declared, would have walked on thorns to hear her, as it seemed to them that they heard and saw a spirit of paradise Something divine was shining in her eyes, which consoled them even when they were reprimanded Charity and zeal joined to majesty in correcting filled the hearts with a holy fear not disjoined from consolation She herself seemed almost trembling, on account of her great humility, in the act of correcting, and she made others tremble by the sacred terror of sanctity transpiring from her countenance This wonderful coupling of humility and majesty succeeded admirably in breaking the hardness of insubordinate spirits, not rare among young persons. She herself performed the penances for her who would not submit to them, and this not sufficing, in her presence she knelt before another novice, begging her to suggest what could be done to help that soul; and in so doing she shed such copious and bitter tears as to melt even a heart of stone; yet her face appeared at the same time as majestically illumined as the sky when Iris appears between the light and the clouds Towards a young maid contumacious in her disobedience, arming herself with stronger zeal, she thought of using the discipline, striking her in a more humiliating than severe manner; and thus she obtained her loyal and sincere amendment. There was not anybody, in a word, who could resist her various and opportune manners of leading souls to perfection She imposed no penance but that which she herself first practiced; neither did she ever order anything without having first consulted Jesus about it in prayer Before reproving any faults in others, she looked at herself very diligently, to see if perchance she was likewise guilty of them, and whilst correcting, she was making within herself acts of profound humility, knowing herself to be (so she said) more imperfect and less virtuous than the one she corrected. Often, after having corrected some one she went to the superioress to humble and accuse herself of having done so, judging herself more imperfect. She always had in her heart and mind the

Rules that God had given her to guide herself and her neighbors to perfection.

Now it behooves us to describe with how much solicitude she instilled in the souls of those who were entrusted to her care the virtues which render the Religious perfect and the Religious Orders spiritually happy Charity, above all, she wished to take deep root in those tender plants of hers, that charity for which the holy founders instituted the so well-deserving Congregations whose members, satisfied with a short sleep, a frugal repast, modest clothing, narrow cells, were to consecrate their thoughts, affections, and cares to the benefit of their neighbors; or to gather, feed, and educate the abandoned orphans, or to teach all liberal and useful sciences to well-born youth, or to go through solitary lands to console the labors of the poor farmers, and to draw from the wilderness and unknown corners savage spirits to the love of humanity and Religion, or again, in the deep snow and ice on very high and inaccessible peaks, to retrace with wonderful arts the lost travelers, and restore their bodies and their souls; or else to redeem with gold, and, where gold does not suffice, with their own person, the liberty of the slaves; or, finally, to assist the asylums of misery, attend those infected with pestilence, and receive the sighs of the dying. That charity of which the Apostles, leaving in themselves so powerful and magnanimous an example, teach us that, without it, the regular congregations of persons would be gatherings of idleness, greediness, and hypocrisy. St. Paul asserts of himself (he being a man of the highest perfection) that if he were to speak with the tongues of angels, had the gift of prophecy, penetrated well into the depth of mysteries, had such faith in his breast that he could remove mountains, were to give all he had to the poor, and throw himself into the flames to burn and be consumed, and yet was without *it* (the virtue of charity), he would be but *as sounding brass or a tinkling cymbal* (1 Cor. xiii)

That charity, therefore, which is the mark of the follower of Christ, the bond of every perfection, Magdalen wished to see practiced in a singular manner by her disciples Every day, and several times during the day, she was wont to repeat to them with St John: "Daughters, love one another, for this is the command of Jesus " She wished them to love one another as if born of the same parents; and she did not wish to see any difference between them, therefore she said always that every one was to regard her companions as daughters of the Eternal Father, as brides of Jesus, as temples of the Holy Ghost, and as sisters of the angels; and that, when together, they were to deem themselves to be as if in a choir of angels, for the virgins are representing them; and she wished their love to be such that whenever they met through the house they were to exult with joy in their heart, as if meeting for the first time, and to salute one another with words tending to the love of God. In order to eradicate from their hearts every root of spiritual envy, or to prevent its taking root therein, she taught them always to wish more good to their neighbor than to themselves. "If you, daughters," (these were her words) " wish for yourselves a degree of grace, ask two degrees of it from God for your sisters;" and, giving the reason therefor, she added, "because you must deem them more worthy than yourselves, and better able to produce more fruit and give more glory to God than you would; and in this manner you will purify your souls from self-esteem and any self-interest, and dispose yourselves the better to receive the same graces " She trained them to confer mutual favors, exchanging their offices and labors; and exhorted them to communicate to one another their spiritual goods. She used to say that she did not like those persons who were good for themselves alone; nay, she affirmed that those who are good only for themselves are not good either for themselves or for others; on the contrary, she liked very much those persons who were spiritually communicative, and she gave the following reason for it " If you bring forth no fruit out of the graces God bestows upon you, by communicating them to others, they might do it "

One day the novices proposed to practice among themselves a particular devotion, which a girl already admitted as a probationer in the monastery wished to join, but they would not accept her. On hearing this, the Saint severely reprimanded the novices, saying that theirs was no devotion, but self-love, since it did not extend to the charity of their neighbor.

One was to bear the vexations and the faults of the other with great deference, and woe to her who murmured; the holy mistress did not tolerate, in regard to that, the least fault She well knew that speaking against a neighbor is speaking against the law, and detractors, therefore, are hated of God; and that there being but one Legislator and Judge of the living and the dead, those who presume to condemn others draw upon their heads the most terrible condemnation. She well knew how the poison of a slanderous tongue is more fatal than that of the murderous steel; for the slanderer by a single act wounds both religion and society, and tends to rob the individual of what he holds most sacred and precious. Hence if any of her subjects incurred even lightly this fault, she would not allow her in the evening to enter the oratory with the rest, unless she had previously atoned for it by some penance, which ordinarily consisted in the avowal of the fault before the other novices; or, if the murmuring was slight, the Saint was wont to impose on the guilty one the making of a cross with her tongue on the floor; and, if more grievous, she would make her lie supine on it whilst her companions would dexterously trample with their feet on her mouth, or else she would make every novice strike her mouth with a discipline. This operation, more humiliating than painful, on account of the discretion with which it was performed, produced wonderful effect. Neither did she allow one who had some ill feeling with another to go to rest herself, unless she had first been reconciled Nay, she had prescribed that twice a day all should mutually ask forgiveness of the bad example they had given to one another, and of the little love they had borne to one another, which was also a very valuable means to beget true love. Moreover, to make them better appreciate the wise restraint of speech, she used to say that had she known one who had never spoken ill of her neighbor during her life, she would have deemed her worthy of being canonized before death. Among the remedies she suggested to them, in order that they might avoid falling into this fault, was the following, viz, to speak little of their neighbor, even for good, "because" (and she often repeated it) "one commences in good but afterwards generally ends in evil." She taught that, whenever it was necessary to speak of our neighbor, nothing should ever be said in his absence that we would find difficult to repeat in his presence.

The other thing in which she wanted her subjects to exercise themselves was prayer, the importance, necessity, and fruit of which she daily expounded to them. Prayer, she said, is a short road to reach spiritual perfection, as in it Christ teaches the soul, and by it the soul detaches itself from created things and unites itself to God. "If you wish, daughters" (she thus expressed herself), "to acquire in a short time great perfection, take the Crucifix as your teacher, and let your ears be attentive to His words, as He continually speaks to your heart, especially after you have received the Most Holy Sacrament Give yourselves to prayer, as the intercourse with God in prayer makes a person care for nothing but God, let God suffice you, and care not for relatives or any earthly thing; as, I assure you, in Him you will find every true good and a perfect fulfillment of all your desires." Every morning she gave them the points of meditation for the day, and if anyone was ignorant of how to meditate, she would place her near herself, instructing her by the practice of her own meditation, made in a clear manner, and during which she was very often rapt in ecstasy and felt sublime sentiments of divine things, to the amazement and profit of her who stood near by Sometimes she called some sister to spend the night with her in prayer, and to all she frequently addressed questions as to how and with what profit they had meditated, and in many other ways she made this holy exercise easy to them On the approach of the solemnities which the Church celebrates during the year, eight or ten days in advance she began to make them prepare themselves by means of some devout practice of prayer or mortification; which she also performed, both to encourage and to instruct them by her example With the same object in view she zealously endeavored to accustom them to be prompt, reverent, and devout in the choir, impressing upon them that the Divine Office is one of the principal obligations of nuns, and that therein chiefly is the Divine Majesty acknowledged, honored, and adored. Sometimes before they went to the choir she called them and said to them: "Daughters, reflect that till now you have been engaged in human acts, dealing with creatures, now you have to perform angelic acts, dealing with God Himself;" or: "Consider that this exercise is so important that the blessed spirits themselves, whose purity is wonderful, scarcely dare with fear and trembling to perform it; with how much greater reverence must we then assist before the Divine Countenance, who are most unworthy creatures?" Moreover, she taught them that, before commencing the Divine Office, they should make acts of humility, deeming themselves unworthy to praise God with the angels; and that, in order that they might be acceptable, they should offer their praises to God in union with those that the blessed spirits offer to Him in the Heavenly Fatherland, "because," she said, "though it is impossible for our praises to attain to the purity of those which are presented by the blessed spirits to His Divine Majesty, we are by no means forbidden to wish to attain to so high a mode of worshiping God."

She also inspired these daughters with the same feeling of God's love that she had in reciting the *Gloria Patri*, thinking she was giving up her head to martyrdom for the Christian faith, and other like devotions. She was also very attentive to noticing whether the sisters in the choir were modest and composed, conforming themselves to the ceremonies and the usual mode of reciting the psalms, and on discovering them wanting in this—now with charity and amiability, now with severity, as the need might be—she corrected them. Once in particular, seeing a novice who was paying no attention to the Office, and who did not even compose herself after being reproachfully hinted at, Magdalen called her out to the middle of the choir and then ejected her, saying to her afterwards that she had seen the devil standing around her, dancing and leaping, while she distracted herself and paid no attention to the beckoning of the mistress

In order that the novices might become attached to the recitation in common of the Divine Office above any private devotion, if anyone asked her permission to leave the choir in order to go and make mental prayer, she answered her: "Daughter, it seems to me that I would deceive thee if I granted thee such a permission, because whilst thinking that thou dost give greater honor to God, and dost please Him more by this private prayer of thine, thou wouldst find afterwards to have merited little, as, compared with reciting the Divine Office in the choir with the other nuns, every other prayer and private devotion is of little merit in the sight of God." Thus she persuaded her to appreciate and follow with love the exercises of the choir, to which she wanted all to be very prompt and attentive

There was in her no virtue which she did not try, as far as she was able, to transplant in the souls of those committed to her care We have already seen how Magdalen had at heart the good intention in working (the root whence an action derives most of its value) Her thought had no aim but the divine honor and pleasure. Hence she took the greatest care to show her disciples how pleasing to God a soul becomes that works with a pure intention; and how this enhances the value and makes meritorious even the least action. She was wont to say that if one performed all his actions with the pure intention of giving glory to God, he would after death go to heaven without entering purgatory. On the contrary, she manifested to her disciples how she detested, like deadly poison, the working at random or for any other end but God, and in order that they might persist in the practice of this exercise, often she suddenly asked one or the other about the intention they had in the work they were then performing; and, on any of them being found somewhat perplexed in giving the answer, this sufficed for the wise and subtle mistress to judge that that sister acted at least inconsiderately Hence she would proceed to correct her in the following words . "Dost thou not see that thou losest the merit of this action? God takes no pleasure in actions done without a good intention." Which spur was very efficacious to promote the spiritual profit of the young novices. Afterwards she taught them that in order to make their works acceptable to God, they should unite them with those that Jesus performed v . the on earth ; and she was wont to say that our actions, though good, of themselves alone are, like lead, of little value; but when united to those of Jesus they become like most pure gold Among the means she suggested for acquiring purity of intention, the principal one was to keep the mind united to God with holy thoughts and affections, for the exercise of which she used the above-mentioned method; hence, she would ask one. "What dost thou think about? Where is thy heart?" and the other: "How many times didst thou think of God to-day? What was thy first thought after waking up? How many times didst thou thank God to-day for having called thee to Religion? What thoughts hadst thou in reciting the Divine Office? What profit didst thou derive from the reading in the refectory?" After they had heard a sermon or an exhortation, she would question them on the profit they had drawn therefrom, and also on the sentiments and resolutions of the meditation, especially on the days they had received Holy Communion, asking them: "What did Jesus tell you within your hearts when you received Him? How many times did you thank Him on this day, Who gave Himself to you in the Most Holy Sacrament?" On Thursday and Friday,—days which she spent in a special feeling of devotion, the one in remembrance of the Eucharistic institution, which therefore she called *the day of love*, the other in memory of the Passion, called by her *the day of the nuptials*,—she was wont to ask of the nuns the following question. "Did you consider what Jesus has done for you on this day?" Thus, according to the times and the occasions, she asked them about what passed within their hearts; so that she not only made them vigilant and exercised them to work conscientiously and keep their spirits united to God, but also accustomed them to lay their hearts and thoughts ingenuously open to her,—a thing she deemed greatly adapted to attain to Religious perfection and free their souls from the frauds of the devil. To this end she also wanted them to present themselves every day to tell her their faults. Sometimes one of them would object that it was impossible to always have the mind united to God; and to her the Saint would answer: "It is true that it is impossible actually to think always of God, as this shall be done perfectly but in the Fatherland; it can be accomplished, though, viz , to be always united to God, by having Him always in view, as, even if we work for creatures, for the good of their souls or of their bodies, and without any other end in view but to give honor and glory to God, so that if it were not for God we would not do it, it cannot be denied that in that manner we are always united to God; and if we labor for the good of Religion, and do it because Religion is God's, and what we do, we do only to please and honor and glorify Him, it must be admitted that all those who do this are united with God "

Furthermore, she deemed the observance of silence very opportune, nay, even necessary to attain to the union of mind with God, as it is prescribed by the Religious that the soul may reenter into itself and gather itself in God; and she was wont to say that a religious person who has no taste for silence cannot by any means taste the things of God Hence she insisted on having silence rigorously kept by all her disciples, and with a true religious spirit; and if any of them failed to do it, besides the penance she would impose on her, she herself, who was a perfect keeper of silence, wou'd remain some time silent during recreation time,

as if to atone for the fault of her disciple, saying to anyone who asked
her the reason therefor: "I want Religion to have its due." She used
also to teach what thoughts and considerations were to be attended to in
time of silence, among which was the following, viz . to consider the
works Jesus wrought from His 12th to His 30th year, whilst He lived a
hidden life, which works the Evangelists have not made known, and she
added that the works done in silence are very pleasing to God—that is,
those which do not appear to the eyes of others; and that it is more
useful and safer to do great works which appear very small than to do
those works which are great only in appearance. But, nevertheless, she
wished all to work with manifest fervor, and that everyone should aim
at the greatest possible perfection. On discovering a nun who was
slothful and without fervor, she reprehended her, and, to sting her, she
said to her that whoever acts coldly in Religion is nothing but a burden
to Religion, being in need of being supported by Religion, which is the
reverse of what should be with nuns, who are themselves bound to support Religion In order that they might not grow up slothful and negligent, she always kept them busy and never permitted them to be idle.

Though the life of her monastery was the total observance of a
perfect religious community, nevertheless, well reflecting on how
easy it was to fail in regard to the holy vow of poverty, on
account of the inordinate attachment of humanity to earthly things,
though these be few and small, she never ceased to enlighten the new
Religious in regard to the beauty and importance of this vow, showing them how the perfection to which they were called depended
chiefly upon the full observance of it. She used to try to find out
to what they were attached, and employed the best means to detach
them from any earthly object. Therefore, she had prescribed for
them that they should examine themselves monthly, in order to see
whether they were inordinately attached to anything, or possessed anything superfluous, on finding which they were to give it up; and she
used to say to them that they should rather love to live in need than to
have anything superfluous, as whatever is wanting a Religious in this
life will be given to her superabundantly in the next. That they might
not entertain any affection even for necessary things, she often made
them exchange habits among themselves, as is done with so much praise
and profit in the Society of Jesus, and on the strength of this example
in several other Congregations, especially in that of the Salesians, where
a nun cannot propose to make use to-morrow of a pin used to-day
Magdalen noticed that one of her disciples had an attachment for a little
book of spiritual exercises, written by her own hand, and she made her
throw it into the fire. She took from another a rosary, because she had
too much attachment for it, and only returned it to her six months afterwards, with the injunction, though, that she should bring it back to her
every evening , which was done for some time, that is, until that novice
learned to hold it as lent to her by the Religion; as this is the way
the Religious must hold all things granted them for their use. By this
means she led her disciples to the love of poverty and, together with it,
to the mortification of themselves. In regard to this self mortification,
considered in its perfect degree, she was wont to tell them that anyone

who expects to find satisfaction and consolation in the giving of himself to the service of God, deceives himself very much, as God is not to be found in the satisfaction, but in the true virtue which has its proper place in tribulations, toils, and hardships, and we are to hold in esteem only those satisfactions and sweetnesses which animate us to suffer willingly for the love and glory of God, and to fulfill His Divine Will She asserted that that soul was unworthy of being called a servant of God that did not endure and strive for this virtue. Hence, she did not trust much to the stability of those souls that appeared to have acquired their perfection in peace and spiritual sweetnesses; because (she expressly said) that is not true virtue which is not tried by its opposite, viz., temptations and tribulations, as God requires of those creatures who wish to serve Him perfect death, without which nothing can be done, and anyone who enters rightly into the service of God does nothing but in a thousand ways and manners give death to himself at every hour and moment. This is the reason she gave for it· "The life of our flesh is the delight and pleasure of sensuality; the death of our flesh is to deprive it of every delight and pleasure, and to conquer it by means of fasts and vigils and austerities. The life of our judgment and will consists in disposing of itself and its things as it pleases, its death, to subdue it always to the judgment and the will of others by means of obedience; and thus death is given to the appetite of our reputation and pride by continually making acts of true humility and contempt of self, and by hiding in order to remain unknown. Such a death must anyone give to himself, who truly wishes to serve God, and he deceives himself who thinks he can give himself this death by holding in his mouth the milk and honey of interior and exterior sweetnesses, as it cannot be that the soul which truly dies in order that God may live in it, does not feel pain." On seeing a novice very quiet and tranquil, giving no sign of troubles or difficulties, she became pensive, and was wont to say to her· "I fear thou mayest have placed thy end in accommodating the exterior and forgetting the interior " She added. "Thou must regret as not having well spent it, the day in which thou hast not mortified thyself"

Humility being the foundation of every spiritual edifice, and Mary Magdalen De-Pazzi possessing it in an heroic degree, well may we believe how much she strove to plant it in the hearts of those girls who were coming to serve God in her monastery. As the height of the edifice derives its strength from the depth of its foundation, she first of all sought to root out of the hearts of her subjects all the ground of self-love and human pride. She pretended to have less regard for those endowed with more talent and ability, and more apt to take pride in their actions, than for others, and when compelled to make actual use of the former, she would put them at the more humble and menial occupations. This she did in particular with two young ladies, over twenty years of age, whom she wished to humble on account of a certain conceit they entertained of knowing more than others She appointed them to read in the refectory the children's A B C book. Others of the same disposition she would order to recite publicly and aloud the *Hail Mary*, or she would have them reprimanded by some of the mothers with words indicating that they were considered as of little capacity When-

ever it was necessary to commit to them anything of greater importance, the Saint used such a prudential way in giving the commission
that it would exclude even the slightest motive for them to grow proud,
and, even after they had perfectly fulfilled the commission, she found in
their action so many and so great faults that in exposing them they
were overtaken with shame rather than elated with vainglory, and
regarded as the mere truth, and not exaggeration, what the holy mistress
would say, so much was she guided by the Spirit of God in directing
these souls. Whenever she noticed that anyone considered herself as
becoming useful, she called her out from the midst of the others, and
said to her· "This daughter thinks that it was great luck for us to get
her into our monastery; but I tell you that she was very fortunate in
the nuns having been pleased to accept and admit her into it." Sometimes those who came to the Religion, before receiving the holy habit,
were made by her, though they had on their silk dresses and jewels, to
wait on the table and kiss the feet of the other nuns. One was very
sensitive at being reprehended and remarked for her faults, and the zealous
mother imposed on all the novices diligently to observe all her faults
and tell her about them, and she publicly reprehended and corrected
her. Let us not think for a moment that this practice of the Religious,
viz., the relating of the faults of others to the superioress, is opposed to
charity, as those evil-inclined persons would have us believe who get
hold of anything to blackmail or criticise others   Truth conscientiously
used can never be opposed to virtue. Paid tale-bearing is a vile thing,
but the lending of light and strength to those who have to lead their
flock to the perfection of the spirit cannot be but a praiseworthy and
useful undertaking

At that time a noble girl of nineteen, with great spirit and desire
for religious perfection, came to the Religion   Having spent a few days
in the monastery, and presuming too much of herself, or transported by
youthful fervor, made it known that she found a difficulty in there receiving the sacred habit, as there were no penances practiced and no
opportunity to suffer for the love of God   On another occasion, she
also said that she had come to the Religion in order to be a nun in fact,
and not in name only, and that she would not perform certain ceremonies
which they are wont to use when the holy habit is received.   The
holy mother noted both these expressions of opinion, and dissembling
as to the first, or rather leaving the correction of it to a better time, in
regard to the second, marked as it was by greater pride and singularity,
she immediately and severely reprimanded the girl, telling her repeatedly·
"These are the girls the people of the world think have so much light
and spirit"   Which words were uttered by her with so much emphasis
that the girl, being overtaken by great shame and compunction, asked forgiveness for her fault, both of the mother and of the novices.   This act
of submission, though sincere, did not make the holy directress relent
any in trying, when opportunity offered, to cure the sick spirit of this
subject of hers.   Too important it is to eradicate from the soul of
youthful persons even the most secret roots of anything vicious,
in order to plant therein true virtue and with profit   One must not
become so easily tired of inculcating in youthful souls those virtues

which are necessary to them; nor must one feel satisfied with some act which they are performing in relation to them, whilst fervor more than reflection moves and transports their operations Shortly after this girl had taken the monastic habit, the holy mother behaved towards her with such severity that, by mortifying and punishing her at every little occasion, it almost seemed as though she harbored some ill feeling towards her No day elapsed in which she did not cast up those expressions to her several times, and, more than that, she caused the other novices to reprehend and reproach her as the most imperfect and faulty one in the monastery. This was serious and hard for the soul of that girl to bear; so that, on seeing herself in such a manner and by all found fault with, she could not refrain from crying and grieving. Therefore, the Saint said to her "Remember, sister, that thou didst find difficulty in selecting this monastery, because great penances were not being practiced herein;" and by this road she led her to the conviction of her own error—to disillusion, humiliation, and amendment. Though in acting towards her with such severity Magdalen's charitable feelings would not permit her to leave that girl in those afflictions without any consolation, but she often said to her. "Sister, anyone that wishes to give herself wholly to God must, before all, give up her own self," and the like things Thus, by pointing out the will of God, the greater spiritual benefit, and the eternal reward, she relieved and greatly encouraged the downcast spirit of that novice

In the civil order, also, it is acknowledged that to start a man on the road to honor and equity, it is necessary from the beginning to put such a restraint on him as will habituate him easily to submit his own judgment and will to the will of others, by the doing of which a person of education is distinguished from an ignorant and uncivilized one This is absolutely required by every educational institution, no matter whether its religious maxims differ from those of pure Catholicism or not Anyone who has not been placed under restraint in the years of his growth cannot prove to be anything but a man of disorder, of scandal, of ruin It is just the yoke of abnegation and mortification that Jeremias the prophet wishes to see imposed on the young people, not so much to make them good citizens as to make them acceptable to God by eternal predestination. But our Lord Jesus Christ imposes it on us more openly by the fullness and perfection of the law, protesting that he is not worthy of Him, and consequently cannot obtain the eternal salvation, who does not renounce even his irregular interior sentiments He declares it to be also morally impossible for him who did not bend to right even from his tender age Hence Mary Magdalen employed a great deal of care and diligence in subduing the souls of her disciples, whom she aimed at leading to the pinnacle of spiritual perfection. She explored their inclinations in every way, and, having found them out, without delay she ordered them to do things just contrary to them. Hence, whenever she found that a person was much inclined to prayer, she sent her to sleep, or to some exterior exercises, or to do some work; and, *vice versa*, if she knew of some who were inclined to exterior exercises, she assigned to them prayer or some other interior practice. Thus she imposed simply a *Pater noster* and an *Ave Maria* on one who wished to practice many

and great penances, and, on the contrary, she imposed heavy mortifications on those who felt a repugnance towards them. Sometimes
whilst the nuns were all in the choir, she called upon one of them and
sent her out to count the rafters of the hall or the cell.   At other times,
she made some of them draw water and throw it back into the well.
She also commanded some to go to the orchard and catch ants or
butterflies.   One day she ordered a novice to go into the refectory with
the little tunic alone   She was satisfied at seeing her promptitude to
obey and her good disposition, and made her dress again   To another
she prescribed going every day into the orchard, there to learn from the
trees the manner of praying, and to keep an account of the lessons she
learned from them.

We have already said how very often she delayed until a better time
correcting the faults of her subjects. It, therefore, happened that feigning not to notice sometimes during the day the fault of someone, she
waited until that one had gone to bed and then had her called, and,
placing her on her knees before her, she, with severe words, reprehended
her for having dared to go to bed without first calling herself guilty of
her fault and humbling herself for it   But correcting the faults of her
subjects was a small thing with her   What she wanted above all was
the effect of the correction, which is amendment   In order to help
them to secure this essential advantage, she ordered them to come to her
every evening and tell her how many times they had fallen into a fault
which had once been corrected by her   If any of them appeared before
her full of shame for her repeated faults, she would cast her away, telling
her with seeming harshness . "I will lose no time with thee when thou
wishest not to profit by my advice " And then, suddenly, she would
call her back and make her confess those repeated faults which she would
not hear of before , and, moreover, she would command her to manifest
what thoughts had passed through her mind whilst she had been so cast
away   She permitted a novice to go to bed, refusing to hear her, and
afterwards she called her to humble herself and acknowledge her faults
Likewise the good, zealous mother once went to the bedside of one who
had lain down to sleep before she had been permitted to confess her
fault, and, having made her rise, led her to the chapel of the novices,
where, after reprimanding her, she commanded her in punishment to
remain and sleep on the floor; and with this order she left her, returning
shortly after to examine her in what she might have said and thought
in view of such a proceeding ; and having reason to judge her humiliated
and well-disposed, she permitted her to return to her bed. A girl who
was on probation in the monastery having risen one morning earlier
than usual, because she was desirous of attending matin with the nuns,
was noticed by the Saint, who told her it was necessary that she should
ask permission of the mother prioress, which she obtained.   Nevertheless, as a mistress of novices, she ordered her back to her bed   The
girl complied, and, having hardly lain down, Mary Magdalen told her in
a tone of satisfaction "Dress and come to the choir with us ; I have
done this to try thy obedience "

She was also wont to impose a penance and then revoke it at the
moment it was to be performed, being satisfied at seeing the prompt and

spontaneous acceptation of the obedience, for which she absolutely required a cheerful disposition, free from all hesitation. Therefore, she often repeated to her young charges that in obeying they should not regard the person giving the order, but God in her, and her they should simply obey as though she were God Himself; "because," she would say, "you did not give up your will to the creature, but to God, and the creature stands there to you in God's place;" hence, she told them to obey the superioresses that were assigned to them, even though they might be lay-sisters, and even if it was a question of things contrary to their judgment, being persuaded that what is commanded is the will of God. She also told them to hold humility in great value, as though it wonders are wrought, which in fact was experienced by several of them, and particularly by the one she had sent, as we said above, to learn the exercise of prayer from the trees of the orchard. She, who found it very difficult to pray, by means of this obedience acquired so much facility and pleasure in praying, that of her own choice she would not have occupied herself in anything else during her whole life.

To a novice grievously tempted she lent her girdle, suggesting to her to gird herself with it, which was no sooner done by the novice than the temptation ceased. She was wont to say to all: "Until you give yourselves into the hands of obedience as if dead, you can never taste what serving God is. Offer your will in sacrifice to God, and you will derive therefrom a sovereign consolation. If you wish to comply with the Divine Will, beware lest by persuasions you draw the will of the superiors to your own, but try to execute, simply and entirely, their orders, and thus will you arrive at a great perfection. If you experience a repugnance to break your will for the sake of obedience, you show that you have very little love for God, as you do not wish to trouble yourself in the one thing by which you can give Him sovereign honor—namely, submitting to the will of others for His love." And she tried to render her disciples not only obedient with a tranquil submission, but also desirous and almost famishing for the yoke of obedience. To this end she imposed on them that they should never do even the least thing without her permission, and as she could not always be with them, she assigned to each of them a companion, of whom, in her absence, they were to ask permission; and when even this could not be done, they were then to ask permission of anyone present, and never to do anything without some submission to the will of others. By accustoming themselves to obey in small things they facilitated obedience in things greater and of strict obligation, as the same disciples avowed that it had so happened to them. She reputed as blasphemy on the lips of a Religious: *I will* or *I will not;* so that if any of her subjects uttered these words, she immediately punished her, and with inexorable severity. Thus removing from the novitiate every attachment to self-will, so inimical to our true welfare and that of a community, she succeeded in introducing therein those virtues which are the precious and essential dowry of a bride of Jesus Christ.

Two facts are worth relating here, as evidence to prove how much light and power God was giving to this, his beloved servant, that she might carry souls along with herself to the highest degree of spiritual perfection.

On the 9th of March, 1591, her eyes assumed an expression of sweetness and wonder at the same time, in her countenance the divine flame showed which was burning within her heart, and the position of her body indicated that she was rapt in ecstasy   While thus alienated from her senses she manifested the sublimity and vastness of her intelligence, drawn by compared visions, the better to communicate them to others. "I see," said she to the sisters, "a column of the most beautiful porphyry, the size of which is such that ten men could not embrace it; it rests on a base of the finest gold, partly covered, and at each of the four corners there is a canal   In the column many precious stones of divers qualities and colors are enchased, and likewise I see four large and most clear mirrors, and many others below them, a little smaller   Three very beautiful ropes are tied to the column—one of gold, another red, and the last of silver—which are held by a great many Nazarites, who follow this column.   There is a pilot, with his helpmate, who with one hand holds the column, and with the other elevates the three ropes that the Nazarites may see them, and the coadjutor holds them out to them, not the three of them at a time, but first one and then another, though each one of them is bound to have the three of them.   Likewise they show to the Nazarites some of the mirrors, but only as they proceed, without causing them to stop   At the top of the column the king of these Nazarites rests his hands on said column, so that it may go straight, without wavering   There is also on the summit a crystal gnomon reaching over a spring.   This column is led by a bright star, which fixes one of its rays upon it, till it reaches the city of Jerusalem, where it has to stop.   It is also accompanied by seven very beautiful trees, on which rest many little birds, giving great delight by their singing to the traveling Nazarites.   Some of these Nazarites throw darts against the column, but as this is of porphyry, they mark it, but only break off some of the precious stones enchased in the same   Some try to unravel those three very worthy ropes, and others to stain and soil them.   Among these Nazarites there is one holding in his hand a little bell, continually ringing it, and more strongly when the others wish to go to sleep   There are others also who hold little bells, but do not ring them   Now behold the explanation of this.   The column signifies our Religion, the golden base on which it rests signifies that it is founded on charity, its being partly covered denotes that our Religion tends more properly to the interior perfection than to outward penance and exterior practices   The four canals at the four corners of the base, and from which issue divers liquors, are four great gifts, benefits, or tastes which are to be found in the Religious state   From the first canal issues the best wine, which is the *union* with God, as Religion is the most suitable and easy place to unite ourselves with God, and this *union* inebriates the soul and makes her one with her loving Spouse Jesus.   From the second canal issues water, which signifies that the Religious partake in a more particular and continuous manner of all the goods of Holy Church, and at this canal those drink who thirst after justice   From the third canal oil issues, by means of which the Religious, according to the saving of the prophet, becomes by participation as another God on earth, for he tastes and feels within himself that interior peace that the Word Incarnate once felt here below ; hence as it was a glory for the Word to suffer, nay, He wished for nothing but this, and for this *He was made flesh*, likewise the perfect Religious regards it as his glory to suffer and to be despised, so that on being assailed by temptations, distress, and vexations he does not become disturbed in the least degree, nor permits himself to be robbed of his quietness and interior peace, as he had already adopted the above-mentioned things for his glory, and wishes and craves for nothing else From the fourth and last canal issues forth a very odoriferous balm, which denotes the fourth gift which is found in the Religions, viz , the counsels and the help which are given to us by the superiors; and this balm anoints only those who are dead to themselves, in the same manner that the material balm ordinarily is only used upon dead bodies, but when employed for the living it is generally used to anoint one of the limbs, never the whole body. Thus then it happens in the Religion, that he who is not dead to his own will, judgment, and understanding does not avail himself of the fruit of the counsels and help of the superiors, as he believes in himself much more than he does in them. The various precious stones signify the virtues which shine in our Rule and Constitution The four principal mirrors are the four principal Saints of our Religion, viz., St. Eliseus, St. Angelus, St Albert, and St Cyril, and the smaller ones denote the other Saints and blessed souls of our Order The three ropes which are attached to the column are the three vows that of obedience, represented by the golden one, that of poverty by the red, and that of chastity by the silver. The Nazarites who hold the ropes in their hands are all of us who promised to the Lord and made a solemn profession to keep the above three vows The pilot of the Nazarites, who with one hand holds the column and with the other elevates the three ropes, is the superioress who directs us, and who must in everything she has to do, treat and order, always keep the Rule in her hands, viz , she must see that all she orders is in conformity with our Rule and Constitution, never departing from it in the least; moreover, she must teach her subjects by her example the observance of the three vows; and yet she trains her subjects, now in the observance of one and now of the other, because, if she wanted to exercise them in the three at the same time, she would not be acting as charity and compassion require her to act She must, therefore, have grace and light from God in order to know well how to discern the nature, the tendencies, and the spirit of each, so as to assign the occupations convenient to each particular case , for instance, in time of sickness, it is necessary to withdraw the *rope of poverty*, in regard to the actual practice of it, and to consign the rope of *obedience*, by which one may peacefully submit to the pains of sickness To the young nuns and the beginners who are not yet well established in the way of perfection, she ought also to hand the *rope of obedience*, and so she changes them from time to time, as she may deem necessary, though each of them must of herself fulfill the three vows The superioresses also point out to their subjects *those mirrors* which are enchased in the column, but this they do as they walk along without causing them to stop, —and this means that they must excite them to imitate the lives of the Saints, but without obstructing the

. interior vocation to which God called them. The *king of these Nazarites*, who keeps his hands on the *column* that it may proceed straightforward, is the spiritual father, who must be always watching and see that we continually and perfectly fulfill the Rule. The *crystal gnomon*, which is at the summit of the *column* and reaches a fount near by, indicates the doctrine which is embodied in the Rule, and which aims at nothing else but the union with God, signified by the rotundity of the *gnomon*. The *fount* is the Eucharistic Sacrament, it being the surest and most efficacious means to employ in order that we may live united to God. The *star* which guides said column is the Blessed Virgin, our Mother and protectress, to whom our Rule is dedicated, and who, by her special protection and grace, assists us to advance towards the heavenly Jerusalem, where we shall finally stop and dwell, if we shall have perfectly fulfilled our holy Rule and Constitution. The *seven Trees* which accompany this *column* are the seven Gifts of the Holy Ghost, the *birds* singing on *these Trees* with sweet melody are the fruits of the same Holy Ghost The *Nazarites* throwing *darts* against the *column* are those who find fault with and murmur against the Rule and the Constitution, it seeming to them as if it were either too austere or not ordained as they would prefer; but their *throwing of darts* cannot hurt said Rule, as it cannot detract even the least particle from its interior spiritual greatness and perfection. By these faults they blunt some of those stones that are joined to the column, as these murmurs being heard by imperfect persons who are not constant in doing good, they pour into their soul a similar opinion and easily fasten it therein, and for this reason, as far as they are concerned, they detract some exterior beauty from the virtues and from the perfection which our holy Religion teaches us and binds us to practice. As to those *Nazarites* who try to unravel the three beautiful ropes, they represent those sisters who willfully break the three vows and shun the practices and toils of the Religion. The *others* who *stain* and *soil* those most worthy *ropes* are those Religious who do not perfectly observe the promises they have made to the Lord, so that if anything is enjoined on them by obedience, they do not execute it with spiritual promptitude, humility, and the other conditions required of truly obedient persons They stain the vow of poverty when they wish to have more than is given to them by the Religion (Religious Order), instead of glorying in poverty and in suffering for the love of Christ Crucified They stain and soil the vow of chastity when they do not guard their heart, thoughts, desires, and words as the most delicate perfection of this vow requires. The Nazarites who have the bell in their hands, and ring it not, are those who have the knowledge of God but do not use it in behalf of their neighbors (She not having announced who was the Nazarite who was ringing the bell continually, the nuns rightly interpreted that she was herself, the venerable mother, so zealous of the spiritual advancement of others, who was now hiding her own name under the veil of humility) The *Nazarites* walking behind the *column* hear the disagreeable singing of a bird; but those who are determined to continue their journey with alacrity pass on as if they were deaf, which signifies the discipline of the Religion, which gives no delight to the sensitive part of the flesh; but we must be as deaf to it,

nay, try to attain to such a perfection, that whatever displeases our
senses may be our glory and delight, and with the spirit we must conquer our flesh and its appetites.   I see the *king* of these *Nazarites* who
sometimes lifts up his hands to heaven, in order that receiving some
dew he may moisten the heads of these *Nazarites*.   This is our Rev. Father
Confessor who, elevating the powers of his soul to God, has them filled
up by God with grace, light, and virtue; and then, by his preaching,
exhortations, and advice, he communicates these to us, leading us through
the road of perfection.   But we must keep our heads uncovered to feel
this dew—that is, we must preserve our minds pure and free from vain
and useless thoughts.   Whilst journeying to perfection, by night we
must go with our heads erect and our eyes turned to heaven, and by
day with our heads down and our eyes fixed upon the ground—that is,
when the soul finds herself in the night of tribulation and toil, she must
turn to God, and trust only in Him, resting and fixing all her thoughts
and affections in His providence.   As to daytime—that is, during prosperity—the soul must humble and annihilate herself so as to become
convinced of being a mere nothing and undeserving that God should so
long tolerate her upon the earth.   The *Nazarites* also, like their *king*,
must often lift their hands up to heaven to receive the dew and refresh
themselves with it.   For whilst we are in this miserable life, preparing
for the celestial and blessed one, we must elevate our soul to God by continual meditation and contemplation, in which the intellect is enlightened, and the will is inflamed and made to burn with divine love.   This
cools the fire of sensuality in the soul, and makes her fly up the road of
perfection, rendering sweet and palatable whatever bitterness may have
to be tasted for the love of her amiable Spouse, Jesus Crucified "

On the first day of Pentecost, 1604, having been already alienated from
her senses for several hours, with the strongest enthusiasm of celestial
affection, among many and wonderful things, she said : " This Divine
Spirit is love and asks for love, and rests not in those hearts that love
Him not, and do not love purely for God .   There are many souls
making nothing but little bundles of hay and straw.   Few are they that
work precious stones and embrace strong columns.   These bundles of
straw and hay are good for nothing except to burn; and when burning,
they make a very light fire, which quickly disappears, leaving soot and
smoke, but the *stones* are of infinite value and enrich those who possess
them ; the columns support the high buildings and those who embrace
them.   The *bundles of straw* indicate those persons who attend to the performance of many manual works with vanity and for human ends . . .
There are many persons working all their lives, but, as they do not work
for God, they derive therefrom nothing more than a light splendor of
human glory, which soon passes away, leaving their hearts full of regret
and pain, and they find no reward for it in the next life.   The Divine
Spirit rests but little in these persons ; but He comes down in great fullness and rests in those souls that work precious stones of solid and real
virtues, of humility, despisement of self and everything created, poverty,
purity, and resignation of their will to God and the superiors. . . .
The souls embracing strong columns are governed by them, and their
edifice will never shake or fall; for, when working for God with purity

of intention, neither tribulation, nor distress, nor any creature can ever
overthrow their constancy, as they are strengthened by the Divine Spirit
and their operations remain forever, because they are founded on the
Divine Truth." Turning to the novices when she was their mistress,
she used to say to them with great emphasis · "Do not make bundles of
straw, but enrich yourselves with these valuable stones, embrace the
strong pillars, if you wish the Divine Spirit to rest in you" And,
having been silent for a while, she added "This Divine Love and pure
Spirit will not rest by any means in those souls that possess cutting
tongues, as He hates and very much abhors a backbiting tongue, and
departs and flees from it. It is true that this Divine Spirit comes down,
for, being communicative, He would like to give Himself to all; but He
does not stop, not knowing where to rest. He rests for a moment in
those souls that make bundles of straw, but He does not stop at all where
there are cutting tongues." Here, with a louder voice, she would say:
"Harm not thy neighbor, as God commanded that we should love him
as ourselves, and it is too great an evil to touch him He is the pupil
of God's eye; and the eye is so delicate an organ that the least wisp of
straw offends it. He who offends his neighbor offends God. Of the
neighbor's faults we cannot, we must not speak, except with the intention
of doing him good, and with those who can remedy the evil; whatever
else is spoken of is murmuring . . . I would like to be able to go
throughout the whole world and get all the souls into my hands, and I
would exert myself so much with the divine help that I would root out all
these biting teeth. Ah! if creatures could see and understand fully how
much God hates these tongues with teeth no one would be found that
would dare to murmur. If God hates murmuring in every creature, He
cannot, He will not, tolerate it at all in the Religious and Spouses consecrated to Him. Some Religions (Religious Orders) are like well-cul-
tivated gardens decked out with beautiful trees, odoriferous flowers, and
leafy plants, on account of the exact observance and the beautiful order
that are found therein. Other Religious Orders are like ugly forests
compared to the former, because in them there is no order of religious
observance; nevertheless, in these the Divine Spirit rests a little, as
there are no murmuring tongues there, and, on the contrary, He comes
to the others and passes on without stopping, because the spirit of
hypocrisy which dominates them, rather than truth, leads them frequently to the vice of backbiting. But woe, woe to them" (she used
to say still louder) "because God will permit the light they possess to be
turned into darkness, if they do not pull out these teeth, and He will
give His light to other Religions O perverse tongues, what wonder of
iniquity are you, that you suffice to overthrow all the good of a Religion!
O my souls" (she used also to say to the novices) "beware of putting on
these teeth, and thank Divine Goodness that at present not one among
you is stained with this vice" Progressing with her deep contemplation,
the Saint so penetrated the mystery of the Most Holy Trinity that, overcome by feelings of amazement, she was wont to repeat· "Incomprehensible God! . . . eternal is Thy greatness . . . ineffable is Thy
goodness. . . I see, and I see with comfort . . . three Divine
Persons imparting to one another their livin. . . . in an ineffable

and inscrutable manner. The Father flows into the Son, the Son into the Father, and the Father and the Son into the Holy Ghost, the Holy Ghost flows in a manner which it is impossible for us to understand Eternal God, Thou art ineffably good; and, by Thy goodness, Thou dost impart to the creature immersed in the knowledge of her nothingness some knowledge of Thy eternal being; but, even granted that this communication is wonderful, yet it may be said with truth that it is as a mere nothing compared to that which passes between God and His creature . . . The three Divine Persons communicate their divine *influxes* to all the blessed in heaven; and the blessed return their *influxes* into the Father, the Son, and the Holy Ghost, with their praise and thanksgiving, magnifying, blessing, and exalting continually and without ceasing the Most Holy Trinity. The three Divine Persons communicate their *influxes* also to the creatures of this world, and the Word Incarnate does it by sending gifts and graces to them, that they may so dispose themselves that all the Most Holy Trinity may be well pleased in them. . . . I see the Father aspiring to the salvation of the same creatures, I see the Son breathing in them, and the Holy Ghost inspiring the aspiration of the Father, which is like an ardent wish for the salvation of creatures. The breathing of the Son is like a rest He takes in the soul, making the creature look up to God the Father. The inspiration of the Holy Ghost is like the enlightening which He gives that the soul may go on from virtue to virtue till *Deus deorum in Sion* may be seen. This is the wonderful work the Most Holy Trinity continually performs in the creature. . . . The Most Holy Trinity communicates its *influx* in a most special manner to the Religious, but in so different a manner that I feel amazed at it, because some receive more and some less, and with such a difference between one and the other that I would never have thought it to be so." Being filled with this feeling of wonder, it seemed to her as if she saw the soul of a Religious not receiving these divine *influxes*, having rendered herself unworthy of them by being willing to remain in mortal sin. Therefore, many devils bound her with horrible chains, and, with insults and contempt, led her to the place of eternal torments; at which sight Mary Magdalen wept for grief, sighed with convulsive agitation, and, emitting plaintive and strong cries, said · "Unhappy soul, and who would have believed it that thou with obstinate will wouldst not only live, but also die, in mortal sin!" She was so frightened at it that for two whole days she was in great anguish and terror. Finally she understood that the devils acquire great power over those Religious who through their own fault do not receive these *influxes*, thereby becoming a source of great scandal in their Congregation and of serious ruin to it. As God for the sake of a good person sends many favors to a place, so also, on account of a bad person, He permits many evils and losses to befall another place. Hence she recommended the most rigid perspicuity when it was a question of admitting a person to the religious state, and that all possible zeal and care should be used to lead such person rightly to the road of perfection. When God calls anyone to Religion, He desires that, in saving and perfecting his own soul, others also may be led to the haven of salvation, both by example and exhortations.

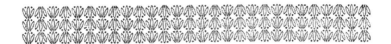

CHAPTER XXX.

OF HER SPECIAL GIFT OF PENETRATING THE HEART OF THE SISTERS COMMITTED TO HER CARE.

GOD assisted Mary Magdalen with a gift which helped her very much in the various and wonderful ways she employed in the spiritual direction of her subjects, which have been described more at length than it was at first intended in the preceding chapter. This gift consisted in enabling her to penetrate the secrets of others' spirits, which we have already seen manifesting itself in several cases. We will here relate in particular those which came under the observation of her young girls and novices, and which have been by them testified to in the processes.

One day whilst Mary Magdalen was at work with her novices, she saw in the heart of one of them a fault or imperfection which was greatly displeasing to God, and of which the novice having no knowledge had not spoken to the mother or the others. She saw that such a fault was rooted in the heart of that girl like a juniper tree (so it presented itself to the imagination of Mary Magdalen), and she said that the Guardian Angel of this novice was trying to uproot it from her heart, but could not succeed, as some devils prevented him. Hence the holy mother, enkindled with zeal, arose suddenly from her seat, and, taking the novice by the arm, led her to the oratory of the novitiate, and there, being rapt in ecstasy, began to strike her with the *discipline*, so as to humble her spirit rather than inflict pain on her body, saying at the same time to the devils: "Depart from her, ye evil ones, and leave this soul." The novice, between the surprise and the humiliation, burst into tears, and the mother, having known her to be well disposed towards docility, manifested to her the fault which had taken root in her interior, and thus enlightening her wrought also her amendment.

Another novice had kept a temptation for five months hidden in her heart and would not confess it. God manifested it to our holy mistress, who, calling the novice to her and reprimanding her, spoke openly to her concerning her temptation. She then impressively told her to beware in future lest she should keep anything hidden, and to consider it a strict obligation to confess to the mistress whatever passed through her mind.

She obtains from God that the spoiled wine in a keg in the
monastery become good (page 158).

One evening, whilst reciting compline in the choir, another of her disciples was troubled by strong temptations against her own vocation. The Saint, whose place it was then to sprinkle the sisters with holy water, when she turned to bless this young lady, made all temptations disappear from her troubled soul, leaving her in the most complete tranquillity. The young lady being amazed at this sudden result, and believing at the same time that the Saint had been the benign cause of it, asked her for an explanation, and Mary Magdalen answered that Jesus Christ had truly manifested to her the agitation of her heart, and that in blessing her, she prayed to God that He might deliver her from those temptations.

The mistress of the young girls had a disciple who was very much afflicted; and being unable to find any way of giving her rest, she recommended her one day to the charity of our Saint, then mistress of novices, that she might help her to that end. Whilst Mary Magdalen was lending herself to the charitable office with all the zeal of which she was capable, one of her novices having come to speak to her, and being unable to do so, murmured within herself, without giving any exterior sign of it, these words of impatience· "It is not enough for that girl to have her own mistress, but she must come and take ours away." The Saint, who, on coming out of the young girl's cell, found her own novice on the threshold, reproached her for this murmuring, and added "When thou shalt be afflicted and tempted, I shall help thee, too, even though I shall not then be thy mother mistress." Hence, the novice, full of confusion, humbly and sincerely begged forgiveness from so zealous and enlightened a mistress.

The sense of pride was troubling the spirit of one of her novices, and, what is worse, she studied very carefully to hide it One morning, when she was about entering the choir, Magdalen said: "*Ave Maria*"— this being the usual answer of respect and devotion when anyone was called This novice who was near her, said. "Mother mistress, nobody calls thee" To this, ·the Saint answered· "Come with me" And, having led her apart, she bitterly reprimanded her for permitting herself to be so much troubled by pride, adding that St Catherine of Siena had suggested to her not to let her come into the choir whilst she remained in so improper a disposition, without first imposing a penance on her; which having been done by the mother, the novice humbled herself, and in the future did all she could in order to be ingenuous and tranquil

One of her disciples, whilst reciting the Divine Office with her, was assailed by strange thoughts and temptations, but all this was interior, and she gave no exterior sign of it. Nevertheless, the Saint knew it, and, fixing her eyes upon her, said to her rather severely "When done with this office, we shall have to call the chapter;" and, in fact, she made her afterwards humble herself in the presence of the other novices, manifesting how, not without some fault, she had had her attention distracted from the Divine Office

A novice was doing what the Saint had imposed on her through obedience, which was to draw daily some pails of water from the well. She thought one day that it would be better to pour out that water into the trough, to be used to water the orchard, but, without following this contrary thought, she did her duty as usual   Having returned to the novitiate, the Saint asked her immediately whether she had done her duty, alluding to obedience, and on the novice's answering Yes, the mother added : " It would have been better to throw the water into the trough Is it not true?" The novice blushed like a child caught in a fault, and, bowing her head, confessed her thought. Then Mary Magdalen told her to learn blind obedience, which leaves no room for human prudence. It is not the deed which gives value to obedience; but it is obedience itself which raises any work to a degree of sovereign value, though the work may be of the humblest and even opposed to reason.

It also happened to this novice that out of her own caprice, without consulting anybody, she girded her body with a knotty rope   A few days after she had first worn it, the Saint one evening went to her bedside and frankly told her: " Sister, see what thou dost, as thou dost not do the will of God." The novice, not understanding what the holy mistress meant, answered with an air of surprise : " What dost thou speak of ? " And the mother " Of that rope which thou wearest , take it off and give it to me." The novice obeyed and thanked God who gave so much light to the directress of her spirit.

Another novice entertained some feelings of contempt (without ever having given any exterior sign thereof) against one of her companions who appeared to her faulty in manners and disposition   The Saint having perceived this, said to her unexpectedly " My sister, if that companion of thine does not possess all the exterior qualities thou thinkest she should possess—'Ipse fecit nos, et non ipsi nos'—' He made us, and not we ourselves ' (Ps xcix, 3)   God made us and formed us according to His liking, and we are not our own makers, that we may be reproached for having one nature rather than another " Through these words the novice corrected her own moral fault, shutting her eyes to the innocent faults of her companion, and opening her heart to an affectionate esteem for her.

A nun of Sister Mary Magdalen's monastery was troubled interiorly by a serious thought and lacked the courage to manifest it to anybody, only praying God with constant fervor that He might vouchsafe to deliver her from it   One day the Saint, being in ecstasy, said to this sister . " Jesus intends to grant thee the grace thou desirest " A few days afterwards meeting her in a corridor, the Saint called her aside and said to her : " The thing thou askest of God is this "   . . (manifesting to her exactly the hidden thought which tormented her), .   " but thou placest this impediment" . . . (which also was by the Saint manifested) The nun acknowledged the truth of all, removed the obstacle, and obtained the grace so much wished for.

On account of the narrowness of the choir, the novices were compelled to remain out of it   One day one of them felt a great desire to enter it to recite the office with the nuns, but she dared not speak of it to anyone. The Saint saw in spirit the desire of this young girl, and being in the choir, left her place, went to her, and led her to the choir, where she remained to her great delight and wondering how the mother could have come to the knowledge of her hidden wish

At another time it happened that this same sister having to assist the holy mother in her last sickness, was unwilling to do it, fearing that death might overtake her whilst she was alone with her at that moment. With this fear wholly interior she went to the bedside of the Saint, who immediately uttered these words, which at once show the gift of prophecy and that of searching hearts, with which she was endowed: "Sister Angela Catherine" (said she to this sister, whose name was such), "come cheerfully along; for when I shall die, all the nuns will be present." So in fact it happened at the time when the happy passage of our glorious mother took place.

What she chiefly discerned, however, in the interior of others, was whether anyone humbled herself truly or not; hence, no matter how much one tried to simulate the interior disposition, the venerable mother was never deceived, neither did she rest satisfied with exterior humiliations. To one who through human respect had asked her to impose some such mortification upon her, she said that God does not value those sacrifices, but rather prefers purity of heart and rectitude of intention. Another who under the appearance of humility came to her to justify herself by blaming a companion, she no sooner saw than she said to her these plain words: "Sister, if thou art silent with thy mouth, be also silent with thy heart; and keep to thyself what thou wishest to say to me." The evidence of these facts dispenses us from further demonstrating to what a degree God enlightened the mind of Mary Magdalen. It gives us also an idea of how much the young girls committed to her care, being continually called to keep a strict watch over their hearts, could profit in regard to their spiritual perfection and eternal salvation.

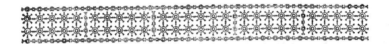

CHAPTER XXXI.

WHAT RESPECTFUL AND BENEFICENT CHARITY MARY MAGDALEN
HAD FOR HER NEIGHBOR.

 *OMINIS officium est homini cuivis benefacere*—"It is man's own duty to do good to every man," said Terence. "Beware of doing to others what thou wishest not done to thee," said Aristotle. "Respect thy image in thy neighbor; by injuring it, thou injurest thyself," thus said Cato. "Nobody does harm to himself by benefiting others," thus said Seneca. And many others, though idolaters, used the same language about the duties we owe to our neighbor. Truth has said: "*What thou wouldst that men do to thee, do thou to them likewise*" (Matth. vii, 12). This truth is the light infused by the Creator into the soul of the first man, that he and his descendants, united to God by charity, might partake in this life of that peace and most perfect beatitude to which they were destined in the next. Adam's error, which threw all mankind into the vile slavery of the rebellious passions, made of this world a theatre of enormous crimes, of guilty machinations, of secret calumnies, of invectives, and all sorts of injustice. Human legislation to check this sad overflowing of evils used all kinds of remedies and punishments. With these coöperated the religious ideas of pagans, which, though false, still had as a principal aim the union of the people in one thought and affection. Moses, the first lawgiver of the chosen people, in the love of God and of our neighbor includes all the precepts of his tables. Jesus Christ, who from the highest heavens came down on earth to rekindle and revive this flame of charity which was nearly extinguished in men's hearts, reduced all the laws, the prophets, the sacrifices, the worships, and, I will say it, for the greater part even the love of God *to the love of our neighbor*. According to the spirit of the Gospel, the love of God is the word of the heart cultivated interiorly, and the love of our neighbor is the complete realization of the social actions, embracing and including all the virtues and all the duties, and touching all the points of every perfection. He who says that he loves God and yet entertains hatred against his neighbor is a liar. He who may even spend all the hours of his life in penance and prayer, in works of divine worship, and loves not his neighbor, is a hypocrite, a Pharisee; "*I*," thus argues the Apostle St. John, "*he who loves not his brother whom he seeth,*

how can he love God, whom he seeth not?" (1 John iv, 20). Like God's precepts, so, also, those of the Church are but means to lead us to the most noble end of fraternal benevolence. "Go," said Jesus Christ to the Apostles, "and announce to the whole world the gospel, the good news, the universal peace, the reunion of all the members to their one only Head!" Choosing Peter to preside over the rest, he only inquired about his charity, of which being assured, He concluded: "*Feed My sheep*" (John xxi, 17) The Holy Ghost dwelling in the heart of the Apostles so diffused charity therein, that thenceforth they lived but for the benefit of their brethren. The image of God, equally imprinted in every human creature, is the most powerful motive which should induce us to love, benefit, and help everybody as much as we can. It not only checks all positively contrary feelings, but also that voracious self-love; and, to use the word now mostly in vogue, that cruel egotism which, whilst wishing that everything should serve to its comfort, extinguishes in the heart the sacred sparks of compassionating charity, and hardens and closes the heart, so that the love of our neighbor has no place therein Having laid down these premises, already mentioned elsewhere but never sufficiently repeated, let us in this chapter look in particular to the acts practiced by Mary Magdalen De-Pazzi in behalf of her neighbors, listening in the meantime to the voice of nature, which, by the regeneration of Jesus Christ, calls strongly upon us to embrace as brothers all people and all nations

St. Mary Magdalen being in the habit of writing down all the acts of virtue in the practice of which she felt greater interest and zeal, among those of charity towards her neighbor, we find the following: "To incline the will to love the creature simply because God loves her, and to rejoice in the love which He bears to her, and in the perfection which He communicates to her." In speaking thus, she manifested the purity of this sentiment: "Even granted (which cannot be) that God Himself *wanted* to permit our neighbor to offend us and cause us grief, nevertheless we must wish our neighbor all the perfection and glory of the seraphim, even if he were to employ it against us." And again. "If God were pleased, and it would redound to His glory, that I should be troubled by a creature having the talents of the seraphim, still I must and will wish her to possess those talents, though they are to be spent to offend me, in order to give delight and glory to God." To this alternate passing from the love of God to that of her neighbor, and from the latter to the former, her most profound humility was not a stranger, as she sometimes said that she wished more good to her neighbor than to herself, thinking that her neighbor would be more thankful to God for it, and would derive more benefit therefrom than herself.

Whilst contemplating one day the grace of God under the image of a fount, she, in the effervescence of her spirit, saw many souls around this fount like many little lambs, and, being overtaken by the desire that all of them should dip in that fount to taste its celestial sweetness, she continued, saying with animated words · "I would like to dip therein all those souls one by one" As if in the act of seeing some of them dipping themselves into the fount, she added with great joy. "O my Jesus, they do very well."

During the five years of her probation whilst God had deprived her
of all spiritual taste, she compensated herself for this privation by
wishing the greatest possible good to her neighbor. This she herself
said during the last eight days of her ecstasy before she entered that horrible and long trial: "I shall stay there in a little corner" (she said in
a low and very submissive voice) "looking at all the other Brides, my
companions, having myself nothing to taste; but I shall do, Eternal
Word, like those little infants Thou hast taken up to Thyself (viz.,
those children who die after baptism before reaching the use of reason),
"who, though they possess not that fullness of glory which they see
many other Saints possessing, nevertheless are satisfied with what they
have; or else I will think that I, too, possess all those things that others
possess; and though I shall not taste them, yet *charity*, which makes
things common to all, will make me taste even while not tasting them,
as if sharing in others' taste."

Her companions of the monastery testified to having witnessed
many a time the excessive joy by which Mary Magdalen was transported
at seeing souls favored by God with graces and celestial gifts. As to
the gifts with which God favored her, she not only wished but also tried
with utmost industry to communicate them to others. This she did on
all occasions, but especially, as we have already seen, during the time that
she had charge of the novices and young ladies of the monastery She
received no spiritual light which she did not try to communicate—now
by example, now by words, in which way, while in ecstasy, she was
sometimes forced by the Spirit of God to manifest the treasures of her
heart more than she would have done of her own will This happened
particularly the third night of Pentecost, during the already recorded
ecstasy of eight continuous days, whilst penetrating with her thoughts
into the humanity of the Word and contemplating it under the symbol
of a most charming garden She said that on the *feet* of Jesus she
found flowers, in His *hands* fruits and jewels, and in His *heart* darts of
love in great abundance. Then, fixing her admiring gaze on the sacred
feet, she said: "He that wants to find many bouquets of flowers and
lilies let him come here, as he can gather baskets of them around the
feet of my Spouse" And, with boundless love, she added: "I would
like with these flowers to make garlands and place them on the heads of
Thy Brides, but I will make a little bundle of them, and give them to
Mary to preserve them" . Contemplating the *left hand*, she spoke thus:
"These fruits which I draw from the *left hand*, O Word, I would like
to have not only for myself, but I aspire to communicate them also
to the whole world" At the *right hand*, she continued: "From this
right hand of thine, O Word, I will gather all the precious gems that I
shall find therein, which my soul wishes to communicate to every
creature." Of the darts of love she found in the *Sacred Side*, deeming
herself unable to bear them, she only said, exclaiming· "O Heart, O Side
of the Eternal Word Incarnate, one cannot correspond to so great an
influence of Thine. Thou dartest too much, one cannot bear it, great
assistance is needed to correspond to and keep so many darts" On the
second day of this same ecstasy, she also gave a sign of this desire of
communicating every good to the souls; whilst contemplating the grace

of the Holy Ghost under the image of water, she uttered these words:
"O Precious Water; oh! if one could become a fountain of it through
charity! Oh, if one could communicate it and scatter it through the
whole world, and become a fountain of it and a river so large and
swift that it would carry and draw along, as if to the sea, all the
souls to eternal life!" Many other things she added, by which she
gave to understand how ardently she wished that the Holy Ghost would
be diffused by His grace through the hearts of all creatures She also
manifested the same desire coupled with grief at seeing the souls remaining deprived of the grace of God

In another ecstasy, understanding how the Divine Spirit wanted to
depart from some souls on account of their ingratitude, she felt for them
so much affliction and anguish that she became pale, as if mortally
wounded, and gave vent to expressions of the deepest bitterness Then,
to appease God and move Him to pity, she formed some most devout
prayers upon these words: "*Protector noster, aspice Deus, et respice in
faciem Christi tui*"—"Look, O Lord, our Protector; look upon the face
of Thy Christ," as if taking for an Intercessor the wounded and bloody
face of her beloved Jesus. Among her morning protestations there was
this also, that she wanted to suffer any extreme suffering rather than
prevent her neighbor's attaining some greater spiritual good

But the most conspicuous mark of heavenly and wonderful truth
in the life of Mary Magdalen appears from her enjoyment of so
many contemplations, ecstasies, and excesses of love and her performance of so many charitable actions for which she was always
ready, and which were so easy to her. Her contemplative method
causes us immediately to liken her to the Magdalen of the Divine
Master, who, finding her delight in sitting at His sacred feet, was
leaving to her sister all the care of earthly things. The activity,
the solicitude, the affection with which our Saint lent herself to all
works of charity convince us likewise that she, in choosing the best
part, neglected in no way to imitate in some manner the busying of
Martha for the social conveniences of human life. For, besides the
spiritual charities of consoling the afflicted and sad ones, encouraging
the tempted and the faint-hearted, there was no work done in the monastery, to which, as far as obedience permitted her, she did not put her
hand. She wanted to partake of all the labors of either veiled or lay
sisters. The sisters endeavored to hide their needs from her, as they
knew it was impossible for her to abstain from coming in some manner
to their relief, at the cost of any sacrifice. Besides the offices she filled
in the Order, frequently she would go to the kitchen to help in the
laborious duties of the cooks—now carrying wood, now drawing water,
now cleaning and putting away the kitchen utensils and crockery;
sometimes waiting on the table, sweeping the cells, washing, making
bread and carrying it to the oven, or doing other similar work, to which
not by obedience, but by charity alone she was drawn Thus voluntarily helping a lay-sister for six years to bake, she arose before the
usual time, heated the water, and commenced to work at the flour In
carrying the bread to the oven upon a board, she would go as quickly as
possible, so that the greatest share of the work would be hers For the

washing of the community, she arose before the lay-sisters, filled the cauldrons with water, gathered the wood, built the fire, and commenced to wash, so that when the others appeared, she had already finished a great deal of work. She would sometimes stay washing linens for five or six hours in the night, that she might not be seen so assiduously at work in the day-time, and that she might during the day perform other labors, according to her various duties. Whilst she was mistress of novices, she sent them through the monastery to look after soiled linens; and having gotten them, she washed them in the night-time, the more to lessen the work of others. Suffice it to say that by reason of this constant occupation at washing, a bone of her right hand became dislocated. O God! what a cause for wonder, shame, and confusion for us to see a noble young lady, delicate, innocent, who overcoming her own weak constitution, is willing to lay down her very life for the love of her neighbors. If any lay-sister out of dutiful respect refused to be assisted in her work by Magdalen, the latter would beg her in such a pressing manner that she was forced to let her help her. "Deprive me not, sister" (the Saint would say), "of the merit of this work; let me do it; thou shalt do something else for me. It is better that we should labor in doing work one for the other, than that one should work for herself alone; as in working for one's self there is self-love, and in working for others there is charity."

When by reason of some occupation she could not be present to work with the lay-sisters, if any spare time was left her, she would immediately go to their cells to sweep and to make their beds, saying afterwards: "I wish those poor sisters, after they have done their work, to have rest." It being the duty of a lay-sister to call the nuns to matins, she asked her the favor (with the permission of the superioress) to attend to this alternately with her, one week each. She having obtained permission, and having attended to it for some time, the lay-sister took sick, and Mary Magdalen continued alone for fifteen years to call up the nuns every night for matins. When the needs of the monastery required something to be done which few knew how to do, she herself tried with the greatest care to learn how to do it, in order to help those who were doing it, and that the monastery might not be deprived of any assistance she could possibly give it, as every Religious is bound to do. She was wont to say that she looked upon that day as lost in which she had not done some act of charity towards her neighbor. But, in truth, not one such loss can be counted during her whole life. The occasions for being charitable in the community life are most frequent, and Mary Magdalen, far from passing them by, hunted them up with great diligence, and she wanted to embrace them all. Sometimes, though very tired from having done some hard work, if occasion offered itself, without showing that she was tired, she seized it as if she were just then commencing her day's work, and being sometimes asked by some sister to take rest, or questioned as to how she could endure so much, she answered: "My body is like that of an ass— I suffer nothing;" or else: "This body of mine is like that of a little donkey, and must carry its load day and night, and it not be given any rest." At the same time, through humility, she said that she was good for nothing, that she knew not how to pray, and that in order that she might not become useless to the Order, she had to occupy herself about these exterior exercises. But the fact was that she exerted herself so indefatigably in behalf of her neighbor, not so much on account of her special virtue, as in order to fulfill the Rule given her by her Divine Spouse, in which He commanded her to thirst, as the deer for water, after the exercise of charity towards her neighbor at all times, without any greater consideration for the weakness and fatigue of her body than for the dust which is trampled upon

So did our heroine work, that the sisters bore testimony that her labors were equivalent to those of four lay-sisters. Because of this, there being no necessity which she did not run to satisfy, no sister whom she did not benefit, she was styled the Mother of Charity and the Charity of the Monastery. Hence, the nuns felt constant admiration for her, for they could not help regarding as a supernatural gift both this over-exertion of Magdalen, with her weak constitution and all her fasts and penances, and the perfect manner in which she attended to one office and the other, as if she were entirely contemplative or wholly active. In the exterior works they would see her always fixed in God, even so as to remain ecstatic some time, and in the interior acts she was never forgetful of the needs of her neighbor, nay, many times it happened, especially when she had charge of the novices, that during the ecstasy itself she performed works of charity, and told others to do what she herself could not then do. As during the days of great solemnities she would generally be rapt in ecstasy, she, in the care and prudence of her charity, anticipated those days, giving orders to the teacher or the senior of the novices for the performance of those works of charity that she herself had been accustomed to perform for the novices, or the sick sisters, or others in need. When that hour came, though she might be in the height of her ecstasy, she reminded them of what she had ordered, and requested its being done. But the manner, the intensity, the fervor of her attendance upon the sick, carried her to such excesses that they seem almost incredible If one of the sisters became sick, she tried to be the first one to visit her, offering her services. According to the gravity of the illness and the disposition of the sick, day and night Mary Magdalen made and repeated her visits. She also studied to anticipate the needs of others, and then she informed the superioress or the officer that these might be provided for, as opportunity permitted She compassionated so much the pains of corporal sickness in anybody, that she prayed to God rather to send them to herself. Several times she was heard to say to some patient: "I wish I could steal these pains from thee" And the patient answering her with the like charity that she would not wish her to suffer them in the least, Mary Magdalen replied : "My constitution is more robust than thine, and I would not feel them so much " With those who on account of sickness felt a dislike for food, she employed all the art that a tender mother employs with her child when it refuses to eat. If there was any sister who had by order of the physicians to take medicine at inconvenient hours of the night, requiring the nurse, Mary Magdalen offered herself for this office, in order to save trouble to others, and to make her act more sincere and acceptable.

Knowing that one was short or in need of something, she deprived herself of it, if she had it, or procured it elsewhere. This she did especially when some of the sisters were convalescent in the infirmary, so that they would not need to be too solicitous for themselves, to the detriment both of their bodies and of their souls. The least thing that might be of some benefit to the sick did not escape her attention. Sometimes, having scarcely come out of a rapture, she would be seen running to the bedside of some sick nun, as if that were her only thought, and as if in atonement for having detained a little. Such was the satisfaction of her heart in doing these things, that she used to say there was no office in Religion she wished so much as that of nurse, and at the mere thought of it she rejoiced immensely. Sometimes she talked about what she would do for the sick, and seeing herself incapacitated from doing it by her other offices, she felt ineffable grief thereat, without losing a moment in exerting herself in every way she could. This charity of hers was unalterably the same for all, the same in all circumstances, always disinterested and always practiced simply for the love of God. Nothing did she wish but the glory of God, the temporal and eternal happiness of her neighbors; seeing in these but brothers and sisters, all children of the same Father, all belonging to the same family, all redeemed from perdition by the same Redeemer, all called to the same everlasting beatitude. She saw the image of the Divine Creator clearly imprinted on the forehead of the rich as well as of the poor, of the superior as well as of the subject, of the learned as well as of the ignorant. No matter how faulty or even loaded with sins one might be, the noble and generous sentiment of Magdalen for such did not diminish. In serving her neighbor she thought that she was serving God Himself; and her nuns in particular she regarded as daughters of the Eternal Father, as Brides of the Word, as temples of the Holy Ghost, or as sisters of the Angels, or else she considered the love with which God had loved and was still loving them, and in this consideration she enkindled within herself such a fire of charity that she said. " I would undertake to bear anything for my neighbor, and especially to obtain rest and consolation for a soul ; as a restless heart gives not true rest to God in itself, and I wish for nothing except to give to God His own creatures " These same reflections she suggested to her nuns, saying to them " You ought to consider yourselves unworthy, and regard it as a great favor, to serve souls that are the tabernacles of the Holy Ghost "

We have already seen that she did not neglect the least opportunity of leading her subjects to practices of charity. When her parents sent anything which she deemed of some use to the sick or the convalescent, with the permission of the superioress, she brought it to them, but as the property of the Religion, for in her modesty she did not wish to appear as if making a present, that the sisters might not have to consider themselves doubly obliged to her. By the intensity of her love for this exercise of serving the sick, once she said that, though she was perfectly satisfied with the state in which God had placed her, yet she would have regarded it as the greatest grace if God had wanted her to be a servant in a hospital "I would like," she said, "to render there to the sick all service possible, as I see that I do not know how to draw souls to the knowledge

of the love of God, neither do I deserve to lead them to it, which is
what would mostly please me.   But if I were employed in a hospital, at
least I would serve their bodies "

Besides the general services and the charity thus far related, she
took upon herself the office of assisting particularly some sick sisters,
among whom were two lay-sisters, one named Sister Charity and the other
Sister Mattea   The first of these was blind and affected with phthisis.
For the whole year during which she kept her bed, Mary Magdalen
waited on her with tireless attention, changing her clothing and assisting
her in all her necessities, which are so frequent and hard to satisfy in an
unhappy blind and sick person   On being asked by the superioress
why she was so solicitous for this lay-sister, she answered that Jesus had
shown Himself to her as poor, and had told her that if she wanted to do
a thing pleasing to Him, she should serve Him in the person of that sick
Bride of His.   The other lay-sister, Sister Mattea, had a sore on her
right limb, from which issued vermin and corruption with such a stench
that it was necessary to keep her in a room apart from the rest.   Mary
Magdalen attended to this sore, applying the remedies to it and cleaning
it from the vermin and corruption and the like, which is far from pleasing
to the human stomach.   But all this was not sufficient to satisfy the
ardent charity of our Saint, as she went so far that, through humility and
for her greater mortification, several times she·put her lips to the sore,
as if to draw the disease all to herself   This, with tears of tenderness
and confusion, was related by the patient herself to the mother prioress,
Sister Vangelista del Giocondo   With Sisters Barbara Bassi and Benigna
Orlandini, Mary Magdalen acted likewise ; as, after the most loving care
bestowed upon them to relieve them of their sickness, she also licked
their limbs which were affected by contagious and offensive diseases, the
heroism of which action was followed by the miraculous cure of both
these sisters.

During the gravity of the disease, when the patient was in danger
of her life, Mary Magdalen redoubled her care.   If necessary, she watched
several consecutive nights at the bedside of the sick, without taking the
least rest ; and if, being overtired, she took a little rest, it was on a chair,
not on the straw-bed   By the bedside of one of the above-mentioned
lay-sisters, she stood watching continuously for ten consecutive days and
nights, and fifteen by the bedside of the other

But it is impossible to tell how ardent her charity became on the
approach of the last moment of some sister   It is not necessary to
repeat that the chief aim of her charity always was the glory of God
and the salvation of souls ; so that the arguments most calculated to
strengthen and sanctify the spirit were brought forward by her at all
times and with all persons, more than those which had only reference to
this material life.   Whilst at the bedside of a dying person, she deemed
it a grievous sin to lose a single minute.   The importance of the passage
from time to eternity, the life of a God immolated for all the souls and
for each of them in particular, the severity of a judgment without appeal,
were subjects which left not Mary Magdalen enough strength to do all
she wished to do in behalf of the agonizing ones.   She wanted always
to be present at the passing away of the sisters of her monastery.   And,

being present, now she read the *Recommendation of the Soul*, now the *Passio*, or the psalms or other devout prayers, now she spoke about God and induced the dying nun to make acts of contrition, of love, of hope, of faith, and especially of resignation to the Divine Will, making a virtuous sacrifice of what necessarily must return to the nullity of its origin. In so doing, it happened that while alleviating as far as possible the horrible but inevitable anguish consequent on the separation of the soul from the body, her charity was so efficacious that the agonizing one with these consolations expired, not sadly but with calm trust in the arms of the Lord; and her companions were so edified by her death that every one of them wished to have Mother Mary Magdalen to assist at their last hours, deeming that blessed were those who expired in her arms. Even to the corpse of a deceased she showed those regards that her highly merciful heart knew how to suggest to her. She did not leave it until it was buried, and, in the meantime, she prayed to God for that soul in the most fervent manner; and whilst doing that, being nearly always rapt in ecstasy, she came to know, supernaturally, the state of the souls for whom she was interceding; and, seeing them in purgatory, besides the prayers, the fasts, the disciplines, and other penances she practiced for them, she offered herself to God, and asked of Him that she might suffer for them in her body as many torments as would be equivalent to the sufferings they were to undergo. This God several times granted to her, so that, in consequence of it, for many days she endured such pains in her limbs as if they had been lacerated by dogs or bitten by serpents. Afterwards she was consoled by the sight of those same souls that, thanks to these satisfactory sufferings of hers, were passing joyfully and happily to the possession of the everlasting good.

This great charity of our Saint was accompanied by, or rather took strength chiefly from the high opinion and esteem that she entertained of all, as she always thought more of the spirit than of the flesh, and all reasoning creatures she called by the name of *souls*. Of everyone she was wont to speak with reverence and affection, and never did the least word that might be offensive to her neighbor escape her lips, and, save the corrections she was obliged to make with her subjects whilst in office, she always excused the faults and failings of others, and advised that as little as possible should be said of them, "because" (she used to say) "as glass which is handled without care is easily broken, so, also, our neighbor, being too much on our lips, is easily offended." When called to the parlor grates to see some outsiders, she would go and remain there with so much modesty and reverence, and show so much respect for everyone, that they would part from her very much edified and happy. The domestic intercourse with her nuns was a continuous exercise of charity and humility. The spiritually important titles by which she called them showed in what esteem she held them, and with what dignity she deemed their souls clothed as Brides-elect of Jesus. She considered herself unworthy to dwell with them, and she was frequently seen to kiss the ground on which they had stood, and to honor them in many other respectful ways, as we shall see in speaking of her humility in particular.

Burning exceedingly with divine love, now she refreshed her breast
with cool water, and now she ran through the monastery,
Crucifix in hand (page 162).

It is useless to say that the spirit of contention, opposition, and domineering was not in her at all; and if, on finding fault with any of her disciples, she was answered with some indocility, she deferred the making of the correction until a more suitable time, cutting off for the present every cause of opposition. Thus envy, rancor, and the like fatal enemies of human tranquillity were wholly unknown to the heart of Mary Magdalen. When she met a nun or a lay-sister in the monastery, she was the first to salute her with a modest and ingenuously cheerful countenance. As to the superiors and the seniors, she always met them with that demeanor that one would wish to see in a novice on the first day of her entering Religion. She called prelates and priests God's *christs*, looking upon them as the representatives of God Himself, and she could not endure that the sisters should speak of them, even when the least occasion was given, with levity or disrespect She always remained on her knees before them until they ordered her to arise. But these were marks of exterior respect, as to the esteem and love of her heart, they embraced in like manner the highest and the humblest of them Finally, we must remark that many a time she postponed her spiritual exercises, most sweet though they were on account of the special favors of Heaven, in order to assist her neighbor in his needs, saying that she most cheerfully left God for God, viz, that as no one could see God in this mortal life, love for Him can best be shown by charity towards our brethren, so that the highest excesses of divine love in the Saints were rather consequences or rewards of perfect fraternal charity

To conclude so important a subject, let us beware of following those who are pleased to consider mankind like a herd of shrewd or foolish beasts, born only to feed, beget, move about, and return into dust. Let us rather learn and practice the maxim of fraternal charity—pure, universal, without distinction of persons—so clearly and strictly commanded us, even from the day when, as the Apostle says, the benignity and charity of our Lord and Saviour appeared, and afterwards practiced after this Divine Model by persons like ourselves, who, sanctifying their own lives, deserved so well of society. Let us render to each other the justice of love, esteem, and beneficence, so that prayer, fasting, the Church, and all the practices of Religion may not become illusory, because not corresponding to the spirit from which they are supposed to proceed. As doing good calls for a return of the same, it wonderfully promotes the happiness of the human family, and brings to our conscience the sweetest testimony of having properly seconded the noblest sentiment of man Though through somebody's wickedness our good deeds may not be well known, and our virtue may be denied its credit and value, yet let us not depart, because of this, from the practice of , fraternal charity , and let this be our consolation, that it is well-known

" To the eyes of Him Who sees everything "

CHAPTER XXXII.

OF THE ESTEEM AND LOVE SHE ENTERTAINED FOR THE RELIGIOUS STATE, AND PARTICULARLY FOR HER OWN MONASTERY.

O make known what esteem and love Mary Magdalen bore to the Religious state, it suffices to quote what she very often said to the novices, the young girls, and all the nuns, the better to make them understand the excellence, the value, and the advantages of this state. She was wont to call the Religion (Religious Life) a paradise on earth, a paradise of delights, the garden of God; and, comparing it to the Heavenly Fatherland, she would point out how there is in the Religion that order which exists between God and the angels in heaven. Very beautiful and profitable were the things she understood about it in an ecstasy, and the similitudes by which God condescended to enlighten her. Once it seemed to her as if she saw the Religious state under the figure of a most beautiful virgin, mysteriously clothed, with various instruments in her hands, from which she understood how the Religion perfects and adorns the souls dedicated to it. Another time it appeared to her under the figure of a fountain and streams of various liquors, and she understood by this the spiritual tastes that God communicates to the true Religious. She also saw it under the figure of various crossways, and she understood by that how the Religious Life is a short road by which to reach heaven. She also saw it under the form of other symbols, which would take too long to enumerate.

Both in her ecstasies and out of them, she spoke of the Religion with expressions of the highest sublimity and deepest gratitude. After baptism, she deemed the grace of having been called by God to the life of the cloister as the greatest of all, regarding a religious vocation as the most sublime privilege God can confer upon a soul after having washed her in the baptismal waters. She was often heard to say that she would not have changed her condition for that of any king or monarch in the world, and that she did not even envy the angels of heaven, as the Religious state professes to imitate the Incarnate Word by the observance of the three vows, which the angels cannot do. She added that even if she were to be used as the dish-cloth of the monastery, she would regard it as a greater favor than the possession of any worldly greatness whatever, and she would always have considered herself unworthy even of that office. Hence she often used as an ejaculatory prayer these words of the prophet

David "*I have chosen to be an abject in the house of my God, rather than to dwell in the tabernacles of sinners*" (Ps. lxxxiii, 11). Hence, whenever any person embraced the Religious state, she felt very great joy thereat, especially if such a person entered an order of strict observance. The least order of the Religion she held in high esteem, regarding it as written and ordered by the Holy Ghost, and she made much of all, even the most simple things of Religion, and would not permit them to be criticised in the least in her presence, nor would she allow any levity or scurrility in those whom the religious habit covered. A novice wondering how the nuns of said monastery could endure its fatigues whilst being nourished with coarse and unwholesome food, thus spoke the Saint. "These meals are sanctified by the Religion, and God places in them a virtue by which they nourish us as though they were of the best food; and when God wants otherwise, He will provide," as the monastery was so poor that it could not then furnish the community better food. If any nun became sick, or grew so tired as to be unable to endure some labor prescribed by the monastery, she would suggest to her to beware of blaming for it the mode of life of the Religion, but rather to say. "I, on account of my sins, deserve not to be able to labor in the Religion," thus accepting from the hands of God with equanimity of sentiment both good and hard living. Likewise she could not endure that the sisters in attending to the work of the community would show any affected tiredness, and if she happened to notice it in any of her subjects, she addressed her as follows. "Dost thou think Religion must be obliged to thee, because thou didst work for it? I tell thee that thou art obliged to Religion that makes use of thee, and the more this costs thee, the more thou shouldst rejoice" From this great esteem for the Religious state proceeded in her a very particular love for her monastery, hence she loved it as a dear mother, and, many a time speaking about it, was by her love for it carried into ecstasy. Often she repeated: "My Religion!" and being one day asked by a novice why she called it "hers," she answered: "Because God made me a present of it, and wants me to keep it; therefore I wish it to appear beautiful and immaculate in the sight of God." Every morning in her prayers she offered her monastery to the Blessed Virgin, begging her to keep it as she kept the humanity of the Incarnate Word and her own purity. Sometimes she showed her predilection even for the cracked walls of the monastery, turning to them with these words: "Though the walls of these cells are half ruined, oh! how good and dear they are, for they keep us separated from the world and prevent us from seeing anything which might give us an occasion for distracting our attention from God" She tried to impress as much as she could in the hearts of the nuns the greatest esteem for the Religious state, and the most loyal affection for their monastery· "Daughters," she often said to her subjects, "love the Religion as a dear mother" At which repetition one day a novice, being almost annoyed, asked her the reason The Saint thus manifested it to her "Because it is of no use to possess a precious gem and not to know its value, for, not knowing this, one does not esteem nor love it," signifying that such exhortation tended to make them know and esteem the benefit they had received by having been called and admitted to the

Religion. To this end she sometimes reasoned as follows. "If we would intimately penetrate the dignity of our soul by the most close union it has contracted with the Blessed God by means of the three solemn vows,—as a little country shepherdess, who, having been raised by a very powerful king to the royal dignity, dislikes anyone reminding her of her former state, so we should despise permitting ourselves by our own thoughts to be drawn to the consideration of worldly things, and knowing that we have been made Brides of the King of the universe, to satisfy our craving for things not earthly nor corruptible, we should raise ourselves with holy pride to the contemplation of the everlasting riches of heaven" She also said to her novices· "As you are called to the Religion, you are called to serve God, to serve Whom is to reign, and to take part now on earth in what you will have to do forever in heaven, viz., to praise and bless Him." Teaching them the manner of loving the Religion, she told them that *this is done* when one obeys and lovingly fulfills everything that the Religion orders in the Rules and Constitutions, and good care is taken of everything.

As to the vows of the Religion, she held them as divine things, as privileges and benefits most singular, which the Divine Goodness grants to dearest souls as a treasure and a prize of paradise, and she loved them as the bonds of union of the souls with God, as roads to God, as glories of God   With these sentiments she spoke of them on every occasion, taking very great delight in seeing herself bound by them, and stimulating her companions to do the same on their part, none of them ceasing to thank the benignity of the Sovereign God for the special grace of the Religious vocation. Every day, between herself and God, she renewed her vows. She once had in an ecstasy this beautiful intelligence about this renewal, which she thus expressed· "Every time that the promises made to God are renewed, a renewal of union with God takes place, and the beloved soul acquires more or less union according to the state of perfection she finds herself in, and the charity she possesses. This renewal of the vows made interiorly by the soul pleases the Most Holy Trinity, as the renewal of the interior complacency the soul experiences in herself and about herself by this offering made to God, which always renews the delight of the first offering with a new complacency and a new consolation. It pleases Mary as much as if she renewed the vow of purity. It gives glory to the angels, as they see the fulfillment of those inspirations which we receive from them. It exalts the Saints, as they see their Creator followed in their own footsteps. It gives joy to the Choir of the Virgins, who sing anew the new canticle, seeing that perfection increasing which they practiced with so much love, and their glory is also increased, as every time this renewal takes place, their feast, so to say, is being celebrated. The soul acquires very great fruit, as grace is increased in her, and the promises made are strengthened, a new peace is born in her, and a new union, and the fruit of that peace appears in her conversation and works   Oh! of what dignity are these vows and promises made to God in the holy profession, when their renewal produces so many worthy fruits! Hence we should not wonder that those who have light about this O World of the Religion of Thy Most Holy Name | she meant the Society of Jesus , celebrate said renewal with so great a solemnity and feast. If the people of the world make so much of their birthday, or the day when they are invested with some dignity, how much more should we celebrate the day on which we united ourselves to God by so close a tie (which can never be untied) with feast and spiritual joy!" If this intelligence (though perhaps the result of the enthusiasm of her heart more than of the heavenly revelation which it closely resembles) is a valid evidence of the esteem and love which she entertained for the Religious vows, let us now see the corresponding facts, that is, the perfection with which she knew how to keep these three solemn promises.

CHAPTER XXXIII.

OF HER OBEDIENCE.

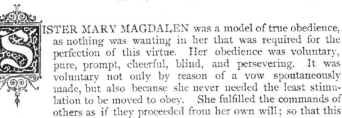

ISTER MARY MAGDALEN was a model of true obedience, as nothing was wanting in her that was required for the perfection of this virtue. Her obedience was voluntary, pure, prompt, cheerful, blind, and persevering. It was voluntary not only by reason of a vow spontaneously made, but also because she never needed the least stimulation to be moved to obey. She fulfilled the commands of others as if they proceeded from her own will; so that this very facility with which she obeyed was a source of grief to her, as she feared she would earn no merit for it. Hence she tried at least to conceal her natural tendencies, pretending to enjoy the hardest and most tedious labors, and, on the contrary, to be annoyed at those which pleased her; so that the latter being forbidden her and the former demanded of her, as often happened, she might have the opportunity of feeling the weight of obedience. This she was wont to call a "hidden capital," because hidden to the eyes of creatures and known only to the eyes of God. Moreover, it seemed so little to her to be subject to the superiors, that she would place herself under her companions, and equals, and even inferiors. Among her companions she selected one especially, Sister Maria Pacifica del Tovaglia, to whom she so submitted herself that she would ask permission of her for nearly all her actions, though necessary and commanded by the Order. This she practiced because she deemed it so acceptable to God to act for obedience' sake, that she did not wish to do the least thing without actually sacrificing it to God by means of this virtue. Hence, when she could not have the above companion, she practiced the same submission to anyone present, and sometimes to her very novices, as if asking their approval of her work. When working in the kitchen with the lay-sisters, she was humble and resigned to obey them no less than she would teachers and superiors. She was likewise always very obedient and of one mind with those she had as companions in the performance of certain duties, never permitting herself to contradict them in the least. She called that day a lost one when she did not break her own will or submit it to someone by obedience to this end. She thought it was better to live in the Order than in solitude; and she used to say, that though the state of solitude is one of great perfection, nevertheless she would always have preferred to live in the Order, as there is always an opportunity to give death to one's self, by means of the abnegation of one's will through the perfect practice of obedience

If pure obedience is that which makes one act without regard to any earthly interest, human respect, or self-love, but solely to please God, such undoubtedly was Mary Magdalen's obedience. Whilst she concealed from the eyes of creatures the hardships of obedience, that the most arduous things might be imposed on her, it is clearly seen that in obeying she sought nothing but to please God, to whom alone her sufferings were known, that her obedience might be truly *pure* She was wont to say, for her own and others' instruction, that she never looked at the person who gave the order, and to her it made no difference if the superioresses were kind or rude, holy or faulty, because in all she always saw God Whom she obeyed. Hence she obeyed with full will and great delight, thinking she obeyed God, Whom she desired to please in all things ; and all the creatures who ordered her to do services, she deemed as God's vicars The manner of obedience, viz , to see God purely in the person commanding, she gave assurance to be the most efficacious means to profit in religious perfection and in all the holy virtues ; hence, in the fervor of her devotion speaking to the novices, she promised that the soul that was convinced that the superioress stands in the place of God, and whatever she ordered and said was ordered and said by God through her lips, had obtained from God the following five particular graces· "1st, that, through her faith, God would communicate Himself more to that superior and that subject having such conviction ; 2d, that all things imposed by obedience would be equally acceptable, both the pleasant and the unpleasant ones; 3d, that the heart of that subject would always enjoy peace and tranquillity, and feel a contentment and great interior sweetness; 4th, that such a subject would be more apt to help the Holy Church by prayer, as Jesus hears the prayers of the obedient, and the most obedient will be granted everything they ask ; 5th, that of these souls God makes a crown to Himself, because as the crown manifests the greatness of a king, so they honor and glorify God in all their works " Free in her obedience from every shadow of self-love, not only was she more willing to do the will of others than her own, but she was always ready to postpone every work of spiritual satisfaction in favor of obedience ; because, she was wont to say, when the superiors forbid austerities, penances, and prayers, it is self-love not to want to obey. On account of pure obedience, she esteemed humble and lowly things imposed by others more than those of great perfection done by one's own will.

Her obedience was also prompt and cheerful. No sooner did she come to know the will of her superiors than she undertook, without the least delay or reply, to fulfill it, leaving unfinished any other thing she might then have been doing. Neither were words of command required with her; but the least hint was sufficient, nay, as far as possible, she tried to guess and foresee the very wish of her superioresses, in order to anticipate its fulfillment Of this her mistresses and the prioresses of those days several times rendered testimony. Not only was she never seen sad or unwilling in obeying, even when excessively tired, but she obeyed with cheerful countenance and spirit, as if the things required of her would be to her greatest liking, and it happened, moreover, that if she found herself pressed by some internal trouble or temptation when anything was commanded her, she was resigned, as if she had received a marked favor from Heaven   Her promptness in obeying was such that, whilst her soul was raised to the most sublime ecstasy, at the voice of her superioress she either immediately came out of it, returning to her senses, or, still ecstatic, fulfilled what had been commanded her. Sister Vangelista del Giocondo, who nearly all the time presided at her direction, noticed several times both the one and the other.   When, in order to obey, she came out of the rapture, as soon as she had done the work commanded she returned to it as before; and the nuns also noticed that, whilst she was in ecstasy, most of the times she neither heard nor understood any other voice than that of the superioress.   The two following cases are singularly remarkable. One is this, that Alessandro de' Medici, Archbishop of Florence, afterwards (as we have seen) Sovereign Pontiff with the name of Leo XI, hearing that she had already passed fifteen days, eating but thrice during all that time, commanded her that she should never let twenty-four hours pass without taking some food. After this, during her long ecstasies, it would happen that when this time was nearing its end without her having eaten, she would come to herself, take something, and then return to her ecstasy.   The other case was the ecstasy in which she remained during Holy Thursday and Good Friday of the year 1592, participating in the Passion of Christ, when, on the approach of the twenty-fourth hour of her fast, turning to her Divine Spouse, she thus said to Him. "O Word, Thou shortenest my time by obedience!" And a little afterwards, returning to her senses, she took some bread and water.   Another case was when the confessor of the monastery, knowing that whilst ecstatic she had walked around on the cornice of the choir without any support, ordered her that in future, whenever she wanted to go there she should take the ladder   Hence, being one day carried out of her senses by the burning desire of going to that Crucifix, as soon as she had reached the choir, raising her eyes to that devout image, she remembered the obedience, and said: "One must go by the instrument;" and, thus ecstatic, she went for a ladder, by which she ascended the said cornice.

The obedience of Mary Magdalen was not exterior and apparent only, but interior and from her heart, that is, practiced in uniformity of will with the person commanding   This appears not only from the promptitude with which she obeyed, but also from her not manifesting any opposition to or displeasure at anything which was assigned for her to do.   Though greatly anxious to suffer, she did not cease praying to God that she might take the same food other sisters did, when after the seven years she had passed on bread and water, she was ordered by obedience, as has been said, to pray to the Lord to grant her this grace, which she afterwards obtained.   When, being sick or convalescent, some delicate food or other things were ordered her to strengthen her body, although in the beginning she seemed unwilling, no sooner was it imposed on her to do it by obedience than, without saying a word, divested of all self ... she could fully and from her inmost heart submit to the will of it ... as to that of God, saying.

"*Benedictus Deus.*" Never did she advance an argument to change the will of the superiors, to which she always conformed herself, deeming it always profitable to her soul

Hence the obedience of Mary Magdalen had also the other quality so much appreciated by the masters of spiritual life, viz., to be blind, that is, that not only should one agree with the will of the superior in doing a thing commanded, but also with his judgment, reputing it right and good, making no opposition to it, nor passing judgment contrary to the same [1] This our Saint practiced with sovereign perfection, as she herself manifested when instructing her disciples She was wont to say to them that one could not obey perfectly without entirely conforming his own judgment to that of the superior, and that it did not seem to her as if she obeyed, though she fulfilled a command, unless she had previously conformed her understanding to it Therefore, when anything was commanded of her which was contrary to her inclinations, she tried her best to invest herself with the feeling and judgment of the superioress, as much as possible, by judging that what was ordered of her was the best for herself without investigating the motive, the end, or the intention ; in a word, without as much as thinking over it, that no particle of her own judgment would be found therein. Of this submitting her own judgment to others, she gave wonderful instances, especially in regard to the things God ordered her in her ecstasies, which, though she heard so distinctly in a superhuman manner, she never practiced without the consent of the superioress or the spiritual father; and, if they made any opposition, the humble virgin gave up her own judgment to follow that of those persons who were for her the safest guide to eternal truth. She totally submitted to the superiors when they imposed on her to conform herself to the common food and habit At the same time, she doubted not but that it was the will of God that she should live on bread and water only, and go barefoot, and dressed in the humblest tunic, as it was revealed to her in the ecstasy, and as afterwards God Himself, by the miracle which we related in Chapter XII, convinced the superiors of what His beloved Bride had been supernaturally enjoined to do. The miracle would not have been sufficient unless the superiors had manifested their own condescension, so much did she prize the *visible direction* to which God wants the human creature to submit Hence, at the end of her life, she felt she had reason to be pleased with it, saying there was nothing of all that had happened her during life which gave her more peace than the certainty she felt of having done nothing of her own choice, but of having been guided in everything by the will and judgment of her superiors. In this exercise she had attained to such perfection that her obedience rather than *blind* might be called *dead*, as her reasoning faculty, when it was a question of obedience, was as if extinct This was the grace she so much wished for, and so frequently asked during her ecstasies, both for herself and for *religious souls*, viz , to wish for nothing, to understand nothing, but to allow herself, as dead, to be led by the hands of others In this state, God often showed her to herself. Mary Magdalen began to practice her religious

---

[1] Unless, of course, it would be evidently wrong *Note of the Translator*

obedience with such perfection when, on the very day she put on the monastic habit, she resigned herself as dead into the hands of the prioress. It being extremely difficult to judge the degree of perfection she had reached in this by constant practice during her entire life, God manifested it by a very wonderful action He permitted to the Saint when she was at her last moment; and it was that, being just about to breathe her last, she was commanded that by obedience she should wait until the father confessor had said Mass and given Communion to the nuns; at which, regaining her lost speech and acquiring new strength, she satisfied the desire of others in spite of the irresistible force of death which faced her.

CHAPTER XXXIV.

OF HER CHASTITY AND THE EXTERIOR EFFICACY OF THIS VIRTUE IN HER.

HE fact of Mary Magdalen's having consecrated forever to God her virginity from her childhood, and her having declared shortly before her death that she knew not what it was that stained chastity, are two things which imply such and so great a perfection that our mind would vainly try to find any traces thereof in the natural forces of the human creature. There is nothing in the order of nature which can bear comparison with the stainless purity of this Saint. The whiteness of the purest snow, that of the purest lilies, the clearness of the most limpid waters, the brightness of the clearest sky, are vile comparisons for the purity of Mary Magdalen. When her parents wanted to make an earthly bride of her, she, faithful to her first intention, resisted them with so strong and constant a will that she concluded to become a nun without delay, in order to remove all worldly obstacles. The very strong temptations against purity which she endured from the evil one during the first two years of her probation, viz., from the year 1585 to the year 1587, served but to confirm her in her resolution, so that they became to her rather a source of merit and a crown. At the age of forty-two, that being the end of her life, with great complacency she could address her Divine Bridegroom in these words: "Thou knowest well, O my Lord, that my heart has never wished anything but Thee." And repeating these words several times to solace her spirit in the fierceness of the malady, when she saw all the sisters present, she thanked God also with great joy because she was dying without knowing, or ever having known, what actions against chastity were or how chastity could be lost. She had already told a sister who was her confidant that she never knew what the devil wanted of her during the impure temptations, and that she had fought with an entirely unknown enemy. She so much abhorred everything impure that she had cast away her enemy before the temptation had actually assailed her; and, though she felt the first attack, yet, her mind and will being wholly free from every earthly affection and fully occupied with God, she could not even apprehend the aim of the temptations. Even from these, after a two years' struggle, she was delivered by the Blessed Virgin, who miraculously covered her with a white veil, so that, like St. Thomas

Aquinas, by a most special privilege, she was not again tempted during her lifetime by the least thought or suggestion contrary to purity, but had become in regard to this like a statue

So great a purity endowed even her exterior with something super-human. Her looks, her gestures were so graceful, grave, modest, benign that they caused good and chaste thoughts in those who looked at her. Her very body when she was still living exhaled such an odor (called by the nuns *odor of purity*) that it greatly excited affection for holy purity. The same nuns attested that during the last three years that Mary Magdalen was sick in her cell, which, by its disadvantageous situation and the continuous exhalations of a diseased body, should have become a source of disgusting and nauseating smell, nevertheless, was always full of that good odor which constantly came out of her limbs and also diffused itself to her habit and the bed-covers. Her words were so powerful to inspire purity that they never fell in vain upon the souls of those who heard them. During her ecstasies, she was given very high ideas of this virtue, and she manifested them in the most wonderful and winning ways, as we shall see in her Works, in Part Second.

She was also wont to manifest with feelings of evident delight that the Lord had granted her from her most tender years a particular love and wish for purity, and that she wished to attain as much purity as one can have in this life, and that to increase this virtue in herself she would endure any pain. Through love of this virtue she held the virgins in great honor and reverence, and treated the girls especially with excessive marks of respect, so much so that one of them who had come on trial to the monastery suspected that all the ceremonies of Sister Mary Magdalen might not be sincere, but she finally felt much amazed and thankful when she knew that the Saint intended thereby to honor virginity. Thus the more of sweet delight the conversing with such persons caused her, the more disagreeable and annoying it was to her to treat with persons settled in the world. She said openly that she felt more love and sympathy for the unmarried than for the married ones, though the latter might be more upright and virtuous in ful-filling their duties. But notwithstanding these natural tendencies to purity, and the most singular privileges with which God endowed her, Mary Magdalen, deeming herself a person of easy capture and exposed to the gravest dangers, used to guard herself with such austerity of man-ners, greater than which could not have been practiced by the most wicked sinner, who, placing herself at the feet of Christ, begins with the greatest fervor to enter the path of justice. To throw herself naked among thorns, like Saint Benedict, is such an act that it suffices of itself to show the force of her zeal for the preservation of holy purity. To protect this virtue she employed as the most efficacious means the fre-quenting of the Eucharistic Sacrament, prayer, devotion to the Mother of Virgins, abstinence from even the lawful pleasures, fasting, and, above all, fleeing from all occasions of seeing, hearing, or treating of things which might furnish the least incentive to impurity. Hence, regarding the cloistered life as the greatest boon, often transported by a live and grateful enthusiasm, she blessed and kissed with great warmth the walls of the monastery, and answered the nuns who sometimes asked her the

She fiercely scourges herself before the Crucifix (page 191).

motive for so doing: "Don't you think, sisters, that I have great reason for doing so? These holy walls separate me from the wretched world, and render more safe the most esteemed treasure I possess on earth" (by which she meant her virginity) And sometimes she exclaimed with great feeling. "Oh! if the people of the world understood how great is the sweetness that in the blissful life is prepared for those who always remain virgins, they would run, like thirsty deer to the fountain, to immure themselves in the most austere Religions, so as to preserve their purity intact, for safer is the vineyard the more surrounded it is by thorny hedges" One day, while in ecstasy, she said that the Religious ought to be as distant with the lay people as the deer; for which Jesus would be much pleased Thus did she act very particularly; not that she would be rude and impolite in her dealing even with lay people, well knowing how to couple gravity with sweetness and religious modesty, but she was never familiar with any person outside the monastery, neither by conversing nor by writing, no matter of what condition or how virtuous such a person might be. Nothing short of an explicit order of obedience was required to bring her to the parlor; and, as often as she had to go there, she went against her will, so much so that on account of this she often could not restrain her tears, especially when she was called there by worldly people, who to the eyes of the true follower of Christ cannot be but objects of commiseration and sadness. She was wont to say that for the time she remained at the parlor grates she would have more willingly remained in the fire of purgatory ; as in those persons she could only see occasions of trouble, cares, distractions, temptations, and danger of offending God Whilst mistress of novices, if called to the parlor, she would say to them. "Novices, pray to God for me, as I am called to the grates," and expressed to them the wish that they might find some motive to soon recall her thence. On account of this so-openly-declared repugnance of Sister Mary Magdalen, the nuns had accustomed themselves not to tell her to go down to the parlor, except in cases of grave importance, relating to her those of less importance, that she might pray to God about them, and no more Frequently people asked for her to entrust to her their affairs. She also felt a repugnance at receiving letters, and never answered them unless compelled by obedience Ludovico Capponi, her relative, having recommended some of his affairs to her, and manifested in several ways his desire for a prompt answer, could not get it until the command of the father confessor intervened. As to her writing, it was short, simple, spiritual, without ceremonies or affected words Here, too, and for the same reason as the aforesaid, most of her letters were communicated to her in a general way by the superioress, who would likewise answer them. Thus the Saint in this also kept aloof from external communications; and, in so doing, she greatly satisfied her wishes, holding, as she did, that it was not becoming a Religious Bride of Jesus to have any dealings outside the monastery, or to write and receive letters, the reading of which recalls to the mind the things of the world.

Such a retirement from the world proceeded also from that sovereign purity of her heart by which, even in the monastery, she kept in solitude, and especially shunned every carnal affection. To this all her

companions were able to bear witness, and she said during the last days
of her life that she never felt the least attachment to any creature.   On
account of this love of purity, she would not allow others to show her
excessive kindness.   Hence, whilst yet a secular, noticing that her mother
was too much attached to her, and that on this account she opposed
her choosing the monastic state, Magdalen did all she possibly could
to detach her from herself   In Religion, if any of her novices became
too much attached to her, she dealt with her with such severity of
manners that the novice felt compelled either to give up or to spiritualize
her affection altogether.   Moreover, she never touched anyone, neither
did she permit others to touch her, and, outside of the excesses of the
love of God by which she was sometimes forced to take her companions
by the hand to invite them to love God, she abhorred even the simple
touch of the hand, face, and the like, which worldly politeness requires,
and which she always deemed unbecoming Religious persons.   During
her last illness, being unable to move herself, and, therefore, in need of
being occasionally moved by the sisters, she said and repeated to them
the following words, which also confirm how she was ignorant of anything which may actually contaminate chastity   "Sisters" (said she),
"if you think that to touch me in this way may be against purity, let
me alone, as I will gladly remain in this torment and permit the worms
to eat me up on this side."   So great was the love she bore the angelic
virtue!

Finally, she deemed as very useful to preserve the virginal purity
never to speak nor think of worldly and secular things, so that, except
in cases of charity, she did not want to know anything of the events
of the world   This method she had adopted for herself, she also wished
it employed likewise by her companions, to whom she often said   "Remember, sisters, that you are consecrated to God, and that you must not
care for others but for Him, and try to please Him alone "   In order to
lead them willingly to solitude, she would make them reflect that the
parlor is a cause of such distraction that a Religious could never leave
it without having afterwards to spend a great deal of time in removing
from her mind the images of things seen or heard, at least those in
regard to her own peace   Another time, enlightened not by experience
but by God, she said that the discourses of seculars often darken the
white lily of chastity; and she took great delight that in her monastery
there was a general abhorrence for the parlor and dealing with the
world.   Hence, whenever she saw a novice rejoicing at the announcement of some secular visit, she was wont to say to her·   "One can see,
sister, that thou hast not yet become entirely ours, as it is customary
with the nuns of Santa Maria degli Angeli to grow sad and not to rejoice
when they are called to the parlor grates."   If any other, subject to her,
would fall into discourses of espousals, marriages, parties, and the like,
she would not omit to correct her bluntly   Thus she tried to lead her
disciples and companions to that chastity (which she possessed in a
manner more angelical than human and which appeared so markedly in
the exterior of her person) by suggesting to them both by her example
and by her words the opportune means of successfully preserving a
virtue as precious as it is frail and delicate.

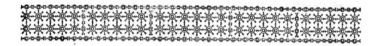

CHAPTER XXXV.

OF HER POVERTY AND THE ZEAL SHE FELT TO SEE IT PRACTICED IN HER MONASTERY.

UR Redeemer had just caressed some children when a rich Hebrew youth, moved by a certain fire of devotion, ran to Him, and, kneeling at His feet, thus asked Him: "*Master, what shall I do to possess eternal life?*" Jesus answered him: "*If thou wilt enter into life, keep the Commandments;*" and, hearing how he had kept them till then and yet wished to *know more*, added, in a loving tone: "*If thou wilt be perfect, go and sell all thou hast and give it to the poor, and then follow Me, and I will reward thee with a better treasure in heaven*" (Matth. xix, 16–21). These words hint at the generous act performed by the Apostles in leaving all earthly things to follow Christ, and at the act which for the same purpose is practiced by those who strengthen their relinquishment by a solemn vow of poverty. From these words it also appears that this vow may be called the compendium, the culminating point, the most sublime effort of human perfection. In truth, he who, to walk in the way of the Lord, abandons not only his substance, but every affection and wish for it, gives during life the most solemn and the most loyal proof of his love for God. Thus he who possesses nothing, and wishes for nothing, can be but wholly God's.

Mary Magdalen De-Pazzi protested to God every morning that she would exalt holy poverty on all occasions. Having continually before her eyes Jesus Christ, who was born poor, lived poor, and died naked on the cross, she loved poverty as a thing divine, and attained to such a degree of love for it that it was to her an unbearable torment to think that the Order provided for her above the strict necessaries; and, on the contrary, she greatly rejoiced when deprived of something necessary to her. Whilst the imperfect Religious are wont to complain of their superiors when their needs are not so promptly satisfied or in the manner they would wish, Mary Magdalen, on the contrary, never complained of anything, except that it seemed to her that the superioress had too much thought for her. For which (imagined by her humility rather than founded in truth), she grieved so much that she wept bitterly many a time. Because what was strictly necessary was not wanting to her, it seemed to her as if she did not keep the vow of poverty; hence she often complained, saying that after having professed poverty, she should have to die without knowing what poverty was; so that the superioresses, in order not to increase her grief, often abstained from manifesting their loving solicitude for her. Sometimes, being more inflamed with the love of this virtue, she addressed to Heaven these words: "O my God, why dost Thou urge me so much to be poor for Thee, seeing that it is not permitted me to go begging my bread from door to door, which would please me so much? Nay, among all the consolations I might experience during this life, this would be the greatest, viz., that Thou, O my Jesus, wouldst grant me the grace that I might die upon a cross as Thou didst die for me." If she heard of any poor who went begging, she was filled with confusion and said. "They are not bound, as I am, to observe poverty, and yet they endure so many inconveniences of poverty whilst I endure nothing," and here, being fired by holy envy, she added: "Oh! if it were given to me to go begging, and that when I asked alms for the love of God, contemptuous words would be said to me, and that in bad weather I should return home tired and careworn and without any comfort, oh! what a joy mine would be! But I am not worthy of it." Exhorting the novices and her companions to the love of poverty, she thus expressed herself. "Sisters, we will be able to call ourselves truly nuns of Santa Maria degli Angeli, if, when being tired and worn out in the evening, instead of getting any rest or comfort, we should find somebody to reprimand us and give us the *discipline* Oh! what a grace, what a privilege it would be for us if, on going to the refectory, we would find nothing to eat, being in need of rest, we would have no bed to rest upon; having to dress or change our clothes, because of the poverty of the monastery, there would be no clothes to be given us I, for one, would greatly rejoice at it, and I would consider myself bound to give my blood for the person who would grant me such a favor."

She did all she could to be deprived even of the necessaries of life, hiding as far as possible her own needs; and, if she succeeded in doing so, her joy was at its height. One day by an oversight of the sister-butler no bread was placed before her at table, and she took her dinner without asking for any, nay, she was filled with so much joy that it being noticed outwardly, the superioress in the recreation hall asked her the reason of such excessive pleasure Sister Mary Magdalen, as if accusing herself, answered that she felt too much pleasure at not having received any bread for dinner. Thus she rejoiced when she had to suffer cold, thirst, fatigue, and other inconveniences of life. Sometimes, returning to the poorest places of the monastery, Crucifix in hand, she knelt down, and, turning to her Lord, with tears and sighs, she gave vent to her ardent desire of living stripped of everything for His love. "Happy I would be" (she was wont to say), "if all that this body needs would be wanting to it; and, instead of being gratified, I should suffer insults and abuses for Thy love, O my Jesus! Then I would deem myself somewhat poor for Thy love"

Like St. Francis of Assisi, she called poverty by the most honorable and endearing names; ordinarily she called it the Bride of Jesus, adding that it should be the best ornament of His Brides. On these points she entertained very sublime ideas, and spoke with the most lively feeling The fifth night of the octave of Pentecost, in 1585, during that ecstasy of eight continuous days, conversing with Jesus, she thus expressed herself: "Happy those who follow Thee only without possessing any transitory thing, as they shall have Thee for a reward, Who art the wealth of every wealth, the treasure of every treasure, and the infinite wealth of paradise! But who shall purchase paradise? Where shall sufficient money be found? What can be given as a price of so great a good? Who would believe it? The nothingness, the nothingness! To possess nothing for the love of God, to wish for nothing of this world, to wish nothing but God: *'Dominus pars hæreditatis meæ'*—'The Lord is the portion of my inheritance' (Ps xv, 5). I say more: Nay, to wish for God only for the sake of God! O most sublime and most rich poverty! Thus those who are poor have money in hand to buy paradise, for the heavenly treasures are purchased with absolute poverty; and the poorer a soul is, the more God infuses His treasures into it, with which it can purchase heaven. Who will not love poverty, which causes God to grant us so many gifts? *'Beati pauperes spiritu!'*—'Blessed are the poor in spirit' (Matth v, 3). *'Quam dilecta tabernacula tua, Domine virtutum Concupiscit et deficit anima mea'*—' How lovely are Thy tabernacles, O Lord of hosts! My soul longeth and fainteth for the courts of the Lord' (Ps. lxxxiii, 23). I say this of the desire of heaven, or of the desire of Thy poverty, which is worth heaven to me, as by it Thou wishest me to purchase heaven, and it is the price sufficient for so great a kingdom." In another ecstasy, she exclaimed: "O happy Religious, who are so honored of God that He Himself wishes to be their portion, because for His love, by a solemn vow, they left everything else! O rich poverty! Thou makest us the possessors of the Sovereign Good! But, on the contrary, woe to those Religious who appropriate anything, trafficking with it as if they were not bound by poverty! Alas! that thus they come to renounce their part, which is God, wishing for and keeping other things besides Him, contrary to the promises made to Him. But God grant that at death, when judgment shall take place before God's tribunal, they may not be rejected by God Himself, and separated from Him Who is the Sovereign Good! O poor Religious, so blind about their own state! O simplicity and poverty, declining so much among the Religious, and so little known and kept by those who profess thee! God knows whether this blindness will deserve any excuse in that Divine Judgment where not only faults but even many things that we regard as virtues, will appear to be faults and vices "

This great love that Sister Mary Magdalen bore to the poverty she professed, she also practiced in a wonderful manner during the whole course of her life, showing evidence of it in her food, clothing, and everything else of which she stood in need about her person. Not satisfied with having chosen a monastery of wholly *common life* and strict observance, she always endeavored to exceed the rigor of the rule and the vows. She not only never kept nor received a thing superfluous or vain, but even what was necessary she tried to reduce to the greatest scarcity; or, if unable to diminish it, she would choose the vilest and the most abject. Of this ample testimony is borne by those ecstasies she had in 1587, during which she understood how God wanted from her an extraordinary and singular poverty, because of which she, whilst in ecstasy, cast off shoes and stockings, threw away the bed-clothing, leaving only the straw-bed, removing from her cell every object except the Crucifix, and went to the old-clothes chest, from which she took the meanest and most patched tunic and put it on. After that she would never put on new clothing; so that, in her person and in her cell, she appeared to be the poorest nun. She always feared that she might possess something superfluous, hence she often cast her eyes around on the things she had. One day finding on her little altar a small piece of cloth for which she had asked in order to mend her habit, and which afterwards she had not used, she brought it back immediately to the superioress, accusing herself with great sorrow for such a negligence, and begging of God that He would grant her time to atone for it. At another time, out of two dozen pins she returned one dozen, thinking she had more of them than she needed.

In 1588, the superioress, Sister Vangelista del Giocondo, foreseeing that Mary Magdalen would pass a very bad winter with the light habit she was then wearing, determined to give her a better one; and, in order that she might not grieve on that account, she employed this stratagem: On the night of St. John the Evangelist, on December 27th, after matin, in the presence of the nuns, she called the Saint out to the middle of the choir, and, making her kneel there, told her that the better to accustom her to poverty, she wanted her to take off her tunic, and she having taken it off, the superioress asked the nuns whether they were pleased that another tunic should be given to her for the love of God; and they having assented, she called out one of them, and making her take off the tunic, she offered it to Mary Magdalen, telling her. "This tunic Religion gives to thee for the love of God; put it on and keep it until thou art asked for it" She accepted it in the true spirit of poverty, cordially answering: "May God reward you for it;" which greatly touched the nuns and increased their love for religious poverty

But the renouncing of property and of one's own things is not always an evangelical virtue. Of some philosophers we read, that to throw off every impediment to the acquisition of wisdom, they gave away all they had; but theirs was not the perfect virtue shown by Jesus Christ, the principal aim of which is to detach our heart entirely from things temporal, from things necessary, and even from ourselves. Thus Mary Magdalen, being penetrated by this spirit, which is the basis, the foundation of the vow of poverty, regarded the habits and other necessary things as objects lent her by charity, ready to give them back at the least hint, loving to be in the monastery like a poor wretch and a beggar, received and kept there for mercy's sake. To show in a few words how perfect her detachment was, let these words suffice which during an ecstasy she addressed to the Crucifix she kept in her cell: "O Word Incarnate, if I thought that the keeping of Thy image would deprive me of the least degree of glory in heaven, I would give it up at once." She seemed to have no attachment but for that Crucifix, and she was ready to deprive herself even of it at any moment. Here is the true poverty of spirit; that poverty which, raising the soul to the bosom of God, makes it enjoy beatitude even in this world.

On account of the same virtue Mary Magdalen experienced great delight when coarse and ill-dressed food was given her; and, on the contrary, she tried her best to avoid eating delicate food, saying that it did not agree with her. More than once did the superioress through religious mortification send her around the refectory to ask bread of the sisters and to eat it at once, and Mary Magdalen used to do this with indescribable joy. It also happened many times that, having been prevented from sitting at the first table with the nuns, she went to the kitchen, where she caused what others had left to be gathered into a bowl, saying she wished it for a poor little one; and similar other contrivances of the love of poverty were suggested to her by the zeal which moved her to the most perfect imitation of her Divine Spouse naked and crucified.

As she well understood the welfare of the Religious derived its greatest strength from the observance of the vow of poverty, she omitted no care that her monastery, which she loved with a most warm and loyal feeling, might be distinguished in a singular manner by its poverty and religious simplicity; hence, whenever she noticed anything having a tendency to alter it, she immediately informed the superioresses and the spiritual fathers of it, warmly begging them to provide a remedy. One of her novices had worked some figures with unusual ornaments, to present them to her relations outside. The zealous mistress reproached her, and would not permit her to let seculars see them, much less to make a present of them. A nun had done some work for the sacristy which exceeded the usual simplicity, and the Saint, one day when the spirit of God kept her out of her senses, seized and tore them. In an ecstasy during which she understood how much this simplicity pleased God, and how, like a watch-dog, it discovers the thieves and enemies of the Religion, and keeps the seculars away from it, making the Religious communities the dwellings of God, she finally concluded: "Let each one guard herself and take care not to draw on herself, under the plea of compassion, the curse of some vanity. Woe, a thousand times woe to her who will draw the curse of vanity on Religion, and especially where a little light of simplicity reigns!" This was her saying· "Let the nun who loves not poverty be shunned and considered as if afflicted with leprosy."

Her ears could not endure any criticism of the things of Religion, and she thought that the poorer and more abject these things were, the more they ought to be esteemed and sought after by the Religious, because they had professed poverty, and the poor appreciated everything, knowing that precious and valuable things were not for them. She was wont to say : "She that loves humility and poverty will never waste words to complain of anything." She also used to say: "She that professes poverty always thinks of the poor Christ, and thinks as little of her body as the king does of the cobweb," and, turning to those who complained of anything, she used to say bitterly "Remember, sisters, that you profess poverty, and that when the poor people go begging, they are very glad to get a piece of bread, even if it be dry and stale " Moreover, she asserted that poverty must be the mark of all religious works; and that, as the people of the world, in order to distinguish and magnify their works, imprint their coat-of-arms on them, so, in order to make the works of religious persons easily recognizable, they must be marked with poverty. Hence, she wanted this poverty to shine in everything in and out of the monastery, viz., that whatever was in it or came out of it should wholly appear as the product of a poor religious house. Though on account of the charitable feeling she entertained for the sick she would have wished that the Order should sacrifice itself, so to say, for them, nevertheless she wanted that even in the infirmary poverty should be kept, and that the difference between a sick Religious and a secular sick person should be manifest. Likewise, though she was very anxious that nothing needful should be wanting to her disciples, she would not tolerate seeing them have anything superfluous, and made them practice poverty on every occasion. If one of them betrayed too much attachment to any object she possessed for her own use, she took it away from her, or gave her another in its place; and, often looking through their cells and little altars, she would remove whatever she found to be superfluous or too much ornamented, saying that the observance of poverty was incompatible with superfluity and vanity. She took from a novice a pair of paper angels which she herself had painted, simply because the extremities were somewhat ornamented. She severely reprimanded another who would not wear a veil because she did not like it, and imposed on her that for sixteen days she should present herself to her begging her for the love of God to give her the most worn-out veil that was in the novitiate. She would cause some of the oldest habits to be given to some who were anxious to have new ones, thus exercising the novices in the holy vow of poverty, the spirit of which, more by her marked example than by her voice, she transfused into the souls of her subjects and companions, so that her monastery made wonderful strides in the observance of so essential a duty.

CHAPTER XXXVI.

HOW MUCH SHE ESTEEMED THE RULES OF HER MONASTERY, AND
HOW SHE REFORMED THEM A LITTLE, WISHING TO DO THE
SAME FOR ALL THE RELIGIONS (RELIGIOUS ORDERS).

THE solemn vows which a Religious person makes are defined by the statutes of each regular Congregation, so that the persons professing are bound to keep the vows according to the Rules, Constitutions, and practices of the Religion whose habit is worn by them; hence, he or she who breaks the vows breaks the laws of his or her monastery. Mary Magdalen held in the highest esteem even the least rule, which she would not have broken for all the treasures and honors of the world. She regarded every rule as the will of God and the dictate of the Holy Ghost. Unless prevented by sickness or works of her office, it was simply impossible for her to omit being present at an act of the community. Even the usages and practices of the monastery had upon her soul the force of law. If she could do no better, at least she tried to stay a few minutes with the community, thus gathering, as she was wont to say, a little of that merit which to the rest was given to enjoy in full. When she was wholly prevented from attending, she tried to make up by the desire and by humbling herself before God and confessing herself unworthy to take part in that observance. During the night or at an extraordinary time she did the works of her choice or of charity, in order to be ready to do those prescribed by the Rule; so that the superioress sometimes seeing her very much fatigued, out of compassion for her would tell her to give up her work at once and rest herself; but she never accepted such a dispensation unless compelled by obedience. In order that this might not happen, she tried her best to hide her fatigue and needs.

Silence was for her one of the principal points of religious observance. She was wont to say that a soul which does not taste the sweetness of silence, can never taste the sweetness of the things of heaven; nay, that it will live always afflicted and troubled, as, by not knowing how to restrain the tongue many evils follow, which cause the soul a great deal of trouble. In regard to silence she was most observing, and even outside of silence time, she was singularly moderate in speaking, and always did so in a low and subdued voice, saying that such was the proper way for Religious persons to speak She greatly disliked the raising of the voice and loud laughing, as things most unbecoming a nun.

She very much appreciated the observance of the constitutions, and when she thought she had committed some fault for which a penance was imposed by them, she performed such a penance without waiting for the order of the superioress, protesting that she would have endured any torment rather than to see the least prescription of the Religion made little of. Every morning she offered her monastery to the Blessed Virgin, declaring to her that she would rather be a firebrand of hell than not to have always zeal for her own perfection and that of all her companions in the monastery. Hence, when she noticed in them some transgression of the rules, if able, she would remedy it herself; if unable, she would have recourse to the superioresses and the senioresses, that they might watch and remedy the disorder, saying to them that by neglecting even the least thing concerning the holy rules, the pupil of the eye of God (which is the Religion, on account of the love He bears to it) was offended.

At most times, the busying of herself in behalf of others was intended to render them more prompt to attend to the community acts; and, to her subjects as well as to her companions, she was wont to give this advice· That they should never prefer their own comforts nor their other actions, no matter how devout and holy, to any order of the Religion, "because," she said, "in performing the common acts of the Religion, we are sure of God's will, of which we cannot assure ourselves when working according to our own will and caprice, nay, we then expose ourselves to a great danger of deception and illusion" She added that they were really in great danger of being deceived by the devil, who, in order to remain in retirement and pray at their will, do not care to attend the exercises of the community, and, being deprived of their satisfaction, they grieve at it, for which they injure the religious observance, which cannot be kept if the sisters do not exercise themselves in it with fidelity and solicitude. She also advised that every one should attend the community practices with as much zeal as if she alone were bound to keep them, and be ready to give up her blood and her life rather than allow the least loosening of the rule and the constitutions of the monastery. But the keen vigilance of her spirit not being satisfied with the present, she exerted all her efforts to obtain the perpetuation of this observance in her monastery, and she said that such an observance and nothing else should be the legacy each one dying should leave to her surviving companions.

Though the monastery of St. Maria degli Angeli proceeded with great regularity and exactness in the fulfillment of its duties, nevertheless the Saint, on account of the great zeal she possessed concerning the religious perfection and the glory and pleasure given to God by a monastery aspiring to the most perfect observance, entertained a strong desire to perfect also its rules and to add some reform to the constitution. One might also take this mania for reforming which fills the soul of nearly all persons of singular piety for a subtlety of self-love, but in reality it is a natural consequence of the greater knowledge they have of the duties, the imperfect correspondence to them, and the importance of often recalling things to their first principles, that they may not be spoiled, viz , returning to the spirit of the lawmaker, in which true and legitimate reform consists. Macchiavelli, even in the political laws, proposes and recommends it to enlightened men; and shall it not be the desire of the good that this may obtain in regard to God's law of which the many passions of the wicked, and the discouragements of the imperfect, oppose the proper fulfillment? But in a matter of so great importance and delicacy, Mary Magdalen De-Pazzi did not fail to have persistent recourse to God, Who afterwards was pleased to reveal to her some points which He would like to have inserted in the constitutions. Of these, some were by her uttered in an ecstasy and taken down by the nuns, and others she wrote with her own hands, and, being near death, she called to herself the father director and confessor, Rev. Vincenzo Puccini, and to him she gave a memorandum of all the things that, by the will of God, were to be added to the constitutions, and warmly begged him to unite them and coordinate them with the same. This, he having promised, was done after her death with the consent of the chapter of the monastery, and this reform was in 1609 confirmed with a special brief by the Sovereign Pontiff Paul V. To dispose the nuns to a stricter observance, she often addressed to them the most cogent reasons, and she would exact from the novices before their profession a promise concerning this matter This zeal of Mary Magdalen was not restricted to her own monastery alone, but embraced all the Religions, wishing to see them all in the highest fervor and purity of discipline in which they were begun by their founders. If unable to assist others proximately with her work, she offered to God for them the most fervent prayers and presented herself to Him ready to endure any pain whatsoever that they might resume their original fervor. She was wont to shed copious and bitter tears on account of the relaxation of the Religions, and she even said that she would not mind being considered crazy if she could have gone around the world to bring back the cloistered families to their original fervor To this end, she often dictated, while in ecstasy, letters addressed to various regular prelates, which were written by the nuns present, but were not sent to their destination The visions she had of the souls of Religious falling down like lightning into hell, condemned to the most horrible torments for their inobservant life, were the strongest motives to enkindle her zeal in favor of religious observance Having once heard of some friars who boasted of observing poverty more than others (as they were scantily provided for by the community), and of trying to help support themselves by appearing lowly dressed, which would not have happened if the Religion had provided for them, the Saint, with sighs and weeping, thus exclaimed: "O blindness of the creatures! O Religious state so little known! O great misery, that they try to cover the very evil with what is really good, to the loss of many souls! These deceived ones think that they will find the merit of their works, but will find instead their eternal perdition, as the inconveniences of poverty will have been the effect of their own self-love " In regard to this point, she used to say that the salvation of the observant Religious who is provided for by the Religion in all needs, is almost assured, and, on the contrary, that of the Religious who is voluntarily a property-holder, though dressing poorly, is almost despaired of; for, if the latter had not the disposition to deprive himself of everything, there will be no heaven for him. About this most important subject of life in common for all Religious, she thus expressed herself: "I cannot see nor understand why those Religious, who by the three solemn vows dedicated themselves to God, do not keep community life, but try by holding property to alter so beautiful an order of perfect life   O accursed property! which carries with it so many pretexts and inventions by which it often makes a thing appear as virtue which is nothing but vice and defect" And again. "I do not understand how Religious can with good conscience have particular revenues, and how the offices of the monastery must be kept with particular incomes and works, so that it ordinarily happens that Religious are more attached to the things of the world than seculars are. O my Jesus, make me suffer any pain that so many Brides consecrated to Thee may return to observe life in common, as Thou makest me see to my great sorrow many of those unhappy ones descending into hell."

She also understood ecstatically how displeasing to the Lord those Religious were who occupy themselves in worldly pursuits, upon which she said, with great emphasis, the following words: "May it please God that this trafficking in exterior things in which the Bride of Jesus indulges, and which takes from her the time and the opportunity of doing her true traffic with God—may it please God that in the end they do not take from her the beatific vision!" Which threat was uttered by her with so great energy that she frightened those who heard her   In another ecstasy, she understood the enormous offense which is offered to God by those Religious who, not being satisfied with being themselves inobservant, prevent others also from fulfilling their duty; and, on the contrary, she understood how much pleasure and glory is given to God by those who, living in a Religion of lax observance, try, as far as they can, though meeting with obstacles, to correspond to the true spirit of their Order, thus becoming a source at once of good example and of reproach to their companions. Feeling compassion for these, she said "Oh! how grieved I am at not being able, by shedding my own blood, to obtain that those enlightened souls dwelling in a lax Religion may enjoy the happiness and opportunity I enjoy, by corresponding to the desire and interior stimulus they feel." Then, thinking of herself, she added: "Oh! how better than myself they would serve God! Oh! much more grateful for such a gift they would be if they would find themselves where I am " Moreover, reflecting on the evil conduct of those nuns who, to please wordly creatures, perform works of fashion and make up attractive ornaments, she exclaimed, in like words of sorrow: "Alas! that those eyes that ought yet to be fixed on Christ Crucified and His divine beauty should busy themselves so unhappily to look upon things vain and miserable, and that those hands consecrated to God should be employed in making snares to catch souls and send them to hell!   O extreme misery! O miserable and ever-to-be-deplored unhappiness!"   One day whilst she was looking with great attention at some flowers wrought with great skill by some nuns, she was asked by some of them why she looked at them so attentively.   And she answered: "O my sisters, I think and consider that God knows whether the nun who made these flowers knew

In obedience to her confessor, she revives and receives new
strength "in extremis" (page 284).

how to take as much time to enter into herself and think of the state of her soul and her obligation towards God, as she knew how to take in doing this kind of work " And she added . "O confusion of ours ! God knows whether I, too, have employed my attention in making acts of love of God as she employed her talent in flower-making O nobility of the soul, especially of the religious soul, that is under such an obligation of serving God, in what art thou wasting thyself? O unhappy Religious, so blind concerning the dignity of their state !" She gave vent to many other exclamations like these when considering the relaxation of the Religious. It was from the expression of these sentiments that the nuns gathered wonderful evidence of religious perfection which the Saint furnished upon every opportune occasion, and of which we shall give an abridgment of no little interest in the Works. Here we shall relate the two following ecstasies as appertaining proximately to the subject we treat of.

One evening, the spirit of Mary Magdalen being absorbed in a celestial ecstasy, she heard the Most Holy Trinity calling her thus "Come, my chosen one, take three victims and consecrate them to us, the Three Divine Persons, though they may be already consecrated " Not understanding what these three victims were, whether they were the three powers of the soul or something else, three souls were particularly named to her, whom God had chosen for the Religion, and she was given to understand that these would not be the last ones, but that before her death she was to consecrate to the Most Holy Trinity six others who were not yet in the Religion ; and that, of these nine souls, she was to consecrate three to the Father, three to the Word, and three to the Holy Ghost Hence, having understood the will of God, she withdrew to a secluded place with the superioress, another mother, and the three souls above mentioned, two of whom were Religious already professed, and the other a girl on trial, who wished very much to become a nun These, then, were the three victims to be consecrated to the Three Divine Persons, one for each, as it was even more clearly shown to her afterwards. Turning to them, therefore, whilst still in ecstasy, she said to them : "Are you satisfied, O sisters of mine, that I should consecrate you to the Most Holy Trinity?" Upon all of them answering in the affirmative, she also asked them whether they were ready to submit in everything to the Divine Will; to which, having received an affirmative reply, she continued, saying to them : "This shows the submission you must make of yourselves to the Divine Will, being ready to suffer everything interior and exterior to fulfill God's Will " Then, kneeling down, she said : "Now adore the unity of the Most Holy Trinity, for yourselves and for all those who fail to do so " Then arising, with hands and eyes lifted up to heaven, she added : "Be always right and sincere in every action and work, keeping your eyes fixed on God." Kneeling again, she extended her arms, saying : "Always have a great desire for your perfection and that of the Religion, and to be kept like the Word on the cross—namely, lowly and despised—and consider yourselves such." Then she crossed her hands on her breast, pronouncing with force these words "Embrace O sisters, all creatures in a bond of charity and love, loving every one of them always in the bond of love and charity." Here she told them to say the *Confiteor*, and made the two who had the veil renew their profession, and the girl the resolution to take the religious habit. She then took the hands of one of the professed nuns and offered her to the Most Holy Trinity, and particularly to the Person of the Holy Ghost, not with the sound of her voice, but with her eyes fixed on heaven, remaining entranced for some time; then she made it known to be God's will that that sister should promise to be always zealous as to herself and others for sublime purity of heart and holy simplicity, trying with all her power always to promote in the Religion the perfect observance of this holy vow of poverty, and she exhorted her to take for this end, as a patron, St. John the Evangelist. She took the second nun likewise by the hand, offering her to the Most Holy Trinity, and more particularly to the Person of the Word Incarnate, and remaining, as before, a little while without speaking, she told her it was the will of God that she should promise to have always a great zeal for the perfect observance, by herself and all her companions, of the vow of poverty and of true poverty of spirit, exhorting her to take for this St. Paul the Apostle, as a patron. The same thing she did with the girl, offering her to the Eternal Father, and she told her that God expected from her that she should reduce to effect the inspiration she had to become a nun; which having done, she should attend with the greatest care to the practice of obedience and self-abnegation, and try with equal zeal to make her companions do the same, taking for a helper the seraphic father, St Francis. The offering up of these three creatures and their correspondence being completed, it seemed to her as if each of the Divine Persons espoused the one that had been respectively consecrated to Him, drawing her spirit to Himself in a manner altogether peculiar; and here ended the first ecstasy.

There was on probation in her monastery a girl by the name of Catherine, who had entered there with marked vocation, but, on the other hand, she was troubled by *our three capital enemies*, which wished to draw her away from the divine call   After having several times assisted and comforted her, one evening Mary Magdalen, whilst speaking with her, was rapt in ecstasy, and, turning upon her a look of encouragement, told her with a firm voice not to fear any assault, but to fight with great strength and to be sure that God wanted her to be a nun in that monastery, and that no sooner would she put on its habit than all temptations would cease and an ineffable peace would fill her heart. Having made this known, the holy mother took the girl with her to the choir, where ascending, as usual, the entablature and taking therefrom the oftenmentioned Crucifix, she gave it to her, and then both passed over to the oratory of the novices. Here, in the presence of the prioress, the mistress of novices, and another mother, she consecrated that girl also to the Most Holy Trinity, and particularly to the Person of the Word, she entering into the number of the nine offerings above mentioned   In offering her, she followed this order: First, she asked her whether she was satisfied that such a consecration should be made of her, and having received an affirmative answer, she proceeded to ask her this question: "Dost thou choose to do this by my advice?" "No," the girl replied: "No, but simply to fulfil" the will of God, which I believe is found in what thou now desirest to do with me " Then the mother made the girl go through a brief self-examination; and, having said the *Confiteor* with her, she offered her in particular to the Divine Word—not with words, but with the effervescence of her heart, as she had done with the first three. After this, she told her what God wanted of her, and assigned to her, as a patron, the glorious St. Ignatius Loyola, and then came to herself from the ecstasy. A few weeks having elapsed, the same girl received the nun's habit with ineffable consolation, but the enemy of mankind the same evening assailed her with new temptations and stronger suggestions. But the holy mother, who was then in ecstasy, ran to encourage her, speaking to her as follows: "I bring thee good tidings, beloved soul, hear me: An archangel, beautiful and radiant, came with a scythe and cut off all the thorns by which thou hast been pressed from the day thou madest thy first covenant with God until now, except some little ones which thou hast to trample upon, that they may not grow and pierce thee. The thorns are the passions; and, when these show themselves at the window, thou must fight or bind them. Thou fightest them by doing the opposite of what they wish; thou bindest them by the recollection of thy obligations towards God. Place two guards over thyself, one at the door of thy soul and the other at the door of thy heart; visit them often and keep them watching that nothing may enter there which may not be able to stand before the divine purity. Give death to self and bury thy own opinion and understanding, and thus shalt thou enjoy the peace of which I spoke to thee If I had all the angelic and all the human tongues, I would still be unable to tell all the glory thou hast given to God, or rather God has taken to Himself out of the oblation thou hast made of thyself to Him. And if thou wishest to walk towards that perfection to which He calls thee, thou must not think of any impossibility in interior or exterior works, but have always a lively faith and a firm confidence in our loving and great God and in holy obedience. As the Divine Spouse chooses thee for the highest perfection, see that all thoughts, words, and works are according to the model He left us in His humanity. Jesus takes much delight in the Brides that are dear to Him, wishing through them to make the places where they dwell perfect " This is what was spoken by the ecstatic Mary Magdalen on the above occasion, but she said more, carrying into the soul of the newly-made bride perfect calm and ample understanding of the worth of the evangelical counsels.

Among the things mentioned in this chapter, the attention of a Religious is called, above all, to what concerns community life, viz , that mode of life which, destroying totally the deliberative faculty about any subject whatsoever, embodies in one all the products of the house and those of the individual, so that, providing for all, it is lawful to none to choose or appropriate or dispose at will of anything. Upon this point I will make but two reflections, for the regulars, more than for the information of others, as the former stand in greater need of the divine grace to elevate them to thoughts and affections more worthy of their vocation. I say, then, first, that the Religious more fervent and assiduous at prayer and in the observance of their duties, have also a great desire for *life in common*, and also endeavor to introduce it where it is not practiced. If their efforts are often useless, the cause of it is in the number of the imperfect, which ordinarily is greater and more powerful, just as the zeal of the bishops is seldom sufficient to put the nuns under this system, which is so essential to the vow of poverty, and consequently the cause of so much peace and profit to those communities which have adopted it; just as, I will also say, even the wish of the Sovereign Pontiffs that all *regular Congregations* would submit to the *community life* has remained almost wholly inefficacious, for the reason which has been advanced that the house had not sufficient income to live the *life in common*. From which I draw my second reflection, asserting that such a pretext, unless we call it manifestly erroneous, cannot be ascribed to want of spirit, to say the least, because, if in private life the individual by his industry provides for all his needs, by doing as much for the *life in common* the same results would be obtained for all and for each in particular. The concurrence of many causes to one end will even give more impetus to the whole—so that it may be shared by each one—than if each cause worked separately and for the individual benefit. Hence we must conclude that a remnant of wordly love and of self-love is the source by which some religious is obstinately opposed to *life in common*, and that he alone shall be able to justify himself who, having embraced the system of private life, does not persist in it because attached to it, or would not care whether the efforts of those who are more zealous and virtuous would meet with a happy result or not; but because it is not in his power to do otherwise.

CHAPTER XXXVII.

SHE WISHES TO SUFFER PURELY FOR GOD, WHICH PROVES HER EMINENT
SANCTITY; WHEREBY, ON ACCOUNT OF HER BEING PRESENT, OR
OF THINGS SHE HAD USED, MANY WONDERFUL EVENTS
TOOK PLACE DURING HER LIFETIME.

IT is the heroism of virtue so to elevate one's self above the
sorrows of nature as to aspire, with joy and longing desire,
to nothing but the desolations and the torments of Calvary,
whilst it is also lawful and proper for just souls to desire the
enjoyment, at times, of the delights of Thabor. Mary Magdalen De-Pazzi possessed this virtue in so heroic a degree
that she seemed never to have suffered enough; and in the
year 1590, viz., at the end of the five years of her trial, she
gave up to God all but spiritual taste, making with Him an agreement,
which she then expressed in ecstasy and afterwards confirmed several
times out of ecstasy. To a sister who offered her congratulations to the
Saint upon the glorious end of her combats, and the promise God had made
her that she would enjoy in return His Divine Presence, she answered:
" It will be so truly, but without any sweetness; it will only be for comfort
and strength in trials;" thinking of this relinquishment of all sweetness. Being also asked by the same nun about the motive of so sublime
an act, the Saint manifested it in the following words: "Wishing to be
able to give and offer to God something, and to remain for the love of
Him without anything, and finding that I had nothing, as by the vows
of holy Religion I have renounced not only every created thing outside
of myself, but even my own self and my own will, I gave up to Him
what he had given me, having nothing else to give Him." It happened,
.therefore, that from the year 1590, though God deprived her not of the
ecstasies, yet, as she was wont to say, these were almost always without
any sensibility of spiritual taste, and rather intended for the strengthening
of her soul and its powers. Hence, one day whilst out of her senses and
feeling her heart inundated with an extraordinary delight, she uttered
these words in a tone of lamentation: "Ah! my God, why dost Thou
break the agreement Thou madest with me when I gave up all delights for Thy love?" Thus, except during these ecstasies, desolation
and aridity prevailed in her spirit, so that frequently, to excite herself to
devotion, she was compelled to have recourse to those means of which

the beginners in God's service stand in need   Sometimes she was wont to say that in thinking of God she became like a piece of wood or stone, without any feeling.   Her own humility made this aridity even more painful, for, though it was a matter of her own choice, she feared lest it might be the consequence of her own fault; and, feeling so much repugnance to the exercises of piety, it seemed to her as if she did not execute them with the necessary promptness.   Of this she often accused herself, to a companion, in these words. " O sister, it is very hard, and a soul must have really tasted of God and be truly anxious to suffer, in order that she may be able to work, in the midst of so much aridity of spirit, as if she abundantly tasted of God."   Thus she spoke to accuse herself, far from realizing that she was the very person who possessed so great a perfection   Hence the exercises of devotion, which she never omitted, no matter how much weariness they caused her, were so perfectly and evidently virtuous, on account of the purity of their beginning, progress, and close, that they brought her to such a degree of sanctity as to cause the most manifest signs and the most wonderful effects to be visible in her own person.   From her eyes, words, gestures, and every movement of her person, it appeared that she was a Saint, and everybody was compelled to adjudge her a Saint who saw her, though not knowing who she was.

We have already seen how she infused into the souls of others hatred of vice, love of virtue, comfort, encouragement, by a word or a look, and sometimes by her own presence alone.   All her companions of the monastery were able to testify to having experienced in themselves most consoling effects by virtue of their holy sister; and this was particularly the case of those who had been under her direction, some of whom affirmed that, being molested by great temptations, these would cease by their simply approaching her, or touching her habit, or just remaining where she was, or looking at her, or, if away in another place, by simply turning their thoughts to her, they felt sweetness and peace descending into their hearts.   As true virtue never compromises with vice, she wrought in the souls of those who were stained with it salutary effects of confusion, shame, and sadness.   Among many others was the case of a Florentine youth, of noble family but licentious life, who, having gone to the monastery to visit a sister of his, who was a novice there, no sooner did she come to the grates, accompanied by her mistress, Mary Magdalen De-Pazzi, than without a word or syllable of courtesy to one or the other, he immediately left   On the day following, the mother of the novice came to apologize for the incivility of her son, relating how he was so terrified and confused at the sight of the Saint that he could not endure it for a single minute   Even brute animals seemed to feel some depression and restraint in her presence.   Once, a wild-goat that had been presented to the monastery began to run here and there, so that it was not possible for the nuns to secure it.   It entered the work-hall, where, on account of its restlessness, it threw those who were present into great excitement and fear lest it might do some damage.   Soon afterwards Mary Magdalen came in, and, approaching it, it immediately submitted to her, becoming meek and tractable, and allowing itself to be seized and led to where the nuns wanted it.

Another time, whilst the nuns were at dinner, by an oversight of the janitress a mastiff got into the monastery, striking terror into everyone by its ferocious mien. Mary Magdalen seeing the anguish of the sisters, who did not know how to chase it away, got up from the table, and, calling the dog (which promptly obeyed) to herself, took it by one ear, and the dog, like a little lamb, permitted her to lead it to the door of the cloister, whence she sent it peaceably away

We have already remarked that, besides her presence, the things that had been used by her communicated some of the superhuman virtue that was in her. Her nuns attested that they derived some benefit both for the good of their souls and for the health of their bodies, either by girding themselves with her cord, or by carrying her hair-cloth, or by touching the habit she was wearing. On Good Friday of the year 1592, Sister Mary Magdalen De-Mori, a nun in the same monastery, was much troubled by pains of gout and sciatica, to which she had been for a long time subject Whilst suffering such severe pains, an inner voice was thus encouraging her· "If thou wilt recover, get somebody to carry thee before the mother, Mary Magdalen" Hence, having conceived some confidence in this inspiration, with the permission of the superioress, she caused herself to be carried to the place where the Saint was, and found her rapt in ecstatic contemplation. With the assistance of two sisters she approached her and touched her with the affected side, and this was enough for God to perform a miracle by means of His beloved servant. The patient felt that her pains had immediately ceased, and without any help she returned to her cell. Another nun was tormented by such excessive pains in the head that she felt as if her brains were bursting out. She went to the bed of the Saint, who then was seriously ill; and, having rested her head with great confidence on her shoulder, she felt instantly that all pains were gone. Some nuns also remarked that when the Saint was working in the kitchen, her hands seemed to possess the virtue of increasing the things; as, with less quantity than that assigned to anybody else, she succeeded in making larger and more abundant dishes; hence, a lay-sister in particular, whenever she noticed that the provision was insufficient for the community, recommended herself to Mary Magdalen, who encouraged her to have faith; which the lay-sister trying to do, she confessed that thereby she herself saw several times that the things were wonderfully multiplied, so that there was something left after she had given to all an abundant portion These things wrought by Mary Magdalen during her lifetime, and which stand as a proof of her eminent sanctity, become accessories to the following prodigies, which, by their notable importance and on account of their being recognized and approved by the Holy Church, deserve that we should believe them to be more than probable.

1. LICKING THE DISEASED LIMBS OF A NUN, SHE CLEANSES AND, HEALS HER —In the year 1591, Sister Maria Benigna Orlandini was in the same monastery sick with such a disease that the physicians judged it to be leprosy and wholly incurable, as evidenced by the inutility of all remedies applied Discouraged by so obstinate and incurable a disease, this nun had recourse to the holy mother, begging of her to obtain

her recovery from Jesus. The Saint promised her to do what she wished, and on the morning of St. Peter the Martyr, both having received Holy Communion, Mary Magdalen a few moments afterwards was raised into ecstasy. Thus ecstatic, she went to the infirmary, where, presenting herself at the bedside of the patient, cheerful in countenance and extremely sweet in the expression of the salutation of peace, she removed the veils from the head of the sister, and with her own tongue began to lick her head, ears, and neck, commanding her at the same time not to speak to anybody in the least about this fact, but simply to trust in God that she would get cured. It happened that after the lapse of a few days, the sick nun found herself cured and cleansed entirely from that pestilential sickness.

2. SHE MAKES THE SIGN OF THE CROSS REPEATEDLY OVER A PAINFUL SORE WHICH WAS TORMENTING A NUN, AND SHE CAUSES THE IMMEDIATE CURE OF THE SAME.—In the same year, 1591, Sister Cherubina Rabatti, already mentioned, for a similar reason was greatly tormented by a sore which was eating through the back part of her head Now it happened that, on the morning of the 13th of December, whilst the nuns were receiving Holy Communion, the Saint, being in ecstasy, by divine disposition, did not approach the holy table ; hence the confessor, having to carry Holy Communion to the sick ones, told her to go for it to the infirmary, which she did, and there having received Communion was again rapt in ecstasy. During this, she approached Sister Cherubina, and thus spoke to her : " Sister, unite with me in asking thy cure of the Lord God." And both having prayed a little while, Mary Magdalen made the sign of the cross three times over the head of the patient, and instantly the sore was healed, leaving her wholly free from the fever and the pains which had afflicted her.

3. THE SAME NUN BEING NEAR DEATH IS CARRIED TO THE STRAW-BED WHEREON THE SAINT WAS SLEEPING, AND RECOVERS PERFECT HEALTH.—The same Sister Cherubina Rabatti the following year, 1592, on account of two sores, was confined to her bed with such violent fever and spasms that by the advice of the physicians, who declared all hope gone, Extreme Unction was administered to her In the meantime, Mary Magdalen, the better to assist this patient, and in order to be certainly present at her death which was thought to be very near, had her straw-bed carried near the room of the sick nun. In this condition of things, without a ray of hope, humanly speaking, a comforting voice thus spoke to the heart of Sister Cherubina · "If thou wilt recover, enter the bed of Sister Mary Magdalen " To which inspiration willingly listening with great confidence, by the permission and in the presence of the mother prioress, she caused herself to be carried from the infirmary to the straw-bed of the Saint; and lo ! what a prodigy ! no sooner was she laid down upon it than she felt better, nay, cured, so that in about one-eighth of an hour she went by herself to her own bed, more out of caution than anything else, and arose the following morning with her usual strength and went with the nuns to recite the Office in the choir, and then followed all the other exercises of the monastery.

4 MARY MAGDALEN MIRACULOUSLY CURES ANOTHER NUN OF A SERIOUS SORE —Sister Maria Caterina Chelli, a professed nun of the

same monastery, had a sore on the right arm near the wrist. With physicians and medicines she had already doctored for two years, without any good result; nay, she was getting so much worse that, a piece of bone being extracted from the sore, the physicians said that either she would be a cripple or would not recover. On the 15th of May, 1595, the poor sister experiencing in her sore arm persistent and most intense pains, presented herself suppliantly to the prioress, Sister Vange-lista del Giocondo, that she might help her in some way to be patient, as all remedies appeared to be useless. The prioress by divine inspiration thus answered her: "Sister, go to Sister Mary Magdalen, and recommend thyself to her, who has granted favors to others and will also grant them to thee." Sister Maria Caterina went without delay to the Saint, telling her first how she had been sent by the superioress, then manifesting the reason, and making her request. The compassionate and good Mary Magdalen on hearing this went to see the mother prioress, and took her with the patient to the choir. There, the three kneeling before the altar of the Blessed Virgin, Mary Magdalen took hold of the sore arm of the afflicted sister, unswathed it, and then turning to the mother prioress thus said to her: "Wilt thou that I take out the lint from the sore?" To which the prioress answered: "If thou hast faith that she will recover, take it out." Then Sister Mary Magdalen having premised a short prayer, took out the lint, and bound up the arm without putting anything on the sore; and the pain immediately ceased. In a few days the sore healed without any medicines being applied to it, and in such a manner that Sister Maria Caterina was cured and as free from any scar as if she had never had a sore on her arm.

CHAPTER XXXVIII.

OF THE HUMILITY OF HER HEART IN THE MIDST OF THE SPLENDOR
AND ABUNDANCE OF HEAVENLY FAVORS.

S humility is greater and more perfect as the subject possessing it is endowed with higher virtue and talents, it must
not be considered improper to mention in the last place
this virtue of humility, which is the root and foundation of
the spiritual life. The profound humility of the heart of
Mary Magdalen cannot be better shown than by placing it
alongside of her other virtues, which all help to manifest
the perfection of humility; and much would be detracted
from the idea that should be conceived of her humility, unless the ornaments of her noble soul had been previously described. After the sublimity of her contemplations, the marvel of her celestial favors and privileges, the perfection of so many virtues, the stupendous miracles wrought
by God in this soul,—her thinking so little of her own self, the low
estimation and contempt she entertained of herself, should more than
convince anyone that humility was so deeply and profoundly rooted in
her heart that words are insufficient to explain it.

Notwithstanding the sanctity of her soul, she nevertheless, on account
of the pride and ingratitude of which she thought herself guilty, regarded
herself hardly better than the devils. She deemed herself unworthy to
serve God purely—unworthy that anything should be imposed on her by
obedience, unworthy to dwell in that sacred college of virgins, to unite
her praise with that of the Brides of Jesus, and to converse with them,
even if they addressed to her injurious and shameful words. She
deemed herself unworthy of every grace and gift of heaven; also of
showing charity on earth to her neighbor, and of partaking of the goods
of all the faithful. She deemed herself unworthy to possess poverty of
spirit and every other virtue; and above all she thought herself most
unworthy to unite with her Spouse Jesus in the Eucharistic Banquet,
unworthy of all celestial light and divine inspiration, and rather deserving to be abandoned by God and left in the darkness of her sins and
errors. Finally, she wondered how God preserved her and tolerated her
on this earth, rather than hurled her down into the flames of hell.
Among all creatures she deemed herself alone unworthy of the care and
providence of God and of the love He bears to all that He created; and
she abhorred herself, as the most loathsome and blameworthy thing in

existence.   These were not flights of diseased imagination, but thoughts
and sentiments of deep conviction, to the practice of which she dedicated
herself with the greatest sincerity and frequency   The better to impress
them on her mind and practice them, she had written down a collection
of them for daily exercise, divided into nine distinct acts, because of
the nine Choirs of the Angels —

1. Thou shalt go to the Choir of the Holy Angels, and shalt beg of
them that they offer to the throne of the Most Holy Trinity the Blood
of the Incarnate Word, asking of them true humility of spirit; and thou,
O my soul, shalt humble thyself so as to deem thyself similar to the
demons, by thy pride and ingratitude

2   Thou shalt go to the Choir of the Archangels, and shalt pray to
them, as above; and thou, O soul, thirsting for purity, asking it of them,
shalt humble thyself so as to consider thyself unworthy to receive the
aureola of virginity and serve God purely.

3. Thou shalt go to the Choir of the Principalities, and shalt ask of
them that they offer the Blood of the Incarnate Word to the Eternal
Father; and begging of them for most perfect obedience and submission
to the Divine Will and to all creatures for the love of the Creator, thou
shalt endeavor to attain to this humiliation that thou mayst know that
thou art unworthy that anything should be imposed at any time on thee
by obedience, and that thou art also unworthy to be counted among
the number of the truly obedient

4   Thou shalt go to the Choir of the Powers, and shalt beg them to
offer the Blood of the Incarnate Word, as above, and thou, O soul, made
slave by thy sensual appetites, shalt ask the grace of being able to
restrain each one of thy sensual appetites, and to the best of thy ability
thou shalt come to this humiliation that thou reputest thyself unworthy
to dwell in this holy college and unite thy praise with that of the
Brides of Jesus

5   Thou shalt go to the Choir of the Virtues, begging them, as
above, and thou, my soul, devoid of every virtue, shalt ask of them
firmness, stability, and constancy in doing good, and thou shalt humble
thyself so as to acknowledge thyself unworthy of every grace and gift of
Heaven, and also of being able, while on earth, to help thy neighbor
with offices of charity, and to partake of the good of all the believers

6   Thou shalt go to the Choir of the Dominations, asking them to
make the above offering; and thou, my soul, begging of them a perfect
control of all thy interior passions and earthly affections, shalt humble
thyself interiorly, acknowledging thyself unworthy to possess humility of
spirit and every other virtue

7   Thou shalt have recourse to the Thrones, who will go to the
loving arms of the Incarnate Word, and there shall offer thee; and thou,
my soul, shalt lower thyself so as to consider thyself most unworthy, as
in fact thou art, of the union which thou dost so often enjoy with thy
Spouse, by means of the Most Holy Sacrament, Who with so much
love comes to sit in the midst of thy heart

8   Thou shalt go to the Choir of the Cherubim, and they shall offer
thee before the most pure eyes of the Word Incarnate , and thou, my soul,
shalt go on in thy humiliations, asking of the Cherubim light to know in

thyself the Divine Will, the graces thou receivest every moment, and how ill thou dost correspond to them, deeming thyself unworthy of all light and heavenly inspiration and of being preserved by the Divine Mercy, whilst thou deservest, for thy ill-correspondence to the divine light, to be abandoned by God and left in darkness and error.

9. Thou shalt also go to the Choir of the Seraphim, that they may offer thee to the most sweet, most pious, and most loving Heart of the Incarnate Word; and thou, my soul, begging of them the purity of the divine love, and that thou mayest burn in those flames of charity wherein they burn everlastingly, shalt continue thy exercise and endeavor to arrive at this humiliation, viz , to acknowledge thyself unworthy that God should have till now preserved and tolerated thee, rather than have sunk thee down into the flames of hell for the coldness and frozenness of thy heart, whilst it is exposed to so many fires of divine charity. Gathering thyself up around the centre of thy lowliness and meanness, thou shalt acknowledge that thou alone among all creatures art unworthy of the care and providence of God and of the love He bears His creatures, and, abhorring thyself as a thing above all else loathsome and despicable, thou shalt ask for grace through these most pure and loving spirits, to be, as was Jesus, purified and cleansed by means of tribulation, so that all the rustiness of thy faults may be taken off thy soul, that it may be no longer unworthy of that most pure love

Such a low estimation of herself, cultivated by these and other similar acts, so manifested itself in all her works and words that she astonished very much everybody that knew her, as they found it impossible to conceive how a soul so favored of God and endowed with so much light and virtue could entertain so vile an opinion of herself. Confessing herself constantly to be the most abject of all creatures, in that ecstasy of eight days during which God showed her the strength and virtue He wished to communicate to her against the devils and their temptations, which she was to endure pending the five years of her probation, with extraordinary feeling, she broke out into these words : "Oh! my confusion, that, being the lowest and vilest creature in the world, still Thou wishest to manifest in me the greatness and immensity of the treasures of Thy liberality and mercy " She was wont to call herself God's poor little one, a little worm, a little maggot of the earth, and similar names indicating self-contempt Though so learned and enlightened in things divine, yet deeming herself the most ignorant, she asked the advice of others, be they superiors to her or not, even in the least things, and sometimes she asked even her very novices. She did not trust at all to her own judgment, and whatever she was doing seemed most imperfect and of no value to her; hence, sometimes in doing or saying anything, she addressed this question to others : " Does it seem to you that I have done or said well? For the love of God, tell me whether I have committed a fault in that?" Upon which the sisters took delight in pointing out to her some faults which in truth did not exist; but she. believing them to be facts, accused herself of them as guilty, deeply humbling herself and asking forgiveness for them. In the matter of spiritual direction, although she was such an

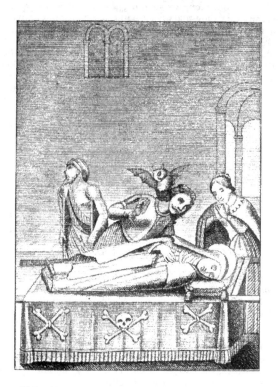

Whilst lying dead in the coffin, she turns her face from a
lascivious young man who was looking at her

(page 290).

excellent teacher, even though the thing might be of little importance, she recommended herself to the advice of others, with this expression of humility: "Tell me, sister, what dost thou think I might do to enlighten this soul?" In manual work, in which also she was very proficient, she thought that others were always doing better than herself. She exalted as so many Saints all her companions of the monastery, and humbled herself as contemptible and a sinner. She was seen several times kissing the ground upon which her sisters had stood. She extended her praise and veneration also to the sisters departed, speaking of them in a manner calculated to make everybody conceive a good opinion of them. Whenever a fault appeared in anyone, she, with humble and charitable manner, excused it, saying: "I would have done worse." And this was the reason why she placed herself below all the sinners of the world. "If God would withdraw His hand from me," she was wont to say, "there is no sin, no matter how grievous, that I might not commit." Thus she deemed each little fault of hers as an enormous one, thinking that anyone else, had she received the like favors, would have corresponded better to them. In the enthusiasm of her humility, she called herself the cause of all the faults that were committed in the monastery, and also of all the sins of the world. In an ecstasy during which some knowledge of the sinner's malice was imparted to her, having first bitterly deplored such malice, she inveighed against herself with these reproachful and threatening words: "I am the cause of every evil, let justice, therefore, come upon me and mercy upon others." Hence sprang in her that feeling of amazement at the thought that God, the angels, and the Saints endured her on the earth, and that the earth did not open to swallow her alive. One day she said to a sister: "What wouldst thou say, sister, if thou wouldst now see the earth open and swallow me?" And in the ecstasy and vision she had of the pains of purgatory, seeing those suffering souls and fearing hell for herself, she repeated several times, with a trembling voice: "Lucky will I be if I do not go lower down!"

In the presence of the superioress, it seemed as if all her limbs were shaking; and on being asked the reason why such a thing happened, she answered that knowing herself to be unworthy to stand before her, it seemed as if she heard herself addressed in the following words: "Depart this holy place, as thou art not worthy to stay in the company of these holy Spouses of Christ." When the superioress called her for anything, she threw herself at her feet as a guilty one, waiting always for a correction or a penance. Where the nuns met, she behaved with such reverence that she dared not raise her eyes, saying that they, having seen her faults, well knew her unworthiness; and she deemed it a singular benefit from God not to be cast away by them. Hence, one day on going to the choir, she said to one of her novices. "O sister, what good have you and I before God that He should grant us so great a favor as to deem us deserving of being admitted to the company of so many mothers and sisters, to praise Him? And in return for this benefit what shall we give to God?" Hence, she declared herself very much obliged to all the sisters who had admitted her, and regarded herself as the servant of all. In token of her humble gratitude she often kissed the walls of the monastery, and said: "O blessed walls! If I had remained in the world outside this sacred enclosure, I would have committed so many crimes that I would have died at the hands of the hangman; therefore have I reason to kiss you." Whilst in the choir with the rest of the nuns, she even thought that those common praises and prayers might not be acceptable to God on account of the gravity and the number of her sins. Sometimes it seemed to her as if she heard an imperious voice saying· "Let the wicked one be removed from the company of the holy ones, as her iniquity prevents their prayers from ascending, like incense, before God." A few days before her death she went so far as to say that she thought God would take her away from this life, that He might spare the earth some terrible punishment on her account; and she had already expressed herself at another time to the effect that she would not have wondered at any scourge that might befall the world on account of her being such a great sinner. These exaggerated expressions in the presence of so much virtue, seemed always the more incomprehensible to the mind of the nuns; therefore one day some of them made bold to ask her whether, when she was saying she feared the earth might swallow her up, that she was the greatest sinner, and the like, she actually felt that way. To which she answered with frank and certain accents: "Truly I do, and I have reason to feel this way; for if I did not commit sins that would have deprived me of the grace of God, it is due to the Lord's having kept me away from the occasion and preserved me; if others had received from God the graces and the opportunities to do good which I have received, they would not have offended Him as I did, and would have honored him better than I did; hence I know that on account of my ingratitude I deserve very great punishment." Having said this, she knelt before her interrogators, and, manifesting to them her past temptations as so many voluntary sins, she added "Do you see whether I have reason to feel as I do or not?" Another day, having been asked by one of her novices how she could think so lowly of herself, whilst she could not ignore the sublime favors with which God had privileged her, she gave this explanatory answer: "Know, daughter, that unless God had favored me with particular gifts, and almost detained me in this manner, I would have thrown myself into the greatest crimes that can be committed against His Divine Majesty With you He has not done so, because you are obedient to His simple voice and serve Him without these particular favors, hence I am more miserable than all of you." In a word, she took occasion from everything to humble herself.

When she led the mastiff out of the monastery (of which we have spoken above) being asked why she was not afraid to take him by the ear and lead him to the door, she answered· "A beast was leading another beast." To a nun who expressed to her the wish to know whether on account of so many graces received from God, she had ever permitted herself to be carried away by vain complacency, she said: "Dost thou not know that nobody should glory in what is not his? and why then dost thou suppose I gloried in the favors God granted me, as they are all His?" Another time, whilst one of her companions was reading to her some raptures and revelations which the Saint had written down, to see whether there were any errors, this nun asked her whether in such works she felt any movement of vainglory. Mary Magdalen answered "I feel in regard to what you have read to me, as in regard to any other book. I simply acknowledge that I have had such sentiments and intelligences as you have read to me." Some note-books wherein the nuns had written several anecdotes of her life having come to her hands, she immediately burnt them; for which being reprimanded by the superioress, and being asked whether she had done it through fear of vainglory, she answered No, but that she rather believed it her duty to burn them, quoting the example of a good servant of God Notwithstanding this she humbled herself before the superioress, begging her pardon, and it having being imposed upon her by obedience never again to act so arbitrarily, she fully submitted to the will of others

The spirit of human self-complacency had therefore no force in her soul. As to how she called herself the cause of the imperfections that were committed in her monastery, she explained it several times in her ecstatic contemplations, thus weeping over the weaknesses of others· "Oh ! if I had been employed in fervent prayer, if I had been recollected within myself, or had done other similar things, it is certain that God would have enlightened me better than He has done concerning my faults, and therefore I might have employed some means to obtain light for these souls, so that they would not have fallen " She similarly explained, during her ecstatic soliloquies, that she was the cause of the sins of the world and the damnation of many souls, because it seemed to her that she did not pray to God, as was her duty, for the conversion of sinners, as we have said elsewhere. Among the Lives of the Saints which were read, she loved in preference the lives of those who, living in community, had so hidden their virtue as to be deemed insane. These she would have willingly imitated; and though the Lord did not want her to follow this path, as she was to be rather an example and guide to the rest, still she did her best to be considered as contemptible and to be treated accordingly She entertained a desire for everything which was lowly in the offices of the monastery, rather than for any honorable position, and she applied herself to the former so cheerfully, that she really seemed to have gained a victory. One day she asked one of her novices whether she would have been willing to be a nun without having a voice in the Chapter, and upon her answering No, as she wished to be like the rest, the Saint added " I would be glad to remain in that condition, lowly and neglected, and with pleasure would I give my place and my voice to another one, who, I think, would make better use of it than myself"

For the same love of her own humiliation, she took very great delight in donning the most worn-out and patched habits, and making use of anything left by others Speaking on this point, it is remarkable how for a long time she chose to eat her pottage from a bowl which was being used by a sister who was suffering from a very loathsome sore Moreover, she frequently engaged in those acts of mortification which rendered her more contemptible, such as being blindfolded, having her hands tied behind, having herself trampled upon and struck, having con-

tumelious words addressed to her, and similar things, as we have already
seen in the course of her Life, and from which she derived so much
pleasure that not a few ecstasies took their origin from them.   At times
she asked one of her novices about her faults, and though the latter could
say nothing about them, yet the Saint knelt down to kiss her feet, and
begged her to trample upon her mouth and strike her with the scourge,
and when the novice was reluctant, she commanded her to do it in
virtue of obedience, bidding her say nothing to anyone about it.   Several
times she caused herself to be scourged by her own novices and lay-
sisters.   One day while she was the mistress of the young girls she cast
herself down on the ground in their midst and bade each one of them
strike her with a slipper on the mouth   Which thing caused her subjects
extreme confusion, and at the same time were to them occasions of being
moved and edified; so that often while doing such things they were all
moved to tears.   The better to induce her disciples and companions to
ill-treat her in the manner she wished, she told them that she was
grievously tempted, and that therefore she needed to be thus mortified, as
this helped her much to check her passions   For nine continuous years
she humbled herself before one of her companions nearly every day,
kneeling before her to accuse herself of the faults it seemed to her she
committed, and then begging her pardon   She had her to inflict the
punishment, sometimes with the scourge   Thus daily for a long time
she acted with one of her novices, whom she commanded to impose a
penance upon her, and as long as she lived she always wanted to have
one in particular to whom she would daily humble herself on account of
her faults, to receive the penance for them, or at least some harsh and
mortifying words   These faults, though, were so light and so imper-
ceptible, that the very nuns to whom she accused herself, asserted their
inability ever to discover in her any stain from those things on account
of which she tried to make herself believe and appear to be the most
relaxed nun in the world.

   What was generally deemed harmless, she would look upon, as
far as she was concerned, as a great fault   For instance, one day while
breaking a pine-cone, she ate two pine seeds which she had not even
extracted, but which had fallen out on the table; this was sufficient for
her to accuse herself of gluttony, and of having transgressed the Constitutions by eating out of the regular time without leave.   At every like
deviation, though she was wholly inadvertent of the orders of the community, she thought she was grievously violating the Rules and Constitutions
of the monastery.   When she heard of the faults of others, she immediately
said that she had greater ones; especially to the novices, after having
corrected them with manifest profit, she said· "I, too, daughters, have
committed this fault, I, too, have this imperfection," or else. "Do not
be frightened; I would have done worse than you did."   On the contrary, if she happened to see or hear of anyone's having performed some
virtuous action, much confused, she would say. "Surely I would not
have known how to do it," and similar other expressions indicative of
humiliation.   She often threw herself down on her knees at their feet,
that the sisters might tell her of her mistakes, begging them most pressingly to comply with her request.   By this she placed them in great

embarrassment, as they knew not how to grant her request, her conduct being faultless.

With those who gave signs of entertaining a great esteem for her, she used all possible means which would not be offensive to God, in order to make them form a contrary opinion. Sister Sommai, one of her novices and a girl of great virtue, loved and esteemed this holy mistress to a very remarkable degree. This being ill endured by the humility of Mary Magdalen, she thought (and obtained permission to that effect from the spiritual father) of making known to this novice the sad picture of the temptations she suffered during the five years of her probation Hence, having led her one day to a remote place, she knelt at her feet, and, breaking into most bitter weeping, amidst sobs and sighs, she thus addressed her. "Sister, I wish thee to know what kind of mistress thou hast, that thou mayest have more merit in obeying me, as thou art bound to do on account of the office I fill though I am unworthy, and I beg of thee to obey without thinking of what I am going to say. Know, therefore, that I have been the scandal and the trouble of this Religion," and, commencing with one of her temptations, she accused herself of all of them, as if they had been most grievous sins. She said that she had been gluttonous, thievish, wasteful, and hypocritical, as she had temptations of gluttony and of taking something to eat without permission, especially at those times when she was fasting on bread and water On account of the temptations of pride and sensuality, she accused herself as a proud and sensual nun ; and because, on one occasion, she had prudently passed over truth in silence, she accused herself of being guilty of lying, and, likewise, she considered as so many sins the suggestions of despair and of abandoning the sacred habit and the monastery, presented to her by the devil. Having thus given to the novice this most unfavorable picture of herself, she added: " If I had remained in the world, there is no doubt but that I would have ended my life at the hands of the executioner, on account of the many crimes I have committed, and if I had been in another monastery where there was less charity, I would have been shut up in a dungeon for life ; and yet these holy mothers and sisters have endured and pitied me with so much patience ! Oh ! how much I am indebted to each of them ! Oh ! what mercy I have received at their hands." Several times during this narrative of humiliation, she repeated : " Behold, sister, what kind of a mistress thou hast. Pray for me to God that He may deal with me so mercifully as not to send me to hell, as I deserve to be sent " The young girl (Sommai), amazed by so unlooked-for a scene, if, on the one hand, she was touched even to shed tears, on the other, she could not cast off the thought that all were true facts which Mary Magdalen had manifested to her so vividly and submissively. Therefore, feeling rather disturbed by being compelled to think that only afterwards had Mary Magdalen attained to that great sanctity with which she then saw her endowed, she went to the choir, and, prostrating herself before the Blessed Sacrament, said somewhat impatiently: "O Lord, let it be what Thou wilt; at present, she is a great servant of Thy Divine Majesty, and I will always look upon her and revere her as such " In saying this, as she afterwards testified, she felt all perturbation vanish, and, as if a veil had fallen from before her mind, she understood that all of which Mary Magdalen had accused herself as guilty had simply been prompted by her excessive humility, and that she had had no other end in view in thus humbling herself than to appear before her as a great sinner. In speaking about this to the nuns, they related to her how the Saint had been grievously tempted by all those things of which she had accused herself, but had won a complete and glorious victory, so that her esteem and love for this her dear mother greatly increased, and she, on her part, never tired telling her "Sister, remember me, thou knowest my needs" Whenever some of these humiliating things presented themselves to her mind, which she thought she had manifested to her, she immediately ran to make them known to her. She repeated them especially when she was doing some work near her. "O sister," she said, "I have already committed so many sins, pray to God to have mercy on me, do me this charity"

The prudent novice had feigned to believe everything as if it had really happened, hence the Saint was exceedingly pleased   But the same young girl once, wanting to convince the mother whilst she was telling her that she had offended God so much, answered her· "Mother, to offend God one must have a wicked will" To which the Saint, almost interrupting her words, immediately replied "This will, by the grace of God, I never had ; in my heart I have constantly desired to honor God, though I find that I have always offended Him   I have always loved Jesus, as He was always very good to me" She showed in this manner and very evidently, though unintentionally, how innocent and holy she was   She thus gives us an opportunity to establish this maxim, that the fact that some Saints called and believed themselves to be the greatest sinners, though amply possessed of all virtues, was simply a consequence of the supernatural operations with which they were favored   As if sensibly touched by the Divinity, the greatness and perfection of the Infinite Being inspires them with such a reverence and esteem for Him that they are dazzled and amazed. In this immense flood of vivid light they know themselves, their natural vileness, faults, and corruption   Necessarily they conceive a supreme contempt of self, a shame, and an excessive confusion; by which comparing themselves to God, their imperfections and sins are so magnified and appear to them in so deformed and abominable a light, that they are unable to bear with themselves, and deem themselves, by a true and sincere judgment, worthy of the greatest vituperation and shame. Hence it was wholly true what these Saints felt about themselves, that no person in the world was worse than they were, and that they looked upon it as a miracle of God's patience that He would tolerate them upon the earth, and other like expressions   Certain it is that to judge thus a special light from God is needed; and those who are wanting in it know not how to form in themselves this judgment, and can hardly believe others capable of it.   But that *contempt* and *most low estimation* of self was the foundation of Christian humility which God was laying in them, and upon which He afterwards raised the edifice of greater perfection—a perfection so sublime as to lift them up to the highest and most intimate union of pure love with Himself cleansing them by the from all self-love and self-esteem, which is the greatest impediment grace may encounter in its wonderful operations To complete this explanatory digression this must also be said, viz , that no one should flatter himself with professing humility by the simple fact of knowing himself to be poor and sinful; as such a knowledge, even supposing it to come from divine light, is but the first of the many steps by which man is united to God; and thus, like the Saints, we shall attain to the fullness of humility, if *from it* we shall proceed to *hope* in God and to *love* Him

Moreover, the holy and noble Mary Magdalen De-Pazzi, through the feeling and practice of humility, not satisfied with making known to everybody anything in her which might have the mere shadow of a fault, made her most luminous virtues appear as deserving of reproach rather than praise. If able, she hid them; if not able to hide them, she rigidly criticised them, so that they might be regarded as faults; and, not succeeding in this, she endeavored to persuade others that the particular deed they wanted to praise was the outcome of natural tendency rather than of virtue. Many acts of virtuous humiliation which she practiced with her novices became known only after her death, as she was wont to charge them not to speak about them to anyone.

During the time she was going around barefooted, when any girls entered the monastery on trial, she, that it might not be remarked by them, used to cover her feet with a pair of shoes without soles. Never did she discourse with others about the heavenly gifts with which she was so highly favored, she wished always to hide them ; so that, at the very time of her ecstasies, she complained very much of becoming so noticed. When she was wedded in spirit by Jesus, she said, as if complaining: "Thou hast promised me, O my Jesus, that as Thou wast hidden so was I to be, yet let Thy Divine Will be done." At another time, being grieved because Jesus made her speak while in ecstasy, so that she revealed all that He supernaturally suggested to her, she broke out into these words of complaint: "Please, loving Word, oh! please, I pray Thee, why didst Thou tell me so many things confidentially ; and now Thou willest that I manifest them?" Thus, at the moment when God wanted to reveal some heavenly operations or future events to her, she was several times heard to say: "Keep to Thyself, O Lord, keep to Thyself these secrets!" To those who recommended to her prayers some of their particular wants, awaiting with great anxiety to hear her opinion in the matter, whenever she had some particular light from God concerning it, she did not manifest it, unless compelled by command or necessity, limiting her answer to general and common words. Of her own will, speaking of herself, she never said anything but what helped to make her appear worthy of contempt and derision, so that nothing would have been known of her celestial communications if obedience or an irresistible force had not, during her alienation from her senses, compelled her to make them manifest. In an ecstasy, during which God revealed to her the mutual complacency He feels with the human soul and it with Him, she uttered the following words "O my God, keep for Thyself, keep this greatness; give no more so much participation to so vile a creature, as I am incapable of doing any good Keep it, keep it, O great God, in Thyself and delight in it. I, too, will draw

delight therefrom; but, on account of my weakness, I care not to understand anything more."

To the command of her confessor that she make known her intelligences to others, she naturally submitted fully and sincerely, but at the
same time with very bitter tears. Even to be simply seen in ecstasy was
for her a cause of great grief, hence the mother prioress, to alleviate her
anguish, was wont to send away those present, whenever the Saint gave
signs of going into ecstasy, that when she came out of it she would
think that there had been no witnesses to it. When by the superioress
herself she was asked to make the sign of the cross on some patient, or
to intercede with God for some grace by her prayer, she nearly always
called upon some of her companions to join her, so that to the latter
and not to herself the success might be ascribed "To the prayer of this
companion of mine you owe this grace; to her you must be thankful,"
she tried to say after a wonderful success; but it was useless, for the evidence of the virtuous efficacy was such as to exclude any doubt that it
might be owing to anyone but herself.

When God was pleased to make known to her the heavenly glory
of Louis Gonzaga, the process of Beatification of the angelic Jesuit youth
was being formed in Rome. The fathers of the Society of Jesus having
heard of this revelation placed it for examination before the tribunal
of the Sacred Rota, and this tribunal commissioned Mons. Alexander
Marzi-Medici, Archbishop of Florence, to inquire into the matter The
Archbishop then, with notary and witnesses, entered the monastery
of St. Maria degli Angeli to examine our Saint, who was then ill, but it
required no less than an express command of obedience to make her
answer the questions put to her, and afterwards she burst into such
copious weeping that nothing sufficed to quiet her. With great grief
and amazement, she repeatedly said. "Is it possible that I, so vile a
creature as I am, should be written about in books and spoken of by the
mouths of men, for these things;" and only the divine maxim, to listen
to the superior as if he were God, succeeded in calming her distress

As she avoided conversing and becoming acquainted with lay
people, so she felt a special pain at being visited by great and renowned
persons, both on account of her wish to remain unknown, and, more
so, in order to shun honors and to follow that evangelical inclination
well rooted in the hearts of the Saints—that feeling which cannot
mingle with the everlasting habits of deceitfulness and ambition, with
which the aristocratic class is wont to go forth on the theatre of the
world, to the special insult of truth and poverty Among the conspicuous
visits received by Mary Magdalen at the monastery, was that of the
Duchess of Bracciano, at the announcement of which, made to her
by the doorkeeper, she pronounced these words: "If the Duchess of
Bracciano knew that Sister Mary Magdalen is the abomination of this
monastery, she would avoid even naming her, let alone calling upon her."
Another visit was that which she received from the Duchess of Mantova,
on which occasion the Saint, weeping disconsolately, thus expressed
herself: "I know not why I should have to go and speak with these
persons, I being but a nun like all the rest nay, even the least of all "
Finally, when the Most Serene Princess De' Medici addressed to Mary

Magdalen a letter in which, asking some advice and spiritual instruction, she said that she intended to visit her soon, Mary Magdalen grieved at it beyond measure; and, being commanded by the superioress to answer regarding what she had been asked, she thus expressed her mind, but not without tears "Mother prioress, thou wishest that I should be esteemed for what I am not, and that I should go to hell for my pride; if I get there, these great people will not get me out" In the written answer which she gave to the most serene princess, she warmly begged her not to visit her, as she would pray for her all the same; and thus she saved herself that time from the proposed visit. She was not so successful at other times, and especially when the princess was called to the throne of France, at which time writing to our Saint that she positively wanted to see her and to speak to her before leaving for France, Mary Magdalen, unable to prevent it, sent word to her, begging that at least she should come alone and privately, to avoid as much as possible her making acquaintances and gaining renown. In this matter the august queen pleased her, as we have seen in Chapter XXII.

A soul so rich in humility could not but nourish a noble sense of this virtue, and consequently manifested it, even unwittingly at times, for the instruction of others; in fact, innumerable were the ideas and maxims expressed by Mary Magdalen about the virtue of humility; and it will be well here to relate some of the most important ones, both to prove in what degree this Saint possessed humility, and for the immediate benefit and profit of our readers. Most beautiful was the definition of humility she gave when in ecstasy; she said that this virtue was nothing but "a constant knowledge of one's nothingness, and a continuous enjoyment of all those things that may induce one to the contempt of self" In another ecstasy, speaking of the causes which moved God to unite Himself to our soul, she said that among them humility held the first place, and that it drew God into the soul that possessed it, like a magnet She continued speaking in the following manner, which shows with what efficacy the divine light wrought on her spirit "God," she said, "looking on the work of His hands, which by humility, self-knowledge, and annihilation has lost, so to say, its being, and sees only its nothingness, gives it a most noble and perfect being, I would almost say a being without beginning and without end; a being (as Thou hast said, O Lord), that is just Thy own; a being divine. '*Qui adhæret Domino, unus spiritus est*'—'But he who is joined to the Lord is one spirit' (1 Cor. vi, 17), not by communication of nature, but by union of will, so that it seems to have no other will and understanding but Thine Thus it works with Thee as if it knew not how to work in itself and by itself, and all it does seems Thy doing and not its own; but it is more Thine than its own, for though it concurs as a creature moved by Thee to the operation, yet the mode of operation is more Thine than its own, as Thou art the beginning, the middle, and the end of such an operation. Thou movest all with Thy grace and love and workest in Thy creature, but not without its cooperation. When the soul reaches this degree of humility, God is so pleased with its annihilation that He enlarges its nothingness and there He permanently dwells." In giving the reason why God does not unite with proud souls, she added "God refuses to unite Himself to that soul which refuses to acknowledge its own nothingness, because, being in Himself and of Himself glorious, and not being in need of anyone, if he united Himself to a soul so unjust and blind, He would seem to be in need of this soul rather than to be what He is in Himself, happy. As in the creation of the universe, nothingness preceded (if that which is not can be said to precede) all that the Creator made in this world, and the union He made of Himself, giving the being and the participation of Himself to all creatures, according to the capacity and the nature of each, whereby every creature becomes united with and dependent on God; so, in order to accomplish this other union with the soul and receive a world of graces, this annihilation must be found in the soul. As in the creation (by grace) of the microcosm which is the reasonable creature, and in the union of the Word with the humanity, He wanted an anterior annihilation in her who was to be His Mother. '*Ecce ancilla Domini*'— 'Behold the handmaid of the Lord' (Luke 1, 38); that by this act she might become more worthy and capable of a glory and greatness so wonderful that neither she nor any blessed spirit or mere creature can fully comprehend it (the dignity of such a Mother being an infinite grace); so, in order that the Divine Word may unite with the soul, this annihilation must precede, and, by means of it or this being done, God comes to do wonderful things in that soul, and of it can be said: '*Quia fecit mihi magna qui potens est; quia respexit humilitatem ancillæ suæ*' But even this annihilation the soul does not know in itself; but, by annihilating itself, it attains to the greatness of God, Who unites Himself to the soul possessed of such annihilation. This soul then acknowledges God as glorious in Himself, attributing to Him all honor and glory, and not to itself. Hence God Himself takes such pleasure in this soul that He remains continually united to it. By means of this union, this soul partakes as far as is possible (remaining in its being as to the nature) of the divine perfections "

Another time, whilst admiring ecstatically the humility of Jesus in washing the feet of His disciples, she gave utterance to these expressions of praise· "O humility, that exalteth the things that are not, and dost lower the things that are, and therefore exaltest man, who is a mere nothing, and dost lower God, Who is everything ! O humility, that being victorious, and raising thyself, reachest the very throne of the Most Holy Trinity ! O humility, how thou producest and nourishest purity with thy breasts ! Thou, as a mother, givest suck to the poor in spirit and leadest them under the shade of the Word, and embracest the ignorant and bringest them to the Bride Church , thou dost nourish the faint-hearted, crown the virgins, give the palm to the martyrs, put the diadem on thy priests in heaven, give satiety of thy vision to the hermits, in a word, to all the Saints; and during the pilgrimage of this life thou renderest us patient and constant, tranquil and merry before the arrogance of the world that would swallow up all in the abyss of a laborious and troublesome career " One day, comparing purity and humility, she preferred the latter to the former, and, to show that purity is not pleasing to God without humility, she concluded as follows "Many virgins will be found in hell: but no humble souls can be sent there, though they may be without this purity." Hence she insisted on the necessity of this virtue, especially in religious persons; and exhorting the superioresses and the mistresses to exercise their subjects in the practice of this virtue, she was wont to say: "Humility must be infused into the young plants of the Religion like oil in a lamp; and as the wick cannot burn without oil, so these young plants will not yield to the splendor of the Religion in sanctity and perfection, unless at every moment a fresh stimulus be given them and they are tried in this virtue of humility." She added: "Let no one rest until death from the practice of humility. Let him that has the care of souls not grow tired of making them practice this virtue as long as they are imprisoned in the body; as humility is a ladder of many steps, the top of which cannot be reached." This virtue during the time Mary Magdalen was mistress of novices she admirably practiced towards her novices and with herself always; as she did not cease until death to humble herself in the most constant and profitable manner, triumphing in the most extensive and radical way over the inevitable and constant instigations of pride, to which, on account of corrupt nature, the human soul is subject. We shall see in the following chapter, which embraces the last period of her life, how she finally conquered.

CHAPTER XXXIX.

THE LAST ILLNESS OF SISTER MARY MAGDALEN, DURING WHICH SHE
ATTAINS TO A *NAKED* SUFFERING. PROLONGATION OF THE
SAME ILLNESS, DURING WHICH SHE IS ELECTED
SUPERIORESS. HER HAPPY DEATH.

S the natural motion increases the nearer it approaches its
centre, so this blessed mother, the nearer she approached
the end of her life and her centre, God, the more anxious
and thirsty she became to suffer for the love of Him Who
was the necessary and vital strength of her spirit. This
strength, which proceeded from the purest and sublimest
love of God, besides experiencing the greater velocity of this
motion from getting nearer the limits of time, felt at the same
time great reluctance to submit to the necessity of inaction. The desire
to suffer, natural to the heart of Mary Magdalen, was subject to the
effects that human nature encounters in its physical condition. Hence,
as a natural lamentation, she emitted more loudly, when near her end,
her own characteristic motto: *"Non mori, sed pati!"*—"Let me suffer,
and not die!" She felt an irrepressible panting to be with Christ in
heaven; but not without having first obtained on earth the fullness of a
wonderful suffering, which it seemed to her she never had reached amidst
the innumerable sufferings she endured in her life. Hence she grieved
excessively; fearing the time might be wanting to her in which to give
God so heroic a testimony of affection. "In heaven," she said, "there
is no place for this glorious suffering; therefore, in order to attain it, I
am compelled to wish for more life. One day, in 1602, hearing while in
the refectory the reading of a treatise on the *naked* suffering for the love
of God, she became so inflamed with the desire of undergoing it, that,
unable to endure calmly that impulse, she rose from the table, and going
to Sister Vangelista del Giocondo, her particular directress, manifested
to her how she felt within herself that God would finally grant her a
true and *naked* suffering. Therefore she begged her not to interfere
with her in this by procuring any comforts for her; and then, feeling
very happy on account of this presentiment, as if it had been the happiest
news she could hear, she went to the choir to express to God all the
gratitude her burning heart knew or could suggest to her. Not many
days thereafter, during the same year, she was attacked and brought low

by a very severe catarrh, which caused a violent and continuous cough and made her lose her strength in a short time, so that she could scarcely keep alive. Notwithstanding this she did not relax in the least her ordinary austerity, neither did she make use of any remedy, fearing lest her self-love might deceive her, nay, thinking that the lassitude caused by the cough, and the fever which at certain times accompanied it, might be laziness or slothfulness of her senses, she was wont to say. "Oh, how one must be on guard on account of these senses, which are so lazy and cowardly, and which want me to regard what is slothfulness in God's service as mere weakness and infirmity, so that they might take rest" With an inexorable accent, she addressed her body in these words: "I know thee well; I will never do thy will, but God's."

It was April, 1603, and the health of Mary Magdalen was about the same as we have described it. One day of said month, whilst she, as mistress, was assisting one of her sick novices, a vein burst in her breast, and she vomited a great deal of blood, but she said not a word to anybody about it, in order to avoid what would naturally have been the consequence of her mentioning it—the compassion of others. The day following, while accompanying a novice to the parlor grates, Mary Magdalen again had a hemorrhage, and, as she could not hide it, she was compelled by obedience to go to bed and take some medicine for it Having taken a few days' rest without getting any worse, she thought she had wholly recovered, and quickly and cheerfully returned to her former mode of life. But the disease was such as not to be baffled so easily; hence, from day to day, Mary Magdalen went on feeling its sad results with notable loss of strength. She grieved at this very much, fearing, as usual, it might be a snare of the devil, and, with tears and painful feelings of amazement, she said continually: " I stop to think whether I am the same one that I was before, when with a resolution I overcame all great difficulties, and now, the more I try, the more I feel weakened " In the month of July of the same year, she again suffered from hemorrhage and in greater quantity; so that the superioress, who, having noticed so many wonders in her and that God was leading her by extraordinary ways, had not dared till then to make her remain in bed, now compelled her to do so. As she grew worse in the following August, she vomited so much blood that the physicians themselves deemed her recovery impossible, fearing, moreover, to see her choked at any moment. Her novices, together with the nuns, were already bewailing her loss; but she, though brought to such an extremity, told them to be of good cheer, as she surely would not die of that malady, it being the will of God that she should complete her term of mistress of novices; in fact, she continued improving so that, on All Saints' Day of the following November, she resumed the charge of the novices, and returned to the community life and the routine of the monastery, to the amazement and joy of all But at times she vomited some blood, at which the novices especially could not give themselves peace. She repeated to them that they should trust in God and not waver, even if she vomited a barrel of blood daily, as she knew to a certainty that it was God's will that she should live to end her term of the office she then filled over them Notwithstanding so poor a state of health, she prevailed on the superiors to allow her to abstain and fast with the community during the following Lent of 1604; but, having rigorously kept it till the Saturday before Passion Sunday, on the latter day she again had a hemorrhage, so that she was compelled by obedience to interrupt its observance, and, weeping, she said that on account of her sins she had not deserved to complete it, though after a few days she resumed the Lenten practices and continued them with the rest till the end.

On the 24th of June of the same year, her spirit having already been subjected for some time to a singular aridity, it was raised above its senses, she understanding, though, that this was to be the last ecstasy of her life   During it, the Lord showed to her the *naked* suffering which He wanted to make her taste, by means of a very serious infirmity with an extreme desolation of spirit, regarding which she thus expressed herself: "O my Jesus, Thou wilt that I become as a very little girl; nay, Thou wilt that I be born again ! O how small must I become again ! These souls will no longer recognize me on account of my littleness." Wholly burning with the desire of being tortured from head to foot, she exhorted, during the same ecstasy, all those present to embrace the *naked* suffering, showing to them how useful to attain perfection it was, and she remained eight whole hours in this ecstasy   As in October following the election of the new superioress of the monastery was to take place, the nuns had a desire to elect her, with a mind to obtain the dispensation from the age of which she was short. This intention became known to her, and immediately putting together all the reasons her humility could suggest to her, she presented them to the nuns, so that they might not calculate on her in any way. Her feeble health, above all, was a great pretext to dissuade the nuns from their project. Finally the matter was compromised by electing another nun as prioress and her as sub-prioress. She resigned herself to the voice of obedience, laying aside every repugnance of her modesty, and displaying at the same time all her zeal in discharging the duties of the office; so that, from the very beginning, she arranged some matters tending to the greater observance of the rules. But after the lapse of eight days, a fever which was continually wearing her out seemed to reach its worst degree, and rendered her so feeble that, being unable to stand, it was found necessary to bring her to the bed on which she was to end her mortal pilgrimage after thirty months of the most severe and cruel sufferings. The torments with which God tried her for so long a time, to second her wish for a *naked* suffering, were partly in her body and partly in her soul. In her body, she was consumed by most burning fevers, with catarrh and cough, and often with hemorrhages. She felt very piercing headaches, so that the least noise, even the subdued talk of the nuns, caused her the most painful sensations   During the last two years of her life, she was troubled with so intense and constant a toothache, without intermission day or night, that it seemed as if, though innocent, she was enduring that gnashing of teeth of which the Gospel speaks as the symbol of the infernal torments, together with the weeping to which she was forced, especially at the time of taking her meals   *And this pain increased with such an acerbity that in a short time it ate up the stumps and roots of her teeth, so that many of them fell out of her mouth.* Those which remained, on account of the excessive torment they caused her, had, nearly all, to be extracted by the dentist, and she was left almost toothless. By the violence of such a martyrdom, she was inadvertently drawn to utter some voice or word of lament which was followed immediately by a strong fear of having thereby offended God; hence, with tears in her eyes, she soon turned to the sisters, saying to them that they should pray for her that she might endure those torments without offending His Divine Majesty. There was no part of her body which was not greatly tortured. Now she felt as if her breast had been cut with a razor; now as if her head had been struck with a hammer; now in this, now in that part of her body she suffered as if one member were being torn off from the other. One day she said that it seemed to her as though she had been fried in a pan. Her body was reduced to such a condition that it was but skin, nerves, and bones. She was also so much flayed, shrunk, and hurt that, being unable to move by herself, she was carried by the nuns from one bed to another, presenting a spectacle so pitiful as to draw tears even from a stone. Some nuns would not even be present at it, as they could not endure such a sight. The physicians themselves were amazed, and used to say that they did not know how it was possible, naturally speaking, that a body so wasted, and tortured with so many and divers sufferings day and night, could keep alive so long and endure such severe pains. They often declared that she would not live the week out; but, nevertheless, the weeks, the months, and the years were passing by, and she was still alive. This, it is necessary to believe, happened in virtue of the strength of divine power, because God wished to satisfy her desire of *naked* suffering, and, therefore, He kept her alive to fill her with suffering. Having lost all taste for material food, she gradually became insensible to spiritual things also, so that no respect or attention which was paid her gave her any comfort, nay, she was wont to say that whatever formerly gave her relief and consolation had now turned into pain and sorrow, and that her heart was capable of but grief and anguish. Sometimes during those sad days, she addressed these words to the Crucifix, though in peace and resignation : "O my Lord, if Thou givest not to me help and vigor, my body cannot endure so many pains." But the pure and complete desolation of spirit followed, and it led her to the height of sadness and anguish. The heavens seemed to her to have become of bronze, and her prayers seemed no longer to reach the ears of God, as if her voice were hushed by the divine clemency. The heavenly sweetnesses were no longer distilled on her, instead of which all was darkness and terror for her, so that she greatly feared for her eternal salvation. She recommended herself to the sisters with a most fervent and pitiful pleading that they might obtain for her mercy from God. This suffering was also wished for by her, and yet, blaming her sins for it of which she desired to consider herself guilty at any rate, she often asked her spiritual father, with a feeling of painful apprehension : "Father, dost thou think I will be saved ?" And, on being one day asked by him the reason of this anxious interrogation, she answered : "Father, this is a very serious thing, a creature like myself, having never done any good, to have to appear before God'" Such was the opinion she entertained of herself, counting as nothing her many and most noble and virtuous actions, but only placing before her own eyes some faults inseparable from human weakness with which she reproached herself continually, magnifying them into grievous sins. Hence she said that God would hasten to remove her from this life, lest He should have cause to send some great chastisement to the world on account of her iniquity At other times she said : "Well do I know, O my Lord, that my sins are so many and so great that they deserve other punishments than these infirmities and desolations!" In a word, she appeared before the nuns so oppressed and abandoned of God that they compared her to Christ on the cross when He said. "O my God, O my God, why hast Thou abandoned me?" It also caused her great pain to find herself confined to bed, both because of the vivacity of her nature and the zeal which made her untiring in acting for the glory of God and the good of others. She was wont to say that it did not seem to her as if God could send her pain for which she had greater repugnance than for this. Yet, fully conformed to the Divine Will, not only could no one see acts of impatience in her, nor hear words of complaint, but often she could be detected raising her eyes to heaven and uttering fervid words of thanksgiving to the Divine Goodness, because she had her life lengthened so that she might taste *naked* suffering; and she ended with this generous offering of herself· "O Lord, if Thou art pleased I should stay in this bed suffering till the Day of Judgment, Thy Will be done." One of her disciples, admiring her in so great and tenacious suffering, for one affliction was scarcely over when another attacked her, told her· " O mother mistress, it is a great thing that the Lord should give thee always fresh occasions to suffer !" To which Mary Magdalen answered that from her youth it had been her desire to suffer purely for God, and that she had always asked of Him this grace, and in a special manner in the act of receiving Holy Communion, and therefore she deemed it an immense favor of God, adding "Sister, the *practice of suffering* is a thing so valuable and noble that the Word, being in the bosom of His Eternal Father, in the abundance of all the riches and delights of Paradise, because He was not adorned with the *stole of suffering*, came down to earth for this *ornament;* and He was God, Who could not be deceived. I have not yet, during my life, deserved to have occasion to suffer, for I have always received good from God and all creatures " Here the disciple reminding her of some particular sufferings, and the five years of her painful trial, the Saint replied that all that had been nothing, and that she could not call that a time of *naked* suffering, because during it she had tasted so many and so great suavities of spirit, that all her bitterness was sweetened by them. "What I now ask of God is, that He grant that I experience *naked* suffering, unmixed with any pleasure; and by the confidence I feel in the Divine Goodness, I hope He will grant me this grace before I die " Another time a nun said to her "Mother, I can bear no longer that God should make thee suffer so much " The good mother was troubled on seeing this want of conformity to the Divine Will, and she appeared to feel more pain for this fault than for her own disease To correct this error, she gave her this advice "Sister, whenever thou art oppressed by tribulations, endeavor to be very watchful and see that thou dost not cut them off from their fount, which is the Will of God; otherwise they will be to thee a heavy and unbearable weight "—a maxim truly divine, which we should all keep indelibly engraved on our soul. The disease having progressed, and Mary Magdalen being asked by the confessor about the particulars of her sufferings, she answered "Father, I want thee to know that there is not a spot in my body that is free from pain; but I feel great peace and rest of heart in God's will" And on the father's adding that he hoped the Lord would console her yet before her death, she immediately protested: "This I do not ask, but I ask only patience and strength to bear these pains." Of truth she bore them heroically; for, at the very time ·the vehemence of the pain wetted her cheeks with tears, she endeavored to smile and appear cheerful to the sisters surrounding her. One day being left alone, as the nuns had gone to hear the sermon, this blessed mother in the midst of these excessive pains began to sing psalms, adding at the end of each those celestial words of St. Francis: "Such is the happiness I look for, that in every pain I rejoice more." A nun who happened to pass by and stop a while for something, heard her, without being noticed by Mary Magdalen, and was greatly amazed, both because of the sweetness and the strength of the voice of that emaciated singer. But what surprised the nuns more was the never-changing sweetness of her countenance, so that the angelic gracefulness and the divine peace which her conscience enjoyed, appearing on her countenance even when her spiritual or bodily pains were at their height, if on one hand she inspired compassion, on the other she comforted and delighted the soul of anyone who beheld her.

Besides patience, which she practiced with so much fortitude during this long and serious illness, she continued till the end of her life to give every possible proof of all the virtues we have already described in the course of this book. As to the desire for Holy Communion and of suffering for the love of God, she gave the highest and most wonderful evidences. At the beginning of her illness she had the courage to get up every morning to go to Communion with the rest of the nuns, to do so, on account of her weakness, consumed a very long time for a short distance, and often she had to be supported on the arms of others. It also happened several times, that on account of the fever which assailed her at that hour, she suffered such strange fainting spells on the way, that it seemed as if she were about to breathe her last. Therefore the confessor, Rev. Francesco Benvenuti, seeing to what pains and dangers this mother was thus exposed, resolved to give her Holy Communion in bed every morning, and he did so. But even this did not diminish her sufferings, for in a few days her stomach was reduced to such weakness that it became necessary that she should be fed with light food every three hours Hence, having to pass whole nights without taking anything in order to receive Holy Communion, she often felt like fainting, and yet she could not be prevailed upon to break her fast To the sisters who, compassionating her, exhorted her sometimes to omit Holy Communion, she answered: "Sisters, if you think I should not receive Holy Communion on account of my unworthiness, willingly will I abstain from it; but if you are moved by compassion at seeing my suffering, know that if receiving would cost me my life, I will not abstain from Communion; because, though I derive no *delight* from this Sacrament which I receive, still I feel thereby strengthened to suffer this disease with patience; and when I am deprived of *It*, I feel that a great help is wanting to my soul and I lack strength to bear the illness as it ought to be borne.

When the Rev. Vincenzo Puccini, who succeeded, as a confessor, the above-mentioned Benvenuti, went to give her Holy Communion, he found her so exhausted that she seemed to lack the strength to open her lips. Sometimes he was in doubt whether he should give her Holy Communion or not, fearing that she might be unable to swallow the Sacred Host; but well did he afterwards perceive the effect of which she spoke; for hardly had she received the Most Holy Sacrament than she so evidently grew in vigor and strength that, the divine help and grace appearing on her countenance, she seemed to be entirely different from her former self. As long as she had sufficient strength to recite the Divine Office, she never omitted it, and when she was unable to say it, she had a sister to recite it daily to her till she died, though it caused her great suffering, for the voice of another, no matter how low, was to her a source of great pain, on account of the constant and intense headache from which she suffered Yet she listened to it with great attention, and sometimes she repeated to herself some verse of it, and, at the end of the Office, with great humility she struck her breast, saying: "*Peccavi, Domine, miserere mei*"—"I have sinned, O Lord; have mercy on me" She added "This is my part" Though so grievously sick, she continued to lie for many months on the hard straw-bed with the woolen sheets and little tunic, and she did not lie on the mattress or use linen tunic or sheets until she was compelled to do so by obedience. If it occurred to her that a certain kind of food or something else might please her, she deemed it a fault to say so or to ask for it, and when a lady, who was much attached to her and the monastery, sent her some delicate and tasty viands, notwithstanding that they were the most suitable to her present need, she experienced much difficulty in taking them, as it seemed to her that they were not suitable food for poor Religious; hence the confessor had to order her to eat of them. This she submissively did then and at other times, when the same lady repeated this kindness. Neither did her many pains and afflictions diminish in any way the ardor of her charity for her neighbor. Whenever she saw or heard that anyone was oppressed by temptations and trials, as if she felt her own no longer, she gave herself up entirely to afford all possible relief to the afflicted sister; and, full of compassion, she thought that others' afflictions were greater than her own. The nuns remarked that during so painful an illness, the most efficacious remedy to make her forget her own sorrows was this, viz, to relate to her the afflictions of others. If another sister was sick, Mary Magdalen tried to send her the superior food with which she herself was furnished To this practice of charity the nuns were so accustomed that once, a lay-sister being sick, she felt a desire for I know not what food, but, without manifesting this to anyone, she thought within herself that if the mother, Sister Mary Magdalen, had any of it, she would certainly send her some; and lo! a sister came on behalf of the Saint, bringing her the food she wished for.

When unable to go to the bedside of the dying ones, as was her wont, Mary Magdalen caused herself to be carried there, to assist them personally at the last moment, and she used to say "As the Bridegroom does not come to me, I will be near *them* when He comes for them" She also practiced zeal for the salvation of souls with great energy, especially in teaching, correcting, and enlightening those who had been left to her care, though she had resigned the office of sub-prioress. Likewise she never ceased making offerings of the Blood of Jesus, and praying to God for the conversion of sinners, for the suffering souls, for persons afflicted, and for all other needs that were recommended to her.

A few days before her death, that her charity might be crowned by an irrefragable proof, God permitted that a person should offer her a grave and notable insult. It is not easy to recount how many tokens of love, affability, and gratitude she sincerely gave to her offender for this insult. To the sisters, who were greatly astonished at it, she said: "My sisters, I have done this to show my gratitude for this benefit which I have received (calling the insult a benefit); and I am glad I did not die before I had occasion to taste this pain."

Thus did she give during this illness the most evident proofs of the faith, the hope, the obedience, the purity, the meekness, and every other virtue with which her soul was richly endowed. But this time was not to pass without her giving a more solemn proof of humility, which was a singular prerogative of her heart; nay, she gave several proofs of it, out of which I select the following, and from them it will be easy to guess the rest. On a certain occasion when the nuns were wont to go to the choir, and there, kneeling before the Blessed Sacrament, ask one after another, publicly, forgiveness of God for their sins, our Saint wished also to be present. She had herself carried there on a litter, from which, when her turn came, she threw herself to the floor in the midst of the choir, and, falling on her knees, all trembling, with deep conviction and words of extreme humility, she asked forgiveness of God, begging that He would show her mercy at the hour of her death, as though she were the greatest sinner on earth. Then, turning to the nuns, she asked forgiveness of them for all the scandals and annoyances she might have given them, carrying her fault, and the contempt she drew on herself, to such an extent that she excited in the sisters the most touching feeling of tenderness in her behalf.

Several times during the course of this illness the physicians had ordered that Extreme Unction should be administered to her, it seeming to them as if she had but a few more hours to live. Finally, on the 23d of May of the year 1607, the father confessor, having given her Communion that same morning, as usual, for devotion's sake, and, seeing that she grew notably worse, resolved to anoint her. Magdalen, consenting with great peace and spiritual joy, prepared herself as follows: She begged the mother prioress to have all the sisters brought to the cell where she was lying; and when they were gathered, in the presence of Rev. Father Puccini, she again begged pardon of all for her faults and bad example, using words indicative of excessive humility. She thanked all for having endured her in their community, protesting that she had been unworthy of that holy place, and she said that by the merits of the good sisters who had departed this life (and who had received her among them), she hoped to obtain forgiveness for her sins. After this, she humbled herself in a particular manner to the mother, Sister Vangelista del Giocondo, thanking her for all the labors she had endured for her, and imploring of her forgiveness for all things in which she might have failed in following out her orders or wishes, and, both to her and the confessor, she warmly recommended the monastery, promising that, if she would get to heaven, she would pray to God for them, that they might have light in order to guide well the religious family. She promised to beg of the Divine Goodness that He would in a special manner grant to Sister Vangelista as many years of life as were lived by the Beloved Disciple St. John. It so happened that this nun, being then about seventy-three years old, reached the age of ninety-two (an age approximative to that of said Evangelist, according to the common opinion), and died in the year 1626, after having much benefited the monastery through her zeal, accompanied by the vivid example of her religious perfection.

Moreover, Mary Magdalen left to the nuns these three salutary counsels first, that they should be zealous in observing their Rule and Constitutions, being ready to expose themselves to suffer anything, even death, rather than to allow the least relaxation in the rigor of the observance; and that to maintain this, they should always choose superiors who had zeal for it; secondly, that in all things, they should look for and love holy poverty and religious simplicity; and she asked that if in these things she had caused them displeasure, by leading a singular life as to dress and food, they would forgive her, as she thought such had been the will of God; thirdly, that they should love one another and continue united in charity, being all of one heart and will, as the love of one for the other must be such that each of them would rejoice more for the good of her companion than for her own, judging all to be instruments better suited than herself to honor God by their virtues. Having thus humbled herself, and given these counsels as a legacy of love and zeal, she received Extreme Unction with remarkable devotion, answering by herself all the prayers ordained for it by the Church. In the meantime, the sisters, having been asked by her to do so in homage to the mysteries of our holy faith, recited the Creed of the Mass, the Preface of the Mass for Trinity Sunday, and the Symbol of St. Athanasius, whilst she listened, her eyes fixed on the Crucifix, which she had caused to be suspended in front of her bed, so that she seemed to be much moved and jubilant in the midst of the celestial glory. The fact is that she became notably invigorated throughout all her person, as soon as she received this Sacrament. Some days previous to this, the above-named confessor, Father Puccini, had decided to go, for an object of his own, to Mount Senario,[1] and he was to have started for it the following day; but, not wishing to leave the mother in that critical condition, he had given up the thought of it, being most anxious to be present at her death. Mary Magdalen knew

---

[1] This is one of the most celebrated *Santuarii* of Italy, ten miles from Florence, it having been ... theatre of ... ... Blessed Florentines, who ... ... 1233, and ... ... there the celebrated Order of the Servi Ets of Mary ... it is the ... belief that they received their black habit from ... ... in memory of her Dolors

this, and, as soon as she saw him, addressed to him these frank words: "Father, I tell thee to go without fear; and I beg of thee to recommend me to the prayers of those Religious, that the Lord may grant me the grace of salvation " On the father's answering that he could not feel reassured, she replied: "Go, without fear, as thou shalt find me alive upon thy return." After which, Rev. Father Puccini, being unable to hesitate any longer, went to the above-mentioned hermitage, where he remained three days; and then, returning to Florence, found the Saint alive, but oppressed by such great and excruciating pains that it seemed as if the Lord kept her alive but to give her the merit of a sovereign suffering. After receiving Extreme Unction, she lived twelve days in the most severe and constant torture, so that these days could well be compared to twelve years of purgatory. As she very much feared lest she might fall into some act of impatience, she recommended herself with the most touching and affectionate expressions to God, the Blessed Virgin, the Saints and to the prayers of the sisters, who, whilst not failing to do for her what they could, hastened rather to confidently recommend themselves to her. Seeing that the departure of Mary Magdalen from this world was certain and near, each nun watched for the most opportune moment to approach her for the sake of taking a sad but inevitable leave, and also to lay before her all the needs and wishes of her heart, that she might see to them in heaven with her powerful intercession. All day and night long, they were running to her, one for this grace and another for that; so that this servant of God in her little chamber seemed a great queen, who was about to leave and go to the kingdom of her Spouse, and was receiving many homages and petitions before starting. She promised all to help them better in heaven than she had already done or could do on earth, and said . "If, whilst with you, I would have laid down my life that each of you might become perfect, simply on account of the love Jesus bore to you, how much more shall I not exert myself for you, if God be merciful enough to admit me to heaven?" The nuns inconsolably shed, for her loss, the most sad and abundant tears; and, now asking her pardon, now advice and instruction, gave vent without restraint to the anguish of their hearts. She, on the contrary, all serene, gave to all a benign answer, humbled herself to them, consoled them, gave to each counsels of salvation and religious perfection, and exhorted all to the love and zeal of the regular observance, and to the love of their neighbor. To the mother prioress, in particular, she spoke at length concerning the evangelical perfection and the rules which she wished should be added to their Constitutions To the girls of the monastery still entrusted to her care, having called them to herself two days before she died, she left, as her testament, fraternal charity, taking as a rule the commandment of the Divine Master, Who wished it impressed upon the spirit of His disciples with this formula: "Love one another as I have loved you," viz, with equality and purity of affection

Though assured of the truth of her ecstasies and revelations, as is shown in her life, still, on account of her deep humility, she could never wholly free herself from the fear of having been deceived and deluded by the devil; and during these latter days, with a most piercing anguish she asked the opinion of her confessor concerning them The Rev.

Father Puccini, starting from a generally safe point, thus answered her.
"If thou hast been guided by obedience, be sure that there can have
been no deception." She, being reassured, gave this answer· "I do not
remember having done anything without obedience; but in all things I
have permitted myself simply to be led by my superiors, and in all my
doings I have had nothing in my mind except the presence of God."
After she had received Extreme Unction, she allowed to her infirmity no
other relief, though the physicians warmly exhorted her to do otherwise
"Christ on the Cross," she answered, "received no comfort " She also
wanted to die on the naked cross of suffering, and this was granted to
her, not only in regard to the body, in which she was evidently so
much afflicted, but also in regard to the soul. Three days before she
departed this life, she said to Sister Maria Pacifica del Tovaglia, with
complete peace and tranquillity of soul, that till that moment she had
found herself desolate and without any taste of God; and she ended her
discourse by these words, which indicate to what degree of perfection
her virtue had attained: "I am satisfied with everything in which God
is pleased, and I thank Him, and again offer to Him every satisfaction
and spiritual delight, provided only that I be saved." It was really a pity
to see this soul, so favored of God with gifts and communications so
wonderful, now abandoned and forsaken in the midst of great sorrows and
without the least consolation. Where human nature trembles and
recoils at the vanishing of those hopes which one never likes to give
up, Mary Magdalen felt her soul open to joy, as she saw that her life was
declining. She spoke of her death as we would of nuptials, a banquet,
a treasure and the like, by which we are so strongly attracted Having,
in fact, reached that *naked* suffering so much wished and asked for, it
seemed as if her heart, like an arrow, plunged of itself into the intoxica-
tion of exultation and delight, and her spirit rose so high towards the
beatific end as no longer to feel anything of earth, body or life.

Thus things were on the 24th of May, the Day of the Ascension,
and last day but one of her life. On the morning of this day the father
confessor wanted to give her Holy Communion as Viaticum; but she
told him to give her Communion simply for devotion, as he had done
every morning until then, because he would still be in time to give her
Holy Viaticum the next day. He did so, and it happened as she said She
spent the day now speaking with those present about charity, God, and
their neighbor, and now pressing and warmly kissing the Crucifix she
held in her hands, and speaking to Him of those things which they
alone knew. During the night, being troubled partly by lethargy and
partly by restlessness, she caused the Passion to be read to her by the
nuns, and the Penitential Psalms, the Litanies, the Symbol of St
Athanasius and other prayers to be recited, whilst she endeavored to
follow them with the most constant and lively attention At the
nearing of dawn the light no longer struck her eyes with its wonted
strength, neither was her will sufficient to lend the action to the tongue
which she desired it to have, so that she herself called for the Viaticum,
begging her father confessor to ... ... light. This
was done at a... ... ... he morning
twilight announce ... to our ... ... on the greater

luminary, and the birds before stretching their wings to fly through vast regions, were giving to their Creator the wonted tribute of their praise. It cannot be told with what sentiments of tender and warm piety she received for the last time the Sacrament of the Body of Jesus Christ; feeling certain that she would soon see Him without any veil, in all His glory Few people, I think, can know the joy a holy soul must feel at such a moment. Having passed some time in acts of love, homage, and burning gratitude to her Jesus in the Sacrament, she turned to the sisters to bid them the last adieu. She wanted to embrace them all, and again ask of all their pardon and benediction; and, as they answered with tears and sighs, Mary Magdalen consoled them, promising to them that in heaven also she would love and remember them. She thanked them tenderly, for the love they had borne her, and not without some tears of charitable emotion on her cheeks,—all this was a most amazing compendium of affectionate demonstrations, which is impossible to be described or even imagined, except by those who took part in it.

The nuns who gathered around her bed, however, if on one hand they felt as though their hearts had been snatched away at the imminent separation from this their dear sister, on the other hand experienced also a heavenly sweetness penetrating into their souls, on seeing her already safely approaching the haven with so much joy that she appeared not as one dying, but as a jubilant bride going forth to the nuptials of the Divine Bridegroom. The habits of the different virtues which were so well rooted in her, especially the virtues of faith, hope, and charity, which she practiced in such a lively and constant manner, and the perfect order there was in her most pure soul, lent her a security and a peace so firm that those present were thereby wonderfully attracted. Therefore the sisters mingled tears of sorrow with tears of joy, and never wearied of being near her, all looking at her with various but devout feelings Mary Magdalen addressing her feeble voice to her father confessor, taking leave of him also, expressed herself most thankful to him, and begged of him in a particular manner his blessing, and then she requested him to go and rest for five hours, and return to her to be present to assist her at her death. The father having withdrawn, and Mary Magdalen having attended to these social duties, a general torpor seized all her limbs, and her senses failed so much under the imperious law of nature, that on his return, after the five hours, a heavy, long, and deep breathing was the only sign that she was still alive The confessor attended to the recommending of her soul, adding psalms and other prayers All the nuns had already reached her bedside, thinking that from one moment to another she would expire, but three hours passed in this condition, and the patient was still agonizing slowly, hence the time having arrived to say Mass and give Communion to the nuns, the confessor left for the sacristy. He had hardly got there and put on the sacred vestments, when he was hurriedly called to return, as the Saint was dying Rev Father Puccini, inspired of God, sent this message by the sister-sacristan to the mother prioress: "Tell Sister Mary Magdalen that, as she has been obedient in life, so she must also be in death, and to wait until I have finished saying Mass and giving Communion to the nuns " In a loud voice the prioress repeated this order to Mary Magda-

len, who was ready to yield up the ghost; then she, as though awakening from a very deep sleep or lethargy,—though she had been speechless
for several hours, the time elapsing between respirations being sufficient to
permit of the recitation of a *Hail Mary*,—now her eyes became brilliant
with a new light, and smiling, she loosened her tongue with these words.
"*Benedictus Deus*"—"God be blessed," and then asked for some jelly
broth, by which being restored (more so by the divine virtue), she continued so till after Mass and Communion The father having finished
these, he returned immediately to her, and found her as when he had left
her. Having called her by name, she answered him with a very grateful
countenance; and on his adding words of hope and love of God, she
appeared to be greatly pleased. All the nuns were already gathered
around in a circle and began to sing hymns and divine praises, as she
had, a few days before, requested them to do at that time. Only a short
while elapsed when, from the livid color of her forehead, which was
covered with drops of cold sweat, it appeared that she was at the point
of death, and suffered greatly. The confessor, seeing that she no longer
gave any sign of life, replaced in her hands the Crucifix, which on account
of lack of strength she had been unable to hold , and she pressed it as
closely as she could with her hand, in token, as we may well believe, of
her faith and love. She kept it in her hands, and after a little while,
trying to invoke the name of Jesus, finally with a slight movement of
her lips, in the midst of the melody of the divine praises she loved so
well, mingled though they were then with loud sobs and abundant tears,
calmly, as though she had fallen asleep, she gave up her soul to her
Lord. This happened between two and three o'clock in the afternoon
of May 25th, 1607, which was on a Friday. She was then forty-one
years two months and twenty-four days old, having lived in Religion
twenty-four years three months and twenty-five days.

Now, let not the reader be unwilling to fix his thoughts for a while
upon the death-bed of Mary Magdalen—upon that bed which must also
be the end of each one of us, and where a voice superior to that of the
earthly passions calls to the tribunal of the conscience the good and the
evil—and let him there address to himself these questions   1 Can I
despise Mary Magdalen, and regard her as a fool, because of the mode
of life she led? 2. Does such a death please me, and would I like a
similar one for myself? 3 Does my mode of life, and that of most
persons of our days, give hope of securing *such a death?*

Miraculous multiplication of oil (page 299).

288

CHAPTER XL.

FUNERAL OF MARY MAGDALEN AND A WONDERFUL OCCURRENCE
AT IT. HER BURIAL AND THE MIRACULOUS
INCORRUPTNESS OF HER BODY.

HE death of Sister Mary Magdalen, instead of giving the sad
and bitter pain which is caused by the loss of those who are
loved here on earth, immediately dried up the tears of the
sisters, who were, instead, filled with so much joy and such
a burning love for virtue that it seemed as if they had
attended a celestial festivity, rather than the death of
a human creature. This gave them such superhuman
strength, working in the same manner and at the same
time in the spirit of each, that it made them all proclaim, with an
exultant and unanimous voice, that their sister was Blessed and a Saint.
The flesh of Mary Magdalen, which, on account of such long suffering
of penances and infirmities, was extremely pale and drawn, assumed so
beautiful and white an appearance that it seemed as if a new life were
commencing to circulate through her veins, and as if the glory of her
soul were already shining through her body. Her countenance in particular presented an angelical splendor, inspired devotion and holiness,
and because of this it was a joy and a great comfort to look at it. That
sacred body immediately began to emit the most pleasing odor, which
has never diminished, and forms to this day the wonder, the enthusiasm,
and the delight of everyone who approaches it.

The nuns having rendered to the body of Mary Magdalen the usual
obsequies of Religion, and, having covered it with flowers in an elegant
coffin, placed it in the chapter of the monastery at the foot of the grate
looking into the church. There the Rev. Father Puccini delivered a
fervent address to the nuns, in praise of this holy mother and the better
to exhort them to imitate her example. The nuns spent the night around
the sacred body, singing religious canticles. The following day, the
26th of May, the body was carried into the church, where it remained
the whole day. The words, "*The Saint is dead!*" immediately passed
from lip to lip throughout the city, so that from all directions people
were seen to hasten, saving : " Let us go to St. Fredian's ; let us go to
Santa Maria degli Angeli's !" The crowd of people was so great that it

was with extreme difficulty that the religious rites could be performed; and afterwards, with the assistance of the military, the church being closed, it became necessary to reopen it soon again, as the impatient crowd threatened to break down the church doors. As the people came in, they gave vent to that devotion which, springing generally from the senses, partakes sometimes of the indiscreet and wild. If the armed guards had not kept them in order, they would have cut and torn to pieces the sacred body, in order that each might carry away a small particle. Several times were the flowers replaced over the body, as the people, being unable to do anything else, snatched them with enthusiastic eagerness and love. Finally, at sunset, it became possible to empty the church of the people and to close its doors. Then the body of Mary Magdalen was clothed in a silk habit similar in color and shape to that which she had worn during life, and, without employing any artificial means to preserve it, it was placed in a simple wooden case and was buried behind the main altar.

During the brief interval after the services, during which the church was kept closed, an event occurred which is deserving of mention A very few persons remained within, among them was a certain Father Claudio Sinpandi, a Jesuit, who, whilst enraptured by the superhuman beauty of the sacred body and fixedly looking at it, saw all at once that it moved the head and turned the face to the opposite side. Seeking the reason for it, he was unable to find any natural cause, as neither the pillow-cushion, nor the vestments, nor the bier had been touched in the least. It was a prodigy of the Divine Goodness, Who wished thereby that the virginal purity of Mary Magdalen should condemn the impurity and lasciviousness of a young man who, among the few others, was standing at the bier. Hence God moved the Jesuit to address the young man in these words "See what this holy virgin has done, I think she did it on thy account." The young man, being already frightened and confused at the sight of so wonderful an event, answered with much compunction: "I think so, too," and, having repented of his past transgressions, began a new life.

The renown of the miracles which were being wrought through the intercession of Mary Magdalen, increased beyond measure the devotion of the people towards her. For this reason, as well as because the place where her body had been buried was very damp, the water penetrating into it from dripping eaves and a well being but at two arms' length from it, the Rev. Father Puccini decided to make the translation of the body. Having, therefore, obtained the faculty from the Most Rev. Archbishop of Florence, on the 27th of May, 1608, just one year after her burial, he caused the body to be disinterred. When they opened the coffin, already covered with mold, they found that a piece of oil-cloth which had been placed over the body was so decayed that it fell into pieces; the vestments were for the greater part eaten away, but the body, which should have been the first to suffer alteration and decay, had only the face and feet blackened, and the extremity of the nose and lower lip reduced to ashes. The nuns brought it to the monastery, and, finding it as sound and pliable as if it had just died, full of joy, they dressed it in new silk vestments and placed it in another case, until a special tomb was made for it. Eight days after this removal, the body of the Saint from below the knees began to distill a pleasant and sweet liquor, which, wetting the clothing like oil, was thus gathered by the nuns and distributed to the devout people, who found it very efficacious in satisfying their desires and needs. This liquor continued to flow slowly on for twelve years, from 1608 to 1620, when it ceased, the body remaining in the same condition, preserving the same fragrance in all its parts, but in a more sensible and acute manner at the pit of the stomach. Ten physicians having minutely examined the body many times, on different occasions, both when the liquor was flowing and afterward, affirmed under oath in the formation of the processes both of inquiry and report, that the body of Mary Magdalen was integral and incorrupt, and did not show any symptom of decomposition; also, that the incorruptibility, the flowing of liquor, and the constant odor were not and could not be in the natural nor in the human order, but were supernatural and miraculous. And this was approved by the Sacred Rota and the Congregation of Rites.

CHAPTER XLI.

MIRACLES TAKEN ORDINATELY FROM THE PROCESSES FORMED FOR
THE BEATIFICATION OF MARY MAGDALEN.

AMONG the many miracles wrought through the intercession of this holy mother after her death, and testified to in the processes for her Beatification, the following have been examined and approved by the Rota Romana and the Congregation of Rites :——

Maria Rovai De' Rossi, a Florentine gentlewoman, widow, having been troubled with high fever for sixteen months, so that, on account of her weakness, she could not move, and being without any hope of recovery, five days after the death of Mary Magdalen was visited by the Rev. Giorgio Ciari, curate of St. Simon's in Florence. He brought with him some flowers which had touched the body of the Saint and gave them to the patient. With faith and devotion she placed them on her stomach, and immediately fell asleep; on awakening, shortly after, she found herself wholly cured and at once left her bed, to the unspeakable amazement of the people of the house. Four years afterwards, in May, 1611, the same lady fell ill again, and continued to get worse for five months. At the end of that time, on the 27th of October, all hopes of her cure being nearly lost, the above-mentioned Father Ciari paid her a visit. He had with him a small feather pillow which had been used by the Saint during her last illness. The sick lady placed it on her breast, and she immediately felt a strengthening heat throughout all her limbs, so that the fever left her, she got out of bed, called her daughter to sing the *Te Deum*, and, the following morning, went without assistance to the Church of Santa Maria degli Angeli.

A daughter of the same lady (Rovai) was in the monastery of our Saint to become a nun. Now, it happened that the mother fell sick again of the same fever, which caused delay in the daughter's taking the religious habit. Two months having elapsed, the daughter sent word to her mother that she wished to receive the habit at all hazards, and the mother answered that in that case she should pray to the holy soul of Mary Magdalen to obtain her cure. The daughter having heard this, sent to her mother a little tunic in which the body of the Saint had been dressed shortly after her death. The same evening the patient put it on, and having recovered instantly, she complied with her daughter's wish, two days later assisting at the ceremony of her taking the nun's habit, and feeling everlasting gratitude to their miraculous benefactress.

Maddalena of Pietro Rondoni, a girl of the Abbandonate of the Ceppo of Florence, for six years suffered from a fierce malady, during which the very smell of food nauseated her   She put on herself a little piece of the Saint's habit, making at the same time a vow to visit her Church, and there to confess and receive Holy Communion, and she was immediately freed from all sickness.

Catherine of Antonio Tosi, a girl of the Abbandonate of St. Catherine in Florence, having been for twelve years continually troubled with excessive pains in the stomach, which had reduced her to extreme thinness and caused her to despair of recovering, put on herself a little bit of the habit of Mary Magdalen, at once fell asleep, and on awakening in less than half an hour she found herself well, and never more did she suffer from that illness.

Andrea Bindi, a Florentine priest, curate of St. Frediano, having suffered for many years from a malignant disease in the leg, which threatened continually to get worse, determined to carry with other priests the body of the holy mother on the day of her burial, and while doing so, he felt notably better, and shortly afterwards was wholly cured.

Antonio Valderama, a Spaniard living in Florence, being seriously sick with fever and pains in the legs, caused these to be bound up with some bandages made out of a towel which had been used during life by the Saint.   Immediately the pains in the legs left him, and gradually he completely recovered his health.

Bernardino Cerboni of Colle, a Florentine citizen, having for ten years suffered with *gravèl*, which menaced his life, found himself cured and completely freed from the disease by simply putting on himself a small portion of the habit of the Saint.

Antonio Mattei of Lucca, a servant of Alessandro Lamberti, Ambassador of the Republic of Lucca at the Court of Tuscany, having quarreled with a fellow-servant, was by him wounded in one arm, and more seriously in the side   The physicians, thinking that his intestines had been lacerated, and consequently that there was great danger of his death while dressing the wound, told him to make his confession at once.   In the meantime the ambassador's wife mixed up, with the lint ordered for the wound, some lint taken from a sheet that had been used by the Saint, and, having applied it to the wound, in a few days the man was healed by a manifest prodigy.

The same ambassador gave testimony in the processes, that having for several days suffered pain in one of his arms even unto spasms, on account of a small black tumor, he was instantly cured of it by his wife's having applied to it, unknown to him, some lint from the above-mentioned sheet.

Lucretia Cenami-Lamberti, mother of said ambassador, drinking of the water in which had been placed some powder from the flowers which had touched the body of the Saint, was delivered forever from an asthma that for several years had threatened to choke her

Alessandra, daughter of Captain Francesco Puccini, and wife of

Andrea Sapiti, was sick unto death with smallpox, and being given up by the physicians, had received Extreme Unction, and the priest was already reciting over her the prayers for the dying. A relation of hers placed around her neck a relic of St Mary Magdalen, and immediately the dying one grew better, and in a few days left her bed entirely cured.

Stella, widow of Taddeo Corradi, seventy years old, having received the Holy Viaticum, on account of a very great pain in her side placed on the aching spot the little pillow which the Saint had kept on her stomach during her last illness, and immediately the unbearable pain began to diminish, and having fallen asleep, shortly after she woke up entirely cured.

Agostino, son of Francesco Cortellini, a boy two years old, was sick with a burning fever and in great danger of his life, and no effectual remedy could be applied to him. His mother had recourse to the intercession of our Saint; and having obtained from the nuns her veil, placed it on him, and the fever immediately left him, the little boy himself saying cheerfully: "Mamma, I am cured"

Father Vincenzo Maccanti, a Theatine, being very sick with intermittent fever in Modena, after spending fifteen days in the application of useless remedies, turned to the intercession of this Saint. At the hour when the fever was wont to attack him, he began to meditate on her glory. In doing so he fell asleep, and it seemed to him as if St. Mary Magdalen appeared to him in company with St. Nicolaus, Bishop, to whom he had a special devotion, and he thought he heard the Saint saying to her companion. "Let us grant him the grace completely," covering him at the same time with her *mantle*. Be that as it may, he woke up full of joy and contentment and wholly free from the fever, which never returned

Pietro Alli, a Roman gentleman dwelling in Florence, was so sick with fever and excessive pains that the physicians feared for his life, hence they said that he should receive the Holy Viaticum The pastor having come to fix the hour, the sick man's wife begged him to apply to the patient the veil of St. Mary Magdalen, which she had procured No sooner did the pastor apply this relic to the man, recommending him to the Saint, than his pains ceased and the fever disappeared, to the great surprise of all, especially the physicians.

Maria del Garbo de-Rossi, a Florentine gentlewoman, making a vow to this Saint, was immediately delivered from a very bad headache.

The same lady, making another vow to this Saint, obtained the grace that the spasm immediately ceased, and the *pine disease* which tormented her very much in one of her fingers immediately departed.

Antonia, daughter of Jacobo Giulianetti of Scarperia, a girl of the Abbandonate of the Ceppo, mentioned above, being by the violence of disease brought to the last extremity, and having already received Extreme Unction, survived over a month with attacks of the falling sickness so severe that, as soon as she attempted to raise her head, she was taken with it in such a horrible manner and for so long a time as almost to rend the rocks with pity The prioress of the institution having placed on her a relic of St. Mary Magdalen, the patient began at the same time to feel better and able to sit up in bed, and the following day she was totally cured, and never more did she suffer from that disease.

Alessandra, the widow of Lorenzo Mugnaj, prioress of the Abban-donate of St. Catherine, being at the point of death and about to receive Extreme Unction, one of her daughters made a vow to St. Mary Magda-len, and at the same time placed on the patient a relic of the Saint. She immediately felt the effect of a wonderful cure.

Giovanbattista Rossi, a noble Florentine, while suffering from palpitation of the heart with fatal symptoms, resolved to recite daily some prayers to our Saint, and to hang a silver votive offering at her sepulchre, and at once and forever his ailment disappeared.

Lorenzo, son of Paolo del Rosso, a three-year-old boy, was affected by *windy thorns*, which had already bent one of his arms and a foot so that they had made seven openings or mouths on each side, and scaled the bone. After four or five years spent in applying useless remedies, it was concluded to proceed to the amputation of his foot; but his mother, the above-named Maria Rovai, placing her confidence (which several times she had experienced not to be in vain) in the intercession of the glorious soul of Mary Magdalen, applied to her son some of the flowers which had touched the Saint's body, and shortly afterwards the wounds closed, and the root of the sore disappeared.

The same processes contain many other instances of miraculous cures, and particularly of women in severe travail being assisted by the relics and the invocations of this Saint. Many miraculous occurrences were related by the nuns, and by them registered in a separate book, in which they noted the corresponding votive offerings. When during the remissorial processes a visit was paid to the sacred body, these votive offerings were found crowning her sepulchre to the number of 626, viz., 567 in silver and 59 in tablets and paper.

CHAPTER XLII.

HOW QUICKLY DEVOTION TO MARY MAGDALEN DE-PAZZI SPREAD AMONG THE NATIONS, AND HOW URBAN VIII DECLARED HER BLESSED.

IN proportion to the multiplying of such wonders through the intercession of the triumphant Mary Magdalen, homage, gratitude, and confidence were drawing the peoples to her sepulchre. After the Florentines, those who most distinguished themselves on account of their particular devotion were the Lucchesi, who flocked to the sepulchre in crowds to fulfill their ardent vows. Some in going to Santa Maria degli Angeli walked a long distance barefooted, the better to declare their devotion to the Saint. Few were the houses in Tuscany that did not possess a relic of her, or at least a rosary which had touched her body. The cast which was taken, and moulded in copper, shortly after her death could be seen everywhere in Tuscany, and even out of Italy. The nuns of her monastery, being greatly pleased with the fervor of different nations, began to solemnize her *transit*, in a particular form and manner, on the second anniversary, viz., in 1609. This ceremony increased wonderfully in solemnity even to the intervention of the most serene princes; and was adopted by other monasteries of the same Order, among which that of Brussels erected and dedicated an altar to the Saint De-Pazzi. Thus did the faithful show how deeply rooted in their hearts was that veneration, the sanction of which by Christ's Vicar was looked for with a strong and general desire. In the meantime, in that same year, 1609, the Life of Mary Magdalen, printed in Florence, came to light for the first time, and the whole edition being taken very quickly, in 1611 a new edition was published, the ecstasies being added to it; a third edition was issued in 1620, which met with most ready sale. Later on another edition was printed, richer in form and information, at Pavia, which was afterwards translated into English by Chevalier Tobia Mattei, and published in Flanders; and into Spanish by Father Marco di Guadalaxara, a barefooted Carmelite of Saragossa, and chronicler to the Spanish king.

In toto, the first petition was sent to His Holiness Pius V, asking leave to form the process of the Life and Miracles of Mary Magdalen De-Pazzi. The nuns, the people, the magistrates, their most serene highnesses—all, in fact, in Tuscany—were unanimous in this desire. The Cardinal Duke Ferdinando Gonzaga acted as intercessor. His Holiness lent a benevolent ear to the pious request, and was not slow to second it, saying to His Eminence that the first informative process might be made by the Ordinary, and that he should, therefore, communicate with the Archbishop of Florence, telling him to attend to it immediately. The prelate, who was Alessandro Marzi-Medici, having received this commission, during the following year, 1611, complied with the pontifical mandate, examining one hundred and eight witnesses in Florence. The year following, still another process was instituted in Lucca by the respective Ordinary examining thirty-three witnesses, on account of the wonderful occurrences which happened in that city through the intercession of our Saint　Another was also compiled in Parma, concerning the graces there obtained　These three processes were sent to the Sacred Congregation of Rites in Rome, which entrusted their revision to Cardinal Orsino; but he, going shortly after to Ravenna as Legate of the Sovereign Pontiff, the cause *slept* till 1624, in which year the same cardinal, on the 10th of February, reported affirmatively to the Congregation of Rites that the cause of the Beatification of Mary Magdalen De-Pazzi was worthy and deserving to be proceeded with. The Sacred Congregation presented this report to His Holiness Urban VIII, who most willingly gave his assent—provided, though, that all the conditions for Beatifications should be kept by rigorously following all the orders and ceremonies that the Church requires in these causes. Commission was therefore given by special Rescript to three Uditori di Rota, who were John Baptist Coccino, Dean; Alfonso Manzanedo Quinnones, Patriarch of Jerusalem, and Filippo Paravano, who sent the *Remissorial* to the Archbishop of Florence, and two canons of the Metropolitan Church, viz., Andrea del Tovaglia, Chevalier of St. Stephen, and Alessandro Strozzi, who was afterwards Bishop of Sammimato　These three Uditori unitedly and quickly completed the process in a juridical form and sent it to Rome, where, being presented to the Judges of the Rota, it was by them opened and carefully discussed. They scrupulously pondered it, and the sanctity of the life and miracles of this mother, both those wrought during her lifetime and those after her death. They then sent new official letters to the Commissioners in Florence that they should again proceed to visit the body of Sister Mary Magdalen De-Pazzi with a greater number of physicians than formerly, the better to ascertain its incorruptibility and fragrance, and the liquor issuing from the same. The Commissioners made the new visit, and sent the process to Rome to the said Uditori, who, having opened and examined it, pronounced the decision that our Servant of God deserved not only to be declared Blessed, but to be numbered among the canonized Saints. Monsignore Coccino wrote the Report, which, being subscribed by all three, was presented to the Pope. His Holiness gave it back to the Congregation of Rites by means of said Uditori, on the 28th of March, 1626. Cardinal Pio was made relator of the cause, and Antonio Cerro, public prosecutor (devil's lawyer), representing the opposing party. There were three meetings held; in the first, the validity of the processes made at Florence was discussed and approved, in the second, the sanctity of the life; and in the third, the miracles wrought during life and after death were likewise discussed and approved. This being done, the said Sacred Congregation defined that, if it pleased His Holiness, he could *canonize* Mary Magdalen De-Pazzi, and, in the meantime, declare her *Blessed*. Finally, Pope Urban VIII, in consideration of these reports and proofs, and relying on the assistance of the Holy Ghost, by a Brief signed May 8th, 1626, declared and distinguished Mary Magdalen De-Pazzi with the title and honor of Blessed, showing himself extremely willing and happy in performing this act. This Brief of Beatification being sent to Florence, an octave was solemnly kept in the Church of Santa Maria degli Angeli, the body of the newly Beatified being exposed to public view, whilst the people ran in surging crowds to render their tribute of devotion and gratitude to Mary Magdalen, and to supplicate her with renewed fervor to grant them her valuable assistance.

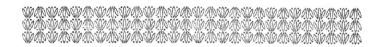

CHAPTER XLIII.

MIRACLES REPORTED IN THE PROCESSES MADE FOR HER SOLEMN CANONIZATION.

N the 23d of May, it being the day previous to the pre-announced feast for the Beatification, the two lay-sisters, appointed for the purpose, wished to prepare the oil for sixty lamps placed around the sacred sepulchre, for the church lamps and for other purposes, and went to the room where the oil was kept. As one of the two approached to finish emptying a jar of thick oil which had been used to light the monastery lamps, she removed the cover and found it full almost to overflowing. At this sight, the lay-sister cried out in great amazement, which made her companion approach, and both of them, most sure as they were that the remnant of oil in the jar could not be over five or six flasks, were overcome by various feelings, and could not assign any reason but a miracle for the great abundance they found of it. The only place where the oil of the monastery was kept was in that room; the several other jars contained the same amount as before; nobody during those days had brought any oil; so that a miracle only, and a miracle, on such an occasion, of their glorious and beloved mother, could have caused the increase. This being related to the nuns, they almost doubted its reality; but God wished to manifest her power more and in such a manner that no one could any longer doubt either the real fact or the superhuman power from which it proceeded. It so happened, then, that with the exception of six or seven flasks which had been taken out the first day, during the days following, whilst many flasks were daily taken out, one could see to a certainty that the measure of the first day was not altered in the least. Only on the fifth day it began gradually and proportionately to decrease according to the quantity which was taken out. The father confessor examined the facts and the persons concerned, and deemed also that beyond a doubt there was a miracle in it. He gave orders that such oil should be religiously kept, and wishing to know how much of it had been taken out and how much actually remained, they found that sixteen flasks were yet filled up, and they counted fifty already taken out, making a total of sixty-six flasks. This proved the miracle to be true, as the capacity of the jar was but forty-five flasks. The Archbishop of Florence took great interest in this

miracle. He had the two lay sisters and three other nuns examined under oath, and they unanimously, through a public notary, affirmed the truth of what has been related above   Afterwards the same Monsignore created a committee of conspicuous theologians to examine the whole matter, and they all asserted and proved with cogent reasoning that the above-described fact was a true miracle; in fact, one of the greatest miracles that God our Lord works to the glory of His most holy name. It seems, then, that we are authorized to conclude that God wished to manifest by this means that He was pleased with the exaltation of Mary Magdalen by the Sovereign Pontiff declaring her Blessed, and with the honor rendered her by the faithful, especially on this occasion.

In 1654, the same oil, prodigiously increased, served to increase other oil.   The monastery of Santa Maria degli Angeli being but scantily provided with oil, on account of the short crop of that year, the person who had charge of it brought an image of the Saint to the place where the oil was kept, and there offered prayer.   She let fall a few drops of the miraculous oil into the other which was in a jar that did not hold over two and a half ordinary barrels.   It so happened that, having taken out of that jar fourteen flasks of oil weekly for the use of the community and the church, no decrease could be noticed for several months, viz., from August to December, when the needs of the monastery could be supplied with new oil.

In the year 1660 all the wine that was in the cellar of the monastery of Santa Maria degli Angeli, amounting to about two hundred barrels, changed color and taste, indicating that it was fast spoiling. The steward having tapped all the casks, almost fainted from grief, and said to the sisters: "Recommend yourselves to the Blessed Mary Magdalen, as you well need it."   Then the superioress and two other nuns took a little vessel of miraculous oil, and going into the wine-cellar, put three drops of it into each cask, repeating each time the invocation and the petition to the Saint that the wine might become good once more Their prayers were heard, for after the lapse of three days, the steward having again tapped the casks, found that the wine had resumed its original color and taste, so that it answered not only for the use of the community, but what was over and above found profitable sale, having regained its former sweet taste.

In the year 1663, about the beginning of May, Sister Angela Maria Angelini was confined to her bed on account of a pain in the knee, which was of several years' duration   It had become so bad as to render the knee stiff, and it was also deemed incurable   As the feast of the Saint was approaching, the patient manifested a desire to be carried to her sepulchre, to pray to her either for recovery or for patience in her sickness.   In the meantime, one evening she caused the knee to be anointed with the miraculous oil, and the gratification of her wish was not long delayed   She was no sooner anointed than she began to improve, and in the space of twenty minutes saw the swelling disappear, and felt free to move the knee without the least pain.   Then she arose from her bed, gave thanks, and would have gone without delay to the sepulchre of Mary Magdalen had she not been kept back by the thought that the Constitutions forbade her going through the monastery

Sixty years after burial, the body of Mary Magdalen was found to
be "incorrupt" (page 329).

at night. Therefore she went to bed again, and there a new miracle awaited her. Unable to sleep, she fell into doubt as to whether the fact of her recovery was the result of the mere natural virtue of the oil or of a superhuman virtue; and, more and more yielding to the bad faith, she anointed herself again with common oil. To her punishment she was soon undeceived, as the swelling immediately returned, and so did the former pains and the paralysis. At which, knowing her guilt, she deeply grieved, passing the remainder of the night in the midst of the pains of her illness and the affliction of her spirit. The next morning, reviving her faith, she asked for some of the Saint's oil, anointed her knee with it, and lo! the miracle of a perfect cure was again wrought; so that she freely left her bed, dressed herself, and went straight to the sepulchre of Mary Magdalen, there to express the sentiments of her devout and grateful heart

In the year 1643, Pietro Caravita, a royal councillor in Naples, being suddenly assailed by fever and pleurisy, accompanied by languor and loss of strength, was given up by the physicians. Father Alberto Colaccio, a Carmelite, at the instance of the wife, anointed with the oil of the Saint the spot where the patient felt the most pain, at the same time invoking her aid. The sick man recovered immediately, and, getting out of his bed, went to supper with the rest of the family, as if nothing had happened Grateful for the grace received, he afterwards offered as a votive token, to Santa Maria della Vita, a Carmelite church, a silver lamp for the chapel of the Saint De-Pazzi.

In the same year, 1643, Giovanni Salgrado, in Madrid, was given up by the physicians. Vincenzo Carlini, who had brought from Florence a small vessel containing the oil of the Saint, anointed him with some, at the same time invoking her intercession. The sick man immediately took some rest; and, on awakening, found himself so much better that the physicians testified that it could only be in consequence of a miracle.

In the year 1660, the wheat of the monastery deteriorated so, on account of numerous insects, that it was crumbling into dust. The sisters turned their trust and their prayers to their glorious mother, and going to the granary, touched all the bags with her image, and made upon them the sign of the cross with the miraculous oil. Great wonder! The insects disappeared, the wheat cooled down at once, and it resumed its wonted perfection.

In the year 1661, the sister-butler of said monastery anointed with the same wonderful oil a great number of stale eggs. They became sweet once more; and, moreover, some of them having been given out for devotion's sake, God made use of them to work other wonders. This happened in Florence to Lady Maddalena Gondi and to Lady Francesca Dei, each of whom was cured of a long and serious malady by partaking of one of those eggs.

Lady Maddalena Angela Gorini, of the monastery of the Murate, in Florence, after two years of great suffering, was reduced to almost total blindness by a disease of the eye called *gotta-serena*. She promised our Saint to fast on bread and water on the vigil of her feast, to have a Mass offered up at her sepulchre, and to send there a silver votive offering. With such a disposition she fell asleep, and on awakening half an hour afterwards, said "I see; praised be God and the Blessed Mary Magdalen Call the prioress for me "—Who, having come, applied to her the *veil* of the Saint, and Lady Gorini added that her eyesight became still clearer. One hour later, being perfectly cured, she went to hear Mass The two attending physicians gave testimony of this miracle.

In the year 1662, Domenico Federighi, being blessed with the *veil* of the Saint, whilst his wife was lamenting him as dead, recovered from a desperate illness.

In the year 1648, Sister Mary Catherine Rinuccini, of the monastery of Santa Maria degli Angeli, who was suffering from a malignant fever and inflammation of the lungs, received the last Sacraments, and, having lost her speech, was about to expire. The mother prioress placed upon her the little pillow of Mary Magdalen, and the patient, having fallen asleep, thought she saw the Saint appearing to her and blessing her on the side, near the heart, saying to her· "Arise ! thou art healed My feast-day is near ; go and prepare my sepulchre " Waking up, she turned cheerfully to the sister-nurse, and said to her: "Sister, I am cured, call in the mother prioress, that she may give me permission to leave my bed and dress myself " This happened the night previous to the 22d of May. The superioress ran to the sister's bedside as soon as she heard of this wonder, still, not unmindful of prudence, she would not permit her to arise until the day following, after the physicians acknowledged that her health had been miraculously restored

Maddalena Vittoria, daughter of Marco Frassinelli, went to bed one evening, in 1661, with perfect eyesight, and awoke the following morning stone blind. In vain did the medical skill resort to all known remedies. In the year 1663, the patient placed all her trust in our Saint, and had herself led every morning to hear Mass in her chapel. Being there on the feast-day of Mary Magdalen in 1664, whilst the panegyric was being delivered, a flower which had been placed on the sacred tomb was given to her She took it devoutly, placed it on her eyes with faith, and, behold ! her eyesight recovered so that without the aid of guide or cane she freely returned to her home, and on the following day came back to the church to attest her everlasting gratitude to the Saint who had restored her eyesight to her.

By means of the oil of the lamp placed before the sepulchre of the Saint, Divine Goodness was pleased to make the merits of this, His holy Servant, well known. Maddalena Boddi, in the year 1659, was contracted and paralyzed by an apoplectic stroke. She recovered the power of her limbs and perfect health by anointing herself with this oil

Costanza, daughter of Luca Misuri, in the year 1664, was given up for dead by the physicians, on account of fever, pains in the stomach, and dysentery She was no sooner anointed with this oil than she was freed from all troubles. She did not fully acknowledge that the grace came from so celestial a source, and fifteen days afterwards she was attacked by most acute pains in the stomach and one shoulder, and nothing afforded her any relief Again she was anointed with the above-mentioned oil, and immediately she felt all pains leaving her and an interior voice saying to her repeated till · "Acknowledge that it was the Saint who obtained this grace for you." She asked pardon, and began to proclaim the miracle.

Tomaso, son of Simon Chiari, and Ginevra, daughter of Jacopo Bertolozzi, in the year 1659, being assailed by fever which made them delirious, were no sooner anointed with the above oil than they felt well, and the following morning went to the church to render thanks to the Saint.

By simply promising her something, or making a vow, or even only invoking her, miracles followed. Don Domenico Caravita, while driving a carriage in Naples, in 1644, fell upon his stomach on one of the wheels, his right leg going under it, after the horses had forced the reins. Unable to speak, he recommended himself with his heart to the glorious De-Pazzi. No sooner did he invoke her than he saw her before him in the Carmelite habit, encouraging him and suggesting to him to draw back the arm around which the reins were twisted. This he did, and the horses immediately stopped, and he, raising himself on the wheel, jumped to the ground. He had but one shoe, his garments were all torn, but he felt only a little pain in the right arm and knee. His brothers, the coachman, and the friends who followed, when they saw him alive and uninjured, were very much amazed at the wonder, and, together with him, rendered due thanks to the Saint. He brought a memorial offering, in gratitude for it, to her chapel in the Church of Santa Maria della Vita

Gaspero Romer, a Flemish merchant residing in Naples, escaped a very serious shipwreck, in 1647, by confidently recommending himself to our Saint.

In the year 1656, the same gentleman, being attacked by the pest, recovered at once from the fever, the carbuncle, and all consequences thereof, by simply applying to himself an image of the same Saint.

Sister Maria Concordia Galletti, of the monastery of St Clement in Florence, being ill with a catarrh, called by the physicians *trama di goccìola*, was confined without hope to her bed She tried in vain all human remedies, and, on the morning of the twenty-first day of her malady, she invoked the help of the Saint In the evening, having very quietly fallen asleep, she heard in her sleep a voice saying to her "Arise and go to the choir, as thou art not at all sick." On awakening, she tried to do it, and, feeling strong, she dressed, went to the choir, where she remained for some time, returning fervent thanks to God and to her patroness, whose image was there.

In the year 1634, Antonio Leoni, chancellor at Forlì, was so troubled with fever and pains in the joints that the physicians had stopped prescribing for him, deeming his malady incurable. A Carmelite monk, his confessor, seeing him so very sad, exhorted him to implore the help of Blessed Mary Magdalen, which was no sooner done by him than he felt himself to be without pain and perfectly cured In token of his gratitude, he caused a portrait of the Saint to be painted and placed in a friend's chapel in the Church of the Carmine, until by his order and at his expense a special chapel (side altar) should be erected therein This altar is an unspeakable consolation to the people of Forlì, because of the graces received in the past and which are still being received at the present time.

In the year 1655, Vincenzo Antonio Ricci, a peasant of Campi, in the Florentine territory, was troubled for three whole years by an abscess in the stomach, and was reduced to such a condition that he could neither stand nor lie down, besides being continually tormented by acute pains. His wife Margherita went to the monastery of Our Lady of Angels to visit her cousin, Sister Martha, whom she told of her husband's illness, which was thought by the physicians to be incurable. The good lay-sister exhorted her to have devotion to and confidence in her Saint, and gave her a small piece of the Saint's habit. Margherita, as soon as she got home, applied it to her husband, who felt all pain immediately cease, saw the wound heal up, and within eight days was fully cured. He went to Florence to visit the sepulchre of the Saint, had a Mass offered there, and left to the sisters a statement of the miracle subscribed to by three witnesses. The Saint did more; Margherita gave a Relic of the same Saint to her husband that he might always wear it. Shortly afterwards he lost it, and though he sought very diligently for it he could not find it. He was in great trouble because of his loss, but three weeks later, whilst in the field breakfasting with others, lo! his dog, with the Relic in his mouth, came swiftly and placed it directly at the feet of Antonio, who, kneeling, took it up from the ground and gave many thanks to the Saint, to whom he felt indebted for its recovery.

In the year 1661, Margherita, a three-year-old daughter of Antonio Cocci, a laborer in the monastery of Santa Maria degli Angeli at Campi, was left alone in the house, and would have been killed by a bull which had escaped from its stable, if she had not been saved from the danger by an invisible hand. Those who, from afar, saw her under the feet of the bull gave her up as dead, and so reported her to her father. He ran to his little darling, and, finding her unharmed, asked her how it had happened. She gave him the following answer. "The Blessed One took me by the hand and told me to pass by here, and thus she saved me from the bull." "How was she dressed?" resumed the father. "In black and white, with a black veil on her head," the child replied. "No," said the father to try her, "the veil was white." "No," replied the child, "it was black, like that which the Blessed One has up in my room where I say the *Hail Mary*." This occurrence was related by her several times without the least alteration, although she was very often contradicted by those who listened to her, in order to try her. In the year 1663, her mother took her to Florence, and, while they were hearing Mass at the chapel of the Saint, the latter manifested herself to the innocent child as she looked in the sacred tomb. The same child related to the nuns how their Blessed One was lying dressed in black and white, with a white veil on top of the black one, and on her head a silver crown covered with pearls. The sisters began to contradict her in order to ascertain the truth, but she persisted in a coherent and firm manner, thus proving beyond a doubt the truth of the grace received. Having left the monastery, the mother complained to her child, saying: "If thou hadst seen the Blessed One, why didst thou not tell me? I would have seen her, too." "Thou hadst her eyes," said the girl, "and I the ones; thou wert looking up there, and I was looking down. The Blessed One told me to be good, and I told her that I would;" and, in fact, she spent all her life in innocence.

In February, 1668, Catherine Nelline Villani, being pursued and fiercely attacked by an insane son, with whom she was alone in the house, invoking the Saint to her aid, heard a voice clearly saying : "Stop; let her alone!" She turned back in amazement, as she knew that there was nobody in the house besides her son and herself, when, behold! she saw Mary Magdalen clothed in her habit, in the midst of a white cloud, and the infuriated son, with his hand raised, was also arrested by the miraculous vision. In the meantime, the mother reached a place of safety, and considered herself indebted to the Saint because she was not struck dead by the blow which was about to fall on her head. She likewise attributed to the Saint the speedy cure of four very serious and dangerous wounds inflicted upon her on the same occasion, and she had several Masses offered at her altar, and also caused a rich and beautiful silver votive offering to be appended to it.

CHAPTER XLIV.

CHANGE OF MONASTERY AND CORRESPONDING DESCRIPTION. DIVERS RE-
PORTS OF THE FEASTS CELEBRATED IN HONOR OF HER CANONIZATION.
AN ACCOUNT OF THE LAST TRANSLATION OF THE BODY OF THE
SAINT AND OF THE MIRACLES WROUGHT DURING
SUCH SOLEMNITIES. CONCLUSION.

DOPTING the words of Marquis Ludovico Adimari, a learned Florentine writer of the last century, I hope to please the reader in giving a full account of the sacred and the popular feasts solemnized in Florence on the occasion of Blessed Mary Magdalen's being raised to the honor of a Saint ; adding, also, to it, the description of the church and monastery, and some particulars of the family De-Pazzi, all tending to increase the esteem of our glorious heroine.

Urban VIII, who entertained a predilection for the monastery of Santa Maria degli Angeli in Florence, both because of the remembrance of Mary Magdalen De-Pazzi by him declared Blessed, and in consideration for the surviving sisters, among whom there were three of the Barberini house—one a sister and two others nieces of his—in 1627 was pleased to give his special attention to the small space of their enclosure. In 1442, with some very limited means given by charity, a small building was erected in Borgo San Frediano, Florence, as a dwelling for the Carmelite nuns, under the title of Santa Maria degli Angeli, with the hope of being able to enlarge it afterwards through additional help from charitable people. These hopes, however, were never realized well enough to relieve the nuns from the narrow limits of their poor convent. The munificence of the above-named Pontiff came to their rescue, assigning to them one of the most celebrated monasteries of the same city. Located in Borgo di Pinti, from 1256 to 1442 it was the dwelling-place of the so-called Convertite under the Rule of St. Benedict; and afterwards of the Cistercian monks, who, being very willing to comply with the wishes of His Holiness, exchanged their dwelling with said nuns. They received from the Pope, besides a rich abbey to be added to their patrimony, the large sum of thirty-five thousand scudi or dollars with which to enlarge and embellish the newly-exchanged building to suit their needs and convenience. This they did at various times, until finally in 1680, when, after the plans of Ceriuti and Antonio Ferii, they rebuilt the church, which in its beauty is still extant, under the title of St. Mary Magdalen the Penitent, and also completed the adjoining monastery.[1]

The nuns for their part, full of joy and gratitude for the pontifical liberality, which handed over to them so great a sum of money to supply their actual needs, moved to Borgo di Pinti in 1628, transferring to the new church and monastery the title of Santa Maria degli Angeli. They also took with them the very same tiles which covered the pavement of the room where Mary Magdalen lived and died, which room has always been held in veneration till our own days, as a sacred Oratory. Many and truthful were the praises unanimously given to the most famous Urban for his tender and warm love of country and Religion, and also for his well-meant sympathy for his own people. Innocent X succeeded Urban in the pontificate; Alexander VII succeeded Innocent, and Clement IX, Alexander, the last two of whom were Tuscans of noble lineage.

In the meantime, the renown of the sanctity of Mary Magdalen and of the great wonders wrought by Almighty God through her intercession in behalf of her devout children, was spread more and more. Italy and Europe were filled with it, and voluntary contributions were collected from the fathers of the Carmelite Order of every province, but, above all, from those of Florence, and many other benefactors, towards the expenses needed for the solemn canonization. Finally, the Sovereign Pontiff Clement IX—to gratify the wish of the entire Christianity, and particularly that of the Most August Leopoldo Ignazio, Roman emperor, and of Theresa d'Austria, the most powerful queen of France, and of the Most Serene Grand Duke of Tuscany, Ferdinand II, who by means of their orators had presented repeated supplications to that effect—was pleased to pronounce the last and final sentence, placing our virtuous maid on the roll of the Saints, together with Blessed Pietro d'Alcantara, a Reformed Franciscan. This took place on the 20th of September, 1668; and on this date the first printed notices appeared in Rome, which were abundantly reprinted afterwards in Florence for distribution among notable persons. The public declaration of it, according to custom, was celebrated in the most spacious Vatican Basilica of St. Peter on the 20th of April, 1669, a memorable and most solemn day, which, that year, fell on Low Sunday, following the Resurrection of our most loving Redeemer. The news of this celebration reached Florence on the 4th of May, it being a Saturday morning, at dawn, and quickly spread among the citizens, whose countenances proved that the happiness was not less than the expectation. Some repeated the news with words of benediction and joy; some with festive fireworks and bonfires, which everywhere during whole nights lit up the streets; and some by firing guns, which were answered by the glad pealing of the bells

---

[1] Here the Cistercian monks remained till their suppression, which took place in 1732. During the following year the parish of St Frediano was transferred to it from the piazza named after said Saint, in which it had existed since 1514. In 1807, it was made a collegiate church, under the title of San Frediano in Castello. The monastery became the first seminary of the Florentine Diocese, and in 1818, on account of the desire for national independence, it fell into the hands of foreigners, who having expelled the seminarians, made it a hospital. But let us hope that it will before long, be given back to its primitive object of ecclesiastical education.

Altogether a great noise was made, which was continually and cheerfully echoed by the voices of the people, who shouted: "*Viva* the family De-Pazzi! *Viva* our glorious Saint! *Viva* our sweet hope! *Viva* our most sweet patroness!" These rejoicings were much greater in the streets surrounding the monastery of Santa Maria degli Angeli, the Murate, and St Peter's, where some nuns of the De-Pazzi family lived, and in all other places where any member of this family dwelt. As all blessings and happiness are to be acknowledged from God, by Whose power and liberality alone they can come down to us, therefore that same Saturday morning the Mass of the Holy Ghost was celebrated in the metropolitan church, and a most solemn *Te Deum* was sung, all the magistrates attending, with a multitude of people—every artisan having left his work, as if it were a regular holy-day. On the following Sunday, after Vespers, solemn services of thanksgiving to the Most High were held in the church of the Carmelite monks. In the meantime, the nuns of Santa Maria degli Angeli, who desired to show their public and private contentment by paying to their happy sister all the possible honor which was due to her innocence and sanctity, resolved to have an eight-days' celebration in their church in honor of the Saint, exposing her body in the most magnificent style.

The prioress then was Sister Maria Minima degli Strozzi, a woman who, on account of her many prerogatives, is deserving of special mention. Born of a most noble family, the only daughter of a rich father, and consequently the sole heiress of a large patrimony, from her very childhood she preferred the virginal crown to everything else Betaking herself away from all chances of a splendid marriage, she shut herself up in a monastery, where she lived long, a wonderful example of magnanimous self-contempt, frequent fasts, fervent prayers, constancy of the hand and heart in ceaselessly scourging herself. Here she finally died, in the constant practice of the most glorious virtues, leaving behind a very marked renown.

This prioress promptly consented to the wish of the nuns, and having quickly gathered in the parlor some members of the De-Pazzi's family and other most noble knights, near relatives to other nuns (for in this monastery, though in its origin very poor, were already gathered nuns of well-known families), asked them to see to all that was required for the proposed festivity Count Philip Bentivoglio, Philip Franceschi, and Luigi Pazzi were charged with the music, which was to be under the direction of that *maestro* whom they considered the ablest to solemnize an octave with a daily variation of music for Mass and Vespers To Senator Marquis Carlo Gerini, Marquis Gabriello Riccardi, Senator Marco Martelli, and Count Pietro Strozzi, curators of the monastery, was assigned the task of decorating the church in the best manner possible, in order highly to praise the name of Saint Mary Magdalen—a name deserving of singular and everlasting esteem, because of the splendor of the glorious images of her illustrious ancestors in the paternal home, the great candor of her innocence, the great merit of her virtues, the great multiplicity of her miracles, and because of the very high degree of never-fading, immortal glory she enjoys and ever shall enjoy in heaven Lastly, the Very Rev Philip Soldani, Archpriest of the Metropolitan Church of

Florence, and director of the above nuns, who was afterwards promoted to the bishopric of Fiesole, was given the commission to invite eight prelates to celebrate Pontifical Mass every morning, and the like number of sacred orators who, from the pulpit, were to satisfy the wish and devotion of the people by eloquent and able discourses in honor of Mary Magdalen. Senator Giovanni Rucellai and the Marquis Luca degli Albizzi were also called in to lend their assistance. This much having been settled by the nuns, the lords of the De-Pazzi family wished also to manifest the great joy they felt, as we shall see presently when proceeding to the description of the feast. The banner blessed by the Holy Father, and on which was the portrait of the Saint, did not arrive from Rome to initiate the festivities until the 31st of May It was received by the nuns with a devout melody of hymns and sacred songs, and was carried by night to the Church of the Carmine, whence, on Sunday, June 2d, it was taken, and, with the honor of a public procession, carried to Pinti, everything having been prepared for its worthy reception The church was already adorned in a wonderful manner with the richest ornaments and sacred articles. All this had opportunely been done at an early date, as the banner had been expected at Florence long before, and it was the common desire to include in this solemn octave the proper feast-day of the Saint, which falls on the 25th of May, or at least begin it on that day, but the circumstances which kept the banner in Rome prevented it. Now let us describe first the monastery, and then the Church of Santa Maria degli Angeli in the true light of those happy days.

THE EXTERIOR OF THE MONASTERY OF SANTA MARIA DEGLI ANGELI.

The monastery of Santa Maria degli Angeli is situated in the street commonly called Pinti, almost at one extreme end of the city It, looking north, has, therefore, the delightful hills of the renowned Fiesole in front, and its most ancient walls, running straight like the public road, end at and join the walls of two other monasteries also of women, the one of St. Sylvester and the other of Candeli, which are on its right and left. In front of it are beautiful mansions, which, proceeding in a parallel line towards the side of the city, are divided for a short space by Colonna Street, which leads to the square of the Annunziata, where it ends. Its beginning is just at Pinti and precisely where, from the walls of said Carmelite convent, hangs, magnificently carved in marble, the coat-of-arms of the Barberini, ornamented with the triple crown, in remembrance of the remarkable benefit received from the great Urban. The main door, or the great church door which one reaches by several steps, leads to a magnificent space supported by stone pillars. On the left is the famous Chapel of the Neri, which in its cupola contains Poccetti's masterpiece representing the abode of the Blessed. The antipendium of the altar of the same chapel is by Passignano. Returning to the first entrance, we proceed to an almost square court, the front of which forms an elegant vaulted lodge, with six stone columns of the Ionic order, three on one side and three on the other, in the midst of which an arc majestically arises on the architrave, which running over their capitals closes afterwards with much grace in the shape of a circle and gives entrance to the church by a door. This main door has two smaller ones on the sides, and corresponds on the outside to the big door on the street, and on the inside to the main altar, with equal elegance and proportion.

On the occasion of the celebration, one could see the public street alongside the monastery covered for a considerable space with white tents, which extended from wall to wall and formed a most brilliant spectacle, on account of the great quantity of tinsel and festoons of fragrant myrtle flying from them, and, underneath, it was a beautiful sight to see the walls adorned with the finest silks and superb paintings of renowned authors representing the most notable events in the Holy Scriptures.

Over the main entrance hung the coats-of-arms of the Rospigliosi (the then Roman Pontiff having been born of that family), the Most August Catholic Emperor, the Grand Duke of Tuscany, the monastery, and the De-Pazzi family. The vestibule of the first entrance and the courtyard were adorned from bottom to top with splendid tapestries and paintings representing the most remarkable events in the life of Mary Magdalen, explained by a short and elegant inscription underneath. In the middle of the court an arch was erected, which was tastefully interwoven with colored serges placed on sharp points covered with damasks These formed a resplendent avenue leading to the church, from the main door of which hung a large placard with a gilt cornice and fine carvings of lilies and roses On it was written in Latin with cubital letters a short *eulogium* of the Saint, composed by the Canon Giambattista Borgherini, which for the information and satisfaction of all is translated here below.

TRANSLATION OF THE EULOGIUM.

"Let anyone who wishes to approach this most grand vision lay down here in the vestibule of the temple all worldly thoughts. Everything in St. Mary Magdalen De-Pazzi is so great and sublime that earthly thought cannot reach it. Nothing in her is mortal. Not even her body, which, though dead, prophesied, and became incorruptible before it arose in the Lord's Day All her counsels from her birth were always full of immortality. In the tenth year of her life, by her offering in advance of her age, she consecrated to God the flower of her virginity, of which gift the Virgin of Virgins from on high wanted to become the tutelar custodian In her tender childhood, loathing the delights of the earth and impatient to seek the ways of virtue, leaving her kindred, she ascended the heights of Carmel, there to feed solely on celestial dew, in the hope of everlasting glory. In the salutary hatred of herself and in the appreciation of innocence, she was always wonderful To her soul, never conquered by any earthly affection, nothing was more agreeable than to feel angry with her own self, to fight against and triumph over herself, subjugating herself by vigils, fatigues, scourges, and fasts. In the estimation of her superiors, of her subjects, and of her companions, she appeared powerful in all virtues, and highly adorned with them. By humility, good example, obedience, integrity of counsels, and wonderful art in commanding and obeying, she accom-

panied all tokens and put in execution all manner of tireless charities
She had no wish, no delight, except Jesus In abundance and in distress, in sweetness and in bitterness Christ was all to her, and she
found all in Christ. By His charity internally wounded, one could see
her languishing altogether, unless she would approach her Beloved and
be upheld with *flowers* compassed with *apples*, and surrounded with
the *lilies* of His graces. In the midst of these delights, girded with a
cilicium, besprinkled with ashes, whitened by abstinences, she pleased
the Son of the Most High, Who chose her as His Bride, giving her in
token of the celestial betrothal the ring and the crown; He enriched her
with the gift of the spirit of His power. Hence she knew how to chase
the devils from bodies that were possessed and how to safely shelter the
innocence that was in danger. Often was she by the Divine Spouse
introduced into His *chamber*, where, opening the treasures of His
knowledge, He taught her fully all that is above the understanding
and knowledge of mortals. Therefore, conversing often in heaven, she
knew not human literature , but in the practice of speaking of God, full
of divine wisdom and intellect, she manifested His hidden mysteries and
brought to light glorious works of His which are neither seen nor understood. She lived as if dead to the world, hidden with Christ in God
Finally, being taken up to heaven, she stole away with her the affections,
the hearts, the homage, and the applause of all the people Enter,
devout soul. Prepare thine eyes for wonders, thy mind for sanctity.
Exult, O Florence, in this thy day. Honor and invoke thy daughter over
thee, because to-day the Sovereign Roman Pontiff made her name most
great among all nations, and by the tongues of all the Church proclaims
her praises."

Two other cartoons of lesser dimensions appeared on the two side
doors, the inscriptions for which were composed by the Canon Matteo
Strozzi (a man of uncommon erudition), and recounted the virtues and
glories of Mary Magdalen.

DESCRIPTION OF THE INTERIOR OF THE CHURCH.

Three doors, then, lead into the church, which the title of majestic
rather than big would suit, though it cannot be called small. It has but
one nave, with twelve chapels harmoniously distributed to the number of
six on each side, one opposite the other. These are all equal in size and
of elegant proportions. They stand back in the shape of a square and
are covered by a solid vault, the entrance to them being by an arch skill-
fully carved with beautiful and various work in *stone serene*. The arch
is supported by two pillars and a capital of composite order, which continues along the two sides to the south, where are three oblong windows,
so well designed that each of them, resting upon the arch of a chapel,
gives the necessary light to the whole church. At the end of this is the
Chapel of St Mary Magdalen, built there as the main altar and inspiring
devotion all around, and, while adding to the sumptuous magnificence of
the edifice, it satisfies, better than one can tell, the eye and the heart of
the beholder. It is raised somewhat from the rest of the floor and stands
many feet back. Spreading out with noble symmetry, it is enclosed by

a balustrade of Sicilian jasper, which joins the two pillars of the same material. Upon this an arch arises forming a magnificent entrance. The marble pavement is distributed and connected in a most pleasing manner   The sides are inlaid with precious and rare marbles, and the centre contains the majestic altar, the front of which, ending in a semi-circle, represents Mary Magdalen kneeling at the feet of Our Lady and taking from her hands a white veil given to her as a protection and security to her purity. The decoration on it is also of Sicilian jasper, with two columns of the same stone, magnificently enriched with gilt-bronze bases and capitals. On them rest the architrave, the ornament, the cornice and the frontispiece, which in all their parts correspond to the beauty of the whole work On the sides of the altar are two like columns, which embellish the wall and present a rich appearance because of two medallions hanging from their bases, which are adorned with beautiful casts of gilt-bronze, and appear to be supported by some small ones of white alabaster. The most wonderful of all, however, is the antipendium of the altar, also of gilt bronze, in which the elegance of the work, surpassing the value of the metal, equals only the diligence and the labor employed therein by the artist. Neither can we leave unpraised a bronze grate, oval in form, which is set in the wall behind the tabernacle, and corresponds to the interior choir of the nuns On two sides of the chapel are also two tables, one opposite the other, ornamented with the same marble, and of the same shape as the main altar, except that these rest upon two doors of gilt bronze, with ebony frames, and are properly located there—one for the Communion of the nuns, and the other for the giving of the religious habit to them. Each of these two tables is flanked by four other columns Between these are placed four marble statues representing the most remarkable virtues of Mary Magdalen, viz, Piety, Affability, Penance, and Religion Affability with the lamb and the dove, and Religion with a veil, are worthy of particular attention, and the last one especially for the ingenious and light carving, the relief of which is noticed through the veil. Under them are seen some bas-reliefs in gilt bronze, representing the most memorable events in the life of our Saint As a suitable finish for this most noble work in marble, an elegant architrave, with its ornament and cornice, runs all around the chapel. From the cornice in all the three fronts start three *lunettes* in the shape of a semicircle, which make three windows elegantly ornamented with cornice and foliage in gilt stucco, and their side corners are of arabesques and gold At the point where these three *lunettes* end, a beautiful cornice in gilt stucco runs all around the building, and from its top begins to arise the cupola, which, round at first, assumes afterwards and closes in an oval shape. Around the sides of the cupola are eight other windows, equally distant, and rich in fine gilt ornaments. Finally, the cupola itself, all frescoed, represents the glory of Mary Magdalen, who, having gone up to heaven, is by the Blessed Virgin Mary introduced to her Divine Son. At the four corners are various and beautiful groups of little angels holding in their hands some scrolls inscribed with sayings from the Holy Bible, the work of Pietro Dandini These paintings among the many that came out of the hands of so famous an artist, are praised as the best Worthy of all

View of the Main Altar of Santa Maria degli Angeli at the time of
Mary Magdalen De-Pazzi's Beatification (page 314).

312

praise are the three tables, the principal one of which is from the brush of Ciro Ferri, and the other two from that of Luca Giordano. The floor of the chapel, the cupola, and the skylight were erected according to the design and under the direction of Pier Francesco Silvani

Such was the church; and, though very magnificent and grand-looking in itself, nevertheless, on account of the many ornaments added to it on that festive occasion, it appeared majestic and gay beyond all description The perfect conception of all things, and their well-understood disposition, attracted the eye to the wonderful sight and elicited praises for those valiant ones who, in embellishing it, had followed the best rules and the most rare beauties of an unexceptionable architecture. The chapels were all hung with silk draperies, divided into compartments by red and yellow strips, which greatly enhanced the loveliness of the altars' canvas. From around the arches in graceful festoons hung taffeta draperies, red and white, which, extending in separate parts from the summit of the cornice, formed a falling drop, with just proportions, towards the ground. At the fastenings of the same there were brackets adorned with gold cords, upon which rested very rich silver vases with silk flowers, looking quite natural These were lilies and roses, to signify the Saint's great purity and her great love for God. The splendor and majesty of the altars, the steps of which were covered with silver candlesticks and silver vases full of silk roses and lilies similar to those outside of it, were fully in keeping with the grand decorations of the chapels. The antipendiums and the cushions were of white satin embroidered in red flowers, with gold galloons and fringes, and the two chapels near the main altar were conspicuous for richness of material and exquisiteness of workmanship All the space on the walls intervening between one chapel and the other was adorned with richest hangings of crimson satin, on which were embroidered ingenious designs of arabesques and flowers. These arose from the bottoms of the arches for about two arms' length, ending in an ornament laid over This hanging ran around the whole church. Immediately above it was an architrave in imitation of marble, frescoed, which, seeming to be worked in the finest carving, matched very nicely the variety of the embroidery. In the space above were four large paintings on each side, between the windows, secured to the walls. Two paintings were also on each side of the main door, over which a stone had been permanently placed with an inscription in praise and remembrance of Cardinal Francesco Barberini, through whose good offices the benefit of the change of monastery had been obtained from his great uncle, the Pope These paintings, which can be seen to this day, represent the greatest works of God in Mary Magdalen, both during her lifetime and after her death. Below them were hung ten gold cartoons with exquisite Latin inscriptions, which were afterwards permanently placed on the wall, and which explained the subject and the imagination of the painter. These inscriptions were the production of the sublime talent of Monsignore Opizzo Pallavicini, then Nuncio at Florence and afterwards Cardinal, who also wished to praise the Saint and show her by his pen the great devotion of his heart. The spaces which remained between the windows and the paintings were filled with six oval figures on each side, representing in *chiaroscuro* some of the many virtues which the actions of the Saint illustrated. (The engravings which adorn this book, designed from said pictures, exempt me from giving a detailed description of them) Above the window-sills were painted some double brackets, enriched with the finest carving, which, seeming to be really fixed in the wall, appeared to carry on their bases the sky of the ceiling, adorned all around with a cornice and over-cornice and various other architectural ornaments, which, on account of the strong tints upon several of the decorations, make the beholder think them at a distance from their resting-place, in order the better to throw out the grand oval placed in the midst of the ceiling. In this oval, with the most exquisite coloring, the brush of Jacopo Chiavistelli had beautifully represented the triumph of Mary Magdalen De-Pazzi in heaven. This work is indeed most deserving of the public praises which it received for the special work in the drapery, the posture, and the finishing of the numerous figures, and also for the design of those many groups of angels which could be seen in progressive distance, and can be seen to-day, for the ornament of the superior part of the church is the same one which the Cistercian monks had caused to be executed many years previous.

The main altar, however, was more richly, elegantly, and majestically adorned, for on it the precious treasure—the body of St. Mary Magdalen De-Pazzi—was to be exposed. On each side of its front arose two fluted columns, apparently of old green Roman marble, with bronze capitals, architrave, and cornice delicately adorned with gold cords, and with the centre ornament of gold arabesques, from the platform of which arose the arch which went all around it. At the corners of this arch were two fresco paintings, one a figure holding a lamb, with eyes cast down and in her countenance and attitude representing Humility ; and the other pressing to her bosom several charming little infants and holding in the right hand a heart in flames arising towards heaven, representing Charity. In the spaces between the two columns were two niches adorned above with some inscriptions to the height of the capitals, and below with graceful decorations. The two corner columns of the front were double. One of them turning towards the centre began on both sides a second order of architecture similar to the outside one, from which started a semicircular alcove divided into three spaces by two pilasters. Above all this, in order to cover the interior, arose a majestic canopy divided into five compartments, which by artistic connection joined in a circular form the arch of the chapel. Nothing was wanting to make this a work of sovereign beauty, as the author of this design, the Volterian, had thought of every possible way to adorn it, placing in the seven niches seven bronze-like statues, larger than the natural size, representing as many virtues, in the practice of which the Saint had indefatigably spent her life. Above the altar was a *double order*, behind which was a prolonged platform, where stood three silver-plated statues representing Chastity, Poverty, and Obedience on their knees, and with expressions of reverence and amazement. They supported with their raised hands another great platform, also silver-plated and strewn with silk flowers, on which rested the venerated body, in a rich gilt case and supported at its angles by four brackets, each of them ending in a lion's paw. The sides of the case were very brilliant with precious jewels. It arose in the shape of a sepulchral Urn, and, ending in a cover of most elaborate carving, held the purest and most costly crystals, which allowed the whole of the holy Relic enclosed to be seen. In order that every part might correspond with the whole in preparing such sumptuous ornaments as were befitting the sacred body, the cornice was adorned with silver vases filled with large branches of silk roses and silver lilies, which looked like natural ones In the lock of this Urn was a label with gold fringes and carvings and the motto. "*Quasi myrra electa dedi suavitatem odoris*"—"I yielded a sweet odor, like the best myrrh" (Ecclus xxiv, 20); and above it was the crowned coat-of-arms of the Carmelite Order, with the monogram below, containing St. Mary Magdalen's name, from which arose a superb canopy of silver gauze with gold flowers and fringes. This canopy opened at the sides, and, falling towards the ground, was slightly gathered at the extremities and held by some little angels, resting on the platform of the arch The sole object of this was that the image of the Saint, raised in the air under the canopy in the attitude of prayer, might appear more majestic and venerable.

The workmanship vied with the richness and elaborateness of such an altar and the precious material of the antipendium. This was of gold embroidery, commonly called relieved, with beautifully worked flowers of the finest silk, on a silver field; so that, though the material cost one thousand dollars, the workmanship was by the experts valued at much more. Of this material were also the chasuble, the dalmatics, and all the other sacred vestments required for the clergy in the Solemn High Mass, with the only difference that these had the groundwork of silver cloth and cost more than two thousand five hundred ducats, including the tabernacle for the ciborium, which during those days was placed in the side chapel on the right. The cloth on the main altar glittered with gold arabesques. The alb and the surplice of the celebrant, with other minor cloths and sacred ornaments, the location of candlesticks and candles,— everything bespoke splendor and magnificence. Before leaving this subject, a word of praise must be said for those nuns, who knew so well how to carry out the vastness of their project by the power of their minds and the skill of their hands, which executed several works truly wonderful

The church being magnificently adorned, on the Saturday previous to the Sunday of the celebration all the nuns gathered in the interior chapel of St. Mary Magdalen at sunset, and having venerated the sacred body, humbly placed it on their shoulders, and forming a procession, two by two, with lighted tapers in their hands, proceeded to a door which from the cloister led into the courtyard. This had been thrown open for the occasion, and there they knelt to receive the blessing of the prioress, and were met by four most noble ladies, viz., the Marchioness Caterina Salviati and the Ladies Clarice Serlupi, Lucrezia Macinghi, and Maria Ximenes They started for the church with their faces covered by black veils, and gave up the inestimable treasure to four priests, that they might carry it to the place prepared for it. After praying a long while, they returned to the monastery At this ceremony, renewed afterwards on the twelfth day when bringing the body back, the director of the monastery, with cope, presided, all being done with the permission of the Sovereign Pontiff, which had been obtained for the nuns by Monsignore Francesco De Neri, Archbishop of Florence, and afterwards a most worthy Cardinal. It was the dawn of the second day of June and one could already see the people, who, overflowing with joy, after going to and fro in the streets selected for the procession, which were strewn with flowers and covered with very rich cloths, began to pour in great crowds into the large church of the Carmelites These nuns, having recited the canonical hours and assisted at Mass, sung with orchestral accompaniment, came out devoutly from the choir, and, kneeling before an altar where the standard had been placed, in a loud voice intoned the Litany of the Saints. On reaching the invocation of the *Saint*, before the versicle, "*Omnes Sanctæ Virgines et Viduæ*," while singing *it* the second time, the solemn procession was begun The six mace-bearers of the Supreme Magistrate, clothed in red velvet, silver maces in hand, went before on horses properly caparisoned, two by two, seeing with noble gravity that the passage-way should not be obstructed by the crowd. They were followed by the standard of the Metropolitan and that of the Abbey of Florence, which in public solemnities enjoys the right to accompany it, both hanging from glittering gilt staffs and made of taffeta of various colors, with a special design on each of its own device Then came, preceded by their cross, the Capuchins of Montughi and of the Conception, the Friars of St. John of God, the Minims of St Francis of Paola and of St. Joseph, the Conventuals of the Holy Cross, the Minor Observants of the Holy Saviour and of All Saints, the Augustinians of the Holy Spirit, of St. Stephen, and of St. James tra' Fossi, the Friars of Our Lady of Mount Carmel and of St Mary Major, the Servites of the Most Holy Annunciation, the Dominicans of St Maria Novella and of St. Mark. These were followed by the Congregations of the monks with their own respective standards, viz., the Regular Canons of St. James Major, the monks of Mount Olivet, the Celestines of St. Michael de' Visdomini, the Cistercians of Borgo San Frediano, the Vallombrosians of the Holy Trinity and of St. Pancratius, the Camaldolenses of the Angels, and, lastly, the black Benedictines of the Abbey. The great number of claustrals from the above-named Religious Houses, then in existence, were immediately followed by the numerous Priories of clerics and priests, vying with one another in neatness, gravity, and devotion. The Canons of St Laurence, and especially those of the Metropolitan Church, distinguished themselves for the grandeur of their habit and for having in their ranks men of high and widespread reputation for birth, knowledge, or virtue. To the Church of the Carmine all the male members of the De-Pazzi family had also come to assist at so great and, for them, so honorable a demonstration of the universal joy; and they occupied a special and convenient place immediately after the clergy, having gone to it two by two with lighted torches in their hands. Among them were the following, according to the order in which they came Clemente and Francesco, of the family of the Commendatore; Captain Cosimo the Commendatore, and Captain Pazzino, of Francesco; Pierantonio and the Canon Renato, of Andrea, the Knight Alemanno, of Chevalier and Captain Girolamo, who, as the descendant of a brother of St Mary Magdalen, though very young, was given, by common consent of the others, who were older, the honor of precedence. The chorus of the singers, placed between two bands of trumpeters, came next; and the trumpeters, with their festival sounds, filled all hearts with singular sweetness After this followed the standard on which was the image of the Saint, and it was carried by the Provincial of the Carmelites of Tuscany, surrounded by other fathers of note, who were also to carry it in turn Its four tassels were held by four little boys of the De-Pazzi family, viz , Agnolo, Antonio, Guglielmo, and Filippo, all children of the Commendatore and Captain Alessandro. They wore pages' suits, with stockings and pants of silver cloth, richly trimmed with gold, cloaks of black silk lined with silver cloth and with gold trimming, and appeared in every way worthy of the honorable office for which the nobility of their blood had destined them. The standard was followed by the Magistrate of the Councillors, who was supreme in the happy Republic of Florence, and all the Senate, with the other eight Magistrates of the Palace so-called It is not easy to imagine how much grandeur was lent to the procession by the splendor of the many knights who accompanied it, among whom, like the light of a most resplendent sun, shone the majesty of the Senate, both in the venerable and yet florid countenances of the Senators, in the beauty of their mantles and their clothes of damask dyed in the finest purple. Thus the procession, going through St. Monica Street, St. Spirito Square, and from St Felix Street to May Street, crossed Holy Trinity Bridge, and, arriving at the square of the Duomo and to the street of the Servites at the square of the St Annunziata, and then, leaving behind the Arc of Innocents, reached, with great pomp, by Laura and Colonna Streets, the monastery of St. Maria degli Angeli The Most Serene Grand Duke Ferdinand II, and the Prince Cardinal Leopoldo, his brother, coming out of the Bentivoglio Palace near by, took their position before the Senate to follow the procession for the short remaining distance As soon as the standard reached the church door, the bearer halted, and then the Apostolic Nunzio, dressed in pontificals, came forward, and, with the usual bows, incensed it three times, and, bringing it into the church, intoned the *Te Deum*. He was followed by eight choruses of musicians placed on two terraces. The harmony of the sweet singing, joined to the incomparable beauty of the decorations and the dazzling splendor of the lights, made one imagine that he was at that instant carried up to paradise. In the meantime, their Most Serene Highnesses, having offered prayer, ascended the extraordinarily splendid throne, where sat alone the Princess of Tuscany, Margherita Luisa di Borbone, for Cosimo III, the reigning prince, was far away, traveling through Europe. The Grand Duke Ferdinand wished the four above-mentioned De-Pazzi boys to be seated on the steps of his throne, thus to honor in them the merit of so illustrious a family. The Grand Duchess Victoria, being in poor health, assisted from a small tribune.

The *Te Deum* being over, the chanters sang " *Ora pro nobis, Sancta Maria Magdalena*" and the responses to it, after which, Monsignor Nunzio recited the *Oremus* proper of the Saint, whilst the standard was raised and safely placed against the wall on one side of the church.

Then the Senate and the Magistrates took their seats, and the Nuuzio
having put on the pontifical vestments for the Mass at the faldistorium,
it was sung by the finest musicians   When Mass was over, as the
panegyrist could not perform his task that morning on account of the
length of the ceremonies, their Highnesses left immediately, waited on as
far as their carriage by the Senate, the Magistrates, and the Cavaliers,
who also returned to their homes, equally overflowing with joy, wonder,
and tenderness   But this did not seem in the least to diminish the
crowd of people, which was so great for the capacity of the church, that,
not only on the first but during the whole of the eight days, the halber-
diers found it very difficult, even in the courtyard, to open a passage-way
for the prelates, the priests, and other distinguished persons, or those
needed for the services   It is impossible to describe the enthusiasm of
the multitudes craving to go to the feet of the sacred remains of Mary
Magdalen, in order to manifest to her the most heartfelt tokens of their
intense devotion.   Many also availed themselves of the night, watching
and praying for whole hours before the sacred Relics, in order to give
vent to their burning piety.   Like the Mass in the morning, so, also,
with vestments similar in richness and workmanship, Vespers were sung
by the same eight choirs of musicians   When Vespers, which were
sung at sunset, were over, the festivities of the first day ended.   In the
evening, there was a repetition of the bonfires in many streets of the city,
and there were fireworks and *girandolas* at Palazzo Vecchio to attract
universal attention to the joyous exhibitions prepared in honor of the
Saint by the Cavaliers of her family   These were conducted in the
manner which I am about to relate, in the belief of pleasing my readers,
renewing the memory of things which have a strict relation to some
customs of our days, and which will the better show the glory of St
Mary Magdalen and the devout tenderness of the Capital of Tuscany
towards this, her most loving benefactress

Description of the Fireworks in the Evening.

The gentlemen of the De-Pazzi family wished to express in common, by some public demonstration, what and how great was their
particular joy because of the canonization of Mary Magdalen, a most
resplendent light and a special pride to their lineage   They concluded
to do it at the same time which was appointed by the nuns of Santa Maria
degli Angeli for the solemn celebration, by exhibiting, during each of the
first three nights, a grand flame of fireworks, which was magnificently
carried out in the following order and arrangement.   After several discus-
sions on the choice of locality, the Holy Cross Square was selected as the
most suitable, both because of its prominent position and because that
church contains sumptuous tombs and chapels of the De-Pazzi family,
among which chapels there was one deservedly held in very high esteem
in the cloister of the Friars for the use of their *chapter*   This work was
not less elegant because of its ornaments than sublime and rare because
of having been designed by the never-sufficiently-praised Filippo Bru-
nelleschi, to whom Florence owes whatever great and rare she in architecture it possesses.   The old practice of holding in the above church the

religious services of this family was also a reason for selecting the square for the object aforesaid. The place then being fixed upon, and having determined what frames were needed, and what, by ingenious allusions, they were to represent, their construction was begun and soon finished, thanks to the skill and energy of a valiant architect, Virgini Zaballi, assisted by the Signor Luigi De-Pazzi, who superintended it in behalf of all the family. As a basis of the frame, they made use of the triumphal car which, being destined for the ceremony of the blessing of the fire on Holy Saturday, refreshes every year the memory of the ancient valor of Pazzo De-Pazzi at the taking of Jerusalem This knight, at the time of the first Crusade, went over to the Holy Land, leading twenty-five hundred Florentines He was the first to scale the walls of Jerusalem and hoist the larger flag of his band. At his return, he carried three pieces of stone from the Holy Sepulchre, and some of his family, followed by an immense crowd of people, went forth to meet him, and made him ascend a triumphal car adorned with precious ornaments and paintings, in which the holy wars, and especially the scaling of Jerusalem, were represented. He entered the city thus, as in triumph, amidst universal acclamations. The memory or symbol of this occurrence was not allowed to perish, but was kept alive in the above-mentioned car, which the De-Pazzi family sends out every year on Holy Saturday, loaded with fireworks, which are lit up in token of joy at the intoning of the *Gloria in excelsis Deo* in the Metropolitan Church, whilst all the bells of the city are ringing. From those stones of the Holy Sepulchre, which at first the De-Pazzi family kept in their palace and afterwards deposited in the Church of the Holy Apostles, is extracted the spark of the *sacred fire* which is carried in procession by the Prior of this church to the *Duomo*, to light all the extinguished lamps and candles, according to the Roman Catholic rite. It was deemed a very proper thing that, as that car was used to revive the memory of the heroic action of the ancestor, so it should be called into service to immortalize the glories and the name of the descendant who forms the greatest honor of all her illustrious family.

As each of the frames, proceeding by degrees, was to represent the three states of the Saint, viz , in the world, in Religion, and in heaven, therefore, beginning with the first, the secular state was represented in the square on Sunday evening The necessary frame was led thereto by six trumpeters on horseback in rich livery, with the very ancient De Pazzi coat-of-arms of six half-moons set up in inverted order, and the dolphins and crosses which they use at present as a noble gift granted by Goffredo di Buglione to the above-mentioned Pazzo De-Pazzi at the conquest of Jerusalem. Over the convent door was placed in public view a very large Latin inscription from the learned pen of Andrea Cavalcanti, a most noble Florentine knight, which set forth the reason for the fireworks, the joy, and the piety of the authors, and the opportune selection of the site. The builder of the frame had repre-sented in it an old fortress of rustic order, with a tower in the middle about fifty feet high, surrounded by four well-designed little forts which at all four corners had little turrets, the whole measuring in circumference about one hundred feet Above and below hung from each tower a large painting

representing some fact in the life of the Saint and some family events,
and in the midst was placed a beautiful scroll, declaring in eight most
elegant verses the events and the relation between them   In oval spaces
over the big tower some fact or virtue of the Saint corresponding to the
subject of the painting was represented in bas-relief; and at the base in
two shields surrounded by trophies were painted two *undertakings*, or
emblems, symbolizing the Saint, and explained in verses from the pens
of the most illustrious lights of Tuscany in epic and lyric poetry —
Dante and Petrarca.   These verses were properly selected by the Abbé
Luigi Strozzi, envoy of the Christian king to the Court of Tuscany, later
Archdeacon of the Florentine metropolitan church, and by the Chevalier
Prior Luigi Ricasoli-Rucellai of the Order of St Stephen.   On the first
façade in the painting above was represented the birth of Catherine
(baptismal name of the Saint); and in the painting below, the origin
of the De-Pazzi family in Florence, to which place they came to live
from Fiesole.   Such is the tradition of its origin, principally deduced
from the half-moons of its old coat-of-arms, which allude to the Fiesole
coat-of-arms, though some writers say, and not without reason, that this
is too weak a proof   However, this amounts to little, and it would be
useless to inquire further into it, as no fact exists which can lead us to
the naked and simple truth.   The Fiesolans firmly holding in their
minds and greatly loving in their hearts this opinion, wished also to
distinctly applaud the canonization of Mary Magdalen De-Pazzi, by
covering the tops of their hills with bonfires during the same three
evenings, when it was solemnized in Florence.   The verses of the above-
mentioned inscription were as follows : —

> *"If a plant, formerly the honor of the neighboring hill,*
> *Came down to adorn Florence,*
> *From the nuptial graft of Buondelmonti and Pazzi*
> *A more beautiful flower springs forth*
> *A flower which, exhaling a sacred fragrance,*
> *Succeeds in pleasing God Himself*
> *Hence Arno bows (rather than to the root)*
> *To Catherine, the immortal offshoot "*

The picture representing a quality in relation to the historical
subject, was *Nobility*.   A more appropriate one could not be found   and
the two symbols were also most appropriate.   The first of these was a
cedar—a tree, because of its nature, incorruptible—which, growing in
elevated places, sends forth its top to sublime heights.   The motto
was : —

> " *Let not the most esteemed be compared to her* "

The second was an oak, from the branches of which military
trophies were wont to hang, and the motto —

> " *Proud of their virtue and of my booty* "

On another façade appeared the Saint, still a little girl, when at
the age of ten, after having received her First Communion, she made a
private vow of virginity and was accepted as His Spouse by the Divine
Word, with the token of the ring, which, then invisible and unknown,

became known and was seen afterwards in one of her ecstasies.   In the corresponding family event was represented the illustrious parentage of the house of the Princess of Tuscany, when Guglielmo De-Pazzi received as wife Bianca, the sister of Lorenzo De' Medici (called because of his munificence the *Magnifico*), and consequently aunt to Leo X, and great-aunt to Lorenzo II, Duke of Urbino, who was the father of Catherine, the Queen of France   The verses were :—

> " *Let Guglielmo boast the royal bed of a noble maid,*
> *And all the most beautiful ornaments,*
> *Let him display before beautiful Tuscany,*
> *For so great a parentage, his great vaunts.*
> *But a gold ring to His humble Servant*
> *Handed in token of love the King of Kings*
> *With her tender hand she takes it in silence*
> *As a pledge of eternal glory and true peace* "

The gift or virtue was *Virginity*   Of the two *undertakings*, one was the perpetual fire, consecrated by the old Romans to the goddess Vesta, which, as it could not be kindled by an earthly spark, had to be drawn by the sun's rays and guarded forever only by virgins, among the choicest for purity of life and nobility of birth , and the motto was :—

> " *This flame could not have any other source.*"

The other *undertaking* was the *emerald*, regarded as the symbol of virginity because it never loses the purity of its color, and the motto was :—

> "*It preserves the green hue.*"

On the third façade was represented the Saint courageously speaking to her parents, persisting in her resolution to become a nun, and, by the efficacy of her arguments, mollifying the hardness of their hearts. The family event represented the embassy of Cosimo De-Pazzi, Arch-bishop of Florence, to the King of France, Charles VIII, in whose presence he, boldly speaking, persuades the king to give back to the Florentine Republic the city of Pisa, which he was keeping against every right and with offense to his royal troth.   The scroll contained the following verses .—

> "*Cosimo arms his speech with intrepid vigor*
> *Whilst addressing the great monarch,*
> *And he tries, to the great amazement of all,*
> *To again subject to his country the wonted gifts of Alphea ;*
> *But Catherine asks, from the paternal love,*
> *And obtains, by insistence, a virginal mantle,*
> *A mantle which, deemed lowly on earth, Heaven appreciates*
> *Above every pomp of royal splendor* "

The virtue represented was *Intrepidity* and the two *undertakings* corresponding to it were: First, a swan, which, though by nature most meek, if provoked sometimes by the eagle, courageously goes forward to meet her.   The motto was —

> " *That I gave so much courage to my heart.*"

Secondly, a dyke which, arresting the flow of the river, turns away the fury of its waves, with the motto :—

" It restrains the course and turns it at pleasure."

On the fourth and last façade appeared the Saint when, in the act of becoming a nun, she receives the Carmelite habit, the sacred veil, and the sacred crown at the hands of the priest   To this corresponded, as an event of her ancestry, the mural crown given by the famous Conqueror of Jerusalem to Pazzo De-Pazzi, as a reward for his having first scaled the walls of the besieged city.   The verses were as follows :—

" With a stately crown the brows are encircled
Of the valiant hero De-Pazzi by the pious Buglione ;
But Catherine covers herself with a despicable mantle
And places herself in servitude
The one undertakes to triumph in the world,
The other proposes to herself to serve God alone.
Now let anyone who chooses compare this world with heaven,
A mural crown with a consecrated veil."

The virtue of the Saint was represented by *Piety;* and, of the two *undertakings*, one was the fish Uranoscopus, which, having but one eye in its head, comes up above water, to contemplate with it the beauty of the heavens, with the motto :—

"For looking thereat my desire finds rest "

The other was the bird of paradise, which always, either balancing itself on its wings or flying through the air, disdains to rest a single moment on the ground.   The motto was :—

" He clothed its feathers for a high flight."

The frame of the first evening was very beautiful, and the fire-works fully corresponded with the beauty of the exterior form.   Filling the air with noise and light, these now went up like stars—now ran along the ground and changed into springs and other very beautiful sights   Not less pleasing and ingenious, however, were the designs that were destined for the evenings of Monday and Tuesday, which I will consecutively describe, returning afterwards to complete the narration of the church festivities.

The second frame represented a delightful place surrounded by walls, the better to express thereby the *religious state*, which, as a most charming enclosed garden, is wont to produce fragrant flowers of sanctity. It began with a large square base, which seemed to be of marble of various colors; on top of it ran an imitation balustrade of lapis lazzuli surmounted with gilt balls   On each of the four corners, which had little pilasters of marble variously colored, rested gilt vases emitting imitation flames. Above this first order was raised the second, in the same style of architecture, which for more artistic finish was gradually narrowed at the top So also the third, from the base of which projected four silver dolphins, supporting a quadrangular pyramid or obelisk of porphyry color, at the summit of which was a globe with a cross, both gilt.   The frame, made in Doric style, was about sixty feet high, and double this in circumference It was everywhere adorned with the handsomest perspectives and pleasing foliage. On its four lower faces were painted in *chiaroscuro* four historical events taken from the pages of the Old Testament, representing events in the lives of the Prophets Elias and Eliseus, fathers and founders of the Carmelites. On the four faces above were described as many events in the life of the Saint, corresponding to those of above-named founders, and all were furnished with appropriate Latin inscriptions. In the spaces between one and the other of these faces were four large placards, each containing an epigram, which, ingeniously explaining the historical facts, connected them together A hard task, but very easy for the talent and erudition of the two renowned academicians of the Crusca, Senator Vincenzo de Filicaja and Lawyer Benedetto Gori, who assumed the writing of these and the other compositions on the same frame.

On the first front of the first order could be seen Elias lying down and sleeping under a juniper tree, whilst an angel, in the act of reproaching him, was pointing out to him with his left hand the hearth-cake, and with his right the ridges of Mount Horeb, extending at a proper distance. In the front of the second order was painted our Most Amiable Redeemer, Who in the Consecrated Host was giving Himself to the Saint. The epigrams of the above-named academicians, transcribed on the placards, had been translated from Latin into Italian by a good poet, and are reported here in the English language.—

EPIGRAM FIRST.

The daughter is greater than the grandfather.
And oh ! how far apart they run on the long road !
He among flowers tends to Horeb,
She by a hard road tends to heaven.
Him a celestial messenger restores
Her the Eternal Love wishes to strengthen.
Two such great events we dare not compare ·
One God commanded, the other God did Himself

On the second front below was represented Elias being carried up to heaven in a fiery chariot. Above it was the Saint in ecstasy, with her body raised in the air, at the foot of a Crucifix, on the entablature of the choir.

EPIGRAM SECOND.

A soul inflamed with the fire of divine love
Lightly flies up to the ethereal regions
Elias, who is burning with such a fire,
Leaves this earth and goes quickly up to the stars.
Not less high, despite her mortal weight,
Does Mary Magdalen upward soar.
And as the flame which continually tends on high,
Her love, which is heavenly, to heaven draws her.

On the third front below was Elias, who, covering Eliseus with his mantle, whilst the latter was ploughing his fields, makes him a prophet and declares him his successor in this high office. Above this was St Mary Magdalen in the act of receiving at the hands of the Blessed Virgin a snow-white veil, to clothe herself thereby with the most spotless purity.

EPIGRAM THIRD.

A rude tiller of the soil receives Elias' mantle,
And lo ! the prophetic spirit through him speaks
A white veil covers a sacred virgin's heart,
And it communicates to her such a virtue,
That her spotless virginal flower
Is worthy to enter into the crown of the great King of Kings.
Let, therefore, Eliseus give way to her, he is not her equal,
To a man he owes the gift, she owes it to Mary.

On the fourth, and last lower face was represented Eliseus, who, by the infusion of salt, was making salubrious the corrupted waters of Jericho. To this historical fact corresponded, in the face above it, that of the Saint, who, at the bidding of the superioress, with her mere blessing, brought back to its former good taste a keg of wine which had become spoiled.

EPIGRAM FOURTH.

The Hebrew was sad and grieved at the sight
Of Jericho's fount giving forth bitter water,
And smiled when he saw quickly flowing from it,
At Eliseus' bidding, waters sweet as honey
And thou, O Saint, on hearing with sad countenance
That the wine had become spoiled by musty taste,
By the virtue of thy heart, candid and pure,
Thou causedst all bad taste depart

On the first face of the third order, which by the same talent had been enriched with sayings from the Sacred Scriptures, on a beautiful label was written the dedication of the car, in the following

EPIGRAM.

Do not disdain this structure inferior to thee,
Which it would be, even if it equaled heaven,
Here a low and humble Muse applauds and praises thee,
Here a perishable brush describes thy deeds.
See what has been the Sun of thy virtues
Within the sacred cloisters, O immortal maiden !
If a bright color suffices to paint others,
Thy works themselves are but the image of thy soul

On the other three faces corresponding to the first were cartoons beautifully worked, with fanciful intertwining of festoons, with inscriptions briefly indicating the interior consolations enjoyed by the Saint in the Religious life. The obelisk or pyramid, placed at the summit of the frame, was, according to the very old custom of the Egyptians, full of hieroglyphics alluding to the various attributes and qualities of the Saint in the same state. In the first of its quadrangular faces were represented the three fundamental vows of Religion— Poverty, Chastity, and

She restores several sick persons to health (page 331).

Obedience. *Poverty* was symbolized by the moon, which, being of itself deficient in light, by looking at the sun's face, becomes at once full of luminous splendor. *Chastity* was symbolized by the girdle with which Jeremias girded his loins by divine command. *Obedience* was symbolized by a cloud moved from place to place by the blowing of the winds, according to the saying of the Holy Ghost: *"And the clouds, since God commanded them to go over the whole world, do that which is commanded them"* (Baruch vi, 61). Three other symbolical figures were painted on the second front, expressive of the several states of the Saint, viz · of Novice, of Professed, and of Office-holder in Religion. The *Novitiate* was symbolized by the sun bursting forth from the bosom of the morning dawn —a thought not less gentle than appropriate, taken from the Canticle of Deborah, Book of Judges, Chapter V, 31, where it is said: *"Let them that love thee shine, as the sun shineth in its rising"* The *Profession* was represented by a tree in blossom near the running waters, an image taken from Psalm 1, 3: *"And he shall be like a tree, which is planted near the running waters"* One of the offices that the Saint filled in the monastery and the one best suited for her to fill with great merit for herself and very great profit for her more heavenly than human virtues, was the office of Mistress of the Novices This was represented by an eagle flying slowly around the nest of her little ones, taking some of them on her own wings to teach them swift and safe flying. As we read in Deuteronomy xxx, 11: *"As the eagle entices her young to fly."*

A like number of symbols were painted on the third face, denoting the three special gifts obtained by the Saint, viz., Contemplation, Prophecy, and Prayer. *Contemplation* was represented by a dove, which, as a symbol of meditation, was seen by King Hezekiah, when, having recovered from his mortal illness at the backward going of the sun dial for ten lines, praising and blessing his benefactor, devoutly sang· *"I will cry like a young swallow; I will meditate like a dove"* (Isa. xxxviii, 14). And *"We shall lament as mournful* (the Latin has *meditantes) doves"* (Isa. lix, 11). And David: *"Who will give me wings like a dove, and I will fly and be at rest?"* (Ps. liv, 7); it being the prerogative of him who meditates to raise his mind to God and there take rest while contemplating. The spirit of *prophecy* was represented by a cloud dropping rain upon the earth, a thought borrowed by St. John Chrysostom, who, in the Homily on Chapter VII of the Gospel of St. Matthew, thus speaks: *"As the clouds carry the rain and let it flow upon the earth, so the prophets receive the words from God and spread them upon the reasoning earth* (mankind)." The strength and ineffable virtue of *prayer* was expressed by the altar and the incense, as prayer, like odorous incense, is most acceptable to God. *"Let my prayer be directed as incense in Thy sight"* (Ps. cxl, 2).

On the fourth and last face of the pyramid were represented the three special and most singular qualities of St. Mary Magdalen—love of God, love of solitude, and tranquillity in tribulations and temptations. The love of God was represented by an iron made red hot in the flames of a furnace, for, as iron placed in the fire is entirely changed into fire, so the soul enamored of God, burning with the fires of a most ardent charity, becomes at once all fire and, consumed by fire, is all transformed into charity. This idea is found admirably developed in the works of St Cyprian and St Chrysostom. A young stag on a mount of aromatic spices represented *Solitude*, in accordance with what the Sacred Bride of the Canticles was wont to say to her Divine Beloved in the excesses of her mysterious love. The *Tranquillity* of the Saint appeared symbolized in a star of the first magnitude, the splendor of which could not be diminished by the thick darkness of the clouds approaching it from all sides, surrounding and trying to obscure it· *"As the morning star in the midst of a cloud"* (Ecclus. 1, 6) Such was the second flame, which, having been previously exposed to the public curiosity in the square, was illuminated on Monday evening to the very great delight of the people, who applauded the various and frequent changes of its fireworks. These showed the truly wonderful talent of the author, particularly those of the ball, which, being left for the last, all luminous, sprang, with its cross in the air, to an untold height, and there, bursting with a crash of thunder, emitted an infinite number of crackers and stars. These, wandering through the dark sky, besides illuminating its darkness by the brightness of their lights, opened in their fall, and each one dropped many other similar ones, though a little smaller, with repeated and brilliant effect.

The third frame, destined for the evening of Tuesday, being intended to represent the state of the Saint in glory, looked like a majestic temple, the base of which, in imitation of Sicilian granite, had on its four façades four cartoons embroidered around with arabesques and with tassels of gold. At each corner was a pyramid in porphyry color, well proportioned in its height and width On this base appeared another order of architecture, which contained, in the middle of every façade, a medallion with pictures of the Saint taken from the world to the bliss of paradise It ended very artistically in four corners, upon which were stationed four gilt vases filled with flames. At the summit of the structure, which gradually became smaller and smaller, were four more pieces, isolated, and resplendent with gold, and which were placed there to support a cornice that ran all around. On this plane were dolphins, covered with gilt scales, grouped together and supporting a crown adorned with golden points and stars, and ending in a silver lily, which was raised above it a little less than two cubits. This flame was of Doric order, thirty-five cubits high and not less than fifteen wide on every side. Carlo Dati, with his admirable talent, assumed the task of illustrating it This ornament of the Academy of the Crusca and of the city of Florence did his work to the full satisfaction of everyone's expectation. To complete his praise, suffice it to say, that Louis XIV, King of France, without having seen him, desired to honor him with a large annual pension, his royal mind being moved by the worth of his works and the greatness of his fame. Here we should record the beautiful epigrams and mottoes which Dati composed in honor of the Saint and which were then placed on the cartoons and under the medallions. But these could not be obtained during his lifetime, he, in his extreme modesty, deeming that this production of his was not deserving of being printed. After his death, though they were several times asked for, the most diligent search by his heir failed to find them. Let the reader, therefore, take the description of this third frame, if not as I wish it to be, at least the best that I can make it; and let him know that, as it surpassed in beauty and skill the other two, so it also was above them in inventive genius and abundance of fireworks, which lasted longer than the others, to the ever-increasing joy and amazement of the immense multitude which had gathered to witness them.

Now, returning to the church feasts, the solemnity of the first day being ended with Vespers, no sooner did the light of the second day begin to break forth in the east, than the church was filled in an instant, for, the people who were waiting in crowds at its doors, were impatient to enter. It seemed to them as if the slowness of the priests did not second the eagerness of their desire, which had even unseasonably antici-pated the rising of the sun. To form an idea of this joyous multitude one must reflect that the country around, the boroughs, the cities, and the chief castles of the nobility for many miles emptied themselves to fill up the city of Florence, and they and the inhabitants of Florence ran to St. Maria degli Angeli. I will not say the church, the courtyard, and the porch, but the very Pinti Street itself was far from being able to hold so great a multitude. Carriages could not approach it at all. Every morn-ing during the celebration more than two hundred priests offered in this church the Divine Sacrifice. The number of lights was the same every day and every hour, and not one of them was ever allowed to be extinguished. The wax, all from Venice, provided for the occasion by the nuns, amounted to twenty-five hundred pounds, besides sixteen hundred pounds contributed by devout people for so noble an object. The Most Serene Grand Duke, with the Prince Cardinal Leopoldo and their Royal Highnesses, the Grand Duke's wife and daughter-in-law, followed by a splendid and noble retinue, came each day to pay their homage to the Saint. The majority of the Tuscan prelates came to Florence for the same object, and many also from outside of Tuscany did the same, the latter and the former being followed by not a few distinguished person-ages. The Oblates of the hospitals, the girls of the conservatories of Florence, who, not being bound by a solemn vow, yet voluntarily pro-fess to observe the monastic enclosure, left their cloisters and came early in the morning to receive Holy Communion at the altar of the Saint. The adjoining nuns of Candeli, having received permission from Rome, threw down a wall which divided the gardens of the two monasteries, and thus came also to pay their respects to the sacred body, kneeling before it nearly two hours, praying and reciting psalms. In the mean-time, Sister Maria Cherubini De-Pazzi, a nun of the Ripoli monastery, and niece of the Saint (being a daughter of a brother of St. Mary Magdalen), was also granted the same privilege—nay, more, for she received permission to leave her monastery and remain a whole day in the monastery of St. Maria degli Angeli, which she did on the third day of Pentecost. She was taken there in a carriage by two ladies, with a nun as companion. She had not been able to get there at the time of the canonization on account of her health and her great age, which was eighty-five years.

Let us now describe the second day of the celebration. At the hour of tierce, the nuns having recited in a low voice the Divine Office, Mon-

signore Roberto Strozzi, Bishop of Fiesole, approached the main altar
with great reverence, and, having knelt before the Saint, went to the
episcopal throne, where he took the pontifical robes.   He then celebrated
Mass with the assistance of many priests and assistant ministers and a
concert of four choirs of musicians, selected from the very best.   The
feelings of the people there assembled harmoniously corresponded with
their melodious voices, and, contemplating the sacred body, they filled the
air with the most fervent sighs, and moistened the floor with the most
tender tears, either to ask for some grace through the Saint, or to offer
their dutiful thanks for a grace already obtained.   Father Francesco Maria
Mancini, Provincial of the Minor Observants of Tuscany, spoke from
the pulpit in honor of our heroine, restricting her most ample praises to
a panegyric, but in language so sweet and persuasive that he won the
hearts of his hearers to make the most enthusiastic declarations of esteem
and love towards our Saint.   At the proper hour Solemn Vespers were
sung, the celebrant being the Archpriest Soldani, who took upon himself this office for the whole Octave.   On all the days that followed, these
same solemnities were carried out.   Not to repeat the same thing,
we shall simply recall the principal points of the other six days.   On
the third day, Pontifical Mass was celebrated by Monsignore Camillo
degli Albizzi, Bishop of Volterra, and a learned panegyric was delivered
by *Father Maestro* Giuseppe Maria Quilici, Prior of the Carmelites of
St. Maria Maggiore.   On the fourth day, Monsignore Francesco d' Elci,
Archbishop of Pisa, celebrated Pontifical Mass, and the panegyrist was
Father Agostino Maria di San Gerolamo, a barefooted Carmelite, Lector
of Theology.   On the fifth day, Monsignore Vincenzo Bardi, of the
Counts of Vernio, Vicar General of Florence, ascended the altar to
pontificate, and Father Basilio Paulicelli, a Theatine monk, was the
orator.   On the sixth day, the Very Rev. Dean Antonio De-Ricci, afterwards Archdeacon and Auditor of the Reformations, enjoyed the honor
of being the celebrant, and the task of speaking was creditably dis-
charged by Father Costantino Fabbri, a Barnabite.   On the seventh day,
the Holy Sacrifice was offered up by the Very Rev. Canon Carlo del
Vigna, who had once been the director of the nuns at St. Maria degli
Angeli; and the praises of the Saint were told by Father Bernardino
Catastini, then Definitor and later General of the Capuchins, a great
man because of the extent of his knowledge and the exemplariness of
his life.   On the last day, which, being the crowning one, could not be
less solemn than the first, especially on account of the commemoration
being made by the Church of the Descent of the Holy Ghost on the
earth, the Mass was celebrated, with eight choirs of musicians, by the
Very Rev. Archpriest Soldani, director of the nuns; and the last
panegyric was recited by Father Giovannagnolo de Benedictis, of the
Society of Jesus, a speaker of great renown for the soundness of his
eloquence and his marvelous delivery.   The Very Rev. Francesco
Zappata, a Canon of St. Lawrence, having about this time returned
to Florence, the Committee of the Feasts, not desiring that an orator
of such great reputation should remain silent on so happy an occasion, pressingly invited him to speak, too.   He, on this same eighth
day, kindly accepted the invitation, and, shortly before Vespers, filled

the whole city with joy by adding to the eight panegyrics a sublime and splendid oration, delivered by him in his usual graceful manner, which was not the least commendable of his many rare gifts
Their two Most Serene Highnesses the Grand Duchess Vittoria and the
Princess Margherita Luisa, with the ladies of their household, assisted
at Vespers from the tribune. The Prince Cardinal (not a priest) gave a
great example of piety. He received Holy Communion in the morning
before the Holy Relic, returned again in the evening, and, having
caused the church to be closed, remained there with his retinue a long
time in most devout prayer.

On Monday morning, the second day of Pentecost, before the rising
of the sun, the nuns came out of the cloister in procession, and, with the
same ceremonies observed when taking out the sacred body of the Saint,
brought it back to their monastery.

Translation of the Sacred Body of St. Mary Magdalen De-Pazzi.

The generosity of the faithful, which had contributed so much
towards the erection of the Saint's chapel, did not cease after the work was
completed. The common desire to see it perfected in the most lasting and
elegant manner caused other works of great value to be added to it, and,
finally, Giovanni Battista Foggini, having been entrusted with its execution (he was a most renowned marble sculptor and metal-worker), made
the magnificent bronze case, into which, under the main altar from the
inside, was translated, and in which remains to this day, that most precious
treasure—the incorrupt body of St. Mary Magdalen De-Pazzi. This last
translation from the old shrine, annually commemorated by the Church,
took place on the 31st of May, 1685, and was then solemnized by the
Church for three days, the sacred remains being exposed to the public veneration, and nothing was omitted which would contribute to make it
universally and fully satisfactory. Innocent XI granted a Plenary Indulgence to all who visited the church with the dispositions required. The
Archbishop of Florence, Giacopantonio Morigia, directed the celebration.
The Grand Duke of Tuscany, Cosimus III, his son Giovan Gastone, and
his brother Francesco Maria, afterwards a Cardinal, assisted at it with singular piety. The Grand Duchess Vittoria distinguished herself by removing
from the head of the Saint the old crown, keeping it as a pledge of
celestial favor and replacing it with her own hands by the gift of a new
one set with most precious gems. Mention should also be made of the
special demonstration of devotion towards the Saint made by Monsignore
Gherardi, Bishop of Pistoja and Prato He was not satisfied with having
offered the Holy Sacrifice, but remained several hours kneeling before
his great advocate He insisted, moreover, in publicly serving as an
acolyte the Mass said by a priest, to the great edification of the people,
who look with enthusiasm on anything which approaches the example
of our Divine Saviour, and easily profit by it. The learned Francesco-
Gregorio-Pio del Teglia published for this solemnity an appropriate
composition, dedicating it to said Prince Giovan Gastone.

Now, supplementing the old knowledge with recent information, in order to make the description of St Maria degli Angeli as complete as possible, we must add what follows.—

Over the door of the church is a fresco by Poccetti, representing St. Mary Magdalen the Penitent.   In the interior, the first chapel on the right contains "The Martyrdom of St. Romolo," painted by Carlo Portelli, of Loro.   The second chapel was lately adorned with gilt stuccos; it has three paintings, representing St Luigi Gonzaga, St. Raphael the Archangel, and St. Anthony of Padua; they are the work of Giuseppe Piattoli.   The third contains a painting by Alfonso Boschi, which represents the Eternal Father and Jesus Christ crowning the Blessed Virgin.   The fourth contains a painting by Pontormo, which represents the Madonna with her Divine Son, and the Saints Giovanni Battista, Pietro, Matteo, Bernardo, Paolo, and Caterina.   In the fifth can be seen an "Annunciation" by Alessandro Botticelli.   Over the door leading to the sacristy is a painting which represents the glory of St Luigi Gonzaga, by Anastasio Bimbacci, restored in 1749 by Agostino Veraccini.   In the sacristy is the Madonna caressing the Infant, St. John the Baptist, with St. Bernard and St. Peter, by Domenico Puligo; the Madonna presenting the Holy Infant to St. Mary Magdalen De-Pazzi, a copy of that of Luca Giordano, which is in the tribune; and the Saints Pietro, Giacomo, and Gerolamo, by the Ghirlandajo school.   The sixth chapel, adorned not long since with gilt stuccos and frescoes by Luigi Catani, contains a Crucifix carved by Bernard Buontalenti.   The magnificent tribune of our Saint is still in the splendid condition above described, and those who have charge of it try with all possible diligence to preserve the cleanliness and the elegance of the ornaments, so that anyone approaching it is filled with unspeakable satisfaction and an irresistible inclination to spend some time there in devout prayer   In the seventh chapel is the painting of Blessed Bartolomea Bagnesi, by Giuseppe Calignon. · The frescoes were executed in 1807 by Giuseppe Servolini, who represented scenes from the life of the Blessed One, whose body rests there   Opposite the sacristy door is the organ, adorned with a painting by Giambattista Cipriani, which represents our Saviour giving Holy Communion to St. Mary Magdalen.   In the eighth chapel is a painting of the Vasari school, which represents the Martyrdom of a Saint.   The ninth is adorned by a "St. Sebastian" in wood, at whose sides are "St. Roch" and "St. Ignatius," painted by Raffaello del Garbo   In the tenth can be seen "Christ Praying in the Garden," by Santi di Tito.   In the eleventh is a painting on a board, attributed to Beato Angelico, representing the Crowning of the Blessed Virgin.   The twelfth contains the Crib with many Shepherds, Angels, and Saints, by Cosimo Gamberucci.   There is a hall in the monastery (where the sacred vestments are kept) in which are paintings by Cosimo Ulivelli.   In the chapter is a painting by Pietro Perugino, of Christ on the Cross, with Mary Magdalen at its foot, and the Blessed Virgin, St. Benedict and St. John.   In the refectory is the "Miracle of the Multiplication of the Loaves and the Fishes," by Raffaele del Garbo· and there are also other paintings by distinguished artists

· Finally, we must say that an inscription at the end of this church mentions that, in 1796, Monsignore Martini, the most deserving Archbishop of Florence, celebrated its consecration, adding to the title of St Maria degli Angeli that of St. Mary Maddalena De-Pazzi. This had been previously adopted with constancy by the devotion of the faithful from the day that Mary Magdalen De-Pazzi, who now had become of common and almost unique invocation, was canonized.

Wonderful Things which happened during the above-described Solemnities.

As on the eve of the feasts of the Beatification of Mary Magdalen in Florence God was pleased to increase the oil of the monastery, so, on the approaching of the solemnity of the Canonization, a similar prodigy was wrought with the flour which the nuns were preparing for the extraordinary needs of those days. From the inquiries made with scrupulous accuracy, and submitted to the judgment of His Eminence Neri, Archbishop of Florence, an evident and miraculous increase of five bushels of flour was proved to have taken place. During the propitious octave, the sick by hundreds came suppliant to the sepulchre of our Saint and obtained the graces wished for. The blind regained their eyesight, as in the cases of Stefano Centeli and Donna Maria Tosci degli Onesti. The deaf had their hearing restored to them, as happened to Carlo Manzi and Luigi Bertieri. Isidoro Bencini, a dumb man, obtained the power of his speech; Angelo Bagni, Francesco Fiaschi, Bartolomea Mugini, and other lame, crippled, and paralyzed people regained their activity.

During the three days in 1685, when the translation was solemnized, many prodigies of this kind also happened, especially that of the flour, a large quantity of which, though already spoiled, not only returned to its primitive state of perfection, but increased in quantity, in a manner altogether wonderful and supernatural. This happened after mixing with it a very small portion of the other flour above mentioned (which was devoutly preserved by the nuns), and making over the whole the sign of the cross with an image of the Saint

Conclusion.

Lofty and celebrated shines the De-Pazzi family from its very ancient foundation, viz , from the year 920. During this year, according to the careful researches of some writers, and chiefly of Gamurrini, who gives the genealogical tree of this family, it takes its start from Buono, father of the Marino who was Governor under the Kings of Italy Beregario and Adalberto, and who was himself the father of Teobaldo the Lord of Classe, a castle four miles distant from Arezzo. This family afterwards divided into two branches, one of Florence and the other of Valdarno, both of which gave legions of illustrious men to the field of glory. They extended themselves afterwards into France, Poland and other far-off regions, and were always distinguished and decorated by the emperors, the kings, and the republics with eminent dignities and splendid honors. From the Cagliano Bridge to the gates of Florence, and in the city itself, they possessed, as independent lords, the strongest

castles and most magnificent palaces. In the Florentine Republic, belonging to the small number of the nobles or magnates, they considerably surpassed others in the number of their titles. This distinction in a free city
was equally as remarkable as it was dangerous, bringing both pomp and
pain. (The authority of the laws in that popular government forbade any
of the magnates taking part in the quinquennial elections. This excluded
them from the enjoyment and the honor of the public offices, and put
also a restraint on the licentiousness of the powerful ones, who, making
too haughty a use of their high position to the harm of others, ruled
their subjects at will and tyrannized over the unhappy people, without
any fear of punishment and with a contempt of the courts.) The De-
Pazzi, however, because of their personal merits, were not without
important offices in this new state of things. Often they held the
balance of power in the Republic. In the first centuries of aristocratic
liberty they, among the ancient fathers, held the consulships; afterwards, in the almost democratic republic, they sat among the principal
rulers thirteen times, and were four times honored with the sublime
office of Doge. Valiant men for wisdom and courage in arms, magnanimous adherents of Italic parties, daring innovators, they reaped
everywhere the glorious laurels of a faithful sword and an incorrupt
wisdom. They became ambassadors, castellians, bishops, and orators
near the Courts or the Pope Cosimo De-Pazzi, at first Bishop of Arezzo,
and afterwards Archbishop of Florence, was closely related by blood, and
more by merits, to Leo X. He was endowed with so high a degree of
eloquence, and enriched with such great learning, that he was several
times appointed ambassador for his country, and turned at will the
minds of the greatest monarchs by the great power of his words, thus
obtaining what he wanted. Not a few orators could be numbered in
the same family, for, at various times, some were found near the kings
of England, of Poland, of Hungary, of Castile, of Aragon and of
Portugal; others near Pius II, Emperor Maximilian of Austria, King
Charles VIII of France, the Roman Pontiff Leo X, and the Venetian
Senate, treating of important affairs for the Florentine Republic, and
they marked most of the days of their lives with victorious labor in
behalf of their country. A certain Stefano was palatine of Troch, a
Cristofano was a great general, and a Michele grand chancellor of
Lithuania.

Not less worthily than elsewhere and in other times, are now
flourishing in Florence the sprouts of the ancient tree, who can feast
their eyes on tokens of the greatness of their fathers within their fatherland, such as magnificent palaces and churches, the numerous styles of
bucklers, the laurels, the mitres, and other marks of honor which are
hanging before the images of their ancestors.

But, beyond a doubt, the one who sheds the greatest splendor on this
most noble and ancient family is St. Mary Magdalen, whose glory, it may
be said, shines forth like a sun, powerful enough to eclipse every other light
in the firmament of her lineage It is true with her that "*Etiam in cinere
virtus*"—"Even in ashes there is strength," as is fabulously said of
the ashes of the Phœnix. Mary Magdalen is the true Phœnix of Carmel,
for her remains still preserve the power of working miracles and prodi-

gies. Her glory, far different from that of this world, crowned with earthly laurels, is a glory ever new, ever celestial. It never perishes, and must be acknowledged by everyone without exception. Her memory shines brightly through the generations and centuries, accompanied by her works of wisdom and love; by the reverence, the gratitude, and the benedictions of antiquity, and saluted by the impartial admiration of posterity. Mary Magdalen, exalted and blessed in heaven, revered on earth by the religious love and veneration of men, who have raised in her honor churches and altars, offered hymns and prayers,—sits now on a throne of glory, which surpasses all earthly imagination. Pure and everlasting is her glory, because pure and heavenly were the means by which she secured it. The knights of her family, like other similar knights, fought with material weapons for temporal ends; Mary Magdalen waged war with spiritual arms, overcoming her passions, triumphing over herself, for an eternal object. They fought to defend the rights of some ambitious men; Mary Magdalen waged war to protect the equality of all. They were ambassadors to kings and republics, Mary Magdalen, contemning human pomps, was mediatrix with God, to implore mercy for mankind. They studied politics, which deceived man; she, with evangelical simplicity, laid bare the deceit of the human passions Animated by the faith of Christ and strengthened by the practice of all virtues, she indefatigably endeavored to unite man to God, and all men to each other; for this is the noble object of the preaching, the labors, the pains, and the death of our Divine Redeemer, and of every one of His followers "No one is so happy, so reasonable, so virtuous, so lovable as a true Christian," said Blase Pascal Hence the Saint, who, living by faith and love, knows how to direct and moderate all his desires, affections, and works to so noble an end, who in meekness and sweetness continues all his works of justice and charity, always amiable, modest, meek, respectful, the same with all, patient with his persecutors, generous with his enemies, cannot but be the most important and useful man in society. A true glory are the Saints and heroes of Christianity. True greatness and true glory emanate only from the humility of faith, hence there is no glory without faith, no virtue without religion, which has its first and only foundation in humility. But it must be the humility practiced and taught by Jesus Christ (the only guide to the happiness of the human heart), by His luminous examples and His divine maxims, that faith which, resting on the Word of God, never lets us tremble with the shocks of any passion, and never permits itself to be carried away by the vortex of opinions and events within the alluring shores of this mortal life. If it were not so, the opprobrious sentence, emphatically directed by Alfieri against the nobles, would also be applicable to us, as it is to all who profess worldly maxims, viz., we would be

> "According to the prosperous or adverse wind,
> Now proud, now cowardly, and always infamous "

Hence the veneration we pay to the Saints, knowing that they had but one countenance, one heart, one tongue, and manner of working, all and always in peace with God and with men, is not the outcome of a superstitious worship or of a natural attraction which easily draws us towards everything that excites our imagination and feelings. Neither is it the effect of human education, which, being instilled in us from childhood, would have us submit in a childish way to the altar and to the throne. It rather proceeds from that conviction which, not unfrequently carrying us out of all deceitful appearances, leads us to elevate ourselves above earthly affections and points out to us our real good in that place where virtue dwells. Let us, however, never forget that this virtue dwells on a mountain, high and difficult of access, so that—

> " He who does not undergo heat and cold,
> He who does not leave the roads of pleasures and comforts,
> Can never reach there."

END OF THE LIFE.

The Incorrupt Body of St. Mary Magdalen De-Pazzi.

THE WORKS

OF

St. Mary Magdalen De-Pazzi

FLORENTINE NOBLE

SACRED CARMELITE VIRGIN

Compiled by the REV. PLACIDO FABRINI

ᴥ ᴥ ᴥ

TO WHICH ARE ADDED SOME OF HER WONDERFUL SAYINGS, A
NARRATION OF MANY MIRACLES WROUGHT THROUGH
HER INTERCESSION DOWN TO OUR DAYS, &c.

BESIDES PRAYERS FOR A NOVENA IN HER HONOR

ᴥ ᴥ ᴥ

Translated from the Florentine Edition of 1852
and Published by the

REV. ANTONIO ISOLERI, Miss. Ap.

Rector of the New St. Mary Magdalen De-Pazzi's Italian Church, Philadelphia. Pa., U. S. A.

ᴥ ᴥ ᴥ

PART II.

Enriched with New Illustrations together with the Reproduction
of those in the Original Work

ᴥ ᴥ ᴥ

PHILADELPHIA

1900

THE COMPILER TO THE READER.

THE strength of the Omnipotent, which animates the weakest creature, continually moved the spirit of Mary Magdalen De-Pazzi, raising her above her senses even to penetrate what mortal man, with all the depth of his studies, could never know. It was then that the Saint uttered those noble sentences concerning the divine mysteries, the celestial virtues and the perfection of the human soul. These lessons were, happily, gathered by the nuns, who took great care to write down what their holy sister used to say during her ecstasies. This is what forms the Works of St Mary Magdalen, and which we put together in this Second Part, as they, too, form a portion of her Life. We need not add that these doctrinal expressions of the Saint, having been submitted to the examination of the most distinguished theologians, were by them approved. Moreover, the prolix scrutiny and the immediate confronting of the person, made by the Very Rev Francesco Benvenuti, theologian and *canon penitentiarius* of the Florentine Metropolitan, and the Rev Father Niccolò-Fabrini, Rector of the Jesuit College in Florence, a man of singular wisdom and virtue, determined them to assure Mary Magdalen that God spoke through her, and therefore to exhort the nuns to hold her maxims in great esteem. We have already seen that all the conditions necessary to judge supernatural things justly were to be found in her. During her ecstasies, she was always humble, obedient, modest, learned, and wonderful, too, as with her eyes fixed on heaven, she sewed, embroidered, cut gold, painted devout images on paper, and did other works which required the attention of the mind and the eyes. The sisters, amazed at the sight of all this, the better to ascertain the nature of those actions, often blindfolded her and shut the windows of the room in which she was working; and she, in perfect darkness, continued the work of her hands. Of these works several paintings, finished with great skill and perfection, were preserved.

Leaving out the narrative and some repetitions, I will confine myself to the doctrinal matter, and, to distribute it for easier intelligence, will reduce and divide it into three sections. In the First Section I will place all the contemplations of St Mary Magdalen on the principal mysteries of our faith, on the Humanity of Christ, and on the Divine Attributes. In the Second Section I will place the moral doctrines concerning different virtues, and especially the religious perfection. In the Third Section, as if in an Appendix, will be found gathered, as precious fragments of the celestial doctrine picked up from different places, the most devout exclamations, the most remarkable sentences, and, finally, the letters of our Saint, and an account of wonderful events wrought through her intercession since her solemn canonization. Yet, notwithstanding such a partition, matters will not be found so divided that they may not sometimes be mixed; for instance, in the contemplations of the Divine Attributes will be found moral sayings, and in the moral doctrines some lofty sentences concerning the Divinity. But this, rather than detract, will add grace, light, and efficacy to the discourses of our almost divine speaker. The circumstances which preceded or accompanied the ecstasies (by me omitted) may be stated in a general way by means of the following remarks. The most simple thought of God or of piety was sufficient to alienate her from her senses, though she might at the time be occupied in the most indifferent action. According to the subject by which her ecstasy was occasioned, she composed her countenance and suited her emotions and her voice. Hence she was now immovable, now swift, now cheerful, and now sad ; sometimes she spoke slowly, and sometimes quickly, whilst some-times she was wholly absorbed in deep silence.   From the sound of her voice and her manner of speaking, it was easy to know what person she meant to represent, whilst speaking.   If she intended to speak in the person of the Eternal Father, her voice be-came majestic and grave ; if in the person of the Son, more meek and pliant ; and if in the person of the Holy Ghost, more sweet and loving.   If she spoke in the name of the Blessed Virgin and the Saints, she did it so as to express their dignity and character ; but if she spoke in her own person, she adopted a voice so humble and low, that it was scarcely audible.   It was, in a word, a marvelous thing to hear from the same mouth so many ways of speaking ; and, more than this, to hear her quote and even compose Latin sentences, whilst of her own knowledge she could hardly read the Breviary.   It is, finally, a very great wonder that, wholly ignorant of those matters, she easily solved during her ecstasies scriptural and theological difficulties ; and all these ecstasies, now brief, now protracted even for forty days, always gave the greatest edification, instruction and consolation to others.

God grant that we learn from them that true wisdom can only come to us not from earth, but from heaven ; and that it more willingly dwells in a meek and humble heart than in a proud and haughty mind.   "All wisdom is from God," says the Ecclesiasticus, who also adds, that vain would be the hope of him who pretended to obtain it without fulfilling the commandments of God, and of all that is pleasing to Him, pointing out (among other things) faith and meekness : *"All wisdom is from the Lord God. . . . Son, if thou desire wisdom, keep justice, and God will give her to thee.   For the fear of the Lord is wisdom and discipline : and that which is agreeable to Him is faith and meekness : and He will fill up His treasures"* (Ecclus. i, 1, 33-35).

The Works of St. Mary Magdalen De-Pazzi.

FIRST SECTION.

OF HER CONTEMPLATIONS ON THE PRINCIPAL MYSTERIES OF OUR
FAITH, ON THE HUMANITY OF CHRIST AND ON
THE DIVINE ATTRIBUTES.[1]

I.

She Likens the Works of Creation to the Operations of the Word in the Soul.

I see and understand that the method our great God followed in creating the machinery of the world is also employed by the Word Incarnate in creating a creature to grace, and in giving her rule and direction till He may glorify her. He completes this work during the same number of days, resting on the seventh. . . . What does the Word rest in? In the complacency of the same work. . . . The creature is a little world made by Thee, O Word, to the likeness and image of the greater one ; and both one and the other represent Thee in the manner in which they exist, as the thing manufactured represents the manufacturer. First, Thou formest the machinery of the world, with its due proportions ; afterwards, taking with the hands of Thy power and wisdom a

---

[1] Balmes' "Protestantism and Catholicity Compared " wisely and truthfully calls attention to the opposite effects produced in Catholics and non-Catholics by visions and revelations, real or imaginary. The Reformers (says he) who believed, or feigned to believe themselves, in the XVIth Century and afterwards, inspired of heaven, committed in Germany, Holland, and England, every kind of disorder and crime. . . . Whereas Catholic Saints to whom visions or heavenly inspirations are attributed, unanimously coöperate to produce contrary results, viz.: of piety, devotion, and love towards God and all the human family. Here are his words: "Nothing is more evident than the diversity intervening, in regard to this, between Protestants and Catholics. On both sides are persons pretending to be favored with celestial visions ; but on account of these the former become proud, turbulent, insane, whilst the latter become more humble and advance in the spirit of peace and love. In the very XVIth Century, whilst the fanaticism of the Protestants was upsetting the whole of Europe, flooding it with blood, there was a woman in Spain (and we might add, another one in Italy—our Saint) who, according to the ideas of Protestants and infidels, must have been one of the worst victims of illusions and fanaticism. But did the pretended fanaticism of this woman cause a drop of blood or a tear to be shed? And were her visions, perchance, orders from heaven to exterminate men, as unhappily was then the case among some Reformers?" And here, after quoting two most beautiful passages from the works of this woman—St. Teresa —this great writer concludes: "Let us now suppose, with Protestants, that all these visions are but illusions, it is certain, nevertheless, that they do not distort the ideas, do not corrupt the morals, do not disturb public order, and if they had only served to inspire these so beautiful pages, we should not be sorry, in truth, for the illusion." Vol. I., Chap. VIII.—*Note of the Translator.*

little clay, Thou formest a creature so much to Thy image and likeness that the angels admire it. But the little love they bear to the truth makes them fall down from heaven. In this little world of the creature, is heaven, like that which has been created, and which is now shown by Thee to me   This heaven of the creature—man—is the free will which Thou gavest to him, and which is truly a heaven when it is conformable to Thy Divine Will   In this heaven are the stars, the moon, and the sun, and some clouds, which are casting a shadow upon it, because in the will, like most brilliant stars, are the many divine inspirations through which good and holy resolutions are formed   Thou givest to the creature the desire to represent the moon; and the moon is not so change-able as the desire of man.   The sun is represented in the will by the grace Thou givest the creature to choose Thee for her Lord and Bridegroom . .   Thou hast given her under-standing, which is discovering and covering heaven   It is the sun of heaven, which is the knowledge of God; because, if the understanding, enlightened by Thee, would not discuss what is to be chosen or done, either she would not know God, or would only know Him lightly and coldly—nay, would offend Him . . .

Thou dost establish in the little world of Thy creature the water, granting her Thy grace.   In this water Thou growest fishes for the service of man, viz, the loving affec-tions which feed on Thy Divinity, and die when they come out of the ocean of Thy Divin-ity, because, no sooner do the affections turn to transitory things than they die   Some fishes are so valuable that they beget within themselves most precious stones and other gems, with which man boastingly adorns himself; and out of the waters also is taken that most beautiful, pure and charming gem, the pearl.   This signifies the loving affection of purity, which begets in itself this precious gem in which the Word takes so much delight, and with which He adorns Himself, not because He is wanting in it,—He being most copiously endowed with it, as the very fountain of purity,—but He is so pleased to see the creature possessing it, that He takes it for an ornament.   Out of the waters grow also some branches, like little flowers, and these are the beads of coral with which they are wont to adorn pure little children   The taste of the wisdom of God delights those who are still children and beginners in the way of God, but those who are past infancy remain no longer in the taste of the wisdom, but in the Giver of it only   Coral shines or darkens, according to the state of health of its wearer, wisdom does like-wise, according to whether it is used to unite with God or to separate from Him, and from this it can be known whether the creature is infirm or enjoys health   For the just, everything cooperates for their good "*Diligentibus Deum omnia cooperantur in bonum*"—"To them that love God, all things work together unto good" (Rom viii, 28)   Others beget in themselves some jewels of much inferior value, wherewith some past middle age adorn themselves, and this is a loving affection that the creature enter-tains for the contempt of the world and of self   Another stone, darker and of less value, is also begotten therein, and this is the loving affection for penance .   In the water other stones are also generated, which are dark, and with these he who has sorrow adorns himself, these are the mortifications that one practices, and, by his example, teaches others to practice . . .

In this little world the loving Word is also seeking the fertile plants, which are the wise memories with which He has endowed the soul, and some of these plants are delight-ful, some fruit-bearing, some useful, and some harmful.   The memory of Thy benefits, O Word, adorns the soul and greatly delights it; the memory of the Blood is that which bears fruit; the memory of the heavenly joys is useful and protective; because, no mat-ter what tribulation, pain, affliction, temptation, or trial may be encountered, the soul, thinking of the celestial joys, which are prepared for those who thus suffer, bears every thing lightly and easily—nay, embraces the pain as a glory—so that is fulfilled in her what Truth has said, viz, that His yoke is sweet and His burden light.   The recollection of the wealth Thou givest to men, and the memory of all other transitory goods, is harmful and offensive   As, however, by grafting, or, like some plants which, though harmful, when transplanted become useful and profitable and bear fruits sweet to the taste,—this recollection also becomes profitable, if transplanted into the valley of self-knowledge   By this it becomes known how vile and perishable and frail is everything that makes us grow proud, and, with a generous contempt, even though one had given up the whole world, he would think he had left nothing, but had simply unburdened himself of a great load   The thought of eternity is sanative, because through it one comes to know his eternal glory or his eternal pain; and, whether one is moved by love or fear, he begins to desire the former or avoid the latter . .

This great God of ours creates also in the little world of the creature large fruit-bearing trees, and these are contained in the most capacious intellect of man, which by its altitude can reach the vision of the Divine Essence, assisted, though, by the light of glory.   Some trees are fruitful, others nourishing, others good light and shade, some must not be allowed to blossom before the soul is set in order . . . . . . ld, as to others, the fruits must be left until well after a long time before they . . . . . . ripe, so that they may grow ripe. . . .   The consideration of the love which made the Word become incarnate

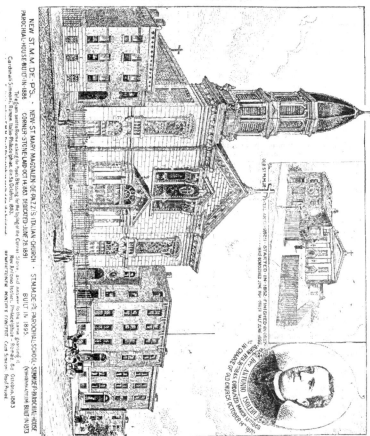

NEW ST. M. M. DE · P'S.

PAROCHIAL·HOUSE·BUILT·IN·1886.

NEW ST MARY MAGDALEN DE·PAZZI'S ITALIAN CHURCH · ST.M.M.DE·P'S PAROCHIAL·SCHOOL·ST·M·M·DE·P·PAROCHIAL·HOUSE

CORNER·STONE·LAID·OCT·14·1883· DEDICATED·JUNE·28·1891   BUILT·IN·1895.   (NEW·GERMANTOWN·BUILT·IN·1873)

is a tree which bears a very nutritious fruit The consideration of the greatness of the most holy Sacraments gives also a nutritious fruit, but it must not be allowed to blossom, because if the flowers fall the fruits will not ripen; hence one must not consider the origin of the Sacraments It might do great harm, and in curious souls occasion some error and deception as to the faith, because it is a terrible thing especially to consider that the whole God is hiding under the appearance of such a small portion of bread It is enough to know that He has said it, and that He can do it Likewise, it is a great and deep mystery that a little water opens paradise to us; therefore we must not tarry with our intellect to investigate how this can be, but, considering the greatness of these Sacraments, we should receive them with deep reverence and humility, and with that love, simplicity and purity with which they were instituted

The consideration of the designs of God in everything, is a fruit we should allow to remain on the tree as long as possible, because the longer we continue in its consideration, the more do we penetrate and comprehend the great harmony of God, and the more do we see that He does nothing without the greatest order and wisdom The consideration of the capacity God grants to the soul, and of His communicating to the same His greatness and goodness, is a fruit not less beneficial than those already mentioned, because it greatly warms and inflames the affection of those who gather it . . .

The Eternal Wisdom ceases not from creating in this little world all those things which may be useful to the soul—some for instruction, others for delight, and others for use He creates therein other creatures, which have being, growth, and feeling, and these are the animals of the earth, some useful and others harmful, viz, the many and various movements of the soul, all of which need tempering Thoughts, deeds and all acts must be directed towards God, doing everything for His honor and for His service, just as animals are for the service of man The passion of concupiscence[1] is the one which can render man great service, for it dwells and feeds itself on desires, and brings to the soul a very great wealth of merits, as the Word says that He is satisfied with good-will when the deed is impossible. The passion of anger or irascibility is also to be found in this little world, and it causes everything to be moderated, restricting the desires and rendering them amenable to God's own service . .

There are also the mountains and the hills Prudence is a high mountain; hence he who dwells on mountains has a more healthy body, as there the air is purer. He can see and foresee what he has to do and provides accordingly, and the fruits he gathers are more rare Thus prudence keeps the soul and the body in better vigor for the practice of virtues, for the many mists and the thick darkness caused by the passions, when they affect the intellect and deprave it, do not reach there. Moreover, one provides there, for he honors God with all his works, he sees and foresees, because he arms himself very strongly against all temptations The fruits are more rare, for what are the fruits of prudence but the works it produces?—which being accomplished through this virtue, though they are few, yet they possess greater vigor and utility, hence a work done with prudence is worth more than many done with imprudence and levity Prudence considers and ponders well before doing anything that is to be done, and thus the works it does are the most acceptable to God and men . .

There is also the delightful valley of temperance, withdrawing by degrees from what the intellect too proudly wishes to understand or the appetite inordinately craves It is neither a mountain, nor even altogether a valley, but a plain on the mount First it withdraws the sophistical prudence of those who want to investigate the works of God The works we do by ourselves we must well consider and perform with the greatest prudence, but those which God makes us perform, we must neither consider nor ponder, but allow them to be directed and judged by Him, without reflecting on them or investigating His will . . Temperance moderates also the levity of those who, in their works, act without prudence It joins together all the virtues, and fixes and establishes them in the soul, so that it may not be shaken by every light wind, nor thrown to the ground . Moreover, temperance moderates and withdraws the soul from all inordinate affections and appetites, preventing their deceiving us under the pretext of necessity, for mere necessity needs so little, that it can hardly be said what it is, as it is next to nothing. The divine grace which helps us, enables us to do and to suffer more than people would think "*Non ego, sed gratia Dei mecum*"—"Not I, but the grace of God with me." But he who is not enlightened from heaven, and dwells not in this valley, is easily deceived, as those are who, with their human prudence, measure the forces of a soul assisted and raised up by the divine grace, hence whatever seems to them an excess, they deem faulty and indiscreet In this work they must acknowledge the author, and thank the Divine Goodness, which communicates Itself to others more than to them, and confess at the same time their tepidity and negligence. .

But the great Builder, our God, is not satisfied with this, for He wishes to complete the work, He being the perfecter of every work; hence He creates in the little world

---

[1] This must properly be understood in a spiritual sense *Note of the Translator.*

of the creatures, other animals, which fly, and which give great delight and contentment
These are in the soul the three theological virtues,—faith, hope, and charity,— and the four
cardinal ones,—justice, fortitude, temperance, and prudence ; and they are various, for
great is the variety of birds.   Faith is represented by the well-known doves, which dwell
together in a certain place, and feed on what is given them by the inhabitants   In order
that some benefit may be derived from those doves, they must be tamed ; and so also
must be the faith in the soul,—that is, it must be intrinsic,—because the more it pene
trates, the greater it is , and it must not come from afar, like the other virtues, but it
must be rooted in the heart . . .   The singing of the dove is plaintive, for in cooing it
sings, and singing it laments.   Thus does the soul that is groaning, seeing so little faith
in the creatures , it sings because it knows the greatness and the goodness of God, and
it laments and sings because it sees how He should be known and loved by all creatures
It rejoices at His greatness, and it grieves at the human ingratitude, which does not `
know it nor love it   . .   The soul must not fly too high to feed, but must keep down,
like the dove, which does not eat those fruits that grow on high, but feeds on the seeds
that are on the ground.   It must not fly too high by wishing to investigate the height of
God, viz , His beginning, which is eternity,—His being, which is a most pure and independent act,—the unity which He has in Himself,—and the communication the Father
makes to the other Divine Persons, Who, with the most simple identity of nature and
essence, are nevertheless really distinct in personality from the Father and each other
It must not seek to understand the immensity of His inscrutable, infinite, and profound
wisdom, because it would soon fail and faint in the attempt ; but it must go for its food
to the Word Incarnate, Who struck His roots into the earth out of the pure bosom of
Mary, believe the words and conform to the works of the Word, which are the seeds
upon which the soul can safely feed.   For some short space of time it may occasionally
use its wings, and raise itself up to these considerations, to revere, adore, and take complacency in the Divine Greatness , but let it return to the earth to take food ; and, if it
sees that it soared too high, let it recollect itself, and in the opposite consideration of
its lowliness, say : "*Bonum mihi quia humiliasti me* "—" It is good for me that Thou
hast humbled me." . . . Other delightful birds, such as goldfinches and canaries,
may indicate the virtue of hope, by which the soul can hope many things ; but it is
not necessary to exercise it so often as the other two, viz., faith and charity, though
the practice of it is useful and profitable   As the creature cannot attain to salvation unless
this virtue is well rooted and infused in the soul, so she is bound, therefore, to make,
during life, frequent acts of it ; either to obtain forgiveness, or the better to acknowledge
her last end   The thought of the eternal beatitude, which is the principal object of
hope, greatly strengthens us to work, and without it we can ill endure the labors and
burdens of this world , and without this hope, "*Miserabiliores essemus omnibus hominibus* "—" We would be more miserable than the rest of men " (1 Cor. xv, 19)   At any
rate, it is necessary to practice the other two more frequently, because we have always
before our eyes the objects of faith, in the Most Holy Sacrament of the altar and in the
other things proposed to us by faith itself.   Charity exercises itself in every good work ;
but hope is principally for the delight and recreation of the soul, that it may be strengthened in its trials.   Moreover, it possesses very great efficacy in obtaining many things from
God, and particularly calmness and strength in our tribulations.   But again I say that the
exercise of it is not so necessary as that of the other two, which are, so to speak, more
united to and identified with God, and without which the soul can hardly work and
attain to the fruition of her God   .   But oh ! what delight this hope gives to the
soul, making her hope for what she is to enjoy later in the Fatherland, and partly taste of
that which in heaven she will eternally enjoy, understand, and possess, viz , her God,
uniting with Him perfectly. . .   There is also the rare and soaring eagle, and this in
the soul is charity, which is not rare because God is sparing in communicating it, but
because it is understood and preserved by few in the soul, and therefore it is possessed
but by a few.   The eagle soars on high, and is not wont to take the bark of the trees,
but their sap, and especially that of the cedar   Charity is as great as God Himself,
because He is charity—"*Deus charitas est* "   It soars so high that it goes to the throne
of the Most Holy Trinity, and there enters the bosom of the Eternal Father , and from
the bosom of the Father it goes to the side of the Word, and from the side to the heart,
and there it rests and gets its nourishment   Hence the soul that possesses charity, seeks
to feed on God alone and rest in Him , therein fed and rested, she retakes her flight
and comes down to the earth, because charity embraces the neighbors by love, loving
them not only as creatures, but as being created by God to His image and likeness
Charity stops not to love the body, which is the bark, but penetrates the interior of the
soul   It does not look at the pain, but at the cause of it, which is the offense, viz , the
object that is offended   It does not regard the glory but the creature who gives it to
Him   It does not stop in the gifts of God but in God   Giver   It does not stop in the
flesh of the Word, but in the soul   It does not consider the pains this Incarnate
Word suffered, but the love with which He suffered them   Finally, it does not stop in

the Word Incarnate, but raised by Him, rests in the Word, begotten of the Father from Eternity; and thus it enters the Divinity, and from it, as the cedar from its sap, draws its nourishment . . .

But there is flying in this little world another bird, which takes rest occasionally in some tree, and there building its nest, begets its delightful and pretty ones, like to itself, feeding them afterwards with the blood from its breast, and this is the pelican, taken into the soul by justice, which rests in the other virtues, as, for instance, in charity, humility, patience, love, and many others, and begets rectitude Justice though it be, it does not refuse mercy. It feeds its little ones with the blood of its breast, and this is the Humanity of the Word, Who feeds them by His words, works and example, but much more by the infinite value of His precious Blood . . . Justice renders also to everyone what belongs to him—to God, the soul, the body and the neighbors It renders to God what belongs to Him, viz , love, worship, and reverence , and, what He wishes above all, the soul created for Him. It renders to the soul what belongs to her, and, as she possesses nothing but herself—nay, not even herself, as she is God's—she is reduced to this, that she possesses nothing which is her own; but, finding in herself the most precious and rare thing that can be, viz , her God, Who for love has given Himself to her, by giving Him to herself, she comes to give to herself the only thing she can call her own, because, outside of Him the soul has no other thing she can appropriate to herself The body has nothing but the earth that supports it high and low, hence it lowers and raises itself , and the soul likewise, regaining the knowledge of herself, arises and falls down by having little or much humility Justice renders also to the neighbor what belongs to him , and what has the neighbor in truth that is really his own? The Divine Word, Who is really born on earth for him, is given to him "*nobis datus, nobis natus* " Hence, the soul possessed of this justice, renders to the neighbor the Incarnate Word, trying to graft It in the hearts of others, by the edification of words and works. . . .

Another bird flies continually through this little world, and its name is turtledove, that is, fortitude This bird laments the loss of its companion , the soul likewise possessing this fortitude, laments her frailty and that of her neighbors , and, having lost her companion, which is the taste of God, by the subtraction of the feeling of grace, does not want to associate with others, no matter what tribulation or temptation may come, but remains still in her strength and position, which is God, though she may not taste Him. .

The hawk is also created therein, not because this bird is good in itself, but it is beautiful and gives delight to anyone who holds him in his hand; and this signifies discretion, which, properly speaking, is not a virtue, but a rule of all the virtues, which, without it, would not be such, as it contains in itself the rule and perfection of every virtue. The hawk attracts to itself all the birds, seizes them and feeds upon them, but does not like to be seen The same is done by discretion in the soul , because, as the mother of temperance, it wonderfully fits her to draw from God the wisdom by which she understands what she has to do in order to please God, and removes from around herself whatever she sees that may be an impediment to wisdom. Thus knowing what she ought to imitate and reproduce in herself, she draws the virtues from her neighbors, as all creatures are copies of God. Hence, if the soul wishes to do the will of God, she must study her neighbors, in whom she sees a variety of virtues, from which, by imitating them in order to please God, she draws and takes as much as may be useful and profitable to her From her neighbor the soul may also learn what displeases God From things transitory the soul also derives the knowledge of their frailty, in order not to become attached to them; and she learns gratitude, seeing how thankful they are to their Creator She learns also from the devil; and what? That which he never knew, viz , humility; for God, on account of his pride, cast him down Hence the soul, knowing that God so hates pride, learns humility and practices it Discretion must also be kept tight in the hand, having continually before the eyes all the virtues, weighing and pondering them so as to practice them. . . .

There are also other birds, the flesh of which is nutritious, and they are easily caught These are the gray partridges, which signify wise prudence. When one wants to catch these birds, he must watch the place wherein they dwell in the daylight, and then go with a particular light to catch them in the darkness of the night. This wisdom is of God and in God, and is by few understood and apprehended, as some search for it with their own cunning, pretending to investigate by themselves the things of God, and what they must do; and truly they lose their time, and these will never acquire prudence But he who really wants to acquire it must go to the Divine Word, wherein this prudence dwells, and by His light he will find it. As we, mortal creatures, can never take it from the Divine Word, we must go to the Word Incarnate, and we will get it by the particular light of charity, which, though it is a light to all, nevertheless is a greater light for those who carry it about, as the lamp throws more light around him who carries it in his hand than around those who are afar. The meat of these birds (partridges) is very delicate, and though all kinds of persons eat it, nevertheless the nobles are those who make the most use of it. This means that, whilst all virtuous persons feed on this prudence, the nobles, viz, the *christs* (priests) and the sacred virgins to whom God more abundantly communicates this celestial gift, do so in a special manner. The *christs* on earth stand in great need of this virtue, in giving counsel, absolving, and instructing, but it is no less necessary to the sacred virgins, because they must accept the advice and counsels which are given to them, and ponder them with very great prudence and alertness of mind. Moreover, they must consider whether they are really from God or from the devil—following them with the greatest diligence, if from the former, shunning and avoiding them with an equal abhorrence, if from the latter.

II.

She Treats in Particular of the Creation of Man and of the other Works of the Old Testament, applying them to the Manner by which God leads Souls to Perfection.

"*Vidit Deus cuncta quæ fecerat, et erant valde bona, et benedixit eis*" I see God creating man, I see God re-creating man, and, in re-creating him to grace, doing in him, who is a little world, what He had done in creating him to the world. God keeps the same order in re-creating, so to say, this little world to grace, that He kept in creating him to nature, and also, in the beginning, bringing him to grace. Three periods of time have been in the world—the time of nature, the time of law, and the time of grace; and these three times are met in man in this re-creation to grace. In the first time, which was that of nature, God created man in the greatest innocence,[1] in which he remained but a little while, for, by sinning in a certain way, he ruined his own nature. Then came the Deluge because of the many sins committed; God commanded Noah to build an Ark, in which eight souls were saved, and wherein clean and unclean animals were placed—of the clean ones *septena et septena*, of the unclean ones *duo et duo*. The Deluge comes and carries away all the things created from the face of the earth; Noah, remaining in the Ark, sends out the dove, which comes back with the olive-branch in its bill, in token that the waters have begun to subside; and the same thing God does in the soul.

In the second period of time, which is that of the law, Moses ascends the mountain, where he receives the law written on stone tablets. In giving it God sends forth lightning and shakes the mountain, whilst Moses' countenance shines so that he must veil himself in speaking to the people, and they tell him that he, not God, must speak to them lest they die. The same thing God does in the soul. I pass by the brier bush which Moses saw burning and not consuming, because it is not necessary now to mention it. The people of God remaining as prisoners in Egypt, God commands Moses to go to Pharaoh and tell him to allow His people to depart, otherwise He will punish him. But this I omit, and will tell how God delivered His people from the bondage of Pharaoh, ordering the Israelites to take the precious vessels and stones of Egypt, making them cross the Red Sea, and drowning therein Pharaoh and all his followers. Then He leads the people through the desert, where they murmur because of want of food, wherefore God sends to them the most sweet nourishment, the manna. The second time the people murmur; and Moses strikes the rock with his rod, and immediately gush forth most abundant waters, whereby not only the people's thirst, but that of the animals as well, is quenched and satiated. The Israelites then proceed towards the Land of Promise, but before entering it they see the fruits thereof, viz, two bunches of grapes; and in punishment of their gluttony they are bitten by the serpents. Then, as a remedy for these bites, Moses raises the serpent in the desert. Finally Moses dies, and two only enter the Land of Promise. But Abraham was before Moses, and God tried him in an extraordinary and very severe manner, telling him to sacrifice his only son Isaac, so much loved by him. This order he complies with, as far as his will is concerned. Then comes the great patriarch Jacob, who wrestled with the angel, and saw that beautiful ladder, the summit of which reached heaven, and upon which angels ascended and descended. But Thou, O Word, wantest me to leave out all these things, because they were shown to him as a figure of the Church more than as things that he should do, and Thou wantest me to look, in this little world of the soul, only at those things that Thou, O my God, hast wrought by Thyself, and also through Thy servants. Then follow the holy prophets who by their prophecies announce the Word, and by their prayers hasten His coming; and by figures they go on showing what He has to do, and this Thou dost in the soul. The prophet Elias, after the long drought, dwells on the mountain and per-

---

[1] Evidently, by *the first time of nature* is meant the preternatural state, which, so to speak, was natural to man, since God created him in it. *Note of the Translator.*

ceives a small cloud arising from the sea, going upward and turning into a heavy rain; but Thou wantest me to leave all this, which for the present does not suit the soul, together with all the other prophecies of the prophets.

But at the time of grace, O Word, God sends Thee, and Thou dost perform all Thy operations, and all this Thou dost in this little world of the soul. I omit those twelve columns Thou gavest to the world. The Antichrist will also come and enter into the soul Thou shalt return, O Word, with Thy power to judge and give glory or punishment . Thou, O Eternal Word, keepest the same order in re-creating the creature to grace and leading a soul to a particular perfection, that Thou hast kept in creating her to the world. But I do not understand nor comprehend this; hence do Thou help me by the power of Thy Blood, that I may understand and comprehend it. O Word, can the soul reach the great perfection to which Thou hast called her and ordained that she should attain? Yes, she can In creating man, first Thou givest him the innocence in which he remains for some time, Thou also givest a companion to him, that he may multiply, afterwards, Thou givest him the precept not to eat the forbidden fruit So does the Word in the soul, for in the place of innocence, He gives her His purity by participation and walking in sincerity, He gives her for companions wisdom and free will, that by wisdom she may know and choose what she has to do to reach perfection, and, by free will, deserve a reward. If the soul experiences some trouble in doing what by wisdom she has chosen, this will be meritorious; for without this free will, all her doings would be the work of God, and therefore she would not have merit But sometimes the soul does not like to possess this free will, as it is very often the cause of separating her from her God . He also wants her to multiply the good works, and to lead many souls to God Then He gives her the precept, and wants her faithfully to keep it, stating to her the penalty for not keeping it The precept is, that He does not want her curiously to investigate His Divine Being more than He may be pleased to let her understand, but wishes her to loiter in the garden of His Humanity, for if she would continue to investigate His eternal and infinite Being, she would faint and fail, because it cannot be understood by any creature . . . Adam remained for some time in the state of innocence, and then lost it. The loss of innocence to the soul is her deviating at some time from that purity of intention infused by God, and her neglect to acknowledge and keep this great gift of purity. Then comes the serpent, which makes her commit disobedience; and the soul, with her wisdom, discusses what her error might be after having sinned, and how great a sin she may have committed that God should go so far from her She grieves, therefore, that God gave her the free will by which she disobeyed, preferring the doing of her own will to God's Hence it will be necessary for the Word to tell her *"In sudore vultus tui vesceris pane tuo"*—"In the sweat of thy brow thou shalt eat thy bread" (Gen iii, 19), viz , He must show her the necessity of suffering to satisfy for the pleasure of sin The Word will say to her also *"Ubi es ?"*—"Where art thou?" (*Ibid* v, 9) "Not in thyself, because thou hast come out of thy rectitude, not in Me, because thou hast offended Me " Consequently, in something more vile than thyself, which is the creature to which one is attached by affection, or the affection for self, whereby one falls to the level of the beasts, to which, by nature, thou art most like, whilst by grace thou wast a much more clear and vivid image of God. As mankind afterwards increased upon the earth, sins and iniquities greatly increased also, so that God was compelled to send the Deluge upon the earth He chose Noah, telling him to build an Ark, *ut salvaretur universum semen in ea*. I leave out all the particulars concerning the Ark, because they are not now to our purpose regarding the soul . . .

The poor little soul continues for a while to deviate from that sincerity and purity which God had given her in the beginning This she does by not following that interior attraction to God whereby she could do great things and walk by great strides to perfection (as, on the contrary, not following it is a great impediment to perfection) ;—the Word sends the deluge, not finding the soul stripped of self, which He requires of her. But who is Noah, in this little world, but the will, which alone has remained enlightened, the other powers and affections being somewhat darkened ? As Noah was not wholly without sin, but was, nevertheless, the most just man that could be found then in the world; so the will, though not wholly perfect, is not wholly stained, but man alone was left with that intrinsic attraction to God . . The ark which she has to build is nothing but the soul's corresponding to the intrinsic light and knowledge God granted her, and the interior movements she gets from the bosom of the Father . . God commanded Noah to enclose eight souls in the Ark , and in our soul must be found eight kinds of knowledge—the knowledge of God , the knowledge of herself—that is, of her non-being as it is of herself, but all from God , the knowledge of the greatness and nobility of the soul ; the knowledge of the particular gifts God imparts to the souls ; the knowledge of the first innocence God granted , the knowledge of the particular providence He exercises over her ; the knowledge that all He does in her is through the affection of love ; the knowl 1 of purity, especially of intention These eight jewels must be placed in the Ark. O sacred Ark, built by the compendium of knowledge ! . . .

God also commanded Noah to enclose in the Ark all kinds of animals, clean and unclean, *septena et septena, duo et duo*   In the soul must be found all the virtues, such as charity, humility, obedience, and others, and, as the clean animals were to be seven and seven of all kinds, so in the soul must the virtues be founded on the seven gifts of the Holy Ghost, and as many virtues to every gift as it shall please the Holy Ghost to communicate A less number of unclean animals were to be in the Ark, because in the soul there is less need of those virtues she must practice in the exterior actions, than of those she must practice in the interior ones. . . . God afterwards sent the Deluge.   So did the Word send the deluge in this little world   And what deluge is this? It is a superabundant grace and infusion of His Blood, in which He causes all the desires, affections, and intentions of the soul, outside of His own will, to be drowned   .   Noah sends the dove out of the Ark to see whether the waters have subsided   The soul sends the dove (which means that she is not wanting anything for herself, but everything that God wants) to see whether the influence of the superabundant grace is spent   Finding that it is, she rests on the mercy of God, which she sees God has shown His creatures, though they have offended Him   The dove returns with a little olive-branch in its bill, viz., with the continuous confession of the purity of God, which purity He strongly wishes to deeply imprint in the soul by His graces   Afterwards, God dismisses Noah out of the Ark , and the Word does likewise with the soul, permitting her to come out of the ark of those kinds of knowledge and to go around expatiating throughout all the world, in which she then walks with every security   Then God comes to try Abraham , and so does the Word try the soul.   God says to Abraham that he must sacrifice his only son, the nearest and dearest thing he possesses ; and what is the dearest thing a soul possesses, but the Word and the sweet feeling of the Word?   He therefore wants her to sacrifice Him to Himself, and leads her to the mountain of the contemplation of the Divinity united with the Humanity, where the same soul, in the depth of that contemplation, consents to cease tasting the Word, to offer Him sacrificed, so to say, in herself, and on the altar of her heart, to the Eternal Father   Hence the Father, seeing this abandonment of the soul, cannot endure that she should remain without tasting His most sweet Word, and, consequently, Himself   Therefore He sends an angel—that is, a supernal inspiration—by which He gives her to understand that she should not sacrifice His Son, viz , His Word, but should take a victim, viz , herself, mortified by the knife of mortification, refined in the fire of tribulation, but not abandoned by the sensible presence of the Word, and that victim she should sacrifice to God

Leaving out all that happened in the meantime, we shall go and look at the Hebrew people whilst under the cruel slavery of Pharaoh in Egypt   Likewise all the sentiments are affected by a servile fear   And, as on coming out of Egypt the Hebrews carried with them vessels and precious stones, so these sentiments of the soul, coming out of that servile fear, take away the vessels and precious stones, viz , the fruits and treasures of the fear.   The Hebrew people cross the Red Sea, and the sentiments of the soul wade through the sea of love   The enemies of the soul, which are the passions, wish to wade through also, but they remain drowned in this sea of love.   The Hebrews go through the desert, where they murmur for want of food , hence God sends them the most sweet food, the manna   The Word gives Himself as food to the soul, when hungry—that is, the hidden manna of the Most Holy Sacrament, wherein the soul finds all the tastes she may wish If she wants Him *Powerful*, He is most powerful, as "*Omnia quæcumque voluit fecit in cœlo et in terra* "   If she wants Him *Immortal* and *Eternal*, here He is, without beginning and without end.   If she wants Him *Temporal*, here is the flesh He took in time for us   If she wants Him *Hidden*, here He is so hidden that by nature He was not even known to the highest seraphim of heaven   If she wants Him *Open* and *Manifest*, behold Him so that what is veiled to the eyes by the veil and band of the sacramental species, is unveiled and without band to the heart by the interior sentiments ; as what one believes by faith, he knows and feels by the warmth of love   In a word, the soul can abundantly find in Him every sentiment, both of sorrow and delight   This bread baked in the fire of sufferings, grieves by its remembrance and refreshes by its taste . .

The people again murmur because of thirst, Moses strikes the rock with the rod, and therefrom most copious waters gush forth, by which not only the thirst of the people, but also that of the cattle, is assuaged   The soul goes on walking by her sentiments through the desert of the subtraction of the feeling of grace.   O my poor little soul, this will befall thee !   Here these interior sentiments justly complain of the thirst which afflicts them, which is chiefly the subtraction of the sensible grace, and the fact that others do not walk in the road of perfection in that strict manner in which this soul leads them   But Moses, viz., the enlightened understanding, strikes the rock with the rod of the promises God made to him ; he strikes the rock, I say, "*petra autem erat Christus,*" and by this rod of the promises that Christ the Word has made him, he strikes the Heart of Christ Himself. He ox i· II's i , ci i ·   , most abundant waters of grace me, whi h not only satire ". s u n' of th   a , but even the senses of the body   Are you satiated now   O Sen im nts . . .

The Hebrew people advancing more and more through the desert, God gives Moses the law written on two tablets of stone, in which were contained all the interior and exterior operations which that people were commanded to do The Word continues His work in the soul; and, whilst this soul walks through the desert of the subtraction of the sentiment of the grace, He gives to her the law written on the tablets and chooses Moses, viz., the enlightened understanding, to manifest it to the people The tablets are the heart of the soul, on which the Word writes, that is, imprints all the operations He wants her to perform—both the interior and the exterior ones, and He binds her so that, in her own opinion, she deems it impossible to remain in such a narrowness, to walk in so great sincerity and purity with God Poor little one! If I but could, I would give thee help, what wilt thou do by thyself? Thus do, thus do, O blessed thou!

God in giving the law speaks with Moses face to face, and this means that the soul must not stop in the Humanity of the Word, feeding herself in the consideration of His Passion or of His Life, but she must pass to the consideration of the Divinity with becoming reverence and sobriety, so that the sentence may not be verified on her "*Dejecisti eos dum allevarentur*"—"When they were lifted up, Thou hast cast them down" (Ps lxxii, 18)—and "*Noli altum sapere, sed time*"—"Be not high-minded, but fear" (Rom. xi, 20) The people who could not stand the splendor of God are the sentiments which, being accustomed to things low and abject, cannot understand the things of God Hence when the splendor of God appears, not being accustomed to taste of God, they faint from fear

The Hebrews then travel on to reach that blessed Land of Promise, and, before reaching it, see the fruits thereof. Moses dies and does not enter it, Joshua and Caleb only enter it. Come now, O soul, go on to enter into the Land of Promise The Word will not lead thee now to Paradise, not now, to enjoy the eternal vision It will suffice for thee if He leads thee to that interior dwelling which is in the mouth of the Word, and before He leads thee therein thou shalt see the fruits thereof, which are the words of the Word, and particularly those uttered by him "*Clarifica me, Pater, apud temet ipsum claritate quam habui priusquam mundus fieret apud te*"—"And now glorify Thou me, O Father, with the glory which I had, before the world was, with Thee" (John xvii, 5). To the dwelling of the mouth of the Word He leads only the will and the love, not the understanding, because it dies before this, as Moses did, for the soul must not understand, so much as to desire and enjoy. Hence she is pleased in working, but without knowing the operation of her intellect in this operation of the Word, receiving in herself the divine illustrations, and practicing them without knowing how they come or how she receives them.

III.

She Applies the Operations of the Word, from the Incarnation to the Passion, to what God does in the Souls.

Then arise the holy prophets who announce to the soul that God will not fail to complete the work He has begun. They announce, and what do they announce? The coming of the Word into the soul These prophets are the Wounds of the Word imprinted in all the souls—in some really, in others by desire, in some by love, and in others by intention. They come with various figures, and this is done by these Wounds of the Word, which imprint various figures and produce various effects These five Wounds are five prophets to the souls, and the largest of them—in the Side—is David, who not only predicted the Incarnation, but the Passion, the Resurrection, and the Ascension of the Word. This is done also by the soul, who, from this Wound of the Side, perceives the coming of the Word to her by loving sentiment, as if He wanted to dwell in her heart She perceives the Passion, seeing the pains He has to endure, and, by the pains of the Word, she measures and moderates all these pains of heis. She perceives the Resurrection—I mean to say, she understands that all her operations must arise again in the sight of all creatures Afterwards she understands by the Ascension that her works will be made manifest not only before all creatures, but also before the Eternal Father, Who, by one of His angels, will have them related in paradise

Then other prophets come, prophesying the Word in Mary, some under one symbol and some under another Mary is pointed out and foretold before she comes The soul, like Mary, must be made known to men Like the sun, by the light of example, like the fixed stars, by firmness and stability of intention, turned to God and united with Him, like the planets, by the operations of charity towards her God, and, like the moon, towards her neighbors "*Omnibus omnia factus sum*" (1 Cor ix, 22), now increasing with the proficient and perfect ones, now decreasing with the incipient and imperfect ones Now full of consolation—"*superabundo gaudio*" (2 Cor vii, 4)—on account of their consolation, now full of sadness for the compassion of their sadness. *Quis infirmatur et ego non infirmor?*"—"Who is weak and I am not weak?" (2 Cor. xi, 29). Always, however, fixed on heaven, on account of the right intention, and superior, as a celestial body, to earthly defects, as is the case with those who are still on earth, and influence all with desires, and, when possible, with words and example, as Mary did, who was "*Pulchra ut luna, electa ut sol*"—"Fair as the moon, bright as the sun" (Cant vi, 9) But, oh! with how great a distance of perfection! Thou, O Word, espousest this soul as Thou didst Mary, and givest her in keeping And to whom dost Thou give her, O Word? To the counsel, the bridegroom of the soul. By means of this counsel, which is one of the seven gifts of the Holy Ghost, Thou keepest in her purity and charity, till by the affection of love she brings forth the Word . . He sends the angel to announce to Mary And He sends to the soul the gift of his right hand, which announces to her that God wants to come to her by grace, and the soul deeming herself unworthy, answers: "*Ecce ancilla Domini, fiat mihi secundum Verbum tuum*" - "Behold the handmaid of the Lord, be it done to me according to Thy Word" (Luke i, 38). Hence the Word, seeing so much humility, descends to her, as to Mary, drawn by humility He not only keeps this virtue in her, but He increases it with all the other gifts and virtues, for, after saying that she is the handmaid, she begins to act as a servant in the house of Elizabeth. She goes to be a servant, who is "*Mater Domini sui.*" The Eternal Father with the Divine Word prepares in the soul that has espoused the Word a lasting and consummate humility, which the soul afterwards shows in her works, advancing more and more in humility the longer the Word remains in her

The Word takes His flesh and blood, and continues producing that holy little body in that most pure virginal bosom, taking great delight in her purity and the practice of charity Mary brings forth the Word So does the soul bring 'Him forth by the affection of love I say that she brings forth His operation, and, like Mary, lays Him down in the manger, and goes on making Him known by His holy poverty She chooses this as her dear lady, according to the example of Blessed Francis, and seeing that the Word, her Spouse, likes it "*Beati pauperes spiritu*" . Two animals keep the Word warm The operation of the soul is not warmed by animals—no; but, through a special grace, by the choir of the seraphim and the archangels, sent to her by the Divine Word. These take up her operation and bring it before the Eternal Father, and offer it to Him, hence by this offering, such an operation is so warmed that it will not fail because of cold, negligence, or tepidity. . The angels come down from heaven singing that beautiful canticle "*Gloria in excelsis Deo*" On account of the offering made to the Eternal Father, of the operation of the soul, the Father sends down with a most sweet distillation of His grace a voice to the heart, which, like a musical concert, goes on singing in the soul. "*Gloria in excelsis Deo et in terra pax hominibus bonæ voluntatis*" I say that the operation must redound wholly to the honor and glory of God, and the benefit of those creatures who shall be ready to receive it The shepherds come to visit the Word Likewise do the little shepherds come to visit the soul, and they are the ignorant and simple creatures, who, by the consciousness the soul possesses of her own ignorance, are by her instructed and consoled . . The Wise Men come and adore the Word So also come the Three Wise Men, to the soul—I mean the Holy Trinity— Who abundantly bring with Them to the soul rich gifts and celestial graces. What gifts? The Holy Trinity gives to the soul strength to keep with all perfection what she promised, and at the same time, if a Religious, gives her merit for the three vows, and if a secular, for all she has done through the three powers of the soul. To all these operations the Holy Trinity communicates the merit of the *power* of the Father, participated in by working in behalf of the neighbors, of the *union* with the Word, participated in, by uniting us, as it does, in fraternal charity with our neighbors, of the *benignity* of the Holy Ghost, participated in and communicated also with bowels of piety and mercy. This is a great gift, viz, that the Most Holy Trinity should make the soul partaker of her union, and work in conformity with this gift But, before all, the Word is taken to be circumcised, and a name is given to Him. So the soul carries her operation to be circumcised, and gives a name to it This happens when the soul is rapt in such sublimity of union, that it must be diminished and lowered, hence she sends out fire of charity, and a name is given to this operation—that is, *it* is written in the Book of Life, whence it can never be erased. Mary carries the Word to the Temple The soul brings her offering, too—that is, she offers her operation in the Consistory of the Most Holy Trinity, in the mind of the Father, where the Holy Ghost takes it up, the Word magnifies it, and the Father takes delight in it Mary flies with the Word into Egypt. The soul flies by hiding her operation from the sight of the creatures, and by her continuous offering of the Word, throws down to the ground so many disloyalties of the incarnate demons

Then the Word is sought after by Mary; and so the soul goes on seeking by her operation the greatness of God in herself and finds it not being deprived of the *internal taste* but, like Mary, su a°a r x r '- t v her of r. 'n is 'l e greatness of God When she does not .ke to work, she has not in d > w , knows that by herself she cannot work, and yet she works, and these are the three do - during which

Mary sought her lost Son Mary finds Him in the midst of the Doctors, and the soul finds Him whilst confounding their human wisdom by His Divine Wisdom. . The Word is led to baptism O Loving Word, O intense Love, whence are this soul and this operation led ? O Loving Word, to baptism ? But if she has been baptized once, how can she be baptized again ? No, the soul is not baptized a second time—no , but the Word with His operation, whom she has conceived within herself, goes on purifying her with His grace, pouring over the head of her intention a distillation of the complacency which the Word feels in His equality with the Father—a complacency similar to the union of the soul with the Word by grace The more abundantly the Word gives grace to her, the more grateful she is towards Him . . .

Afterwards the Word changes water into wine. This operation, so much experienced and practiced, of changing water into wine, Thou dost, O Word, and thus dost Thou show Thy omnipotent wisdom What corresponding operation wilt Thou, O Word, perform in the soul ? Thou wilt change into fervor the tepidity of the soul But, alas! I see that t us change is wrought by Thee in but a few, through man's fault, so great is the amount of this evil tepidity and coldness in the world !

The Word goes on preaching and performing miracles, and the operation of the soul continues—announcing, magnifying, and preaching the ineffable wisdom of the Word, casting the demons out of the creatures, healing the infirmity of vainglory in herself and in others

The Jews wish to stone the Word, and the operation is also led to be stoned This comes when the soul is led to such a perfection that it seems that the demons, with all the creatures, arise against her , and, what is worse, those who seem enlightened begin, as if conspiring together, to contradict that soul But few are those who attain to such a perfection

The Word, before His preaching and performing miracles, was led into the desert, where He fasted forty days and forty nights Thus the operation of the soul is led into the *desert* of the union by the enlightening of merits and the warming up of the love of the Deity by the Most Holy Trinity *There* she abstains from every other food to taste only the fruit of the union, and then the devil comes, by means of some *instruments* of his, seeking to make her believe that there is within her more disunion than there is among the devils themselves, and that *she is the cause* of it But the soul, being founded and established in the union of the Word, hides in this same union and sweetly tastes Him. . .

After the preaching and the great miracles wrought by the Word, He at the end shows His great love by leaving Himself as food to His creatures, by the institution of the Blessed Sacrament. The Word, at the Last Supper, uttered those loving words: "*Desiderio desideravi ,*" and the soul can say the same words, as the Word is led to love this soul so much that He gives Himself as food and nourishment to her. He makes her a present of His Humanity, and gives her by participation His own pure desires and loving affections, those truthful words and most holy works He performed while on earth, and finally He wholly transforms her into Himself By these gifts the soul reaches such a perfection, that every aspiration of the mind which she makes towards God seems to draw the Word from the bosom of the Father into herself Thus, having the Word within herself, she becomes by union and love like another Word , and as the Word with desire wished to give Himself wholly to His creatures, so the soul with an ardent desire goes on wishing to communicate herself to the creatures—I should say, to communicate to them the Word She holds Him within herself, with all His graces and gifts, so that she can also say truly with the same words : " With desire I have desired to eat my Pasch with you "

Then the Word comes to the washing of the feet, wherein He so much lowers and humbles Himself that He does not leave unwashed even the feet of the traitor. Likewise the Word inclines and draws down the operation of the soul, washing and purifying with the aspersion of His Blood all her affections and desires, infusing into her a most heartfelt disposition to humble herself. Now what is this Word going to do? Where does He go? To the sermon, to which he leads the soul, in order to be glorified even here on earth He leads her, I say, to the secret of His heart where, face to face, He holds a most sweet colloquy with her , telling her how He is the Way, the Truth, and the Life, and makes it known to her how He is the true Life, and His Father the Husbandman, and how she will be persecuted, and the world will rejoice thereat . . .

The Word now starts for the Garden of Olives, and the soul follows Him The garden to which he goes, being still in heaven, is the Church , and by the offering of himself, O Word, the priest points out to us how Thou didst conform Thy will, in that prayer, to the will of Thy Eternal Father. Thou takest along three disciples, infusing in the Church the faith, manifesting the truth, and continuing the mercy. The soul too goes on following the Word in the Garden of the Church, to give Him the body as a prey, that the soul may breathe and the spirit may be confirmed by the ardent desire for the salvation of the neighbors.

The Word goes towards Judas to be captured, and I wish to go—(oh! what a favor this is!)—not towards a traitor, but towards my Love, to receive Him in the Most Holy Sacrament, and to receive from Him the kiss of peace.

IV.

Of the Operations of the Word, from the Passion to the Ascension, teaching how We may imitate Them.

The Eternal Word is captured by the Jews; and this operation also takes place in the soul, as she, too, is seized, and in this little world of the soul what took place at the capture of the Word is renewed Behold Judas, the traitor, and the crowd of soldiers. The perverse temptations which the devil suggests to the soul are the soldiers who would take away the good work of the soul, but the Word does not allow her to be seized; nay, He takes her up with His hands, with that love, so to say, whereby He begets Himself in the soul, and with the kiss of peace makes her a captive.

The Word is bound by the soldiers, so also the soul is bound Yes, she is bound with a certain triple rope, viz , with faith, hope, and charity The Word does not allow Peter to prevent Him from suffering. Likewise the soul does not wish that operation to be prevented whereby she unites herself intimately with her God. Oh ! how many Peters there would be, who, lacking wisdom and consideration, would seek to blind the soul with things transitory, but the soul, enlightened, says, that he who inordinately loves transitory things must perish with them, as the Word told Peter that he who uses the sword shall perish by the sword But this soul permits herself to be led, like the Word, where she sees it is the will of the Word Himself, without ever adding of her own either "I will" or "I will not," following constantly the will of the Word

The Word is led to Annas and Caiphas, and the tribunals of the other judges. The soul, too, is conducted by the persuasion of diverse temptations, now to hell and now to paradise ; now they make it appear to her as if she had done no good, thus confounding her, and now as if she were like the great Saints. This and other numberless things they suggest to her, that she may grow proud. But the Word does not permit her to get lukewarm. He protects her, and does with the soul as the Eternal Father did with Him at the time of His Passion, taking away from her the feeling of His grace, to try her and render her more perfect .

The Word is taken to be scourged at the pillar. The soul, too, is led to receive the scourges, which are the many offenses committed against His Divine Majesty, that are shown her, as to a soul who loves God. These offenses, when she sees and understands them as it behooves her, are like so many hard blows As the scourges of the Word were great in number, so much so that many took their turn to scourge Him at the pillar, so the same offenses, shown to the soul, take their turn in scourging her, so to say, at one time being the offenses offered to God by Religious that are shown to her, at another time those offered to Him by bad Christians, and at still others, those offered to Him by heretics and infidels. . .

The Word is crowned with thorns, and the soul, proceeding with this operation, is also crowned with thorns, when the devils in scorn go on representing before her the enormous blasphemies which pierce her like sharp thorns; for, instead of hearing her Spouse, the Word, praised, she is compelled to hear so many and such odious blasphemies.

The Word is derided ; and the derisions offered to the soul are these, that being afflicted and tempted by the devil, in speaking about it with some creature, she is told, instead of being comforted, that those afflictions and temptations befall her on account of her defects and sins, as his friends told the most patient Job . . .

The face of the Word is veiled, and the same thing happens to the soul when human help is taken from her and the divine is denied her, and she is scourged when the light she possesses is somewhat obscured

The Word is shown to the people with the words: "*Ecce Homo*"—"Behold the Man " And so it happens to the poor soul, when by the abundance of the great light she possesses she confers with others about certain things, which afterward she is reproached with ; as it used to happen to the seraphic Francis, when he was told in contempt—"See heaven ! See heaven!" To the soul they say : "See thy Love ! See thy Love !" And they do not perceive that by despising her they make her appear more glorious, as the Word by those words, "*Ecce Homo*," appeared not less glorious than if it had been said "*Ecce Deus*"—"Behold God." . . He is compared to Barabbas—as the soul is many a time, to persons less perfect than herself, because of her not being known Hence those persons are honored and acceptable ; and she is despised and thrown aside, as one loaded with imperfections

The cross is laid on the shoulder of the Word To the chosen soul it is a heavy cross when another chosen one does not believe her, and her words, sentiments, and works are rather despised And yet it is by Thy permission, O Word, that such a trial, as gold in fire, comes to the virtue to purify it The soul goes on carrying the cross with the Word as often as she patiently endures these things, not throwing herself down into hell by discouragement, nor up into heaven by elation, but remaining all quiet under God's protection, permitting herself to be led and judged by Him—entertaining an upright intention towards Him and a deep knowledge of her own nonentity   .

The Word is led to be unrobed, and the same thing happens to the soul when she is prevented from walking in the way of God according to the interior inspiration and enlightenment which the Lord imparts to her, and she is urged on in a manner contrary to what she feels in herself. She, like the Word, helps herself to unrobe when she keeps humble and contradicts herself She stretches on the cross when she ceases investigating what will become of her, but leaves it to God to dispose of her according to His good pleasure

The Word is nailed to the cross by three nails, and the soul, too, is nailed on the hard cross by three nails. One nail is when she considers those things which appear to be an offense to God, as being permitted by Him. She does not trouble herself because they are a punishment inflicted on her, but simply because they appear to be offenses against God; and she submits to the Divine Will The other nail is, that in her operations God leaves the interior delights of the soul for her neighbors, and for the spiritual help of her brothers and sisters The third nail which keeps the soul fastened to the cross is, that she glories in being despised, seeing that thereby she becomes like her Spouse, the Word, and fulfills His will . . .

The Word dies on the cross; and so the soul dies by means of that perfect relaxation she makes of herself in God, understanding, knowing, and willing nothing except so far as the Word wishes it should be done in her, for her, and by her

And now the side of the Word is open; so is the heart of the soul open when, pierced by the wound of love, she desires with an anxious desire that all creatures be converted to God

Afterwards the Word is taken down from the cross, and this happens to the soul when God makes her return somewhat to her former happy state and taste the Divine consolations, and shows her in particular the mystery of the Most Holy Trinity, making her taste the union with the Same.

The Word is laid with the ointments, and the soul, too, is placed among the sweet odors of the ointments, and is wrapped, like the Word, in a pure white sheet, every time she begins to feel any indication of possessing in herself (but by His favor) some virtue—particularly purity, which, though she possessed it before, yet she was deprived of the sight and feeling of it

The Word is laid in the sepulchre, and the soul also is laid in the sepulchre when God keeps her with Himself, making her taste the sweetness of His grace She also goes with her Bridegroom from the bosom of the Father, whence she never departs, into the sepulchre—into limbo, into hell—confounding the demons and taking from them some soul they might have snatched and tormented   . .

The Word arises with glory and triumph; the soul arises every time God removes from her every adversity, temptation, and pain, and gives her peace with a tranquillity of mind wholly conformable to His Divine Will . . .

The Word appears to His Mother; and the soul appears to the Mother when she is forced with an ardent wish to reveal her operation to the Holy Church She does not permit herself, like the Word, to be touched by Magdalen, because as soon as the soul has attained a certain perfection she is averse to mixing up her spiritual and meritorious works with frail, earthly, and perishable ones What is more, she does not esteem, nor does she care to perform interior or exterior acts of any virtue, in order to possess it and exercise herself in it, except the virtue of *love*, though she always performs virtuous works and exercises herself in every act of perfection. Possessing God, she possesses all the virtues, and in Him she delights and rejoices. . . . The soul makes the other apparitions with her Bridegroom, the Word, when she manifests her operations to those creatures that have in themselves the knowledge and light of God, and this she does only for the honor and glory of God, and to comfort and console them. The soul, like the Word, is invisible after her resurrection, because she performs her operations invisibly, that is, unknown to every creature; so that some deem her faulty and she is not understood except by God and by those creatures who are like herself . .

The Word then gives the peace to His apostles, and so does the soul give the peace to her neighbors when she seeks and endeavors to unite the creatures in holy peace

The Word ascends into heaven, and the soul, though yet living on the earth, ascends with Him, raising herself above herself with every affection, wish, intention, and work Hence, if she now is any counsel she takes it from God, more than from creatures, if she must work, she does it with God, and in God In this assumption of the soul into heaven, the Word embraces and presses her to Himself, making her partaker, in an act of love, of the power of the Father, the wisdom of the Son, and the goodness of the Holy Ghost She is overshadowed by a cloud resulting from the distillation of heavenly sweetnesses, graces, and divine gifts, which God pours into her, and wherein all sentiments are absorbed, not knowing how a soul can attain such an altitude

The Word, ascending into heaven, leaves to His Bride, the Church, the twelve apostles; and the soul being thus taken up with the Word, though still conversing on earth, permits the shining in her actions and conversation of the twelve fruits of the Holy Ghost, which are to said soul like twelve columns which support and strengthen her in all her operations

The soul afterward gives praise with the Word to the Eternal Father, which praise is a constant thanksgiving to the Father for having given His Word as a Redeemer to creatures and a Bridegroom to the Virgins.

The Word sends the Holy Ghost, and the soul together with the Word does likewise, when drawing the Spirit to herself by aspiration, she goes on infusing Him by spiritual communication and admonition into the creatures who are fit to receive Him

The Word sits at the right hand of the Father; and with His five wounds draws the blessed souls, as if to a beatific object, not a primary but a secondary one; and on earth, by means of those wounds, and by the virtue of His merits, and as an object of contemplation He draws all the creatures to Himself   Likewise the soul, remembering these five wounds the Word kept for Himself, draws to herself, as if by five darts of love, all the creatures, wishing by charity to inflame them all with the love divine, and desiring to spread everywhere that fire which the Word came to enkindle on the earth. *"Ignem veni mittere in terram, et quid volo, nisi ut accendatur?"*—" I am come to cast fire on the earth, and what will I but that it be kindled?" (Luke xii, 49).   The Word is the Head of the Church, and the creatures are her members. " *Vos autem corpus Christi, et membra de membro"*—"Now you are the body of Christ and members of member" (1 Cor. xii, 27)   "*Unum corpus sumus in Christo"*—"We are one body in Christ " (Rom xii, 5)   Thus are in the soul all the states of creatures that are found in the Church, some by election, others by participation, and others by desire and will.   The state of the Virgins and Religious is found in the soul by election, I say, for having chosen to serve God and walk to perfection in said state   The wishes and superior loving desires of the soul are conformable to those which are required in the priests, viz, just, wise, perfect, and holy.   The memory of the soul represents the state of the hermits, of constant abstinence, because memory itself must abstain from every recollection of anything secular and vain.   The patience of the soul represents the state of the contented ones   The affections of the inferior ones may be referred to the state of seculars, because as these generally practice exterior works, so such affections excite the soul to exterior works of charity and mercy . . .

The little boat of the Church is assailed by the waves of heresy and infidelity, and the soul is warred against by constant temptations and contradictions; but she always remains immovable and strong, because God keeps her in constant motion, without any motion; but this is given by special grace and *gratis data*. Faith can never fail in the Church, as the Word said, thus its foundation can never fail in the soul, by a special divine grace, she having built *it* in the knowledge of her nonentity.

The faith of the Church must go on spreading to all parts of the world, and in this little world of the soul the knowledge of God goes on increasing, together with the knowledge of what God requires of her in the states of her age

At the end of the world the Antichrist comes, seeking to destroy the faith of the Holy Church   But Enoch and Elias will come afterwards to convert those that shall have been perverted by him, and the Word, by the spirit of His breath, will overthrow him.

After this all flesh shall arise and the Word will sit in judgment, giving glory or punishment to each one according to his works   When the soul comes to the end of her (mortal) life, the devil himself comes forth as the Antichrist, with his perverse suggestion seeking to rob her of the Holy Faith, but Enoch and Elias, viz, the virtue of the Blood of the Word, and the recollection of the continued operations done in state of grace, *arise*, and, consoling her, deliver her from the diabolical vexations; and the Word, by the spirit of His breath, and His divine promise, so efficacious, grants her a complete triumph

The soul then arises for the particular judgment wherein the Divine Word, together with the Word of the same soul—by which her operation is meant—sits in judgment. The Divine Word, in the final judgment, will continue recounting the works of mercy performed by the just and neglected by the reprobates. The Word of the soul relates all her privations, trials, and works of mercy   and thus the reward is given to her by the Divine Word, by ad, itting l r to the b st f v si n   behold ! the Incarnate Word has assumed this so l, and made in her a little world   Everything which God made in the whole machinery of the whole world both in creating all things, and in creating man,

Main Altar and Painting above it in St. Mary Magdalen De-Pazzi's (Italian) Church,
Philadelphia.

THE GLORY OF ST. MARY MAGDALEN DE-PAZZI IN HEAVEN.

The New Carmelite Monastery in Florence (?) ... St. M. M. De P.'s Church and Parochial Buildings.
VIGNETTES:
I.   She made ... of M. ... ... delphia
II. Blindfold ... ...
III. St. Augustine ... ... am Esb.
IV. Whilst in ... ... nds of the
        Blessed Virgin.

is there. He gave to her, instead of innocence, virginal purity, which is a communication of His Being by divine participation Such a purity represents the primitive innocence—Who creates everything to His image and likeness, and governs and supports
everything —"*Portans omnia verbo virtutis suæ*"—"Upholding all things by the word
of His power" (Heb. i, 3) He makes her multiply the good operations, and shutting
her in the Ark of the compendium of the knowledge of God—her works and herself,
tries her like Abraham, delivers her from the Egyptian servitude, leads her through
the desert of the subtraction of the sentiment of grace—but always guided by the Divine
Escort, so that she may work without knowing that she does right—where He gives her
the law of the operation that he wants her to do, introducing her, finally, into the land
of promise, in the interior dwelling of the mouth or the heart of the Word.

Afterwards came the prophets announcing to her the coming of the Word, and the
Word, descending into her, works spiritually in her by similarity what He did in His own
Humanity from the Incarnation to the shedding of His own blood. Thus the soul afterwards dies with Him, arises and ascends into heaven (though living on earth), sends in
a manner the Holy Ghost, comes to judgment, and is judged at the end of her life, and,
if found worthy, is by the Word glorified and led to a place where she has no longer any
fear of her past enemies, and enjoys and possesses God for ever and ever.

V.

Of the Unity, Essence, and Trinity of the Divine Persons, Applied Mystically to the Souls.

There is in the Most Holy Trinity a union of power, wisdom, and goodness, and
such a union the Holy Trinity wishes to accomplish in Its brides, so that they may sing
"*Ecce quam bonum et quam jucundum habitare sorores in unum !*"—"Behold how
good and how pleasant it is for *sisters* to dwell together in unity !" (Ps. cxxxii). *Power*
will unite in God those who possess *it*, the same will be done by *wisdom* and *goodness*
with those who possess *them* And so the Congregation of Mary (she meant her monastery) will be made on earth, in spirit, an image of the High and Sovereign Trinity. So
great is the depth contained in the words ' *O altitudo divitiarum sapientiæ et scientiæ
Dei !*"—"O the depth of the riches of the wisdom and the knowledge of God !" (Rom
xi, 33) that it cannot be fathomed by any creature, no matter how sublime, as in *it* is
contained the being of God, Who is eternal, without beginning and without end I
would like to be able to say as much, in proportion, of Thy brides : *O altitudo!* O
depth ! It would be a great height if all the hearts of the Congregation of Mary were
united But, alas ! there can be no union where there is no compassion for one another
"*Alter alterius onera portate*"—"Bear ye one another's burden" (Galat vi, 2)
"*Divitiarum*"—"Of the riches"—and what does it mean but riches of the wisdom and
knowledge of God ? The Father possesses riches because of the delight He takes in His
Word The Word, because of the delight the Father takes in Him. The Holy Ghost
possesses riches because of the delight He takes in the Father and the Word. Riches will
also be found here below in this soul representing the Trinity, riches not of wisdom and
knowledge, but of charity and peace, which will cause the good of one to be shared by
all, and the good of all by each. The power will delight (as in a good of its own) in the
wisdom, the wisdom in the power, and the goodness in both of them The uncreated
Trinity is the riches of this new and, so to speak, created trinity by the communication
It makes to the latter. The created trinity is riches (Oh ! Infinite Goodness, Who takest
so much delight in the good of others, which, after all, is from Thee and through
Thee !)—it is riches, I say, of the uncreated Trinity, because the latter sees in the former
the gifts and perfections It communicates to it, and in this created trinity It loves Itself
and Its own gifts, hence by the communication that must take place, giving and receiving again what It has given, It takes delight in Its creatures, because It receives from
them what It previously gave to them Thus It communicates Itself to creatures, and
especially to the souls favored by grace Hence the communication of the uncreated
Trinity consists in infusing Its gifts and graces into creatures, and the communication
of the created trinity is made not by the infusion, but by the return, with thanksgiving
and gratitude, of the gifts and graces to the Giver. The riches of the uncreated Trinity
consist in assuming the soul to Itself, and the riches of Its creatures consist in drawing
the Word by grace into themselves The riches of the eternal and inscrutable Trinity
consist in showing mercy, and the riches of the creatures in corresponding to this grace
Oh ! what great riches are these in which the eternity of the Trinity takes delight ! The
eternity of the Trinity is and consists in the continuous and unfathomable Being of God
But our trinity made by participation, by feeling of love and consent of will, must be
under whom ? " he to prope tion and the mantle of Mary But we should see to it
that as the Father is not discordant with the Son, nor the Son with the Father, nor both

with the Holy Ghost, nor the Holy Ghost with both, so the daughters of Mary should be united (and not discordant in opinion or will with one another), not only in words, but even, if possible, in intention. *"Unum sint, sicut et nos unum sumus"*—"That they may be one, as we also are one" (John xvii, 22) *"O altitudo divitiarum sapientiæ !"*— "O the depth of the riches of the wisdom !" (Rom xi, 33). Wisdom flowing, wisdom reflowing, and wisdom flowing abundantly to Its creatures Flowing from the Father, reflowing from the Word, and flowing to creatures in abundance from the Holy Ghost This wisdom flows from the Father, and the infusion of it begets in the soul a desire to adhere to God's greatness. The wisdom reflowing from the Word begets a loving hunger to understand God And the Holy Ghost with His constant and most steady motion influences creatures, draws them to Himself, and communicates to them a wisdom which begets a most ardent desire to understand how one can be always united with God *"Et scientiæ Dei "* The knowledge of God is different from that which He imparts to the creatures The knowledge of God is to understand with a most perfect and simple act all the things that have been, are, and shall be. A most subtle penetrating of every intention, desire, and work, of every word, of every winking of the eye, movement of the lips and the hands Oh! scientific knowledge of our God! *"Quam incomprehensibilia sunt judicia ejus, et investigabiles viæ ejus!"*—"How incomprehensible are His judgments, and how unsearchable His ways" (Rom xi, 33) About this incomprehensibility of the knowledge of our God, I do not know how to draw or understand anything except a loving admiration for the same God Who considers and, with a moment's look, judges all the universe Oh! if this were penetrated into! How can creatures perform so many works without considering them? Yet one must render an account of all the intentions (even the least) which he had in performing them, even those which seem good and holy, and must be judged for them in that terrible day of the great judgment. O God, so great! and shall so strict be the account of the good works and the intentions one had in performing them? How strict shall be the account of the express Commandments broken? *"Et investigabiles viæ ejus."* I said, O great God, that Thy ways are investigable, they do not seem so to me, nay, they seem known to me, because Thou hast been willing to show them to us They are capable of investigation, yes, to those who possess not Thy light, but who turn not their eyes from it. *"Judicia Domini vera justificata in semetipsa "*—"The judgments of the Lord are true, justified in themselves" (Ps xviii, 10) Didst Thou not make them say that Thy ways are beautiful? Yes, if they are beautiful, I do not think Thou hast shown them to the creatures without cause The Word is the way, and He manifests these ways by the blood He shed over them for those who wish to walk through them. It is true that it is a thing that cannot be investigated, how one should want to come to Thee without the way, as Thou art the way itself Those things cannot be investigated which are opposed to this way, for one cannot understand how so much ignorance and malice could be found in Thy creature, that she should refuse to walk through them after Thee, following Thy footprints marked with Thy blood This cannot be understood ; but the way in itself is not hidden—nay, it is all lovely, and lined with most sweet vines and various fruits By the strength of these, like Elias by hearth-cake, we not only reach the summit of the Mount Horeb of Thy knowledge by creatures, but by loving intelligence and penetrating affection—more by love than by knowledge—we reach the very throne of the Most Holy Trinity

Behold how the loving Word comes to rest in this created trinity of His creature, which is like the uncreated Trinity, by the three powers of the soul He comes to rest in the trinity of His brides, who resemble Him by the union, and causes in this what takes place in His Trinity He makes the will do what the Father does, the understanding what the Word does, and the memory what the Holy Ghost does ; and all this is done in the soul by affection of love and participation The office of the Father is to beget and to give the glory and communication of His being to the other two Divine Persons, and the will, which does the work of the Father, when it has forgotten and wholly denied itself, by a new strength of affection regenerates itself It is the will that gives glory to all the sentiments, and if it is pure, the understanding is more capable of seeing God, one in essence and triune in person Oh! what tongue could ever explain, or cease crying, that one possesses a God so great, and is created to His image and likeness!   . The Word gives delight to His Father and to Himself by the being He receives, and which is eternally communicated to Him by the Father, and from one and the other, by a tie of love, the Holy Ghost proceeds Thus the understanding gives delight to the will as the Word to the Father, completing the works that the will begins, by consenting to these works Moreover, the understanding takes delight in itself, as the Word does ; that is to say, it takes delight in the work that the will has performed, by concurring also in this work, for the understanding and the will are the same, such as the Father and the Word are the same God. The Holy Ghost proceed from th Father and the Word, and as He is one and the same thing with the Father and the Word, so I concurs in the operations of the Divine Persons, so also the memory must concur in the works of the will

and the understanding. All the effects and affections which are born in the Three
Divine Persons are also born in this trinity of the soul by participation and in an act of
love   In the Trinity of the Three Divine Persons a communication and an equality of a
Being—eternal and most perfect in Himself, Who cannot have any disparity or division—
is born   Thus It is undivided in Its operations, *ad extra*, because all the operations
are alike common to all the Most Holy Trinity   I say not this of the Incarnation, as to the
Person ; because, though all the Three Divine Persons cooperated in this Divine Operation, it was, nevertheless, fully accomplished in the Second Person, that is, the Incarnate Word , because this operation fully ended in the person, and afterwards in the
nature, by a necessary consequence , for the person cannot be divided from the nature,
it being the same thing   Therefore all the Blessed Trinity ordains every thing in the
whole world   It ordains in heaven all the movements which take place among the
blessed in glory ; and on earth all the motions and natural operations which take place
in the creature   In It they receive the maintenance and permanency of being, just
as they receive the being and the life   But it can principally be said that It ordains
from heaven those things which are supernatural, viz , the grace and the interior inspirations to our profit ; because God alone can work and enter the depth of the human
heart, change it and turn it to His will   He that was the Author of it has given to
us the liberty which cannot be forced by anyone but Him, even *necessarily*, unless
He shall so choose, though He moves it always most sweetly and freely.   All the holy
operations and motions in the secret heart of the responsible creatures, by which they
feel themselves drawn to God and turned to Him, proceed immediately from the Most
Holy Trinity.   The fact is, that all is done by God with sovereign wisdom, and we, at
most times, do not understand those operations and motions , or, if we do understand
them, do not want to understand so as to follow them.   Ah ! do Thou, O Most Holy
Trinity, change our hearts !   Thou Who hast made them to Thy image, recast them—so
to say—that they may be wholly conformed to Thee · *"Et spiritum rectum innova in
visceribus nostris"*—"And renew a right spirit within our bowels" (Ps 1, 12). So it
happens to this trinity of the soul   In her, too, is born the communication which communicates to her neighbors the gifts and graces received from God, so that they, being
partakers of it, may bring forth fruit with Him   If a soul wishes to see how much
delight God takes in her, let her see how communicative she is both of spiritual and of
temporal goods, not only of those she possesses, but also of those she desires ; not only
of those she understands and sees, but of those she does not see but believes by faith
From the purity, that is, from being a most pure act without any imperfection of deficiency or dependence which may denote a defect in the divine nature, the equality of
the Divine Persons proceeds.   Hence the soul, preserving or regaining the primitive
innocence, becomes like and equal to God, not by nature, but by participation and grace
She also becomes like the angels by union of love—nay, superior to them—by the *happy
sin*, whereby we are sprinkled with the Most Precious Blood of the Incarnate Word   O
Eternal Word ! what more can man want than what Thou hast given him to bring himself to love and enjoy Thee ? And though he should have to endure a thousand hells to
enjoy Thee, it should not seem hard to him   In reality, little does he suffer in this
world, and that little is mingled with many sweetnesses of Thy consolations, and seasoned with the most delicious love of the consideration of Thy Passion   Moreover, the
Eternal Trinity goes on glorifying and dispensing grace , likewise this trinity of the soul
glorifies and dispenses grace , and how ? The uncreated Trinity glorifies man, and the
created trinity glorifies God, by desiring—and rejoicing at it—that he should have all the
glory He possesses in Himself, and in seeking in all her works the divine honor and
glory, being always ready to give up life for this glory of His Divine Majesty   Moreover,
the Individual Trinity goes on distilling and dispensing Its grace to all the creatures
who are capable of receiving it.   The trinity of the soul distills an anxious desire for
the neighbors, and infuses a strong will that creatures should return to their Creator
This distillation is so intrinsic that it succeeds in penetrating the very Heart of the Word,
Who is well pleased at this effect . . . After the Eternal Trinity had taken delight in
the created trinity, It sent the Word to become flesh and redeem man. So much, I
dare say, the soul does, too ; and not being able to re-create man, what does she do ? O
my Lord Jesus, I will say it, she re-creates God. And how can she re-create God, Who
is Author of everything ? She re-creates Him in those souls who have lost Him , for it
is said that God is re-created whenever a soul is regained. The Individual Trinity is not
an accepter of persons, but rather of anxious desires and loving affections ; and likewise
this trinity of the soul is not an accepter of persons, but of the truth   This was made
manifest by him who was sanctified in the womb, I say, St John the Baptist, and by St
Angelo the Carmelite, who is so little known, and who died for the truth.   Men should
glory in the dignity of being created to the image of God, and in the fact that God Himself became a man to restore a man this divine image   O greatness and dignity of man !
After all, for a title it is lost a'·' ·'   Trinity in person, and one in essence, is my
God. To the unity of the Individual Trinity belongs the judgment of Its creatures,

because It created them, though on account of what the Son of God Incarnate has suffered for His creatures, it is said that the Father has delegated the authority of judging to Him "*Constitutus judex vivorum et mortuorum*"—"Appointed by God to be judge of the living and of the dead" (Acts x, 42). And man living virtuously passes judgment, he judges himself, and by his virtuous way of living he judges those who lead a virtuous life. . . . The angels wish to look into the Eternal Trinity, Whose vision glorifies the souls. Into this created trinity not only the angels, but God also looks He works in it, and continues to extend the work the more He takes delight in Himself and in His work. "*Lætabitur Dominus in omnibus operibus suis*"—"The Lord shall rejoice in all His works" (Ps. ciii, 31) "*Deliciæ meæ esse cum filiis hominum*"—"My delights were to be with the children of men" (Prov viii, 31) O Great God, One in Essence and Triune in Person ! The same Individual Trinity, being Sovereign Purity, despises altogether every vice, wherever it may be found, and particularly pride, which is more opposed to It. This was seen from the beginning, when It cast out of heaven the apostate angel with all his followers The same does the soul who truly loves this great God, that is, she despises all the vices, and especially that of pride, both in herself and in her neighbors . . .

Man is so much like unto God that one cannot look at God without seeing man, nor look at man without seeing God. Let no one say he loves God if he does not love the Truth, because how can we say we love the Lord if we do not love that thing which is nearest and dearest to Him ? O Truth, which art abandoned on account of every light temptation, every breath of reproach, the creature does not want to acknowledge thee from God and in God Himself : "*Ego sum Veritas*"—"I am the Truth (John xvi, 6). Yet the Bridegroom brings to His brides a garment of Truth, and, moreover, the ring, which is tantamount to saying to them· "I am the Truth, I give you the Truth, love the Truth." And as the ring has neither beginning nor end, or, as He says, it is God Himself, hence in this ring is enchased that precious gem which is the Word If thou art not satisfied, O soul, with this gem, because thou canst not understand it, take up the strong stone of the purity of the same Word, because Truth and the Incarnate Word are one and the same thing, and there is no Truth without purity, nor purity without Truth . . . To the Word all power is given in heaven and on earth "*Data est mihi omnis potestas in cælo et in terra*"—"All power is given to Me in heaven and on earth" (Matth. xxviii, 18). Likewise in the trinity of the soul all power in heaven and on earth is given to the second power, which is the intellect To the Word is given the power in heaven to glorify the angels and the blessed spirits, and the intellect has the power to raise itself to the throne of the Most Holy Trinity Here it receives those rays and influxes of loving light proceeding from the same Undivided Trinity, neither can the intellect be restrained by any earthly power. To the Word is given the power to make the creatures choose that vocation which pleases Him, and to the intellect is given the power to compel the submission of all the intrinsic and natural appetites of the soul to the illuminations it receives from God As all power is given to Thee, O Word, in heaven and on earth, can we doubt that Thou hast dominion over us also ? Can it be that power is given to Thee over the universe and not over our hearts? Yes, because, though Thou hast this power, we take it from Thee by the free will Thou hast given to us But if I could, O Word, sometimes I would grieve that I have this liberty in me, and that others have it, too, but Thou art a good God and dost everything with sovereign providence Thou sayest that power is given to Thee, and in *this* Thou showest Thyself less than the Father, and that Thou hast assumed humanity, for man by himself has no power whatever, except in so far as God gave it to him Hence, by saying that power was given to Thee, Thou showest Thyself a true man But, alas ! that men seem to have greater power than Thou, because they usurp it, taking the fame, the property, and even the life of their neighbors ! O Word, Thou sayest that power is given to Thee in heaven and on earth, and after it that Thou art merciful. Oh ! if one could fathom the great mysteries that are hidden in these words !

VI.

She Begins to Contemplate the Mysteries of the Life of Christ from the Incarnation to the Flight into Egypt.

"*Nolite multiplicari loqui sublimia gloriantes*"—"Do not multiply to speak lofty things, boasting" (1 Kings ii, 3) And I with a different meaning, but with a like spirit, if granted me by Thee, O my Spouse, shall say with a loud voice (and so could I be heard by the whole world)! Do not, O prophets, speak and raise your voices any more; do not multiply your discourses, do not go on too far as in promises made to you Let hope cease, now that we possess and see it. Do not count as great any of the things that have been done in the past ings pleasant since God lowered Himself to us Please speak no more of the performers of Egypt, of armies defeated, of seas opened, of waters springing from dry rocks, of manna raining down from heaven Other things we have to speak of "*Recedant vetera de ore vestro. quia Deus scientiarum Dominus est, Ipsi præparantur cogitationes*"—"Let old matters depart from your mouth ; for the Lord is a God of all knowledge, and to Him are thoughts prepared" (I Kings ii, 3) Yes, yes, let all your tremendous speeches cease, because it is no more *Deus ultionum*, but *Deus misericordiarum* It is for Him to prepare the thoughts , words pass through the ear, but the thoughts stop in the heart This He wants, and as in this He wants us to remain, so He wishes also the thoughts to remain which prepare for Him the place. He wants the Old Testament to go no further, except in so far as it serves for the fulfillment of the New, that the veracity of the divine promises already accomplished may be made known O Word, always the new things have pleased Thee · "*Ecce nova facio omnia*"—"Behold I make all things new" (Apoc. xxi, 5). And what thing is newer than this, that Thou, Eternal Word, hast become man, taking human flesh from the pure bosom of Mary? And this for no other reason than that *Deus scientiarum Dominus est* The sovereign plan of the Most Holy Trinity for the Divine Incarnation, reconciling justice and mercy, Thou, O Word, hast renewed in us, when Thou comest down to earth, and every hour returnest to Thy dear souls to prepare thoughts of the great love Thou hast shown us in the Incarnation Thou dost not infuse these thoughts , no, Thou dost prepare them , for Thou hast given us the free will, and desirest that we should learn them , but all come from Thee. "*Ego sum via ,*" Thou hast said O Word, how necessary it was that Thou shouldst come to prepare Thy thoughts full of mercy, for the prophets did not announce to us anything but justice, as our sins deserved. How many times does David mention Thy justice? Oh ! how true it is . "*Justus es, Domine, et rectum judicium tuum !*"—"Thou art just, O Lord, and Thy judgment is right" (Ps cxviii, 107) Now "*Deus misericordiarum Dominus*"— ' Now God is the Lord of mercy " And to this mercy Thou dost invite and call us In the bosom of the Father, I dare say, Thou preparest for us thoughts of wisdom, of purity, of truth , for to these three virtues in particular Thou invitest us when thou sayest · " *Estote perfecti, sicut Pater vester perfectus est*" (Matth. v, 48). In the bosom of the Father . . . for if this is the bosom in which Thou, Son, hast been begotten and from the Father and from Thee proceeds and is breathed the Holy Ghost, therefore will it be the primary object of our beatitude Hence it is meet that thou shouldst now by imitation prepare in us that which we must enjoy for eternity by vision in Thee, Sovereign Good. "*Tunc similes ei erimus, cum videbimus eum sicuti est*"—"(Then) we shall be like to Him, (when) we shall see Him as He is" (I John iii, 2) But we must be like unto Him in this life first, and prepare for *that* by thoughts of *wisdom*, in order not to follow after and be caught by the deceits of the world , of *purity*, in order not to be soiled by the filthiness of the senses ; and of *truth*, in order not to be taken in the nets of 'the father of lies But Thou, O Incarnate Word, goest further, preparing thoughts also in the bosom of Mary ; and these are thoughts of love, goodness, and meekness. In being born, what thought dost Thou prepare for me? Oh ! it is the thought of what I profess, and which by so few is loved and known, *poverty !* O Word, Thou takest it as a nurse, later as a sister, and finally, on the cross, as a bride, espousing it with Thy blood To me Thou first gavest the Rule which fled from so many others of the world, and Thou gavest it to me first by deed and then by words, first by examples and then by precepts ; and as to Thyself, working and teaching the rest of Thy life, Thou hast given the Rule to the whole world. Oh ! what great power and love Thou showest to me O little Infant, wanting to be silent and in need of everything Even the first voice Thou madest me hear of the Scripture joys was that of weeping, to show me my misery "*Primam vocem similem omnibus emisi plorans*"—"And the first voice which I uttered was crying, as all others do" (Wisd. vii, 3) Thou dost refuse to feed except on milk which comes as a gift from the Eternal Father, yes, "*ubere de cælo pleno* " Likewise the soul that wishes to be similar to Thee, must not feed except on the milk that comes from Thee But before the milk nourishes Thee, Thou wishest to give me nourishment by Thy example. What nourishment dost Thou give me? Reclining Thy tender limbs on the straw in the manger, and resting Thy head upon a stone, Thou givest me the nourishment—so useful and necessary—of Thy humility and poverty Mary dissembled Thy greatness , she acknowledged it in her heart, and in her heart she adored Thee ; but outwardly she treated Thee also as her son , because by only adoring Thee, she could not have rendered those services, of which, humanly speaking, Thou stoodest in need Taking the milk, Thou showest me Thy great love, in making Thyself needful of nourishment—Thou who nourishest the universe . O Word, Thou art but eight days old, and Thou givest me Thy blood , and what thought dost Thou prepare for me, by the Blood? of that other virtue, which is also my profession, obedience ! Three things Thou showest me in Thy circumcision—obedience to God, meekness with Mary, justice with us Then Thou didst go to the Temple, where she offered Thee—she who had not one like herself before her, neither had she have one after her , she, who by the mouth of Wisdom was called by Thy Father so beautiful and handsome ; the one who in all Thy works was always with Thee, or in Thy mind before Thou didst create the world, and for Whom, as the noblest of all creatures, Thou hast made the world After she was born, she was always with Thee, being holy and very far from every stain of sin ; and after she conceived Thee in her virginal womb she was always with Thee, adoring Thee as God, and loving and serving Thee as the Son of God ; neither did her mind and heart ever withdraw from Thee and Thy divine will, she even going so far as to offer Thee in sacrifice, in order to conform to Thy Eternal Father's will

And here, O my Lord, Thou didst describe also to me the reverence I owe to the Law, first to the Ten Commandments and then to the Rule of my Religion ; so that I must see that it may not have to complain about me and repeat what Jeremias, the prophet, says of the synagogue: *"Ego te plantari, vinea electa , quomodo conversa es mihi in amaritudinem ?"*—"I planted Thee, a chosen vineyard, all true seed , how, then, art Thou turned unto me into bitterness ?" (Jerem 11, 21). Alas ! the rule turns into bitterness, when one does not live up to it , and we cause bitterness to *it*, when we do not fulfill the obligations *it* imposes upon us, and so easily break the ordinances which, after all, are God's Oh ! how well might the Rule repeat what Thou hast said, O Word : *" Non vos Me elegistis, sed ego elegi vos "*—"You have not chosen Me ; but I have chosen you" (John xv, 16) It is true, yes in a sense, that I have chosen the Rule ; for voluntarily to it, and not to another, I did submit myself, but it is also true that the Rule has chosen me, because on my part I did nothing but arise and consent to the call which the Word gave me to this place, and not to another, to this Rule and not a different one The Rule, already existing before me, chose me, accepted me, revered me, and told me : *" Hoc fac et vives "*—"This do, and thou shalt live " (Luke x, 28) In this manner Thy Spouse, Jesus, wishes to be served by Thee. Beware (moreover says the Rule) that Thou shalt not offend me, breaking me, without offending at the same time Him Who called Thee to this Rule and commanded Thee to obey it The superioress, who is the *Rule animated*, is not by any of us chosen, except in the hope of good results What tree does not in the beginning give sign of becoming fruitful ? O holy desires, O blessed fervors of novitiate, how useful you are, and how much more so you would be if you would continue to be always alive and fervent ! The soul would increase from virtue to virtue, until *" Videretur Deus Deorum in Sion "*—"till the God of gods would be seen in Sion " (Ps. lxxxiii, 8) In this life, in the Sion of peace and interior tranquillity of conscience, which would be in charity and meekness with all, in modesty, and in every action of ours being peaceful and composed Thence from peace to peace, from present to future, from the transitory to the eternal, one would pass into the celestial Sion, a copy of which, O Lord, the dwelling of Thy beloved brides should be Oh ! how many loving thoughts this Eternal Word prepares for us *" Usque ad consummationem sæculi ! "*—"To the consummation of the world " (Matth xxviii, 20)—So they will pass from generation to generation in this our monastery, as I hope and trust in the mercy of Him who chose them for Himself

VII.

From the Flight into Egypt to the Baptism of Christ.

Thou didst flee into Egypt by Thy own will, O my Jesus , and I can say that Thou didst flee another time, when Thou didst leave the bosom of the Father, to come down into this world, which is a dark Egypt, Thou dost flee also into another Egypt, viz , into the souls that receive Thee in the Sacrament of the Altar, of whom many are an Egypt of idolatry, because they are grievously given to the concupiscence of the eyes, of the flesh, of avarice, or the pride of life , which all cause idolatry What stupendous effects are wrought by Thee ! Thou ascendest into the clouds white and light, viz , into those white sacramental species, and entering into the Egypt of the souls, behold, *"Movebuntur omnia simulacra Ægypti "*—"All the idols of Egypt shall be moved" (Isa. xix, 1). All bad habits and all perverse desires of yore fall to the ground in Thy presence, by Thy grace, from those who worthily receive Thee Instead of the many idols adored by her sins that poor soul builds up so many altars in each of her faculties, whereby she adores Thee In her will, only wishing to serve Thee and follow Thy will ; in the intellect, only aspiring to those thoughts which are pleasing to Thee , in the memory, remembering her faults to detest and punish them, and Thy benefits to be grateful for them But different are the effects and the operations that are wrought by Thee, according to the dispositions of those who receive Thee A great desire is followed by great gifts, and a great love by great delight Sometimes Thy mercy overcomes our negligence, granting us consolations, even when we are not apt to receive the fullness of the graces of Thy Sacrament O my God all good and all sweet ! O Word, *"quam magna multitudo* ⸱⸱⸱⸱ *tuæ* ⸱⸱ ⸱⸱ *quæ* ⸱⸱ ⸱⸱ *timentibus te !"*—"O how great is the multitude of Thy sweetness O L—— w————— that hidden for them that fear Thee " Ps xxx, 20 On the w——— t——— w th such a fire, either is not alive, or has no sense I write what am I ? . .

Thou hast fled from Herod to save Thy Humanity. In the day of judgment, when Thou shalt say "*Ite, maledicti, in ignem æternum*"—"Depart from me, you cursed, into everlasting fire" (Matt xxv. 45). Herod will want to fly, with the rest of the wicked like himself, the rigor of Thy Humanity and Divinity, but in vain . . . In Thy flight into Egypt, O my Spouse, Thou dost dictate to me thoughts of prudence and love Of love, because of the affection Thy foster-father Joseph bore Thee, enduring the trial of that journey Of prudence, because that—not being yet the time for Thy Humanity to be cut off by the sword—Thou didst withdraw, preserving Thyself for greater pains and our greater advantage Thou didst remain in Egypt seven years, but I do not know what Thy operations were there, except that Thou didst overthrow many idols, and didst prepare for me thoughts of Thy power. But I dare to say Why didst Thou not prepare for us, also, the words which are so efficacious? Ah! I understand Thee; Thy answer is in my heart—because we ourselves were too quick in preparing the words to our disadvantage; for ordinarily we utter them without premeditation. Thou hast furnished us the thoughts, that when we utter the words we may be more considerate, and that the expressions may be more efficacious "*Vir linguosus non dirigetur in terra*"—"A man full of tongue shall not be established in the earth" (Ps. cxxxix, 12). Oh! how true it is! I conceive many thoughts, but because there is not previous efficacy of reflection and affection, they amount to nothing and perish, not having well taken root in the heart If the thought was well considered, it would have stability and firmness, and would not be thrown to the ground by any light wind, as it befell unhappy Eve, our first mother, who conceived the thought, and spoke, but did not reflect This many do, especially among those of our sex, who utter words without considering them. Eve conceived in her mind to invite her consort to eat the fruit, but she did not reflect The contrary was done by Mary, who first considered when the Fruit of life was offered to her: "*Benedictus fructus ventris tui;*"—"Blessed is the fruit of thy womb (Luke 1, 42)—"*Cogitabat qualis esset ista salutatio*"—"She thought with herself what manner of salutation this should be" (Luke 1, 29) And afterwards she uttered the word. . .

Then, O Word, Thou departest from Egypt, suggesting to us thoughts of honor towards Thy Father by returning to the place destined for His glorification, by the complete sacrifice of Thyself Nothing should keep us from following the will of God, especially in things appertaining to His honor, threats and dangers are nothing, provided His divine will is accomplished; then let the world do as it will But on our part we must avoid the occasions of scandal, for this is the meaning of going to Nazareth Very praiseworthy is prudence, which accompanies the spirit to do the will of God, not the will of the flesh, which separates from God "*Prudentia carnis inimica est Deo*"—"The wisdom of the flesh is an enemy to God" (Rom viii, 7). . . .

Then Thou goest in the company of thy dear Mother to the Temple, and dost arrange so as to remain therein to dispute with the doctors O my young Jesus, O my grateful Spouse· "*Speciosus forma præ filiis hominum*"—"Beautiful above the sons of men" (Ps xliv, 3) It seems to me that I see that beautiful face of thine, so meek at that age, and grave, and venerable Afterwards Thou didst prepare for us new thoughts of providence, of wisdom and of counsel, when Thou didst answer Thy Mother "And why did you seek Me? Did you not know that I must be about my Father's business?" Then, O Divine Word, Thou didst begin to divide Thy attention between Thy heavenly kingdom and the questions put to Thee by the doctors, and addressedst Thyself to them at once in a gentle and heroic spirit But how is this, O my Jesus? Thou Who hast made Thyself so humble and abject as to liken Thyself to a worm, for our sake, wouldst manifest Thyself, now, to the doctors, people esteemed by the world; in the Temple, the most celebrated place, and on the occasion of the Pasch, as I believe, viz, when there was the greatest concourse of people . But I know and understand that Thou didst do it for my example, so that I might learn to know what Thou wouldst of me and of everyone that loveth Thee Thou dost not wish, O my Lord, that we shall bury the talents which Thou hast given to us, but rather that we shall use them with noble pride, to humble the proud for Thy greater glorification

Then Thou returnest home and lendest Thyself to Joseph in the trade of a carpenter; Thou, Who out of nothing hast built the universe! Who can say how Thou didst stay recollected in Thyself, hidden from the eyes of men, and humble in Thy obedience? At the time fixed by the Eternal Father, Thou makest Thyself manifest to the world; whereby Thou gavest me the example of what I should do, viz, to seek, as far as I am concerned, silence, retirement, and to remain hidden, because, oh! how well retirement and humility join together! And when it is pleasing to Thy will that I shall come forth and show myself to others, or better still that I shall manifest Thee in myself to others, I shall do it courageously in Thee, without fear of making known, when Thou shalt order it, Thy gifts—Thou Who gavest them to me and orderest me to manifest them, wilt know how and wilt be willing to defend me from vainglory, pride, and all' other evils to which on account of such a manifestation I might be tempted.

VIII

Of the Baptism of Christ, and of His Sending His Apostles to Preach.

The Blessed Christ goes to His servant John on the shores of the Jordan, and there begins between them that heroic contrast which should move each one of us to sadness, joy, and amazement at the same time. To sadness, for our confusion, to joy, for the acts of Christ and John, and to amazement, for the example which we can take from them   John withdraws and trembles, and Christ goes forward and comforts him   John acknowledges Christ God and man, and Christ holds John as His dear and beloved friend   John follows Christ and goes before Him   He would like to withdraw and cannot   How wilt thou be able, O John, to raise thy hand over Him Who has built the universe? How wilt thou take the water and pour it over Him Who is an immense and never-failing ocean of all the graces? How wilt thou stretch thy hands over that Head, wherein are placed all the treasures of the Divinity? But Thy power and Thy will, O blessed Jesus, overcome the humble resistance of John. He baptizes Thee, and, in this act, Thou preparest for us thoughts of love, of purity, and of humility   Of love, as by the words of the Eternal Father: "*Hic est Filius meus dilectus, in quo mihi bene complacui, Ipsum audite*"—"This is My most beloved Son, in whom I am well pleased, hear ye him" (Mark ix, 6), we are made to see for how strong a reason Thou must be the object of the love and complacency of our own hearts, too   Thou, O Word Incarnate, hast prepared for us thoughts of humility by submitting Thyself to John, wishing to humble Thyself as if Thou wert a sinner and needed to be purified and cleansed by such a baptism, Thou, Who receivest the sinners and infusest into their hearts the grace of repentance and grantest them forgiveness   Finally, by receiving baptism, Thou preparest for us thoughts of purity, as Thou seemest to cry out loud by Thy example   "*Lavamini, mundi estote, auferte malum cogitationum vestrarum*"—"Wash yourselves, be clean, take away the evil of your devices from my eyes" (Isa i, 16)   Oh! how necessary it is to plunge often into the waters of repentance, to acquire the purity which Thou demandest of us. Purity of body is not sufficient, there must be purity of mind and heart; and he who does not often wash himself in this baptism will not be able to preserve it long, as the purity of the heart, though a gift of Thine, cannot be preserved intact, unless by many efforts of our own. So Thou hast ordained   . .   Thou, O Word Incarnate, hadst to dwell in the desert, praying and glorifying, and for me praying to Thy Eternal Father—praying that Thy creatures already born in the world might be converted, and that we, who were in Thy mind already born for Thee before Whom all is present, might perfectly praise and love Thee   Whilst dwelling in the desert I cannot think that Thou dost perform any other work but this, viz, praying for us to Thy Father in the sublimity of Thy love and the depth of Thy mercy and compassion. But, when Thou dost permit Thyself to be tempted by the devil, Thou who hadst come to crush, overawe, and conquer him, O Infinite Goodness! .   Satan tempted Thee, and Thou wast God! And he was not satisfied to tempt Thee once only, but three times he attempted it, as if to destroy the adoration of the Most Holy Trinity   I do not believe that he took Thee for the Son of the living God   I do not believe he penetrated so high a mystery, because, if he had, he would not have dared to attempt what he did   Neither do I believe—nay, I know that, in that conflict, Thou wast not pained as we are during the time of temptation; because, being God and man at the same time, the darkness of hell cannot reach the splendor of that light which "*est candor lucis æternæ*"—"is the brightness of eternal light" (Wisd vii, 26)   I imagine, though, that as a man Thou must have suffered great pain, on account of the love Thou bearest Thy Father, when Thou didst hear Satan saying to Thee   "*Hæc omnia tibi dabo, si cadens adoraveris me*"—"All these will I give Thee, if falling down Thou wilt adore me" (Matth iv, 9)   O impudent Satan! Horrible blasphemy! I believe thine ears could hear it without horror   But, "*Non est sapientia, non est prudentia . . . contra Dominum*"—"There is no wisdom, there is no prudence . . . against the Lord" (Prov. xxi, 30)   Thou didst believe, O spiteful one, that thou hadst to deal with a mere man, and thou wast deceived   Thou didst try to find out whether He was a true God, and thou didst fail   O greatness of my God! All that Thou dost allow of temptation in us to Thy glory, all redounds to our profit, and Thou dost so act that if we only remembered Thy goodness when tempted, this would amply suffice us to overcome every temptation   O Word, by Thy divine language Thou dost confound the demon, who departs in confusion, knowing not whom or what Thou art   I speak not of Thy lofty, mellifluous, and salutary sermons, for what Thou didst say, and the thoughts Thou didst prepare, the Gospel narrates to me, but what thoughts didst Thou prepare for me whilst in the desert   except those of constancy, of faith in Thee, true and living God, and in how little estimation we must hold the devil?

All The sacred miracles cause me to think but the acts of the power, of Thy greatness, and of Thy love   Who would not be moved and   seeing by how many inscrutable and deep ways Thou art trying to draw this soul to Thee! "*Sicut aquila provocans ad volandum pullos suos*"—"As the eagle enticing her young to fly" (Deut xxxii, 11). Now, like a deer, it is necessary to jump over hills and mountains, and I must stop to consider the greatness of Thy love. Thousands upon thousands of years I would need, were I to go over, point by point, all the thoughts Thou didst prepare for us by casting the people from the Temple, by speaking with the woman of Samaria, by granting the prayer of the woman of Canaan, by forgiving Magdalen, and absolving the adulteress. But I must pass over these things, remembering them in my mind and musing over them with the swiftness of an eagle.

Now the Eternal Word, Who always *does new things*, wants to do something worthy of Himself. He calls His twelve Apostles and sends them to preach, giving them the model of all they have to do. Likewise does He with His Brides, but not all understand Him aright. He tells them (the Apostles) they should not take anything for the journey— no scrip, no bread, nor two coats, nor a purse, and that from those who should not receive them they should depart, shaking off the dust from their feet. He gives them the same power and the same orders to cast out the devils, to heal the sick, and do many other things. He chooses them by interior drawing and by external voice. The same thing He does with His Brides, calling them, so that they may know the offenses they have committed, as to know them is to remedy them. He gives them the power to heal all the sick, to cast out devils, and to resuscitate the dead. How must they cure the sick? By means of the power of Thy Word, which heals, O Word, all the ailments of the soul. It heals the fever of pride, when it says that he who does not humble himself shall not enter the kingdom of heaven. It heals vainglory, by saying that without Him one can do nothing. It heals the reprobate feeling of insubordination with that salutary medicine He gave out when He said: "I did not come to do My own will, but the will of My Father that sent Me." And, again: "*Non mea voluntas, sed tua fiat*." "*Factus obediens usque ad mortem*"—"Not My will, but Thine, be done" "Made obedient even unto death" (Luke xxii, 42; Phil ii, 8). It heals the continuous fever which soon leads to death, viz, avarice, by the words and by the example: "*Filius hominis non habet ubi caput suum reclinet*"—"The Son of Man hath not where to lay His head" (Luke ix, 58). It also heals accidental diseases by those words. "*Quidquid petieritis Patrem in nomine meo dabit vobis*"—"If you ask the Father anything in My name, He will give it you" (John xvi, 23). And what are these accidental ailments? The several passions of the soul, which are conquered and overcome by means of prayer made with faith and confidence. The devils are cast out by the cross, by fasting, by prayer, and, above all, by humility, for Thou, O Word, hast said to Thy good servant Anthony, that no one can escape the many snares of the infernal enemy, except the humble one. Life is restored to the dead by the Blood of the Only Begotten Word, for, by offering It, and infusing It in a certain manner through Him into His creatures, by such an influx He raises the dead soul to His grace and reunites her to her Creator, giving her new life. He says and commands that His disciples shall go without carrying a staff, viz, self-defense, so that if they are struck on the right cheek they shall offer the left one. They must not carry provisions, nor two sets of vestments, viz, we should not load ourselves with temporal provisions, but, free from all care and affection for these perishable things, we should put all our trust in Thee, O Lord, Who clothest the birds with feathers, the wild beasts with hair, and even the lilies of the field with those bright colors, so that even Solomon in the greatest pomp of his wealth could not equal them in beauty and ornamentation. Neither dost Thou want them to have vestments, as Thou takest Thy delight in their having the vestment of innocence which Thou hast given them. If they wish to put on another one besides, Thou dost grant it to them, provided it is charity. Oh! what ornaments, oh, what riches! '*Circumdata varietate*' At any rate, there must be but one intention—one end only. Every work must begin in Thee, and be completed by Thee, Who art the Truth. But oh! how few understand this Truth! It seems as if everyone shuts his ears to it, and on the contrary opens them to falsehood. Well did that servant of Thine understand the Truth, who was sanctified in His mother's womb, because for the Truth He laid down His life. Finally, Thou wishest us to have but one vestment, which is the knowledge of Thee and Thy goodness, stopping not in anything created, nor in riches, nor in beauty, nor in strength, nor in pleasures, nor in creatures, nor in anything which is outside of Thee, but wishing only the salvation of all creatures in Thee, and by Thee, which is the most perfect charity. Thou dost not want them to carry either purse or money, or other transitory things, because they are too much opposed to Thee, and he greatly deceives himself who wants to mix them up with the things divine. Instead of earthly things, Thou wishest to give us the gifts of the Spirit, and the kingdom of heaven, which Thou sayest suffers violence, and, therefore, a constant violence to ourselves is necessary in order to acquire it. Thou dost not wish that purse or money should be carried; because Thy Apostle says that there is no proportion between the sufferings of this world, which by you are thought so much of, and the future glory. So much less should we think of the treasures of this world, which Thou so much despisest and which obstruct the road to heaven. These are not for those souls who wish to run to Thee, nay, they are an impediment, as Thou dost not want anyone to come to Thee in their company. Our soul should be so filled up with Thy wealth, as not to leave in it any space whatever for transitory things, either in the heart or in the understanding, or in the memory, or in the will Everything must be filled with Thee, and intent in holding Thee, Who art He that makes rich anyone who approaches Thee. And the more lightly dressed one is, the better is he apt to run. But woe to them who possess these transitory things, woe to the rich in affection, who will be cursed by God, the angels, the saints, and scorned by the world and by hell !

The Divine Word says also to His disciples, that they must stay in all those places which receive them ; and, in another place, He says that if they are persecuted in a city, they should fly to another one. So much Thou, O Word, dost for the soul, that Thou wishest to render her equal by participation, to Thee, Who art unchangeable . *"Ego Dominus, et non mutor"*—"I am the Lord, and I change not" (Mal. iii, 6) Thou wantest her to fly, because she must not remain nor rest where she does not find Thee, lest she lose Thee Thou wishest Thy disciples to remain in all the houses they enter, likewise must the soul do ; remaining firm and stable in all the virtues, being founded on Thee, the Living Stone Woe to him who does not consolidate himself in virtue, and builds instead like the house badly reared on the sand, because the winds will come, and he will shake and fall, causing to others, with his own ruin, great havoc and damage Oh ! what great harm the fall of a person, once regarded as a servant of God and spiritual, causes. And one must really strengthen himself, otherwise he will fall from precipice to precipice, from bad to worse, from worse to worst . Thou dost command, also, that when they are not received in certain dwellings they should shake the dust off their feet O divine words, wherein so many mysteries are hidden ! They must shake the dust off their feet ! Ah ! let all those tremble who fear Thee not, O great God, because Thou dost not want anything of them, not even the dust which fastens itself to the feet. But on the contrary Thou dost number, weigh, and measure the least act and thought of Thine elect , as this is what is meant by numbering the hairs of their heads *"Nam et capilli capitis vestri omnes numerati sunt"*—"For the very hairs of your head are numbered" (Matt x, 30). So that it may be asserted that with the elect everything cooperates for good, and with the former everything turns into evil, on account of their depraved will. Thou dost despise even the dust, viz , what is left of them, and what can be seen with the eyes , because they often give away what is superfluous to themselves, and which, generally speaking, is good for nothing, as the dust is , and afterwards they boast, it seeming to them as if they had wrought great things for Thy love. Such ones Thou dost despise, as Thou wishest that what is done for Thy love should be of *some value* and *secret* Hence, those who fear Thee give much, and of what they have acquired with labor To them it seems as if they gave nothing, and they would not like the creatures to see it, but Thou alone, Who art the Rewarder of all good works. . . Thou dost wish us to shake the dust off the feet, because, as we have to learn the path of virtue, and the manner of serving Thee, Thou dost wish us to go and learn from people that are experienced in these virtues, and not from those who boast of having them, but in reality have them not These do not know them, and yet wish to teach others, that they may appear to have a desire to honor Thee, whilst it is they themselves who aspire to be honored Thou dost not wish us to approach these to be instructed, but rather wishest that we should leave even the dust of their words

IX.

Of the Institution of the Blessed Sacrament

Behold, now we have come to the excess of Thy love, the most sure token of Thy love, the most extensive and certain token of Thy affection towards us , to that institution which forms the object of Thy delights, and the motive of all our consolations and hopes One should have John's purity to be able to contemplate the greatness of the treasures and the innumerable meditations Thou hast prepared for us by instituting the Sacrament of Thy Most Holy Body and Blood Thou alone hast been the worker , and nothing else had anything to do with it but love, which made Thee leave Thyself and remain with us *usque ad consummationem sæculi*, telling us also to always commemorate Thy Passion For which gifts, I would say, we are more indebted to Thee than for that of creation itself How is it possible to find anything more sublime and profitable than the Eucharistic union ? Oh ! what a colloquy of love is entered into with Thee by the soul almost deified by union with Thee ! Who can explain the feelings of a soul who, having received Thee, corresponds to Thy voices and inspirations? Oh ! happy the soul, though oppressed by all the passions and torments of the world, who receives her compassionate and r Consoler ! O firm charity of our g o l f, s ! W at graces and treasures can t e Eterna Father r use us se ng with m rs H, O e P gotten Son, His Beloved, Who is the only object of His complacency ? The Etern al Father would not now permit the just to exclaim, as those of the Old Testament *"Rorate cœli desuper et nubes pluant justum"*—"Drop down dew, ye heavens, from above, and let the clouds rain on the just" (Isaiah xliv, 8), and the like, since at present we have the Word, Who said that we can get all we want by asking rightly and with confidence in His name, for He Himself became for us the Way and the easiest Ladder by which we might ascend to the possession of all treasures and graces Happy will I be, if I shall know how to make use of this Ladder, and walk in this Way His Humanity is that little cloud which raises us to Him like dew, to lay us down in the Father's bosom, which is an infinite ocean of graces and riches As the waters falling into the sea lose their former nature and name, so what happens to us entering this sea, which is God? *"Ego dixi Dii estis"*—"I have said you are gods" (Ps lxxxi, 6), *"Qui adhæret Domino, unus spiritus fit cum illo"*—"But he who is joined to the Lord, is one spirit" (i Cor. vi, 17) . . Moreover, in the union with this Most Holy Sacrament the Bridegroom comes to us, sups with us, *sets in order charity in us* (Cant ii, 4), and many pure and chaste embraces take place, which can be offered up in union with the most intimate ones of the Three Divine Persons in the unity of the essence of the Most Holy Trinity, of which they are like an image and a symbol. Oh ! what sweet embraces ours are, which we make in the complacency of the Three Divine Persons ? And oh ! what divine embraces and bonds are those which are all unity and identity of substance, being, perfection, nature, and attributes Oh ! what a grand thing ! *"Collocavit me in osculo oris sui"*—"He placed me in the kiss of His mouth" (Cant i, 1) But I say again, it is better to rest our thoughts on this excess of divine love in the Eucharistic Banquet, than speak words about it, which will always remain inadequate to express it

X.

Of the Leave-Taking of Christ, the Saviour, from His Holy Mother.

Behold, Abraham's faithful servant going to look for a bride for Isaac. As he finds her at the fount, she gives him to drink This is my Spouse, Who can be called the Servant of the Father, as it was the form of a servant which He acquired in the Humanity And what does He seek ? He seeks to give all mankind to His Eternal Father, like children whom He will adopt by grace, they being sons and servants by nature The bride He is looking for is Mary, who by her consent to the Passion of her Son will cooperate with this spiritual generation Mary gave Him to drink by her conformity to the Divine Will that the Word should suffer Oh ! what a sweet fount this was, which assuaged at that point the anguish of the Passion of the Son Behold the union of the Sun and the Moon, in order to make the Moon more resplendent in that night—so dark—of the Passion. The Word treats to-day of three excesses in Mary · 1st, of love ; 2d, of suffering ; 3d, of the capacity for celestial things Three loves made Thee speak, O good Jesus, of this excess of the Passion to Mary The first was the love Thou didst bear for her, and her Immaculate Conception and sanctity The second was Thy love for Thy Eternal Father, in submitting to His decrees The third was the love Thou didst bear for the angels, whose empty seats Thou didst want to fill, opening by Thy Blood the gates of heaven, that the souls of the just might enter there and fill them

Mary had three sorrows She conformed herself to Thy will, O Word, but she suffered first that grief which was to overflow in Thy Humanity, when Thou didst say *"Spiritus quidem promptus est, caro autem infirma"*—"The spirit indeed is willing, but the flesh is weak" (Mark xiv, 38). Her second grief was on account of the knowledge she had of the greatness of Thy Divinity, which would have withdrawn a little of her support to Thy Humanity, on account of love—to suffer more for the creature Her third grief was a feeling of compassion for the Apostles, Mary Magdalen, and all mankind, and that Humanity, too, Thou hast taken from her, and in order to take from her or diminish somewhat this grief, Thou didst grant her distinctly to feel the effects of Thy death and the glory of Thy resurrection, with all those great events which can never be related But with all this, alas ! Thou hast granted to Mary a very great grief What wast Thou doing, O Mary, when Thou didst wish to proceed in Thy requests? Among the first things Thou didst treat with Mary, I imagine, O Word, was the most tender charity which Thou didst bear to all mankind How many were to be without this charity of Thine, not availing themselves of the price of Thy Blood, which Thou wast to shed for them a few hours later, and which was of so much value that with it Paradise could be purchased for numberless persons ! The complacency of the Divinity and Humanity made a bond, and bound all mankind to the Most Holy Trinity, and all this Thou hast made known to Mary. When Thou didst manifest Thy Being, which is nothing but love and charity, oh ! may it be permitted me to say it, Thou couldst not find a more fitting receptacle than Mary in whom to transfuse the liquor which was in Thy soul, viz , the affection of Thy most ardent charity It was not convenient that Thou shouldst manifest it to the angels before manifesting it to Mary, because, though they burn with love and are flames of fire, nevertheless, their charity cannot be compared to that of Mary, and also because it was principally to be made known to men, for whom Thou wast to die . . Thou didst not condole with Thy Heavenly Father, but with Thy Mother, who is inferior to Thee, as, not wishing for any consolation, the cross and sorrow Thou didst read in her soul were rather a new torment to Thee, and another cross. Neither was this a condolence, but a narration of Thy sufferings and of the benefits that would accrue from them to us, who would be almost deified by the garment of Thy Blood, hiding our sins, that Thy Eternal Father might see in us nothing but Thy merit .

Proceeding in Thy colloquy, O Spouse of mine, I imagine Thou wast making known to her how Thy scourges, and thorns and nails were to obtain for the souls that beatific vision, fruition, and communication of the glory which is given to the blessed ones by the Most Holy Trinity. What this imports cannot be understood, and is not given to know If by an impossible supposition every other delight had failed to make the blessed ones in heaven happy, to make the angels rejoice, and to satisfy Thy Father, humanly speaking, Thou gavest Mary the knowledge of the happiness which Thy Humanity was to cause to the Eternal Father, the angels, and the blessed souls, and of the contentment that Humanity would give them, which, after the Divinity, was to form the object of the everlasting beatitude. But, reflecting always on what Thou wast suffering at the present time, the heart of Mary was pining away and distilling tears of love I could never be satiated with contemplating that colloquy of the capacity of the height of heaven Thou wast to lay open to Mary, the Beloved, whom the Virgins, her followers, and also followers of Thy Humanity, would receive when, in heaven, they would have followed Thee, Lamb Incarnate, and on earth they would have been inebriated and kindled with Thy Blood, and this delight would have been of some alleviation to Thy Passion. . . . What shall I say of Thy Sacred Wounds? They must have been similar to that rainbow which God gave Noah to see, as a guarantee that He would never again send the waters of the Deluge upon the earth, and such will be Thy Wounds, O Word, between the Eternal Father and mankind, that not only they will obtain mercy for our sins, but they will also cause God to be no longer called a God of vengeance, but a God of mercy and love Oh! what a joy must have been that of Mary at seeing that the Blood which the Word had taken from her was to be the stole of all the elect!

But let us come down to what is more proportionate to our understanding, viz, the narration Thou hadst to make to her of every act and smallest suffering Thy Holy Humanity was to endure. The sight of Thy Humanity, so delicate and so beautiful, having to suffer so much and to die amid so many torments, aroused in Mary great compassion Every word of suffering Thou didst speak to her was like a sword passing through her heart; let, then, love cease Thy faculties, O Mary, were like three channels which sent to the heart of the Son those loving words Thy heart was filled with sorrow because of thy compassion for thy Son, hence from thy mouth proceeded words all full of compassion. . . . The Heart of the Son, and that of the Mother, are moved to rain down tears And these ought to suffice to calm every heat and distress of our passions Ah! who amongst us will not be moved to tears, thinking that one is God and man, and the other is the most just and holy creature that ever existed, or may exist at present or in the future? And yet they have to feel passion! He, Who by a drop of His grace washes away every passion, and she, who is called the Mother of Grace .

Whither shall I see the dignity and beauty of Thy face going, O my God? and thine also, so beautiful, O holy Mary? Tears will fill thy eyes, O Virgin of sorrows, and thy face will grow pale! How wilt thou remain, O Mary? and how wilt Thou take leave O Word, from her who has begotten Thee? But love led Thee to accomplish the sublime testimony for which Thou hadst come to earth Let the Son ask the blessing of the Mother, and the Mother of the Son Thou, O Word! wilt give her that blessing which Thy Eternal Father gave to Thy Soul when He infused It into that 'little Body so well *organized* in the bosom of Mary And thou, O Mary! as He so wants and thou dost not wish to differ in anything from His Will, wilt give Him thy blessing, and in it thou wilt renew, in the name of the Eternal Father, the promise which God made to Abraham, that his seed would multiply as the stars of the firmament Oh! what an ample blessing the Son afterwards gives to His Mother, in whom Thou, O Word, infusest all the graces and gifts, and to whom Thou shalt give also all the blessings which the Eternal Father gave to the just of the Old Testament, together with that which Isaac gave to his son Jacob And thou, O Mary, what dost thou include in thy benediction? Thou includest us also, who shall be thy children regenerated by thy Son and by thee, on account of thy conformity to His Passion Thus thou shalt be doubly our Mother, and shalt give us too, thy efficacious blessing

Blindfolded, she draws the "Ecce Homo."

XI

Of the Prayer in the Garden.

My Christ goes to Mount Olivet, and what does He say? "*Tristis est anima mea usque ad mortem*"—"My soul is sorrowful, even unto death" (Matth xxvi, 38) He Who is the gladness and the joy of the blessed, is sad "*Consolationes tuæ lætificaverunt animam meam*"—"Thy comforts have given joy to my soul" (Ps xciii, 19) Oh ! if Thy consolations, or even the least drop of them, which Thou dost enjoy in infinite abundance in Thyself, give joy to the souls of others, how can there be any sadness in Thee? But Thy Divinity goes on, little by little, withdrawing the comfort of the superior from the inferior part, that Thou mayest suffer for us And how can I keep what St. Paul says, "*Gaudete in Domino semper, iterum dico gaudete*"—"Rejoice in the Lord always, again, I say, rejoice" (Phil iv, 4), if my Spouse, Who is my crown and my glory, is sad, *usque ad mortem?* But if my gladness and joy, like the glory, is not to be found in tribulations and in sadness, "*gloriamur in tribulationibus*"—"We glory in tribulations" (Rom v, 3), how can I see the verification of what the Angel said to Mary? "*Et Filius Altissimi vocabitur*, "Son of the Most High, Who, by the strength of His Word, bears and supports everything, if I now see Him fallen to the ground? "*Et procidens in terram*" And how can I see the verification of the other word, that the throne and the kingdom of David shall be given to Him, if He now says : "*Tristis est anima mea*"—"My soul is sorrowful" (Matth xxvi, 38)? Where is Thy kingdom, if Thou awaitest death? Oh ! how well do I now understand that the throne and kingdom of David, Thy father, were to be given Thee, because He had two kingdoms, one after being crowned in Jerusalem, peaceful and quiet, and this he left to Solomon The other, whilst Saul was living, which was full of troubles, during which he fled and hid in caves, and all the troubled and afflicted ones, of whom he was made chief, had recourse to him, this is the kingdom he leaves to Thee, O my Jesus, of which in Thy affliction Thou takest possession, and wilt shortly be crowned with a crown of the most piercing thorns. This kingdom was due Thee from the Son of David, because no one but Thyself would have taken it. Hence I wonder not that Thy soul is sad, but I rather wonder at what the angel says, that Thy kingdom shall not come to an end ; and yet Thou showest just now that Thou art nearing death, which is the end of all reigning . . . Yes, Thy kingdom begins with death, and by death increases, hence Thou didst liken Thyself to the grain of wheat, which grows and brings forth copious fruit, only after having died and been decayed in the ground with water Thus, by shedding Thy blood on the earth and dying, Thou didst grow and draw everything to Thyself "*Et si exaltatus fuero* (on the Holy Cross) *omnia traham ad meipsum*" (John xii, 32) This happens also in Thy members, the martyrs, who were such perfect imitators of Thy patience, and whose blood has been the seed of so many others. How can we bring forth fruit unless our passions shall have been previously well mortified, together with our desires and appetites? Alas ! the cause of bringing forth so little fruit springs from the lack of mortification in him who wants to draw souls to God . .

Thou art also the Light of the World, and now Thou sayest Thou art sad How can it be that Thou art light with sadness? But I know that by the darkness of Thy sadness Thou wantest to cast away and destroy the darkness of our sadness, and render us that gladness which the prophet asked of Thee : "*Redde mihi lætitiam salutaris tui*" (Ps 1, 14) Or else Thou wantest to render us that salutary *sadness* of true contrition and sorrow for the offenses we offer to Thee, and from *which* springs the light of true gladness Thy being troubled causes in us the same effect which Thy voice had on the sea, when, commanding the winds and the storm, there came a very great calm, likewise Thy trouble gives us perfect and tranquil peace, and we are even consoled, when we feel some trouble within us, to think that Thou didst submit for love of us to that sadness, and to even greater ones ; Thou didst wish to take upon Thyself and carry all our iniquities, viz, all the pains which, on account of our sins, *we* deserved What shall now be the love by which I may make Thee a return ? O Eternal and Divine Word, nothing can compensate for Thy love. So great are Thy sufferings that at the mere thought of them Thou dost sweat blood, and for me alone dost Thou suffer, because so great is Thy charity that what Thou dost for all, Thou wouldst do for each soul For so great a charity why shall I not be prepared to endure for Thee one thousand and a thousand more deaths? The Eternal Father sent the scourge which was due me, and Thou, my loving Spouse, didst place Thy shoulders under it, the strokes of the *Divine Anger* were raining down most justly upon us, and Thou didst lay Thyself as an anvil, between *It* and us The strong one armed with sin and iniquity, was everywhere in the world, had seized everything, and was almost in peaceful possession, but when stronger one I u he came, armed with love he was overcome and conquered not with struggle, but with pain and blood.

Ah ! if I could but embrace and kiss some of Thy sacred limbs so tortured, O loving Word , ah ! if I could but gather up some drops of Thy Blood, which are like so many rubies falling to the earth , ah ! if my *heart* were the earth receiving them, how rich and how happy would *it* be ! Ah ! pray come to me, O my Jesus, I wish for nothing but to sleep and rest in Thee ; in Thee shall I rest, but not as the Apostles, whom Thou didst reproach for being unable to watch one hour with Thee Thou art the ship taking us to the port, and this thought refreshes me and gives me peace. O happy ship, that though I sleep, takes me peaceably to the port of the greatest safety. But I must first become inebriated with this Blood, and by conformity or transformation throw myself afterwards into this ship, where, going to sleep, I shall not fear, like Jonas, to be awakened, or to be assailed by the waves. There is no storm for one resting in this ship I shall sleep placidly , and one who sleeps feels no pain, and answers not the voice of anyone shouting, unless he should shout so loud as to awaken one from sleep But I, if inebriated altogether with this Blood of the Word, shall not awaken at any voice, except the divine . . . Full of love didst Thou pray, compassionating Thy just ones and all their tribulations and pains, which they would have to endure until the end of the world By the communication of Thy afflicted Humanity Thou hast obtained that Thy elect, when persecuted and oppressed, consider it an honor, and glory in nothing but Thy cross and suffering ! Oh ! what anguish was Thine, whilst Thou didst obtain for us so many consolations Oh ! what a compassionate shuddering this must have been ; and not only compassionate, but painful ! He saw that many would not profit by His most precious Blood, and yet He wholly offered Himself in sacrifice, though still praying that the chalice might pass away from His lips Oh ! what pain ! and yet, if it had been granted to His soul and Humanity, He would have suffered all His Passion for each one in particular , and well did He suffer it, for, seeing the great multitude of sins that many thousands of persons would commit, He wanted to atone, individually, by His own sorrow, for their defection, and feel the pain that each one should feel who offends God mortally O Divine Word, who can explain Thy sorrow, and fathom the abyss of Thy love and of our ingratitude , the abyss of the charity towards us of a God Who created us, and, whilst we offend Him, sustains and benefits us ; the abyss of the pains which are prepared forever in hell for our sins, and the abyss of sorrow which we should feel, to satisfy so good a God, so unjustly offended ! He who can fathom such abysses, can also understand the painful abyss of our good Jesus, Who sets Himself to satisfy and feel sorrow, in order to obtain contrition for so many Through this, by means of Thy sacraments, we pass from *attrition* to *contrition*, and are by them justified, because Thou hast taken upon Thyself our condition Thou hast satisfied for that internal sorrow, wanting in us, by the anguish, sorrow, and contrition Thou then feltest in Thy most afflicted and sorrowful heart Oh ! if we would consider the pain we caused Thee, Eternal Word, we would rather choose hell than sin mortally. The Paternal communications and the loving looks ceased, Thy Divinity was hidden in the Paternal bosom, leaving Thee as if Thou wert a mere man, that Thou mightest suffer for us the most horrible torments I would like to possess numberless tongues, that I might curse sin, which is the cause of so much pain to my God   .   I see that Countenance growing pale, which is more beautiful than that of all the children of men I see those lights growing dark, which light up Paradise I see Him hardly able to stand, Who alone by the strength and virtue of His Word bears all this structure of the universe Thou hast suffered more pain in the garden, O my Spouse, than Daniel did in the lions' den. Thou dost lie on fresh grass, and art more burnt up by love than the three young men in the furnace. O Blessed Christ ! Thou, whilst in the garden, didst pray to the Father, Who has begotten and is always begetting Thee, being loved by Him, and yet not heard by Him But Thou hast not been heard, O my Spouse, in order that we might be heard

XII.

Of the Seizing of Our Saviour and His Being Taken to Divers Tribunals.

Behold Him Who rules the universe and holds the world in the palm of His hand, turning it at pleasure ! He is seized by a traitor My Spouse is seized ! Ah ! that I, too, might be seized with Him ! Who will follow Thee, O my Spouse ? Ah ! that I should see Thee alone ! But Thy love permits not that anyone should suffer for Thee, or with Thee, for me Alone, alone, Thou wishest to drink the bitter chalice which Thy Father offers to Thee, as alone Thou didst accept it , " *Calicem quem dedit mihi Pater, non vis ut bibam illum ?* ' —" *The chalice* which my Father hath given me, shall I not drink it ? " (John xviii, 11) We, too, are for Thee, but not with Thee neither is our Judas wanting, th ͏ ͏ ͏ traitor of our souls that is, the ͏ ͏ ͏ of love, that does exactly like ͏ ͏ is kissing an ͏ ͏ betraying I ͏ ͏ ͏ ͏ traitor, this self-love , and l ͏ ͏ ͏ ͏ ͏ conquers all O my Christ make m ͏ know it well, for it covers itself with a lamb's skin, and one needs to have eyes well enlightened by Thy grace, in order to see and discern it Who can dispel it ? The thought of Thee, O my God, and of me, miserable creature. And here my Christ left us thoughts of meekness, affability, and love, by which He is always accompanied Oh ! how beautiful He is ! See how merry and smiling He is, and how He rejoices in manifesting Himself to us He holds in one hand a banner, on which is written · "*Fortis est, ut mors, dilectio*"— "*For love is strong as death*" (Canticle viii, 6) In the other hand He holds all the instruments of His Passion, and He goes around through the universe calling with a very pleasant voice, but, while one hears Him, the other turns a deaf ear to Him He would like to hand to all some instrument of His Passion, but with so much meekness, that it causes joy and not sorrow O loving Jesus, never depart with Thy love from me !

Then the Blessed Christ goes from one to the other Pontiff, from Annas to Caiphas, from Caiphas to Pilate, from Pilate to Herod, and from Herod again to Pilate, but I wish to reduce them all to one "*Omnes adversarii congregati sunt in unum*" They are collected in one, and against One, and know not that this One is God; and yet they deemed themselves religious and servants of the people, but they did not understand the operation of the Word, Who was not known by them, because they were blinded by their ambition and malice "*Excaecavit eos malitia eorum*" (Wisd ii, 21) But He is well known by those who love Him "*Electus ex milibus*" (Canticle v, 10) . . And ah ! how many thoughts and examples Thou hast left us here, O my Christ—of love, of patience, of meekness, of humility, of silence, of truth, and of manifestation of truth, by saying what Thy kingdom is, and, consequently, who are Thy faithful subjects "*Regnum meum non est de hoc mundo*" (John xviii, 36) Thy kingdom, O loved Word, is not of this world, but whence ? Thy kingdom is eternal, and Thy throne is immortal, and beneath it the Angels adore Thee, the Dominations tremble, the Thrones become Thy footstool, the Virtues praise Thee, the Principalities invite Thee, the Cherubim and the Seraphim vie with one another to render Thee glory and honor Thy beginning cannot be described, and Thy end cannot be understood, because it is eternal "*Et regni ejus non erit finis*"—"*And of His kingdom there shall be no end*" (Luke i, 33) It is eternal, and not like those here below, which are full of miseries, calamities, and dishonors, it is full of tranquillity, contentment, and infinite joy The beauty of Thy kingdom, O Bridegroom mine, cannot be narrated There was wanting a fount to irrigate it, and behold, Thou givest existence to it by Thy Blood Oh ! what a beautiful Fount, irrigating first the earth, and then heaven ! The same is for us a torrent of salvation, of comfort, of pleasure ! O Fount inexhaustible, for all our good !

XIII.

Of the Scourging of Christ.

Afterwards Thou didst go of Thy own will to the pillar, and, to loose me, Thou didst permit Thyself to be bound ' *Funes peccatorum circumplexi sunt me* "—" *The cords of the wicked have encompassed me*" (Ps xviii, 61) "*In columna nubis loque batur ad eos*"—"*He spoke to them in the pillar of the cloud*" (Ps xcviii, 7) Much more dost Thou speak to us, O Word, in this than in that pillar of the cloud, because Thy suffering caused a great raising of Thy voice, and oh ! how easily and distinctly is Thy voice heard by those whose hearts' ears are purified ! Thou didst emit three voices, keeping silence Thy patience was one voice, which appealed to the Eternal Father, praying that all our sins might be washed away, and Thy voice was so efficacious that "*Exauditus est pro sua reverentia*"—"*He was heard for His reverence*" (Heb v, 7) And far from the just lamenting the sin, I hear also one voice saying "*O felix culpa*"—"*O happy sin !*" Thy other voice was Thy silence, and this put the seal to every fault of tongue, and especially to that of poor Eve It was Thou, too, O my Christ, Who didst want to be born from the same sex, and didst save by Mary what the first woman had unhappily ruined. . . . The greatness of the sin came to be meritorious Great prodigy of Thy goodness. . The sin became meritorious, in so far as God, to show the excess of His love, makes use of the same sin to increase our glory and communicate to us greater graces. Unable to find in the creature anything but demerit, of *this*, which is truly *hers*, He makes use to manifest His eternal pity, by forgiving and remitting sin at the cost of the life and Blood He made His Son shed for us The sin also merited punishment in a certain manner, in so far as the creature was bound to satisfy the Divine Justice, and God alone could give *It* adequate satisfaction, hence the Word became man and paid the debt of our sins The third voice, which thou didst send forth at the pillar was that of the interior joy with which Thou didst endure so many cruel scourges for me, so as to obtain for me what is read of Thy disciples "*Ibant gaudentes '* ' *And they went forth rejoicing* from the presence of the council, that they were accounted worthy to suffer reproach for the name of

Jesus " (Acts v, 41)   And this was a voice which went on interceding, I say not before
the Father only, but before the Holy Spirit, too, and obtained from Him grace that we
might be enlightened and assisted in every tribulation, temptation, and discouragement
So that, ascending Thou up to heaven, O my Incarnate Word, and sitting at the right
hand of the Father, the Holy Spirit looking on the many scourges and pains endured by
Thy *Humanity*, and the communication *It* has with Thy Divine Being, cannot refrain
from sending His grace into our souls

Seeing that we all are His members, as the Apostle also says, He sends to vivify us by
grace, a breath of life much more perfect, because it is the life of grace, some of which,
we read, has been infused into the human body formed by the Divine Hands at the
creation of the world   And if then "*Factus est homo in animam viventem*"—' And
man became a living soul" (Gen 11 7), now with *this breathing* he becomes more
perfect, and it is said "*Factus est in spiritum vivificantem*"—" Was made into a quick-
ening spirit" (1 Cor. xv, 45)   In the same place He left the lesson of exclaiming, viz ,
of prayer, of patience, of meekness, and also of love, which must always be found
there.

XIV.

Of the Crown of Thorns of the Saviour.

Thy crown of thorns will be the helmet to our heads, as we shall be able to say of
Thee , "*In capite ejus coronam de lapide pretioso*"—" Thou hast set on His head a
crown of precious stones " (Ps xx, 4)   How precious are those thorns which have
touched and pierced Thy Most Divine Head, in which are the treasures of Thy Divine
Wisdom, infinitely greater than all precious stones that can be imagined to exist in the
world   Or, *de lapide*, on account of those flaming rubies of that most pure Blood, which
falls from Thy Head, and flows from the wounds of the thorns, dropping from a hundred
pores   O rubies, more resplendent than all the stars of the firmament!   O jewels,
wherewith one can purchase heaven! . . .   This, Thy crown of thorns, placed on our head
the crown of glory which Thou hast prepared for those who love Thee   Thou dost
invite all the souls enamored of Thee to look at *It* · "*Egredimini, filiæ Sion, et videte
Sponsum in diademate, quo coronavit eum mater sua*"—" Go forth, ye daughters of
Sion, and see the *Bridegroom* in the diadem wherewith His mother crowned Him "
(Cant iii, 11), but we must rejoice principally on our account, because thereby we
acquire an eternal crown, which Thou Thyself wilt place on our heads with Thine own
hands   But, why do I stop?   I see that Thy Head is to me as a most large river, or fount,
irrigating heaven and earth—heaven with glory, earth with grace, so that the seed of
Thy Divine Word being afterwards scattered on the earth, this irrigation causes *It* to
bring forth fruit, makes the plants bud, blossom, and bring forth the desired fruits

Though the Eternal Father saw Thy Head so ill treated by us, O my Word, He did
not cease to love us; because, as in the brier bush and the thorns of old the flames
appeared, so *here* He saw the burning flame of Thy charity surrounding them   This great
distilling of Blood gathered all the good which Thou, Blessed Jesus, poured upon us
The Father poured all His treasures and sweetness into Thy Humanity, so that in
Thy discourse with us here on earth there was never found any bitterness   The Holy
Ghost, too, gathered all His goodness into Thy Humanity, O my Spouse ! and all this
sweetness, and all this honey, by virtue of Thy Blood, like streams from a most
abundant fount, came into us   There was never found any bitterness, O my most sweet
Spouse, not only in the conversation Thou hadst with the Jews, but not even in the
conversation Thy Soul held, is holding, and will hold, with Thy Divinity , because,
though Thy Soul had to suffer much, wanting to follow Thee, yet, no matter what
tribulation It may have to meet, It does not call it a pain but a comfort   "*Omnia possum
in eo qui me confortat*"—" I can do all things in Him Who strengtheneth Me "
(Phil iv, 3)   And how dost Thou comfort It, but by the power of Thy most precious
and sweet Blood? . . .

Thou dost continue to leave us a thought of love, of peace, and of self-contempt , but
this by few souls, O good Lord, is understood.   This crown then gave pain to the
Bridegroom, and yet *It* gives comfort to the Bride , and the sharper the thorns were
to pierce Thy Sacred Head, O good Jesus, the more consolation they procured for me,
Thy Bride   Not all the thorns of the crown pierced the Sacred Head of the Bridegroom ,
as some remained on the outside   These, O God, Thou hast kept for Thy elect, that
they might partake of Thy suffering, and their suffering joined to Thine might acquire
merit and value.   Of those thorns which did not pierce Thy Head, but remained outside,
Thou didst wish that some would be on the right and some on the left, that they might
fall to Thy┄┄┄
in Thy Hea┄┄┄
would have┄┄┄

Sacred Head But the thorns which pierced Thy Sacred Head made the openings through which the souls might see the treasures and the secrets of Thy Wisdom there gathered Neither is the place wanting where the souls might rest and remain in peace and quiet ; and this was the space between one thorn and the other Thou also didst want that some of the thorns should point towards heaven, for the ornament and glory of the blessed souls that were to be placed there. Though only those thorns that pierce Thy Head are fixed on Thy Bride, who must be like to Thee, nevertheless she goes on partaking of all Hence, this crown is her glory, consolation, and fruition. .

Now my own eyes, O my Jesus, are given to see Thy most beautiful and Divine Head, that in *It*, together with Thy other beloved souls, I may understand and know Thy great Goodness O beautiful and precious crown, which hast touched the hair of the Incarnate Word, which hast been wet by His blood, which hast penetrated the brains of my Jesus with so much pain and anguish ! O my Spouse, how beautiful Thou art with this crown! O Love, O Sweetness of my soul ! This crown of thorns has made in Thy Divine Head, among the other openings, six most worthy ones , and though the punctures of the thorns which pierced Thy innocent Head were without number, yet six very large ones, like caverns, could be seen there, three of which were in front, viz , one in Thy beautiful forehead, the other on the right, and the other on the left, and the other three on the back part of the Head, viz , one in the centre, and the other two on either side, surrounding Thy Divine Head like a garland

XV.

Of the Rest of the Passion.

Not so fervently did they cry out *"Benedictus qui venit in nomine Domini"*— "Blessed is he that cometh in the name of the Lord " (Matth xxi, 9), as they do now, saying *"Tolle, tolle, crucifige eum"*—"Away with Him, away with Him, crucify Him " (John xix, 15). For which words my God will be compelled to exclaim in the day of judgment *"Ite maledicti in ignem æternum"*—" Go ye cursed into everlasting fire " (Matth. xxv, 41) They are right (oh ! that they had understood it !) not to want Barabbas crucified, because his blood would have availed nothing, whilst the blood of the Lord, if they had known how to use it, would have been of infinite benefit to them Even in heaven, O my Jesus, before Thou camest to suffer for us, Thou hadst been postponed to Barabbas, because Thou, O Word, Who wast to become Incarnate for us and our sin, wast proposed before Thy justice Thou wast proposed, O Word, to the Eternal Father by the mercy which asked that man should be forgiven, and the Father granted it. Hence Thou camest to assume human nature and wast crucified for us, and thereby sin died in Thee, and thus Thou didst satisfy both justice and mercy Justice undertook the office of comparing Thee to Barabbas , love and mercy were the crowds who cried out, not *crucify*, as the Jews did, but mercy. O most happy voices of mercy ! in this you differ, that the Jews were moved by hatred to cry out *"Tolle, tolle,"* &c (*"Away with Him,"* &c), and mercy was moved only by love. The Pontiff said it was expedient that Christ should die for the people and the Eternal Father said likewise to His justice that it was expedient Thou shouldst die, O Word most innocent, to wash away the sin of man

The Eternal Word is on the road , He arrives at Mount Calvary How couldst Thou bear the weight of so big a cross had not love lent Thee assistance ? But I see a man who carries the cross with Thee—yea, Thy own cross And what is this ? It is the love Thou bearest us, whereby Thou wishest to honor us by Thy very cross, giving us a share in Thy glory , and, by accepting *this service* from us, Thou wishest to show that it is Thy desire to be obliged to love us. . . .

No sooner did He reach the summit of Calvary than He wanted to show *in act* what the Apostle relates as His own saying *"Beatius est magis dare quam accipere"*—" It is a more blessed thing to give, rather than to receive" (Acts xx, 35) He does not here sit at the well, as He did when He was tired and waited for the woman of Samaria, because He does not wish to receive any comfort, neither does He seek any drink—nay, He refuses it, as His only comfort is to suffer as much as He can for us. Or it may be said that even here He sat by the fount of His wisdom And immediately He began to give. And what ? Himself—offering Himself as a live holocaust to the Eternal Father, not for Himself, but for all His creatures Yes, He sits by the fount of His wisdom If Thou hadst not been *sitting*, my most beloved Spouse, I tell Thee Thou couldst not have endured so many and such violent torments, and especially the ignominious death of the cross , but, sitting by Thy wisdom and seeing the benefit that would accrue unto us, this cross seemed to Thee so small a thing that Thou didst count it as nothing, wishing it to be much greater Thou didst sit by the fount of wisdom, making Thyself as a fool *"Prædicamus sum Christum Crucifixum, . . . gentibus quidem stultitiam"*—" But we preach Christ crucified . . unto the Gentiles foolishness" (1 Cor. 1, 23), and, by means of this foolishness, to the eyes of the crazy world, Thou didst confound their foolish wisdom .   The Apostles had gone to look for other food, having left Thee, O loving God, and, all disconsolate, could not find any.   And as Thou wast by the fount of the cross, behold the Samaritan woman asking Thee for a drink—nay, Thou dost ask her for it, saying· "*Sitio*"—"I thirst" (John xix, 28), which is the same as to say . "*Mulier, da mihi bibere*"—"Woman, give me to drink" (John iv, 7).   Thou dost show her the fount, which is Thyself , the channels, which are Thy wounds , and the water (of which he who drinks continually shall not thirst forever), which is Thy life-giving Blood Moreover, whilst crying out that Thou art thirsty, those around Thee are laughing at Thee.   And Thou, O Word, how dost Thou pay them?   Instead of what Thou didst say to the woman, that if she had known who Thou wast, she would have asked Thee for a drink, on the cross, Thou continually repeatedst in Thy Spirit these words and prayers· "*Pater, ignosce illis*"—"Father, forgive them" (Luke xxiii, 34)   They well agreed in saying that the Jews and the Samaritans did not agree whilst rejecting Thee as their king, they protested they would recognize no other king but Cæsar, and rejected Thee as the usurper of somebody else's kingdom, saying that Thou didst not want tribute to be paid to Cæsar   But for this Thou dost not stop , Thou dost invite also the Samaritan woman to ask a drink of Thee, so that feeling in herself, too, the great virtue of Thy water, of which anyone drinking would not thirst any more, behold that an-other one would ask Thee for a drink   And what does he ask for his beverage but Thy kingdom?   "*Memento mei, Domine, dum veneris in regnum tuum*"—"Lord, remem-ber me, when Thou shalt come into Thy kingdom" (Luke xxiii, 42)   He asks Thee that he may be with Thee in Thy kingdom, and Thou dost promise him this, saying "*Hodie mecum eris in Paradiso*"—"This day shalt Thou be with Me in Paradise" (Luke xxiii, 43).   And well couldst Thou say to him, O Word, that he had not one hus-band only, but five, as he had offended God not with one only, but with all the five senses.   He was not a Samaritan by birth, but by deeds   And as the Samaritans had abandoned the law, so had he, too, because he was a thief . . He wanted to go and tell the other Samaritans, turning to his fellow-thief   He leaves the water-pot and the well, as he did not heed the voice of his companion , he did not mind nor resent his own sufferings nor anything else ; he did not ask Thee to make him come down from the cross, but simply turned to his fellow-thief, who was cursing Thee, and said that they were suffering deservedly for their crimes, and the Lord suffered unjustly .   Thou wast, O my blessed Christ, with this Samaritan woman, viz , be-tween these wicked people for two days, which were a great deal more than two days, if we consider the suffering of the three hours whilst Thou wast agonizing on the cross . . Thou didst go on preaching, not with Thy own voice—no , but by Thy will Thy creatures preached, so that the earth that trembled, the sun that was darkened, the sepulchres that opened were nothing but Thy voices, at which many became converted, and could say to the Samaritan, viz , to the thief, that they did not believe on account of his confession, but on account of the wonders which they saw "*Multi percutientes pectora sua revertebantur*"—"And the multitude returned striking their breasts" (Luke xxiii, 48).   Behold, O my Spouse, that Thou hast become unto me a fountain where I can allay my thirst ; a rivulet or river, pure and calm, where I can fly in safety, as a dove, when the infernal hawk wishes to grasp me.   Behold, my Love, that Thou hast turned Thyself into an Ark, where I may be sheltered from the waters of the Deluge in this great and tempestuous sea of the world.   Noah was in the Ark with eight souls , the paternal love was enclosed in this divinest Ark with the eight Beatitudes.   Noah sent out the dove as soon as the Deluge ceased ; when the pains and the torments of the Word ceased, He sent out the Spirit.

XVI.

Of the Resurrection of the Saviour.

The Mother of the Word, with a pale countenance, awaits the rising of her Son from the sepulchre.   Oh ! how great was thy faith, O Mary !   Turning to the right and to the left, thou wast looking to see whether thy sweet Jesus would appear all glorious.   Thou didst know He was most powerful, and that whilst someone was returning from the sepulchre in tears, to this very one He might appear alive and glorious, He being every-where.   Let therefore this strongest Lord arise soon, and confound all those armed ones who guard the sepulchre   John and Magdalen went there to find their Master; but He already triumphant had risen.   They teach us that when our Lord departs from us with His grace, as dead, with great desire we should seek Him, and with most ardent sighs penetrate to the right hand of the Father never stopping until we shall have found Him We must ll. wi·, call Him with murior voices, shooting at her so many darts continually with the bow of love , and He, a charitable wound b it the ground, will allow us to take Him.   It is then dutiful for the soul to be satisfied with its nothingness,

Interior of St. Mary Magdalen De-Pazzi's (Italian) Church, Philadelphia.

since the Eternal Word permits Himself to be moved by a sigh, or by an interior voice, when this is sent with that straight aim to the bosom of the Father or into His right side Oh ! how much more should the soul permit itself to be moved by the interior voice of the Eternal Father ! O Mary, every instant must have seemed to thee like a century, when thou wast waiting for thy Beloved Son ! Pray, then, O Word ! come to Mary, and come to me, O my Bridegroom ! Oh ! how beautiful Thou art ! . . . Thou didst wish to appear to Mary first, because she had conceived Thee, because she was Virgin, because she had kept the faith, because she had awaited Thee with the greatest desire, because she had been the humblest of all creatures, and also to give her first the participation of Thy glory Likewise, he who wishes to be visited first by Thee, O Lord, must have, like Mary, conceived Thee with anxious pain, and must afterwards have brought Thee forth by a continuous operation of his own He who wishes to ascend to the sublimity of Thy union, must have so much faith that, being almost a certainty, it ceases to be faith But when the soul proceeds to forget itself and unite itself with its Creator, it is the first to partake of His union and to be confirmed in the faith As God is excellent, infinite, immense, and inscrutably good, the more the soul believes this, the more it becomes partaker of His goodness In order to be the first one to receive the visit it is necessary to be virgin not only in body, but in mind also, so that nothing may impede the purity of the heart, and thus such a soul will be first consoled and obtain the promises of the Word The Blessed Virgin was the first to be consoled also on account of her humility, by which she drew the Word from heaven to earth , hence, humility, O Word, hastens Thy visit, as Thou canst not refrain from visiting a soul adorned with this virtue

Thy Mother was deservedly the first to be consoled, because she was also conformable to Thy will ; likewise the soul wishing to be consoled must possess this conformity of will O Soul of the Word, do return to glorify the body which is in the sepulchre ! O Most Holy Flesh, which hast received so much glory, that Thou mightest afterwards glorify us' We had to go underground, and therefore Thou, too, didst wish to remain in the earth, to be placed under the earth, in order to raise us up from the earth Most Sacred Soul, reuniting though Thou wast in the same union, Thou didst resume the Body, and didst glorify It with a *glory* which would have been in part invisible to those blessed souls in limbo, if Thou hadst not strengthened them with Thy beatific light ; because if they had seen it immediately they would have been reduced to nothing at so much light Thus dost Thou do with Thine elect, not giving them all Thy glory to taste, as they could not endure it . The Soul of the Word, united to the Divinity, is reunited to the Body, assumes It, and gives It a new name, which cannot be pronounced but by those who follow the Lamb and receive It from the Lamb The Soul of the Word takes up again its flesh and gives it a glory, glorifying and communicating, and gives it, moreover, every power in heaven and on earth The Holy Ghost is reunited to this Body (though He was always united), and gives It a light above every light, so that of said Humanity this can be said *"In lumine videbimus lumen ; oculi nostri sint semper in lumine Humanitatis verbis "*—" In Thy light we shall see light , let our eyes be always fixed in the light of the Humanity of the Word " (Ps. xxxv, 10) Yes, certainly, in Thy Humanity we see light . *"De vultu tuo video procedentem splendorem gloriæ tuæ"*—" From Thy countenance I see the splendor of Thy glory beaming forth " The Humanity of Thy Word becomes the crown of the Divinity, the ring of the virginity, the garland of the martyrs, the splendor of the apostles, the mirror of the confessors, the book of the doctors, sun and light of all creatures O Humanity, Thou art all we wish or can desire For so great a gift as Thy Humanity, who can adequately thank Thee? The thanksgiving we can offer to the Same will be ' *"Calicem salutaris accipiam et nomen Domini invocabo "*—" I will take the chalice of salvation, and I will call upon the name of the Lord " (Ps. cxv, 13)

XVII.

Of the Ascension of Christ the Saviour.

O happy gathering of yours, holy Apostles, in which thou particularly, O John, with alternate speech dost ask and understand a great deal Where Jesus is, there is paradise , it is then very meet that the angels should be in such a place where Jesus is O great multitude of happy spirits, so bright and resplendent ! Who could enumerate them? Oh ! what a great preparation they make for the Word ! Oh ! what a sweet shade ! . O Word ! what colloquy is that which Thou hast with Mary ? Thou leavest Mary separated from Thee as to the body , but Thou didst comfort her afterwards, not that she was in need of comfort, because though she was clothed in mortal flesh, yet she was in everything so confo .'. to Thy will that she would have been satisfied to remain forever on earth 1 . had so pleased Thee Thou didst comfort her that she might strengthen the will of the Apostles in attracting the Virgins. Thou didst so comfort her that now anyone looking at her is consoled in all his anxieties, tribulations, and pains, and comes out the conqueror of every temptation   Hence, let him who looks for mercy have recourse to Mary , let him who is fainting away from weakness trust to Mary, who is all pitiful, strong, and powerful   Let him who is in constant conflict turn to Mary, who is a peaceful sea , let him who is choked by the pastimes of this world, wish for Mary, who is the bitter sea , let him who is tormented by the devil invoke Mary, who is Mother of humility—as nothing chases away the devil more quickly than humility   Let, then, everyone have recourse to Mary.   Great and marvelous are the secrets confided to her by my sweet Spouse.   O Mary ! the colloquy thou hadst with thy Son when He went to suffer, was of conformity, and that after the Resurrection was of joy , but this of the Ascension, being the last, is the most glorious   But in what didst thou take delight, O Mary, in this colloquy? Was it in this, viz , that the Word was the Spouse of the Virgins, and that He had chosen the Virgins for His crown ? Yes, yes ; because thou wast Virgin, and the same Word had become so enamored of virginity, that it was just that this last delight should be of the Virgins   These are they who manifest all His power, in abandoning everything , His liberality, in abandoning their very selves , His wisdom, in abandoning their parents and others   They manifest the wealth of the Word, in leaving all created things , and they do not wish to love, neither do they wish to hear any other named, but this, their own Spouse.   Oh ! how the Word did love the virginity and honor it in Himself !   .

    When Thou didst go to the Passion, O Word, Mary was left all sorrowful , when Thou didst arise, she remained all confident , when Thou didst ascend to heaven, all admiring   Likewise the soul, Thy Bride, when Thou dost visit her with Thy tribulations, remains all sorrowful, but not impatient ; she grieves not for the pain, but that she should deserve it   In the Resurrection, Mary remained confident , and so, too, the soul remains confident on account of the grace received, being able to say   *"Omnia possum in eo qui me confortat ,"* *"Nunc cujusvis manus pugnet contra me"*—" I can do all things in Him who strengtheneth Me ," "And let any man's hand fight against Me" (Phil iv, 13 , Job xvii, 3).   Moreover, in this colloquy Thou dost confirm and strengthen the Apostles, O my Jesus, because they were destined to be the columns of Thy Church , and Thou dost exhort them with Thy presence   In Thy Passion Thou gavest them the example , in Thy Resurrection, peace ; in Thy Ascension, joy , promising them the gifts of the Holy Ghost   In Thy Passion Thou gavest them the example, to show that Thy servants and faithful lovers must give example in suffering ; as many know how to talk, but not how to act   O blessed, happy, and glorious, he who suffers for Thy love, O Word ! because it is a greater thing, I shall dare say it, to suffer for Thy love, than to possess Thee , for when we possess Thee we may lose Thee, whilst if we suffer for Thy love, Thou dost write us down in the Book of Life, which suffers no loss   In Thy Resurrection Thou gavest them peace, because no sooner wast Thou arisen, than peace was made between God and the creature   In the heart where peace is, there is paradise, because Thou art there , and this peace does not wish to offend anyone—does not speak of the neighbor, except in so far as Thy honor requires it.   The peaceful and humble heart looks up always to the union . .   In this colloquy of Thy Ascension Thou givest them joy, promising the Holy Ghost , Thou dost teach and show them the way to receive it, so that they will work wonders, and afterwards Thou dost promise them Thy Own Self, saying that Thou wilt be with them till the consummation of the world

    Mary sees the Humanity, taken from herself, formed by her most precious blood, and nourished with her milk, arrive in heaven   She sees the multitude of the angels, and the beautiful and numerous company of the holy Fathers, among whom stands particularly John the Baptist, through whom she was praised, and whom she caused to leap for joy in his mother's womb.   Mary had prophesied of the Word, but nobody penetrated the glory He possessed, so incomprehensible it was   O Eternal Word ! what did the creature do for Thee, for whom Thou hast wrought so many things, and for whose greater glory now Thou dost ascend to heaven? O Infinite Goodness ! O Love ! little known, less loved, and by few possessed ! O Love Incarnate ! O Word Humanified ! O Eternal Wisdom ! Oh our ingratitude, the cause of all evil ! O my Spouse ! now that Thou art with Thy Humanity in heaven, sitting at the right hand of the Father *"Cor mundum crea in me Deus, et spiritum rectum innova in visceribus meis "*—"Create a clean heart in me, O God, and renew a right spirit within my bowels " (Ps 1, 12).

XVIII.

Of the Descent of the Holy Ghost, of His Marvelous Effects, and of What in us Opposes Impediment to Him.

    O pure God, the Word reminded Thee, O Father, of the promise made to His Apostles, by means of His Passion, by showing to Thee His five Wounds   That of the Side was the nearest to Thee because near the Heart, the nest of ... ove, it moved

Thee most to send the Holy Ghost, and this also because *it* is opposite Thy bosom, and because, there being His divine Heart in the Side, Thou seest therein that excessive desire for the salvation of the world. If the Infallible Truth said that where the treasure is there is the heart, the treasure of the Word being the creature, there was also His Heart, and consequently Thy treasure, O Father, as the Word Himself is . . . I have seen a Guest dwelling on a high throne, and the throne was formed by a number of converging clouds, artistically arranged and fixed, surrounded by splendors, and lightly shaken by a gentle wind. On this throne rests this most noble Guest—the Holy Ghost—and, with the weight and lightness of His goodness and charity towards us, He moves swiftly to all those places which are suitable and prepared to receive Him Who can tell what He does where He is worthily received? He speaks, and yet He is silent, and, in His sovereign silence, He is heard by all. He is at one and the same time immovable and most agile, and, in His immovable mobility, He infuses Himself into all—is always quiet and always working, and, in His restfulness, He does the greatest and most wonderful things With the steps of His firm stability, He is always firm and goes always around, and, wherever He puts His foot, He fixes, preserves, and yet melts everything. By His immense, penetrating power and hearing, He hears and penetrates everything, and yet He hears nothing, and, though not hearing, yet He penetrates and hears the least thing that hearts may utter interiorly. He bends and lowers His head with a compassionate movement, and, in lowering Himself, He raises those who are low, and who, in their humility, become still lower This Guest, so noble and so gentle in every soul, never resting, rests and is always moving, though always most stable; neither does He ever so rest in the Father or the Word, nor in the blessed spirits, nor in the creatures, that He does not also communicate Himself to others by grace He does not communicate Himself so much to a creature that He would not at any time be ready to communicate Himself even more, if He would find in that creature the disposition required to communicate Himself This throne goes on surrounding the universe, filling heaven, encircling the earth as the sun does, so that this Divine Spirit is in heaven, on earth, and everywhere If Thou dost regard the beginning of Him, Who sits on said throne, Thou shalt first see the end without end of the eternity, which is the same beginning If Thou dost wish to regard the eternity of His beginning, Thou shalt see the end This Divine Spirit rests in people of a certain number, and united; but they must remain, like the Apostles, in union and prayer, and in interior fear, imperfect yet good The number of the Apostles is a perfect one, and the others also that are numbered, but these were not the only ones that received the Holy Ghost All just souls and dear to God received on that blessed day a very great increase of graces and gifts communicated by this Spirit It was a shower that poured over the whole Church—that is, over all the souls just and holy that were in the world, and each one partook of it according to its own disposition These were numbered; and, after the Apostles received the Holy Ghost, they were certainly numberless, though also counted by thousands upon thousands This Thou dost seek in the soul, in the Congregation—in a word, in the whole Church, viz, that there should be a certain number, as it was with those who received Him on that day In the soul, a number of virtues, in the Congregation, a sweet wisdom, in the Church, a number of people Thou seekest in Thy Church the number twelve These are the Religious, their heads, Thy true *christs*, the charitable preachers, the mystic religious, the mortified hermits, the contemplative anchorites, the merciful workers, the valiant fighters for the faith, the prudent princes, the obedient subjects, the just judges, and the patient pupils. Thou dost require in the soul this perfect number of twelve, because Thou wishest to find in it twelve dispositions or virtues, in order that Thou mayst be able to do Thy work in it: An intrinsic humility, a resigned will, a dull memory, a dead understanding, an indifferent affection, a charitable will, an intrinsic meekness, a persevering patience, a sincere mind, a strengthened justice, Thy love and the neighbor's, which is the fulfilling of the law.

Then Thou seekest this fixed number in every Congregation (Religious Order) First, the three vows by many emitted and by few kept, a sound doctrine, a simple and hidden life, a deep-rooted discretion, a right justice, a union untold for its closeness, a constant praise, a strong vigilance, a conspicuous wisdom, a safe solitude, a holy silence, a stable, firm, sincere, truthful, just, and holy rule From all these, viz, the soul, the Church, and the Congregation . This Divine Spirit goes on infusing His gifts and graces in every creature; but in how few He succeeds in being fully efficacious! The perverse self-love, fountain and origin of every sin, is the cause of this The world is all submerged and drowned in this self-love But woe, a thousand times woe, to that soul living in peace with this world, especially when it is covered and hidden by the cloak of piety and Religion! Oh! how I see, O Word, the creatures stained by this abominable self-love! If I go to Thy *christs*, as to the leaders, I see rooted in them exteriorly and, worse still, interiorly this self-love, and, to feed it well many go seeking—with human, nay devilish, means -not Thy benefits but those of the earth I also see Thy Brides so busy with self-love that they love more themselves and their own will than

Thee, most sweet Spouse. Self-love acts in the soul as the little worm, which, with its light and constant gnawing, goes on consuming the roots of the tree, depriving it not only of its fruits, but also of its life, making it wither I see self-love caressed by every creature more than the babe by its nurse when it is sucking her breast But who will be so strong as to remove such a stench from the creatures, and such abominable dirt from Thy souls? The Holy Ghost will do *this* at His coming down He will commence first by purifying the hearts of the creatures, so that, being purified, they will afterwards exalt in themselves the Word, Whom they had lowered by their self-love ; thus by the same word, love, one despises and exalts. .. The Holy Ghost will flow like a river of living waters, but our self-love and this, our will, will not cease to check the course and the impetuosity of His grace I see this accursed self-will and self-love fighting and equaling the strength of Thy Omnipotence, O Word, it is omnipotent to its own harm, this, our self-will and self-love, because by its dykes it can check this river (more swift and violent than the sea, or any other river) of Thy divine grace, preventing it from overflowing and reaching the soul Is it not a wonder of Thy Omnipotence that the little grain of sand on the shores checks the fury and the haughtiness of the waves, when the sea is most swollen? Who checks those waves and makes them retreat broken into themselves? The dyke of sand, or the force of Thy omnipotent hand that so wills? Small grains of dust and sand can resist the great force of the sea, because Thou dost so order, O Lord! Shall a thing so weak and light and small as our own will and self-love is, have force to resist the torrent of Thy grace, and check its course, which is so rapid as to be able, without any difficulty, if no resistance is offered it within us, to draw along with it all mankind to heaven? But, alas! resistance there is, and we experience it every day! So let us not deem the disorder of our self-love and our self-will a small thing If it appears to us as small as a grain of sand, alas, it is big beyond measure to our ruin! Neither mountains nor cliffs are needed against the sea , the sand is sufficient to check and repel the waves Mountains of enormous sins are not required, the sand of those faults which appear to be small, and are not, when opposed to God, is sufficient to arrest the course of this rapid torrent and ocean of grace

Oh! how many and many Brides of the Word, who fled from the spiritual life at the beginning of their turning their hearts to God, on account of their fatal self-love, turned back and found themselves still in a most miserable state! What checked and is still checking them? That self-love, small in appearance, yet very great in strength ; therefore *"Iterum dico vigilate"*—"I say it again · watch " Great care is necessary first to know it, then to eradicate and extirpate it, so that it may never sprout in the soul and take root therein *"Omnia in sapientia fecisti, sapientia ædificavit thronum Altissimi"*—" Thou hast done everything wisely, wisdom has built the throne of the Most High ; on which throne the Word rests " *"Et Verbum erat apud Deum"*—"And the Word was with God " With an eternal wisdom He sits on this throne, sweetly forcing, without depriving them of their liberty, the reasonable creatures who wish to receive this gift of the Holy Ghost. He knocks at everybody's door, but does it gently, and tries to make everybody disposed to receive such a gift. He goes on singing softly, in a sweet, plaintive way He continues rejoicing, weeping, seeking. . . .

Let the understanding admire, the will take notice, and the memory realize this gift of the Holy Ghost, Who infuses Himself and His gifts into the soul This Spirit proceeding from the Father and the Word, infuses Himself in a most sweet manner into the soul, and brings therein, besides His goodness, the power of the Father and the wisdom of the Son And the soul, being made so powerful and so wise, becomes capable of entertaining this worthy Guest, delighting Him, and making Him loth to depart Thus the Holy Spirit, by His descent, makes the earth like heaven, and men like angels, and by the bond of most perfect charity unites all to God He Himself gathers the scattered ones to Himself, and scatters from Himself all the gathered ones. Yes, all the scattered ones, and the despised of mankind, Thou dost gather and draw to Thyself! *"Venite ad me omnes qui laboratis et onerati estis"*—"Come to Me all you that labor and are burdened" (Matth. xi, 28)—with the load and weight of privations and contempt, because *they* are despised as most vile beasts, and deemed as nothing, and oppressed by the world. All those who are engaged and rest wholly in transitory things, placing therein their happiness and final end, are foolishly esteemed, by the world, as happy Or else they are gathered together by malice and perverse operations, united in evil doing, but divided among themselves by their wishes and appetites, and very often united by a very great discord, and divided by a most wicked union These, O Lord, Thou dost scatter and cast away from Thyself, but they persist in this miserable and most dangerous state! .

The same Spirit, like a high-flying eagle taking and assuring the souls that have received Him, brings them before the Word, and some of them He places in His sacred head, others in His sacred mouth, and others, because they are so pure and beautiful, He is pleased to place in His resplendent eyes, that is, the light of those eyes, even the pupils of those eyes, where the go on perceiving what the Word perceives, with due proportion convenient to a creature. Of these souls in particular He said. *"Qui vos tangit, tangit pupillam oculi Mei* "—" He that toucheth you, toucheth the apple of My eye" (Zach ii, 8) And when *they* are *therein*, who can touch them? The Word looks into Himself, *they* look into Him, the Word looks into the Father, and *they* too, the Word looks also into all the creatures, who afterwards become inebriated in the wine-cellar of love. The soul looks at God every time she sees Him in any object; she also looks at the creatures, but in God, and cannot see them but in God, not even in themselves, except as they proceed from God, in the same manner that our eye, which, having looked fixedly at the sun, sees everywhere, and in everything, the same luminous orb. But, does a soul look at the creatures? She looks at them every time that, by reason of charity, she aspires to their salvation, ardently wishing to see in every one of them, through grace, the living image of God. She has such a burning desire that she would, for their salvation, and that of every most low and abject person in the world, give her life a thousand times, if it were necessary, bringing them forth in her heart before God, with longing desire and most fervent sighs, like that soul, all burning with charity for her neighbor, that was wont to say and wish "*Anathema esse pro fratribus suis*," "*Filioli quos iterum parturio donec formetur Christus in vobis*"—"To be an anathema from Christ, for his brethren," "My little children, of whom I am in labor again, until Christ be formed in you" (Rom ix, 3; Galat iv, 19). And what were the pains of labor, pains so intense and so deadly? "*Quis infirmatur et ego non infirmor? Quis scandalizatur et ego non uror?*"— 'Who is weak and I am not weak? Who is scandalized and I am not on fire?'" (2 Cor xi, 29) Neither do these pains of labor last but a little while, nor does one come to the end of giving birth, for, no sooner is a soul brought forth, than one, by desire, conceives not thousands, but millions of them Because this aspiration is so great that one is not satisfied with one, or two, or three cities, but looks to the whole world, and not only to the present ones, but to the creatures to come, so great becomes, by charity, the capacity of this heart, whereby the soul brings them forth

What more? The soul sees in an instant all the things that God sees, as God Himself is present to her. O Eternal Word! O pure and great God! there is no desire adding strength, understanding, or will, that may comprehend how great is the coming of so high and noble a Being! Hence it is necessary that it should hide us in Thyself, and thus it will to a certain extent prepare a dwelling for so worthy a Guest At the coming of this Holy Spirit the countenances of the angels were bowed down, those of the holy Fathers were raised up, and by love and grace they united together in an untold manner. Thy Humanity, O Word, exalted above the hierarchies, moved also at the coming of this Spirit, to confirm the work done in the strengthening of the Apostles, and to dispose creatures to receive the faith. I see Thee, O God, Word, and Spirit, and I understand that Thou dost continue seeking out Thy creature with sovereign wisdom, with eternal goodness In fact, it seems that Thou hast no glory nor complacency whatever, except in this, Thy creature, who yet is so lowly; and this, Thy Spirit, is the fish-hook whereby Thou dost try to catch it

That heart that receives the Spirit is like the bush seen by Moses, which burned without being consumed With a sovereign purity it burns with desire that God may be honored, though one cannot see it consuming . . In the effusion of the Holy Spirit, remember, my soul, His effusion; and thou shalt never rest in thy spirit and will, but shalt relax thyself wholly in God. Sometimes this Spirit comes with such sparks and rays of splendor that He makes purity shine in the soul, and even produces a light in the body, indicative of that which is within In some creatures this light shines only interiorly, but in others interiorly and exteriorly, though not always necessarily Certain it is that this light cannot exist in the exterior, if it is not in the interior, which alone causes the Word to be pleased and take more delight in the soul in which this Holy Spirit dwells. Who can know which and how many are His influxes? They are so many that infinite is the number of channels whereby they come to us here below. Oh! if one would but wait for them! Mary still awaited the coming of the Holy Ghost so often promised, and yet she had received Him so many times, and was filled with Him. In Him she had nourished the Word, to give example to the soul, that though it has received the Holy Spirit, and by love nourishes the Word within, again it must desire Him with a loving desire Mary dwelt with the Apostles to strengthen them and encourage them to ask for Him, but I shall not believe that Mary, during those ten days she was waiting for the Holy Ghost, was deprived of His particular gifts and influxes Nay, I believe that every moment the Divine Spirit diffused Himself in her with new gifts and graces, though He did not appear exteriorly, and that in Thy new coming she received a new superabundance of divine union Mary might as well have said · "*Recogitabo omnes annos meos*"—"I will recount all my years" (Isai xxxviii, 15), not in bitterness, no, but in the joy and exaltation of all the elect, and in the relief of all that labor in journeying Even John, who had tasted whence and where he had received his Being, and whence this Spirit proceeded, waited for Him with greater desire, and received Him with more intrinsic fruit than others. though all received Him in a wonderful manner. Likewise the soul, after tasting God interiorly, more easily understands His works

Hearken, dearest Bride (she speaks here in the person of the Word), various and great are the impediments which prevent the advantages that My Spirit, breathing and bringing forth fruit everywhere, would produce in the soul of everyone Know that an impediment, for those who are far from Me, is the malice of which men have their hearts so full, that My Spirit cannot rest in them. Some others oppose the impediment of their will , others, too, that of their seeing and knowing, so that they wish to serve Me in their own way. They wish for My Spirit, certainly , but in the manner which pleases them, and when it seems best to them, thus becoming incapable of receiving Him. Others, who are nearer to Me, oppose an impediment, which does not displease Me less than the others ; and this is accursed tepidity , for it seems to them that they serve Me, and they see not that they serve themselves. And when they believe they have commenced to serve Me, then it is that they are in a most dangerous state , for, though they serve Me, they measure with the measure of their low self-knowledge what I deserve, and yet they think they serve Me properly But, they deceive themselves ; for I wish to be served without any selfishness, with sincerity and humility ; and this humility must be such as to sink the soul to the very centre of the earth. My Spirit acts as the lightning, which, coming down from on high, does not stop except at the contact of the earth. Likewise, the Spirit does not rest except in those souls which He finds in the centre of their own annihilation, passing by the haughty and proud ones.

But, O loving Word, I would like to know what I must do against all these obstacles, because, what would it avail me to have known them, if I know not the remedy?

Most beloved Bride, know that against the first impediment, which is *malice*, thou must oppose a simple intention, which cannot exist in malign hearts Thou shalt consider it all in thyself, feeling thereat an intolerable pain, and then offering said pain to Me in union with Mine Thou shalt be as the wind, which rarefies the clouds By means of this desire and pain thou shalt weaken the malice of the heart of My creatures Against self-will, thou shalt take up a dead will, so as not to wish even Myself, except in so far as it is My will And this dead will of thine, thou shalt offer up in union with the act of resignation to My Eternal Father which I made while praying in the garden , and by this means, as the watchful gardener, thou shalt somewhat uproot the bad herbs which sprout in the garden of the Church. To proud knowledge, which destroys virtue, and to the disposition to serve Me according to one's caprice, thou shalt oppose a disposition to will, understand, and know nothing according to thy preference And thou shalt offer Me this disposition in union with that desire I had that the Father should be honored ; and thus thou shalt succeed, on thy part, in softening the hearts of My creatures, which being thus softened and moved, will become anxious to receive My Spirit As to tepidity, which, by so false a judgment, makes it appear to the soul that whilst serving herself she serves Me, I tell you, daughter, that when one *knows* he is serving Me, at that very moment he ceases serving me. Hence, against this tepidity thou shalt take up the ardor of charity, which likewise thou shalt offer in union with that loving charity whereby I left to you Myself And this charity re-offered will act as fire, which, descending into their hearts, will warm up their tepidity.

XIX.

She Shows how the Blessed Virgin offered the Word Loving Obsequies to counteract the Affronts and the Pains He endured during His Passion.

When the time came, O Word, for us so happy and by Thee so much desired, in which the Eternal Father wished to send Thee to fulfill the great work of our Redemption, He made use of one of the most noble and excellent among the angelic spirits, sending him to Mary , and when the time came for Thee to do Thy Father's will that Thou shouldst give us Thy own Blood, He made use of *one* who, by imitation, was almost a diabolical spirit ; and by the same word which gave commencement to our life a commencement was given to Thy death ; both were words of salutation · "*Ave*"— "Hail " Mary asks of the angel how that can be , and the Word asks of the traitor what he came for. As soon as Mary gave her consent, Thou didst immediately become Incarnate in her bosom , and as soon as Thou didst manifest Thyself to Judas, saying   "*Ego sum* "—"I am," the soldiers seized Thee as their prey Mary kept Thee for nine months in her womb ; and in nine hours Thou didst suffer the greatest pains of Thy Passion It was necessary that Thou shouldst become incarnate in Mary by the Holy Ghost , and it was expedient that Thy Pass n s' ou'd be the work of the s e st r t Mary in spirit of charity, and the impious Jews killed with hatred and T. t an to it to the other Mary manifeste l Thee not to s out hat st to the c h s be capable of knowing Thee , and the Jews proclaimed and despised Thee as a ma t i ot and a seducer.

Mary clothed Thee with the clothing of Humanity, and they with scorn, dressing Thee with a white habit, showing, in spite of themselves, Thy innocence Mary, whilst she carried Thee in her womb, was careful not to fatigue Herself, in order not to hurt Thee; but they, scourging Thee at the column, did not mind being tired, provided they gave no rest to Thee. Mary crowned Thee with the desires and affections Thy Brides were to have in the Church, and the Jews crowned Thee with piercing thorns They put in Thy hand an empty reed, and Mary continually reminded Thee of the frailty of mankind that the Eternal Father might continue to have compassion on men. Mary veiled Thy Divinity, clothing Thee with mortal dress, and they veiled Thy resplendent face Mary, melted with pious love, looking at Thy beautiful countenance, and those wicked ones contaminated It with their filthy expectorations Mary constantly offered supplications to Thee, thus manifesting Thy power, and they reviled Thee, calling Thee a king! The earthly judge showed Thee to the creatures as a man, all abject and wounded, and Mary presented Thee to the Eternal Father all beautiful and resplendent The ministers of malignity placed the cross on Thy shoulders to cause Thee greater pain, and Mary laid on Thee all her virtues, thoughts, desires, and affections, which gave Thee so much delight The Jews raised Thee high on the cross, whereon Thy side was opened to make way to Thy Heart, and Mary with the same dart whereby she wounded the Heart of the Eternal Father, wounded Thee hanging on the cross; and Thou didst wound her. By her humility she drew Thee from the bosom of the Father, and looking at Thee hanging on the cross, and seeing Thee so afflicted and reviled and humiliated, Mary was wounded by thy profound humility Likewise, looking from the cross on Mary, standing at its foot, so sad and sorrowful and humiliated, Thou wast wounded by her inmost sorrow and humility; so that she was wounded by Thy humility, and Thou by hers While on the cross Thou dost not forget to appoint a custodian for her who had kept custody over Thee From the cross Thou didst send forth seven great voices, and whilst in Mary's bosom Thou didst not omit to make with Thy own interior voice seven petitions, which were as follows The first was, that having brought Thee forth she should lay Thee, so little and so tender, on the hard straw in the crib, for Mary never would have dared to lay Thee down in so hard a place, unless Thou first hadst requested her with Thy own inmost voice to do it The second was, that as soon as she would see Thee born she should adore Thee, and then nurse Thee at her breast, for Mary would not have dared to give Thee her milk unless Thou first hadst asked her to do it, for she well knew that Thou art He Who feeds all the creatures The third was, that she should show Thee to the shepherds and the Magi, that they might adore Thee, as Mary would not have shown Thee to them unless Thou hadst so directed her, for she would have been afraid that, not believing in Thee, they would have despised Thee, seeing Thee in so humble and abject a place The fourth was, that at the tender age of eight days she should have Thee fulfill the law by shedding Thy Blood The fifth, that she should save Thy life when the wicked Herod sought to kill Thee, so that Thou mightest live to do Thy Father's will The sixth was, that when Thou wast to perform Thy first miracle by changing water into wine at the nuptials in Cana of Galilee, she should ask Thee to do it Finally, the seventh was, that when Thou wouldst go to die, her will should be perfectly like Thine and Thy Father's, and she should willingly make an offering of Thee, for, unless Thou hadst made her understand it whilst in Her womb, she would not have had such a conformity and courage In fulfilling Thy first petition by laying Thee down in the crib, Mary showed a deep humility By putting Thee to her breast she showed Thee a pure love By making Thee known to the shepherds and the Magi she manifested a great liberality. By being willing that thou shouldst, though but a babe, shed Thy Blood, she gave a token of prompt and exact obedience. Carrying Thee into Egypt to save Thy life, she practiced great patience Begging of Thee to manifest Thyself to the world, she showed great mercy. And being satisfied that Thou shouldst suffer, she manifested a perfect conformity to Thy will.

XX

She Speaks of the Power of the Divine Word, of the Congruent Reasons of the Incarnation, and of the Divers States of God's Servants.

Thy speech, O Word, is our instruction, our rule, and the compendium of every perfection It is a nook where the soul should rest, a fixed and most solid stone on which that high and very deep edifice should be constructed, high on account of the knowledge of Thee, very deep on account of our own self-knowledge It is the food of the soul; for Thy Word, coming from Thee, is no less required that Thou mayst be with us in Thy pilgrimage than Thy own self. As a most loving Father when he wishes to go into very far countries, Thou hast provided for us Thy children, our delight, our nourishment, and our protection also Thou hast begun, even from Thy infancy, to provide for us, Thy children with Thy wise and inscrutable words, from which we derive all the good that can ever be desired. He who is contaminated by unbelief should remember that sentence "He who believes not is already judged" (John III, 18), and the other one "He that hath faith let him command the mountains, and they will obey him; and whatever he shall ask in the name of the Word it shall be given to him" (Matth xvii, 19, John xiv, 13) He who is full of hatred toward his brother should remember that "*In hoc cognoscent omnes quia discipuli mei estis, si dilectionem habueritis ad invicem*"—"By this shall all men know that you are My disciples, if you have love one for another" (John xiii, 35) And those who are tired of their labors and troubles should remember this "If you shall have suffered persecution during this short time, you shall be rewarded hereafter with an everlasting reward," (1 Peter iv, 13) Let him who considers his will to be under restraint, remember the words said with so much liberality· "*Qui fecerit voluntatem Patris mei, ipse meus frater, soror et mater est*"—"For whosoever shall do the will of my Father that is in heaven, he is my brother, sister, and mother" (Matth xii, 50) And let him who grieves because he gets not his due, and because evil comes to the good, and good to the bad ones, remember that sentence: "*Reddet (Deus) unicuique secundum opera ejus*"—"And then (God) will render to everyone according to his works" (Matth xvi, 27) Let him who cannot keep his patience in adversity remember that "*In patientia vestra possidebitis animas vestras*"—"In your patience you shall possess your souls" (Luke xxi, 19) And he who thinks it hard to be put down and humiliated should remember these words "Unless you become as little children, you shall not enter the kingdom of heaven" (Matth xviii, 3); and the others· "*Qui se exallat humiliabitur, qui se humiliat exaltabitur*"—"Everyone that exalteth himself shall be humbled, and he that humbleth himself shall be exalted" (Luke xiv, 11) And let him who feels that it is hard to serve and be subject, remember the following, and keep it well in his mind "*Ego in medio vestrum sum, sicut qui ministrat*"—"I am in the midst of you, as he that serveth" (Luke xxii, 27) Oh! what solid shields, what safe arms, Thy divine words are for our defense, O Word! Speaking to herself in the person of the Eternal Father, she continued thus O my beloved One, dost Thou not see, conceive, and understand that the utterances of My Word are that ladder seen by Jacob, by which the angels ascended and descended, and the summit of which touched heaven, and the other extremity the earth? But this ladder of the words of My Word is even longer, because it rests in the soul that by humility and self-knowledge is lower down and deeper than the abyss, there is this difference between these two ladders, that the former just touched the surface of the earth but the latter reaches above the stars, the more the soul humbles herself It reaches high up, even to Me, so that its sinking down gives it elevation, and the more it sinks down at the foot, the more it rises at the top There is more—because the soul will not ascend this ladder alone, but will have triple company, being in the midst of those personages who descend and ascend for her. The first of them is My Word, who descended to fulfill the promise made to My faithful servant Abraham, and to the other one whom, from the pasture and herdship of the sheep, I raised to the royal dignity The second is the Archangel Gabriel, who carried the tidings of the Word going to be Incarnate by love. The third is not one only, but thousands and thousands—that is, an infinite number of angels and blessed spirits of all the heavenly hierarchies, who, descending by the ladder, come down to encourage the souls of the faithful to ascend by it

The Word ascends and returns to My bosom, according to those words which He Himself uttered: "*Ascendo ad Patrem meum et Patrem vestrum*"—"I ascend to My Father and to your Father" (John xx, 17)   Now listen, My daughter, for thy consolation I wish to reveal to thee some profound truths Know that the first sin committed by Eve, when she consented to the lying words of the infernal serpent, was not principally of gluttony or disobedience, but of a vain and proud desire to be like unto Me, otherwise than in conformity to My will. "*Eritis sicut Dii, scientes bonum et malum*"—"You shall be as gods, knowing good and evil" (Gen iii, 5). She wished for this likeness in the knowledge of good and evil, an operation of the intellect, understanding and discerning the good and the evil Know that this, My gift of *understanding*, is communicated to the responsible creature, and this is what gives it being, and, likewise the intellectual substances are such, because they are by Me made partakers of this gift, viz, this *power of understanding* And though the will is also from Me, and is an essential power, because by it one has the liberty to will one or the other thing, yet if by the intellect one conceives a creature deprived of this will, he still preserves the idea of her being, though not so perfect And thus man is man by the understanding and the will, but in such a way that if he conceives the power to will without the understanding, he is not a man, because *this* does away with responsibility, and, *vice versa*, if he conceives the power to understand without will, *this* preserves the essence of a reasonable being, though not so perfect as when en? ? ? ? ? ? ? ? ? ? be understood of the angels who are more perfect than ? ? ? ? ? ? thou to Me, understand as the cause, ? ? ? ? of My ? ? ? ? ? ? though most simple, as the purest act, without any mixture of potentia ? ? ? ? ? tion, except of persons, yet in My most simple Being first thou must know the intellect, and then the will, according to thy mode of understanding In the intellect, or power of understanding with a most *pure act*, principally consists the idea thou must form of My most perfect substance. Not that the understanding and the will are in any way distinct from one another, or from Me, or that one is superior to the other, for in the purest act of My Being there is no distinction ; but apprehending, as thou mayest, this simplicity of Mine, thou must consider that first is the understanding in Me, and then the will, as if this were born from that Thus, the idea thou shalt form of Me, as God, must be that of knowing and understanding all, then of willing and being able to do all, and of communicating Myself to all And this power of the intellect in the reasonable and intellectual creatures is what gives them the *distinctive character*. Hence, My Word and Son is called My Image, because He represents Me perfectly (as the Holy Ghost does), because He proceeds by the operation of the intellect, in which principally consists the idea of the being of intellectual substances. Hence, He is called My Image, because a thing intellectual cannot be conceived or deprived of the power of understanding, without destroying its very idea ; which does not happen in regard to the will. Eve, then, and the first man, wished to be like unto Me in the understanding to acquire that perfection which is My own , but on this account she and Adam lost very much and became like unto the animals. It was necessary, therefore, that My Image by the understanding, as proceeding from Me through the intellect, should come to reform that image which by this inordinate desire had become deformed , and, as in the print of wax the first figure cannot be better imprinted than by the first seal, likewise it was necessary that by My Word and Wisdom man should be reformed, who by his vain appetite for knowledge, and the desire by this knowledge to be like unto Myself, had become so dissimilar from Me. The Word, then, according to those words by Him uttered in His Humanity. *"Exivi a Patre et veni in mundum , iterum relinquo mundum et vado ad Patrem"*—" I came forth from the Father, and am come into the world ; again I leave the world and I go to the Father " (John xvi, 28)—descended and ascended by said ladder

The second, viz , the Archangel Gabriel, as I told thee, came down to announce to the Virgin, and ascended as soon as he received her consent The third personages, viz , the hierarchies, ascend said ladder by virtue of those words uttered by My Truth · *"Regnum meum non est de hoc mundo"* – " My kingdom is not of this world " (John xviii, 36). And so, pointing to what and where His kingdom was, who were His subjects, and where they resided, He showed plainly that His dwelling-place, and that of His chosen subjects, was not in this world below , and, therefore, the angels returning by the same ladder gave evidence of their determination to stay in the kingdom of their Lord, which is in heaven Dost thou not think that My Word has built a sweet, and beautiful, and easy ladder, to lead souls to His kingdom? Does it not seem to you that each word is like a step, easy and agreeable, to lead them up to the top? And there is even something better—to make the ascent easier —inasmuch as My words are like darts penetrating the souls, and moving, waking, and encouraging them not only to ascend themselves, but to lead with them other creatures also My words are, moreover, like so many feathers, forming wings to fly up with the greatest ease, without feeling the least fatigue in the ascent: *"Assument pennas ut aquilæ , volabunt et non deficient , current et non laborabunt"*—" They shall take wings as eagles , they shall run and not be weary , they shall walk and not faint " (Isai xl, 31) And mark, My daughter, that this voice of My Spirit says that they shall walk and not faint from the fatigue of the journey , they shall run and not be weary, as it is easier and less fatiguing to go up quickly, as if flying, and to run very swiftly up this ladder of My words, than to go up slowly ; because there is nothing more annoying on the road of the Spirit and of My counsels than slowness, or laziness, or cowardice Thou well knowest, My daughter, what My Servant said : *"Nescit tarda molimina Spiritus Sancti gratia"*—" The grace of the Holy Ghost knows not slow means," and that the man according to My Heart is he who, when he abandons himself wholly into My hands, and I enlarge his heart by charity, runs, as if it were nothing, over all the long and tedious road of the holy precepts: *"Viam mandatorum tuorum cucurri, quum dilatasti cor meum"*—" I have run the way of Thy Commandments, when Thou didst enlarge my heart " (Ps cxviii, 32) Who, therefore, can excuse themselves from ascending? And who can plead that they do not understand the sayings of My Word, but those whose hearts are full of pride, and, therefore *"Obscuratum est insipiens cor eorum"*—"And their foolish heart was darkened "? (Rom i, 21) O unhappy souls, living in the midst of sins, will you think you can excuse yourselves from ascending by this ladder? You say that you live in the world , but anybody who *wills*, finds this ladder easier than he imagines or his senses paint it for him Sin, O souls, keeps you , but who bound you by sin, except yourselves? If your sins deserve one hell, by excusing yourselves you deserve many more *"Ad excusandas excusationes in peccatis"*—"To make excuses in sins " (Ps cxl, ; Be ashamed of your excuse, since even children have ascended by this ladder so swiftly. The sweetness and beauty of this ladder is so great that it draws anyone who wants to ascend by it, as the load-stone draws iron And if My Word had not uttered other words than these "*Ego sum via, veritas et vita*"—"I am the Way, and the Truth, and the Life " (John xiv, 6)—they would have been sufficient to prove it. Dost thou know, Daughter Mine, how I regard those who ascend by this ladder? I regard some of them as so many little children, who hardly move one step , others, as those who move but slowly , others, as people who walk ; and others still, as people who run , but I look upon them all, by My goodness, as the pupil of My eye .

The pusillanimous are those little children who hardly seem to move a step , as they are so timorous they hardly appear to recognize in Me the God of Goodness that I am, and their Creator and Maker. Hence, such people cannot say with their hearts truly, because, in fact, they show they do not feel it "*Manus tuæ, Domine, fecerunt me et plasmaverunt me*," "*Et oculi mei semper ad Dominum*"—"Thy hands, O Lord, have made me and formed me ," " My eyes are ever towards the Lord " (Ps cxviii, 73, Ps. xxiv, 15) They do not regard Me as a Father, but as a Judge. As to those who move on, but go very easily and slowly, they are the thoughtless ones, who in one moment wish to jump, and in the next find themselves behind These, if I would not obstruct their way, nay, cut their legs, could never be led ; they never acknowledge My wisdom, but fall now to the right, now to the left. The others who walk, but do not run, are those who walk in charity, but are not *dead*, because they wish for something else outside of My will, pure and simple, seeking themselves in something These do not deny My goodness, nor My wisdom ; but in seeking something out of Me, or with Me, which is not Myself, pure and simple, they deny, in a measure, My Being of purity, which is a Being without beginning and without end, and without any mixture of a created thing. They love Me above everything, they acknowledge Me as the First Truth, trusting to My promises , but they are not wholly pure and divested of them-selves. There are some, but they are very few, who *walk dead*, because they seek not what God is, nor the angels, nor the Saints, nor creatures, nor purgatory, with a feeling of self-interest, or to acquire any good, or for any spiritual complacency whatever, but with the understanding and desire to wish what I wish absolutely Thus they find Me, and yet seem not to seek Me , for their affection, though they may not be conscious of it, is all centred in Me, as if they had neither life nor senses. Their senses, their lives, and operations are all absorbed and fixed in Me "*Et vita vestra abscondita est cum Christo in Deo*"—"Your life is hid with Christ in God " (Col iii, 3) These acknowledge My goodness, wisdom, and purity, and in a manner so painful, though to themselves un-known, that it gives them a true and lasting death Such, O daughter, I wish thee to be , and that thou mayest acquire this life of death, My Word wishes to deprive thee of the feeling of My grace, so that thou mayest be able to say "*Vivo ego, jam non ego*"—"And I live, yet not I " (Gal. ii, 20). The testimony of those who are thus dead in Me, is such, that if you would ask them What is God? they would be unable to tell you. But you might hear them speaking of My greatness and immensity, without being able to say God is such a thing, and produces this and that effect. With a fervent confession they continually confess Me, even though it may seem to them that they are silent about Me Does not this seem to thee a grand, easy, and beautiful ladder? (Here she answered in her own person Certainly, yes ; O Eternal Father . . .)

XXI.

She is instructed by the Eternal Father about the Essence and the Effects of the Divine Peace.

" *Pacem relinquo vobis, pacem meam do vobis , non quomodo mundus dat ego do vobis*"—"Peace I leave with you, My peace I give unto you , not as the world giveth, do I give unto you " (John xiv, 27) But how many things are contained in this peace? How, and to whom dost Thou, O Word, give this gift so grand and safe, breathed by the Three Divine Persons, conferred by the Incarnate Word, received by the creature regen-erated? This peace was given in paradise (she continued speaking in the Person of the Eternal Father), on the throne of the Most Holy Trinity Afterwards it passed from the Divinity to the Humanity, from My Word to Mary, and from Mary to the Word, and finally from the Word to the creature, and from the creature to the Word The peace of the throne of the Most Holy Trinity is, so to speak, an affectionate breath-ing that was given from eternity, is, and shall be given forever In this peace was conceived from eternity, and decreed, the design of creating in time those noble spirits, the pure an.'s and this pe'', we m'' ''   ''' f'' ''''s 'ut once, and yet many ar l m.'v tim' s, 'w c are it was 'A ''' ''   '' ',' ' '   ''' l'' given among Us, the Thr'' l'''ine l'' '''s l' ''' r'' '' ''   My daughter, that this pe''ce was given when in l'''' at '''' .'''''' W'' r - lved to create man, whose type We had already conceived in Our Divine Mind , and that was not a peace of breathing, but of contemplating In so doing, We were so enraptured with Our greatness and goodness, that, without desiring, We desired immensely to communicate this, Our goodness, to some creature in a more perfect manner than to another ; and not finding any capable of receiving it better than man, in whom, as in a compendium, all creation is united, on account of the most high destiny for which We created him, and the design We conceived to unite the Person of the Word to him—Who is infinitely communicable for Himself —We decreed to create man to Our Image and Likeness, and to unite him to Our Nature in the Person of the Word

And this as a remedy for sin, yes , but principally for the glory and exaltation of the human nature and of Our goodness that wished, by this means, to communicate Itself to the creature in the most perfect manner, showing thereby the greatest possible love We first gave Our likeness, which We did not do in any other creatures here below ; and afterwards raised it to so great a dignity, that it is said "*Et adorent* EAM *omnes angeli ejus*"—"Adore Him, all you His angels" (Ps xcvi, 7) Hence, it was determined to create a new trinity, in order that this peace might be conferred upon it As the first peace was given on the throne of the Blessed Trinity, so this second peace was given in My bosom, and in My Word, not yet Incarnate, but decreed to become such, and in the Heart of the Word, Who was, by election and the promptitude with which He accepted the command, as if He were Incarnate, before any creature was made by the Blessed Trinity.

The Word is the first-born, as it were, of all the creatures, foreseen before any other in the essence and the idea of the Holy Trinity, as the Head of the elect, the Saviour and Glorifier of all men, the hope and crown of all created things And it was meet that such an ample way should be laid out for this new, created trinity, that it might reach the enjoyment of the uncreated Trinity This ample way the Incarnate Word was to teach, more by deeds than by words , so that everyone might walk in it freely It was not enough for the Word to teach this way ; but He made Himself the Way, saying "*Ego sum via*"—"I am the Way" (John xiv, 6). The peace was then given between the Word and Mary, not by breathing, or by looking, but by complacency , as the Holy Trinity, looking at Mary, was so well pleased with her, that My Word commenced to become Incarnate in her , and thus assumed the Humanity by the operation of the Holy Ghost and the power of Myself, the Father, overshadowing Mary This was the fruit of the Heart of the Word before He became Incarnate, as He conceived a boundless desire to find His complacency in the creature, proceeding from the complacency in Himself And such was His love of complacency in the creature, that it superabounded and overflowed, with a distilling superfluency descending into Mary Well did Mary give this peace to the Word, re-creating, so to speak, the Uncreated One, completing and restoring the angelic ranks by the people sent to heaven, and re-creating, by grace and glory (cooperating with the Incarnation of the Word), the creature already created The angelic nature was restored by the restoration of the human nature, made by My Word, through the substance He received from Mary, viz , the Humanity And the wish of the angels was satisfied through Mary ; because on seeing the creature, through the Incarnation and suffering of the Word, made so apt to praise and honor Me, they made a great feast thereat, their desire for the extension of My glory being fulfilled, and they gave one another more peace, because of the union of the angelic and the human nature Hence it was that men were called angels, and angels bore a special love and reverence for men Moreover, the former deem it a great privilege to be given to men as guardians , for this reason they were heard to sing at the Nativity of My Word "*Gloria in excelsis Deo, et in terra pax hominibus*"—"Glory to God in the highest, and on earth peace to men " (Luke ii, 14) Then a perfect union between the angelic and the human nature took place, and angels and men, meeting, gave one another the peace with great joy ; and all this through Mary But they gave one another this peace even more when My Word returned to heaven with His Humanity in great triumph and glory, bringing along with Him the blessed souls of the holy Fathers, the first fruit of the Incarnation The angels then joining those souls already made blessed and glorious, felt a peace of sovereign fullness and perfect joy, and wished to communicate it to the earth, appearing in white garments, not only to manifest their joy, but also to denote the purity which the creature had regained by the restitution made to it by the Word, of the primitive state of innocence Moreover, every time a soul enters heaven, or a sinner is converted, this joy of the angels is renewed, as they see the fruit of the Word Incarnate ; and in this joy they again communicate the peace to one another   . Mary also gave that peace that was given among the Three Divine Persons, which was of reflection In this peace, man, already conceived by nature, was conceived also by grace, and a new trinity of the three powers was restored in him Another one was made and joined together, of soul, body, and divinity, in so far as she furnished the body to the Word in the restoration of the creature, by the grace and likeness of virtue, in which the likeness of man to God consists, as the image consists in the nature and power Hence it may be said . *to the image and likeness*, to denote these two similitudes , of nature, which is the *image*, and of grace and virtue infused, which is the *likeness*. . . Afterwards this Eternal and Incarnate Word gave the peace to the creature—a peace of union—through Mary. This union makes you, creatures, capable of receiving the communication of the Divinity, and as many gifts and graces as this Divinity confers This Divinity was so bountiful in this communication, that, not only was It not satisfied to assume the Humanity, and in It walk on earth for thirty-three years, and shed its Most Precious Blood for your redemption, but also wished to do more, leaving Itself in the Blessed Sacrament, to be with you till the consummation of the world

Yes, the Word gives you peace ; but not as the world gives it, viz., with delights, riches, pleasures , for this is not true peace, but rather very real war, because the enjoying of it leads to an atrocious and lasting war And this a soul well knows, who, being enlightened by Divine grace, in some way loses it Out of the state of grace this war is well known , as whilst one is in the world he seems to enjoy peace, but really does not If it seems to you that you possess it, it is because you have become slaves of your passions and the world, and, I will also add, of the devil, who holds you as slaves chained, and will not even permit you to think of your liberty—that real liberty in which you would find true peace with God and with yourselves. The peace, on the contrary, which the Word gives is full of pain, tribulations, and persecutions, but in the end it leads to a quiet and tranquil peace I will say more In the midst of this pain the Word gives His peace, because, finally, the Spirit Himself gives you testimony that you are children of God And this is what is meant by the *"Beati qui lugent, quoniam ipsi consolabuntur"*—" Blessed are they that mourn, for they shall be comforted " (Matth v, 5) Not only will they be comforted in the future, but their very weeping is, for them, consolation, and the very war which they endure for God's sake is, to them, peace. O peace ! O peace ' What is this peace? It is a tranquillity of heart, a serenity of conscience, a light, and a participation in the celestial light and splendor, that makes you understand, as far as is possible on earth, that you are children of God. And, whoever possesses this peace, lives secure and leaves everything to God . The creature then returns this peace to her Creator, viz , peace of praise and thanksgiving for the peace the Word gave to the creature, and in which the soul and the body participated Thus, the peace which man renders to his Creator must be intrinsic and exterior The latter is the praise of the lips, provided it is accompanied by the heart , the former is the interior thanksgiving which proceeds from the love of God, with the knowledge of the gifts and graces received from Him , and it renders us capable of receiving them in greater abundance from the sovereign liberality of the Incarnate Word.

XXII.

She speaks of the Divers Properties of the Word, and the Various Effects He Produces in the Souls.

Woe to thee, my soul, if thou dost not leave thyself and remove from thee all self-love ' Not only the Word, but Satan himself will hold thee in abomination Thou art most powerful, O God ! and yet, I dare say, that with all Thy omnipotence Thou couldst not prepare, neither could be found so many torments in hell, nor so many hells as could suffice to punish me, miserable creature ' Woe to me ! Woe to me ! a vessel of imperfections and all iniquities ! How shall I endure my abomination any longer? Yet, I shall not cease trusting in Thee, O Word, My Spouse ! Thou shalt be all in me, and for me ; as I cannot find in myself, out of Thee, anything but infirmity, abomination, and filth O my Spouse ! Thou wishest, and I wish, that all offenses offered to Thee by others should be punished in me, but what shall I do, if in hell itself I do not find as many torments as may adequately punish my faults? I dare not call the creatures to my assistance, knowing they should justly be, on account of my sins, my deadly enemies *"Recogitabo tibi omnes annos meos, in amaritudine animæ meæ "*—" I will recount to Thee all my years in the bitterness of my soul " (Isai. xxxviii 15) Oh ! what bitter sea this is in which I plunge, when I consider the years of my life so badly spent ! Yet, I will enter it, and Thou shalt throw me in it, that being immersed therein, I may know what I am *"Et in profundum maris demersit me"*—"As into the depth of the sea (He) overwhelmed me " (Ps. lxviii, 3). Stop ! Stop ! O Lord ! I would suffer less, were I in hell, provided this could be without offense to Thee Alas ' *"Narrabo prcprietates* (O Father) *Verbi tui "*—" I shall recount the properties of Thy Word " Those Thou dost manifest to me, and communicate to Him, the Only Begotten of Thy Intellect, and Thy Very Heart, are *"Pulchritudo mirabilia, sapientia scientia potentia, æternitas, impassibilita ...* ' Beauty, wonderment, wisdom science, power, eternity, impassibility union, no communication O ... es' O infinite treasures contained in Thee, O Word ! Thou art the Fountain of all beauty . Beautiful in Thy

Humanity, in a manner incomprehensible, inconceivable. Thy beauty of Soul and Body cannot be described, and the beauty springing from Thy words and works is delightful But the beauty of Thy Divinity despises the malignity of many creatures, and that wicked intention to harm others, to judge rashly, and to look always at the worst side of other people's deeds Better will it be for me to be mistaken through judging well of my neighbor, leaving to Thee, O Spouse, the judgment of his intentions, than that resting on my evil judgment of others, I come to offend Thee, Who dost not wish I should judge the servant of another, who is Thy servant

Lies and backbitings show contempt for the beauty of Thy Humanity The lazy and the hypocrites, against whom Thou didst make use of such burning language, despise the beauty of Thy soul On the contrary, the goodness of Thy chosen ones exalts the beauty of Thy Divinity, and delights therein Those who thirst after Thy Truth exalt the beauty of Thy Humanity. The pure and simple of heart exalt Thy beauty Oh ! beautiful band of virtues, which draws beauty and splendor from Thy beauty "*Mirabilis Deus in sanctis tuis*"—"God is wonderful in Thy Saints" (Ps lxvii, 36). And, how much more wonderful must Thou be, O Word, in Thyself, and in Thy Divinity, whence proceeds all that is wonderful in the Saints? Wonderful in the Father, wonderful in all Thy operations, which the more they are employed in some work appearing to us abject and low, the more wonderful they are Wonderful Thou art in Thy Father, to incline Him towards us, sometimes by an act of humiliation of the creature herself Wonderful in the Holy Ghost, causing Him to infuse Himself in the soul, so that being thereby united to God, it conceives God, tastes Him, and delights in nothing but God And the soul that would be without this infusion would become a demon. Oh ! how many such incarnate devils are found to-day, from whom so many dangers arise to Thy poor servants ! Dangers on the sea, dangers on land, it is true, but, I believe, greater dangers from "*Falsis fratribus*"—"False brethren" (2 Cor. xi, 26), who do not spare those whom the sea and the earth have spared Let Paul, Thy most faithful servant, say which he found more cruel—the waves of the sea, the vipers of the earth, or his false brethren, who grieved him so much ! Ah ! grant, O Word, that this gift may be diffused in all, that the Holy Spirit may be diffused in all, and, though, to try the elect there must always be evil people in the world, grant that these may not be always wicked, but that they may be made good by means of those whom they grieve Chastise them in this life, and forgive them in the next

Wonderful art Thou, also, O Word, in Thyself—I mean, in Thy coming down to us, and communicating Thyself to us with so much charity, that we comprehend and possess Thee Oh ! Wonderful Being of My Word ! By many so little known, and by so few acknowledged ! O my God ! Thy Wonderful Being is like unto the sea, which, receiving the waters of all the rivers, deprives them of their names, so that they are no longer called rivers, but the sea, which afterwards produces precious stones and gems We go on continually sailing in this infinite sea of Thy Wonderful Being, in great danger of drowning, unless the favorable wind of Thy faith comes to our aid, and we are willing to be governed by the chart of the Holy Writ, which indicates Thy successor on earth, and all other *christs* of Thine (priests) We must remain always in the boat of Thy Church, which Thou hast entrusted to Thy Peter and his successors This is the safe ship, that cannot be lost, nor be shipwrecked, because "*Portæ inferi non prævalebunt adversus eam*"—"And the gates of hell shall not prevail against it" (Matth xvi, 18) But, still, in this world of Thy knowledge there is sometimes danger, on account of the restless waves, for we do not well know the wonderful tread of Thy Loving Being, that wishes to save us, whilst we become unworthy of the salvation Thou wishest to grant us . . "*Et sapientiæ ejus non est numerus*"—"And of His wisdom there is no number" (Ps cxlvi, 5) Thou dost possess, O Word, that wisdom which cannot be understood except by him who becomes altogether *foolish*, as that *vessel of election* who understood nothing but "*Jesum et hunc crucifixum*"—"Jesus, and Him crucified" (1 Cor ii, 2) Hence, he was wont to say "*Nos stulti propter Christum*"—"We are all fools for Christ's sake" (1 Cor iv, 10), and in this foolishness, which is the true wisdom, He was chosen as the Teacher of the world Those who seek and follow after human wisdom, which is foolishness before God, abhor this wisdom And, how numerous are these now ! Thou, O Word, knowest it, and they can well say in the end, on settling their accounts. "*Nihil inveni in manu mea*"—"I have found nothing in my hand" (Ps lxxv, 6), except shadow, wind, smoke, and vanity, such as everything is outside of Thee

This wisdom is also abhorred by anyone who deprives himself of Thy union as those who offend Thee deprive themselves of Thee and of themselves O wisdom ! who causest the soul to be dilated, the will to be kindled and warmed, the intellect to be enlightened, the love to be purified, who excitest the hatred of sin, the fear of the Divine Judgment, the hope of paradise, the desire of heavenly glory ! And, how is this wisdom acquired ? Not by words nor by arts, not by riches nor by anyone's intelligence, but by a deep knowledge of one's nothingness, and by an enlightened understanding of the Being of God, with a constant hatred of self, and of self-love, in so far as it is contrary to God. This wisdom is experienced by him who tastes it, and is understood by him who knows nothing . . . "*Scientia Dei abyssus multa*"—"Thy judgments are a great deep" (Ps. xxxv, 7). O wisdom! thou art like that most beautiful palm tree that brings forth most sweet fruits, and does not grow everywhere, but only where the ground is prepared and suitable for it! And the palm tree gives also a most pleasing shade So this knowledge of Thee, O Eternal Word, produces fruit in those who are well disposed ; but, as for those who are not so disposed, let them acquire other sciences, as much as they wish, they shall never possess nor be able to secure even the least part of Thy knowledge, without which every science is most foolish and stupid ignorance. O science of my Word ! who can ever tell of Thee ? Who can ever reach the height of this palm tree ? Oh ! how it surpasses in height all the heavens ! And who shall ever comprehend it ? All the cherubim rest under thy shade, neither can they reach the altitude of thy branches, for they cannot (unless Thou, O Word, wouldst reveal them to them) penetrate Thy most profound secrets This knowledge of Thine Thou dost infuse into us with a complete communication by the grace of Thy soul in us , and this causes our soul to become as an ox continually ruminating the food he takes. Likewise, whoever possesses this science continues meditating, till he at last understands, by the light Thou givest to him, what is convenient for him to know of Thee, Sovereign Good, in this life and in the next. In this life, the splendor, a little dimmed, of the faith ; in the next, the open vision, whereby, as a glass illumined by Thee, he will be transformed into the object seen. O science, mother of justice, companion of mercy, nurse of love, light of the intellect, guide of the will, life of the memory ! And could we live in this world without Thy help? Thou givest everyone his dues, thus endowing him with a just being, as justice means nothing else but to render to everyone what is due to him ; to God, honor, and to the neighbor, love This science is a companion of mercy , for without it charity is extinct. It is the nurse of love , for he who knows, loves, and one cannot love the unknown

Thou art the Light of the Intellect, O wonderful science of the Word , and I am always in darkness, alas ! and fear that my darkness, like black and thick clouds, may spread through the world, on account of my sins, darken the atmosphere, and cause so much blindness in the world. Alas ! how lame is this will of mine, and how often it trips ! And, yet, Thy science is its guide. So many faults, so many sins—always returning to commit the same I feel like an ass tied, by the miller, to the mill, going always around, pacing, growing tired, and never moving out of that place But, I am not tied ; "*Vinctus non ferro, sed mea ferrea voluntate*"—"Bound up not by iron, but by *my* iron will "; as that great servant of Thine was wont to say at the time he did not know Thee

This chain, and this bondage, will be broken ; and I will certainly go by another road If I possess Thy science, I will remember nothing but Thee , because Thy science is the life of the memory Do grant, O my God, that I may remember Thee only to love and thank Thee, and to rest fully in Thy will Sweet sleep, beginning of the true life, not to remember, nor to think, of anything but one's God ; to wholly give up self, not to care for anything, and to sleep and rest all in God. "*Ego dormio et cor meum vigilat*"—"I sleep and my heart watcheth" (Cant. v, 2), with my heart and mind remembering always who I am, and to whom I am so much indebted

O power ! Powerful is the Word in all His works Great power I see in the Word, in assuming our souls to Himself , great power in supporting and glorifying them, and in all the works He does. I see creatures, in nearly every motive and action of theirs, denying in deeds, not in words, Thy power, O my God ! In their evil intentions they deny Thy power, and also in their deceitful words and lukewarm works ; because, did they believe Thou art so powerful, they would live in fear and trembling always, so as not to offend Thee, and would keep watch in the expectation of Thy coming, thinking Thou hast said "*Vigilate quia nescitis qua hora Dominus vester venturus sit*" —"Watch ye, therefore, because you know not at what hour your Lord will come " (Matth xxiv, 42) The foolish virgins did not understand this, Thy power , otherwise they would have prepared themselves better Oh ! what sweetness is felt by the soul that possesses and tastes the fruit of Thy power, knowing that by possessing it neither devil, nor any creature whatsoever, can separate her from Thee.

Eternity ! Eternal in Thyself, O Word ! Eternal in Thy designs to glorify the angels, and in Thy will to conceive and create other creatures. Eternal in Thy operations And, what more? Eternal, O Father, in begetting Thy Word, I will not say like, but consubstantial with Thee, from Thee, and in Thee, without beginning, and without end Eternal, O Word, in breathing with the Father, the Holy Ghost, who is a most perfect bond of love Eternal with the Holy Spirit, in uniting thereby the Divine Persons. O ... Word, I ... and Omega. Thou hast no beginning and art the end of all thing Or ... of my Word Wl ... no beginning ... from the Father, and it was a beginning without a beginning because He is eternal ; eternal before, eternal after. But, in eternity there is no before nor after; all is a uniform, invariable, and everlasting Being. O my God, eternal, immense, impassible, infinite! and who shall comprehend Thee? Impassible, yes, and from whom can that Being suffer, who is independent of everybody but Himself? He is a most simple act, most pure, without any mixture of act and *potentiality*, without any variation or change. But, as to the impassibility, one must consider Thy Humanity, making Thee appear passible, though Thou art impassible. As soon as Thy Humanity, O Word, was united to Thee, It necessarily acquired impassibility; but this Thou didst not wish, because of Thy desire to suffer for us. Now Thou art impassible both in Thy Divinity and in Thy Humanity.

O wonderful union, in heaven, on earth, and also in that intimacy, and in the most secret and perfect bond of the Divine nature, whereby the Holy Ghost unites in an unspeakable manner the Three Divine Persons! Oh! how united is the Most Holy Trinity, in the unity of essence, substance, and love! Moreover, there is another union, caused by the preference Thou, O Word, hast shown for us here below. Thou hast so well united Thy Divinity to our humanity, for Thy glory and our benefit, that we receive therefrom all our good, viz, Thyself. But this union does not suffice me, the Eucharistic communication of Thy Body and Blood, O my Spouse, this is my sweetest bond. O Union! who shall be able to understand it? Only to say that the Infinite unites to Himself the finite, to make it equal to Himself, is enough to amaze all the angelic hierarchies. So much did the Eternal Father love and does love these His creatures, that it was not enough for Him to give His Only Begotten for our redemption, but He gives Him to us continually for our help, relief, and consolation, that He may always enkindle and inflame our hearts with the divine love, and grant us His light to discern ourselves and His goodness. The Word ceases not to look upon us, and, by His look, causes and begets in us piety, mercy, and love. O God of love and union, Thou art the One Who grants every peace, and without Thee there can be no true peace nor union! The peace and union among sinners are false ones, which cannot last long, because, being ruled by the tyranny of sin and the passions, the frail bond uniting them soon breaks, as a thread of tow. From Thee alone comes the perfect union, and, where there is no union, there is confusion, on account of sin and the devil. Where there is union, there is all good, there is abundance of everything, of all heavenly and earthly riches. Where this union is wanting, every good—the grace of God, the benevolence of the creatures—is wanting, and there is dearth of everything. . . O my loving Word, Thou art also the Good Shepherd who unites His Sheep with Himself, and keeps them also united among themselves. And how many are the things required in the good shepherd? First, that he love his flock more than himself; then, that he go before his flock, rod in hand, and, with a dog, to protect them. He must find fresh and green pastures, springs of fresh waters, a warm or a cool sheepfold, in which to enclose his sheep according to the seasons. Behold Thou, O Word, dost possess all these qualifications of the good shepherd. Thou didst begin in the bosom of mercy to love Thy flock more than Thyself, by desire, laying down Thy life before the time arrived to give it up, and then on the cross Thou didst make known fully the same desire, and didst fulfill it, by actually laying down Thy life for Thy sheep, showing thereby how much Thou didst love them. Thou dost go before the flock, as, being from eternity without beginning, Thou didst go into all those souls that pleased Thee from the commencement of the world, and, dost go into them now, and shalt go till the end into those who shall please Thee, and whom Thou wilt wish to make Thine. Where is the one Thou wouldst not like to make Thine own by Thy preceding will, since Thou art He *"Qui vult omnes homines salvos fieri?"*—Who will have all men to be saved?" (1 Tim. ii, 4). Thou givest him Thy grace first, and thus Thou goest before him with the rod, enlightening him with the light of Thy internal inspirations. Thou dost always place in every soul within Thy flock the stimulus of conscience the dog. Thou Thyself dost lead the flock into the verdant and safe pastures of Thy holy doctrine, viz, of Thy Gospel. Thou also dost lead Thy flock to drink Thy overflowing grace, and, having assumed our flesh, givest them to drink at the most limpid spring of Thy most loving side and sacred wounds. Thou dost watch in the night-time (for Thee, O Word, it is always daylight, but for us it is night). Then Thou art resting and communicating to the souls an interior and an exterior light, watching unceasingly over Thy flock.

According to different needs, Thou dost infuse now a security and pledge of inconceivable love, now an interior, tremendous fear. Thy pastures, O Word, are in Thyself; but it is necessary, according to time and place, to go and find them out. *"Per vicos et plateas"*—"In the streets and broad ways" (Cant. iii, 2). So delightful are these pastures, that whoever shall find them shall be unable to restrain himself from entering them. Oh! how many fruits do I gather from the sweet head of the Word's Humanity, and His sacred wounds! But, I would not have them for myself alone, I aspire to communicate them to the whole world. Well do I know that were I to offer them to many, it would seem to them too sweet and mean to *Nos insensati vitam illorum æstimabamus insaniam*" "We fools esteemed their life madness" (Wisd. v, 4). But woe,

woe to them ! I shall offer them again to Thee, O Word ! for they are Thine, and Thou canst make anybody partake of them as Thou wilt. O Heart ! O Side of the Eternal Word Incarnate ! It is not possible to correspond even once to such generosity Thy darts are too many ; one cannot endure them , great help is needed to correspond and keep so many arrows "*Ego sum Pastor bonus, ego sum ostium , per me si quis introierit salvabitur, et ingredietur, et egredietur, et pascua inveniet*"—"I am the Good Shepherd ; I am the Door; by Me, if any man enter in, he shall be saved, and he shall go in and go out, and shall find pastures" (John x, 14 , John x, 9) Where do they enter, and where do they come out, O Word, but into the pasture of Thy wisdom, and out of it ? In this pasture not only do we feed, but Thou, the archangels, and all the blessed spirits also Hence, in saying that they entered and came out, Thou didst manifest the secret of secrets, viz , the Divine idea of the Father, of Thyself, and of the Holy Ghost ; the secret of Thy most loving Heart, the secret of the angels, and of the blessed spirits The secret, which was in the Father's mind, manifested itself, coming out of the Father and begetting the Word ; for, by the Father understanding Himself the Word is begotten. And the Word being thus begotten by way of the intellect, which is in its nature similar, is called the figure and image of the Father, and, by the purest bond of love, the Father and the Word breathe the Holy Spirit, Who is Love itself. The more this manifestation is multiplied, the more it is communicated to the multitude of creatures

The angels and the glorious spirits enter into said pasture of wisdom, and by the force of the union they are almost compelled to raise themselves above themselves They enter it by the sentiment of love, and come out by the greatness of the Trinity, incomprehensible to them and every other creature They come out, *never coming out ,* as they see more and more, and there remains infinitely more of the divine perfections to be seen than they can ever actually see But great study is necessary, O Word, to learn this wisdom of entering in and coming out of Thee, whilst remaining always in Thee It is necessary that the creature should always enter into Thy Divinity, and come out through Thy Humanity, in every movement she has to undertake She should enter into Thy Divinity to please Thee, and come out through Thy Humanity, to imitate Thee. This is the doctrine that must be practiced by any creature who is desirous of learning how to enter into Thee and come out of Thee.

There are also other pastures, as the virtues, which shine in Thy Humanity, wherein some enter without tasting Thee at all , and others endeavor to enter, and it is granted to them, because they go by the right road Happy is he who knows well how to enter into Thee and come out of Thee ! Wonderful wisdom, which is an aspiration to Thee, a sweet and quiet restlessness in Thee, wanting nothing, understanding nothing in anything, grieving to see Thou art so little known, and repining because Thou art so little loved. O God ! Wonderful in the selection of the souls, wonderful in the communication of Thy Divinity to the lowliness of our humanity.   .

God is so good to His sheep, because of three things · First, by nature, He being a God of Sovereign Goodness, Who cannot but be just and holy Good by operation ; because all His works have been to us so many causes of merit Good, because of the inheritance He leaves us—that everlasting inheritance of His beatific vision, and His endowing with gifts the soul and the body, when they shall be glorified "*Bonitatem fecisti cum servo tuo, Domine*"—"Thou hast done well, with Thy servant, O Lord" (Ps. cxvii, 65) These are the good things He has done unto us ; and then, what follows? "*Secundum Verbum tuum*"—"According to Thy Word" (*Ibid*) The term *Word* may be understood in two ways : Word, according to the Word He had given to the prophets, and Whom, afterwards, He sent ; and also according to the word that the same Word, while in this world, spoke to us by His sacred lips, viz , His heavenly, divine Doctrine. Since this Word came down upon the earth, God has dealt with us more in mercy than in justice The shepherd holds in his hands a something to call his sheep, and, to some of them, he gives a name and feeds them sometimes with his own food At night, he keeps them in his own sheepfold, or within certain enclosures, and he keeps the dog to waken him up, and loves him for the sheep's sake Before sending them to the pasture, he keeps them in his own house This means that God keeps us first in His own mind, and afterwards sends us into this valley of tears and miseries, that, feeding herewith, we may give Him milk The dog means the preachers The Holy Ghost is the sound that goes on ringing songs of love, calling the sheep The symbol and the articles of faith are the enclosure The little shepherds, by staying around the sheep, seem unable to speak or treat of anything but them. Thus our Word, when He became a man, seemed to be unable to think of anything else but us and our salvation We are of those sheep called by their own name and fed by His own food, as He communicates Himself to anyone who renders himself capable of His complacency and the knowledge of His bounty And the place wherein the shepherd rests is not different from that of his flock The place of rest for the soul is her own heart, where all her powers and desert, and there God condescends to come and dwell ! Man's life in this but a cross, and so it is a constant warfare. Christ also ascended the cross, but His was far different from ours, and there will never be one so heavy as His own   Shepherds never choose soft garments, but rough and lowly ones.   And what did the Word say concerning John ?   "They that are clothed in soft garments are in the houses of kings" (Matth xi, 8)   What garment could be more lowly for the Word than to take up our humanity?   A shepherd, as a rule, does not defend himself by means of arms, but with small slings   Well did Christ say to Peter "Put up again thy sword into its place" (Matth xxvi, 52)   Since the roaring lion had entered this big flock of sheep to devour them, the Word came, as a most loving Shepherd, to fight for the sheep, not by arms, but by sufferings and the passion   The Gospel and all its words are the slings whereby the Word protected us, His beloved little sheep, from the voracious, infernal lion   And those seven words He uttered from the cross, whereon He manifested such an ardor of charity, were nothing but seven slings that crushed the head of that roaring lion   Those sweet words He uttered during His mortal life viz , that we should learn from Him to be meek and humble of heart (Matth xi, 29), and that we should follow Him and love one another, and so many others ; what were they but slings He was flinging against that ferocious beast of hell ?   A truthful word is more powerful than an unjust stroke   Christ always carried the rod in His hands to denote His strength, and sometimes to strike His sheep   The rod indicates His Divinity, whence strength came to His humanity, which fact became evident in that mystery when He cast out of the Temple those who were selling therein, and when He wrought miracles   The rod is also His cross, which He took up from the moment of His conception and carried till He said   "*Consummatum est*"—"It is consummated" (John iv, 30)   He leads His sheep to the pasture of His humanity, where is to be found   that fine and fresh grass of the seven gifts of the Holy Ghost and of Himself   Nay, He feeds them with Himself, giving them His own Body and Blood, and those, to whom it is granted to attain a greater nobility of grace, taste the sweet grass of the interior communication which God infuses into the soul, and also that of His innumerable benefits   Others partake of the taller grass, viz , the celestial happiness —here below, by participation , up above, by everlasting possession   And what is, O my Word, the limpid spring Thou dost lead them to, that they may drink ?   Thou Thyself art the Spring   "*Fons sapientiæ*"— "Fountain of wisdom" (Ecclus 1, 5)   And Thou dost cry always   "*Si quis sitit, veniat ad me et bibat*"—"If any man thirst, let him come to Me and drink."   Thou didst say also to the Samaritan woman that, from the soul that would drink of the water, a fountain of water should spring up into life everlasting (John iv, 14)   After having led the sheep to drink, Thou washest them   "*Lavit nos in sanguine suo*"—"He washed us from our sins in His own blood" (Apoc. 1, 5) , and then He takes the shears and shears them, which happens when the soul is in a state between fear and suffering, or between temptations and discouragements   God takes away from the soul its appetites and desires—from one, the passions ; from another, self-love—according to His own divine will and pleasure   Then He ties them by the feet and makes them lie down   God binds all our sentiments and affections, so that the soul remains desolate, being deprived of taste and all exterior feelings , and interiorly, the feeling being bound, the soul seems unable to say anything else but   "*Eripe me de ore leonis*"—" Deliver me from the lion's mouth " (Ps xxi, 22)   The soul lies down in the consciousness of its desolation and misery, at times only raising its eyes to plead for help and relief   No matter what soul it is, it cannot reach perfection unless it be previously sheared by the Lord   One suffers interiorly another exteriorly , but only the one who shall have suffered for the love of God shall be able to say : "*Ego dormivi et somnum cæpi, et exsurrexi, quoniam Dominus suscepit me*"—"I have slept and taken My rest ; and I have risen up, because the Lord hath protected Me " (Ps iii, 6).   It is necessary, before all, to sleep, if the Lord has to raise one up, and it is also necessary to do what a sleeping person does   One who sleeps does not hear one who speaks ill of him ; does not see another working, and is not annoyed by one who is asleep or awake   When a soul has reached a state of perfect humiliation and annihilation, then it is permitted to her to rejoice, and to know the graces and gifts His Divine Majesty has granted to her , because she acknowledges them from God, she derives consolation always from what is written, that good works should be performed in the sight of men .   "*Ut glorificent Patrem qui in cœlis est*"—"That they may glorify the Father, Who is in heaven" (Matth v, 16).   First it is necessary to contemplate God, and know His interior illuminations, and then rise—that, is work   He does not say   I raised myself, that is, I worked by Myself, without the will of my Father, but   "*Quia Dominus suscepit me*," because the Lord has protected me , because such was the will of My Father and God , not a man, but God , for if all men would join together, they could not make one *work*.   If the Holy Scriptures would be studied for a thousand years, without God's grace and His *working*   "*In vanum labora-verunt*" —"They labored in vain " (Ps cxxvi, 1)   Then the shepherd continues milking his sheep , so the Word takes the milk from us when we are in the act of love and divine charity   Moreover   He takes our milk and is, our good works—to feed other chosen ones, to insinuate the heat of he with against the poor sinners and sweeten the bitterness of the wicked   Happy are those sheep that   ear the voice of his Good Shepherd

But, oh ! many are the voices whereby He goes on calling these little sheep ! The first is by means of the prophets , the second, by His own voice , the third, by the Holy Ghost. Then He.Himself, goes on calling by another interior voice , and happy is the soul that hears this voice. He calls her by her own name, as He does with all believing souls, according to their various vocations By the same voice, and by her own name, He calls every sheep, according to her own vocation The sheep follows the shepherd, and He leads her with the rod, not allowing her to feed on that which is the food of creatures more noble than herself, that is, man When the soul follows the Word, He leads her by the works He performed in His humanity The rod means His commandments, and if the sheep happens to run off, with the rod He makes her return, not permitting her to take the food of anyone greater than herself, because, when we wish to usurp the glory of the Divinity, and feed on it, which is the divine glory and honor, He drives us away by the rod, so that we are compelled to say "*Non nobis, Domine, non nobis sed nomini tuo da gloriam*"—"Not to us, O Lord, not to us, but to Thy name give glory" (Ps cxiii, 1) It is necessary,—O my God, that we should acknowledge Thee, and this, our acknowledgment on earth, must be endowed in particular with fine qualities (or conditions) The first is that we should acknowledge Thee with so much faith that, by its certainty, it may appear to be true evidence, so to speak, as in heaven faith ceases to be such The soul must believe in Thee, as if she saw with her own eyes If this were the case, it no longer would be faith, Thou being present, because faith ceases where there is evidence of the senses With this condition I must confess Thee, O my God. In the second place, faith must be founded on Thee, and always supported by Thee, who art the living *stone*. The third condition is the intention of benefiting our neighbors The fourth is, that this confession should be made with so much fortitude, and such a manly heart, that if all torments and pains a creature could endure, and even a thousand hells were prepared, the soul would fear nothing, and regard them as nothing, in order to maintain this truth. The fifth and last condition is, that this confession be made with such constancy that, though we had persisted in it without ceasing, still we should persevere in confessing this truth for all eternity In heaven this confession is made without conditions , because there is no danger of deceptions. "*Confessio et pulchritudo in conspectu ejus*"—"Praise and beauty are before Him" (Ps xcv, 6) In heaven we, too, will be beautiful, partaking of Thy immense beauty, by which we will please Thee, and will ourselves be pleased Here below very few are they who are so beautiful in Thy sight that Thou carest to look upon them with delight There are four things that, during this life, make us appear beautiful in Thy sight The first is meekness, and this is such a beautiful thing that it draws the soul to Thee, and Thou dost feel immensely pleased in her because of the likeness she bears to Thee The second is the beauty we receive from Thy Blood, being purified and adorned by It The third thing which, in this life, makes us appear beautiful in Thy sight, is the frequenting of the Holy Sacrament , I mean confession. The fourth is Baptism, which cleanses the soul and washes it of every stain of sin All other Sacraments, also conferred on us by the Holy Church, make us appear beautiful before Thee The holy virtues practiced by us—faith, hope, and charity, humility, patience, and others—are, as it were, our garments and adornments, so that of the soul can be said "*In vestitu deaurato, circumdata varietate*"—"In gilded clothing, surrounded with variety" (Ps xliv, 10) How beautiful in Thy sight appears the soul in the state of grace, clothed with Thy charity and that of her neighbor, and the precious gems of holy virtues These *conditions* infuse into the soul a prudence, which, to the ignorant and blind, seems imprudence Whoever shall persevere, here below, in this beauty, will afterwards go and rest himself in that place which Thou, O Lord, hast gone to prepare for him , but Thou art sufficient unto me "*Vado parare vobis locum*"—"I go to prepare a place for you" (John xiv, 2), Thou hast said , but the place was already prepared from eternity Thou rather goest to prepare us the means to secure it, by infusing Thy Holy Spirit in us, that, enlightened and strengthened thereby, we may reach where Thou dost call us Thine is a place of peace, and we must secure it by constant warfare It is a place of rest, and we must acquire it by labor. It is a place of contentment joy, and cheerfulness, and we must merit it by anxiety, pain, weeping, and, above all, humility, as the proud will never reach it Woe to that soul that has not its understanding and all other powers, resting upon humility ! Woe to that congregation (Religious Order) wherein pride dwells ! Woe to that city where are proud subjects and princes! Woe to the Church, where so many proud ones dwell, but greater woe unless the pride in the Church be surpassed by the humility of Thy servant ! It would be as a boat sinking in the sea The Church is assailed , yes, by some stormy waves, but the gates of hell will never prevail against her; and she, like a firm rock in the midst of the waters, directs her faithful believers to the port of eternal life

XXIII.

She Speaks in the Person of the Eternal Father about the Equality of the Divine Persons, and then about the Value of Charity.
Mercy, Truth, and Justice

Thou knowest, daughter, that my catholic faith teaches, We are Three in person and One in essence, the Father communicating from eternity to the Word, and with the Word, to the Holy Ghost, the Divinity, and all the divine perfections. And as We are One in essence, so We are also as to the external operations, for all the Divine Persons work together. But as to the Incarnation of the Word, though all the Three Divine Persons concurred in it, Thou must believe and confess what I have often taught you, that it was a work ending only in the Person of the Word, without change or alteration whatever of the Divine Person, but simply of the human. This mutual, interior communication of the Divine Persons is the cause of the equality in the Divinity. And this other communication of the Person of My Word to the reasonable creature, in other words, the link binding and joining together all other creatures among themselves, and consequently with all creatures, is the cause of a certain equality between creatures and the Creator—after this benefit of the Incarnation. As you, when you take two things and join them so that they work together, say that is equality, so likewise the works performed by My humanity and My Spirit, are equal, because we are One and the same thing. This, O daughter, is truly the equality. My Only Begotten left you the first and noblest fruit of this equality of mine that you could hope for, when He left you Himself in the Most Holy Sacrament. The fruit, so to speak, of my equality, is Himself, both as to the origin in my Divinity of the Person of the Word and of the Holy Ghost. This Divinity is first, as to origin, but not as to time, because there is one nature and one divine substance equally shared by all the Three Divine Persons. But as to origin, the Word is before the Holy Ghost; because I and the Word breathe the Holy Ghost, whilst the Holy Ghost does not beget, with Me, the Word, for He that begets One cannot proceed from Him Whom He begets. Hence I call Him the first fruit, of Whom you partake in a wonderful manner, understood by Me alone. By showing to you the boundless love with which He burnt, and still burns, for you, He has granted to you that you may, every time you so desire, feed on Him, and, consequently, on Me, and on all the Most Holy Trinity, that, by concomitance, is in this Sacrament, and He being the fruit of my equality, receiving Him, you receive every time Myself too. . . As to charity, my daughter, it is a golden bond, so to speak, proceeding from Me, and causing the souls to be with Me, and among themselves in Me, for in Essence and Divinity are all the Three Divine Persons united, according to the request My Word made with ardent prayers, in that, His last sermon of charity. "*Unum sint, ut nos, unum sumus*"—"That they may be one, as We also are One" (John xvii, 22). True it is that it is not, in you, intrinsic and essential, as it is in Us; because, though it is My gift, and I never take My gifts back, neither do I leave you, unless I am first offended and left by you, still you are liable to lose it, and through your fault and weakness nothing do you lose so easily, and with so little regret, as this, because you know not the value of this gift. But, oh! what grand effects does this charity produce! See, daughter, if a fire, no matter how great and ardent, falls on a little bit of straw or stubble, it cannot make a great flame, on account of the light material receiving it. On the contrary, if a small piece of burning coal falls on a great quantity of gunpowder, what wonderful effects are produced! My charity is so ardent a fire that We alone can understand it. If it falls upon human hearts, and is diffused therein by My Spirit, it cannot, of course, produce the effects it produces in Me, because *you* are like straw and grass: "*Omnis caro fœnum*"—"All flesh is grass" (Isa. xl, 6). Hence it is that it cannot manifest itself in all its strength, and yet Thou dost see, daughter, the force of this fire working in you. Continue to recount, in thy memory, the deeds of the Saints, and see all they wrought by means of this charity.

They rejoiced in the midst of torments, and were glad when confronted with crosses. Strength rather failed to the tormentors, than courage to the tormented. The limbs destroyed by the torments suffered rather because of the victims' desire to suffer, and their unconquered and cheerful patience. Human malice could not invent more ways to torment, neither could more instruments of torture come out of hell—as that beloved of Mine, Ignatius, was wont to say—but that they did not wish for more, on account of this charity. See how it acted in so many little virgin girls! With what constancy it armed them! How they conquered and triumphed over all the strength of human malice and diabolical suggestion. All this was the consequence of this fire kindled in straw. Stop and think of the many little children who, hardly able to untie their tongues, had, nevertheless, the courage to suffer for My Love the most atrocious torments tyrants could inflict! They suffered even death itself in such a painful manner, that even the most courageous would find it frightful and horrible. Acknowledge that all this was in virtue of the power of this flame of ardent charity which fell, as I was just telling thee, in a little stubble. Go even further with thy memory and thy thoughts, go into the wilderness and the solitudes of Thebes, Nitria, and Scythia, in many places of Egypt and Syria, penetrate into those cells looking like sepulchres of the dead, not dwellings of the living,—those places, either burning like furnaces from excessive heat, or freezing from excessive cold, those mountains, and those horrid and squalid sands, bare of any of the comforts which your frail nature requires   Consider how they lived there, apart from the world, all by themselves, in the flesh, yes, but as if they were all spirit, without garments, exposed to the rays of the sun and to the icy winds; entering frozen lakes, girded with the coarsest haircloth, iron belts, and chains.   They were wont to pass their nights without sleep, and to eat, I will not say how much, but not enough to support their bodies, which looked like dry mummies, rather than living bodies—so little that it would not be possible to live on it, except by the strength of My charity

See, some of them constantly standing on pillars, exposed to all the inclemency of the seasons, others, with insupportable weights on their shoulders, to mortify themselves; others, singing night and day, and as if they were angels, who "*Semper vident factem Patris*"—"Who always see the face of My Father" (Matth xviii, 10), remaining always fixed with their soul and thought in perpetual contemplations   And know, My daughter, that as the things which My Beloved Son did for your love in secret are far more numerous than those which were recorded in writing, so also the works of the Saints, known to Me alone, are, without comparison, more numerous than those written of them

Go also with thy thought into the monasteries and cloisters of My servants of both sexes, in the olden times. Look into the works performed by the Religious in the beginning and fervor of the Religious Orders   How great ! how stupendous were they not !   What ardor of charity !   What fervor in My servants !   And whence came all this, but from the power of My charity ?   Now raise thyself in thought to Me, and consider within thyself, if this charity, which is less than a little spark dropping on straw or stubble—comparing creatures to Me—produces such effects, what will be the effect of an infinite and eternal fire in My bosom, which is like the strongest powder, breaking and destroying every obstacle it may meet, such as the ingratitude of My creatures?   And know, O daughter, that the reason which moves Me to do good to My creatures, and to man, so unmindful of My benefits, is not the correspondence I meet with in him, as he is most ungrateful; but that the strength of My charity is stimulated by his ingratitude and offenses; and, the more he offends Me, and the greater his demerits, the more the strength of this fire increases in Me, and moves Me to help him.   The more man fled and moved far away from Me, the more did I resolve to run after him, and unite him to Me, so that (causing My Word to become Man) he could never separate himself from me.

Charity moved Me to create you, and to send you My Only Begotten Word to re-create you, so to speak   Charity is the cause of My giving all good to you , by charity you become partakers of Me, and in so wonderful a manner the Word again unites Himself to you in the Holy Eucharist, and I shall grant you in heaven the fruition of Myself.   This charity is a bond binding the soul so closely to Me as to make it one thing with Myself, because, whoever is in charity abides in Me, and I in him   This, properly speaking, is the participation you have with My equality, of which one fruit is mercy; so that, as My own essence is charity, it is also mercy   And this is made manifest by My Truth , that in order to show you mercy He took on Himself all justice, satisfying it in all rigor for you   Could He manifest better and more clearly His mercy to you by deeds and example, than He did when He was nailed to the cross, whereon He prayed to Me that I should not lay the offense to the charge of those who crucified Him, and that I should not regard your iniquities?   See how He excused them, that I might be moved to show mercy to them, and not punish them as they deserved , and then He uttered that other word· "*Sitio*"—"I thirst " (John xix, 28), showing His burning love, which produced in Him the thirst for the salvation of souls   Know, O My daughter, that to know My Truth is a fruit of My mercy, as, whoever does not know the latter, neither does he care for My promises, nor does he like them, nor is he afraid of My punishments, nor does he give himself a thought to avoid them   From this Truth of Mine comes also the *equality*, because it begets the esteem and appreciation one must entertain of My grace, whereby this *equality* is acquired   If thou dost wish to know who are those who despise My *equality*, I will tell you· they are those (and there is such an abundance of them to-day on the earth) thou dost call *My Christs*, and justly so   These in My Church look for places and honors through deception, hypocrisy, and mendacity , and as these, excepting the good ones, are dissemblers and liars so they even do worse, by allowing their subjects to serve Me with less hypocrisy, and dissimulation Daughter, does it not look so to you ?   they seek to keep with gold in   in the tabernacles and sacred vessels, which I like and am not as it is, h, it shows   reverence and honor due Me. But I wish they would try to adorn their interior, wherein I would like con-

She receives the sacred " stigmata " (page 437).

stantly to dwell; yet, instead of doing so, they keep it full of all kinds of dirt—so dirty and filthy is it, because of the multitude of their sins, that, I was almost going to say it is even more foul than hell itself. And, after all, they dare, with so much effrontery, to come to My house (the Church), and touch Me with their hands, and receive Me in their breasts. How much this offends Me thou canst, in a measure, imagine, but fully comprehend it thou canst not, as it is known to Me alone. . .

Another fruit of My equality is justice. Did not My Truth manifest it when He said: "*Beati qui esuriunt et sitiunt justitiam, quoniam ipsi saturabuntur*"—"Blessed are they that hunger and thirst after justice, for they shall have their fill" (Matth v, 6)? Whence could the beatitude of justice, and the desire and craving for it come, if not from My *equality* ? "*Justitia et pax osculatæ sunt*"—"Justice and peace have kissed" (Ps lxxxiv, 11) Peace and justice go together. I have praised this justice of My Word in all His life; all His words and works being nothing but a perfect justice. I praised it in Him, that in Him I might praise also your justice, which, if by imitation, shall be by you, and in you, expressed; the soul shall be praised with My Word, and crowned afterwards with everlasting joy and contentment in paradise. I have praised this justice in My Word, giving Him a power and a name which is above all names, and to which heaven and earth must bow, and hell, too; and this on account of the insults which He had endured for you, and the obedience which He rendered to My commandment: "*Factus obediens usque ad mortem . . . dedit illi nomen quod est super omne nomen, ut in nomine Jesu omne genuflectatur, cælestium, terrestrium et infernorum*"—"Becoming obedient unto death . and God hath given Him a name which is above every name, that at the name of Jesus every knee shall bow, of those that are in heaven, on earth, and under the earth" (Philip ii, 8-10)—bowing to Him, and acknowledging Him as Judge, Lord, and God. I gave Him, moreover, all power in heaven and on earth; because His Humanity was afterwards to judge the world. As He received this power, He, in turn, gives it, in a measure, to all His true and loyal brides, so that His dearly beloved will also judge the world.

I also raised this justice, in the person of My Incarnate Word, when He was raised up on the cross, that I might raise thee and all creatures on the same cross, and there all justice was consummated. Hence He said "*Consummatum est*"—"It is consummated" (John xix, 30) Then did He consummate love, justice, sin, scriptures, prophecies, and figures, and could well say "*Consummatum est*," having fulfilled every thing in divers ways. He consummated the love wherewith I created you, and the love wherewith I re-created you, when I sent the Word Himself to you. He consummated that infusion of justice I made for Him; He consummated the love wherewith I wished to save you, and that wherewith I wished to glorify you. My Word consummated on the cross the love wherewith I sent Him to you, satisfying My justice for your sins so fully that I received more satisfaction, without comparison, than I had received offense. Hence it is that I am so easily appeased with the sinners who return to Me and are converted, and I receive them in the arms of My Love, because I have been so well satisfied by the obedience of My Word. In this world, or in an infinite number of worlds, so many sins could not be committed, for which My Word had atoned, that I would not be satisfied with the reparation He made for the sins and the offense. Hence, the Royal Prophet, foreseeing this satisfaction, has said "*Copiosa apud eum redemptio*"—"With Him plentiful redemption" (Ps. cxxix, 7) He consummated the love, shedding also what little Blood was left in His Divine Heart, which was a sublimity of love for our souls; as He shed it to decorate, embellish, and adorn them. This Blood was shed to adorn the countenance of the Church, and make her appear more beantiful; I say, of the Church, which He had taken for His Bride, and I for My Daughter, and, as He removed every wrinkle and stain by stretching Himself on the cross, so the Blood of His Heart was shed to give her, so to say, gracefulness and color. Blood and water came out of His side, that the Church might be, like her Bridegroom, clear and ruddy—clear as the waters of His side, and ruddy as the blood . .

My Word consummated the love wherewith I wished to give you glory, by that transformation men wrought in Him through the shedding of His Blood, for, seeing you with and in Him, and seeing that He had acquired the glory for Himself and you, I consummated that glory which from all eternity I had prepared for you. I consummated in My Word, and My Word consummated on the cross, that love wherewith I wished to give you the glory, and He consummated this glory in a manner most sublime. Oh! how great, how great, O daughter, is the glory that by this means I give you! Oh! how much, how much was increased the river and torrent of the pleasure of paradise with the Blood of My Only Begotten!

XXIV.

Of Some Effects of the Divine Union and the Sweet Kisses the Heavenly Bride-groom gives to the Soul.

The first fruit, My daughter (she speaks in the Person of the Eternal Father), of My Union is the inheritance I cause the soul to enjoy by means of the Incarnate Word, the Spirit breathing in human hearts , and this inheritance I am Myself Though the Word has shown it to you in a shadowy way, when, dwelling here below amongst you, He was asked by the mother of the sons of Zebedee, that one might sit at His right and the other at His left, and He answered her that they knew not what they asked, and that it was not His to give the right or the left, showing thereby the greatness of this inheritance, because they did not and could not understand it "*Nescitis quid petatis* "—"You know not what you ask " (Matth xx, 22), and because it was so great that His own Humanity could not give it And dost thou know how this immense inheritance can be acquired ? It can be acquired by you, in virtue of the Incarnate Word, by the sprinkling and infusion of His Blood This outpouring He made copiously on the cross, and makes it now at My right, whilst by the channels of the Sacraments, the grace He merited, is infused into you and communicated by this Blood And take notice, daughter, that this infusion produces in you many and various effects First, it causes to bud, then it nourishes, inebriates, transforms, and glorifies It causes the lilies of jocundity to blossom around a beautiful fountain, and among these lilies the Word hides and feeds: "*Qui pascitur inter lilia*"—"Who feedeth among the lilies " (Cant ii, 16); breathing into the souls, His brides, an ardent feeling of love, whereby He constantly infuses into them the virtues and graces, so that some are always drowning and dying, for love, therein, whilst some survive in the same Blood A soul dies to herself for love, living only for Me and in Me, and seeking nothing in all her operations but My honor and the salvation of the creatures, all of which proceeds from charity Others die also all along the way , for, by the infusion of this Blood they remain so absorbed in God that they are as if dead, and, ceasing from all works, they attend but to commune with and enjoy Me, and, though still here below, they are absorbed in the sublime and divine contemplation The fountain is of blood and water , of water, to cleanse ; of blood, to embellish , and from the water and the blood they receive that most sweet odor which is afterwards felt everywhere : "*Christi bonus odor sumus*"—"We are the good odor of Christ " (2 Cor ii, 15)

The soul, too, produces there a most delightful fountain of tears, which mixes with that Blood ; tears which are shed because of the love and desire of the Bridegroom, and because of contrition caused by self-knowledge Hence the Word gives the Blood, and the water is given by the Soul-Bride. This is a fountain wherein the soul washes herself altogether, and sees herself ; and to which all the pure souls go, like doves, to bathe and purify themselves fully, pure and spotless though they may be ; for, by constantly bathing in this fountain, they acquire a candor of purity which makes them more and more acceptable to the Bridegroom Plunging and bathing therein constantly in this manner, they absorb so much of the efficacious strength of this Blood that they send out flashes of it to the other creatures, so that they, too, beget and acquire other souls, bringing them forth to Me. . . After this infusion of Blood has caused it to bud so well, it also nourishes the soul And with what does this Word nourish it, O daughter? It nourishes it with the inmost marrow of its divinity, viz , with the loving knowledge and the grace derived from the same divinity, whence it receives an untold taste The same infusion inebriates the soul in such a manner that the Bridegroom and Bride, being both inebriated, remain in a state of most pure and sweet union and delight in the pain of love which causes such inebriety. This is followed by the transformation of the lover into the loved one caused by this infusion I am He, dearest, Who transforms And what do I transform? You in Me and Myself in you. I transformed My Being into yours in the Incarnate Word, when My Word—Who was, is, and always shall be God—took, for love of you, the form of servant , and this transformation, so to say, made by the union with you, causes the other transformation of you in Me, which you can accomplish : "*Et qui adhæret Deo, unus spiritus fit cum illo*"—" But he who is joined to the Lord, is one spirit with Him " (1 Cor. vi, 17) When the blacksmith places the iron in the forge and the iron becomes red-hot, it shines and burns and sends out sparks, so that it can hardly be distinguished from a live coal Likewise the soul is plunged into the forge of His love, into the fire of charity, and is united to My Word, Who is fire. He came upon earth to set it on fire, and wishes nothing but that it should burn The Holy Spirit also breathes into it with the breath of His inspiration This soul   n so that she no longer seems what she was b fore, but a n different thing a ther t reformed in Me, and made, by the bond of charity, one thing with Me, so that an ne looking at her recognizes her as Mine and recognizes her in Me -the Author and Cause of such transformation. By this I make it possible for you to reach that perfection with which you were created, according to My idea, and made to My likeness, and that of the Most Holy Trinity, as We are the same thing. You already know that the image of the same Holy Trinity is to be found in all the souls. In the memory, the Word is represented; in the intellect, the Holy Ghost; and in the will, the Eternal Father Himself Memory represents the remembering Word, reminding Me of that love which moved Me to make you My creatures; and thus, by this transformation, you can and do move the will and the intellect to love Me, remembering the love I bore you in creating you to my image and likeness The intellect represents the Holy Ghost; because, as the Holy Ghost is a light proceeding from *Me* and My Word, so your intellect, enlightened by said Spirit, enlightens your memory and will, that they may know this love of Mine, and, by a bond, unite these two powers to Me The will represents Me, because, as I am the origin of the whole Trinity and communicate all the perfections to the Divine Persons, so this will imparts all the perfection to the intellect and the memory, because, without this will, there could not be any goodness or perfection pleasing to Me in these two powers The reason is, that the memory is moved by the will to always remember me, and the intellect to discourse about Me; but what I like most in a soul is the will, without which nothing, as I have told thee, can please Me. . . From this union another fruit proceeds This is My vision, which you partake of in this world I infuse into you a vision of constant renovation, which I make you taste on earth, and later on enjoy fully in heaven Here below I grant you the vision of My Incarnate Word by means of most pure and enlightened faith and perfect living charity, the greatness of which vision was manifested to you by My Word when He said *"Beati oculi qui vident quæ vos videtis"*—"Blessed are the eyes that see the things which you see" (Luke x, 23). But those creatures make themselves unfit and incapable of enjoying this vision, who are full of malice, for this malice blinds the eye of the intellect. . . To the soul purified and adorned (she added in her own person), the Heavenly Bridegroom gives the kiss of peace and love And what kiss dost Thou, O Word, imprint on the soul, Thy Bride? *"Osculum pacis, osculum unionis, osculum sapientiæ, osculum ordinationis, osculum amoris, osculum salutis, osculum scientiæ Dei, quam incomprehensibilia sunt omni carni!"*—"Kiss of grace, union, wisdom, ordination, love, salvation, knowledge of God; how incomprehensible to all flesh!" In these delightful and sweet kisses, all those who have suffered and now suffer pain and anguish, because of the offenses offered to the Word, congratulate and console themselves It is a practice of the Word to give and receive the never-heard-of kiss Hence Thou hast permitted Thyself to be kissed by Judas, that Thou mayest continually be kissed by Thy chosen ones with the kiss of peace Peace proceeds from Thee, the head and beginning of everything The kiss proceeds from the head, whence life comes to all the members, and we cannot possess true peace but from Thee, Who, in truth, art peace itself *"Ipse est pax nostra. . . . Osculum unionis"*—"He is our peace" (Ephes ii, 14) . . . Kiss of union Oh! what a wonderful union this kiss has produced! It united peace and justice, the Eternal Father with the human-kind, Mary with the Word, the Word with the creature, mankind with the angels, and constantly unites the Bride with the Bridegroom, the Bridegroom with the Soul-Bride, with the Church-Bride, and also with the Bride of Thy Doctrine. Oh! what a worthy Bride this Thy Doctrine is, O Word! So strong, firm, and unchangeable is this Bride that no one can conquer and overthrow her Hence heaven and earth will pass away before one jot of this Bride will pass away She gives nourishment to the Church-Bride and delight to the Soul-Bride; confounds malice, brings down all the pride of perverse heretics, condemns and punishes every hypocrisy, dissimulation, vain and false opinion; reduces to nothing all ungrateful and mendacious Religious, and contemns the hatred of all the kings and princes, together with that of all their subjects Oh! Thou art truly a Bride of great value to our great mother—the Church—and hast a right to boast of it . *"Osculum sapientiæ et ordinationis tuæ"*—Kiss of wisdom and of Thy ordination, wherewith Thou dost dispose all things according to Thy wisdom and sovereign charity, passing afterwards to the kiss of love—"*osculum amoris"*—which draws the soul to love, and leads it to that love which has neither beginning nor end, and which is found in all the divine operations, and, I will say, in Thy very justice *"Osculum salutis"*—Kiss of salvation Thou dost grant salvation, O Word, preserving the soul from all dangers and pains, and the Eternal, Individual, and Incomprehensible Trinity also constantly works salvation. Thou dost save the body, free the soul, and fulfill the desires. I invite all the angelic choirs, all the blessed spirits, all the elements, heaven and earth, with all the creatures, to come and hail this salvation. "*Osculum scientiæ*"—a kiss which imparts knowledge and maintains it *"Ecce venio, cito venies Incomprehensibilia sunt omnia"*—"Behold I come, Thou shalt come quickly. All things are incomprehensible."

XXV

Under the Symbols of Twelve Canals, the Saint Discourses of the Various Operations of the Word, now in the Person of the Eternal Father, and now in Her Own Person.

The redundance of the glory I communicate to My elect above belongs to that operation of glorification which I largely cover them with as a river of delight *"Fluminis impetus lætificat civitatem Dei"*—"The stream of the river maketh the city of God joyful" (Ps xlv, 5) This same river of delight floods also the souls on earth which are dearer to Me, by means of twelve canals proceeding and flowing from My living Word, Who died for you Now the understanding of this operation by the soul imports the participation of His glorification, and the desire to correspond to this operation imports her salvation. Very large canals—very ample and copious springs. *" Haurietis aquas in gaudio de fontibus Salvatoris"*—" You shall draw waters with joy out of the Saviour's fountains " (Isa xii, 3)

The first canal proceeding from the Word, dead in My bosom, because here from eternity He accepted death, means the words of the Word Himself, uttered by Him or by the mouth of His prophets. Some of them manifest the operations which take place in heaven, and others those which take place on earth *"Dixit Dominus Domino meo"*— "The Lord said to my Lord" (Ps cix, 1), inspired words of David, indicating part of the operations which take place in heaven *"Cum autem venerit ille arguet mundum de peccato, de justitia et de judicio"*—"When He (the Paraclete) is come, He will convince the world of sin, of justice, and of judgment" (John xvi, 8) These words point out some of the operations taking place here below, as the words of the Holy Ghost are also those of the Word. The same Spirit will convince *" de peccato "* Oh ! how this horrible monster encumbered and still encumbers the world ! Blindness not in the Jews alone—*"qui non crediderunt in Me"*—"who did not believe in Me ," but in others who so act as if they did not believe in Me. O Word ! and how is it that so much ingratitude is nowadays found in the world? Do Thou cause them to ask Thee : *"Domine, adauge nobis fidem"*—"Lord, increase our faith " (Luke xvii, 5), but the faith, *"Quæ per dilectionem operatur"*—"That worketh by charity" (Galat v, 6), not the faith which is dead, or extinguished, even *"Dæmones credunt et contremiscunt"*—"The devils also believe and tremble" (James ii, 19). Grant that the faith of Thy followers may conform to their works, and their works to the faith How many shipwrecks in the faith ! How many sins ! What will follow? Faith follows the route of the sun ; here it arises, there it sets, there it goes high, there it goes down , and what do the shadows of sin, everywhere visible, indicate but the setting of this sun of faith? He will convince the world of *justice* so despised, and finally of *judgment*, because, He having freed us from the slavery of the devil, men return, through their own fault, to place themselves under the yoke of so cruel a tyrant They, fleeing the yoke of Christ, which is sweet and light and brings eternal rest, submit to the yoke of the world, which, by its weight, in this life is unbearable and allows us no rest at all, and in the next will bring us eternal torments . . .

The second canal means the operations of the Incarnate Word during His childhood, which manifest also the operations of heaven and earth Sitting in the midst of the doctors the Word shows the operations of heaven, whilst He is asked questions by the wisdom of the world, and He overcomes this same wisdom And, what is more, He overcomes even the heavenly wisdom , as all wisdom is centred in the Word, and all the wisdom that creatures may possess is but a spark of the superabundance of the Word's wisdom He excels the wisdom, because the wisdom is in the Word, and not the Word in the wisdom And, standing in the centre, He shows that He should be adored, and can command He sits at the right hand of the Father, in the midst of the Father, in His bosom , and whilst there He shows Himself to be the Judge of the universe. He shows the operations that must be constantly performed upon earth, in His circumcision, which is shedding of blood, pain, sorrow, and the diminution of His limbs ; by which He teaches us that pain and sorrow, and in many the shedding of blood, is indispensable during this, our mortal pilgrimage. I do not add diminution of limbs, but of our own will, which, by far, surpasses the pain of exterior limbs

The third canal signifies the operations performed by the Word in His youth, for conversing on earth and being at the same time in the bosom of the Father, He shows by His miracles the operations which are performed in heaven, as by one word *"Adolescens, tibi dico surge"*—"Young man, I say to thee, arise" (Luke vii, 14), he was raised ; just as it happens when it is in God's mind to do a certain thing, that the thing is done immediately, and to will and to do are one and the same thing *Dixit et fr. i in H. statu ed they were m it "* (Ps xxxii, 9) In raising Lazarus He manifested the operations which are performed in this miserable time and to accomplish them many things have to be done. One must move his feet, repeat words, shed tears, groan within himself Perseverance is also necessary, and a discreet self-reproach , a frequent confession, not only with tears, but also with the shedding of blood And it is a laborious task to accomplish this, on account of the incessant warring between the soul and the body, the reason and the sense, the world, the flesh, and the devil

The fourth canal, flowing from the Word, is the love He manifested for us from the wood of the cross, that love by which He gave paradise to the good thief. He points out that eternal day, in which there is no variation, by saying "*Hodie*"—"To-day " By this word He likewise shows that He has the power to give paradise and the happiness to be found therein . "*Hodie mecum eris in paradiso*"—' This day thou shalt be with Me in paradise" (Luke xxiii, 43) He shows that the operation is performed hiddenly; as He was then hidden He shows, moreover, that we cannot, by our offenses, prevent His operations and His giving beatitude and glory to whomsoever He pleases In the other words· "*Pater, ignosce illis*"—"Father, forgive them " (Luke xxiii, 34), He shows the operations of the earth Saying "Father," He makes Himself a subject; saying, "forgive them," He shows the charity and compassion we should feel for our neighbor ; saying "for they know not what they are doing," He shows our ignorance in doing our works and discerning His

The fifth canal is the power Thou hast manifested to us in Thy Resurrection, O Word! In the Resurrection of Thy Humanity Thou dost show the power Thou dost possess and wilt give, afterwards, to Thy elect, raising their bodies from their graves, endowed with movement and all other properties, and the glory which is Thy supreme reward and our final end Saying to Magdalen "*Noli Me tangere*"—"Do not touch Me" (John xx, 17). and questioning the two disciples on their way to Emmaus, Thou dost indicate the operations which are performed upon the earth, and that we should be retired, and not relaxed Saying, "Do not touch me," Thou showest that we must not permit ourselves to be touched by anyone so as to be led by their evil example, and that we must not share Thy gifts with everybody By questioning Thy two disciples Thou dost teach us, that whilst we journey here below, we can always learn to work with the greatest prudence, always seeking to teach by means of our actions

The sixth canal shows Thy heavenly and exalted operations , and it is Thy wonderful and glorious Ascension wherein Thou dost manifest the operation constantly going on in heaven, where Thy power in a moment assumes Thy body, and can, if Thou willest it, assume and lead into heaven (as was the case with Thy Mother) the body of any one it may please Thee to draw unto Thyself, and in a moment, nay, a thousand times in a moment, Thou dost assume to Thyself, if not the bodies, the souls of Thy elect Reprehending Thy disciples, and ascending the mountain, Thou dost show the operations which are performed on earth , for, whilst we are here below we must ascend the mountain of Thy knowledge, reproaching ourselves with our faults and our little faith. Moreover, in preserving Thy wounds, Thou didst wish to show to Thine elect that what was cause of confusion and shame here below, will be, hereafter, in heaven, cause of merit and glory . . .

The seventh canal, which manifests these operations, is the offering made to the Eternal Father by the Word, of His Divinity and Humanity , offering which He made on His entering and leaving, and all the time He remained in this world On entering into the bosom of the Mother. on leaving from the arms of the cross, and constantly during His mortal life, when "*Erat pernoctans in oratione Dei*"—"He passed the whole night in the prayer of God " (Luke vi, 12). And how fervent was He then, when the blood being fired by the heat of love, could not contain itself in the veins, but oozed out The offering of the Divinity, then, is the operation performed in heaven , because it shows the greatness of the Father, which is not possible nor convenient for man to understand The offering of the Humanity shows the operation performed on earth , as we here below must offer all our works, either actually or habitually, in union with said Humanity, that they may be acceptable to the Eternal Father

The eighth canal, manifesting this operation of heaven and earth, is nothing else (so I understand it, and I believe I am not mistaken) but that praise of glorification given by the Word to His Eternal Father, when He actually overcame all who wanted to prevent the work of the redemption This is the most worthy work *ad extra*, and gives the most glory in heaven—I mean the praise given by the Word to the Father, by which, praising Him for the glory given to His Humanity and all His elect, He increases the glory, but not the essential glory for Himself or others, for there can be no essential increase in heaven where one cannot merit anymore, and the reward is given according to merit, in the beatific vision Neither does He increase the essential glory for Himself; because all the essential glory was communicated to His soul when He was created, and to the soul and the body nearly all the accidental glory was given when He was placed at the right hand of His Father. But He increases the glory of all the angelic choirs and blessed spirits , so that we must not believe that there is in heaven a higher or more worthy operation than the praise of this Word . . .

The ninth canal manifesting to us the operation of heaven and earth, is the petition of the Incarnate Word to His Eternal Father to grant and communicate His equality to the blessed spirits, viz., that they may be, according to their capacity, blessed, as He is, in soul and body ; and to communicate His mercy to mortal creatures, that in time they may all partake of this equality : "*Ut ipse sit omnia in omnibus*"—"That He may be all in all" (I Cor. xv, 28). . . .

The tenth canal is of conferring ; hence, it shows an occult and manifest glory in heaven, and a despised work on earth. The Eternal Father confers; the Word confers His Individual Being, and the Holy Ghost confers His Unitive Being. The blessed spirits confer their being—subordinate and purifying, and in heaven the Divine Being of our God is constantly conferred. Oh! what a gift! What a conferring! The Father confers all His Being, Divinity, and perfections to the Word ; and the Word with the Father confers these to the Holy Ghost. Ah! all I might understand of it would be but a shadow ; and all I might tell about it, nothing! On earth charity, love, benevolence, are conferred ; and these virtues are despised by the inhabitants of the earth. I am unable sufficiently to praise charity ; but this St. Paul can well and does do : "*Perfecta charitas, nulla cupiditas*"—"Perfect charity leaves no desire." . . .

The eleventh canal is of counsel ; which manifests the works constantly done in heaven, and which ought so to be done on earth. Counsel from all eternity to create the angels and, after their fall, to create man, and then, on account of his disobedience, to send the Word upon earth to satisfy the divine justice. And now a loving counsel is decided upon, which is to confer and give sublime gifts and graces to the creatures ; glory, beauty, agility, vision, communication, immortality, eternity (as to duration), and others. This counsel manifests the work which is done upon earth ; the counsel to give the power to the Word, Who will come at the end of time to judge, and give to everyone the glory or punishment which his works deserve. This should enlighten us as to what we should do, viz., to judge ourselves, lest we succumb in the tremendous judgment which the Word will make at the end of the world. . . .

The twelfth canal, which is the last, is the definitive one, and gives completion to all the operations which are performed in heaven and on earth. The Word in the bosom of the Father performs with the same Father all the operations, manifesting them to us by His Blood ; not only those which are done in heaven, but even those which are performed in the bowels of the earth.

SECOND SECTION.

OF THE MORAL DOCTRINES CONCERNING DIVERS VIRTUES, AND CHIEFLY THE RELIGIOUS PERFECTION.

I.

Of the Nature of the Divine Truth and the Incarnate Word under Various Symbols, and how One Should Seek God.

He who is of the truth speaks the truth; he who loves light possesses the truth; and the truth in the Church is a sea most calm. This sea leads from earth to heaven, and from heaven to earth; it leads the soul that is on it whithersoever the soul wishes. In this sea the eagles sail—I mean certain angelic creatures in the flesh, but living as if they were out of it. They look like men, but are not men, though made of flesh, and all those who are, swim by love, like our burning seraphim. The depth of this sea is so great that no eye can penetrate it. The water of this sea serves to carry the ships and the merchandise from earth to heaven, and from heaven to the earth. It also gives delight by reason of its soft and pleasant murmur. It serves as nourishment for all it begets in itself, and by its crystal clearness it becomes a glass in which to see one's self. O truth! O sea! Must this truth be proposed with such a condition? O sea of truth, how sufficient thou art! O truth! how lovable and how indispensable, but how little known, and still less embraced! How few embrace thee! Man labors to row that he may guide his little ship throughout this sea, and in it he afterwards learns the alphabet of love. The A signifies (*amore*) extensive love; B, benign; C (*cieco*), blind; D, desirous; E, elevated; F, (*fervid*); G (*geloso*), jealous and generous (the Word was generous, and such it behooves also the Bride to be); H (*umile*), humble; I (*intero*), entire; K (*kallido*), intelligent in every operation, and full of light; L, lucid; M, mortified, remembering the blood, and dead; N, negative; O (*ozioso*), idle, thinking nothing of self, but only of God: "*Optimam partem elegit sibi Maria* "—Mary hath chosen the best part " (Luke x, 42); P (*pietoso*), compassionate; Q (*querelante*), complaining, like the bride who could not endure for a moment the absence of her bridegroom; R, ruddy with the Blood of the Word; S (*sapiente*), wise and foolish at one and the same time; because love must be wise in choosing, and foolish even, to draw the soul out of herself, all rapt in God; J, triplicated, towards God, the neighbor, and self, but with that love which begets a holy hatred: "*Odit animam suam in hoc mundo* "—"Hateth his life in this world" (John xii, 25); V, vehement; X (*schietto*), sincere; Z, zealous; Con, counsellor; Ru, ruminating, always within herself of her lover. . . . All this alphabet must be learned by anyone who wishes to possess charity. Truth is a sea, and the Word is a sea also. The Word lies in the truth, and the truth in the Word. God is in this sea of truth. The Divine Word, the Incarnate Word, and everyone who adheres to the truth is in it: *Leva in circuitu oculos tuos et vide* "—"Lift up thy eyes round about and see " (Isa lx 4). God plunges into the truth, and hides therein, and draws everything to it. Truly the Word became incarnate, truly He arose from the dead, and truly He gives us either glory or hell; as truth is all that is, and falsehood all that is not, viz, sin itself. But as truth has its being from God, so it is permanent: "*Et veritas Domini manet in æternum* "—"And the truth of the Lord remaineth forever" (Ps. cxvi, 2). But, alas! that on account of this truth man is hated by other men, and for falsehood he is loved by men and hated by God. But what does it matter to be hated by man, who is vanity? All those who rest their thoughts in man, in created things, and in themselves, do not love truth. Who can explain thy greatness, O truth, and thy precious worth? Thou art the nourishment of charity, the sister of patience, the daughter of humanity, the help of love, the mother of faith, the doctrine of the ignorant the discipline of the unwise, the bridle of the proud, the prison of the lukewarm the ladder of the enamored. the repose of the

tired, the looking glass of the virgins, the security of all Thy elect . . Various are those who go on swimming and fishing in this sea of truth, and various are the results they produce Some, as Peter and the other Apostles, do not catch what they seek, whilst others succeed in doing so , and others again do not catch what they seek, nor anything else. Those who enter in and submit to that Religion so loved by Thee, are those who do not catch what they seek, but get it afterwards in a much better way .
Those who run after the Commandments are they who catch what they seek. Those who do not catch what they fish for are those who keep Thy Commandments, but because they think of some exterior works, which appear to be good, but are not, not being performed in state of grace, are not good enough to attain the sovereign good, viz , they a e lukewarm and negligent concerning the most important affair, Thy service and their salvation. As the Apostle St James says, "They do not find, because they ask amiss" (James iv, 3) , they do not obtain, because they do not ask But to all who seek Thee, particularly in Religion (*Religious life, Religious Order*), Thou, O my God, givest all Thyself for them to possess Happy lot of the brides consecrated to Thee, who love Thee above everything, and in everything serve only Thee, for they possess Thee all and in all, not wishing anything but Thee Those who seek something else together with Thee, though they partly possess Thee, still they do not possess Thee wholly, for Thou art divided, so to speak, because their hearts are divided. Thou dost become like one spoken of by the prophet: "*Cum sancto sanctus eris . et cum perverso perverteris*"—"And with the elect Thou wilt be elect, and with the perverse Thou wilt be perverted" (Ps. xvii, 27). Everyone finds Thee, as he is in himself, hence in such, as St Paul says "*Christus divisus, est*"—"Christ is divided" (1 Cor. 1, 13). Others go about and seek; but because they seek not as they ought, they do not find. They do not seek Thee as Father, Lord, and Spouse, and do not care to find Thee, but seek after Thee with selflove and pride; and consequently they find themselves without Thee, without themselves, and without all the things of this world , because, loving these much, and seeking Thee with them, they lose themselves, Thee, and everything . Next, there is the calm sea of the Word's Humanity, which is truth itself. In this sea some people purify themselves, others dress, and others feed themselves The Church feeds, the soul dresses, and all mankind purifies himself in it The Church feeds with the Blood, the soul dresses with the same Humanity, and mankind is purified by the water gushing from His most sacred side The Church feeds with Blood ; because this, our Christ, like the pelican, who picks his breast with his own bill, and gives life and food to his little brood with the blood that comes therefrom, has done The soul dresses by uniting intimately with Him, as the garment to the body : "*Induimini Dominum nostrum Jesum Christum*"—"Put ye on the Lord Jesus Christ" (Rom xiii, 14) She dresses also with Him by love and imitation, and this is that nuptial garment without which one cannot gain admittance into the nuptial banquet-hall; for he who is not dressed with Christ's Humanity, by imitation and merit, cannot enter the nuptials of eternal life Likewise in this vast sea of the Word's Humanity not only does the soul dress, but all mankind is purified Every soul continues purifying and washing away her crimes and sins in it For those who may not be able to get into this sea so quickly, there is the shore to rest on where there are many trees giving a sweet shade. Hence whoever cannot enter the Blood and the water, and nourish and purify himself in the Divinity and Humanity of the Word, let him stay on the shore; that is practice the humility, obedience and patience which the Word taught us in His Passion This being done, who shall have a right to complain of not being partaker of the Passion suffered by the Immaculate Word, and of not being able to enter therein ? He suffered for all, and accepts not persons nor conditions, but anxious desires Or can this be said, that the creature suffers any temptation or tribulation which the Word has not suffered in Himself for us ? Every creature can enter under these shades of Thy infinite gifts and graces, O Word , because, if there were nothing else but the eight beatitudes the following of these would be sufficient to enamor us of Thee, and lead us to union with Thee Hence let him who cannot be poor in spirit, be meek ; and he who cannot be meek, let him be just ; and he who does not understand justice, let him follow purity; let him be peaceful who has no peace or at least, let him endeavor to possess mercy O magnanimous and eternal Word ! Thou, after all, art the Way along which we must walk, and Thy Humanity is the sign pointing out this pathway, that we may not be mistaken Immovable and unchangeable sign given us from eternity, as Teacher and Guide for all those who wish to ascend to the Father "*Nemo venit ad Patrem nisi per Me*"—"No man cometh to the Father but by Me " (John xiv, 6), the Eternal Truth said, that Truth which is plain and sweet, and an easy road for us creatures, shortening the path which leads us to our perfect and sovereign God But many there are who do not take to this easy and delightful rea... ...follow i... ...se of th... ...reason, f... ...d by self love and regard for... ...by... ...trength of the human reaso... ...hes us to be en tirely dead, simp... ...ithout f... ...Moreover, one must

not tarry on this road, but must walk quickly, for the Word, our Guide, and Escort, strides like a giant, and, lest we lose sight of Him, we must walk along with Him with equal velocity Neither should we fear to become fatigued, for, in this running and flying, so to say, we shall rest; and He will give us strength to run quickly, nay, to fly. Those who only walk are they who begin with great fervor, and soon fail, as this fervor is not genuine Hence it comes that they wish to stop for everything they hear or see along the route, and they lose time They taste not the sweetness and purity of this road, and, what is worse, through paying attention to other things, little by little they lose their fervor, which is not genuine, because it is not yet founded on the living stone of the Divine Saviour; that is, according to His will, without following in anything our own will and appetites, even though they appear to us good and spiritual For, if we follow after what may be called spiritual consolations, when these fail us (God in His judgment sometimes depriving us of them) we fall away from all fervor, and give way to lamentations and regrets, forsaking even the very way of truth But those who run on the same road are they who are already well founded on the living stone, so that they are never a source of scandal to their neighbor, or of offense to God; and these run fast, but do not fly. Those who really fly are they who are no longer wise, reasoning about truth, and no longer care to understand it, but simply with a burning desire run to embrace all truth, and with a love all inflamed with it, looking only to God, they go to Him These do not stop while on the road of truth in any virtue, to practice it, as an act of it, and to form the habit thereof, though this would be very well done; but go on simply with the desire to be united with God, looking to nothing but the end Because of the ardent wish to reach it, they do not consider or look to the means as such, but only to the end, so that, soaring away at once, they reach the highest degree of perfection. . .

The Incarnate Word is also a looking-glass for our souls, but one must have his eyes well purified in order to be able to look at Him O blessed soul ever looking at Him ! O Divine Spouse, Thou also art Love ! And how canst Thou help showing Thyself as such ? Show me, I beg of Thee, what Thou hast done with that publican. Magdalen was also a sinner, when Thou didst manifest Thy clemency to her But, pray, show me what Thou didst with that so-much-loved Zacchaeus But, behold, I feel in my interior that I must ascend, as he did, if I wish to get Thee. This Spouse of mine passes along the road, but one must raise himself up to take the cross the Lord gives him. Zacchaeus would not have seen Thee, my Lord, if he only considered his small stature; but everyone must take up the cross, large or small, which Thou givest to him. This Divine Word shows Himself to me in thick darkness Wonderful thing ! the light is found among the darkness But what does this indicate, except that the soul filled with darkness—that is, her own passions—finds the Divine Word ? Blessed the soul that, possessing and conquering her passions, finds the Word But one must conquer and hate them—conquer them, because they must be subjected to reason; hate them, because we must hate all things hurtful to our souls This Word is found in the darkness; shall I contradict the beloved John, who says "Et tenebræ in eo non sunt ullæ" —"And in Him there is no darkness" (1 John 1, 5) ? No, because the darkness in which I find this Divine Word is His most bitter Passion The soul looking into this looking-glass, viz., the Divine Word sitting at the right hand of the Father, sees nothing to imitate, but everything to adore and admire, but, seeking Him as the Incarnate Word, she finds Him in the darkness of the Passion Here He is found with great profit, as He can be imitated, having said to Himself, "Discite a me, quia mitis sum et humilis corde"—"Learn of Me, because I am meek and humble of heart" (Matth x1, 29) In this looking-glass can be seen all the extent of heaven— its adornments, gifts, and graces. What else is this but His loving Side ? But when we look into it, He causes us to receive every gift and grace, because "Oculi Domini super metuentes eum"—"The eyes of the Lord are on them that fear Him" (Ps. xxx11, 18)

This communication of His brings to me four kinds of knowledge—one concerning God, one concerning myself, another concerning my neighbor, and another, Religion. O glass without stain ! if thou wert more known, thou wouldst be embraced and loved. The knowledge He will give me concerning God, when I look into this glass, will be as to the greatness of the love He bore, bears, and shall bear all mankind, shown by the constant commemoration He gives me of His Passion Whoever possesses this knowledge, is always burning with love for his God The knowledge concerning myself has reference to the benefit not only of the creation, but also of the redemption and the vocation That concerning my neighbor has reference to the manner of dealing with various kinds of persons, in which one must exercise a hidden prudence, using this knowledge in joining those characters in the bonds of peace Many there are who know how to converse, but in the inmost recess of their hearts, know not how to compassionate and endure The knowledge concerning Religion consists in knowing how useful and necessary it is to keep the Religion and the Rule according to the first spirit and rigor of its foundation, observing faithfully all promises and vows which a religious soul makes to God, and constantly keeping the mind away from the world as much as possible Thus, O my Jesus, I ask for all that they may know how useful it is to keep their eyes fixed on Thee in the choice of the state they wish to embrace. The nurse of this knowledge of the Religion is interior mortification or simplicity. These seem two different things, but they are united in one   Behold the glass I must look at in the Side of the Incarnate Word .   I will also take from My Spouse a model of all I should do , and, being unable to copy it fully on account of my frailty, I will at least show Him my gratitude and thank Him because He wrought so many wonderful works for love of me. From Him I will draw the rule which will show me how to walk in the virtuous path From His humility I will learn to lower myself and know my nothingness. From His obedience I will draw a resolution never to do anything according to my will, but to submit always to the will of others   From His charity I will learn how I must love my neighbor In this glass I will see also that boundless love He wished to show us by leaving Himself to us in the *Blessed Sacrament*, which is the *compendium* of all He has done for us in His life, Passion, and death   Here I will see also the Blood He shed to prepare a bath for us, in which we can at all times wash our souls and adorn them, that they may appear all beautiful in His sight . .

The Incarnate Word is also a book, in which I must read three kinds of knowledge, which He wishes to impart to me   The first regards His Divine Majesty, and is nothing but a most clever illumination, which He vouchsafes us by His bounty, concerning that so high, admirable, and adorable communication that passes between the Three Divine Persons, and which ought to be more loved by creatures than related to them . . .   The soul that possesses such a knowledge is delighted with those loving complacencies which take place *in divinis* (among the Divine Persons).   But here words fail to express every sentiment, and it is necessary rather to meditate and admire than to speak about this matter.   The second knowledge this book gives me regards the greatness, the dignity, and the beauty of the soul.   How I must acknowledge in myself the beauty of my soul ! Who would not become enamored of it ? O great and inexplicable beauty ! This knowledge of her greatness begets in the soul a tranquil and constant union and peace of heart, and a pleasing meekness with her neighbors.   Blessed and happy is the soul to whom, O my God, Thou dost go on communicating this knowledge , because, as soon as she has learned her greatness, she continues reflecting on what she is of herself—that is, her nothingness   As to the third kind of knowledge—that of the Religion—how fruitful it is, no tongue can explain,   Oh ! what delight not only the Word, but also the Father and the Holy Ghost, take in the Religion, which almost adapts its order to that of heaven.   There is no tranquillity in the Religion, where there is no tranquillity partaking of the Most Holy Trinity !

To the Father belongs the power, also the government ; to the Word, wisdom, with the communication , to the Holy Ghost, goodness, with its influxes of tranquillity.   The first office in heaven is to render glory and praise to God, the principal office in Religion is to praise God   In heaven there is the communication of the Three Divine Persons , and *we* partake of this communication according to our capacity, given us by Thee, O Word !   In heaven the angels are , and in Religion all should be like unto the angels   The first office we remark in the angels, after the adoration of the Most Holy Trinity, is submission to God ; and in Religion, after the same adoration, there must be submission to the superiors, and even to equals   In heaven it is never night, and all blessed spirits follow the little Lamb , so we must always follow Him—Christ Crucified—by imitating His Passion   We should always so act that it will never be night, but always daylight , and we should never lie down and rest without being first reconciled to our neighbor   As the Evangelist says . "If thou offer thy gift at the altar, and there thou remember that thy brother hath anything against thee, leave there thy offering before the altar, and go first to be reconciled to thy brother, and then coming thou shalt offer thy gift" (Matth v, 23, 24).   We must keep God in our midst, He being the light *"Quæ illuminat omnem hominem venientem in hunc mundum "*—"Which enlighteneth every man that cometh into this world" (John i, 9)   *"Qui sequitur Me non ambulat in tenebris "*—"He that followeth Me walketh not in darkness" (John viii, 12). . . .

The foolishness of the cross is an infinite wisdom, and to deny one's self is sovereign prudence   What a wiser foolishness than to take up the cross with my Word and follow in His footsteps !   Prudence is a virtue having special reference to the end , hence a person is called prudent when he or she considers, in every work, what may be the result to him or her, and always acts with mature reflection.   Hence, he who denies himself is very prudent, because he looks to the end for which he does it, viz , the future reward, and knows well that he who wants to go to God must walk in the narrow road, as the wide one leads to perdition.   One must carry the cross and not drag it   Oh ! how numerous are those who drag it ; and how many are also those who do worse, because they throw it off !   Those drag the cross who complain when they meet with some tribulation or sorrow which God sends them sometimes, for their greater profit.   They throw it away who, as far   b y   . . noern   l la . air v. v a'must to rid themselves of every tribulation and s . .i . ' ich th y sen is them.   P t or to these ' for they shall perish under the very cros. '   ' s is intended to be their salvation

II.

She Treats of the Divine Love and the Means of Acquiring It; and Unravels Many Subtleties of Self-Love and the Malice of Men.

I see Mary as a little one, and I see her at the right hand of her Son! O Mary! how well do I see thee, holding in thy hands a beautiful vase of sweet liquor! And where was this vase? In the wound of the left side, the sweet Side of the Only Begotten. This liquor is given to those who give up human wisdom and prudence , and they draw it who, with great zeal, thirst after the justice and purity of their hearts, and have become foolish for Christ's sake. The meek ones and the humble of heart delight in it, and those who really love their neighbor, feed and fatten upon it Those who possess the perfection of charity are nearly drowned in this liquor , as are also those who know they are nothing and delight in being nothing This liquor satiates all desires, heals all infirmities, consoles in tribulations, pacifies the soul with God, so that she does not rest until she sees in her neighbor this peace also. This is the peace *"which surpasseth all understanding"* (Phil iv, 7). O sacred Side of my Jesus, Thou art truly that *"Cellar of Wine"* (Cant ii, 4), into which the soul being introduced, Thou dost inebriate and satiate her with the *sweetness of every taste* But those who are introduced therein are pure and virgins ; so that it can be said of them : *"Hi sunt qui cum mulieribus non sunt coinquinati"*—"These are they who were not defiled with women" (Apoc xiv, 4). . . .

Thou, O Word, dost point out to me three particular ways, or steps, by which to reach this wine-cellar—humility, justice, and love ! Humility is the first step, bringing forth a holy hatred of self, and consequently a true love for the neighbor, nourishing the ignorant, and attracting, by the sweetness of its walk, infidels to God Humility is that virtue compassionating all, deeming itself inferior to all, and it can truly be said of those who possess it, that *"Spiritus Domini requiescit super humilem et quietum"*—"The Spirit of God rests upon the humble and peaceful " The second step is justice, for, when one is just and acts rightly, this virtue proceeds from Thee, O God ! It is nourished by humility, and holds the scales in hand, giving to all what is just, rewarding the well-doer, rendering honor to the great, due reverence to superiors, charity and all that is due to the humble and inferior , the poor, rich, ignorant, or learned, as it may be ; giving to everyone what is justly due, having nothing else in view but Thee, O my God! Justice begets truth, which is but a constant act of sincerity towards God and our neighbor. Love is the third step, which contains in itself great power of motion, so that in an instant it takes us into the wine-cellar of the Divine Side But there are three kinds of love obstructing this holy and pure love ; first is the great and disordered self-love ; secondly, the great and solitary love for material things , thirdly, the great and restless love for creatures. Oh ! how much the disordered love of creatures interferes with this pure, divine love ! Would to my Spouse that this were not found upon the earth, or, at least, among the Religious ; for, I dare say, there is no Religion where someone does not love with particular affection not only relations, but even the Religious Though not a great offense, this is, nevertheless, a fault , not being altogether devoid of self-love ; whilst in Religion one must love everyone equally with charity and the bond of love divine But, who can recount the harm and subtleties of self-love? I see a multitude of souls, among whom I discover one, O sweet Word, who, in the act of uniting with Thee, remains all recollected, seeing and hearing nothing, so that she does not appear to be upon the earth, but all absorbed in Thee But sometimes not one hour elapses, until she is vexed because she meets with something not in accord with her will She no longer appears as one filled with divine love, but as one in whom self-love reigns.

I see another *soul* (a priest), who, when offering the mystery of my Spouse to the Eternal Father and in Thy praise, sparkles so with the divine love as to resemble a seraphim , but, no sooner has he departed than, if a fault is discovered and pointed out to him, he will not believe it, and will excuse himself in a thousand ways, to make himself appear innocent There is another soul, than whom, in the exercises of charity, no bird ever flies more swiftly, when it is a question of leaving all that is comfortable and useful to herself, in order to serve her neighbor When done, however, it seems to her she has a right to, and she would like to be shown gratitude and rendered thanks by the one benefited What is worse, she knows and delights in her deed, and wishes to be praised by all Behold the seat of self-love There is another soul who is engaged in all her exercises like a simple little girl, happy and fervent, wishing to see or know nothing; but she delights in being noticed by her companions, as one happy and fervent It seems to her that she does more than the rest, and she aspires to be known for her zeal She does not perceive that she does less than all others, and derives no profit whatever from her work.

I see another soul, who, in the austerity of her life seems to equal a St. Anthony (the Abbot) Thousands upon thousands of instances of the old Fathers come up in her mind, for her imitation, and every hour she makes a thousand resolutions, but, if obedience forbids her this austerity, she stubbornly refuses to obey, as if she had discretionary powers in her own hand Another one behaves in the refectory with fixed gravity and mortification, but delights in it and likes to be deemed holier than the rest Though aspiring to abstinence and mortification, she would like, nevertheless, to be shown by others every consideration, and is not satisfied, many a time, with what the poverty of Religion can afford Thus she never rests , for, when some consideration is paid to her, it seems excessive to her , and when it is not given to her, it seems as if no consideration whatever was paid to her Hence, not wanting to practice abstinence by taking the little that Religion can afford to give others, she does not see that by her will she wishes to have more than the rest Here self-love greatly prevails. Another one in the recreation hall, seems to hold the scales in her left hand, and the emblem of justice in her right, and, like another St. Paul, thinks that nothing whatever can separate her from the charity of God. She takes no care to guard the senses, it seeming to her that she is so interiorly united to God, that nothing can harm her. Likewise, in the place of dissipation, to so call it, viz , in the parlor, she wishes to show so much wisdom, that she appears desirous to surpass that of St. Augustine. She uses such prudence in conversing, as almost to make it appear that she, of her own wisdom, chose the Religious vocation, instead of acknowledging it from God What is worse, hearing of this world's miseries, it seems to her as if the world, because of her holiness, did not deserve to hold her Thus she manifests her own perfection, and, more still, she thinks she must make known to others their goodness also, and with sweet talk she allures the creatures and makes them feel too confident By this they lose much time in which they might praise and bless God more and more Here is a subtle and hidden pride ; and self-love is its seat I will say with Paul, "Perils in the wilderness, perils in the sea, perils in solitude, perils from false brethren " (2 Cor. xi, 26), moreover, I will say, perils in myself, if I do not deny myself, by lowering and reputing myself as nothing , perils out of myself, if I do not flee self-complacency in these abasements and humiliations.

O man, how great is thy malice ! O Eternal Father, I pray Thee, grant me light and strength to know, abhor, and avoid it ! . . Know, My daughter (speaking in the Person of the Eternal Father), that the malice of the creatures is so great that, but for the elect and My Brides, who pacify Me, thou wouldst see so much justice and vengeance, that thou couldst not endure it, and shouldst wonder at it Hence, do not fall asleep, but, as an instrument of Mine, together with My elect, do thou endeavor to appease My anger for so many offenses which are offered to Me. And know, that all those who do not reprehend the offenders, almost prove that they consent to their offenses. The malice and iniquity in the hearts of the creatures cry for justice and vengeance more than the blood of Abel ever did The malice lurking in the hearts of creatures grieves My goodness so much, that were I to make you understand and see how it is, thou couldst never endure the anguish it would cause thee But I will show thee as much thereof as thou canst endure, which is nothing compared to what it really is, and yet it seems great even to thee Dost thou know what malice and iniquity in the hearts of creatures is like? It is just like a rust—nay, it is an impregnable wall, standing between them and Me, which allows them to receive no grace of Mine or of My Truth Offer constantly, daughter, My Truth and His Blood to Me ! Offer also to My Truth His own Blood, so that We may thereby be appeased. See how men by their own malice are in the hands of the devil, who keeps his mouth open to devour them , so that if My elect, by their prayers, did not snatch them from him, they would be devoured by him, and deservedly, because they themselves provoke him to do so. I write in a book all the wicked actions and works of these malicious and malign ones , and, opposite this, I put down all the assistance rendered them by My elect I will present this book on the Day of Judgment to My Truth, to Whom I give the power to judge them, that they may see that they are justly condemned to eternal torments Know thou, also, that if in Me or in My Truth, sitting at My right hand, there could be any pain, I would grieve at seeing so much malice and iniquity in the hearts of creatures

Again, if I could receive consolation from you, My elect would give me so much of it—that is, if this could be said, that it would make me gloriously happy Hence I tell thee, join My elect also, in order to give Me this solace. The sinners are in so deep and large an abyss that nothing short of My power and goodness can draw them out of it This is why My elect are more persecuted to-day than they have ever been, and the time has come when My creatures sin more by malice than frailty The more I help them with My gifts and graces, the more they increase in malice Dost thou . . see that the garden of My Church is so laden by thorns and brambles, and the flower of good desires are so choked and squeezed that with difficulty they can bring the r l.t) to see maturity? So much opposed to-day is the good as I inspire in My creatures a human wisdom, that, in many, it brings forth very little fruit   Your mode of living is entirely reduced to ceremonials and excuses , and when people approach the Sacrament of Confession, which My Truth instituted for the regaining of the lost grace, it seems that, instead of accusing themselves, they go to excuse themselves   Hence it is, that instead of having their sins forgiven, they commit more sins ; and all this proceeds from that accursed human respect and self-love   Even My *christs* do not attend to their duty as they ought, and do not open their eyes to see the things which it is their duty to correct and observe   They let their souls run into faults, sins, and blindness, so that they fall headlong into the depth of all miseries   And all this comes from human respect and from permitting their eyes to be closed by pride   I gave you My Incarnate Word, as a most strong sword, to defend yourselves and oppose your enemies , and malicious men, thinking they offend you, My elect, do you no harm—nay, they do harm to themselves, and bring unto themselves death As it is a most horrible thing to kill one's self, so it is much more horrible for one to kill his own soul . . .

This malice is so great that it changes works of perfection into works of condemnation   This malice consists in wanting to investigate the judgments of God and in contradicting His works , it is a thinking and speaking of falsehood and lies.   Those who are imbued with this malice explain what happens in their own way, present everything according to their own ideas, and take everything according to their own caprice   They always make excuses, offend the creatures, and contradict Me   They never speak the truth, having one thing in their heart and another on their lips. .

Who can ever remove so much malice from the hearts of creatures (she adds in her own person)?   Surely nothing less is required than Thy goodness, O my God   O charity ' Thou art a file, filing away, little by little, the soul and the body, and nourishing them both at the same time.   Alas ' these malignant men seem to me not creatures, but demons   For what are the demons doing but practicing malice, so as to deceive the Truth?   Who will oppose so much malice?   Whither shall I go?   Where shall I turn so that I may not see, O good God, offenses committed against Thee?   Everywhere, everywhere, I see malice abounding   O Father, O Word, O Spirit ' O God, One in Three Persons, grant that Thy light may be given to each one in particular, that by it everyone may know and partly penetrate his malice ; and to me do Thou grant the grace that I may satisfy for them, by laying down my life, if necessary   O malice of the creature, how little and by how few Thou art understood '   Good God, it is not understood '   Many say Thou art offended, but they know not and do not realize what offending God means Many know Thy goodness, Thy power, and Thy glory , but the offense offered to Thee by the sinners is not penetrated   . .   If I turn to the prelates, I see a great part of them full of injustice, with a feigned mercy , if to the princes, I notice them full of avarice and vainglory , if to the subjects, I see them full of hatred and lies , if to the Religious, . . . many seek to buy dignities at the price of Thy Blood, O my Christ, and then they affect to convert people by their words, full of dissimulation, hypocrisy, and ambition.

Woe ' woe ' to him who dissembles, or, to express it better, pretends not to know nor understand the offenses offered to Thee by sinners '   Sometimes these appear small to us, because we do not penetrate deeply the great goodness of God   O immense goodness ' diffuse Thyself, I pray, into the hearts of Thy elect, few though they are   See ' see ' my soul, that Incarnate Word in the midst of a great multitude, scourged and bantered by all '   See how they scoff Him and how they ill-treat Him by signs, by words, and by blows '   I see some who would like to deliver Him , but, from fear, self-love, and human respect, they leave my Spouse in the midst of that rabble, to be so maltreated This self-love is, like a moth, consuming the soul little by little, and by its gnawing reduces it to nothing.   O soul ' so worthy and noble, why dost thou make thyself so base as to permit thyself to be robbed of thy dignity ? and whilst thou art made capable of enjoying everlastingly the wisdom of God, why makest thyself the slave of the devil? Oh ' how Thy *christs* (priests) abase themselves '   Being made ministers of invaluable treasures, sometimes they act like incarnate devils   O Father ' yes, no more malice, no more ignorance, no more ingratitude—no more '   I feel my life fainting away from this horrible sight , so that, whilst living, I die an unendurable death, seeing that I cannot afford any remedy to it   I wonder not at Thy elect laying down their lives in expiation, though I wonder that men could be found to make this necessary.

III.

Of the Earthly-and Worldly Prudence, and of the True Prudence of God's Servants ; of Pride and Other Vices, and their Remedies.

People of the world wish for a youthful and perfect prudence , but the lovers of charity, and Thy servants, O my God, must have it very little, that they may hide it, as the fire is hidden under the ashes   The lovers of the world place their confidence in a human and carnal prudence, and put no trust in God, but good Religious do the reverse, for they trust altogether in God, and then little by little show their prudence, and keep it   Like a little child, they can manifest it when they please. The garment of prudence is nothing but foolishness   *"Nos stulti propter Christum"*—"We are fools for Christ's sake " (1 Cor. iv, 10)   From His mouth honey and milk came forth. O Divine Word, in Thy foolishness (for, because of Thy love Thou dost not mind being so regarded by people), I feel like raising my voice, for, looking at Thee on the cross, I see this prudence, and I see it followed by every Saint, but some loved it, and others became enamored with it   .

Pride acts like a very strong wind, which shuts and re-shuts the door, and penetrates everywhere, if it only finds a crack   This wind of pride is very harmful, therefore one must be very careful and fix himself in Thee, O Word, for a long time, so that the soul may be well grounded in humility   The wind, raising a leaf, carries it where it wills, so does this wind of pride in worldly people, it leads them where it wills, and, like grass seeds, soon drops them to the earth, nay, even to hell   Pride is an elevation of the mind above its own being, nay, we may say its *nonentity*, because we, of ourselves, possess nothing, and pride also objects to being subject to any creature   Pride is also the taking of delight in things worldly and transitory, which to the worldlings appear great, and yet are nothing   The soul, the mind, the body, possessed by pride, I will not, I know not, how to compare to anything except a bundle of straw, good for nothing but to make a little fire, which soon dies, leaving ugly black ashes   Such is pride   But let us come to the remedy for this vice, with which Divine Goodness supplies us. This is to look steadfastly to Thee, O Word, hanging on the cross   By doing so the soul thinks of Thee, and Thou, seeing her so humiliated, art moved to look at her   This look acts like the sun upon the earth, which dries it up, and prepares it, by its heat, that it may bring forth fruit   It dries it up, by drawing up all its humidity, so that it becomes more capable of bringing forth its fruit   Likewise Thou, O Word, with the ray of Thy look, drawest to Thyself all the pride which is in the soul, not to draw it into Thee, but to consume it with Thy heat   Let no one dare say that he acquires humility, if he does not look to Thee, O Word, on the cross   I know not, and will not, compare humility to anything but a well-sharpened sword, self-defending and carrying victory against all enemies   By its strokes the devil flees, and the creature with all her strength falls to the ground   .   •

Then comes that accursed vice of avarice, which is rooted in so many hearts, known only to Thee, O my God!   I will not compare it to anything but a very thick mist, which blinds and obscures the clear, bright sky, viz., Thyself, O Word!   The mist comes down low around the waters, and this worst of vices—avarice—fattens upon those who are low and mean, because of the love they bear earthly things, and their walking beside the waters of sensuality   The more they possess of these vain and earthly things, the more the avaricious crave to possess of them   Such also is this wicked vice, that, like pride, it enters even into Thy gifts, O Lord, causing them to be withheld, because the soul possessed by the vice of avarice loses the virtue of liberality, so pleasing to Thee, and spoils, as far as it can, Thy being in her, which is communicative of all Thy gifts   For such a vice, the remedy is a disregard and contempt of self, and I will call the virtue opposed to this vice the knowledge of Thee ; for, from this comes liberality, which would like to die, that it might communicate all Thy gifts unto others   But what do I say—*cease being?*   It would like to possess a thousand beings, to be able to give itself not only for Thee, and to Thee, but also to its neighbors and for their benefit   Thus, as the avaricious would like to have and keep everything for himself, Thy liberal servant, on the contrary, leaves everything to whomsoever wishes it   Liberality is like the olive tree bearing fruit, and as from the olive comes that useful oil which seasons food, and feeds the lamps, so also the souls possessing that liberality which comes of Thee are enlightened and also enlightening   They give a seasoning, which imparts a taste to all their works   *"Quasi oliva speciosa in campis"*—"As a fair olive tree in the plains" (Ecclus xxiv, 19), that soul can be said who is adorned by Thy goodness with this virtue divine   ,

Anger is nothing but a kindling of the blood, and is caused by pride ; hence pride is the mother of anger, so that one feeds and the other receives, pride, as the mother, feeds anger, and this, as an offspring, is inseparable from pride   Anger may be compared to a ferocious wolf, and makes the creatures become like this animal, devouring the meek sheep   Anger may be called a self-knowledge and complacency, whose right name is self-love   It draws everything to itself, because of the least trifle loses its temper, and is unable to endure anything it may imagine to be opposed to itself   What do I say?   A look saddens the soul possessed by this vice, and she does not wish to be at peace with anyone, but rather at war   To this accursed beast of anger is opposed the delightful and benign virtue of meekness   'twas accompanying us like a dove fleeing, lamenting, delighting in the waters, and drawing everyone to itself by its pleasing and plaintive cooing . . .

Afterwards the accursed vice of gluttony comes, which is so common. Those who are tainted with it are like houses built on sand, or, to express it better, on water, which soon fall and are carried down the rivers. This vice proceeds from a great foolishness and blindness, because God's creatures use the things which He has made for their needs, as the beasts do. What is given men for their relief thus makes them become subject to even the lowest and meanest creatures, viz., the unreasoning animals, and, although these were made for men's service, the latter become slaves to them. The remedy for this vice is holy abstinence, and to satiate it, Thy infinite goodness, O my God, has given us Thy Flesh as food, and Thy Blood as drink. Abstinence, or continence, is a constant reminder that we belong to God. Thy Flesh and Blood, O Word, keep us always satiated with Thee, and enjoying and tasting Thee, the desire of being satiated by Thee, and of Thee, ever increases in us, but this can only be understood by one who lives in purity and continence.

Accursed envy is that vice which wishes and craves for what is not its own. And are not those creatures, who are envious of brother's and sister's welfare, like the birds of prey called the hawks, that say always, "Mine, mine"—"*Mio, mio*"—and steal what belongs to others? Envy is the *carnal* sister of avarice, because, like it, she is always stealing what belongs to the neighbor. The virtue opposed to envy is that of charity, so beautiful and acceptable to the Word. Charity is like the loving pelican, giving her blood not only for her children, but also for her enemies; and, verily, he who possesses charity, does not hold or regard anyone as an enemy, but looks upon all as the dearest friends, and for all would give his blood, his life, and even his soul.

IV.

Of the Vices Predominating in the Religions, and their Remedies ; also of Simplicity and Purity.

Now, I wish to discourse on things nearer to myself. The above-mentioned vices are material things, and ordinarily thrive more in the world than in the Religion. Now, let us come to the vices of the latter. Oh! how much is there to be said, O Word, of the vices of negligence, tepidity, and self-love! Negligence is born of tepidity, and they are like mother and daughter, the former feeding, the latter receiving. Tepidity, which is so abominable in Thy sight, O Word, constantly feeds the negligence of lukewarm Religious, and negligence holds tepidity, that it may not depart from them. As water surrounds a land, and penetrates gently and quietly, so also tepidity enters the hearts, particularly of Religious, who feel it not, and do not avert it. Water undermines great buildings, softening and destroying by degrees their foundations, so gradually as not to be noticed, likewise tepidity ruins and destroys every large spiritual edifice of the soul. Water also dampens and produces other effects; so also tepidity dampens us all, causes us to become very sensual, and produces other consequences in us. Water purges; so also does this tepidity, but what does it purge? Not negligence, because it likes it too well, nay, one cannot exist without the other, but it purges the fervor of the soul. Not being able to live in its company, it purges it, viz, throws it off and extinguishes it altogether. Water quenches thirst; so also does tepidity, but in whom does it quench it? Not in the soul, wherein it rather enkindles a thirst for worldly things and sensuality, but in the devil, for, from a tepid and negligent soul he gets all he wishes. And who are they that are marked by this tepidity and negligence? Alas! how many are they! and especially among Religious there are many who are filled with it in the highest degree, and few are altogether free from it. The remedy for it is a fervent heart, that wishes for and knows nothing, and, not wanting, nor knowing anything, knows and wants all. Everything is to him earth—heaven, God, union. All appear to him to be Saints, and more just and perfect than himself. He has compassion for errors, gives prudent correction for faults, loves solitude, rejoices in the multitude gathered for good exercises, endures injuries with patience, and excuses them with benignity and meekness.

Now tell me, Spouse of my soul, where dost Thou want to place this bride-purity of Thine, so loved? I find no place worthy of her. But, dear Spouse, I would like to know what prevents this delicate bride of Thine from finding rest in me, and in us. I will tell thee, my soul; as I cannot make others understand it. It is kept off by the least look not given for God; by all the words not uttered in praise of God or for the benefit of the neighbor. Thou dost chase it away from thy intention whenever thou hast not the pure aim to honor God and help thy neighbor; whenever thou wishest to cover, hide, and excuse thy faults, not thinking that God sees the heart and reveals it to His servants. If thou didst believe this, thou wouldst not act so. Such persons are like the leaves of the trees. When the wind blows they are carried hither and thither, and you cannot see to which side they are blown. But woe to him who will seek to justify himself in this world, knowing that at Thy Judgment, O my God, everything must be unraveled, not only before Thee, but also before all creatures   Blessed is he who hides not his faults, for then they are covered by the Blood of the Word, and, he who accuses himself will not suffer any confusion, but will give glory to the Blood that washes them off   Why should I justify myself before creatures?   Does not my pure conscience suffice me?   It is wrong to excuse one's faults to one's self, it is worse to excuse one's self to creatures, and worst of all, to excuse one's self to God's minister in the Sacrament of Penance   I almost dare say, that it would be better to leave a sin, even of a more grievous kind, unconfessed (not a mortal sin, though), rather than to confess a less grievous venial sin with excuses and palliations, because, by excusing a sin, one makes it more grievous, especially when excusing it deliberately.   In doing so sometimes, one, by trying to excuse himself will aggravate the fault of his brother   O purity! thou art beautiful! and thou art ever accompanied by that intimate companion of thine, simplicity   This is very gentle, too   Like a little dog, it follows constantly this beautiful bride, guarding her, and, by its barking, keeping off the evil-minded ones, who would like to harm her and it also leads creatures to her   Those who wish to capture wild beasts, send forth their dogs to bring them out to them   Likewise simplicity leads many creatures to this purity, and they adopt it and wish to follow it, but when they discover that they cannot easily embrace it, they forsake it, not because they do not want it, but because they see it joined to simplicity, which carries with it self-contempt and abasement   Whoever wishes to embrace the one must embrace the other as well   Purity is so delicate a thing that it cannot dwell in a heart too much attached to itself   It is so pure that I cannot take it up, unless I drop all my self-love and opinion.   O purity! O simplicity! dwell amongst us.   There are not wanting some who artfully cast thee off under the pretext of natural necessity, of preserving health, the difficulty of keeping thee, or other excuses, yet thou art so charming and pleasant, and dost possess beautiful, golden hair, which is like so many tongues crying out: "Take me, take me!"   Oh! wilt thou not dwell at least in monasteries, oratories, and devout and pious places?   And yet, even there, thou findest no room, for many, under the appearance of honoring the Saints, do not see that they do things displeasing to them.   They do many things to honor God and the Saints, but God sees the intention and knows whether their work is to honor Him or His Saints, or to show their own talent and be praised by others.   Hence it is, that often, instead of honoring God, they offend Him   They are wont to say they act so as to draw other minds to the contemplation of God, alleging that so the Saints did   As to this, one could answer, that the Saints did it because they had a simple and pure intention, or, because the people of their time were so ignorant that they needed to be drawn to the contemplation of God by external things.   It may be said also, that all times are not alike   Whilst the Word was in the womb of Mary, the Eternal Father did not require that He should perform great miracles, nor that He should preach, and, when He was in the midst of the Doctors, He did not expect Him to shed His Blood.   But the time came, at last, when He shed His Blood and accomplished everything the Father required of Him   This is no longer the time for the Word to remain in the bosom of Mary, viz, it is not the time to feed the understanding and the heart, but to dispute, like the Word among the Doctors, asking and answering questions, so that the sweet Mother Mary may find us with an enlightened intellect and an inflamed heart, showing the fruit of the milk wherewith she had previously nourished us   The same fruit is not gathered at all times . . .   O purity and simplicity! come and tell me how the creature can acquire thee inwardly and outwardly.   These virtues cannot be acquired except by one who possesses interior love. Love is found in many, but not the interior kind.   To know this, let every soul reflect and see whether she is quicker to tell the faults of her neighbor than his virtues, and whether, when commencing to speak of anybody, she is more inclined to manifest his faults than his virtues.   This is a great evil, and the listener also partakes of it; for, by his keeping silence, he appears to approve of what is said by the speaker   Whilst if one's eyes, I do not mean only the interior eyes, but even the corporal eyes, were clear, he would see how the love of our neighbor should be practiced.   A person who is guilty of a fault, if he possesses this love, with wise prudence, would go to his neighbor, also stained with the same fault, and, feigning ignorance of it, would ask his advice   He would beg to be instructed in order to understand in what way it is a fault, and how one should guard against it.   Then his neighbor, wishing to answer him, will meditate on the same fault, to be able to advise him, and not to appear wholly ignorant, thus he will come to know that he has the same fault, too, and they would be mutually instructed   Ah! what a sweet love this is, whereby one who has a clear eye, and possesses this internal love, wins his neighbor. For, if I love my sister, I am bound, O my God, though I were chanting Thy praises, to stop and go to assist her in her needs.   And if I am bound to do this in things external, I am much more bound to enlighten and advise her of her fault concerning the soul, which is much more important than the body   If I should remain with her one or two nights, or as long as necessary in order to assist her in her bodily needs, how much less (if I possessed this interior love) should I regard it as necessary to watch one or two nights, weeping bitter tears over even the least fault of my sister!   I should be obliged to wish her the possession of all virtues, and to labor that she may acquire them, and not only to wish her every virtue and the salvation of her soul, but also many merits and divine favors. He who does not possess this intrinsic love, does not act thus, and many times, instead of helping his neighbor, he injures him He deals with him so subtly, talks so artfully, and, under the guise of helping him, tries to know and understand only what pleases him, and not acting with simplicity, he hurts himself, and his neighbor also. What is worse, this is sometimes the case with Religious persons in dealing with those who, compared to the paradise of their own Religion, live in the hell of a miserable world. When it is necessary for the former to converse with the latter, in order not to displease them, they hide their simplicity, and though this virtue may be possessed by them, they make it appear as if it were absent from them, for by not condemning the talk of others, even when it is contrary to simplicity, by their silence they consent to what is said by them

To-day Religious do not practice the rules which the Word required His servants to teach us by word and example What did these servants teach? Not that Religious should recount to those who dwell in the world their own goodness and simplicity, but that neither should they consent to what worldlings might say—nay, that they should flee from them, as that man, Bernard, enamored with Mary, fled from his own flesh, I say his own, because it was begotten in the same womb The truth must be spoken to them, showing that those things are not tolerated which interfere with the Religious profession. Great care should be taken that the young plants entering Religion should do so with great simplicity. They should be made to understand what they must promise and observe, and how important these promises are, lest they find themselves in great disturbance and restlessness of spirit O purity! O sweet simplicity! pray, come; thou dost always make me understand profound things concerning thee . . O Spouse, Thou dost truly require a great perfection in Thy Religious brides But tell me, beautiful bride, sweet simplicity, why they do not want to take thee, though thou art so beautiful? Alas! I see a ferocious lion coming from the other side, with another big, ugly beast This lion is vainglory, always seeking to swallow this beautiful little bride of purity, and to hinder and steal away all her good works.

Self-complacency dwells always with pride, so that what one does not take away the other one will That ugly beast is the difficulty of an action, trying to prevent this pretty little dog of simplicity from accompanying it Ah! thou art truly beautiful! Come to me, O simplicity! as I cannot endure to see action without thee. I wish to tie thee to my belt. Thou art more persecuted than purity, because that is in the heart and is not seen, but simplicity, which shines in all works, both interior and exterior, is much more persecuted . . . O purity, thou art so beautiful that the Father plunges into thee, the Son feeds on thee, the Holy Ghost glories in thee, Mary is well pleased in thee, the angels delight in thee, the Saints find their bliss in thee Purity is a thing so sublime that, unless God infuses it into the soul, we cannot attain it by our own efforts, but simplicity we can acquire, though with many labors and difficulties . . .

In order that the soul may possess this purity (the Saint went on in the Person of the Divine Saviour) four things are necessary The first is that the soul be altogether dead and out of herself, so as not to have any understanding, knowledge, or will. She must be totally deprived of her being, taking on Mine as far as possible The second is to try and have all her thoughts, affections, and desires well purified and ever directed towards Me, her God and Creator. She must never let anything enter the heart, or the mind, that might stain her; remove every imagination of any earthly or base things that might separate her from Me and leave a blot on her, and avoid as far as possible every sin, even the least. These are they of whom it is written "*Beati mundo corde, quoniam ipsi Deum videbunt*"—"Blessed are the clean of heart, for they shall see God" (Matth. v, 8) The third necessity is cleanliness and bodily purity—I mean, holy virginity, in which state I placed all the Religious, as they vowed to Me to preserve it They must preserve it very strictly, keeping it as a precious treasure, for they become apt thereby to receive My purity The fourth and last is holy humility, which pleases Me so that I do not care for any other virtue in the soul that is without it, for humility is the mother of purity, and *vice versa* This purity is offended by the least degree of self-will, by the least disordered affection, by the smallest grain of the dust of earthly things This purity is tarnished by a word not well pondered, and it condemns every look of the soul into her own being, which is a nonentity. This purity abhors every taste, sentiment, and imagination outside of God .

Many are the Religious who possess it (she now speaks in her own person), but, alas! many also there are who have not joined it with the other two virtues, humility and charity. The splendor and candor of virginity is without ornament, and almost tarnished, without the practice of the other two virtues Virginity is not acceptable to Thee at all, O my God, without humility and charity Many souls are now in hell, who have kept virginity, but no one will ever be found in the heavenly Fatherland who has not possessed during this life humility and charity . . . Humility was perfect in thee, O beloved John (it was the feast-day of St. John the Evangelist); it was holy humility, and not such as is found to-day in the souls wishing to possess it. Some wish to be humble in themselves, but will not submit to God or creatures These will never possess humility. Others submit to God, obeying His Commandments, but do not wish to submit to creatures for God's sake. Though these, to some extent, partake of this humility, they are as if dressed in a very contemptible and abject garment Some seek humility by submitting to God and creatures for the love of God, and beseeching for it in fervent prayer; and these are they who acquire it, but not perfectly. Thou, O beloved John, makest me understand that if the soul will not sink herself down, even into hell, sincerely deeming herself worse than the very infernal spirits, not by nature, but by sin, she cannot truly declare herself the possessor of humility. Then she can rest with thee on the breast of Jesus, drawing therefrom those deep secrets and that delightful taste of love. As we cannot, like John, rest visibly on the breast of Jesus Incarnate, we must rest on the Holy Gospel, for this, after all, came out of the Heart of the Incarnate Word The seat of life is in the heart, so the life of the soul lies in the observance of the commandments and of the evangelical counsels.

V.

Self-Love and Charity Compared.

Self-love is ugly, but holy charity is beautiful and wise They seem to be disposed to fight one against the other, but charity is so well armed as to regard the blows of the other as a breath of wind St Catherine teaches me how to overcome in this struggle, viz , by taking the side of humility. This fight against self-love lasts the whole of our lifetime; for self-love pursues us all the time, beginning in the cradle, ending at the grave. When did charity begin to love us? Charity is eternal, because *"Deus charitas est"*—"God is charity" (1 John iv, 16). Charity began to love us when we were still in God's mind, and will last as long as eternity will. It exclaims and says *"Congratulamini mihi"*—"Congratulate with me" (Phil ii, 18). It invites everyone to rejoice and make merry, and says *"Lætare, Jerusalem, et conventum facite omnes qui diligitis eam, gaudete cum lætitia"*—"Rejoice, Jerusalem, and gather together all ye who love her, and rejoice with gladness " Invite her to a gathering in thy soul, viz , see that there is order and union therein, and that the powers be subject to charity When all the powers, wishes, passions, and concupiscence are quiet and subject to charity, nothing is to be feared from self-love; because, if it attempts to enter the soul, charity comes forward and repels it, opposing it as a wall and a *trench*. The fight we must carry on with this self-love all our lifetime consists in never doing anything for our own honor or comfort We must never rest by day or night, but repel it always. Our own reputation and comfort are the two eyes of this accursed self-love, and we must leave nothing undone to pluck them out and blind it altogether. Hence, with heart burning with divine charity and true love for our neighbor, we should incline our ears to him, as the Prophet says, and not our eyes, or lips, or anything else , because many look to their neighbor, but hear him not, as was the case with Dives in regard to poor Lazarus. We should incline our ears, so that, by hearing, the understanding may be reached, and the will bent to listen to and grant the request We must incline our ears to the little ones, the poor, the needy of soul and body, answering them peacefully and meekly; but that silly old fellow, Self-love, or Sensual-love, desirous that the ears be inclined to the kings of the earth and their riches, should be despised and destroyed by our mortifications and sufferings Divine love cuts off the head of sensual love by two kinds of knowledge, one of which is to prepare a seat in the soul for this love divine; and the other, the knowledge that sensual love is opposed to divine love *"Amicitia hujus mundi inimica est Dei"*—"The friendship of this world is the enemy of God" (James iv, 4). O love divine, thy words are but a new canticle *"Cantate Domino canticum novum, Mandatum novum do vobis'* —"Sing ye to the Lord a new canticle ," "A new commandment I give unto you " (Ps. cxlix, 1 , John xiii, 34) This is the new canticle, and what else beside love and charity is contained in this commandment? The love of God and that of our neighbor go together, kissing one another, and to a distant beholder, whose sight is not very clear, they seem to be equal ; but, on closer inspection one finds a great difference between them The love of our neighbor makes us fulfill the law, performing our works in God, and for God, ' it the love of God not only makes us fulfill the law, but also deifies us in God.

VI.

During an Apparition of St. Ignatius de Loyola and St. Angelo, the Carmelite, She is Instructed concerning Humility and Poverty.

I, Ignatius, was chosen by the Mother of thy Spouse to entertain thee about humility, hearken, then, to my words · Humility must be infused, like oil in the lamp, into the tender candidates of Religion, and they will never shine with sanctity and perfection, unless, every moment, they are taught humility, and are exercised and tried in it, being shown how this virtue is indispensable to the true Religious Humility is nothing but a constant knowledge of one's nonentity, and a constant enjoyment of all those things which tend to produce self-contempt. But one must see to it that in all the humiliations to which the young plant is submitted to attain that end, it remains immovably fixed, reminding *her* that for no other purpose did she receive the habit That the devil may have no part in it, their nurse must use a holy artifice, that is, when she desires to keep down their judgment or will, and they resist or show signs of impatience, she must reprehend them severely, and make much of it, though the thing may be small in itself Exterior humility must be found in all their words, gestures, and works, and must shine through them Every word must be forbidden which savors not of humility, and, also every gesture which is opposed to it, such as blasphemies and gestures against any person's honor or reputation All that is done without humility must be abhorred, as a king would abhor the sight of his son if dressed as a guardian of cattle Let the Religious be, in the edifice of the spiritual perfection, like the stones used for Solomon's Temple, about which not a sound of hammer was heard Let all those who would open their mouths while being fitted for the edifice, be taken to the fountain and there inebriated partly with acts of love and partly with acts of mortification, so that they may be unable to speak, but, like inebriates, be overcome by a sweet sleep

If such humiliation be repugnant to anyone, let her Crucified Spouse be given into her hands, reminding her that she must follow Him Let none rest from this practice of humility until death, and let those who have care of souls cease not from exercising them in this virtue as long as life lasts, because it is a ladder one is never done ascending, and its steps must be mounted many times by multiplying the acts. Being nourished with humility, go now and feed on poverty.

I, Angelo, wearing the livery of the Mother of the Incarnate Word, say to the dearly beloved brides that poverty, the Bride of Jesus, must be the breast they suck and at which they must constantly feed. Not a day should elapse without speaking of this poverty to these young brides; now praising it, now magnifying it, now making efforts to have them love it, and now trying an experiment to see whether they really do love it Efforts should be made that their children, viz, their works, be dressed up with nothing but poverty. This poverty you must love greatly in the food, make it shine in the habit, and magnify and sublimate it in everything God so loves poverty that, to a soul possessing it, He cannot help giving possession of Himself and His kingdom The soul that possesses poverty secures for herself the crown of the martyrs Those who come to Mary's dwelling must be embalmed with these two virtues, humility and poverty, that they may preserve the innocence they possessed when taking the habit

By the exercise of these two virtues, obedience, our first vow, is made perfect Souls possessing humility and poverty confound hell, and have the power of carrying in their hands the head of Holofernes The Word also makes them the bulwark of His city Whoever loves these virtues does not waste any words in complaining, always thinks of the poverty of Christ, and makes as little of her own body as the king does of the spider's cobweb Humility should be practiced with gravity, and poverty with hilarity The soul that cares not for riches and transitory goods, but wishes rather for poverty, confounds and conquers all human wealth, despises all vain delights, rejects and abhors all pleasures She possesses withal a sovereign peace, a perfect tranquillity of spirit, and a security of conscience, which the tongue of man cannot explain "*Beati pauperes, quoniam ipsorum est regnum cœlorum*"—"Blessed are ye poor for yours is the kingdom of heaven" (Luke vi, 20) In a word, by interior and exterior *poverty* of spirit everything can be acquired; and yet, few know *it* and still fewer love it

VII

She Sees Religion under the Appearance of a Most Beautiful Virgin, etc.

Religion said to a soul Do not put on any ornament whatsoever, unless thou hast previously seen that it looked well on me—that is, wish not for anything and do nothing that is not according to the Rule and the Constitution by thee chosen Then she began to purify the eyes of that soul, giving it a most splendid light by means of the breath which issued from her mouth, and flooding it so with light that everything around it seemed turned into light. With the same breath she removed from its eyes some motes, shutting them at once, so that they might see nothing but Jesus Christ This light, communicated to the soul by Religion through her breath, means that the Religious who keeps the Rule and the Constitution acquires an internal light, whereby she removes from herself the motes of every imperfection, even the least one. From everything she hears in conversing, she draws some good and spiritual profit, even from what are faults. Religion has a file in her hand, whereby she purifies the lips and the tongue of this soul. This is nothing but the fear of God. Not satisfied with purifying her words, she gives her a balm so sweet that, in order to relish it, she does not speak, except when compelled by necessity, and this balm is silence Religion fastens to the feet of her children two spurs of gold, because, though the religious soul walks quickly by herself, Religion wishes, notwithstanding, that she should spur herself, and the more slowly she walks, the more she is pressed to walk faster The spurs are the examples of the holy ones of the past and the present They are golden, because they consist wholly of charity, for in every Religion there is some soul inflamed with charity. But those who did not previously put on this garment, have no eyes to see the past and the present ones We must give place to Religion in our own heart, that this high perfection may abide therein The soul receives four tastes in Religion, which appear to come out as from four springs The first of these distills perfect wine, which is the union of God with the religious soul, as Religion is the most suitable and convenient place to unite with God, and this union is likened to wine, because it inebriates the soul with celestial love Water comes out of the second spring, and it signifies the participation of the Religious in the benefits of the Church in a more particular and noble manner than others, on account of the greater opportunities they have to live in the state of grace, which is necessary in order to be able to partake of the benefits signified by the water A most sweet liquor similar to oil comes out of the third spring, and it means that the true Religious becomes, by participation, like another God on earth, enjoying within himself a sovereign peace, and aspiring but to suffer and be despised From the fourth spring odoriferous balm flows, symbolizing the counsels and helps of the superiors; and this balm anoints only those who are dead to themselves, even as the natural balm is generally used only for dead bodies . The faithful Religious are like unto the Innocents in purity and martyrdom They follow the Lamb Immaculate, surrounded also with ineffable light and splendor. The Innocents actually gave their life and blood for Jesus, but their martyrdom was over in a moment, whilst that of the Religious is of long duration, and is a constant martyrdom . Moreover, their martyrdom was not voluntary, whilst that of the Religious is accepted and welcome . . . Moreover, oh ! how few are they who reach this altitude of merit ! Jesus is delighted when the Religious offer the Blood He shed in His Passion, just as He was delighted in the blood distilled from the Holy Innocents. O God of sovereign good and mercy ! Let the Religious sing that new canticle · "*Ante sedem Dei*"—"Before the throne of God " (Apoc xiv, 3), when they sing psalms in the choir with that pure and always upright intention to please Thy Divine Majesty Oh ! how delighted is God with the praise of the true Religious : "*Rectos decet collaudatio*"—"Praise becometh the upright" (Ps xxxii, 1).

VIII

She Speaks of the Efficacy of the Three Religious Vows.

"*Vias tuas, Domine, demonstra mihi, et semitas tuas edoce me*"—"Show, O Lord, Thy ways to me, and teach me Thy paths" (Ps. xxiv, 4) Various are the ways and the paths, O Lord, which lead to Thee, and these ways are beautiful, sweet, and delightful— these paths peaceful and decorated It seems to many that they are on the right way, though they have not yet entered it ; and to many it seems as if they had reached the end of the road, though they have not begun to walk upon it And these are they Thou spokest of, O Word, they are that *unsavory salt* (Mark ix, 49) which is no good and must be thrown away Those who keep the Ten Commandments truly, walk by those roads, for they do all that God has commanded. They walk through the paths (which are narrower than the roads) who are under a more particular obedience, such as the Religious, who walk in the paths of the observance of the counsels, viz, the three vows The first is holy obedience, without which one cannot rightly walk in these paths ; and this is why so many walk therein so tepidly, not knowing the value of obedience, and not practicing it But woe, woe to them who embrace Religion with a will of their own ! Some also walk in these paths so beautiful, with that poverty so little known and less practiced, nay, despised, so that no one can be found who wants it as a companion, not even among those who are bound to practice it, which rise . . Like we . . . e walk through these paths with their purity, which none . . . The O Word . . . keep all the ceremonies, rules and customs of the holy Religion, in which Thou O Word, hast made

Thyself a plant, growing along those fresh and sweet paths, of which plant we are the branches. "*Ego sum vitis vera . et vos palmites*"—"I am the True Vine . . . you the branches" (John xv, 1-5). . .

But as to those who keep not the promises made to Thee, I would wish, if I could, to tear off their habits with my hands, because they are so unworthy of them They do injury to Thee, O Word, and indulge in hypocrisy and dissimulation, pretending to be what they are not, and causing other Religious to be despised What shall I say of those who are more worthy of blame, viz, Thy *christs*, who bear this name so unworthily? Not only would I deprive these of their habits, but also wish that Thou wouldst deprive them of life, if this would be according to Thy pleasure; because, if Thou wouldst take life away from them, it would be giving it to others, for others, if not led by their bad example, would have no occasion to commit sins These who, as Thou hast said, O Word, should be the light of the world, are more darksome than others O infinite goodness of a God, in bearing with so much ingratitude in the human creature! Ah! if it were a lord who, in his kindness, gave a hearing to his servant and granted him all the graces and favors he asked for, this would seem a great thing, but if he were to grant the same graces and favors likewise to another servant who, in return, offended and persecuted him, this would certainly be deemed a greater thing Yet, what comparison can there be between God and the creature? Notwithstanding this ingratitude, O my Lord, Thou lovest this creature so that Thou ceasest not to shower constantly upon him graces, gifts, and benefits By Thy infinite mercy not only dost Thou incline to us, who are so low and ungrateful, but even goest after those who offend Thee, and believe not in Thee, O Sovereign Goodness! O Infinite Mercy! And in what does this infinite mercy show itself greater? I dare say, it is greater in enduring these constant and grievous offenses offered to Thee, than in the shedding of Thy Blood

O my Spouse! how great is Thy liberality! Thou art to us Father, Spouse, Lord, and Brother "*Pater noster, qui es in cœlis*"—"Our Father, who art in heaven" (Matth. vi, 9) Right was he, that enamored servant of Thine, Francis, to *dwell* so long on that word, *Pater*. But I will not dwell on it, but proceed to the consideration of Thy Being, of Thy greatness, and that Thou art a God of sovereign power, wisdom, and goodness, that Thou art immense, incomprehensible, inscrutable, and infinite But seeing Thee also so beautiful, so pretty, so lovable, benign, meek, and graceful, I will not even dwell on Thy greatness and Divinity. I wish to call Thee Spouse, and, regarding Thee as such, to love and embrace Thee as my chaste, pure, and loving Spouse, knowing that without Thee one could not rest, nor live, nor be happy. Without Thee I am nothing, and even if I could, and Thou wert to enrich me with all the gifts of heaven and earth, I would not desire to be anything without Thee.

IX.

On the Day of the Feast for the Canonization of St. Diego, a Franciscan, She Spoke thus.

Happy and blessed art thou, O my advocate Diego, as thou art constantly in the company of the Word and looking at Him Now I see thee going about making merry, and following the Immaculate Lamb with the holy Virgins, in the midst of four beautiful queens, and having under thy feet a flying eagle To three of those queens thou hast made thyself a servant whilst on earth, and one thou hast taken for a spouse; but now all four of them wait on thee in heaven Obedience and poverty are at thy right hand, purity and charity on thy left, and humility is thy diadem and glory In this world thou didst choose as thy queens, obedience, poverty, and purity, and to them didst become a servant Likewise every Religious, who makes profession of obedience, poverty, and chastity, chooses these three virtues as his *queens*, and binds himself to their service But what service do *they* require of us? Purity requires many things, and purity of heart, in particular, requires detachment from all things under God, and from self (here is the difficulty), and to rest only in God. Obedience requires that one should have no will of his own in anything, however holy, and that one should make virtue cheerful to his neighbor, entertain fervent love and reverence for his superiors, make himself blindly obedient to superiors, and also to equals and inferiors *Poverty* requires that one should abandon the riches and delights of this world, because, whilst we deprive ourselves of transitory things, *it* gives us the immutable and eternal. If purity imposes the giving up of transitory things, poverty imposes even more, viz, that we should not only give them up, but distribute them to the poor of Christ Many do not keep that strict poverty that my advocate was wont to keep—speaking in general But, does not the Rule command all the Religious to keep it strictly? Poverty consists in sincerity, rectitude, and simplicity, which all should keep, and which are known to so few in these days O my glorious advocate, how happily dost thou stay in the midst of these queens! At times they are on his right and left, at times they surround him, making a circle. But what capital shall I make of these things which I have heard? I will not avail myself of them, I fear, because, though I understand many things, I put so few into practice. Purity of heart seems difficult to us; obedience we do not understand; poverty we know nothing of, as we are not compelled to practice it

The lot of poverty is to suffer, and it seems to everyone in Religion that he suffers enough, and that consequently he practices poverty.   .   What shall I say of humility, which was so deep in my advocate? Though he was humble by nature, he nevertheless changed nature into virtue   And, now in heaven, all is credited to him as virtue; and this makes a shade for him, that he may endure the great heat of the knowledge and power of the Incarnate Word, for the more one shall have been humble on earth, so much the more knowledge and acquaintance he will have with the Word in heaven. As this virtue brings with it only lowliness and abasement, it is difficult for the great ones of this world to possess it. Hence it is that, as they possessed this virtue, while on earth, only in a less degree, they are assigned in heaven to inferior places, there being a difference in heaven between a greater and a less knowledge of God . . . But thou, my advocate, wast father, mother, brother, sister, and spouse of humility Father, because thou wast not possessed by humility, but didst possess it; which is a much greater thing   Mother, because thou didst beget it in thyself, and, by deeds and words, didst incline souls to wish for it and secure it. Brother and sister, because as the brother succors the needs of a sister who, when abandoned by all, by him is cared for and assisted, likewise thou didst take this virtue from thy father, holy Francis, who left it to thee by such luminous examples, and obtained by thy exhortations, that thy fathers and brothers should exalt and honor her in themselves. Perhaps I may not be able to explain how thou hast been a spouse to it   But as the spouse does nothing but what is according to the pleasure and wish of the bride, so thou didst not say a word or perform an action wherein humility did not shine. . . . Now I would like to understand the meaning of that eagle which is under thy feet   It denotes contemplation, prayer, or love, I may say, which did not make thee walk, nor run, but fly   All other virtues helped thee to arrive at the contemplation, because purity made thee fit for it, poverty raised thee, obedience gave thee peace in everything, and charity united thee to God, for "*Deus charitas est*"—" God is charity "—(1 John iv, 8)   .   In this world thou didst need prayer and contemplation, but now in heaven thou dost constantly see and enjoy God. And how thou didst partake of this great work of charity! The beginning and the end of every action of thine, both interior and exterior, was by charity and for charity   I do not know thy worthy queen, charity, neither do I wish for the present to try and understand it, as I am too far from the other virtues leading to it   Oh! how many deceive themselves, thinking they possess it, and yet know it not! Behold the proof Thou wilt sometimes hear something of thyself with a certain amount of regret, under the cloak of charity, and a desire that God may not be offended, but do thou, my soul, look well into it and thou shalt see it is not zeal that God may not be offended, but sensitiveness lest thou be offended. Ah! would to God that there was always this true zeal! But it is not so, for, truly, charity is unknown and not understood, though it is so great that tongues of angels would not be sufficient to describe it But, O my soul, what wilt thou do with the greatness of the virtues which thou hast understood? Thou wilt not avail thyself of them, for the door of heaven will be shut, and those virtues will remain in heaven and thou on earth; and, though they be on earth, thou wilt look at and praise them, but not take them.

X.

At the end of Matin, the Night preceding the Feast of St. Augustine, She Expressed these Sublime Ideas of her Rule and the Religious Perfection.

O Eternal Word (she began, on seeing an image of Jesus, which she took in her hand)! O Inscrutable Word! Thy servant, and my advocate, Augustine, calls Thee "*Old and New Truth*," and says, too late he knew and loved Thee   He says so of Thee, but I will say it of that truth, the words of which are, like so many chains, to lead me to Thee, Old and New Truth, and well can I say that, until now, I have not known it—I mean my holy Rule—which is, indeed, truth, as it teaches me the way to come to Thee, the Truth.   Happy would I be, were I to do what it counsels me, because I would thereby surely bring myself to Thee, Infallible Truth! . .   It is old, because it was made and ordained of old—in the Old Testament, before Thy Incarnation   It is new, having been con____ al and ke nt in t e New Te st amr nt ____ct Thy cor ·· It is ancient; because in its ____ nning it w ss ker ' 'g th· anm··t l i·._r·· ·· 'l· ·e· r·· ind rectitude It is also new ·· ____·· · (· Wor' · kr·t pl· is ···· ·r·· ·· w····· ·· ·· hserved by us with great exac tit ar le and perfection . . . . M n over the soul -bride -hould be old and new truth, old in prudence, and new in the contempt of self, old in mortification, and new in abandoning herself in God, seeking nothing of or for herself. It is a great thing to seek neither place nor comfort for one's self, but a much greater thing it is not to seek self, not even God, except for God's own sake, abandoning one's self entirely to His will. . . Even the words of the soul-bride must partake of the old and new truth, of the old, in speaking of Thee, O Truth, viz, of the love Thou hast borne and dost bear us, of the glory and happiness of heaven, or any other thing that may excite our hearts to comtemplate Thee, O God Eternal and without a beginning. Its words partake of the new truth, in discoursing of the ways and means we must adopt in order to reach that perfection that God requires of us, and to which our old and new truth—the holy Rule—binds us; in speaking of the virtues to which it binds us more strictly, as obedience, for instance, to which it engages us so, repeating what Thou hast said, O Truth "He who despises the superiors, despises Me" (Luke x, 16)

We must flee from idleness, so much detested by the Rule, which calls it the receptacle of all vices We should arm ourselves against it with holy silence, observing it perfectly in all places, and at all times prescribed by the Rule, and seeing to it that our words are always fruitful . . . Our words should also be of the ancient and new truth, even with those we left in the world, ancient, because we should converse with them of the kingdom of heaven, and the way to get to it, new, reminding them of mercy due to the poor, both as to body and spirit. As Thy servant Augustine says, our words should be few and of God ; Thy brides should only speak to ask advice, or to help the neighbor, or for Thy love and glory Oh! how hurtful too much talk is! How many advantages do I miss for the soul, while I waste the time in useless words! . . .

I see, by similitude, a young girl to whom the Bridegroom, passing by with carloads of gems and ornaments, throws, almost into her hands, many precious objects, whilst she, amusing herself, sees and hears nothing, but the blackest chancellor, our adversary, notes down everything, to bring it up on Judgment Day The Bridegroom writes down also the good thoughts and resolutions, but, as they are not carried into effect, they are canceled from the Book of Life; so that the devil puts down to his own account even these good resolutions, because of their not being made good in deeds . Oh! what perfection God requires of the Religious! Whoever does not save his own soul in Religions where the Rules are regularly kept, can never expect to save his own soul elsewhere O sweet little Infant, if we would but hear and comprehend Thy voice! Thou art in the Most Holy Sacrament, and at the same time at the right hand of the Father! If I had that lively faith which I should possess, Oh! how many times I would come to visit Thee, to make myself worthy to hear Thy voice! There is no lively faith, hence we do not hear it.

XI.

She Draws various Lessons from the Conversion of St. Paul.

"*Domine, quid me vis facere?*"—"Lord, what wilt Thou have me to do?" (Acts ix, 6). What, O Lord, dost want Thy servant to do in this world? God is pleased to have His elect in His hands, like a royal sceptre ; because the sceptre indicates that he who holds it is a king, and by it he shows his servants what his will is, that it may be fulfilled He wishes His servants, in like manner, whilst they live, to manifest His greatness and glory to His creatures, by examples of virtue and good works, and to show them that He is the Supreme King, Who is to come with great majesty to judge the world His servants likewise, if they are like a sceptre in the hands of God, manifest to the creatures the will of God as it is, viz, that they should practice what He has taught by word and example . When God introduces the light into the heart of a sinner, as He did with St Paul, though this light enlightens him, being perfect in itself, because derived from a most perfect God, still its effect in the sinner is not perfect at once, on account of the indisposition of the receiver The divine light meets that obstacle n ost opposed to it, namely, sin, which dominates the sinner Hence the Apostle becomes blind, because, as the sinner receives this divine light in a dark heart, he becomes at once surrounded by it, and does not then know what he wants or what he must do But, once this light is infused into this sinner, if he is disposed, by corresponding to the first light, he makes himself worthy of a greater light, not on the part of it, which is always clear in itself, but on the part of the sinner, already disposed by the first, to that he becomes capable of knowing the divine mysteries, and is so enlightened that he goes throughout the world manifesting the glory of God to all creatures, preaching with efficacious words and exemplary works This is what this holy Apostle did, who, having been cast to the ground by the light from above, and blinded by it immediately forgot himself, and seeing himself no longer because of the supernatural blindness, was raised up to the throne of the Most Holy Trinity where he understood those most deep secrets of the Divinity and the Humanity of the Word, and learned that sublime doctrine of the Gospel, which he afterwards taught the whole world And why did this light become perfect in him? Because he received not only the interior light, but also recovered the sight of his bodily eyes, for by the first light he gave up his own being. Thus the sinner, on receiving the first light, must give up his own being entirely, if he wishes, after the first grace, to receive also the second, which enlightens the soul as to the will of God.

After this comes the cooperation, which makes him do such great things for the honor of God, like St. Paul, who, having renounced himself, and seen "*Arcana Dei, quæ non licet homini loqui*"—"Secret things of God, which it is not granted to man to utter" (2 Cor xii, 4), said "*Gratia Dei sum id quod sum, et gratia Dei in me vacua non fuit*"—"By the grace of God I am what I am, and this grace in me hath not been void " By the first grace he confessed his nothingness, and that whatever good he possessed was from God, Who anticipated him with His grace, and gave him afterwards His light, and made him a vessel of election to manifest His name to the whole world. "*Et gratia ejus in me vacua non fuit,*" because St Paul cooperated with this grace of the Lord, laboring much for His honor, preaching to the Gentiles, enduring much, and working hard for the salvation of the souls redeemed by the Blood of the Word Saying those words of Psalm lxxiv, 2, 3 "*Narrabimus mirabilia tua, cum accepero tempus ego justitias judicabo*"—"We will relate Thy wondrous works; when I shall take time I shall judge justice;" she added St Paul related the wondrous works of the Lord when he saw that the time was fit to manifest them, and judged justice—that is, all virtuous works—for by justice not only the divine, but also all the holy virtues—as faith, charity, humility, obedience, and others are understood These become acceptable in the divine sight, even by way of gratitude. The Apostle says "*Narrabimus mirabilia tua,*" as if he meant to say · So many are the favors and graces, O my God, Thou by Thy goodness hast granted to me, that I do not wish them to remain shut up in me, but, even on the most risky occasion, I will manifest to every nation and people the wonderful things Thou hast wrought in me, and still dost work and wilt work in all ages in every creature   . . As to justice, St. Paul here means that whenever he saw the opportunity in his neighbors to exercise charity in their behalf, he judged whether it would be advantageous for them or not, and, if God's honor and the salvation of this or that soul demanded it, he would not allow all the obstacles that might be opposed to him to withdraw him therefrom If he observed his opportunity to practice patience, he judged whether practicing it would redound to the honor of God or not, after which, he would expose himself to the torments and to death, with intrepidity Likewise, in all the virtues, he pondered well whether he was to practice them in this or that manner, and, once knowing what God's honor demanded, he would undoubtedly put it into practice As this holy Apostle did, so must they do who serve God in the Religions (Religious Orders) God has communicated to the Religious His gifts and graces; also their high vocation, the opportunity for doing good and frequenting the sacraments, and other numberless favors They must see, therefore, that they do not remain useless in them; but, cooperating with them, they ought to progress from virtue to virtue. . . . Religious are also bound to relate the wonderful blessings which God by His goodness has granted to them, whilst they have lived in the religious observance and the holy fear of God, so that, hearing of the favors and graces of the sacraments, the word of God, and special benefits granted by God to Religious souls, those who might have it in mind to relax the holy religious life, may take fresh vigor on account of the marvels they hear Religious must also pass judgment on justice, not only in their own heart, but also as to their Religion, in order that if it were offered to them, by one who had power, to adopt another mode of life or exercise, before they would consent to it, they must judge and see whether it is for the greater good or only a pliable relaxation of said Religion If they judge the latter to be the case, they should never give their consent to such a changes being introduced, even if this should cost them their life This is truly passing judgment on justice. . . They will also relate the wondrous things of the Lord, and judge justice, who, at all times and occasions, will put into practice all the virtues and good works they possibly can, and they will judge justice, when an action proposed to them as a virtue, whilst it is not so—nay, is contrary thereto, is unmasked by them and rejected, as not being what it pretends to be, thus showing before all the heavens and the creatures that they have not received the grace of God in vain

XII.

Words on the Gospel of the Vineyard.

This Fe. . . of family ʼ me an the Holy Ghost comes out and sends laborers to work in the v . . . yard of the Most Sacred Humanity of Jesus, I say to work, according to His own word · The Holy Ghost is one and the same thing with Jesus as to the Divinity, but here He is . . . Master o. the vineyard who is Jesus Himself because the Holy

Ghost possessed that Holy Humanity as His, according to the words of Isaiah xi, 2 *"Et replevit eam Dominus spiritu sapientiæ et intellectus, spiritu consilii "*—"And He filled her with the spirit of wisdom, and of understanding, the spirit of counsel " . . It is His vineyard, for the Holy Ghost sends laborers to work therein, inviting and calling them with His divine inspirations to perform all those actions which Jesus did whilst in this world, and put into practice all He has commanded and counseled us to do in the Holy Gospel He calls at various hours, the conditions of creatures being different, in this variety we see the greatness of this Father of the family, and His benignity, Who never fails at any time, or in any condition in which we may find ourselves, to call us by His divine inspirations Those whom this Divine Spirit calls at the first hour are the beginners, to whom He gives the knowledge of themselves, whereby they are moved to go and work in this vineyard, and they work in the left foot of Jesus These, who stop in the sole knowledge of themselves, without progressing, are people of little fervor, having little heat of God's love. Those of the third hour are other lay people called by the Holy Ghost to work in this vineyard, by the knowledge of God, and these work in the right foot of Jesus, and possess a greater degree of God's love, passing from self-knowledge to God's knowledge, which draws man out of the imperfect state. Those who are called by the same Holy Ghost at the sixth hour are sent to work in the vineyard by wisdom, and they work in the left hand of Jesus Though this state is somewhat more perfect than the two above mentioned, nevertheless, these souls have attained to a small degree of perfection, because the wisdom they possess is not what is called the gift of the Holy Ghost, but simply the virtue called wisdom, whereby man delights to study and learn a great deal, in order to teach others These possess a certain greater degree of the fervor of love, just as the sun, when it begins to warm up, but has not yet reached its greatest degree of heat, which is felt at noon, at which hour the fourth class of laborers is called by the same Divine Spirit to work in this vineyard, by charity, which is the bond of perfection These latter are working in the right hand of Jesus, and are in a more perfect state than the other three classes, though they have not yet attained the height of perfection possible in this life These have an ardent love for God, and all their works are directed to God, and all performed for His love. They also love their neighbor, and the great zeal they feel for the greater glory of God renders them solicitous to labor much for the salvation of others. The last ones are they who are called to the sovereign degree of perfection which can be reached and secured in this world, viz, to penetrate God's purity and love These operate divinely in the sacred side of Jesus, and are said to come at the eleventh hour, which is the end of the day, because they are called by the Holy Ghost with a particular vocation, much higher and more sublime than that of all others, so that, without any other means, but simply through purity and the love of God, they attain the highest degree of perfection without really knowing it or passing through the degrees already mentioned above. The Holy Gospel says these were standing idle in the market-place, which means that they were in the state of relaxation in God that the perfect enjoy, whereby they only do what God wishes, think of nothing, seek nothing, care for nothing, trouble themselves about nothing, except what God wants These are the first to receive their wages from the Householder, leaving all to Him, for they made no bargain with Him about reward or wages; and as they do nothing to get heaven or any other payment, they are the first ones to be paid off, though they were the last to come, because, being by grace nearer to God, they come to be nearer to Him in union, which union with God is our sovereign reward. The fact that these last came to work at the eleventh hour, when the sun had lost nearly all its heat, means that, by that relaxation in God, they have, so to say, lost the use of the interior sense, that is, they walk on God's road like dead people, indifferent to tastes, sentiments or any other things, without which, others less perfect, seem unable to find God And though it seems to those who are less perfect that they should not get the same reward, as they did not see them working in the vineyard so long and hard as they themselves, viz, laboring by the way of self-knowledge, and the knowledge of God, and through wisdom or charity; nevertheless, the Father of the family well knows that they, in a short time and secretly, have acquired more by the way of purity and God's love, through that relaxation in God, than they did through all the labors they have borne Hence it is that God should never be judged by the creature in regard to any of His doings, "The Lord being just, and His judgment right " (Ps cxviii, 137), and He can do as He pleases, being good, as the Gospel says of Him "Thus the last become the first, and the first last "—*"Sic erunt novissimi primi, et primi novissimi "* (Luke xiii, 30)

By the vineyard we may also understand the Religious Congregations to which the Householder, viz, the Holy Ghost, calls those creatures who come to them in various ways and by divers roads We may put these down as five, corresponding to the five hours in which he Father of the family chooses the creatures for the Religious vocation. At the first hour those are sent who join the Religion by the way of poverty, and these have very little heat of God's love. Still it is by this road that the light of the sun of grace manifests itself to them ; and if they do not stop at this imperfect beginning, they may go on, always increasing more and more in warmth, through God's love, which is found in the holy Religion At the second hour those come who are induced to embrace the Religious state by their parents; who, many times, know not what they are doing ; and, this notwithstanding, they are more easily warmed up with God's love than the first, as they come in with a simple intention, without any malice At the third hour they come who enter Religion to avoid the labors of the world , and this is a very imperfect beginning. At the fourth hour those are called who enter Religion for fear of not being able to save their souls if they remain in the world. This is a much better beginning, and these are more apt to receive the fire of God's love than all those mentioned above. At the fifth hour, which corresponds to the eleventh and last one, all those come who are moved to enter Religion by the sole desire to honor God , and these are they who derive much fruit therefrom, and deserve, at the setting of the sun, viz , at the time of death, to receive a great reward from the Father of the family. All these persons introduced into the vineyard of the Lord, both by holy Religion and the Most Holy Humanity of Jesus, can repeat that verse of Ps. xxii, 2 : *"In loco pascuæ ibi me collocavit"*—"He has set me in a place of pasture."

XIII.

Words on the Gospel of the Kingdom of Heaven being like to a Man who Sows Good Seed in His Field.

The kingdom of heaven is likened to a man who has sown the good seed in his field. This kingdom is the Word, hidden under the sacramental species, Who comes into the souls to reign therein The Word is the kingdom, because the kingdom has dominion over many things ; and the Word is likened to the kingdom, because He has dominion over all things, having been constituted by His Eternal Father, King and absolute Lord of the whole universe, with all the creatures and everything that is contained therein : *"Rex regum et Dominus dominantium"*—"King of kings and Lord of lords" (Apoc. xix, 16). . The kingdom of a king does not consist simply in palaces, possessions, and other things ; but his dominion is called his kingdom, and he is called the king of all he has under his dominion and in his kingdom. But our Word is the Lord of all things, even the souls of His creatures, and He wished to make Himself like unto man : *"Simile est regnum cœlorum homini"*—"The kingdom of heaven is likened to a man" (Matth xiii, 24), in order that, before His Father, He might make us appear like unto Himself by our deeds enlivened by grace . . . The good seed this Man-God has sown in His field is the sacred Gospel From the lips of my Spouse comes the divine seed of His holy words, like very small grains of the finest gold. The ground in which my Beloved sows this golden seed is the soul of every creature. This divine seed, which is constantly and abundantly scattered by the preachers, causes the seed of the Divine Word to fall on the souls. As the material seed, once sown, belongs more to the earth than to the husbandman sowing it, so the word of God—I say His *word*—belongs more to the hearers than to the preachers; because the preacher has for his principal object to teach, and the hearer must have as his object to do and practice what he hears . . This earth peopled with our souls was wetted by the precious Blood, O my Jesus, abundantly gushing forth from Thy sacred wounds, that it might bring forth copious fruit *"Cum autem dormirent homines, venit inimicus homo et superseminavit zizania in medio tritici"*—"But while men were asleep, his enemy came and oversowed cockle among the wheat" (Matth. xiii, 25). This cockle is sown in the soul by the infernal enemy, when the powers of the soul, that should have kept guard, were asleep. Because, when these powers are awake, and diligent, and watching, especially after having received the seed of the Word—that is, of the Word of God, the ancient adversary of human-kind is not slow to come upon the soul with his diabolical temptations, sowing therein the cockle, which is his seed, over the perfect seed of the Divine Word This cockle is self-love, self-opinion, so hateful in the eyes of God, Who cannot bear to look upon the souls which are dominated by it . . . These faults of self-love and self-judgment are the obstacles which prevent God from uniting and taking as perfect a delight in the souls of His creatures as His immense liberality so ardently would wish . . But the Lord does not wish the cockle to be rooted up and removed—no, because He said . *"Ne forte colligentes zizania, eradicetis cum eis simul et triticum"*—"No lest perhaps gathering up the cockle, you root up the wheat also together with it" (Matth xiii, 29). This good God is not satisfied and does not always allow the removal of this self-opinion and self-love from certain souls whilst they live in the world, though these faults displease Him ; because He the Eternal Wisdom sees that, without this interest of self-love and self-judgment, many souls would not perform the good works, in a extreme they do Hence He does not root them up nor destroy them lest these good works, for the edification of their neighbors and the advantage of Holy Church, fail But, at the time of the harvest, viz , at the end of their lives, these souls that love themselves and their judgment too much will be punished. Though God tolerates the cockle a long time in the soul, let no one think that He will ever put it in the barn of life eternal, with the good wheat, unless all evil seed is first burnt out in the fire of purgatory. . . . This most wise God also permits, with sovereign providence, that some souls do not advert to the fact of their having in themselves this cockle of self-love , as He knows that, if they realized it, they would fall into such discouragement that they would do no more good Hence, being ignorant of it, they cannot root it out, and thus it grows in them along with the wheat till death. But even to these souls, at the time of the harvest, which will be their death, God will make known that He did not like this cockle, because it was their fault that they did not know it, as they made themselves incapable of such knowledge on account of their having cowardly and pusillanimous hearts. Consequently, by the judgment of the Supreme Judge, they, too, will be sent to the flames of purgatory, to burn out the cockle which has grown with the good seed in His field. The Lord, Who is the Man of the Gospel, Who sowed the good seed in His field, will say "*Colligite, primum zizania et alligate ea in fasciculos ad comburendum* "—"Gather up first the cockle, and bind it in bundles to burn, but the wheat gather ye into My barn" (Matth. xiii, 30). Do not allow, O my God, that to some souls especially chosen by Thee, this self-love and judgment may remain unknown, for Thou seest their anxiety to find it out. To such, by interior inspirations, do Thou give light and knowledge, that they may up-root and destroy it Thus freed, in this life, of such an evil seed, at the time of the har-vest the Lord of the field and the seed will take these souls without any delay, and place them, with great joy, in His barn of life eternal Yes, yes, O Lord! "*Triticum autem congregate in horreum meum*"—"But the wheat gather ye into My barn" (Matth. xiii, 30).

XIV.
Thinking of St. Agnes, She gave Expression to these Thoughts.

The deep love which St Agnes bore her Spouse had opened for her the door to enter, at pleasure, the nuptial chamber As the confidant, the friends, and secret grooms of the great lords can go and treat familiarly with them, so she had the privilege of entering into the intimacy of God, and did enter therein at will, as the bride into the chamber of her royal spouse, treating with Him freely and with a loving familiarity Hence she drew therefrom those deep, divine secrets of the eternal wisdom, which she afterwards mani-fested to the world with that divine eloquence which filled with amazement all who heard her Oh ! how full of wisdom and sweetness are the words uttered by this bride of my Word ! "*Quem cum amavero casta sum, cum teligero munda sum , cum accepero virgo sum*"—"Whom when I love I remain chaste, when I touch I remain pure, when I receive I remain virgin ,"[1] "*Mel et lac ex ejus ore suscepi* "—"I drew honey and milk from His lips" (Cant iv, 11) , as I hear the blessed Agnes saying "From the mouth of my heavenly Spouse I received milk and honey, that is charity, which, in this sense, ex-tends more to the love of the neighbor than to that of God " Honey, though sweet, is a little rugged ; which means that in loving the neighbor one suffers much , especially when one really loves God and leads a perfect life , because, seeing creatures offending God, which is so unlike his ideas, he finds it hard to love them, on account of the love one bears to God, Who is so much offended by them And yet this God wants us to love the sin-ners as much as the just, and those who offend and persecute us, as well as those who love us Hence, charity having been infused into the glorious Agnes, both for God and her neighbors, she, like honey, was well able to endure its ruggedness in suffering so many ignominious injuries from creatures. Hence, she could well say ' "I received the honey from the mouth of my Spouse, that is charity, which enabled me to love my enemies, who otherwise would have incited me to hatred, as they offend my God in me " St Agnes also received the milk from the divine lips Milk retains a sweetness more delicate than that of the honey , it strengthens and nourishes, and is taken at the breast, coming from the inmost life of the giver, and partaking of her sub stance Hence the milk of the divine will is very delicious, and nourishes and strengthens the soul receiving it, as has been said It is taken by the mouth at the breasts of the Word's Humanity , but what dost thou mean, holy Agnes, by saying thou hast received it not from the breasts of the Word, but from His mouth ? This means that the Word imparts to the soul that delicate feeling for His Divinity by the mouth of His Humanity, and the soul draws Him to herself by the mouth of desire The milk originates from the inmost part of the giver, and belongs to the substance of

---

' From the Office of St Agnes.

the same , and likewise the feeling and the taste which the soul gets in taking delight in the Divinity, comes to her through the Word Incarnate .   It may also be said that the Holy Gospel is a most sweet milk given to us by the mouth of the Church, through the Evangelists and the Doctors who preach and explain it   And how full this Gospel is of the sweetness and delight of the Divinity and Humanity of the Word, let, O my God, whoever loves Thee, and has some knowledge of Thee, say !   This milk nourishes the soul who, by faith and desire, places her lips to the fruitful breasts of the Divinity and Humanity of my Spouse, as they are manifested in the Holy Gospel, and she (this soul) is thereby strengthened by His power.

XV.

With her Thoughts fixed on Jesus Christ and the Blessed Virgin, she expresses Loving Sentiments.

The Divine Word, become a little Child, sings   "*Ego sum in sinu Patris sine principio*"—"I am in the Father's bosom from eternity ," and, to the little Child, Mary sings "*Ab initio et ante sæcula creata sum*"—"From the beginning and before the world was I created" (Ecclus xxiv, 14)   Behold the Word speaking to the soul, and saying "*Quam suavis crux mea rectis corde !*"—"How sweet is my cross to the righteous of heart "   ' *Recti diligunt me et ego diligo eos*"—"The righteous love Me and I them, and their souls are like these little children." . . .   The hands of the Word on the cross distill honey for the lovers of the cross, and myrrh to those who are far from Him   The ears of the Word lend themselves to the pure and righteous of heart, who love their neighbors, and those of Mary incline themselves to the souls consecrated to her Divine Son   The eyes of the Word pierce the souls that submit to obedience, and those of Mary the souls dwelling between purity and humility   The feet of the Word walk in search of the lost sheep, and those of Mary follow the Word's footsteps to obtain mercy for sinful souls, she being   "*Mater gratiæ, Mater misericordiæ*"   "When Thou shalt be on the cross, O Word, Thou shalt draw everything to Thee by Thy Blood (John xii, 32) , and Mary, when raised to Thy right hand, will remove all the sins of the creatures, appealing Thee by showing Thee her breasts   Thou speakest to the soul , and what dost Thou say, O sweet Word ? "*Nihil scias, nihil velis, nihil possis, nihil sis et omnia possidebis*"—"Know nothing, will nothing, be unable to do anything, be nothing, and thou shalt possess all "   Thou shalt believe everything, do and know everything, be capable of anything in Me Who strengthens thee   Thou art so little, and askest of Me so many things   Now that Thou hast spoken to me as a little Child, speak to me from the cross   As a little Child Thou dost tell me to know, will, do, and be nothing, and that I thereby will possess everything , from the cross but one thing Thou dost require of Me, viz , that I shall conform to Thy will   As a little Infant, Thou dost promise me that I will believe, know and be enabled to do everything in Thee , and from the cross Thou dost promise to transform me in Thee   Heavy is the cross, if carried here without the Crucifix, as I must do , but it is also true that greater then is the reward   Give me strength, sweet Infant, that I may be able to carry it.

XVI.

Considerations on the Assumption of the Blessed Virgin applied to the Reformation of Life, and Account of a Vision.

Whoever wishes to reach Mary must be light of body, joyful of heart, free of will, pure of intellect, mindful of past benefits, pure of intention, simple in action, true in words, and mortified in his senses   The heart wishing to receive the gifts must be pure, resplendent, and strong; pure in the faithful obedience of the Commandments and religious counsels , resplendent on account of the peace it must feel in itself, and of the remembrance of the Blood it received in holy baptism   Purity can be acquired by the humble lowering of self in the sight of God and creatures, and also by a humble confession   The splendor can be acquired by conformity with the will of God, and that of the superiors   Strength can be secured by means of hope, constant prayer, and confidence in God   Oh ! how many are the gifts and the graces Mary wishes to grant to creatures who are desirous of them !   O Mary, how pure and beautiful art thou !   By thy looks thou dost wish the angels to rejoice   thou dost strengthen sinners, and render all creatures h----- and f astf-l   In heaven thon, with th looks on ---st the anger of God towar   · ·   · ·! · · ·   ight   Going to heaven, O .   ·. ·t   e ⁊ · ·   ·   ι that unheard-of example   ··· \ _·'   ·. ι .r . t · . . .. ~ · ·] .   .   As all perfections are found in heaven, with all graces and virtues, so every perfection of virtue is centred in virginity, not because this is the perfection of all the virtues, but because it is the most fitting instrument to acquire them   O Mary, loving Mother, now thou hast been raised up to heaven, but thou art now even more solicitous for our welfare, and the more glorious thou art, the more loving towards us   Pray, teach us, thy daughters, that, conversing with our minds in heaven, we may not perform negligently the works of the earth, especially when there is a question of relieving the neighbor   Mary is the fountain sealed up with the immaculate seal of the Word, wherein she is proclaimed Virgin and Mother   This fountain irrigates the whole of heaven, makes the earth bear fruit, the angels rejoice, and the souls in purgatory feel relief   O Mary, thou art that door through which we were led into our heavenly country when God came down upon the earth   Mary leaves the most chaste mantle of her body to take on a ruddy one, viz, the merits of all the martyrs that had been or were to be, because she, in the Passion of the Divine Son, had suffered more than all the martyrs put together   These graces, O Mary, came to us through thy admission into heaven   O glorious Mary, glorious is he also that follows thee!   But to follow thee we first must die to ourselves, then we must crown Mary spiritually, offering all merits to her, together with all the praises that have been given to her blessed soul, and the merits of all the saints, having a great desire to increase her glory as far as we can   This offering is very acceptable to the heart of Mary   As our Mother goes up to heaven, there must be in us a burning desire to follow her   O most great Mary, take my soul and my will, and give me thine   O most glorious Mary, our Mother, do not suffer that, whilst thou goest to heaven, our hearts should remain upon earth   During the portion of life which is left to me I wish to enjoy thee, and do nothing else but admire thee

In another ecstasy, on the eve of the Epiphany, Mary Magdalen said that she saw the most blessed and glorious Virgin showing a great desire to draw to herself the brides consecrated to her beloved Son, to adorn their souls with gifts and graces, thus making them pleasing and acceptable to her Only Begotten Son   The Mother of God intended to favor these brides by purifying the three holy vows they made at their profession, hence the Saint added   "Though Mary sees the essence of the virtue of the vow imprinted in many, still there is much need of purification, on account of the many imperfections into which they constantly fall   Hence this loving Mother, who wished that, like the wise men, they might offer these three holy vows, as three precious gifts, to her Divine Son, by ratifying them every morning, performed this purification in an ineffable manner in the heart of every one of them"   Our Saint also saw the most blessed Virgin placing these, her daughters, with motherly love, under her sacred mantle   She noticed some of them approaching her with such negligence and coldness that they remained outside this mantle, whilst others were running so swiftly, with such ardent fervor, that they entered under it

.   .   .   .

And the Blessed Virgin told her, so great was the love she bore these brides of her Only Begotten Son, that though they approach such a Mother with negligence and coldness, she receives them, nevertheless, with love, and seeing them walk toward her with slow step, she goes forth to meet them, and approaches them, so that they, too, may enter under her mantle   Even if they, persisting in their ingratitude, go farther away, the Mother of Mercy is not angry with these discourteous and ungrateful daughters, but extends her arms more and more to gather them under her mantle, but they, making themselves more unworthy of so great a love, go still farther away   Our Saint noticed also some that ran away very quickly, and some who made light of so much love, and showed contempt for it   This most holy Mother wishing to draw them to herself, withdrew her gifts from them, to impart them to other brides, who returned for them not only fruit of gratitude, but of good works as well   The Blessed Virgin complained much to them, that her gifts and graces were not much esteemed by the brides consecrated to her Son, especially her most precious gift of obedience, as the value of this gift was little thought of   But at the end she understood that the protection and the love of this great Mother of Mercy towards her monastery, which was consecrated to her, was most special.   After which, all consoled and full of joy, our Saint came out of this ecstasy.

THIRD SECTION.

MAXIMS AND EXCLAMATIONS OF THE SAINT, HER LETTERS, AND
MIRACULOUS EVENTS AFTER HER CANONIZATION.

§ I.

Sayings of General Application.

1. That soul is most perfect which most truly wishes to honor God, and to do in everything and at all times His Most Holy Will.

2. The eye of our good intention draws to itself the Divine eye.

3. The sacrifice most pleasing in the eyes of His Divine Majesty is that of a good will; as the works are the more meritorious, the more willingly they are performed.

4. One must offer herself to the Eternal Father as a daughter, to the Son as a bride, and to the Holy Ghost as a disciple.

5. Happy those souls that continually repose, and dwell, and build up all their works in the open Side of Jesus Christ !

6. All our strength, ability, and industry are derived from the Blood of Jesus Christ, which changes the old Adam into the new man.

7. We must not walk, but run ; we must not run, but fly, to perfection.

8. Fervor is the flame that incessantly enkindles all our spiritual exercises, and the practices of our life, which we must never follow by habit or natural propensity only.

9. Our soul being united to God, and all bound to Him interiorly and exteriorly, makes us appear with a serene countenance, and never allows us to be troubled by anything that happens.

10. The bride of Jesus Christ must be like the wise ones of the world, who keep their money hidden. She must amass in her heart treasures of good works, concealed from men, and manifest to God alone. And this is the surest way of laying up treasures for heaven.

11. The shortest and most efficacious exercise to draw God into the soul, is to keep an infinite distance from every imperfection, flying from the very shadow of sin.

12. Alas ! we ought to die of horror at the simple mention of the word *sin*.

13. We must condole with God for the offenses which are committed against His will.

14. The least imperfection, even were it to be as small as a hair of the head, prevents notably an intimate union with God.

15. The soul must have two interior eyes ; the one to know the enormity of her faults, the other to see continually the benefits she receives from God, the little profit she derives therefrom, and how anyone else would derive greater utility.

16. In all things divest yourselves of your own reputation, and in what concerns your interior, seek only after conformity with the Most Holy Will of God.

17. In your exterior occupations do not value your body more than a broom, or a kitchen rag, showing yourselves everywhere indefatigable, humble, and resigned to the will of others.

18. In all your actions remember to turn to God with lively and loving looks, imploring the succor of His graces. And pray to His Divine Majesty that He may be pleased to think, work, and speak for you in everything that you shall be commanded to do. Offer, also, all your actions and sufferings in honor of all that the Incarnate Word has done and suffered on earth.

19. We must fly, as much as possible, from any exercise which savors of greatness and show, as pride is often hiding therein ; and it is the more dangerous, the more hidden and concealed it is.

20. The actions which earn credit for us, easily draw us away from the love of our neighbor

21. Exterior works must be performed promptly and diligently without detriment to the interior life.

22. When one has satisfied himself in the beginning as to the righteousness of some exterior action, to finish the remainder without so much curiosity is a rare manner of preserving humility.

23 In whatever Religious Order one might be, five things must be asked of God, which are most necessary for help and support Union between the Religious; charity with God, punctual obedience, superiors like unto David, according to the heart of God, that will maintain simplicity and the regular observance, and that the vow of poverty may never be relaxed, and that all those who shall be called to Religion, may be enlightened with efficacious light, that God may make them know of what importance are the abnegation of their own will, and the full, punctual, and exact observance of even the smallest rule.

24. The officers of the monasteries must provide with charity and diligence for the wants of the Religious, having regard, though, to necessity alone, and having no other consideration or thought

25. Never refuse anything you may be asked to give, if you have leave to grant it.

26 We must continually offer ourselves and all creatures with Jesus Christ to the Eternal Father; and this is an excellent preparation for the Most Holy Communion

27. Go often to salute and pay your respect to the Most Holy Sacrament of the Altar

28. I would rather die than remain a single day without Communion, unless it be on account of obedience

29. The holy and triumphant Eucharist is our capital and our arsenal.

30 Christians, remember, when you go to the confessional, that you go but to wash yourselves, and to wash in the Wounds and the Blood of Jesus Christ

31 Try to make your confession frequent, exact, diligent, humble, and full of sorrow.

32. When priests lead a bad life, the sun is eclipsed, and the light is turned into darkness, filling everything with disorder

33 We must envy the land of Calvary, wet and soaked with the Blood of Jesus Christ

34 The good examples, past and present, must stimulate us, and force us on.

35. Accursed human respect is a hungry wolf, a furious lion, that devours and eats up the greatest part of good works

36 Virtue makes the human soul so perfectly good, that she converts everything into good, never believing that her neighbor has done any evil action

37. Every temptation can be overcome by the grace of God, by fidelity and mortification, invoking the holy patrons, and discovering everything to our superiors

38. Imagine that everything you do is the last act of your life, which will bring an eternity of bliss, or an eternity of pain.

39 The durability of a building depends upon the solidity of the foundation. Likewise a Christian soul cannot persevere, except by founding all her actions in the simplicity and truth of God

40. To die to one's self and be lost in God is the purest guarantee for eternity.

§ II.

Sayings Applicable to Religious.

1. Vocation to Religion is the greatest grace, after baptism, that God can grant to His elect.

2. Religion (a Religious Order) is an earthly paradise, but one must enter it with the most pure intention, and not be drawn into it by coercion, or for a worldly object or interest

3. Oh ! how much better it would be to stay in the world, than to be lost in Religion !

4 A novice must abandon Herself, and be as dead in the hands of her mistress

5 Religion is a traffic, a business One earns *one hundred on one*, when she knows how to use her talent

6 The shortest, the clearest, and the surest road to heaven is that of Religion

7. The two foundations of Religion are fervor of spirit, and contempt of the world and of self

8 Religion purifies, enlightens, and perfects all the interior and the exterior man

9 The eyes of a Religious must be shut to all the things of the earth, and open only to those of heaven

10. Once clothed with the religious habit, adopt as a maxim and a general principle, that you must never think, say, or do anything that is not worthy of the nobility of the religious state

11 Whatever will be wanting to Religious in this life will be granted to them in the next.

12. No matter how sick you may be, never take anything which may not be in keeping with holy poverty

13. Fables, jests, vain discourses, gifts, and presents are to the souls of Religious as so many snares, to catch them and draw them down into hell

14 Woe to anyone who will introduce vanity and property-holding in holy Religion, especially in that in which simplicity and poverty reign !

15 Examine yourselves, once a month, in order to see whether your heart is attached to anything, and, if you find this to be the case, renounce it immediately into the hands of the superioress

16 Oh ! how much human and worldly little traffics, found sometimes in monasteries, prevent the Religious from trafficking heaven and earth with Jesus Christ ! And, may it please God, that in the end they may not prevent Religious from attaining the Beatific Vision !

17 Chastity is a rose which does not blossom except in closed gardens and among thorns It is that which erects for the soul of a Religious a throne of ivory up in heaven Oh ! if its merit and excellence were known, it would soon shut itself up in monasteries ! We should kiss the locks and the walls of the monasteries, as being the custodians of so white a lily.

18. Purity and chastity must be universally found in all the parts of the body and the spirit.

19 Purity can only be found in those souls that lead a spiritual life , and the countermark of such a life is never to speak nor to hear evil of our neighbor, but to love him as ourselves

20 Do not delude yourselves , no one can enter the temple of purity, except by that of simplicity.

21. The Bridegroom of pure souls preserves His faithful brides in the midst of impure temptations, no less than He did the three young men in the Babylonian furnace

22 Even the smallest imperfection is a great stain to internal purity

23 Godlike purity is acquired by means of interior and exterior mortification, the custody of the heart, the purity of the body, and humility

24 Obedience is the mystic bed of Solomon.

25. Perfect obedience requires a soul without will, a will without judgment, a spirit without eyes, and blind to everything else but obedience to all the world

26 Your obedience must be accompanied by cheerfulness, humility, simplicity, promptness, and perseverance

27 A Religious has not given up his will to men, but to God , and all of it. Oh ! what a sacrilege, then, it would be to retake it from Him, even if but in part !

28. Look upon the day you have not obeyed anyone, as a lost day

29 A small drop of simple obedience is worth a million times more than a vessel full of the most subtle contemplation

30. Oh ! how desirable it would be that all our actions, and each one of them, would be actually commanded us by obedience !

31 Oh ! good Jesus ! how much sweetness is enclosed in this naked expression *Will of God !*

32. We must have a horror for all sorts of singularity, no matter how small it may be , as the punctual observance of our Rule is the straightest road Singularity is the shadow of death

33. A Religious must hold his Rule in esteem, as much as God Himself, for from Him it proceeded , and he must live and die in the exact observance of the same, not caring whether it is kept by others or not

34. We must strive to supply and make amendment for all the faults which are committed in the monastery or Religious House

35. Religion (a Religious House) is a sacred place, representing the Apostolic College

36. A Religious fulfills the office of the angels, and therefore should possess angelical purity

37. Good example is one of the greatest honors that can be rendered to God

38. The ambition of a Religious must be to become the master of his own passions

§ III

Sayings Concerning Superiors.

1. A Superior must be ... ... pattern of virtue, in which two rich colors ... ...

2 The Subject is ... ... the Divinity ... ... have as many eyes as there are ... ... to his care

3. He must take counsel and permission from Jesus Christ, before giving any advice or issuing any order.

4. A Superior must never reprimand or chastise any fault, unless he has previously obtained full and entire knowledge of it

5 The offices of Religion must be distributed with discreet equality, having regard but to the capacity and the forces of the subjects, not to the nobility of the blood, or any other consideration, which savors of the world and vanity

6. Superiors must not allow any opportunity to pass whereby they may exercise their subjects in virtue.

7. The only way to close a quiet life with a happy death, is simply to permit ourselves to be guided by our Superiors, and to act always in the presence of God

8. It is a great artifice of our enemy to rob us of our confidence in our Superiors, and to prevent our going to see them in order to unfold our temptations to them

9. Oh! that Religious House is truly happy, to which God grants Superiors that are good to work and to speak!

10 Oh! loving Word, I see in the furnace of Thy Heart a note, in which are four things Thou dost require of the perfect Religious 1. An ardent zeal for the salvation of souls 2 Study and diligence in attending to the interior man 3 That they add study to study, diligence to diligence, in rendering themselves fit for the frequenting of the Most Holy Sacrament, returning love for so much love 4 That they be perfect in the virtue of humility and poverty.

§ IV.

Sayings Concerning Various Virtues.

1 A closed and shut-up virtue, which does not communicate itself to others, is no virtue.

2. In all actions and practices of virtue, we must propose to ourselves Jesus Christ as a model.

3. Oh! souls desirous of making great progress in virtue in a short time, choose for your teacher and guide Jesus Christ on the cross, or in the Sacrament of the Altar

4 It is but too true that we, in everything and always, must imitate Jesus Incarnate, Who appeared on earth but in servitude and abasement

5 Oh! what a beautiful virtue humility is! It is the virtue which opens the gates of heaven, atoning by one of its acts, for any debt contracted by our sins He will see the Divine Essence more clearly, who shall have more humbly abased himself God creates a world of perfections on the nothingness of humility

6. To criticise our own virtues and excuse the sins of others, are two good effects of humility, and altogether befitting a Religious soul

7. The soul that, accusing herself, discovers her own faults, deserves that Jesus Christ, forgiving her, cover them with His own Blood

8. To excuse one's self, even when wrongly accused, is to cease being a Religious.

9 Oh! how profitable it would be, if there were a companion that would accuse us of all our faults, without sparing any of them!

10 Our perfection revolves on these two poles. The desire of being subject to all, and the horror of being preferred even to the least of all

11. The brevity of this life, which puts an end to all sufferings, helps the practice of patience.

12. Virtue without trial is no virtue, and patience without suffering is a weak tincture, which often possesses nothing but the appearance of patience

13. Afflictions answer for purgatory in this life, and deliver us from it in the next

14 As far as I am concerned, I feel no great desire to go to heaven, as there is nothing to suffer there; and I regret that this one thing be wanting in the perfection of beatitude

15. Oh! what a shame! To solace ourselves among roses, whilst Christ walks among thorns!

16 The affronts, crosses, and torments are the caresses and delights of our Heavenly Bridegroom

17 Cheerfulness, contentment, and peace are the arms and hands by which to accept humbly all mortifications

18 The most excessive pain becomes glorious and tastes agreeably, when one looks at Jesus on the cross

19 A rose can only be gathered from ... But ... is seldom found among sweet thorns ... delight ...

20. The death of Je ... is the life ...

21. Prayer must be humble, fervent, resigned, accompanied by perseverance and a most profound reverence, considering that in prayer we speak to God, in Whose presence the heavenly virtues tremble

22. Prayer is the spirit of Religion , but it must not become a pretext for any dispensation, for all the exercises of obedience are so many prayers

23. The fruit of prayer is mortification , and we must ask for nothing but the Will of God

24. Interior peace is an effect of mental prayer, and the reward of a union contracted with God.

25 Ah ! my God ! How can a creature endowed with reason offend Thee deliberately? . . Let us love one another, as this is Christ's new and own Commandment.

26 Compassion is the daughter of Charity All things must be done in charity and for charity, serving our neighbor as we do God Himself, Who regards as done to Himself whatever is done to His members

27. A soul clothed with charity is all-powerful

28 A day spent without mortification is a day lost .

29 The silence of the lips suffices not, if the silence of the heart is not kept.

30. One of the principal fruits of our Communions must be a horror of the grates and the parlor

31. A Religious should never speak but humbly and modestly, and for necessity alone , as one of the points about which a strict account is to be rendered to God, is the speaking of idle and useless words.

32. Never open your lips to discourse, unless you have previously considered whether you do it purely for the love of God, the profit of your neighbor, and whether it is *then* necessary to speak

33 The words of a Christian must be of truth, of meekness, and of justice.

34. The words of a Religious must be an attraction of hearts, and a model of virtues

35 Let your conversation be sweet, cheerful, humble, patient, prudent, and considerate ; thinking that your sisters are angels on earth, images of God, brides of Jesus Christ, daughters of the Eternal Father, temples of the Holy Ghost, sisters of the angels , deeming yourself unworthy to dwell with them

36 Esteem others and speak of them as you would like to be esteemed by others and spoken of by them

37. Nobody's faults must ever be made public

38. Oh ! if we would but reflect on the great obligations of our state, we would never stop to listen to any backbitings, nor to say even the least idle word !

39. With our superiors we must act with humility, with our equals with modesty, with our inferiors with suavity, and towards all with meekness and gravity.

40. We must regard our neighbor by the side on which the image of God is imprinted on him, so that, when we notice any imperfection in anybody, we must not think that God ceases on that account to take delight in him, as there is an interior perfection we do not see. Keep your eyes always open to the virtues, and closed to the imperfections of your neighbor.

41. Those who do not save their souls in Religions (Religious Orders) must never hope to save themselves anywhere else

§ V.

Exercises of Some Exterior Acts, of which the Saint left us a Record written with Her own Hand.

1. To hold dear, enjoy, and take delight in the divine attributes, viz., the wisdom, the omnipotence, and the goodness of God, and the infinite love with which He loves Himself and all creatures.

2. To wish to God all that good, glory, and honor that He has and shall have throughout eternity.

3. To be delighted at those mutual communications which the Three Divine Persons make among themselves

4. To rejoice that God is so great and infinite that He cannot be comprehended by the creatures.

5. To rejoice at that infinite love wherewith God loves Himself, has loved and will love Himself for eternity , to delight in the thought that all creatures and the blessed spirits are not sufficient to love Him as He deserves to be loved , and to thank His Divine Majesty that He loves Himself infinitely

6. To rejoice at all those treasures and infinite grace wis   the Eternal Father granted and communicated to the *Him* o s of th Word, the gra   He had of performing miracles and of gi   n to H s ti   lo rt on   se

7. To rejoice at the Eternal Father's having given us ea   the Incarnate Word

St. Augustine engraves on her breast "Et Verbum Caro Factum
Est" (page 437).

for our inheritance, and to delight in the pleasure which He takes in it, and in the complacency which He finds in the souls of the just

8. To rejoice at the love which the Word always bore to virginity.

9. To offer to God, God Himself, in thanksgiving for all the glory, honor, and beatitude which He possesses, and in thanksgiving for all the gifts and graces ever communicated by Him to all creatures

10. To say to the Lord · "Could I at this moment give Thee all that glory, honor, and praise that all the blessed spirits, together with all the just of the earth, give Thee at present, willingly would I do it ; but, as I cannot, accept the good will I bear towards Thy Divine Majesty "

11. To offer one's self to God, and to wish for all that perfection that He delights us to have, as He wishes it

12. To incline our will to love the creature, simply because God loves her, and to rejoice at the love He bears to her, and at the perfection He communicates to her And supposing (what cannot be) that God Himself wished to grant to a creature power to offend us, or cause us displeasure, still to desire that such creature may have all the perfection and glory of the seraphim, even if she were to employ it in offending us—keeping ourselves in accord with God, by not wishing for anything except what God Himself wishes.

§ VI.

Invocation.

"*Protector noster, aspice, Deus, et respice in faciem Christi tui* " O Divine Spirit, our Protector, behold with what love the Eternal Father has given us His Word, that He might come into the world and suffer so cruel a death to save our souls ! Therefore, we beg of Thee, Spirit of Love, do not deprive us of Thy presence ! Look also, O Most Loving Protector of ours, on the Face of Thy Christ—I mean the *Humanity* of the Word , behold that Face of Thy Christ, now become so disfigured on account of the blows and stripes and the ignominious spittle ! And as the Divine Word, with that unmeasured and infinite love which Thou Thyself art, wished to give this Spirit to us, pray, do not depart from Thy creatures, O Holy Ghost ! O Divine Father, Protector of Thy creatures, look upon Thy Only Begotten Son, Who, together with Thee, is the same only God, and, for obedience' sake, became man Look, therefore, O Father, upon Thy Son, God and man, all wounded , and, for His sake, I beg of Thee, to forgive us Look again, O Father, upon the Face of Thy Christ, and see how the soul of every creature is Thine by creation, and His by redemption, He having ransomed her by His own Blood, His Passion and death His she is also by likeness, His by the gift He made her of the Sacraments, and especially of Baptism , and His by His espousals with her in the union of grace, by the merits of His Blood, which He shed for her , His, finally, in many and many ways Therefore, O Divine Father and our Protector, do not permit Thy souls to perish , but forgive them by Thy grace and mercy, and do Thou vouchsafe that they may never be abandoned by Thy divine grace ! Ah ! pray, O my Jesus, give Thy Blood to Thy brides, and write with It in their hearts Thy most lovable Name, which is sweet and powerful, and is not understood or comprehended by any creature All the hierarchy in heaven seem like one body, so much are they united to bow at Thy sweet Name , and those of hell, who are not capable of doing it, nevertheless, when this Name was imposed on Thee, felt a somewhat of fear, and were compelled to bow And yet the creatures that have received the fruit of this Name are so ungrateful ! Thy Name appeases the Father, gives happiness to the angels, cheers up the just, and makes the demons tremble. By Thy Name we receive from the Eternal Father all graces , hence, do not fail to write It in the hearts of all Thy brides with Thy Blood That love which moved Thee to come down on earth and give Thy life for us, that same love may move Thee to imprint Thy most holy Name in the hearts of Thy creatures Well do I know that Thou dost not fail to infuse the virtue of this Name in them, but they derive no benefit therefrom ; and what is the cause of it ? Our ingratitude Ah ! please, O my sweet Spouse, in Thy dearly beloved souls, in the brides especially consecrated to Thee, imprint in their hearts, and stamp in every sentiment of theirs, a letter of Thy holy Name ,[1] for, as Thy enamored Bernard said : "It is the joy of all our senses, and honey to our mouth " Oh ! how sweet are the words of those who have Thee in their hearts ! What more exquisite and sweet melody than to hear Thy sweet Name pronounced, as by means of Thy Name we induce the Eternal Father to turn His eyes towards us, and the pure angelic spirits to wish, so to speak, that we go and join their company, and by this Name we render ourselves terrible to the devils !

---

[1] In the Life of the Saint it is related that on the eve of the Annunciation of the Blessed Virgin, in the year 1585, St Augustin appeared to her, during an ecstasy, and wrote on her heart in golden letters, "VERBUM CARO FACTUM EST " *Note of the Translator.*

LETTERS OF ST. MARY MAGDALEN DE-PAZZI.

1. To a Nun of St Giovannino of the Knights of Malta.

Very Rev in Christ, Mother, health in the Lord.

JUNE 1st, 1588.

These lines will tell you that last Sunday your business lady came, and I learned from her that the sister of our sister-in-law was among those who made their holy profession   Not having known it previously, I did not do what would have been my duty and desire to do , but now I send her these few little things, begging of her to excuse me, and accept my good will , and may God reward you for the loving consideration you were pleased to use towards me   I did not fail that morning, just as I am, to recommend to God all those who were to make the holy profession, having heard about it, though I did not know she was one of the number , and I will be pleased if she has done the same for me   And even if she did not do so in particular that morning, I beg of her to do it now, during this octave , because, having consummated so great a union with the Lord, as the religious profession is, He will be very much pleased with the prayers that she will offer up to Him, and which I find myself so greatly in need of   I recommend myself to your holy prayers and hers, whom I cannot name, because I forget it, though my sister in-law Hyppolita told me it. Be pleased, also, to recommend me to our cousin, Sr Selvaggia, and to Sr. Maria Francesca, together with all the others, of whom I beg that they offer up prayer for me, whilst I, such as I am, will not fail to do the same for you all   There being nothing else, I will finish this, begging the Lord to keep you always in His holy grace

From our Monastery of S. Maria degli Angeli da S. Frediano of Florence.

Your Sister in Christ,

SR MARIA MADDALENA DE-PAZZI.

2. To Sister Diamante Mazzinghi of St Giovannino of the Knights in Florence.

Very Rev in Christ, most Beloved Sister, health in the Lord.

MARCH 15th, 1590.

In the Name of Christ Crucified   With loving compassion I rejoiced very much at what you wrote me, in your last, from which I understood that it is now nine years since the Lord granted you the favor of keeping you at His table, giving you to taste that food of which He Himself partook whilst with us on earth, and which was nothing else but pain, contempt, suffering, and the cross, of which He made you partaker   I exhort you, most beloved sister in Christ, to follow the Lord cheerfully, according to what He says in the Gospel   "*Qui vult venire post me, abneget semetipsum, et tollat crucem suam et sequatur me*"—"If any man will come after Me, let him deny himself and take up his cross and follow Me" (Matth xvi, 24)   This shows us how much He delights in trying His elect, among whom you are numbered , as tribulations are but a forge, purifying the soul of all its imperfections   I confidently hope you may be able to say with David the Prophet   "*Secundum multitudinem dolorum meorum consolationes tuæ lætificaverunt animam meam*"—"According to the multitude of my sorrows, Thy comforts have given joy to my soul " (Ps xciii, 24)   According to the greatness of your sorrow and affliction you will be consoled , and the greater the suffering, the greater will be the reward, most certainly, if not in this, in the next life   On the other hand, Sr in Christ Jesus, I could not with pen express the sorrow I have felt, and the great compassion I feel for you, as I believe it to be a sweet martyrdom to be prevented from practicing with peace of mind those acts of virtue and piety according to your desire   I exhort you to take all this from the Lord, and by His permission, and as a special grace, knowing that He is a most clement Father, and does not permit us to be tried above our strength   Thus you will reach a greater degree of virtue, and will be able to say with the Apostle Paul (Gal vi, 14) that you will not glory in anything but the cross of Christ   You complain to me that you can no longer carry   . . . . your memory (Rom viii, ... ared with the glory to com. . . . . In regard to what you tell me, viz , that you are almost deprived of the conversation of your sisters, offer up what you suffered in the past to your Spouse, together with all He suffered from His dearest friends at the time of His Passion, so that He was forced to cry with a loud voice to His Eternal Father "Why hast Thou forsaken Me?" (Matth xxvii, 46) Now, concerning that sister who causes you this affliction, you may proceed in this manner, viz , by strongly thinking that she is an image of Jesus Christ, a soul redeemed at such a dear price as His precious Blood ; and, considering this, you will feel like being under great obligation to her, on account of her being to you the occasion of so much profit Moreover, I beg of you to do as our loving Christ did at the time of His Passion First, when the rabble went to seize Him, He gave them sufficient time to repent ; secondly, He was silent in the face of all their accusations , thirdly, he offered up prayers for His persecutors at the time they had taken from Him property, fame, name, and, finally, life itself. You, His bride, must lend her the light given to you, in imitation of Him, exhorting her to change this mode of proceeding, telling her that the Lord is ever present and is a just Judge, Who, as He will not leave any good unrewarded neither will He leave any evil without the punishment it deserves When you notice her in a passion, saying of you something displeasing to you, pass it over in holy silence, not ceasing to pray to God for her ; and in this I will help you, asking for her the grace to return to the true religious life, which is your desire and mine for the love I bear all of you In regard to what you tell of the conversation of Sr Maria Fedele, I do not think there is any offense to God therein I presuppose you do not seek it for any other purpose than to encourage yourself to serve your Spouse Jesus with true love and more fervor Beware, though, lest you conceive a particular affection for her, or feel any more pain for her absence than for that of any other sister, or regret her conversing with others, and others with her, in order to conform with your God, Who is no receiver of persons On finding yourself despoiled of such an affection, you can, in all security, enjoy her conversation, uniting in charity to help her This is all I have to say concerning what you wrote to me. Together with this I send you a little Treatise on Spiritual Life, suitable for us Religious. It will please me much if you read it, as it is very useful, and I think it will please you too You may lend it to others, if you see proper I will simply add that I recommend myself to you and Sr Maria Fedele, whilst I assure you, on my part, that, just as I am, I will not fail to offer up in my prayers your just petitions and desires , again begging of you to remember my miserable self The Reverend aunt of our Mother Prioress salutes you, too , asking you, in her behalf and mine, to salute the Reverend aunt of your Mother Prioress, and the Reverend Mother Vicaria, and all of your community, as I love you all *in the bowels* of Jesus Christ, Whom I wish to be always with you, inflaming you with His holy love

Most humble in Christ Jesus, most affectionate sister

* * *

---

3. To Sister Maria Fedele Soldani and to Sister Diamante Mazzinghi, of the aforesaid Monastery of St. Giovannino.

Very Rev. in Christ Jesus, Sisters, health in His Most Precious Blood.

AUGUST 12th, 1592.

This present will be in answer to a pitiful one of yours, from which I understood that your tribulation grows daily , wherefore I compassionate you so much that it is impossible to express it with a pen , and to remedy it, if it were needed, I would be ready to give my own blood You complain to me, in your epistle, that you have pretty nearly lost all hope, seeing that the tribulation is constantly augmenting , but I counsel you to remain firm and unshaken, as it is perseverance alone that receives the crown Consider, most beloved sister, how short is the present life, which is a constant warfare and battle, and we should not deem it hard work to fight for the great reward promised to us, viz , everlasting bliss, in the possession of those things that eye hath not seen, nor ear heard, neither hath it entered into the heart of man (1 Cor 11, 9) , . and this great good cannot be attained except by much suffering Whenever, by the constant and fierce battling, you feel like failing in the midst of tribulations, have then recourse to the health-giving tree of the cross, and you will thereby be strengthened in the virtue of the most precious Blood of Jesus Christ And think, moreover, that the merciful Lord never permits His elect to encounter temptations or tribulations which are above their strength Hence, when we find ourselves in such plights, we must place all our hope in the help of God, thanking His Divine Majesty for giving us the opportunity to conform ourselves to our dear Crucified Spouse offering to Him those tribulations in union with His most bitter Passion. Do right ̇ ̇ ̇ ̇ ̇ d ̇ ̇ ̇ ̇ ̇ of your consolations. In order not to ̇ ̇ ̇ ̇ ̇ ̇ ̇ ̇ ̇ hat you are deemed worthy to suffer contumelies for the Name of Jesus Christ And if you meet with difficulties and impediments in your spiritual exercises, call to mind that sentence of our Lord in the Gospel "*Arcta est via quæ ducit ad vitam*"— "Strait is the way that leads to life" (Matth vii, 14). Recall also the persecutions of the Saints, who were made to suffer in so many ways, in their honor, in their worldly goods, and in the loss of their own life They endured all with so much patience, in order to render to their Redeemer love for love, and blood for blood When it seems to you, dearest sister, that the little boat of your soul is about to sink, throw into the sea the anchor of hope, placing all your confidence in the Divine help, and have no fear lest God will fail to meet your confidence. He so loves our souls that He grants more than we ask

I was much pleased with those things you sent, and I thank you much therefor With this I send a *Jesus carrying the cross*, and hope that by looking at Him you may carry with more cheerfulness and contentment this, your own cross I will not tell you to recommend me to my cousin, as I do not know whether you want her to hear you wrote to me If it is not inconvenient for you, I would like you to remember me to her, telling her to pray to God for me Having nothing else to say now, I will end this by recommending myself a thousand times to you May God grant you His grace.

Yours in Jesus, Minor Sister.

*   *   *

4. To a Sister of San Giovannino's.

Very Rev. in Jesus Christ, Beloved Sister, health

SEPTEMBER 1st, 1592.

This present will be in answer to one of yours, which was very acceptable to me, and by which I discovered the great love you bear me in Jesus Christ. And I would like to be such as your confidence in my prayers presupposes But even such as I am I did not fail to pray to the Lord to be pleased to console you, and grant you those petitions and graces you recommend to me, particularly the cause of that niece of yours For the taking of such a resolution is a thing of the greatest importance, and, in order to take this step rightly it is necessary to pay much attention to the inspiration of the Holy Ghost, endeavoring to choose a place where she may keep what she must promise, and wherein light and regular observance may be found. Should her desire be to enter your own monastery, do not dissuade her from it, as I suppose that, with God's help, this will come to pass The bearer of your dearest missive was Mary Magdalen De-Pecori, whom I very gladly welcomed, as she is the mother of Sr Virginia, and, having been sent by you, it seemed to me as if I saw, in a manner, your own Reverence, which, by the affection I bear you in the Lord, so pleased me, that I could not fully express it with the pen I send you back with this The Representation (Drama) of the Prodigal Son Excuse me for keeping it longer than I intended, as we could not copy it sooner Together with it I send you a *Jesus carrying the cross*, and wish that you and I may stop to listen to His sweet voice calling us and saying "*Qui vult venire post me abneget semetipsum, et tollat crucem suam et sequatur me*"—"If any man will come after Me, let him deny himself, and take up his cross, and follow Me" (Matth. xvi. 24) Please return, duplicated, the salutations to my cousin, and tell her I wish her to pray to the Lord for me. And, in order not to be too long, recommend me to all the sisters, particularly to Sr Virginia, Sr. Innocenzia, and Sr Ortensia I suppose you know we surely expect your dear Sr Leonora, and that she is by us greatly desired I did not fail, lukewarm as I am to pray with more persistency, on the feast of the glorious St John the Baptist, for your Religion (Religious Order), as this Saint is your Special Advocate and Patron near the Divine Majesty There being nothing else to say, I recommend myself to you as well as I can, and so does the Reverence of our Mother Prioress. May the Lord always be with you, adorning you with His holy graces

Yours in Christ Jesus, most affectionate sister

*   *   *

5. To Sister Carità Rucellai, Prioress of the Monastery of San Giovannino.

JULY 26th, 1593

I received yours of the 22d inst , from which I understood what Sr Maria Francesca had already notified me of, viz , that the Lord was pleased to choose you as the guide and keeper of that, His little flock And truly can we believe this to have been His will, as the election has been determined as is usual Though the burden seems heavy to you as it truly is do not doubt but that He Who placed it on you will also help you to carry it, if you will trust wholly in Him, as I hope you are doing Do not be frightened at having to provide for the monastery, knowing it is written that those who fear the Lord God want for nothing And though something will be wanting to your daughters, rejoice that they have the opportunity to practice, in part, what they promised by a solemn vow, viz , holy poverty, which our Spouse so loved and exalted in Himself You say in your epistle that the burden that the Lord placed on your shoulders seems heavy to you also for the reason that you have to please all of the nuns At this I will remind you of something of which I just now think. It is what St. Louis Bertrand did when he was elected prior He wrote over the door of his cell, and, I think, much more deeply in his heart, these beautiful words of the Apostle *"Si adhuc hominibus placerem servus Christi non essem"*—"If I yet pleased men, I should not be the servant of Christ" (Galat 1, 10) The same, it seems to me, should be done by anybody upon whom such a burden has been placed, viz , to set first the honor and glory of God, doing all that is due to Him, and not minding the rest I also think your proceeding will be according to the will of God, and for the salvation of souls, whenever you do anything in holy charity, the name of which you bear, and in the practice of which, together with the other virtues, I feel sure you have so far advanced, that you will show it with great ease to your daughters and subjects, not only by words, but much more by example You do very well to ask for help, knocking at the door of the Divine Mercy, but, as for myself, I grieve that I am not such that I can help you and implore of God what you so much wish for But, to make up for my tepidity and negligence, I will not fail to recommend you always to these Mothers and Sisters. I will say no more except to beg you constantly to keep before your eyes the welfare and perfection of the Religion, and all those things of which oftentimes you had light from God and incitement in yourself Forgive me if, by my words, I annoyed you, and whenever you find yourself in the most intimate communications with your Divine Spouse, remember me a most vile sinner I beg it of you with all my heart I beg you likewise to be pleased to recommend me to our cousin, to Sr Maria Eletta, and to the nieces of our Rev Mother Prioress, who also recommends herself to all your community.

Of Your Reverence,

*   *   *

---

6. To the Same.

Very Rev Mother in Christ, health

OCTOBER 20th, 1598.

By this present I answer your very welcome letter, which afforded me as much consolation as you can imagine As the former one caused me extraordinary sorrow, because I grieved that a servant of God, such as I hold this venerable father to be, should suffer so great a tribulation, so this last of yours changed my sorrow into joy Blessed be the Lord, Who does not abandon His servants, though saddened and afflicted—nay, He then delivers them when they least think of it And it seems as if the Divine Majesty wished to illustrate in this, His servant, the words of David *"Cum ipso sum in tribulatione eripiam eum et glorificabo eum"*—"I am with him in tribulation I will deliver him, and I will glorify him" (Ps xc, 15) ; and that, not only God was with him in tribulation and delivered him from it, but that he glorified him besides, making thus known to all his patience and innocence Concerning what you tell me, to pray to our Lord to take away from your mind a little of the desire you feel that those who accused him unjustly should suffer therefor, I answer you that I think this is not the case ; but that, in my prayers, I do beg of the Lord to grant you a heart conformable to the name of charity you bear, and feel certain you have such a heart I believe further that we, who are Brides of Christ, are under a special obligation to love and do good to those who displease and offend not only us, but also those we love , and this in order that we may be followers of Him, Who, whilst hanging for us on the cross, said to His Father *"Ignosce illis; non enim sciunt quid faciunt"*—"Forgive them, for they know not what they do" (Luke xxiii, 34), and I feel most sure that you know and do all better than myself In my prayers I continually remember your Religious community, and particularly I recommended the affair you mentioned to me, viz , the changing of your offices You should trust that God will dispose these changes for His greater glory, and that you will not be wanting in subjects that may be suitable to keep up and increase every good in your holy Religion, and I hope He will grant this to you Having nothing else now to say, I will end this by recommending myself an infinite number of times to you and your holy prayers I was forgetting to tell you that the Rev Mother Prioress recommends herself innumerable times to her very dear nieces. May Jesus fill us with His holy love

Yours, in Christ most humble.

*   *   *

7. To Signor Camillo Pazzi (Father of the Saint).

Very honorable and very dear Father, health in the Lord

MARCH 23d, 1596.

As it is not yet pleasing to the Lord that we should see one another again, I concluded to write you these lines to learn something of your present state, and to exhort you at the same time to be patient and conform to the will of God in everything, whether it pleases His Divine Majesty to keep you ill or well. Short is the time we have to remain in this valley of miseries, everlasting is the glory we shall enjoy in heaven, prepared for us by our own good God, and merited through the Passion and Death of the Incarnate Word, commemorated during these holydays by our Holy Mother Church I pity you much for not having been able during this holy Lent, and not being yet able, to hear the Word of God, but I think Geri (her grandfather) will perform the office of charity by telling you of it I fail not to recommend you all the time to the Lord, as is my duty, and think that, on the solemnity of the Annunciation, you will confess and receive Holy Communion By doing this, dearest father, you will be better disposed to receive again the Most Blessed Sacrament on the most solemn day of Easter In the meantime, during these fifteen days, I beg of you to exhort Alamanno, my dearest brother, to approach the Sacraments of Confession and Communion, as becomes every faithful Christian, so that, as you are his father according to the flesh, you may also beget him in the Lord according to the spirit. I beg this of him with all possible affection I send you a *Jesus carrying the cross*, which you asked of me some time ago. Excuse me if I did not comply with your request before now, and if you ever need anything that I or this our Community can give, it will please these mothers very much if you will feel sure of it. As I have nothing else to say now, I recommend myself with all my heart to you, to our dearest brothers, to Hyppolita and dear nephews, Rev. Mother Prioress does the same. May the Lord be with you.

Your most affectionate daughter

*   *   *

----

8. To a Nun of San Giovannino's.

Very dear in Christ, sister, health in the same Christ Crucified

AUGUST 5th, 1598.

My unusual act of writing will, perhaps, cause you to wonder, but the love I always bore, in the Lord, and still bear, the holy College in which I have been and conversed, moved me to do it And as God gave me this thought (I certainly have it from Him) several months ago, nay, years, to write to you, finally I must carry it into effect. As I was moved by the love wherewith the Lord is pleased I should love your soul, therefore I beg of you to receive this, my letter, in the same love and charity I tell you, then, most beloved sister, and I beg of you, in the *bowels* of Jesus Crucified, that you keep on exercising yourself in a constant, sincere, and true contrition of your sins, if you wish to please God and do good to your soul And the greater our sorrow and tears are for them, the sooner shall our sins be forgotten in the sight of God The iniquity of sin is so great, that the grief and tears of all creatures would not suffice to destroy it. But the compassion and mercy of our most benign Lord is so boundless, that He is satisfied if we are sorry for it, and abhor and hate it with a sincere heart; He attends to the rest. But this notwithstanding, it behooves us to be always in holy fear, "*As man knoweth not whether he be worthy of love or hatred*" (Eccles ix, 1). And if St Mary Magdalen, who heard from the very lips of Eternal Truth those sweet and loving words "*Remittuntur ei*"—"They are forgiven her" (Luke vii, 47), remained afterwards so many years in the horrid wilderness to do penance, what should we not do, who have not yet received such a grace, and who should not even deem ourselves worthy of it? Hence I exhort you, dearest sister in the Lord, by the Blood Jesus shed for you with such fire of love, to do cheerfully and patiently all the penance that has been imposed on you by your Superiors; as the sufferings of this life are not worthy to be compared with the glory to come (Rom viii, 18), prepared for us by the Son of God, through so many sufferings, sorrows, and His most cruel death And see how all the Saints, who are enjoying that ineffable glory which we hope for, reached it, "*per magnos labores*," for it is good and a happiness so great, that it can only be acquired by pains and labors If so many Saints who, while on earth, led an innocent and pure life, tormented and scourged themselves with so many hard penances, what should we not do to r   ·   ·.   l .·l. . rue t': Divine Goodness? Hence you ·   · s. ·   ·   · · ·. r·' · · · ·ir   ·· which to offer up to Him · ·   · .   i · ·:   · ·   · l .an·' il '·:. ne Majesty. I send you a *Jesus carrying the cross*, that you may often look at Him, and meditate on His bitter Passion—a most efficacious means to correct every imperfection, and kindle in the soul love for its Creator   I also exhort you, dearest sister, to seek, when permitted by your Superiors, to unite with Jesus in the Most Blessed Sacrament, with an entire abandonment of yourself and all created things, as this is the means to regain the time lost, and become just and pure in the sight of God, Who is constantly knocking at our hearts and sweetly calling us   Hearken, I beg of you, to His voice telling you *"Revertere, revertere, Sulamitis"*—"Return, return, O Sulamitess" (Cant vi, 12), return, return, My soul, to Me, as, outside of Me, thou shalt not find contentment or delight whatever, because I created thee only for Myself   And our God wishes nothing else from us, but our heart   Therefore, delay no longer, but offer it to Him a thousand times a day, giving up yourself entirely to Him, for by His infinite goodness He loves you more than you do yourself   Ah ! if we could but penetrate this love ! it would seem a pleasure to suffer, so to say, a thousand deaths every day for the least offense committed against so great a goodness, in order to make some return to the same   With these considerations and spiritual exercises you might turn your dwelling-place into a paradise And, the better to succeed in doing what I recommend, have recourse to the Blessed Virgin, the Mother of Mercy, by saying daily that beautiful prayer composed by the devout Doctor, St Bernard, which, I think, will afford you spiritual consolation.   I never failed to remember you in my holy prayers, and I promise that now I will do it even more   I beg of you to be pleased to do the same for me   Having now nothing else to say, I very heartily recommend myself to you, praying the Lord to fill you up with His holy grace.   Jesus be with you

Yours, in Jesus, Sister.

*   *   *

9. To Sister Maria Angela Guidi of San Giovannino's.

Very Rev in Christ, Sister, health

JULY 10th, 1599.

I think you will wonder at my delaying so long to answer a letter of yours which pleased me very much   This was not caused by the fact that I did not take to heart what you tell me, as I love you and all your Religious Community very much in the Lord   You tell me you are much urged by the Lord, with constant inspirations, to serve Him perfectly, whilst you remain doubtful and irresolute about the manner of corresponding to such inspirations   Now, I think, it will be very useful for you to follow those inspirations which you more frequently feel in your interior, but only when you are quiet and free from affliction, for, when the soul is troubled, it cannot well discern the movement of God and His holy Will   Be very careful to observe, also, as much as you can, your Rule and the Constitution, despising and withdrawing, as much as possible, from all transitory things, and placing all your trust in the Lord, Who will not forsake you, as He promises to help whomsoever puts his hope in Him   You may be sure that this is what Jesus expects of you, as He expects from everyone according to the vocation which has been given to him   Be pleased to salute for me Sister Carità, and all your Mothers and Sisters   Sister Angela Caterina, too, salutes her sisters, as also does Valenzia her own dear sisters.   She is well, and it seems to her a thousand years before she will take the habit of the holy Religion   Having nothing more to say   I recommend myself to you heartily.   May the Lord be with you and keep you in His holy grace

Your sister in Christ.

*   *   *

10. To Father Virgilio Cepari, S. J.

Rev in Christ, Father   *Jesus, Maria*

JULY 22d, 1599.

To obey you I write as much as I remember concerning your demand, and this is First, that you accept the charge to govern with that love wherewith our Lord took up His cross   Secondly, that you remain in office with the same love and contentment with which our Lord remained on the cross   Thirdly, that you do not seek anything else in the office except what our Lord Himself sought whilst hanging on the cross, viz, to suffer, love, and give glory to His Father, and pray for those who crucified Him   Anything else I may have said to you I have forgotten, because, as you know, I have no memory. *Benedicite*   Pray to God for me, that He may enlighten my soul about something which causes me uncertainty and worry   May Jesus fill us up with His real

Your, as in Christ devout daughter.

*   *   *

11. To Sister Carità Rucellai, of San Giovannino's.

Very Rev in Christ, Mother, health in the Lord.

AUGUST 9th, 1599

I have received the most pleasing letter of your Reverence, which consoled me, because it gave me your news, but even more so, because I could see your own writing ; for I love you very much   I hear how you and some of your sisters are tried by the Lord , for which I pity you much, and exhort you all to take this trial from the hand of our Lord God, by Whose permission you may be sure it comes   I just now remember a thing I wish to tell you, which I read in the Instruction of Giovanni Taulero, which is to the purpose   He says that "God is pleased and delighted that a soul, whilst in this world, should suffer tribulation , because it, thereby, becomes like unto His Only Begotten Son, Who, whilst on earth, led a life of labor, suffered persecutions, and afflictions, and, finally, dying on a cross, in the midst of so many pains and sorrows, cried out to His Father, saying, 'My God ! My God ! why hast Thou forsaken Me?'" (Matth xxvii, 46). He is so delighted, I say, to see a soul suffering, that, if there were no other means to cause it, He would send an angel from heaven for that purpose. This being so, you should thank the Lord for calling you by the royal road of the cross, on which He Himself first trod for love of you   As to the prayer you ask, we will not fail   Valenzia recommends herself to her dear sisters, Sister Angela Caterina to hers. The Rev Mother Prioress salutes her niece   I will not compose litanies, as the saying is ; but I recommend myself to all, from the greatest to the least one   May Jesus inflame you with His love.

Yours, as a daughter most affectionate.

*   *   *

12. To Maria de' Medici, the Wife of Henry IV, the Great King of France.

Most Christian Queen, health.

JANUARY 12th, 1600.

By these few lines I wish to manifest my joy to your Majesty upon your happy arrival, of which I was informed, by the grace of God, in order that you may see that though absent in body, you are, nevertheless, present to me in spirit.   I never forget your just petitions, which I hope the Lord, in His goodness, will grant , therefore, I would not now fail to do what I did in former years, when you were in this city of yours, viz , send you the *Saint*, on the solemnity of the Epiphany, begging with faith to keep you during the present year   St John the Baptist was drawn for you, as you will find in the enclosed, together with the motto   Your Majesty may be sure I will always keep you in my memory, as I know this to be your wish. But knowing myself to be unable to help you, I placed you under the protection of the most holy Virgin, and wish you to cooperate in this by having a special devotion to her, as you bear her name

Not wishing to annoy you, I end this by saluting you in the Lord   The Rev Mother Prioress does the same, with all my other Mothers and Sisters, all of whom keep your memory in their hearts, on account of your very kind and courteous visit. And they never fail to recommend you to the Lord, together with the Sacred Majesty of the King, your spouse, begging for you from the Lord every complete happiness

Of your most Christian Majesty,

Most humble servant.

*   *   *

13. To Sister Margarita Medici, in the Monastery of Candeli in Florence.

Very Rev. in Christ, Sister, health.

JANUARY 10th, 1601.

I understood by your letter what your wishes are ; and, such as I am, I have not failed, and will not fail in the future, to present such petitions to God ; it being just and holy that every creature, and particularly we Religious, should aspire to obtain them. But we hope the Lord, Who has given us the desire, and can do so, will also grant us the graces   For this reason He sends forth the desire first, because He wishes to grant the graces afterwards. And He is delighted when we ask them with fervent prayers, as He said with His most holy lips "*Petite, et accipietis* "—"Ask, and you shall receive " (John xvi, 24). I see also from your letter how our good God, through your illness, makes you partake of what He suffered here below, of tribulations and pains. Hence you must be satisfied and cheerful, for you in on the royal road which leads to heaven, viz , suffering , in fact, it was necessary that the Son of God Himself should suffer in order to enter into His glory as He Himself said Luke xxiv 26   You also know that He is with him who suffers, as we say every evening at Complin (Ps xc, 15), hence I exhort you to take everything from the benign hand of the Lord. Thus every pain and tribulation will become sweet to you, when you think Who sends it to you, and with what love He does it, viz., with an infinite love I send you an image of Our Lord Crucified, which you asked of me, and I beg of you to recommend me to Him, our Spouse, on the cross, asking Him to grant us the grace to keep us hidden in His loving wounds Having nothing more to say, I recommend myself to you. Your most affectionate sister.

* * *

14. To Messer Luigi Ardinghelli, in Villa.

Much magnificent and honorable as a Brother, health

FEBRUARY 9th, 1601.

I received your very welcome letter, but delayed so long to answer it, because I was busy celebrating the feast of the novices Now I write you these few lines to thank you for the charity and benevolence you have shown me, which has not been less agreeable on this feast than if I had received it for St. Mary Magdalen's, and it gave me a reason to think of you more and more in my prayers, such as they are, as I know you desire I remind you, as a very dear brother in Christ, that when the Lord has given Himself to a soul, granting to it His light and particular graces, helping it directly and through His creatures, that soul is under much greater obligation to Him and bound to render Him a stricter account And when this soul does not persevere in the good begun then, it does not make a return for gifts and graces received—nay, it repays the Giver with ingratitude (from which may the Lord deliver us), and this, as you know, dries up the spring of mercy What could we do if we found this never-failing spring dried up? We would find ourselves without way, truth, and life. I beg of you to ask the Lord for me the grace to correspond to His light, that I may not fall into the abyss of ingratitude, and I will do the same for you, that our God may be glorified in you and give you, finally, Himself as a reward, for this is the only object He had in dying for us on the cross. Having said this much, I recommend myself very heartily to you; and your very dear sister, Mother Sister Evangelista, and the Rev Mother Prioress does the same May the Lord grant you His holy grace and keep you in it.

Yours, as a sister in Christ.

* * *

15. To Sister Giulia Sommaj, of the Monastery of St. Catherine in Florence.

OCTOBER 18th, 1602.

I received the very acceptable letter of your Reverence, from which I understood how you desired that we should send you the *cilicium* and the *discipline* of the Rev. Father Alessandro, of good and holy memory As we have already written, we have not the *cilicium*, but the *discipline* we have and this we send you, the Rev. Mother Prioress being satisfied. That you may see how much we desire to please you, instead of the *cilicium*, we send a *tunic* of the same Rev holy Father. These things we beg of your Reverence to send back to us at the end of four or six days, as they are relics to be held dearer than any precious earthly treasure We hold them very dear and in great veneration on account of the sanctity of said blessed and holy father, and the affection and obligation we feel towards him I fail not, such as I am, to remember your Reverence in my prayers, and recommend you to the novices, as you wish, and I desire you to do the same for me Sister Maria continues to enjoy good health, by the grace of God, and to progress in the holy virtues cheerfully. May the Lord ever be with you, granting you whatever you desire most for the glory of His Divine Majesty

Of your Reverence, daughter in Christ.

* * *

16. To Geri De-Pazzi, her Brother, in the Country Residence at Palugiano.

Very honorable and very dear Brother, health

DECEMBER 25th, 1601.

With these few lines I wish to rejoice with you for the coming of this new King and God, born into this world for us sinners, Whom I trust you have received in the tabernacle of your heart, as He did not become a man but to become the possessor of the man's heart He leaves the delights of His Father's bosom to come and load Himself with our sins, and take on Himself the just punishment due for them. He comes all sweet and meek, not in His Divine Majesty but in His Humanity and lowliness. He comes as an indefatigable Shepherd to seek out His sheep and press them to His bosom, as said the Prophet Isaias (liii), and bring them back to the fold of our Heavenly Fatherland But, with all His mercy, we must not forget that He is most just, and will render to everyone according to his works Hence it is necessary, very dear brother, that we should try to act so that our works may be found to be of proper weight in the divine scales; and the fear of God will help us to accomplish this I thank His Divine Majesty that you do not love with excess persons and things created , but I beg of you to be pleased weekly to examine yourself as to this point, by doing which you will give glory to God and benefit your own soul I send you the book of the Life of Father Francesco Borgia, of the Society of Jesus, for I think the reading of it will give you great pleasure and consolation Having nothing more to say, I heartily recommend myself to you Be pleased to salute sister-in-law and nephews for me Sister Maria Grazia is well and recommends herself to you. May the Lord be always with you

Your most affectionate sister. 　　　*　　　*　　　*

17. To the Same.

Very honorable and very dear Brother, health.

MARCH 7th, 1602.

These lines are addressed to you to salute you and give you news about my condition, which is good, by God's grace, except that I feel a little weak. But what principally moved me to write these few lines is that, as you have returned to Florence during this holy time, I persuade myself and wish to believe that you went to confession , though, on the other hand, I doubt it Hence, if this doubt should be found to be true, I beg and press you, by *the bowels of Jesus*, to delay no longer, and it will also please me that you go to the Fathers of Jesus Holy Lent being a season of penance, during which commemoration is made of the Passion of our Lord, I wish, most dear brother, that it should not pass without your detesting all things you know to be displeasing to His Divine Majesty, for it is a terrible thing to fall into the hands of God, He not being under any obligation to us. I cannot refrain from begging you by those nails and the lance which pierced the sacred hands, feet, and side of the Saviour, to be watchful in seeing that what is the temple of the Holy Spirit may not become that of the adversary, thus turning you, a member of God, from our Divine Head—Who is so noble and worthy Excuse me, dearest brother, if I have let the pen run too far ; blame for it the love I bear you, not only as a brother, but as a beloved creature of God, created by Him to enjoy forever the sovereign good , and believe me that, if it were possible, willingly and more than once would I lay down my life to see you walking on the right road to the fruition of the sovereign good I will say no more. I wish you to send an answer to this of mine, and rest assured it will not be seen, as I received permission not to show it In fine, I recommend myself to you May the Lord keep you in His holy grace

P. S.—I would like you to send me, if it does not inconvenience you, some oil of nutmeg, with four walnuts and some fenugreek. Excuse me

Your most affectionate sister 　　　*　　　*　　　*

18. To the Lady Catarina Minorbetti, Daughter of the Godmother of Our Saint.

Very Magnificent, and very dear in Christ

MARCH 13th, 1602.

I received your letter, and I thank you and the Rev Fathers for the prayers you have offered up for me, which were acceptable, as, by the grace of God, I now feel well Beg of the Lord, that as it pleased His goodness to restore me to my former health, so He may also grant me the grace that I may do His holy will always, not desiring nor wishing anything else In regard to what you wish to know for the peace of your conscience, I will tell you just how I would conduct myself I say, then, that if you feel at peace, and nothing in particular troubles you, and yet you resolve to make a general search of your soul for a more than ordinary satisfaction, but without any necessity, I say that to me it seems that you should forego it Nay I say more I would consider it a special grace if I felt I were in peace , and I know that Fathers so enlightened as those you mentioned to me, would advise me to desist from doing it But I say this, though, that if you fear that at the point of death you may not be happy on account of not having 　　·　　　·　　　　　:　　　　·　　·　··　　　　for you to make this genera　　　　　·· | 　　　·　· ·− † ·　　　. to Himself, you may; with |　　 ·　　　·　　· ·　　　··∼ ··· ··· ·· · I r −t w ·h P ··　Again I exhort and tell you that if there is nothing important, you may abide by what the Spiritual Fathers tell you, as they know what is best for you I salute Father Michele Girolamo, and thank him for the prayer he offered up for me All of us fail not to recommend him to Jesus, that he may do all the good that God wills Sr Maria Maddalena salutes you, and so do also Lady Violante, her aunt, and myself And thus I end this, wishing to you from the Lord God every contentment and spiritual grace That is all.

Most affectionate, in Jesus Christ.

* * *

19. To the Brother aforesaid, Geri De-Pazzi.

Much Magnificent and Honorable Brother, health

DECEMBER 11th, 1604.

By request of the Rev. Mother Prioress, I write to you these lines, to tell you that we would like, if it is not inconvenient for you, that you should send us those seventy scudi (dollars) in payment for the lumber furnished your daughter, as we need them. I also send you the list of the things that were made here, so that you may see how much was spent, and we would like you to send us this, also I remind you of the daughters of Sr. Maria Grazia,[1] your own daughter, who asked me to tell you she would like you to send them as soon as you can She is well, and salutes you, together with her Honorable Mother And the Rev Mother Prioress does the same Having nothing else to add, I recommend myself to you and sister-in-law May the Lord be with you.

Your most affectionate sister.

* * *

20. To Rev. Father Giovanni Battista Rabatti, Hermit Priest of the Sacred Hermitage of Mount Senario, of the Servants of Mary.

Very Rev. Father in Christ, health

MARCH 20th, 1605

Your very welcome letter afforded me spiritual consolation, as I saw therein that you remember me in your prayers This pleases me very much, for I stand much in need of them Such as I am, I fail not, and never will fail, to do the same for you in particular, and for all of your Congregation, that the Lord God may always advance it in every perfection In regard to what you make particular request of in your letter, I am very sorry that I am unable to afford you any relief in your affliction and perplexity, concerning which (on hearing of it) God knows how heartily I compassionated you And so I answer your request most simply, as I feel about it, viz, that should I find myself in such perplexity, I would just throw myself entirely on the obedience of my superior, doing, without a doubt, what he would judge and think I should do, because, as you understand and know better than myself, when we rest in holy obedience we can never be mistaken If the superior would allow me to adopt all the means needed for the preservation of health, I would do so at once with great calm and interior peace, and, on the contrary, I would persuade myself that the Lord permitted this to try me about that matter, and I would acquiesce therein, for I feel every day more convinced that the Lord delights more in a peaceful heart than in any other work Moreover, I believe you would honor God none the less by taking that food which I think your holy rule allows you in the case of a weak constitution, for, by strictly observing the rule for a little while, you may get sick for a long time and be unable to do anything Sickness is not to be made little of, it being something useful to our souls, still one should never give cause for it, as you well know And if His Divine Majesty has called you to such a state, as we can certainly believe, you would not be the first, this notwithstanding, that the Lord has called to a Religious Order, and then, for reasons known to Himself alone, has not given the strength to follow such a vocation, which is so pleasing to Him Hence we should be fully resigned to His holy will, and this, with all my heart, I ask you to pray for constantly, that I may fulfill it perfectly Having no other object in writing this, I recommend myself to your holy prayers, and ask of you the paternal blessing

Most affectionate, in Christ * * *

[1] This Sr Grazia, niece of the Saint, was one of those nuns who, in 1603, went to Rome to found the Convent of the Barberine, by order of the Sovereign Pontiff Urban VIII The others were Sr Innocenzia and Sr Grazia Barberini nieces of said Pope, and daughters of Don Carlo, General of Holy Church

21. To Sister Cherubina De-Pazzi,[1] Nun in the Monastery of St. Jacopo in Ripoli, of the Order of St. Dominic, in Florence.

Very Rev. and Dear Niece, health in Jesus

SEPTEMBER 26th, 1605.

In answer to your very pleasing letter I will not leave this unsaid, viz, that I constantly recommend you to the Lord in my prayers, such as I am, that this most benign Spouse, by His mercy, may grant you the grace to worthily prepare for the nuptials you will celebrate with His Divine Majesty, and go to meet Him with your lamp burning, as a prudent virgin   You, dear niece, must see to it that your heart be like a well-trimmed lamp, open from above to receive the lights, gifts, and graces the Lord will be pleased to communicate to you, and closed below, that no earthly and sinful thing may enter it to displease the eyes of your spotless Bridegroom   Then there must be the oil of charity, with the fire of divine love, that you may cast light around by your good example to all your sisters, and be acceptable to the sweet Jesus   If you do this, dear niece, I am sure you will find yourself prepared for those great nuptials you are to make with Jesus, and I beg of you to remember me in that holy act   About my ailment—I feel the same   I wish also to know whether you will make your profession only, or will receive also the black veil, and, this said, I recommend myself much to you   Sr Maria Grazia, your sister, salutes you, and recommends herself to you, also.   May Jesus grant you His grace and His love.   Your dear Aunt,

*   *   *

22. To Lady Violante Medici (about the Coming of the Holy Ghost).

Much Magnificent, and honorable Lady

MAY 11th, 1606.

I cannot and know not, dearest in Christ, how to say anything worthy of this Heavenly Comforter, according to your wish, because I am wholly incapable of speaking, not only of the Holy Spirit, but also of His effects   But, in order not to disappoint you altogether concerning your request, I will present to you just these three considerations, which, if you will ponder during these days with profitable meditation, I know and believe will render you apt, to a great extent, to receive this heavenly fire   In the first place, I wish we may go on considering that this Spirit, Who descends upon the earth, is a *Spirit of purity*, causing all earthly and carnal hearts to become totally spiritual and heavenly, so that, if we crave to receive Him within ourselves, we must endeavor to purify our hearts from every affection for created things, and detest whatever is contrary to this cleanliness and purity   He is likewise a *Spirit of truth* and we should strive that our will may want truly and sincerely no one else, but God alone, tearing ourselves from every personal interest, which oftentimes appears to us as if wanting God, and hiddenly seeks and wishes but self   And, finally, this is a *Spirit of holiness,* therefore we should endeavor to so sanctify ourselves with the holy virtues and exercises pleasing to God, that we may merit to become worthy temples of this heavenly Spirit   And pray for me that I, too, may have the grace to entertain some thoughts worthy of Him   With this end in view, I recommend myself to you, as to all

Your most affectionate,

*   *   *

23. Account in Form of a Letter, given by the Saint to Her Confessor, Rev. Vincenzo Puccini, of the Sacred Stigmata She Received, and of the "Verbum caro Factum est" (the Word was made Flesh) Engraved by St. Augustine on Her Heart, and the Bridal Ring given Her by the Divine Redeemer.

Very Rev and Venerable Father, your Blessing

By the obedience I owe you, as to one who speaks to me by order of the Lord, I answer your request, as far as my memory supports me and the occurrences are remembered by my good sisters in Jesus Christ, who took down my words

On Holy Monday, April, 1585, whilst I, with the other sisters, was in the garden, I heard the Lord calling me with these words   " *Veni et vide operationes animæ, quas ego*

---

[1] This nun, the daughter of Geri De-Pazzi, was much beloved by the Saint from whom, having gone to take leave before donning the habit, she received some precepts of true religious perfection and the Saint even told her she would not die before passing through all the offices of the monastery, as, in fact, happened, she ...... to a better life at the age of 81 years in 1611   This is the sister who received leave from Pope .... canonized, and whose body was ...... published ...... this letter was religiously kept ...... made by the very hands of the Saint who gave it ....

facio inter me et ipsam, quod nemo intelligere potest, nisi qui mundus est corde"—
"Come and see the operations of the soul, which I do with the soul, and which no one can
understand, except him who is clean of heart" At this call I nearly fainted, and
was compelled to lean against a tree, with my eyes fixed on heaven, and my face all on
fire The sisters, noticing this, led me to a cell, where, no sooner with great difficulty had
I arrived, than I threw myself on my knees, looking fixedly at a Crucifix, just in the
same position in which St Francis received the holy stigmata Then I asked Jesus that
I might enter by meditation into the wounds of His Humanity, repeating five times these
words: *"Absconde me in vulneribus humanitatis tuæ"*—"Hide me in the wounds of
Thy Humanity" At that time it seemed to me I saw truly the Humanity of Christ,
hence, being more kindled, I placed all my sentiments in those of the dead Jesus, and
spoke thus: "Nothing it would be, O my Jesus, to have placed all myself in Thee,
if I did not interiorly strive to remain in Thee" And here, looking more intently
into the face of my beloved Jesus hanging on the cross, I saw, falling from it, drops of
blood, in very great quantities, to the ground, wherefore I exclaimed "My Lord is
sweating blood O Love, it is not enough that blood is oozing out from all Thy body, but
that even from the eyes Thou wishest to shed it, instead of tears! O love, had I at least
been in the land which received this blood! O Love, grant, at least, that the hearts of
the creatures may receive it! Thou didst wish to be crowned with thorns, in order to
crown Thy brides with glory in heaven, O Love, but nowadays Thou canst not say that
Thy delights are to be with the children of men, but rather in the midst of torments and insults." I remained still for some time in this contemplation, and, later on,
with a voice stronger and more plaintive, and with tears, I said: "Pilate pronounced that
iniquitous sentence He Who will sentence all creatures now must submit to be sentenced O God! my Love strips Himself. . . . The cross is laid upon the ground, and
my Love goes on stripping Himself Alas! would that they, at least, strike Him with
light blows . I see them killing the Innocent Alas! I cannot stand it longer .
Give me strength, O Love, to endure the pain I feel! Jesus mine, I can well say '*Tristis
est anima mea usque ad mortem*'—'My soul is sorrowful, even unto death' (Matth.
xxvi, 38) After remaining about two hours with interior and exterior pain, in the contemplation of the most holy Passion, I saw Jesus giving me His holy wounds, for He
sent certain rays into my hands and feet and right side, that seemed to be of fire, and
penetrated to the centre of the places where the wounds are, so as to leave their imprint
therein. After this all pain and sadness suddenly left me, nay, I felt glad at seeing in
myself the wounds of my Lord, which always, even at this time, it seems to me that I
see, though exteriorly they appear not, which I like very much I saw then that the unitive
love united me to Jesus, and, being all united to Him, I did not know what else to do,
except to plunge myself into the goodness and love God bears to the soul I remained
in this ecstasy until the fifth hour of the night; but what joy I tasted I could never even
begin to explain.

The other occurrence was that on the eve of the Annunciation of the Virgin Mary,
in 1585, meditating on those words of St John *"Et Verbum caro Factum est"*—"And
the Word was made Flesh," I felt rapt out of myself, with a burning desire to receive a
particular intelligence of this divine mystery Whilst in this state St Augustine appeared to me, and I begged Him to write on my heart said words. For this purpose I
sat, arranging my person in position, and with hands and arms, pointing to him the
place of the heart, so that he might write thereon those words, and said to him "Here
is the blood, the inkstand is open; delay not, O Augustine!" Then the Saint wrote in
my heart *Verbum* in golden letters, and *caro Factum est* in letters of blood—to denote,
by the *gold*, the Divinity, and, by the *blood*, the Humanity of Christ, and he assured
me that, through this favor, I would always retain in my heart the memory of the Incarnation of Jesus

Finally, after a few weeks, viz, on the eve of St Catherine of Siena's feast (*April
29th*), having passed three hours in great sorrow and anguish, on account of seeing the
many and grievous offenses committed by men against Him, which God showed me, the
benign Jesus consoled me, appearing to me in glory, between St Augustine and St Catherine of Siena, with His hands and side full of most precious rings, and indicating that
He wished to espouse me Then I felt an ineffable consolation coming to me from this
sight, and began to burn with desire to be wedded by Jesus I at once asked Him for
one of those rings, begging Him to grant me such a favor, and that such a gift should remain hidden from the eyes of creatures After this I deemed myself most unworthy of
such a favor, and offered, in preparation to receive it, the most precious Blood of the
same Lord. The benign Jesus wished to favor me, and, as I stretched out my hand, He
placed a precious ring on the ring-finger

This is all I am able to say in answer to your request And, begging you for your
blessing, I also ask you not to cease recommending me to God

Yours, in Jesus Christ, most devoted daughter,

* * *

The following three letters were dictated by the Saint whilst she was in ecstasy :—

1. To the Very Rev. Frat' Angelo, of the Order of Friar Preachers.

To the Very Rev in Christ, Father, and to all the Coadjutors of the intrinsic work, health in the Sweet Truth and the Uncreated Wisdom.

I, unworthy handmaid of the Incarnate Word, compelled by Sweet Truth, write to your Reverence, the chosen instrument of said Truth, to help the intrinsic work ordained from eternity. The time has now come when He wants His servants to carry this work into effect, viz , to reunite to Himself His brides, who are scattered, and all other Religious living to-day in the cloisters, so opposed to the vocation God gave them, because they keep not the vows they made to Him Hence I write to you, to make you understand how said Truth has chosen you, not exactly as the doer of this work, but as the co-operator and coadjutor, to help the real and principal operator of said work. On the part of the Incarnate Word, I press you, together with the other coadjutors, to strip yourselves of every self-love, human respect, and dissimulation, and to walk always in righteousness, with naked truth and sincere speech, having before your eyes the stainless Lamb, Jesus Christ   . . Let all remember that sentence the Word uttered, viz , " That He would give His beatific vision to the clean of heart "—"*Beati mundo corde, quoniam ipsi Deum videbunt* " (Matth v, 8), especially to you possessing the name of those pure and immortal spirits before us creatures. Purity cannot exist where one does not proceed with rectitude and truth The clean of heart cannot be deprived of Thy vision by the simple angry look of anyone, though he be in dignity. . . .

Know, your Reverence, dearest Father in Jesus Christ, that purity is nothing else than not to have a thought, a desire, or the least aim contrary to rectitude and sincerity. Hence we should walk always with all frankness and tell the truth See that your works, like your name, are *angelic*, and deal with your fathers and brothers, who will concur in this work, with that wisdom and prudence which God has bestowed on you . . Remember also the words of the enamored Paul, who gloried in his being separated from God and was deemed insane on account of his telling the truth Proceed with the doctrine you possess , see that this is the first offering you make in the Sacrifice of the Mass which you offer up so often, and fear not, afterwards, if you meet with some opposition, placing before your eyes the slain Lamb. . . . And if, at times, in giving advice to your *christ* (priest), and telling him the truth, you will have occasion to see that his irascibility is stirred up, remind him, with sweetness, of those words of St. John, the Virgin (John viii, 7) " He that is without sin, let him first cast a stone " But never fear to tell the truth always, though you must not uncover to your brother at once all the faults he is guilty of, and which place such an obstacle to this work . . .

Ah ! let my Father put on *Him* who left for us garment and body, I say, the slain Lamb ! Oh ' let him clothe himself, let him clothe himself, let him clothe himself with Him ' and let him not fear to tell the truth ; and let not the zeal of which he makes profession fail him .   Let not the fervor of the first followers of the Truth cool in him ; and let him ponder well the work of God   . . Let him remember the very holy Moses, who, on account of a single transgression, was excluded from the promised land . . Let not, therefore, any negligence in this work so pleasing to God, as God is pleasing to Himself, reign in him, or in those to whom this light shall be vouchsafed. . . .

But, I notice in my Rev Father a fear of all his community , hence he is silent, not because he lacks the knowledge of its error and the goodness of God , but that he lacks confidence. . . . And what remedy should he adopt against this fear, though he has some reasons for it ? Let him take as help some of them he is afraid of—I say, of his own fathers, but some of those who are better grounded in the zeal of their enamored Father   . . Let him take for counsellors some of them whom he knows to be already instructed by the Sovereign Truth, and enlightened by the Same . .   Ah ' let not my Father find excuses, let him not offer me excuses , let him forgive me my apparent disrespect for his dignity, and that great Sacrifice he offers. God does not like, wish, nor accept these excuses ; therefore, let him not excuse himself ; but let him place before his eyes and look at the Lamb slain on the cross, whence He saw His Eternal Father dishonored, but, for this reason, He did not retard His work, but hastened it to the greater glory of the Same, His Eternal Father. Thus you shall cooperate with this work, which, though it will seem to redound to the dishonor of your Religion (Order), will not do so, but will on'y can . . . . . nfu . . f . . . . . . afterwar's, . eater honor will come to God . . the Religio. . .

· Do not become asleep, nor lukewarm nor negligent ; and do not despise, nor judge the words of that slain Lamb, though uttered by her who is all ignorance. . Remember and ponder well those words you read, when discoursing through the garden of Holy Writ, viz., "That He Who sits on the throne always makes things new"—"*Ecce nota facio omnia*" (Apoc xxi, 5) Though this work has ever proceeded, and proceeds from the Ancient and New Wisdom, through anyone He chooses, remember that God does these things anew every time, for these things are upon the earth, as many iniquities and sins without number are to-day. . Remember also, and penetrate well, those words you have, perhaps, just said at matins, on account of your bodily weakness "*Calicem Domini, biberunt et amici Dei facti sunt*"—"They drank the chalice of the Lord and became the friends of God"

It is not said they were *friends* before drinking the chalice, but after it Let not my Father find excuses, let him not offer excuses, saying I am not an Apostle Let it not seem to him an exaggeration, if I compare him to the Apostles, for I know it is not; whilst I do know that he has the same power to administer and give out the Blood of the Lamb slain, as the Apostles had. In virtue of that Blood, all that he will bind and loose upon earth shall be bound or loosed also in heaven (Matth xvi, 19), as my Truth promises "*Quodcumque ligaveris super terram erit ligatum et in cœlis, et quodcumque solveris super terram, erit solutum et in cœlis*" O goodness! O goodness of my Truth! . God would not have given unto you such a degree of grace, if He did not want to make use of it and dispose the heart of His *christ* (that is the priest), with the wish to do such a work. . Oh! let the Blood penetrate so that this *christ* may be so disposed! . If Christ in heaven is satisfied to loose and bind all you will bind and loose on earth, can it be that His *christ* on earth will not endeavor to reunite here on earth, according to His example, His brides? Nay, I deem, he would go on if it were possible, seeking them, as the Bride seeks the Bridegroom, did he know how pleasing this work is to Him . .

My Father keeps the precious gems shut up in his breast, but let him be pleased to show and give them also to his brethren and children, and if he also possesses the most precious and naked poverty, let him not fail to communicate his *wealth* to others who share his vocation, as all this work is to be performed is expressed in these words "*Vos qui reliquistis omnia et secuti estis me, centuplum accipietis et vitam æternam possidebitis*"—"You who have left everything and followed Me, shall receive an hundred-fold, and shall possess life everlasting" (Matth. xix 28, 29) You know it better than myself, on account of your learning, but the Word is pleased that I should tell you what He promises us Please pay attention to what my Christ promises us What does He promise us? Not the human glory, which is vanity and nothingness, nor the riches, which cannot satiate our desires, and, as Paul says, should be counted as dung (Phil iii, 8), but He says "an hundred-fold" *One* is nothing, but *one hundred* is a perfect number by which you can count to the infinite When the Word said He would give "an hundred-fold" He meant by it *His beatific vision* and my Word does not forget even that *one*, though it is nothing to Him, but to you is something, and this means earthly things, which are possessed in this world, and which help us to acquire the possession of the eternal goods, and that full "hundred-fold" of said vision but please take notice, *take notice!* He does not say "*habebunt*"—"they shall have"—but "*possidebunt*"—"they shall possess" Hence, to have and to possess is not the same thing; and if I have a thing in my hands I do not, therefore, possess it But pray, O my Father, note this! The thing I possess is subject to me, and cannot be taken away from me Prizes are things we may lose or gain, they may be ours or not, according as we work or not, and according as to whether God is pleased or not to grant them to His creatures A thing which is possessed is the eternal life And what is the eternal life but the True Life? Thou hast lowered Thyself, O Lord, below us, and cannot prevent our possessing Thee. We possess Thee! we possess Thee! yes, because Thou art of us, and we cannot, will not lose Thee, since Thou hast submitted to us, and were we to lose Thee, the True Life, we should be deprived of the paradise Thou hast opened to us with Thy Blood, O enamored, slain, and crucified Lamb!

I tarried with your charity, dilating in certain things, but let us come back to the first beginning of my Truth Keep well in your mind those words uttered by the First Truth, Whom we would know, were we His friends, pray, tell me, by what?—by love And what greater love can there be, than to lay down one's life for the neighbor? If there does not exist greater love than this, neither is there greater work than to help the creatures to return to God I will give you another spur before returning with you to the first beginning. I will—nay, Truth wills to do with you as is done with little infants needing milk, and with too timid servants who are promised a reward Remember Truth said that he who should confess Him before men, would also be confessed by Him before His Father and His angels, and, on the contrary, he who would not confess Him . . (Matth x, 32, 33, and so . . . of my Word, and let him constantly confer with and relate truth of the Truth

I recommend myself earnestly to the holy prayers of your Reverence, whilst humbly asking your holy blessing. My loving Jesus! Uncreated Wisdom! Sweet Truth! Tranquil Love! Jesus, Jesus, Jesus!

From our Monastery of Santa Maria degli Angeli at San Frediano, July 25th, 1586

The humble handmaid of the Incarnate Word,

SISTER MARIA MADDALENA DE-PAZZI.

---

2. In the Name of the Ancient Truth, the Incarnate Word, the Lamb Slain on the most hard Wood of the Cross.

To the Most Illustrious Lord Cardinal, her Father most Reverend.[1]

The useless servant of the servants of Jesus Christ and His dearest daughter, most obedient in desire and fact, compelled by the Ancient Truth, by all the blessed spirits, by all the just, and, so to say, by heaven and earth, and, if I am permitted to say it, even by hell, to remind you, encourage and invite you, to be pleased to come and hear the very important, pleasing, and necessary will of God And if you would tell me . What matters, so contemptible a creature, my coming, that they should so desire it? I would tell you that the anxious desire is felt so that you may not delay your coming so long I see so many, almost numberless, souls in constant danger of their salvation, that, though you may not at present free them all, you must at least in part begin to relieve them of their danger. If you have any business or work which might seem to you of greater importance than this, I tell you this is the greatest work any creature on earth may ever do If you do not, as yet, see it, I beg of you, because of the Blood that was shed with so much fire of love, that you may be pleased to come and hear it from one who has received some idea of it, and will make you, to some extent, understand it I say, be pleased to come and learn the will of God , and also to try and see whether it is the will of God Please do not look at the labor and inconvenience of the body , but remember that he who loves himself in this life loses the eternal life. "*Qui amat animam suam, perdet eam , et qui odit animam suam in hoc mundo, in vitam æternam custodit eam* " (John xii, 25). Do not look at the lowliness and meanness of the one who tells you these words , but fix your eyes on and look at Him, Who makes her say them Come ; come and see the truth for yourself , do not close your ears any longer, so that God's goodness, in giving to you the singular gift of choosing you for this work, may not be changed against you into wrath and vengeance. Because . . woe! woe! to him on whom God turns His back ! And you, who so familiarly treat, and, I will say, with so much *gusto*, handle this very God Incarnate, and can give Him to, or withhold Him from, the creatures, be not ungrateful for the privilege of such familiarity to the extent of falling short of executing God's will, which is to strive and bring souls back to Him . . Do not take these words as the outcome of presumption or frivolity ; but take them as from one who is compelled to speak them by the Truth—as, in fact, is the case. And I repeat to you that if you do not believe it to be so, and fear or doubt that it may be a deception, you should come and satisfy yourself about it, as I will no longer bear that a soul should remain in such a danger Come , and, as a loving father, you shall do your duty and free one of your daughters from such a thought and undeceive her Thus far there have been many enlightenments (as I truly cannot call them otherwise) of which I will not speak now, preferring to do it at your coming, by which God has often forced me to compel, incite, and invite you, though I was not permitted to do so by those whom I am bound to obey. But now, again, I am compelled to do it (being forced to it by the Blood of the Lamb slain, Christ Crucified), by familiarly uttering these few words, and taking with your most illustrious lordship the liberty, as of a daughter with a most loving father, not wishing to fear you any longer as a servant, but rather to love you as a most benign father I beg of you to look at everything that might seem presumptuous therein, in the light of the Lamb slain, Christ Crucified , and forgive with that mercy wherewith He forgave those who offended Him , though these words are not uttered to offend, but I feel as if compelled to utter them, to make you understand the will of God I doubt not but that, as a lover of this God and most zealous for the salvation of a soul, you will not mind the inconsiderate expressions of your handmaid, and will come to find out the truth for yourself, without any delay, as time is not waiting for us, but we for it. Let us not feel sure of the uncertain ; but let us, from hour to hour, from moment to moment, ask what God wants in His Church, given to you in special keeping . I will not incite you further, nor provoke you, by adding more words ; but, putting an end to this, I

---

will humbly ask of you the holy blessing   Jesus, Jesus, Jesus ! Infallible Truth ! Tranquil
Love ! Jesus, Jesus !
From our Monastery of St Maria degli Angeli, at San Frediano, August 24th, 1586.
The humble handmaid of the Incarnate Word

                                             *   *   *

---

3. In the Name of the First Truth, the Loving Word, and the Love united with Mankind.

To the above-named Lord Cardinal, her Most Rev Father.

The useless daughter of the First Truth is drawn, by the love which moved Him to
leave Himself to us, to repeat the information already given, though unknown to you,
concerning the importance of the great and God-pleasing work and His sweet will   I am
forced, I say, by this love which compelled Him to leave Himself to us in the Blessed Sacrament, and by Him Who gave you such a dignity that you can so easily handle Him with
your own hands   I am forced to beg of you and incite you to be pleased to raise yourself
above yourself, fixing your eyes on this Loving Word, knowing for a certainty that, if
you do so, you will burn, as a most ardent flame, with a desire to love the little sheep
committed to your care, as the Incarnate Word showed us on the last evening   Ah ! let
my Rev. Father be pleased to do what the Word did on that evening, what our Creator,
Ruler, and Sovereign Monarch of the universe, Jesus Christ, taught us by giving Himself
to us, not for a while, but till the consummation of the world   And let my most dear Father
(to call you by the sweetest name that may be permitted to me) leave himself in the place
of God, even as the Word left Himself wholly for us, going to the Passion and submitting
His Humanity to the will and pleasure of His Eternal Father,—as He gave Himself to us
in the Most Holy Sacrament, for the nourishment and food of our souls, so be you pleased
to give your services to His creatures   And how will you leave all yourself in God?   You
will do it when you will condescend to learn the sweet will of God, even through a contemptible medium, and will thereby receive light, plunging in the never-failing light,
so that you may be able to say . *"In lumine tuo videbimus lumen "*—" In Thy light we
shall see light," (Ps. xxxv, 10)   Then you shall not fail to be enlightened , and I see
that you already, placed in such a light by God, understand His wishes , and, with a
sovereign and quiet will, put this work into execution
You will also give yourself to creatures, as the Sweet Truth did this evening (Holy
Thursday) , and, being unable to give yourself as food, as Truth did, you will give what
God Himself has given to nourish you and the creatures subject to you, viz , the temporal
substances and goods, leaving all, as to the attachment, and only possessing them so as
to relieve them of their needs and to nourish and feed these creatures, members of Christ,
who, being in want of the *necessaries* of life, depart sometimes from the beautiful and
handsome body of the Holy Church, and this is very painful to those who have relaxed in
the love of God.   You will also leave yourself to the creatures in this other manner—by
not failing to nourish with doctrines and examples your subjects, given into your keeping , and by acting with the wisdom and prudence which God will inspire you with   If you
consider well, and ruminate, on those words uttered by the Ancient and New Truth   that
He would be with us till the consummation of the world, you will think nothing of leaving off a certain habit contracted, which is somewhat difficult to do ; as it is difficult also
to resist the temptations which may come from the enemy   Neither should you mind
the tongues of the creatures who assist you, who, oftentimes, moved by charity (which is
not charity, no, they only put on its mantle), might speak words that would prevent
such a work and will of God   Remember that God will be with you always, giving you
help and light concerning what you have to do ; which *light* you will, no doubt, secure
when you will make a firm and true resolution to leave altogether the things created by
God , and, what is more, to give yourself to the service of creatures   But you should not
esteem it more than is necessary to honor God and help his creatures   Please, Father,
please take this resolution , as, after doing so, God will infuse into your soul so much
light that you will be enabled to fathom, understand, and put into execution His holy
will , and you will not fear the talk of the creatures assisting you, nor the very devil, so
to say, who makes them talk , but you will desire to give up your own body to any kind
of death, in order to see the will of God accomplished and be able to repeat with the enamored Paul   *"Mihi mundus crucifixus est, et ego mundo "*—" The world is crucified
to me, and I to the world " (Galat vi, 14) .
I speak no longer with your most illustrious lordship as with one who does not
understand God's will, because I deem you already enamored of it , and, such being the
case, you must consider those sweet words the First Truth used in commending to His Apostles,
viz., that they would be known as such from the love that would bear one another   My

understanding will not be capable of believing that My Most Rev. Father loves his neighbor, if he will suffer to see him to slip down into the abyss of sins, and walk, so to say, on the road to hell Neither can my affection feel that you love your neighbor, if you do not mind that many rest so much in the vanities and transitory and perishable things of this miserable world, as to be deprived of God This miserable will of mine shall never be able to admit that you love your neighbor as long as you dissimulate and allow the other *christs* and the brides consecrated to God, to play with the promises and vows they made to God, by trying to make themselves believe (notwithstanding that in their hearts they know it is not so) that God is satisfied with but the promises made, without their being fulfilled I will not be able to believe that you hold in proper estimation the Blood that the Lamb slain has shed, so long as you suffer souls redeemed and adorned with this most precious Blood, to run so precipitously to hell

And please do not forget, either, those words uttered by the Virgin-John, viz , that (John iii, 9) *the light came into the world, and men loved darkness rather than the light* Though it is impossible to fully understand, let alone tell, except by divine assistance, what this darkness is, and what this light, and how resplendent the latter, and how black and thick the former. God alone knows it, and he only in part understands it to whom God is pleased to make it known , as this knowledge comes from God, Who is the Father of all true light—*a Patre luminum* As the sun cannot be seen by any other light than its own, nor through any other ray than that which proceeds from the same, which is the fountain of all rays , so, likewise, this heavenly light cannot be known by means of any other light than the divine No light of learning, or natural understanding, no matter how acute and penetrating, can succeed in it, nay this would rather turn it into a shadow and confusing dazzling, when it is a question of understanding the secrets of God, concerning which His light alone can enlighten us . *"Et revelasti ea parvulis"*—"And hast revealed them to little ones" (Matth xi, 25)

So much did the Eternal Father love, and still loves, this His creature, that He was not satisfied to give His Only Begotten for our redemption, but He still gives Him to us as a help, relief, and consolation , and not for this only, but also in order that He may constantly enkindle and inflame our hearts with His divine love , and He gives us this, His divine light, too, that we may know ourselves and His goodness But many, I repeat it, love darkness rather than light So immense, O Lord, is Thy greatness and Thy love, that it extends all around the earth, among the blessed spirits up above and here below among men and all other creatures! I tell you then, that though on account of our corrupt natures we are in darkness, still, if we wish to profit thereby and dispose ourselves well, the light is in the world, because the loving Word, Who is the True Light, dwells in our midst by our reception of His Body and Blood Your most illustrious lordship knows that His delight is to be with the children of men, and He will find His delight to be with you also, since you, too, are one of the children of men, though surpassing many of them in office and dignity, for you can dispense unto others His Body and Blood I say that the Word will find His delight to dwell with you, when you will wholly detach yourself from all the created things God gave you, that you might help His creatures .

After you shall have considered so many sweet words of the Ancient and New Truth and tasted the delicious fruits of the living garden of the Holy Writ, you must look, fixing the eyes (as I told you in the beginning) on the Lamb slain upon the cross, with a great desire to imitate Him, in what He regarded His honor For He wished to die the most ignominious death that could be imagined, and, considering Him also in all His life, you will see that if He had had any riches, willingly would He have parted with them, by abundantly distributing them to His creatures But, in order to give us the example, He never wished to possess anything, though He was most rich, as St. Paul says *"In quo sunt omnes thesauri absconditi"*—"In whom are hid all the treasures . . . " (Coloss. ii, 3), He gave all His most precious Blood, shedding it from all His limbs, to cleanse our souls He also willed that all His limbs should be disjointed from His body, that He might reunite us, His dear members, to Himself, our True Head This will be a constant stimulus to throw off, according to His example, all self-love, and deprive yourself of the things God gave you, to come to the relief of the necessities and wants of the creatures subject to Him, not making anything of your honor, when it is a question of helping to reunite those members who have rambled from their True Head, Christ Crucified , particularly the men and the women consecrated to Him And if you shall keep on considering this loving Word, you will see how He, being enamored of His creatures, became Incarnate, assuming our humanity, in which He gave us all His most precious Blood, with such fire of love that He went to the extent of dying the opprobrious death of the cross, whereon with seven words He consummated our redemption and manifested the greatness of His love And you, with the Seven Sacraments, must urge the creatures . . . . the Religious, according to t' w' f d \ W r . . . . made known the thirst He took for our souls . . . . ly and Blood,

Whose keys you possess with full power, must show the thirst we should feel for God What can better assuage the thirst of the souls than this Sacrament? And with the same Sacrament you must quench in your subjects the thirst for these transitory things, showing them the preciousness of the Body and Blood of Jesus Christ, and endeavoring to make these souls live so that your soul may rest confident of their not receiving Them unworthily, as might be the case with some Ah! yes, try to understand the value and power of this Blood, and make others understand it i And if the blood of a wild beast had such power as to make Jacob say, when he saw the bloody garment of his Joseph, that he would ever remain sad till he should again see his son, how much greater power with you must not the Blood of the Incarnate Word have, Who proceeds from the very essence of God? It must cause you to give yourself no rest till you see reunited and renovated the dearest members of your body—Christ—especially of those given into your particular keeping. Permit not yourself to be outdone by a contemptible animal, such as the pelican, which opens its breast with its bill, and with its blood feeds and nourishes its brood I invite you not to give your blood, but rather to make known the Blood of the Lamb slain, and see that it is not despised I beg of you not to disregard the words of so low a creature, but to carry out the important work of God and His sweet will.

Now, I wish to bring this to an end with my Most Rev Father, reminding him to consider what moved God to re-create us The greatness He gave to all His creatures, who might be capable of His vision, the dignity He gave you in the office you hold, the brevity of time, and its value, the goodness of God Himself, and the benefit that has to result from so great a work, and one so pleasing to God I will not speak any longer with your most illustrious lordship, but I will only tell you and counsel you, on the part of the Ancient and New Truth, to put into execution His sweet will, prepared to undergo a thousand hells, and any manner of death you might meet with by any kind of torture, rather than to see God offended any more I beg of you to have no consideration for property, honor, body, or life, but only to do the sweet will of God And, as a useless daughter of yours, I ask your holy blessing Jesus, Jesus, Jesus!

From our Monastery of St. Maria degli Angeli at San Frediano, September 4th, 1586
The humble handmaid of the Incarnate Word,

* * *

END OF THE WORKS.

APPENDIX.

§ I.

Miracles Wrought and Graces Obtained through the Intercession of St. Mary Magdalen De-Pazzi after Her Canonization.

In the month of August, 1669, Mary Bernieri, a noble lady of Parma, aged thirty-six years, fell so seriously ill, and in so strange a manner, that the physicians, astonished beyond measure, were about to diagnose the illness as preternatural and absolutely incurable by human means. They were almost going to say that a superhuman power was taking delight in tormenting that unhappy creature. Fever, vomit, catarrh, convulsions, and other ills had reduced her to the point of showing no life except by a painful breathing. Being so prostrated about the end of the eighth month of her sickness, a religious person suggested to her the devotion to St. Mary Magdalen De-Pazzi, whose canonization had lately been celebrated in Parma with solemn pomp. The patient accepted the suggestion cheerfully and considerately, and caused the Most Serene Highness, Margherita de' Medici, to be asked for a *relic* of the Saint, which she preserved as a most precious treasure. Being blessed with *it* twice, she was not cured at once, but received a prompt and certain token that the glorious St. Mary Magdalen would be her benefactress. Cultivating thus devotion and confidence in her, at dawn of the eighth day of April, 1670, she thought she saw somebody standing at her bedside, on the right; and, looking attentively, she recognized her Deliverer, who, with an air of paradise and in the most loving and gentle way, touched her attenuated body, and then lifted her from her bed with a sudden and entire recovery of her health.

Ginevra Salvini, after thirty-four months of a most painful malady, was so swollen in the throat that she could no longer breathe; but, no sooner was the *veil* of the Saint placed over her, than she perfectly recovered.

By the application of the same *veil*, a boy seven years old, the son of Lady Maria Maddalena Albini de' Bonsi, was instantly cured of excessive pains.

Giacinto Zanetti, of Romagna, keeper of the Leghorn Lazzaretto, having received Holy Viaticum and Extreme Unction, and being already in his agony, was cured through a relic of the Saint.

Pandolfo di Silvio Spanocchi, a Siennese gentleman, recovered his health by just praying with confidence to our Saint.

A Neapolitan young man, falling from a steeple with evident danger of being killed, remained unhurt by simply invoking St. Mary Magdalen De-Pazzi.

The Sisters of the Charity Monastery in Naples succeeded in stopping a terrible fire in their monastery by throwing an image of the Saint into it; and the image itself, in the midst of those burning flames, remained intact.

The daughter of a great lady of Madrid recovered her health, almost entirely lost, by touching the car of the Saint, that was to be taken around in the procession.

Luigi Campacini, a Florentine priest, falling down a rocky precipice with the horse he was riding, invoked St. Mary Magdalen and escaped unhurt.

The Marquises Giovanni Battista Pucci, Ferdinando Capponi, Pierantonio Guadagni, and Pierantonio Gerini, whilst returning from their embassy to England, where they had been sent by the Grand Duke of Tuscany, Cosimus III, no sooner reached Florence than they immediately betook themselves to the tomb of St. Mary Magdalen De-Pazzi, to fulfill a vow they had made on the sea, when, by the intercession of St. Mary Magdalen De-Pazzi, they were delivered from a very fierce tempest.

Signor Manfredi Macinghi, having fallen into the Arno and being almost drowned, was saved by a manifest prodigy, on recommending himself to St. Mary Magdalen De-Pazzi.

Two persons, who were holding a licentious talk by the road, and otherwise became converted on kneeling at the feet of Monsignor Alessandro Strozzi who had with him a relic of St. Mary Magdalen, and they ascribed their conversion to the intercession of St Mary Magdalen

Simone, the four-year old son of Francesco Forcelli, fell from a terrace and was so badly hurt that he was about to expire, when his mother, in the excess of her grief, took him up in her arms and invoked St Mary Magdalen thus "Help me, and restore my son to me," and then fell into a swoon Shortly after, she heard her little son calling out to her very cheerfully: "Mamma, I am cured, a little nun dressed in white and brown, the one to whom I say every night the *Ave Maria*, healed me." On the following day, the parents took this boy to the church of our Saint, to give expression to their sentiments of gratitude.

Caterina Giusti, stewardess of the Signori Tempi in Valley of Pesa, being bitten by a viper, and sure of her death, was anointed with oil from the lamp burning before the Saint, and immediately healed

Quinzio Vettori, of Fermo, an employé at the Court of Tuscany, had a son who was leading a very scandalous life, but, on recommending him to St Mary Magdalen De-Pazzi, he had the consolation of seeing him so changed and converted that, leaving the world, he joined the Capuchin Order and persevered therein with exemplary fervor

Our Saint appeared to Margherita Cornelio, a dame of the Duchess of Parma, and cured her of a mortal sickness by blessing her

Another woman of Parma, falling downstairs with a child in her arms, invoked the Saint, and escaped unhurt with the child

Tomaso Querini, of Pistoja, being fatally wounded, recovered through the intercession of St Mary Magdalen De-Pazzi

Giovancarlo Tavoletti, of Arezzo, recommends himself to the Saint, and immediately recovers his health and the sight of both eyes, which he had lost in a powder explosion.

A nun of the Monastery of St Maria degli Angeli in Florence, having fallen into a well, is miraculously taken out and saved from death, after coming to the surface the third time, through the Saint

Monsignor Bonacorsi, Bishop of Colle, sent twenty-five pounds of wax to the sepulchre of the Saint, in token of gratitude for recovered health

Antonio Prestevoli in the service of the Grand Duke of Tuscany at Portoferrajo, having been cured of a gangrenous sore in the right leg, through the intercession of the Saint, caused a silver leg to be appended at the sepulchre of the Saint

Don Ferdinando, Duke of Mantova, having recovered his health through the intercession of the Saint, offered a token of his gratitude in the shape of a golden heart with this inscription "*Signum cordis Ferdinandi, Ducis Mantuæ VI et Montisferrati IV, Beatæ Mariæ Magdalenæ De-Pazzi dicatum*"—"A token of the heartfelt gratitude of Ferdinand, VI Duke of Mantova, and IV of Monferrato, offered to Blessed Mary Magdalen," &c

A rich silver *vow*, gilt-plated, bears witness to a prodigious cure obtained through our Saint, by a Florentine gentlewoman, Maria de' Bardi in the Arrighi

Another votive offering, for a similar reason, is the gift of Fabio Serragli, a Florentine gentleman.

From Palermo were sent to Florence five silver offerings, corresponding to as many graces received there, one being that of a nun who instantaneously recovered her sight on simply promising the votive gift to our Saint

A tablet of gratitude relates how Signor Domenico Orsini, of Bagnione in the Lunigiana, and his wife Settimia dei Franceschini obtained wonderful favors for themselves, and the recovery of the sight of a young woman of their household, through St. Mary Magdalen De-Pazzi

Several tablets hanging at her sepulchre and around her image, are witnesses of special graces obtained through her intercession Two large tablets immured on either side at the entrance of the sumptuous chapel where the body of the Saint is kept, contain a large number of gold and silver votive offerings for the most remarkable graces received by those who had a special devotion to the Saint in more recent times And the number of these votive offerings daily increases, as the arm of God is not shortened in doing wonders in behalf of the faithful and to the glory of His Saints. Every year are registered several graces which have been secured through the intercession of this Saint

The devout practice of the Five Fridays, dedicated to consider and honor the five principal virtues of St Mary Magdalen De-Pazzi, has been and is always of marvelous efficacy By means of this devotion, or by recommending one's self to our Saint in any other form, or by making a vow or promise to her, in various parts of Italy and elsewhere, not a few, sick of incurable diseases, recovered their health during this century in which we live. From the year 1830 to 1854, this happened more particularly in Tuscany, to Giulio Franchetti, Leopoldo Trinci, Annunziata Sereni, Ersilia Conti, *et al.* In the Pontifical States, to Sister Maddalena Pesci, Enrico Valli, Vittorio Ceccherini, *et al.* In the Kingdom of the two Sicilies, to Fra Bernardo Bracciolini, Giuseppe Nerli, Angelo Formigli, *et al.* In Piedmont, to Pietro Guerrieri, Lucia Angelini, Margherita Sannini, *et al.* In the Lombardo-Veneto, to Luigi Anzidei, Francesco Bartolini, Ottavio Testi, Caterina Federighi, *et al.* In many cities and villages are churches and chapels erected in honor of the Saint; and wherever her image is exposed to veneration, *it* is adorned with votive offerings in thanksgiving for graces received. Many monasteries are built and founded anew with her rules by the grateful munificence of her devout clients. Parma, Bastia in Corsica, the four principal cities of the Kingdom of Naples, and Palermo have chosen her for their mistress and patroness The spiritual helps, the consolations, and the counsels obtained by those who have had recourse to her, are as innumerable as they are unfailing, verifying constantly the saying of an ecclesiastic of high rank, that "*no one ever placed his trust in the intercession of St. Mary Magdalen De-Pazzi in vain.*"

Lucky Florence ! who hadst from heaven the privilege that one of thy noble families should give to the world a virgin, who, by a life of singular sanctity, obtained from God splendors of superhuman knowledge ; and, by *preserving her body incorrupt to this day*, secures to thee a pledge of the Divine Mercy. Thou canst well see, by the graces granted through the intercession of so great a Saint, that Heaven regards thee with favorable eyes, and that thy just petitions will always be met with a prompt and generous response.

§ II.

The Devotion to St. Mary Magdalen De-Pazzi in Philadelphia.

The devotion to our Saint—who gives the name to this, the first Italian Catholic Church built in this country, in 1852, by the late Rev Gaetano Mariani, and now replaced by the magnificent edifice, the corner-stone of which was laid October 14th, 1883, and the Dedication of which took place June 28th, 1891—has increased wonderfully here Among other things bearing witness to it, are the solemn annual procession on the last Sunday of May and the well-nigh numberless votive offerings in gold watches, chains, necklaces, bracelets, earrings, rings, &c., made for graces received
Here we insert a few of the many occurrences of what may be regarded as miraculous cures and graces obtained through the intercession of the Saint , though, mindful of the decree of His Holiness Pope Urban VIII, we claim for them nothing more than human credence.
I   On August 29th, 1879, the translator, in company with the late Rev. Joseph Alizeri, C. M , visited Mount Hope Retreat, and found there a Carmelite nun, from Guatemala (Sister C de J——), furiously insane most of the time, and with little or no hope of recovery On my recommending her interiorly to St Mary Magdalen De-Pazzi, as one of " her own," with great confidence, intending to say a Mass at her altar on returning home (which was afterwards done), this Sister at once gave signs of great improvement, and in one week after the above date was pronounced cured, wrote a beautiful letter to translator, and returned to her Sisters
II   In the summer of 1880, S S (a convert to the Catholic faith), middle-aged, was at the point of death from great debility and a sore leg, which, as the doctor said, should have been cut off, but that the man was too weak to stand the operation The patient was blessed several times, and some Masses were offered for him in honor of St Mary Magdalen, to whom he and his wife had a great devotion. He recovered, as if by a miracle, and is well and strong to-day
III   A D 1881, in the month of March, whilst a smallpox epidemic was raging in Philadelphi. ... ... boy, was very low with this ... one disease ... ... One day, seeing his mother cr ... ... her with ... I'm and assuring, t ... of voice, " Do not

cry, mamma, but take a gold ring to St Mary Magdalen De-Pazzi, and have a Mass said in her honor " The mother did so, and the boy soon recovered, whilst many, apparently less sick, died.

IV A D 1881, in the month of May, C. C , a young Irish lady, 29 years of age, was at the point of death from what appeared to be the worst kind of consumption, and an ulcer on a leg, and another in the throat, which latter threatened to choke her from one moment to another She could only whisper, and very faintly She had received the Holy Viaticum and Extreme Unction , and the attending physician thought her so near death, that he told her sisters he would pass by in the evening and give the death certificate Translator being sent for, he blessed her and recommended her to pray to St Mary Magdalen De-Pazzi, whose Novena had just begun The sick lady did so, and recited three *Our Fathers* every day of the Novena, and was cured for the feast of the Saint, like one who comes from death to life For several years two of the largest and most costly bouquets seen on the altar for the feast of the Saint, were her offering, as a token of gratitude for her wonderful recovery This same person married some years later and had children, enjoying good health

V In the same year, 1881, a little girl, S M , in our Orphan Asylum under the title of St Mary Magdalen, was very low with smallpox Translator blessed her, and said a Mass in honor of St. Mary Magdalen De-Pazzi, and she recovered almost instantaneously, and none of the Sisters nor orphans in the asylum took the smallpox

VI In May, 1883, an Italian young man, M T , was taken sick in Florida, with a malignant fever and an abscess, which tortured him for six long months He then made a vow to St Mary Magdalen De-Pazzi *of Philadelphia*, to present her candles and a gold chain of $10 value, if she would obtain for him the grace of recovery He was cured soon after , and his mother and sister came on the 27th of May to fulfill the vow

VII On the 9th of December, 1883, Josephine L , a Neapolitan, brought a votive offering in thanksgiving for a grace received, and in fulfillment of a vow made when she encountered a fierce storm in the Gulf Leone, while going to Italy, in March, 1883 On returning, she brought a golden cross and a pair of earrings to St Mary Magdalen, to whom she had recommended herself in the imminent danger of shipwreck The captain of the steamer, the day after the storm, had told the passengers that the night previous they had escaped a watery grave by a miracle

VIII On April 4th, 1884, Antonio De-M——, brought a gold ring to St Mary Magdalen De-Pazzi, in behalf of his wife, who was then in labor, and suffering greatly A few hours afterwards she happily gave birth to a child, without the need of any medical assistance.

IX During the first five months of the year 1884, Maria Rosa T——, mother of the above mentioned M T , fell very ill at Savannah, Ga , and could get no relief from doctors or medicines She at last recommended herself to St Mary Magdalen De-Pazzi, and immediately got well Grateful for the favor received, she brought to the Saint a beautiful pair of gold earrings

X In 1884, Christina M——, a German lady, in New Jersey, who had been sick unto death, and had been given up by the doctor in March, was cured by recommending herself to St Mary Magdalen De-Pazzi at the suggestion of the late Rev Antonio Cassese She had promised to visit the Church of the Saint, with some relatives, in Philadelphia On the 15th of August, 1884, she came to fulfill her promise, accompanied by her husband and seven other people, witnesses of her miraculous recovery through the intercession of St. Mary Magdalen De-Pazzi

XI In the month of October, 1885, N N was at the point of death, but, under the circumstances, no Sacraments could be administered without a separation and a reparation In the meantime the man was at the foot of the bed, swearing he would never part with her (Terrible and obstinate blindness of a sinner! Had she died then, would not the separation be forcibly made? except, perhaps, to be followed a few years later by a reunion, unless he would repent, in the abode of everlasting torments!) Well, I asked the people in the Church to say one *Our Father* to St Mary Magdalen De-Pazzi, and three *Hail Marys* to the Blessed Virgin , and on the following day the sick woman was removed to the hospital Translator visited her there, and found her still so obstinate, that when she could no longer say No to my exhortations to make her confession, she shook her head , and I could do nothing After two or three visits, the sick woman being *in extremis*, I again asked the people to pray, as above, and behold! on the following day she was wholly changed, as if by a miracle She made her confession, and received all the Sacraments, with the most evident signs of contrition I ever noticed in sixteen years of pastoral ministry *Deo gratias! et B M V , et St. M M De-P !*

XII On the 2d of November, 1885, T V , who had been ill with a malignant fever for five months and had obtained no relief from the attendance of two physicians—after making a vow to give . . . . St . . . . len . . . . were cured, began to improve at on . , and her . . . . Church.

XIII   F G and wife brought, as a votive offering to St Mary Magdalen De-Pazzi—a gold star—because their child, who was very ill, immediately recovered and was cured after they made the *vow* to the Saint

XIV.   Maria Teresa S——, on May 3d, 1887, brought a gold ring and cross as a votive offering to St. Mary Magdalen De-Pazzi, after recovering from a serious illness through her intercession.

XV.   At the end of the Novena, N. N , for a grace received, brought a gold ring to the Saint , and P G , to fulfill a vow made by his wife for the recovery of their child, who was sick for a year, brought the Saint, as a votive offering, a placque, a little cross and a star, a pair of earrings, and five gold rings

XVI   Antonia B——, a widow, was four years on crutches. She made a vow to St Mary Magdalen De-Pazzi to have a Mass said every year of her life, in her honor, if the Saint would obtain for her the grace to improve so as to need no crutches.' She soon recovered, and was able to walk without them. August 5th, 1887, she came to have the first Mass offered up in fulfillment of the vow.

XVII   Carmela M——, 20 years old, married, fell sick , and, having tried five physicians with no benefit, was pronounced dying by the attending one. Her mother made a promise to give a gold ring to St Mary Magdalen if her daughter would get over the sickness. The daughter recovered very quickly, and came herself to bring the ring, August 21st, 1887

XVIII   Luigi A——, two years old, was very low for ten days, and apparently dying, when the mother and the aunt said· " St. Mary Magdalen, if you obtain his recovery, we will bring you a golden cross and placque " The child grew better at once, and was quickly cured ; and they came, bringing the votive offerings, June 2d, 1889.

XIX   In the year 1889, Maria C—— was very sick and despondent for some time, whilst two physicians and plenty of medicine were doing her no good   She prayed to St Mary Magdalen De-Pazzi on the approach of the feast, and when this was celebrated she promised to give her a beautiful breastpin, an heirloom from her mother   She grew better in a few days, and came to fulfill the vow on the second Sunday in June of above year

XX.   Maria S——, married, 26 years old, was so very low, in consequence of puerperal fever, that the doctor said she would surely die before 5 A. M. of the following day   On the following day the patient listened a little while to the reading of the Life of St Mary Magdalen, made by the midwife, who, recommending to the patient to have great confidence in the Saint, detached from the book the image of the same and placed it on the breast of the sick woman, both praying and crying at the same time   The patient soon began to improve, on the day following she was pronounced out of danger, and five days later was out of bed.

XXI   Michael M ——, Irish, 18 years old, was very sick with dropsy, and pronounced not only incurable, but near his end, by six physicians, who thought he could not survive five or six weeks; so sure of it were they that, on meeting the attending physician afterwards, they would ask him, in turn, if the boy was dead yet? He made the Novena and the five Fridays more than once, at the suggestion of Translator, his confessor, and grew better, to the great surprise of the physicians and everybody else, going to Church and about for *nearly a year*, until he met with a happy death June 1st, 1890 Sunday within the Octave of St Mary Magdalen De-Pazzi's feast   The four physicians who held the post-mortem unanimously manifested great surprise that he had lived so long   This prolongation of life, and more than that, the happy ending of it, his parents, myself, and others firmly believe were due chiefly to the intercession of St Mary Magdalen De-Pazzi.

XXII.   In the month of October, 1892, Carolina M——, 32 years old, mother of five children, gave birth to another child, and in the following month became very sick with typhoid fever   She was attended by three physicians, and they all gave her up. Translator gave her the last Sacraments, and for a week she was expected to die every minute. Her husband and sisters had no hope of her recovery, neither had I, nor anyone who saw her then   She made a vow to St Mary Magdalen, and so did her two sisters She vowed two gold rings and a box of candles , one of her sisters vowed to buy something for the Church to the amount of $10 or so (two candelabra) ; and the other vowed to bring candles for the feast of the Saint In about a week after this the sick woman began to improve, and soon was out of danger, and is now as well as ever. She and her two sisters fulfilled their vows on the eve of the solemn celebration of the feast of St. Mary Magdalen De-Pazzi, 1893 , all acknowledging that the recovery was due to the intercession of our Saint. The last doctor who attended the sick woman (Dr B ——), a Protestant, said that not he nor his medicine accomplished the cure, but God.—Statement read to the three sisters, who were ready to confirm it under oath

XXIII   G ——y G — had an infant son who was very sick and was given up by the doctor in the fall of 1893. H made a vow to St Mary Magdalen De-Pazzi to go barefooted in her procession, if his boy got better. The boy was cured the day following, and the father fulfilled his vow by walking barefooted behind the statue of our Saint, in 1894 The policemen noticing him, thought him crazy, and were about to remove him, but were told by Translator not to molest him, as he was fulfilling a vow

XXIV Emilia H——, an American lady, was afflicted with scab on the face for four years, and was told by four doctors that it might last for ten years or more . and she might never be cured of it At the suggestion of Mary W H ——, a convert, she made the *Five Fridays* in honor of St Mary Magdalen De-Pazzi, and came, perfectly healed, . May 25th, 1895, to the Church, to return thanks to our Saint

XXV. Rosa G——, from St Stefano di Rogliano (Cosenza), being very sick, out of her mind most of the time, and given up by the doctors after three months' attendance, made a vow to St Mary Magdalen De-Pazzi She grew better, and sent as a votive offering a golden chain to St. Mary Magdalen, with a statement of the above

XXVI. Bridget McG——, 48 years old, had been suffering from a malignant cancer in the left breast for ten months, and had no hope of ever getting better. She put on a piece of the *veil* of the Saint, given her by Translator, and began at once to improve. At the end of seven weeks she was well, and ascribed it to the powerful intercession of St Mary Magdalen De-Pazzi. This account was read to her and approved by her, in the presence of three witnesses.

XXVII. On the solemn feast of St. Mary Magdalen De-Pazzi, Sunday, May 30th, 1897, a woman in tears dragged herself, publicly, on her knees, with face to the ground, from the door to the sanctuary railing, to fulfill a vow for a grace received through the intercession of St. Mary Magdalen De-Pazzi , but I could not get details, except that she had recovered her eyesight

XXVIII Alfonso G——, about 45 years old, had been imprisoned on a very serious charge, from April 10th to May 28th, 1898, and was then acquitted After having been set free, he was fired at five times, but escaped unhurt On the 29th of May, at 9 o'clock Mass, barefooted, on his knees, with tongue on the floor, he dragged himself up from the main church door to the sanctuary railing, in fulfillment of a vow for deliverance, acquittal, and escape, through the intercession of St. Mary Magdalen, who, he said, appeared to him in the prison the night after he made the vow, as she is represented in the Church by her statue, and bowed to him, as if to say, "Thy request is granted." Above statement read to him, and he was ready to swear to it

XXIX F B. (a German convert) was very sick with what bore all the evidence of being the last stage of consumption, and looked like a mere ghost of his former self He had no hope of recovery, and was given up by two doctors. He was told (by the writer) to make the novena to St Mary Magdalen De-Pazzi, then about to begin, May, 1899 Of course, he could not think of going to the church, but his Irish wife offered to go in his stead, and did so On the eighth day of the novena, having greatly improved, he was able to come to the church himself He continued improving and is now better than he ever was. This statement having been read to him, he entirely approved of it, and was ready to swear to it (October 14th, 1899)

XXX. R. R , forty five years old, had been very sick, and the physician told him that if he was taken sick again in the like manner, he could never get well He went to Italy and again became very sick ; his wife made a vow to give St Mary Magdalen De-Pazzi in Philadelphia two gold rings, if he recovered He got better, came back to Philadelphia, and his wife brought the rings to the church, January 23d, 1899. . . .

XXXI A C., a young girl (Germantown), was dying, and had no longer hope of recovery. Her aunt made a vow of a gold necklace to St Mary Magdalen De-Pazzi eight days before her feast ; and, on the ninth day, the girl became better and recovered fully. On Sunday, June 11th, 1899, at 2 30 P. M , the aunt brought the votive offering to the Church of St Mary Magdalen De-Pazzi, in fulfillment of her promise

XXXII C F., the mother of four children, was given up by the doctor as an incurable consumptive. Her mother made a *vow* to buy a five-pound wax candle, and that her daughter would carry it barefooted after the statue of St. Mary Magdalen in the solemn procession, if she recovered She did recover and fulfilled the vow, May 28th, 1899

XXXIII May 28th, 1899, being the Sunday of the celebration of St Mary Magdalen De-Pazzi's annual feast, just before eight o'clock Mass, two little girls walked into the sacristy, each carrying a candle, with a dollar note attached, for St. Mary Magdalen De-Pazzi I asked them what special grace they had obtained from the Saint, and they answered that they did not know I sent them over, with an altar-boy, to place their offerings before the statue of the Saint, telling them to go home after Mass, ask their mother, and then return to let me know what had happened. When they returned and told me in their innocence what their mother in guarded language had told them, my eyes filled with tears. Here is the story : "Papa was here in America , a woman tole him , mamma came here, prayed to St. Mary Magdalen De-Pazzi , and, instid of three months, mamma got papa back, and had us two and a little brother brought here together "—Surely, *as man does not live by bread alone*, THIS is even a greater grace than a wonderful cure of a fatal disease

And—not to mention several other special graces—should I not gratefully attribute to the intercession of St. Mary Magdalen De-Pazzi my wonderful recovery from the very painful and serious illness which kept me on the brink of the grave from June to December, 1878?—· *Translator.*

¿ III.

Extract from a Letter of Sister Maria Maddalena Costante of the Blessed Sacrament, in Behalf of the Mother Prioress, Sister Maria Maddalena Deodata,

To the Rev. Translator, touching upon the removal of the body of St Mary Magdalen De-Pazzi to the new Carmelite Monastery in Piazza Savonarola, the old monastery having been expropriated by the Government for city improvements.

J. M. J.   FLORENCE, October 9th, 1889

Very Rev Sir.

. . . . . You cannot believe how much your letter pleased us, and how much we feel we should thank the Lord for what you say. But the comparison between the devotion to our Saint in America, which you describe, with what we see here, where her body is preserved incorrupt, wounds the heart   Oh ! how much we grieve in seeing the fulfillment of those prophetic words uttered by our Holy Mother in one of her ecstasies, as follows   "Thy faith, O Word, travels as the sun , there it arises, here it sets "   It is truly so, let us pray. About this time a year ago we were expelled from the monastery that had been given to us by Pope Urban VIII, and where St Mary Magdalen had a magnificent church and a very rich, large, and much-admired altar   At present, we are in a monastery built by the alms we received, and hope to be able to finish paying for it with what Providence will send us, as we had nothing left after our suppression

St. Mary Magdalen in a Protestant country goes out in a glorious procession , and here, in her own country, to have *her* with us, we were compelled to carry *her* in the night-time on a cart without any accompaniment   Some of us followed her from the choir to the door, and others were at the new monastery to receive her   Her body as well as that of the Blessed Maria Bagnese, also incorrupt, was encased and sealed by the archiepiscopal curia till the poor chapels where they were to be placed were completed

In May, for the feast (25th), and two days previous to it, the body of the Saint was left exposed to the public veneration , and the same was done with the body of the Blessed Bagnese, whose feast is on the 28th of May   It seemed, then, as if the devotion of the people had been rekindled. But, alas ! it was not so ! You tell us of her glories, and we of our sorrows   Let us pray that all may redound to the honor of God and the triumph of the Church in the whole world   .

Tell St Mary Magdalen to maintain in us her spirit, and to obtain for us the grace of glorifying God and saving souls, as she did   In this world there is nothing else to be done.

Excuse this poor writing , it was done at different times, and I have so little leisure

Accept the regards of my Rev Mother Prioress and mine   Bless us, and allow me to sign myself

Your devoted and humble

SISTER M. M. COSTANTE OF THE BLESSED SACRAMENT.

From the Monastery of St Mary Magdalen De-Pazzi.

Very Rev. Antonio Isoleri, etc.

She receives a bridal ring from the Divine Redeemer (page 437).

§ IV.

OFFERINGS AND PRAYERS

SUITABLE FOR THE

Forty Hours' Devotion, Carnival Time, Lent, and the gaining of the Indulgences and the Holy Jubilee, whenever Prayers are required to be said for the Holy Church, the Conversion of Sinners, etc.,

TOGETHER WITH THE

PRAYERS FOR THE NOVENA OF ST. MARY MAGDALEN DE-PAZZI AND THE FIVE FRIDAYS IN HER HONOR.

A

Offerings to the Divine Word Incarnate, of His Own Most Precious Blood, for Persons of Various States. Selected from those which St. Mary Magdalen De-Pazzi made during Her Ecstasies.

1. O Word most Divine, I offer to Thee Thy priests, and for them I offer to Thee whatever is most dear to Thee in heaven and on earth, in union with Thy Most Precious Blood, and I beg of Thee to grant them that they may conceive the proper esteem for the sublime dignity with which they are clothed, and a supreme horror for all those things which may either abase their dignity or contaminate their lives. *Our Father, Hail Mary, Glory be to the Father*, etc.

2. O Loving Word, I offer to Thee the Virgins, Thy Spouses, and for them I offer to Thee that Most Precious Blood which Thou didst sweat during Thy agony in the garden. I place these *doves* in their nest, and these *lilies* in their garden, viz., in Thy most lovable Heart; and I beg of Thee to grant them that they may well understand the happy lot for which Thou hast chosen them, and correspond with fidelity to Thy love. *Our Father, Hail Mary, Glory be to the Father*, etc.

3. O Eternal Word, I offer to Thee all the faithful children of the Church, Thy Bride, and members of Thee, their Head, and for them I offer to Thee, that Most Precious Blood Thou hast shed during the scourging at the pillar; I beg of Thee to grant them that they may remember the solemn renunciation they made at their Baptism, of the devil, the world, and the flesh, and lead a life that may not contradict the faith, which they profess. *Our Father, Hail Mary, Glory be to the Father*, etc.

4. O Divine Word, I offer to Thee all the poor sinners, and for them I offer to Thee that Most Precious Blood and that Water which Thou didst shed from Thy Sacred Side, when pierced with the lance I beg of Thee that with this Blood and this Water, Thou mayest wash the stains from their souls, and grant them that repenting in time, they may atone with much love for the offenses they have committed against Thee. *Our Father, Hail Mary, Glory be to the Father*, etc.

5. O Eternal Word, I offer to Thee all Heretics, and for them I offer to Thee that Most Precious Blood which Thou didst shed from Thy wounded Body, when the Jews tore away Thy clothing to crucify Thee. I beg of Thee to have compassion on those sheep which, being separated from the fold, run to perdition by the road of error and obstinacy; and to bring them back into the bosom of Thy Church, where alone Truth and Salvation can be found. *Our Father, Hail Mary, Glory be to the Father,* etc.

6. O Divine Word, I offer to Thee all Infidels, and for them I offer to Thee that Most Precious Blood Thou didst shed from Thy Most Holy Head, crowned with thorns. I beg of Thee to remember that these souls Thou also hast created. Enlighten them that they may know their true and only God, and their Saviour, so that they may also become partakers of the grace of the Sacraments, and of the common Redemption. *Our Father, Hail Mary, Glory be to the Father,* etc

7. Eternal Father, I offer to Thee that intense pain which Thy Only-Begotten Son suffered during the three hours of His agony, when He was nailed to the cross for the love of us, and particularly when, on account of the vehemence of His pain and abandonment, He uttered these words: *"Deus, Deus meus, ut quid dereliquisti Me?"*—" God, My God, why hast Thou abandoned Me?" I offer it to Thee for all those who are now dying, together with the Blood Thy Son shed from His five Wounds, that by the power of this Blood they may be strengthened and shielded against all temptations, and may reach the happy port of eternal salvation. *Our Father, Hail Mary, Glory be to the Father,* etc

8. O Most Compassionate Word, I offer to Thee all the blessed souls in Purgatory, and for them I offer to Thee Thy Most Precious Blood. I beg of Thee to grant that this Fountain of Refreshment may incessantly flow to mitigate their flames and hasten their deliverance, so that they may ascend, without delay, to be united with Thee in the glory for which they are destined. Amen, Amen, Amen. *Our Father, Hail Mary, Glory be to the Father,* etc.

9. O Eternal Father, I offer to Thee the love which Jesus Christ, Thy Son, showed to mankind in all His Passion, and especially in the interior pain which He endured by the beatific joy being subtracted from His sensitive part. I beg of Thee that the complacency of *that love* may so occupy Thee that Thou wilt not look at the many offenses which, at this time, are committed against Thee in all the world. *Our Father, Hail Mary, Glory be to the Father,* etc

And this the Lord promised to the Saint would be the case, if this Offering were made to Him during the Carnival time.

B.

Aspiration for a Holy Death, and Preparation for the Same.

In the name of the Most Holy Trinity, in Whom I believe, Whom I love, Whom I adore, for Whom I wish to live, think, speak, act, suffer, and die, Father, Son, and Holy Ghost. Amen.

1. O Jesus, I come to Thee, diffident of myself, and abandoning

myself wholly in Thy Blood and in Thy Charity. Ah! pray, save me for the sake of that love which transfixed Thee on the cross: *Our Father, Hail Mary, Glory be to the Father*, etc

2. And now, for that hour of my death, I detest all the sins of my life. Oh! would that the love of Thy offended Goodness would distill these eyes of mine into tears of blood! *Our Father, Hail Mary, Glory be to the Father*, etc.

3. With Thee, then, O my Jesus, I unite and crucify myself, I desire to suffer, I desire to die for the most pure glory of Thy Holy Name, in union with Thine open Heart. *Our Father, Hail Mary, Glory be to the Father*, etc

4. And, full of confidence and of love, I unite my death to Thine, my sorrows to Thy Passion, my body to Thy torn Body, my soul to Thy Soul Most Divine, expiring on the cross for me. *Our Father, Hail Mary, Glory be to the Father*, etc.

5 O most merciful, most clement, O Father of mercies, by that charity and obedience which brought Thee to suffer and to die, I supplicate Thee for the love God bears to Himself, and for His great goodness, pray, make me die in the merit of that last breath, which saved the world, when *bowing the head*, for my glory, *Thou gavest up the Ghost. Our Father, Hail Mary, Glory be to the Father*, etc.

6. Father, I have sinned against heaven and before Thee, I am no longer worthy of being called Thy son

I believe, love, and adore my Jesus and my God.
Into Thy hands I commend my soul, Thou, O Lord, God of Truth, hast redeemed it.

> Soul of Christ, sanctify me.
> Body of Christ, save me.
> Blood of Christ, inebriate me.
> Water from the Side of Christ, wash me.
> Passion of Christ, comfort me.
> O good Jesus, hear me.
> Within Thy wounds hide me.
> Permit me not to separate from Thee.
> From the malignant enemy, defend me.
> At the hour of my death call me,
> And command me to come to Thee,
> That with all Thy Saints I may praise Thee
> For all ages of eternity. Amen.

Let us pray:

O Lord Jesus Christ, Who, for us sinners, whilst on the cross, wished to have Thy Side and Most Sacred Heart pierced with a lance; grant, we beseech Thee, by the bowels of Thy mercy, that washed in the Blood and Water of Thy Side, we may merit to live, act, suffer, and die in union with Thy Heart and love. Amen.

C

Seven Offerings of the Most Precious Blood of Jesus Christ to the Eternal Father.

1 Eternal Father, I offer to Thee the merits of the Most Precious Blood of Thy Beloved Son and my Divine Redeemer, Jesus, for the propagation and exaltation of my dear Mother the Church, for the protection and prosperity of her visible head, the Sovereign Roman Pontiff, for the cardinals, the bishops, and pastors of souls, and for all the ministers of the sanctuary. *Our Father, Hail Mary, Glory be to the Father*, etc.

May Jesus be always praised and thanked, Who saved us by His Blood

May the Blessed Sacrament be adored, praised, and thanked by all every moment

2 Eternal Father, I offer to Thee the merits of the Most Precious Blood of Thy Most Beloved Son and my Divine Redeemer, Jesus, for the peace and harmony among kings and Christian rulers, for the humiliation of the enemies of our holy Faith, and for the prosperity of the Christian people. *Our Father, Hail Mary, Glory be to the Father*, etc

May Jesus be always praised and thanked, Who saved us by His Blood

May the Blessed Sacrament be adored, praised, and thanked by all every moment

3. Eternal Father, I offer to Thee the merits of the Most Precious Blood of Thy Beloved Son and my Divine Redeemer, Jesus, for the enlightenment of unbelievers, the extirpation of all heresies, and the conversion of all poor sinners. *Our Father, Hail Mary, Glory be to the Father*, etc.

May Jesus be always praised and thanked, Who saved us by His Blood.

May the Blessed Sacrament be adored, praised, and thanked by all every moment.

4. Eternal Father, I offer to Thee the merits of the Most Precious Blood of Thy Beloved Son and my Divine Redeemer, Jesus, for all my relatives, for my friends and my enemies, for the indigent, the sick, and those who are troubled, and for all those for whom Thou knowest and desirest I should pray *Our Father, Hail Mary, Glory be to the Father*, etc

May Jesus be always praised and thanked, Who saved us by His Blood.

May the Blessed Sacrament be adored, praised, and thanked by all every moment.

5. Eternal Father, I offer to Thee the merits of the Most Precious Blood of Thy Beloved Son and my Divine Redeemer, Jesus, for all those who on this day will pass out of this life, that Thou mayest free them from the torments of hell, and admit them, with the greatest speed, to the possession of Thy glory. *Our Father, Hail Mary, Glory be to the Father*, etc.

May Jesus be always praised and thanked, Who saved us by His Blood

May the Blessed Sacrament be adored, praised, and thanked by all every moment.

6 Eternal Father, I offer to Thee the merits of the Most Precious Blood of Thy Beloved Son and my Divine Redeemer, Jesus, for all those who are lovers of so great a Treasure, for all those who are united with me in adoring and honoring the Same, and for those, finally, who labor to propagate the devotion to It. *Our Father, Hail Mary, Glory be to the Father*, etc.

May Jesus be always praised and thanked, Who saved us by His Blood.

May the Blessed Sacrament be adored, praised, and thanked by all every moment

7. Eternal Father, I offer to Thee the merits of the Most Precious Blood of Thy Beloved Son and my Divine Redeemer, Jesus, for all my spiritual and temporal necessities, in suffrage for the souls in Purgatory, and especially for those that have been more devout to the Price of our Redemption, and to the sorrows and pains of our Most Holy Mother, Mary. *Our Father, Hail Mary, Glory be to the Father*, etc

May Jesus be always praised and thanked, Who saved us by His Blood.

May the Blessed Sacrament be adored, praised, and thanked by all every moment

Viva the Most Precious Blood of Jesus, now and forever, for all centuries of centuries. Amen.

By the recitation of these seven Offerings, one may gain a three-hundred-days' Indulgence each time , and after reciting them daily for one month, and going to Con fession and Communion on any one day at choice, and praying according to the intention of the Sovereign Pontiff, one may gain a Plenary Indulgence , and such Indulgences may also be applied by way of suffrage to the holy souls in Purgatory.— *Pius VII, 22d day of September, A. D. 1817.*

D

Prayers and Offerings made by St. Mary Magdalen De-Pazzi, while in Ecstasy, for the Conversion and Salvation of Erring Souls.

O Love, O Love, give, I pray Thee, give Thyself to Thy creatures Grant Thou, O my Jesus, that those who with so great a desire are awaiting Thee (viz., *the Jews*), may not remain longer in this error, because Thou hast come once Grant Thou, O my Jesus, I beg Thee, that they may know this, and how vain and fallacious is their expectation. And to those who have departed from Thee (viz , *the Heretics*), I pray Thee, grant that they may return to Thee like lost sheep returning to the fold, and that they may love and revere Thee as their Shepherd. Do Thou grant that all those who believe not in Thee, may return to Thee, O Love, for they also are Thy creatures O Love, if a soul could see what she is without Thee, not by one, but by a thousand deaths would she remain annihilated.

I beg of Thee, O my Jesus, that Thou mayest condescend to grant
me as many souls as I will walk steps this day. O my Jesus, pray, give
me a voice so strong that I may be heard by all in all parts of the world,
in order that this Love may be equally loved and esteemed by all But
that worst of poisons, self-love, deprives us of this high knowledge, in
order to oppose the Divine Love.

O Love, Thou art great, and worthy of all praise ; but who is of
himself sufficiently capable of praising Thee ? If all the tongues of men
together with the angels,—if all the glory of the firmament, the most
minute sands of the sea, the trees of the earth, the drops of water,
and the birds of the air, would become so many tongues to praise Thee,
they would not in any way be sufficient to do it.

I offer to Thee, Eternal Father, Thy Son, Whom Thou hast begotten from eternity, and sent down to earth.

I offer to Thee, Eternal Father, Thy Son, Whom Thou hast kept in
Thy bosom from eternity, hast begotten in Thy wisdom, and sent down
to the earth, on account of my misery and because of Thy mercy.

Eternal Father, I offer to Thee Thy Son, Whom, after His Resur-
rection, Thou hast attracted to Thyself and placed at Thy right hand
O God, our Protector, look down upon us, and look at the Face of
Thy Christ.

1. O Divine Father, Protector of Thy creatures, look at Thy Only
Begotten Son, Who, together with Thee, is One and the same God, and
Who, to obey Thee, became man. Look at Him all wounded, and for
His sake, I beg Thee, forgive us. Look also and see how the soul of
every creature is Thine by creation, and His by redemption ; He having
purchased it by His own Blood, and by His Passion and death. Therefore, O Divine Father, do not permit Thy own souls to perish, but grant
that by Thy mercy and grace, they may never be forsaken by Thy
divine grace.

2. Everywhere, everywhere, I see malice abounding O Father, O
Word, O Holy Spirit, O God Triune, do Thou grant that to everyone
in particular, Thy light may be vouchsafed, so that by it everyone may
know, and in part penetrate, his malice. And grant to me that I
may atone for it in their behalf, by laying down my life for it, if
needs be.

3. O Word, how can I endure to see a being, created and re-
created by Thee, not be partaker of Thee, Who art Sovereign Goodness, and of Thy Blood ? I wish that thousands upon thousands, and
again thousands and thousands of millions, would be found to say
always these words : "*Not to us, O Lord, not to us, but to Thy Name
give glory!*" O my Jesus, Thy Blood also cries out ! O Love, hear
Thy Blood !

4. O Word, I will not leave here, unless I see first some soul enlightened. I am not myself worthy of being heard, I know ; hear not me,
who am too presumptuous, but do hear Thy Blood I offer to Thee all
the Blood Thou didst shed in Thy Circumcision, whilst praying in the
Garden in so much agony, and that which Thou didst shed at the
Pillar and during all Thy Passion, all the works Thou didst perform,
during the three-and-thirty years Thou didst remain with us, and all

that Thou didst do and suffer during Thy life, Passion, and Death; I offer to Thee, O Word, that most sweet and tender love which Thou didst bear Thy Holy Mother, and I also offer to Thee that love which she bore Thee, and all her holy merits and privileges.

5. I offer to Thee, O Eternal Father, all the blood of the Martyrs in union with *that* which was shed on the cross by Thy *Incarnate Word*. I also offer to Thee all the wisdom, the diligence, the words, and the labors of the Holy Doctors, in union with the Blood of the *Word Incarnate*. I offer to Thee all the wishes, the tears, the prayers, and the devotions of the Holy Confessors, in union with the Blood of the *Word Incarnate*. I offer to Thee the purity, the beauty, and the union of the Virgins, in union with the Blood of the *Word Incarnate*. In a word, I offer to Thee all the merits and the just and holy works of all the creatures, the humility, obedience, charity, mercy, and all the virtues of the elect, in union with the Blood of the *Word Incarnate*

O good Jesus! good Jesus! good Jesus! Let us raise up our hearts and conceive an ardent desire for the salvation of souls! Look down from heaven, O Lord, and see how they all err in their ways! There is not one to be found who does good, not even one. Oh! that the hearts of those who believe not in Thee may be converted: Hallowed be Thy Name for all ages to come. Amen! Amen! Amen!

The above prayers may also be used for the

DEVOTION OF THE FIVE FRIDAYS,

or, this may be performed by simply prefacing the prayers of the Novena with.—

O God, incline unto my aid, etc.
Glory be to the Father, etc.

O Lord, I offer to Thee this devotion of the Five Fridays of St. Mary Magdalen, intending on the First Friday to commemorate and honor particularly her great love for Thee in Thy Passion and the Blessed Sacrament,
Second Friday—Her great love for her neighbor, especially her apostolic zeal for the conversion of sinners;
Third Friday—Her angelic purity;
Fourth Friday—Her profound humility,
Fifth Friday—Her martyr-like penance;—
in order to obtain from Thy mercy, through the merits of our Lord Jesus Christ, the intercession of the Blessed Virgin Mary and all the Saints, and especially that of our St Mary Magdalen, the grace to imitate her in this particular virtue, and to obtain also *this* or *that* special grace, etc,—if it be according to Thy Holy Will.

E.

PRAYERS AND ORDER FOR THE NOVENA OF ST. MARY MAGDALEN DE-PAZZI.

Rosary.

Litany of the Blessed Virgin.

Lord, have mercy on us.
Christ, have mercy on us.
Lord, have mercy on us.
Christ, hear us
Christ, graciously hear us
God, the Father of heaven, have mercy on us.
God, the Son, Redeemer of the world, have mercy on us.
God, the Holy Ghost, have mercy on us.
Holy Trinity, one God, have have mercy on us.

Holy Mary,
Holy Mother of God,
Holy Virgin of virgins,
Mother of Christ,
Mother of Divine Grace,
(Mother of Mercy),
Mother most pure,
Mother most chaste,
Mother inviolate,
Mother undefiled,
Mother most amiable,
Mother most admirable,
Mother of our Creator,
Mother of our Saviour,
Virgin most prudent,
Virgin most venerable,
Virgin most renowned,
Virgin most powerful,
Virgin most merciful,
Virgin most faithful,
Mirror of justice,
Seat of wisdom,
Cause of our joy,
Spiritual vessel,
Vessel of honor,

Pray for us.

Singular vessel of devotion,
Mystical rose,
Tower of David,
Tower of ivory,
House of gold,
Ark of the Covenant,
Gate of Heaven,
Morning star,
Health of the sick,
Refuge of sinners,
Comforter of the afflicted,
Help of Christians,
Queen of Angels,
Queen of Patriarchs,
Queen of Prophets,
Queen of Apostles,
Queen of Martyrs,
Queen of Confessors,
Queen of Virgins,
Queen of all Saints,
Queen conceived without original sin,
Queen of the most holy Rosary,
(Queen, Beauty of Carmel),

Pray for us.

Lamb of God, Who takest away the sins of the world, spare us, O Lord.

Lamb of God, Who takest away the sins of the world, graciously hear us, O Lord.

Lamb of God, Who takest away the sins of the world, have mercy on us.

To the Eternal Father.

1. I adore Thee, O Eternal Father, together with the First Hierarchy, and I thank Thee on the part of Thy beloved Daughter, Mary Magdalen, for all the graces by Thee granted her, and in particular for having chosen her as the resting-place of Thy Divine Being, in that manner, and as far as mortal creatures can become capable thereof, and for having promised her to grant her whatsoever she would ask Thee, saying to her "Bride of My Only-Begotten Word, ask of Me what thou wilt "

I beg of Thee, for the sake of her merits and prayers, to infuse into my heart a true humility and conformity to Thy Divine Will *Our Father, Hail Mary, Glory be to the Father*, etc.

To the Eternal Word.

2. I adore Thee, O Jesus, Word Incarnate, together with the Second Hierarchy, and I thank Thee, on the part of Thy most loving Bride, Mary Magdalen, for all the gifts by Thee granted her, especially for those five with which Thou didst adorn her. 1. With Thy most sacred *stigmata*. 2. When Thou didst place *a ring* on her finger, as to a bride. 3. When Thou gavest her *Thy* own *Heart*, as to a true lover 4. When Thou didst crown her with Thy *most sacred crown of thorns* 5 When Thy most holy Mother covered her with *the veil of purity*, and Thou didst grant her that *naked* suffering so much wished for by her

I beg of Thee, for the sake of her merits and prayers, to grant me the grace of imitating Thee and her, and particularly of being willing to suffer for Thy love; and grant me also, I beseech Thee, a perfect observance of Thy divine law and counsels *Our Father, Hail Mary, Glory be to the Father*, etc.

To the Holy Ghost.

3. I adore Thee, O Spirit Paraclete, and I thank Thee, together with the Third Hierarchy, in the name of Thy dear Disciple, Mary Magdalen, for all the gifts granted her by Thee, for having chosen her for Thy agreeable dwelling place, and particularly for the seven times Thou didst infuse Thyself into that most pure soul, under seven various forms —of cloud, of fire, of column, of river, of dove, of wind, and of flames, in order to strengthen her in the temptations and sufferings she was to endure during the five years of her probation, having made her victorious over hell itself.

I beg of Thee, O Spirit of Sovereign Goodness, to grant me strength in all adversities and temptations in life and death, and to enkindle in my heart a burning flame of Thy Love. *Our Father, Hail Mary, Glory be to the Father*, etc.

To the Blessed Virgin.

Behold me prostrate before thee, O most holy Virgin, Mother of God, to thank thee on the part of our St. Mary Magdalen, with all the Saints of heaven, for all the gifts and graces thou hast obtained for her, and especially for *having given into her arms thy Divine Son*, the Infant Jesus, and covered and protected her with the *veil of purity*, putting also into her bosom thy most pure heart, and then adorning her with a most beautiful *gold necklace* on the day which commemorates thy glorious Assumption into Heaven; and for many other marked favors granted to her.

I beg of thee, O Mother of God and of us poor sinners, that for the sake of the merits of this our Saint, thou wilt reconcile us with thy Divine Son, and render us thy worthy children, leading us constantly, till the end of our days, through the path of grace and justice.

Three *Hail Marys*, etc.

Supplication to the Saint.

To thee, glorious Mary Magdalen, to thee I confidently address my supplications and the sighs of my heart, making known to thee all the wounds which sadden and distress it, and I invoke thy powerful patronage, hoping thou wilt benignly lend me thy hand, to draw me out of the misery in which I find myself But, from heaven, thou dost see my misery, thou hearest my moans, and thou measurest perhaps my afflictions, with that immense charity which distinguishes thee ! Ah ! pray, stretch forth also the arms of thy beneficence over the storms which surround me and which make me sink In contemplating thee, so rich in virtues and merits, so powerful with God in behalf of thy fellow-beings, I take complacency in thee with the most lively and grateful affection which a human creature is capable of, but with as much warmth I beg of thee to admit me to all the efficacy of thy intercession. With the powerful and unfailing depth of thy compassion, see how the passions have disfigured me Not only have I lost the character of a true follower of Jesus Christ, but almost the human character itself, and yet, there was a time when I, too, tasted the sweetness of the celestial peace There was a time in which devotion to thee made me long to imitate thee, turn my back on the world, and plunge into the contemplation of heavenly things. Then my heart, filled with God's grace, during those happy years of innocence, rested tranquilly in the intimate consciousness of right-doing. But furiously assailed by the infernal enemy, tossed about by evil suggestions, and especially by that self-love which, unhappily, predominates in us—forgetful, on the other hand, of what a thousand others likewise have done, or rather, too weak in my will to follow thy example, I lent ear to the malicious tempter. I answered his accursed calls, and, soon becoming their victim and target, found myself cast about on every side by violent incitements to evil, lost in the tortuous ways of error, a slave to darkness, running after deceitful phantoms, which vanished at every step, like an abandoned ship, which the winds and the waves are seeking to swallow. Such has been and is my unhappy lot! Without truth in the soul, without charity in the heart, I go on hoping where there is no ground to hope, and fearing where there is no reason to fear, a toy to vain desires, the satisfying of which is immediately followed by ennui which, in its turn, is followed in succession by a thousand other desires, that disturb and agitate me more and more, either because of the impotency of satisfying them, or by the rancor and envy of others, or by like unfavorable circumstances Such is the case with human desires, which continually alternate a momentary delight with incessant restlessness and anxiety And what reminiscences have I of all worldly enjoyments but bitterness, remorse and confusion? The world, of which I made myself the vile servant, now despises me; my friends delude and defame me; the very shadow of man disgusts me, betokening to me deception and seduction , and with my heart ill-used on all sides, scarce enduring myself, bound at every setting of the sun, to confess that all is vanity and affliction of spirit, nothing is left but a horror of the sepulchre, which indicates to me the terrible and irrevocable account which I will soon be called upon to render. And yet these causes of terror, these prostrations of spirit, are still voices of paternal affection, by which God calls on me to repent and do penance. And I, tired and annoyed by so many afflictions, disabused and burning with a desire to set my heart at rest, would like to correspond to the Lord's voice, would like to return to the arms of so loving a Father, Who, for so long, and in so many and such different ways, stretches them forth to offer me forgiveness I desire to follow the maxims thou hast practiced, and by which (instructing me at the school of Bethlehem and Calvary) thou declarest to me so eloquently that the true triumph of human strength and power is to conquer one's self; that he who suffers and abstains, lives more happily and tranquilly than he who, letting loose the reins of the carnal appetites and pride of the spirit, amuses himself in the midst of the voluptuousness and the haughtiness of this world. I would desire, well convinced as I am and oppressed by my own experience, to draw back from vice and set forth, instead, upon the path of virtue. But being too weakened in the spirit by so many irregularities of the senses, wholly incapable of arising of myself, I need a special grace, a prodigy of Divine grace, to draw me out of this profound misfortune. This is what I ask and hope for from thy patronage Thou canst do it. God hears thee Oh ! delay not to come to my rescue ; let not my demerits keep thee from doing it. Transfuse into my understanding a portion of that light which was wont to reveal so plainly to thee the monstrosity of sin, and then strengthen my will that it may detest and abhor it, and, with true contrition, and works of severe and humble penance, go on purifying my heart from all stains which contaminate it. Quench in me my sinful appetites, calm my restless wishes, and work in me, in one word, my reconciliation and peace with the Father of Mercies. Once free from the irregular and excessive affection for creatures, animated by thy example, obtain for me that I may elevate myself to the love of the Sovereign Good, and progress in It so that, never checked by the power of the great ones, or paralyzed by the abasement of the lowly ones, I may, with evangelical freedom, overcome all human miseries so far as to know and see in every creature nothing but God; to have God alone as the beginning and the end of all my affections and actions Do thou grant that my heart, being inflamed with that fire with which thou didst burn, may become wholly enamored with the Divine Bridegroom, Jesus; serve Him with all its powers, follow Him with all its strength and sentiments; that it may never know or speak of anything but Jesus, that it may never think or live for anything but Jesus. Finally, obtain for me, that the rest of my days being constant in the practice of every virtue that goes to make the good Christian and the good citizen, I may be crowned with the precious death of the just, and thus guided to the possession of that heavenly beatitude, where, in the grateful admiration of thy glory, I may sing for everlasting ages the benignity and mercy of the Divine Saviour. Amen.

Chapter (2 Cor. x, 17-18).

Brethren, he that glorieth, let him glory in the Lord, for not he that commendeth himself, is approved, but he whom God commendeth. *R*. Thanks be to God.

Hymn.

Thou Crown of all the Virgin choir!
That Holy Mother's Virgin Son!
Who is, alone of womankind,
Mother and Virgin both in one.

Encircled by Thy Virgin band,
Amid the lilies Thou art found;
For Thy pure Brides with lavish hand
Scattering immortal graces round.

And still, wherever Thou dost bend
Thy lovely steps, O glorious King,
Virgins upon Thy steps attend,
And hymns to Thy high glory sing.

Keep us, O Purity Divine,
From every least corruption free;
Our every sense from sin refine,
And purify our souls for Thee.

To God the Father, and the Son,
All honor, glory, praise be given;
With Thee, O Holy Paraclete!
Henceforth by all in earth and heaven. Amen.

V. Pray for us, O St. Mary Magdalen
R. That we may be made worthy of the promises of Christ.
V. Lord, hear my prayer.
R And let my cry come unto Thee

(*V.* The Lord be with you.
R. And with thy spirit.)

Let us pray:

Grant, we beseech Thee, O Lord God, that we, Thy servants, may enjoy perpetual health, both of mind and body; and, by the glorious intercession of Blessed Mary ever Virgin, may be delivered from the present sorrow, and attain unto eternal joy.

O God, the lover of virginity, Who didst inflame the breast of Saint Mary Magdalen with the fire of Thy love, and enrich it with heavenly gifts, grant that we may imitate, by our purity and charity, her whose festival we celebrate [or, whose commemoration we devoutly make].

Through our Lord, etc.

N. B.—It is recommended to approach the Sacraments, if possible, after the Novena or the Devotion of the Five Fridays.

" God is wonderful in His Saints: the God of Israel is He Who will give power and strength to His people. Blessed be God."

PSALM LXVII, 36.

NOTE.

In perfect submission to the Decrees of His Holiness Urban VIII, and of the Sacred Congregation of Rites, we declare here that, for the facts related in this book, we claim nothing more than a purely human and historical authority, except as to those upon which Holy Church has already pronounced judgment.   A. I.

INDEX.

PART I.

THE LIFE OF ST. MARY MAGDALEN DE-PAZZI.

PART II.

THE WORKS OF ST. MARY MAGDALEN DE-PAZZI

FIRST SECTION.

OF HER CONTEMPLATIONS ON THE PRINCIPAL MYSTERIES OF OUR FAITH, ON THE HUMANITY OF CHRIST AND ON THE DIVINE ATTRIBUTES.

SECOND SECTION.

THIRD SECTION.

LETTERS OF ST MARY MAGDALEN DE-PAZZI.

LETTERS DICTATED BY THE SAINT WHILST IN ECSTASY.

APPENDIX.

LIST OF ILLUSTRATIONS.

CPSIA information can be obtained
at www.ICGtesting.com
Printed in the USA
BVHW040339140621
609171BV00012B/79